Napoleon's Cursed War

Napoleon's Cursed War

Spanish Popular Resistance in the Peninsular War,
1808–1814

RONALD FRASER

VERSO

London • New York

First published by Verso 2008
© Ronald Fraser 2008

All rights reserved

The moral rights of the author have been asserted

1 3 5 7 9 10 8 6 4 2

Verso
UK: 6 Meard Street, London W1F 0EG
USA: 180 Varick Street, New York, NY 10014-4606
www.versobooks.com

Verso is the imprint of New Left Books

ISBN-13: 978-1-84467-082-6

British Library Cataloguing in Publication Data
A catalogue record for this book is available from the British Library

Library of Congress Cataloging-in-Publication Data
A catalog record for this book is available from the Library of Congress

Typeset in Times by Hewer Text UK Ltd, Edinburgh
Printed in the USA by Maple Vail

For Aurora

Contents

Acknowledgements

I wish to thank the Leverhulme Trust and the Cañada Blanch Foundation for grants which enabled me to carry out a considerable part of the documentary research on which this book is based. Without their generous aid, the work's scope would have been much diminished, especially at the local level where the grants enabled me to engage a score of individuals to scour provincial and other archives for relevant material. I gratefully recognize the contribution to this book made by the following though none, of course, is responsible for the use I made of their research:

Juan Ballesta; Gonzalo Butrón; Julia Cifuentes; Monica Ferrer; Ines Gómez; Leonor Hernández; Germán López; Isabel Martínez; José Manuel Pelaez; Marcel Poblet; Elena Quirós; Gonzalo Rodríguez; Pilar Rovira; Pilar Salomón; Ma. José Sánchez Pravia; Julio Sierra; Sonia Turón; and Miguel Vázquez.

I am especially endebted to Professor Josep Fontana, an outstanding Catalan historian of the period, for his continuing encouragement and knowledge on which I could always call; Professor David Sven-Reher led me gently by the hand through some elementary demographic procedures and his invaluable suggestions have added considerably to the book's range; Antonio Moliner and Richard Hocquellet kindly made available their doctoral theses and the marquesa de Marañón allowed me to consult the private papers of her Bertrán de Lis forebears; William Christian's deep anthropological understanding of popular Spanish religious practices was always instructive and María Tausiet's permission to use her work allowed me to probe a case of village religious 'possession' during the war; in researching the period, Isabel Aguirre, head archivist of the Simancas archives, was exceptionally helpful, as were Fernanda del Rincón, archivist of the Valencian Cortes and Chris Woolgar of the Hartley Library, Southampton University. I wish also sincerely to thank Perry Anderson and Tariq Ali for their constant friendship and counsels during some difficult moments in this book's production; and Fred Halliday for his unremitting efforts on my behalf from his new Barcelona base.

A considerable number of historian-demographers provided me with much valuable information. As their names will be found among the sources at the end of Appendix 5 I shall not repeat them here. But I wish to take the opportunity of thanking them collectively.

Many historians whose names do not figure helped me at various times and in ways too varied to enumerate; I am particularly grateful to the following: Celso Almuiña, Rafael Aracil, Manuel Ardit, Marc Baldó, Xosé Barreiro, Antonio Bernal, Robert Brenner, Esteban Canales, Raymond Carr, Julián Casanova, Francisco Díaz Torrejón, Fernando Díez Rodríguez, Juan Francisco Fuentes, Mario García Bonafé, Salvador García Jiménez, Antonio García López, Carmen García Monerris, Ana Ma. García Rovira, Ramón Garrabou, Carlo Ginzburg, Nigel Glendenning, Manuel González Portilla, Richard Herr, Eric Hobsbawm, Herminio Lafoz, Emilio La Parra, Alicia Laspra, Francisco Javier Maestrojuán, José Martínez Carrión, Tom Mertes, Jesús Millán, Encarna Nicolás, Madalena de Pazzis, Ma. Antonia Peña, Manuel Pérez Ledesma, Vicente Pérez Moreda, José Manuel Pérez García, José Antonio Piqueras, Paul Preston, Joaquín Recaño, Ricardo Robles, Isabel Rodríguez Zurro, Ma. Cruz Romeo, Pedro Ruíz Torres, Jorge Sánchez Fernández, Antoni Simón Tarrès, Ignaci Terradas and Ramón Villares. (I apologize in advance to any I may have inadvertently overlooked; a last-minute computer crash lost for ever the original list which I have had to recompile from memory).

I owe great thanks to Paloma Botella for her outstanding statistical work and to Carla and Blanca Marín's mathematical skills in elaborating demographic figures. Without Amparo Hinarejos, who classified and kept track of thousands of documents, the research effort would have ended in chaos.

Far exceeding an agent's normal duties, Rachel Calder saw this book through to publication for which I am truly grateful.

It has become almost an authorial platitude to thank wife and family for their support during the long years of researching and writing. In this case it is far from platitudinous. My wife, Aurora Bosch, patiently and lovingly supported long absences physical and mental over the past ten years and as a professional historian gave me invaluable advice. My son, Mark, in the antipodes, deprived himself of much needed sleep from his demanding work to read and criticize successive drafts; and my daughter, Jessica, provided me with some invaluable suggestions. To all I owe immense gratitude and love.

Foreword

Amid the vast compendium of histories of the Peninsular War, the appearance of yet another book requires some explanation. It would, of course, be vain to hope to add anything new to the overall map of this well-charted conflict; but within it one area has remained virtually unexplored: the unremitting popular Spanish resistance to Napoleon's attempted seizure of the Spanish homeland.

Over six long years in a nation still proud of its tradition as an age-old Catholic monarchy and defender of the true faith, the bloody struggle was unique in French-occupied countries. (Anti-Napoleonic revolts at different times in other largely Catholic areas – Naples, Sicily, the Tyrol – were by comparison minor, surmountable regional affairs. Even Napoleon's Russian disaster in 1812 owed more to snow and disease than to pitched battles and guerrilla resistance.) Elsewhere in Europe, however, local elites and populations accepted the French imperial system; but not in Spain, France's ally which Napoleon had treacherously invaded and where he had proceeded to depose its new young Bourbon king in favour of his own brother. Reaction to the emperor's attempt to take over the nation, unlike his policy in other defeated countries, aroused a popular Spanish resistance which continued unabated even during the two and a half years when Wellington did not once venture from Portugal into the Spanish interior.

It is sometimes forgotten today that the Peninsular War began in Spain over the nation's immediate destiny as France's ally. In 1808, both sides stumbled – Napoleon aggressively, the Spanish Old Regime's rulers more than reluctantly – into war. Neither expected an armed conflict and both shared a similar view of the necessary outcome should one occur: Spain would inevitably go down to defeat in the face of Napoleon's superior might. And so it would and should have been, had not the Spanish people risen in their country's defence and new patriotic governing bodies seized power from the old rulers; and had not Britain, eager to exploit an anti-Napoleonic struggle on France's southern flank, come to their aid.

From the resistance sprang a political revolution which deeply fissured, without destroying, Spain's Old Order, enunciating the principle of popular sovereignty and heralding the (male) population's entry into the political arena. It was Spain's first step into the modern era.

The causes and experience of the Spanish civilian resistance and revolution form the theme of this book. Its major concern is to elucidate the common people's initiatives and responses to the war while simultaneously taking account of their commoner superiors who initiated the anti-Napoleonic risings in 1808 and used them to seize regional power in the people's name; and among them those who carried the political revolution forward. In short, the book embarks on a social history from below of the resistance and an account of individuals' lived experience during the war.

This dual aim is the cause of some of the book's idiosyncrasies. In the first place, widespread illiteracy among the lower orders made for a scarcity of written sources, and even when these were discovered, they were of a fragmentary nature, difficult to generalize unless repeated in distinct places or regions. And their shard-like character also made it virtually impossible to follow the same individual through distinct experiences. Often I would have given an arm and a leg to have been able to interview a sample of the survivors; instead I was obliged to create new sources – frequently as databases, built out of the fragments – to explore important areas of the resistance and the social changes (or lack of them) that the war induced (or maintained alive).

In those aspects where the fragments were too few to create a new source, I preferred to array them in a mosaic of narrative detail rather than generalize on the basis of insufficient evidence. Some may object that I haven't seen the wood for the trees. I would reply that the trees *are* the wood (or more usually a copse) seen in close-up. If any readers get lost, they'll soon see on which side of the trunk the moss grows. At other times, however, where the specific conditions of a particular form of resistance – the guerrilla, for example – demanded it, the focus was widened beyond the trees to explain the geo-social and historical context in which they could grow. To those discomforted by the narrative break, I can say that these explanatory interludes may be passed over lightly without losing the general thread.

In the course of the book, a number of Spanish myths concerning the war are laid to rest. The 'spontaneity' of the initial popular risings; the uniform patriotism of all social classes; the lower orders' trust in their 'natural' superiors; even their voluntary commitment to the defence of their country. And much else, like the Church hierarchy's immediate and total commitment to the war against 'atheist' France; or the wealthy's financial support for the cause.

Some of these myths are themselves a Spanish historical legacy used for political ends: contemporary with events, in the first instance cited; and later, recycled in mid-nineteenth-century liberal attempts to create a modern nation around the myth of national unity in the war's 'glorious epic'; and again in the mid-twentieth century, to a diametrically opposed, and more sinister political purpose: the early Franco regime's constant invocation of popular resistance to a foreign aggressor (now communism, a judaic–masonic international conspiracy) in defence of Spain's 'eternal values': religion, the fatherland and the natural authority – a return to the absolutist monarch – of the dictator himself.

The reality of the war for the population in general was very different: death, illness, hunger, flight; suffering enemy razzias for food and contriving wily stratagems to prevent the loss; resistance and passivity; and fear, always fear: of all armies, French, British and Spanish; of marauding bandits in the guise of guerrillas; of a treacherous present and – should the French win – an uncertain future, bereft of tradition, altar and throne. In this flux of fears only one constant stood out: popular hatred of the repressive imperial occupation forces which thieved a living off the land (to which they had no alternative under Napoleon's dictum that war feeds war), laid waste to villages, vandalized churches and wantonly killed, nominally to support a usurper Bonaparte king.

*

While the book follows the war's chronological course, though avoiding all but the decisive battles, it will be immediately apparent that a great part is devoted to the first two years of the war, from the summer of 1808 to that of 1810. There is a good reason for this. In wars which unleash in self-defence a popular rising, revolutionary or not, that overthrows or nullifies the existing state apparatus, a power vacuum is opened up in the latter's place. For the struggle to continue this has to be filled and a new regime consolidate its power. But until it does, in the general chaos, all sorts of previously unexpected social and political opportunities are seized upon, whether in actions or words, that demonstrate the people's ideas and wishes formerly repressed either directly by the prior regime or through social conditioning (or more usually both). This is a fertile moment to study popular social realities which largely lay obscured in the immediate past; and which, once some sort of order is restored, tend to subside again into the undergrowth.

These first two years, moreover, were, until the starvation year of 1812, the most tormented of the war. They witnessed the multiform anti-Napoleonic risings and the popular resistance's early victories, followed by crushing military defeats at the hands of the *Grande Armée*, led by Napoleon himself; the worst hardships and the greatest population losses; the creation of a new patriot central power, and almost the largest territorial extent of French military occupation; the beginning of the South American colonial revolt; the decline of the Spanish armies' effective fighting strength; and the rise of the guerrilla. These events in themselves explain the need to devote a large part of the book to these two years.

For want of a better word, I have called *patriots* those who resisted Napoleon; it was the term they used of themselves. But their monopoly of the word is not historically justifiable: those Spaniards who supported Napoleon and the regime he installed in occupied Spain considered themselves equally, if not more, patriotic in their desire to avoid a fratricidal conflict which could only thwart the pursuit of much needed reform – a pursuit that the more progressive of the anti-Napoleonic resistance was also bent on. The clash of 'patriotisms' was but one of the many ironies of the Spanish war.

On a different terminological level, I use the word *villager* in place of – but also in a wider sense than – peasantry, while recognizing that the former is neither an accepted historical nor sociological category. There are two reasons for this: the foremost is the fact that Spanish landworkers never referred then (or now) to themselves or others as 'peasants', but always by the category of their relationship to the land (day labourer, sharecropper, tenant, and so on.) This is not to deny that Rodney Hilton's definition of the peasantry applied to them: 'those who possess but do not necessarily own their subsistence's means of production, and whose basic unit of work is the family. Day labourers and rural artisans are included in this definition. All are obliged by the dominant classes to produce a surplus over and beyond their subsistence and reproduction needs in order to sustain these classes'.* However, in using the alternative *villager* I wish to indicate a broader sense of the population of a village or rural township: an (inter-classist) community that includes, but goes beyond, the definition of peasantry, and which, despite its inner conflictivity, adopted certain common cultural attitudes which to no little extent shaped all those who lived in it, including the better off. In this extended meaning villagers can be read as the rural population.

Two other words will not be found in the book: 'bourgeoisie' and 'class'. The former did not enter the Spanish language until a great many years after the war and then only in a translation of a French work; and during the period under consideration here, the most that can be said is that a proto-bourgeoisie was in the process of forming. I preferred therefore not to use the word. As to 'class' in the modern sense, the word was unknown. Classes, on the other hand, meaning groups or kinds of people whose occupations (or lack of them) were broadly similar, was frequently used and I have followed this precedent.

For place names and proper names I have used the spelling of the time with two exceptions to make the book more readily comprehensible to the English-language reader. Regions' derivative names (which in Spanish can vary considerably from the original) have been left in an anglicized form (Galician, for example, instead of the formally correct Gallego). In place names, I have substituted the former initial 'X' for the 'J' in current Spanish usage (Jerez therefore instead of Xerez). For the rest, I believe that if today we can manage Beijing instead of Peking, it is surely not expecting too much of the reader to identify Zaragoza or Sevilla. (However, lest there be any doubt, Castilla la Vieja and Castilla la Nueva are Old and New Castile respectively).

Finally, to any reader who may come across the Spanish edition of this book, I should say that the two, while broadly the same, vary in their chapter structure – this edition combining a number of chapters into one – and more importantly in the extent of their exposition. This was because in the Spanish version I have included material which I believed would interest mainly or solely a Spanish readership.

---

* Hilton, *The English Peasantry in the Later Middle Ages*, Oxford, 1975, p. 13.

Prologue

Spain's Old Order on the Eve of the Napoleonic War

The six-year conflict, Spain's War of Independence (1808–1814) as it later came to be called, was deeply and inevitably conditioned from its outbreak by the ancien régime's social order; at the same time the war itself marked the first political rupture with that order. An overview of pre-war society may, in consequence, assist an understanding of the war and the issues involved.

ABSOLUTISM, CENTRALISM AND THE DISPERSION OF POWER

Like his forebears, Carlos IV was king by divine right but not – as his decrees' preambles made clear – King of Spain; he was the sovereign of the kingdoms of Castilla, León, Aragón, Valencia, Navarra, Count of Barcelona, Señor (Lord) of Vizcaya, Molina and a long *etc.* Seventy-five years of Bourbon centralism, culminating in the reformist absolutism of his father, Carlos III, had in other words not forged a legally unified Spanish kingdom. The map of Spain was a palimpsest of kingdoms, principalities and provinces, many of them with islands adrift in alien territories, where considerable differences (in such elementary matters as weights and measures, terms for money, not to speak of laws, customs and language) pertained.* This cartographical palimpsest can stand as a metaphor for the ancien régime's overlapping of functions and powers.

As in all Old Orders the king united in his being all legislative, executive and judicial powers. These could be delegated to a single person or a corporative body without distinguishing precisely between the different functions. The geo-political confusion was thus replicated in the overlapping administrative, judicial and political roles of the principal state institutions and official posts. As the highest organ of central government, the Consejo de Castilla, apart from

---

* Despite this territorial confusion, common to European feudalism, the thirty-one provinces into which Floridablanca, Carlos III's first minister, divided Spain in 1785, had by the end of the eighteenth century become the major administrative and taxation units, though by no means were they popularly accepted as defining place of origin or residence.

being a state consultative council, enjoyed executive, legislative and judicial powers.

At the regional or provincial level, this imbrication of powers was reproduced in the functions of the captain general who was as much a civilian as a military power. Supreme army commander of his region – though he did not necessarily lead his troops in time of war – he also presided over the audiencia in the supreme regional organ of civil power, the Real Acuerdo. Simultaneously a court of justice and a political administrative council, the audiencia's duties ranged from maintaining public order and food supplies to providing army recruits and soldiers' billeting, while the intendente, a civil servant appointed by the king, held a power parallel to the captain general's: this official controlled all treasury matters and local finances, but was also responsible for a wide spectrum of judicial, fiscal, political and economic matters, the latter especially in relation to military affairs.

This overlapping of powers, a legacy of medieval feudalism, served to maintain the social order. The role of the judiciary in the affairs of government, for example, created 'a formidable instrument at the service of political power,'[1] in other words, of the dominant social order: Church, nobility and state. In the eighteenth, as in earlier centuries, this unity of powers seemed quite natural, and it was their division, brought about by the American and French revolutions, which appeared 'an enormously artificial construction'.[2]

But it also blocked the state's centralizing aspirations. It was one thing for the crown to decree laws and another to see that these laws were put into effect. When they ran counter to the local oligarchy's interests they were quietly sabotaged. Despite the intendentes and state-appointed local corregidores, the monarchy lacked an adequate administrative machinery in the regions to back them up, and relied on local powers to carry out its orders. The result was a 'dispersion of power in a multiplicity of . . . hierarchies, each relatively auton-omous in relation to the crown, although subordinated to it as the supreme power'.[3]

Alongside the overlapping, there lay the clear legal demarcation of the social order. The organization of society by estates, each with its own laws, was hierarchical and distinctly defined. With the exception of the clergy, where there was choice, everyone else was born into a pre-existing estate. In real life things were more complex: by the eighteenth century belonging to an estate was often more a juridical than a functional matter, as the untitled nobility's situation demonstrated (see below).

Within the social structure there was also some movement. By the late eighteenth century a service nobility existed, created by the monarchs to reward special services to their persons or the state. Lower down the social scale, economic expansion in mid-century had created a stratum of the new wealthy: colonial shippers, señorial dues-farmers, government contractors, grain mer-chants, large land-leasing farmers, among whom some had become members of local oligarchies. Even more important for the political revolution that broke out in 1808, the basic tenets of a laissez-faire ideology had evolved in some important sectors of the enlightened classes.

Until the first decade of the nineteenth century, these internal social movements were of no immediate threat to the Old Order, for in this hierarchically organized society, nobility and Church played a dominant role. The Church was the more important of the two. Spaniards inhabited one of the oldest political units in Europe which had spanned almost identical borders since the early sixteenth century; if they had a collective identity it was that they shared the same religion. 'The whole of the ancien régime's legitimising discourse and the vigilant eyes of institutions such as the Inquisition had left a seemingly indelible Catholic legacy.'[4] Alongside allegiance to the crown, this religious identity, the sense of being defenders of the true faith, 'God's chosen people among gentiles', and the 'spiritual reserve of the West',[5] was without doubt the most important national foundation of a society which tended in general to look back on its heritage rather than forward to an innovatory future. Beyond these two national loyalties, at the popular level, there was little or no sense of belonging to more than a local community, or at most a region, which was hardly surprising given the poor communications and the lack of literacy.

The absolute monarchy rested then not only on the interlocking foundations of nobility and Church, but more widely on acceptance of their leading role in society. *Status* (of the individual as member of a recognized grouping) and *stasis* (of the social formation) were two essential characteristics of this patrimonial society. The weakness of absolutism, its insufficient centralization and bureaucracy to bypass provincial powers and popular local loyalties would, paradoxically, turn out to provide much of the country's strength in fighting Napoleon.

THE CHURCH

As the sole effective national institution, the Church did its utmost to ensure that everyone accepted his or her place in the hierarchical order of things: in educating the young and in sermons and private admonitions, it stressed the obligation of submission and obedience to authority and each individual was instructed to observe 'the obligations which correspond to his estate and occupation.' At the ideological level it controlled the expression of ideas and personal and social behaviour – a role in which the Inquisition, as guardian of orthodoxy and morality, and as ecclesiastical censor, was widely involved: here the Holy Tribunal's secrecy and its capacity to destroy a person's life – if not literally, then morally and financially – created 'a pervasive psychology of fear' which gave the Inquisition its special power;[6] and lastly, in the Church's function of administering public charity through its management of beneficial foundations. The clergy was well-placed for these tasks because its leading role in society was uncontested, and at times of calamity unfailingly predominated. 'Drought, hail, frosts, infestations, the saving of life itself in times of scarcity or illness – the Church was always called upon.'[7]

The Church was a state within the state, the monarchy's single wealthiest institution, with its own judicial and tax-raising system, the latter generally more efficient than the state's. Its total annual income, in mid-eighteenth century, has been calculated at just over 450 million reales per annum or one-fifth of gross domestic income. Its lands in the kingdom of Castilla* produced one-quarter of all produce, it received nearly three-quarters of all mortgage interest and almost half the dues from feudal rights, tithes and rent on land and urban property; it was an urban Church living off the land, in which it had invested heavily in the eighteenth century at prices it could easily afford but which were too expensive for the ordinary villager: clerics were well aware of the land's profitability at a time of inflationary agricultural prices.† The Church's economic weight in the kingdom of Castilla, 'bore down on the population with relentless uniformity'.[8] But as a territorial organization it was no more uniform than the monarchy itself, a palimpsest of historical accretion: Madrid, capital of a world empire and with a population of nearly 200,000, did not have episcopal status or a cathedral, while a township like Sigüenza, with 4,000 inhabitants, was one of Spain's richest dioceses.[9] Unequal diocesan divisions resulted in an institutional multiformity and an uneven distribution of ecclesiastical wealth: prelates took seventy percent of tithes and parish priests, who were the Church's loyal tax-collector, eleven percent on which they had to live and keep up their church. Many rural priests were often so poor that they had to have recourse to their parishioners.

Unlike eighteenth-century France, the Church was not the preserve of the upper nobility. High ecclesiastical office tended to be filled by university-educated commoners or untitled nobles – many of them reform-minded prelates – in the same way as the royal administration; while at its lower levels it was an avenue of social ascent for the labouring classes' sons. Although the clergy numbered in 1787 just under 134,000 or about 1.3% of the total population, of the 60,000 ordained priests only approximately one-quarter served as parish rectors or curates. This left over 2,000 of the country's 19,000 parishes without spiritual assistance.

The intellectual and spiritual level of parish priests varied from the virtually uneducated to the enlightened. The vicar of Ciudad Real reported that in his district 'many priests were to be found who were so stupefied and ignorant that it was a triumph for them to understand the canon of the Mass'. In the isolated Andalucian vicarates of Huéscar and Cazorla priests were found living with their mistresses, gambling and hunting, engaged in smuggling, and some who refused to wear clerical dress when they performed their sacerdotal duties.[10]

On the other hand, there were those who 'identified with the interests of their flocks . . . [and] defended the poor against the powerful and the señores'. This was certainly the case of some Andalucian parish priests who were among the leaders of their municipal councils' legal battle over their señorial lords' usurpation of village lands.[11]

In addition to the secular clergy, the religious orders had just under 40,000 monks, friars and novices in 2,000 houses; and just over 24,000 nuns and novices

---

* The two Castillas, Andalucía, Extremadura, Galicia and Murcia.
† By comparison the pre-revolutionary French Church held between six and ten percent of the land. (Michel Vovelle, *Introducción a la historia de la Revolución francesa*, trans. Barcelona, 1981, p. 12.)

in 1,000 convents. The majority of the male orders were mendicants (monks represented only one-tenth of the orders' numbers); and because urban centres provided the easiest pickings for alms the friars, alongside the ordinary clergy, were concentrated in towns and cities.* In Sevilla the religious orders outnumbered the secular priesthood, alone providing 1,600 members for the great religious processions.[12]

Like the secular, the regular clergy presented a gamut running from 'ignorance and superstition' to spirituality and erudition. A well-educated elite held high office, presiding over a large body of friars whose 'intellectual quality and religious commitment left much to be desired'.[13] Some friaries and convents were in a state that left more than something to be desired, as the diocesan visitor sent to inspect the Dominicans in Villanueva de los Infantes, a small township in the Mancha, reported.

> The nuns and friars mingle daily together for indecent purposes, from which vile coitus two children have resulted . . . I saw with my own eyes the nuns leaving their convent at night and making for the friary. And in the daytime, the friars scandalously entering into the enclosed convent.[14]

However unruly the behaviour of a minority, most friars and parish priests enjoyed the lower orders' respect. Great numbers of them were recruited from the same social strata; and if their religious observances did not meet the Church's highest demands, the same could be said of the majority of their flock who evinced a common trait, 'ignorance, and an evident superficiality of theological knowledge, a defect which made it easy to fall into superstitious practices far removed from religious rectitude'.[15]

In its determination to control all aspects of society, including the ecclesiastical estate, Bourbon absolutism had wrested from an ineffectual papacy the right to appoint Spain's bishops, and it ensured that a number of enlightened clerics were put in place. These were generally in favour of expanding royal intervention in Church affairs in order to secure the reforms they believed necessary because the state alone had the authority to confront Rome and deeply entrenched religious customs in Spain. These enlightened reformers and their lay supporters were, by the late 1780s, opposed to the religious orders, the Inquisition, and papal temporal authority over the Spanish Church. They believed in a personal, more interior religion, in 'knowledge of the religious truth, and in the practice of a simple liturgy'.[16] They were as hostile to superstitious 'popular' devotions as they were to the extravagances of the official cult. One of their earliest and greatest achievements, no doubt, was to secure the Inquisition's agreement to the Bible being read in the vernacular, though this met strong opposition from ultramontane members of the clergy.

The Inquisition was a state within the ecclesiastical state, but also a power within the temporal state. Under Carlos III it was, however, a power in decline.

---

* Unlike the friaries, many monasteries were in the countryside and exercised ecclesiastical lordship over surrounding villages. Their oppressive reputation seemed frequently worse than that of secular lords.

After exiling one inquisitor general for obeying Rome rather than the monarchy, Carlos III appointed an enlightened bishop to the post. In 1782, the latter admitted that fear of the Inquisition's censorship, now regulated by the state, was 'nearly extinct'. But this did not prevent the Inquisition from banning virtually the entire range of foreign enlightened thought, from Montesquieu to Rousseau, Voltaire to Diderot, Adam Smith (*The Wealth of Nations*) to Defoe's *Robinson Crusoe*. The Inquisition's proscription, however, did not thwart the enlightened securing and reading clandestinely these authors' works in the original. What it did, rather, was to prevent their translation and publication in Spanish.[17]

But the Holy Office's structure – permanent tribunals in the different regions, inquisitors, prisons, *familiares* (lay informers and inquisitorial police force) – remained in place. The Inquisition, with its long history, was arguably a more centralized and effective power for repression than the state itself. And, as always in the past, it could be called upon in defence of the state.

The central role allotted to the Holy Office by the government during the panic of the French Revolution reinforced the threat that hung over Spaniards' heads, and many at all levels of society – from government ministers to obscure parish priests – would suffer the attentions already recently known to others. On being charged in 1797 by the Valladolid tribunal for possessing proscribed works, Juan Antonio Posse, a young rural curate in a remote mountain village of León, believed himself 'doomed'. Before setting off, he hid with great difficulty under rocks on the roadside the works of Pedro Tamburini – 'the Inquisition's most formidable opponent' – taking with him only a relatively harmless dissertation by the Italian professor, whose enlightened Catholicism was the pole star of Spanish Catholic reformers.

> I knew only too well the conduct of this *Holy* Tribunal and of its satellites who, excited by the most frenzied superstition, persecuted without moderation, examination or formality [those who had spoken] indiscrete words or other trifles . . .

The tribunal commissioner, who appeared not to know of Tamburini, demanded the forbidden works. Posse gave him the dissertation. The commissioner looked at its cover, read his orders, and told the curate that he must hand it over. 'Happy to make the sacrifice and to be freed of this henchman's claws, I left.'*

Posse, a Galician smallholder's son, was fortunate; though other prisons awaited him later in life, he would not see the inside of an Inquisitorial prison.

*

There were two important consequences of the Church reform movement. The most significant was that the reformers believed that the forces opposed to change were too strong to overcome without state intervention. This discouraged

---

* He was denounced to the Inquisition by a clerical colleague to whom he had made an outspoken comment against the Holy Office for having proscribed Tamburini's works (Posse, 1984, p. 69).

reforming self-reliance within the Church, and encouraged a too-ready dependence on state legislation. The imbrication of the state in the Church's internal affairs led opponents of eccelesiastical reform to lay the blame on the state – or rather the state's political structure – at crucial moments of shaping a new constitutional monarchy during the war. Opposition to Church reform – especially, but not solely, the Inquisition's abolition – reinforced clerical resistance to political change.

The second consequence was that many university students who, as adults, took part in the war were exposed to – and espoused – the reform movement, particularly at Salamanca university where the curriculum had, after long resistance, been finally modernized. The trajectories of many of these reformers during the war would criss-cross one another's as some stayed loyal to the patriot cause and others served the Bonaparte regime. The conflict tragically split the enlightened, young and old, as it split the governance of Spain in what, effectively, became a civil war within the larger Napoleonic war.

THE NOBILITY AND THE FEUDAL LAND SYSTEM

With one important exception, that of the army officer corps (see below), the Spanish Bourbons excluded the aristocracy from any dominant role in the affairs of state. Unlike in France, by the end of the eighteenth century the old Spanish titled nobility had lost most of its political influence, which had fallen into the hands of commoners and minor untitled nobles.[18] Nonetheless, the nobility was the essential vertebra of the social order and its apex. By its status alone, the aristocracy enjoyed honour, dignity, esteem. 'To be a noble was the secret ambition of every Spaniard.'[19]

In 1797, according to the not always very reliable Godoy census, the 'nobility' numbered just over 400,000; but of these only 1,323 were titled nobles. The remainder were hidalgos – the children or descendants of those who claimed nobility. As the entire Basque-born male population of Vizcaya and Guipúzcoa claimed *hidalguía*, just over 100,000 hidalgos were to be found in those two provinces alone;* and, for historical reasons, a very large proportion of the remainder also lived in the other northern regions where their way of life was often virtually indistinguishable from the lower orders. South of Madrid, however, their numbers fell sharply, they tended to own land and their social status was higher.

The fact that hidalgos could be found in every walk of life did not mean that they were an insignificant social grouping. On the contrary, in their educated middle and upper echelons, they represented an important – arguably indeed one of the most important – strata of Spanish society. They were a working nobility and their very numbers, especially in the north, made them a large

---

* Whereas in England, a noble's children were legally commoners, in Spain, as in France, they were legally nobles. The Basque claim to 'universal hidalguía' was based on the notion that, never having been conquered by the Muslims, all native-born Basques could trace their descendancy without 'contamination' of Muslim or Jewish 'blood' back to noble Basque Houses.

pool of potential recruits to a series of positions and professions. From their ranks came high government officials and prelates, merchants and bankers, lawyers and writers, and virtually all army and naval officers, since hidalguía was a condition of entrance to the military colleges. In the regions their wealthier members, who were usually medium-sized landowners, often with an entailed estate, were almost always to be found among the local elite. In Galicia, for example, though relatively few in number, they *were* the elite.

It was, however, the titled nobility, especially the thirty or so grandees, who were the large landowners and principal *señores*.* Thanks to strategic marriages and fortuitous inheritances, the magnates had become a national, inter-related nobility with domains in different parts of the country. Even so, this tight-knit aristocratic grouping had no real political coherence, some of its members' only desire being to enjoy once again a determining role in the country's government.

How much land the titled nobility owned has never been satisfactorily calculated,† and for a reason: their predominance rested not solely on their own landholdings but as much on a feudal structure for extracting the surplus of those who tilled land which the señores did not own. It was yet another case of overlapping rights; the system was known as *señorial* and the lands and rural municipalities over which it was exercised a *señorío*.

In the main, the system's widespread usage arose from bankrupt Hapsburg monarchs, the Bourbon's predecessors who, to raise money, sold their jurisdictional rights to crown property; these covered the exercise of justice – including on occasion capital punishment – and local administration under the royal prerogative of appointing magistrates and town councils in crown domains. Apart from these, the monarchy also sold its feudal dues and rents, which could include a part of the crown's taxes (and not infrequently a portion of tithes), its rights to levy tributes and tolls and to exercise monopolistic feudal privileges over mills, bakeries, smithies, even brothels and, of course, hunting rights. But the monarchs did not sell the land itself.

Though for historically distinct reasons señoríos, notably in Andalucía and Cataluña, included landownership, the vast majority were jurisdictional only. While the titled nobility occupied the largest single number of these lordships, the Church, monasteries and military orders also exercised and profited from them. In Spain as a whole these different types of señoríos outnumbered royal domains.‡

---

* Grandee was Spain's highest noble distinction after that of infante, which was reserved exclusively for the monarch's children. Although most usually awarded to a duke, persons of lesser or even no title could be raised to grandee.

† By way of an approximate order of comparison, the English peerage in 1790 numbered about 135 individuals (excluding baronetcies but including peeresses) out of a population of approximately nine million, and owned of the order of seventy to seventy-five percent of the land. The French aristocracy, totalling perhaps 230,000 (just under one percent of a population of 28 millions), owned not more than thirty percent of the land.

‡ Compared to the crown's 11,921, there were, according to the 1797 Census, 8,681 secular *señoríos*, 2,591 belonging to the Church, 1,325 to monasteries, and 712 to the military orders. The heaviest concentrations of señoríos were in the two Castillas, Galicia, Extremadura, western Andalucía and Valencia (Anes, 1976, p. 58).

By the end of the eighteenth century it was estimated that more than one-quarter of the Spanish population and over sixty-five percent of cultivated land was under secular and ecclesiastical señorial rule.[20] Another estimate had it that nine-tenths of all wheat on the market, which in normal times kept the urban population in bread, came from noble and ecclesiastical señorial rights, rents and tithes extracted in kind from those who worked the land.[21]

Throughout the second half of the eighteenth century, the increasing belligerence of municipalities which challenged the lord's legal rights led to court cases that could and did drag on for generations, to the señores' considerable cost. Though townships and villages usually lost in the end, unchallengeable ownership became a matter of importance to the nobility. During the Napoleonic war, it was to no small extent this material interest which kept most of the latter – and other would-be landowners – aligned with the patriot reformers, who wanted to introduce a free market in land. The more aware nobles were prepared to exchange their constantly contested señorial rights for a more profitable and less troublesome ownership; and this, as will be seen in the book, they achieved when, under certain conditions, the Cortes of Cádiz turned señores into outright landowners.

With very rare exceptions, the grandees did not invest in new agrarian methods to increase agricultural productivity on their estates. The money went on sumptuary spending, especially in maintaining vast numbers of retainers, or at best – if the Dukes of Medinaceli and Infantado were representative – into reorganizing and centralizing estate administrations to make them more efficient to ensure that they benefited from rising agrarian prices.[22]

Agriculture progress in the kingdom of Castilla was further blocked by the nobility's use – the Church had its own variant (mortmain) – of the legal artifice of entailment to protect their holdings from being squandered by indebted heirs. The entailed secular estate (*mayorazgo*) was indivisible, inalienable and not liable for debt, and inheritable exclusively by the oldest son.* More importantly from the agricultural point of view, the entail could not legally be let on long leases, thus making the improvement of the land of no interest to tenants. And since it could also not be sold, the mayorazgo was especially galling at a time of land hunger at the turn of the century, and was generally criticized as leaving the estates poorly farmed. To Floridablanca, the reforming first minister, entail was 'a seminary of idleness'.†[23]

* It was the equivalent of the English 'strict settlement' which was one of the factors in the rise of the great British landed estates. (Cannon, 1995, p. 71.) In the kingdom of Castilla, where partible inheritance was the custom, it had the effect of creating the right of male primogeniture.

† In Castilla la Vieja, for example, the eighteenth-century dispossesion of smallholders and tenants in favour of noble and Church entailed estates, with the consequent increase of rents and taxes on remaining tenants, short leases and the state's increasing fiscal pressure, took from tenants a higher proportion of their surplus than in the sixteenth century but left agricultural output at little above the levels of the expansionary second half of the 1500s. In the later nineteenth century, with hardly any intervening agrarian technological advances since the previous century, but under a capitalist rather than a señorial system, agrarian production in Castilla la Vieja more than kept pace with the growth in population. (Alberto Marcos Martín, 'El mundo rural castellano del siglo XVIII a la luz de algunos estudios recientes' in VV.AA. Madrid, 1990, (1),pp. 981–996.)

Each municipality also had large tracts of commons which could not in principle be sold. Estimates of the total amount of inalienable land varied from half of the entire territory of Spain (of which only forty percent was arable) to sixty percent of the country's productive land.[24]

Finally, one further point about landownership needs to be made. The question of who owned the land was not always as relevant as that of who controlled and benefited from it. One reason for this was again an overlapping of rights: title to the land and its hereditary use could be vested in distinct individuals (or corporative bodies, in the case of title-holders). In a wide swathe of northern Spain stretching from Galicia and parts of Castilla la Vieja through the Basque country, Navarra and Aragón to Cataluña, different forms of hereditary leases were common, with the result that tenants felt themselves to be 'owners' of the land they worked. During the war, the sense of protecting their own 'property' became an important factor in fomenting popular resistance, especially the guerrillas.

THE ARMY – PRESERVE OF THE NOBLES

[The standing army had] a corps of generals sufficient to command all the armies of the world and who, if they had the soldiers, could conquer all the regions of the Universe; a multitude of regiments short of men though hardened veterans in the fatigues of curling their hair, whitening their uniforms with flour, marching like dancers in a quadrille; wasting powder in salvos in the meadows, and serving to oppress their fellow citizens. (León de Arroyal, 'Pan y Toros', 1793)[25]

The most acerbic critic of Spain's Old Order in the eighteenth century's last decade, Arroyal's irony undershot the mark: the army's situation was more critical than he perceived. Many of its failings were the outcome of social and political decisions which, uncorrected, still affected it at the beginning of the Napoleonic war. Absorbing (with the navy) seventy percent of the royal budget,[26] one of the fateful practices originated by the early Bourbons, who needed the nobility's support, was to turn the officer corps into the latter's preserve, restoring the nobility to their original feudal status as the 'sword' of the realm. This process grew so intense during the latter part of the eighteenth century that the corps became exclusively noble in character, 'turned in on itself', a typical feudal social pyramid: at the base, the soldiery made up of the lowest of commoners, a middle stratum of hidalgo officers, and an apex of titled nobility who dominated the top commands.*

Since social status counted for more than professionalism and personal valour, and promotion was by seniority and normally slow, the officer corps' average age was high: sixty-one for colonels, fifty-nine for captains and fifty-eight for lieutenants.[27] These were hardly likely to be innovative officers; and with a few outstanding exceptions, they were not well trained in the art of war.

---

* The few commoners who rose from the ranks rarely reached higher than lieutenant; at the turn of the century less than five percent of captains were of non-noble birth, and no lieutenant-colonel or higher was of commoner origin.

The second Bourbon innovation was to turn officers into all-powerful political functionaries as the supreme military and civil authority of regions and provinces. Almost inevitably the higher echelons of the officer corps became 'politicized' as they were called upon by different court factions to support their power struggles. Promotion was the usual form of reward for support. The army became top-heavy with officers: one for every twenty men, twice the number of the Prussian army. (Only the pre-revolutionary French army exceeded the Spanish figure: one officer to every sixteen men.[28]) In the four years from the start of Spain's war against the French Revolution (1793–1795), the royal favourite, Manuel Godoy, increased the number of generals by nearly sixty percent, one for every 290 other ranks – or two generals per infantry battalion.[29]

The late eighteenth-century reformers, more concerned about the state of the treasury than the military, whose political power they had, moreover, come to fear, compounded the problems. They had not planned on an army to fight in peninsular Spain. The main enemy, Britain, was a *naval*, not land, power; neighbouring France, with a large army, was an ally; Portugal represented no military threat. The role of Spain's regular army was conceived of as defending the colonies, *in situ* or as an ancillary of the navy which was the first priority. The 30,000-strong militias were thought sufficient to defend metropolitan Spain.[30]

Manning a standing army at least cost to the treasury was another problem. Volunteers and the levies of vagrants, vagabonds, beggars and the like, who were periodically cleared from the major towns and condemned to serve, proved insufficient. Obligatory military service for one in five of the able male population, decreed in 1770, was highly unpopular and generally ineffective in raising the standard of recruit, since those in danger of being selected by lot 'absented' themselves from their villages or, if chosen, could pay another to serve in their place; in either case it was the poorest, least able villagers who were conscripted. There was a constant shortage of men.* Unsurprisingly, the proportion of Spanish military to the civilian population was below the European average and significantly lower than Prussia, Austria and even Russia.†

A soldier's life was harsh in the extreme: subject to very severe discipline, poorly paid (when paid at all), always hungry on meagre rations, wearing tattered uniforms that had worn out before their allotted time; it was little wonder that, as the Inspector of Infantry wrote at the beginning of 1802, many rankers deserted,‡ or committed crimes and acts of indiscipline 'with the premeditated idea of improving their lot in penal servitude'.[31]

---

* After 1784, there was an annual shortfall of 17,500 men for a standing army of 59,000, which meant that only six of the forty-one line regiments could muster the two battalions laid down as the military norm; and a number of foreign mercenary regiments had to be disbanded for lack of volunteers. (Esdaile, 1998, p. 14.) The army's numbers on paper, moreover, hardly ever corresponded to its fighting strength.

† The Spanish proportion was 1:160; Prussia, 1:29; Austria, 1:96, and Russia, 1:120. (Roura i Aulinas, 1993, p. 157.)

‡ Between 1797 and 1801, the desertion rate in Spanish infantry regiments increased from five percent of the total infantry strength to over nine percent. Deserters outnumbered fatal casualties in the same period by thirteen percent. (Andújar Castillo, 1991, pp. 93 and Table 1, p. 94.)

In attempting to maintain a larger standing army than Spain's economic resources could adequately equip and maintain, the army declined seriously in quality in the last quarter of the eighteenth century.[32] Over and above officers' low level of technical instruction and recruitment problems lay the profound contradiction of a professional army organized in its chain of command on feudal social lines which bore no relation to the functions to be carried out.[33]

A secondary, but highly important effect of enlightened military policy with its colonial–naval and cost-cutting emphases, was the reduction of the cavalry's role: only dragoons, still considered mounted infantry in Spain, and thus able to fight on foot, were valued.* The Spanish patriots went into the Napoleonic war desperately short of cavalry, especially of the light cavalry which Napoleon used to such effect as the advance screen of his armies, while the lack of well-trained heavy cavalry more than once turned their disadvantage into staggering defeats by Napoleon's generals.

In time of war, there was no general staff to plan campaigns – though such had existed in France since 1763;[34] and the army had no baggage train of its own but had to hire (or commandeer) mules, carts and their drivers (if any of these scarce items were to be had) from villagers or contractors. In short, before a field army could move considerable time was taken in resolving administrative and logistic problems.

The War of the Convention against revolutionary France revealed these failures.† The army's humiliation brought on an identity crisis among officers who, on the one hand, had admired the French army with which some had trained and alongside which others had fought as allies while, on the other hand, intensely hating the revolutionary ideals that had come to inform it. Their accepted view of the world had been overturned: yesterday's allies, the French, were today's enemy, and the former enemy (Britain) now an ally.[35] In 1808, they had again to confront such fundamental and disorientating changes. Given their state, the Spanish officer corps in general went through the Napoleonic war 'without being able to understand or support either the new strategy of mass warfare or the tactics of guerrilla warfare. They had been trained for very different suppositions than those it was their lot to live through.'[36]

With an officer corps like this, it was hardly to be wondered at that so many of the new recruits who had enthusiastically enlisted to fight Napoleon deserted or took up the struggle on their own as guerrillas.

SPANISH ENLIGHTENMENT AND LIBERALIZATION

The Bourbons' determination to reform and return Spain to a position of power in the world, necessary to strengthen the state and defend its colonial empire, led them to appoint enlightened men to their bureaucracy who tried to put into governmental practice the lessons of 'reason' learnt from France and elsewhere. Thus, many of the major figures of the Spanish Enlightenment from mid-century

---

* Horse-breeding had been neglected from mid-eighteenth century in Spain by the adoption of the mule as the main source of animal traction and transport, used even by the nobility and wealthy to draw their carriages.
† See Chapter 1, pp. 19–24.

on were high state functionaries.* The questions they raised on how best to develop the country, and on the individual's rights, continued to reverberate throughout the Napoleonic era.

One of the main questions posed by these reformers was a question still familiar today. To what extent should the state regulate the lives and activities of its subjects in the interests of their 'felicity' (i.e. well-being) and the country's economic progress? To the early reformers of Carlos III in the 1760s and 1770s, exemplified by Campomanes, the Consejo de Castilla's attorney, there was no doubt: they believed they could – indeed, had to – use the absolute monarchy to reform the absolutist state without undermining its bases. A series of gradualist reforms were put in hand to free Spain of the 'obstacles' to progress.† The thinking behind them, however, was state 'productivism' rather than a generalized opening up to 'free enterprise'. It was a case of using certain market mechanisms for the benefit of the state, and, not least, that of the treasury. But the reforms did not have the desired effect.

Within twenty years, the earlier strategy was radically challenged by some of the second 'generation' of enlightened thinkers, most notably by Gaspar Melchor Jovellanos. Under the influence of Locke and Adam Smith, among others, Jovellanos came to believe that 'the first objective of social laws' must always be 'to protect the individual's interests', which were the stimulus to progress and the source of a nation's wealth. By denying self-interest and relying on government laws and regulations, the earlier reformers had put the cart before the horse. Each citizen must be 'independent and free in his actions, as long as these do not contradict the law', and each citizen must be 'equal in the eyes of the law and have the same right to enjoy its protection'.[37] Taking these views to their logical conclusion became one of the progressives' ideological aims during the war. But Jovellanos, an admirer of England's constitutional monarchy, blended reform with monarchic traditionalism;‡ and in this mix, it could be said, he more closely represented popular wartime sentiment than that of the third generation whose progressives believed in a political rupture with the past since in their view the major obstacle to Spain's advance was absolutism itself.

* This was not to say that Spain's Enlightenment did not have its own trajectory and 'generational' differences. Those born around 1720 – most notably Floridablanca and Campomanes – formed the generation of Carlos III's reforming politicians. Those born in mid-century, men like Gaspar Melchor Jovellanos, usually considered the Spanish Enlightenment's supreme representative. And finally those born around 1770 – Manuel Quintana, Rev. José María Blanco, and the free-thinking cleric José Marchena to name but these – who participated in the Napoleonic war on one side or the other and represented the change not only from the eighteenth to the nineteenth centuries but from 'one Spain to another'. (Domínguez Ortiz, 1984, p. 477.)

† These included abolishing state or municipal intervention in fixing grain prices – thus ending the past three centuries' custom of subsidizing bread – and in determining wages and tenancy contracts. Equally, if not more, significant was the proposal to rent plots of municipal commons annually to the rural landless with a sufficient number of draught animals to till them, a proposal that local oligarchies in general managed to obviate.

‡ He was, for example, largely responsible for fostering the myth that the 'fundamental laws' of medieval Spain had stood guarantor of the country's traditional liberties and 'general will' through the power shared in the Cortes by the three estates with the king. What was needed to guarantee these liberties anew, he believed, was a return to those laws which absolutism had eviscerated.

This last generation came of political age with the French Revolution and the enthronement of Carlos IV in Spain; 'unquiet spirits' like the poet Manuel Quintana and the clerical free-thinker, José Marchena – later to confront each other as the early 'ideologues' on either side of the Napoleonic war – owed much to their immediate forebears. As the son of the Enlightenment Quintana was perfectly aware of what he owed to its great French thinkers. But he refused, like many others, to embrace France because of it: Spain had her own great past which would, in political and civilian matters, reassert 'the place nature has assigned to our character and circumstances'.

Quintana, and others of his generation, took the social commitment of their elders' literary output and radicalized their thinking: they saw their country as presently subjugated to a 'despotic', absolutist royal favourite, Godoy, and as a result their fatherland reduced to a 'deathly counterfeit';[38] they translated their elders' economic liberalization into *national* as well as individual liberty from 'tyrannical' oppression; and they set themselves the literary task of awakening educated people.*

The progressives believed that 'the people's freedom, the good of the fatherland, is the first law'.[39] And that the people themselves must be those who put into effect and carried out this law as the only guarantee that the 'general will' would prevail. They believed Spain needed a constitution to secure individual liberties (not least freedom from the Inquisition's censorship), and to end the arbitrary use of absolutist state power. The 'general will', as will be seen in the book, found its ultimate conclusion during the war in the adoption of national sovereignty by the first liberals of the modern political era.

MONIED COMMONERS

The wholesale merchant classes, who numbered little more than 6,000, a miniscule total in comparison to Britain or France at the time, were among the richest commoners; and, alongside those of Madrid, the large colonial merchants in the Atlantic and Mediterranean ports were the wealthiest of these. Before the Napoleonic wars, the Spanish trade monopoly with its colonies had been highly profitable; and these merchants did not seriously question the Old Order. Their single greatest number was to be found in Cádiz, the top ten percent of whom had fortunes of more than fifteen million reales each.† Madrid

---

* A patriot *avant la lettre*, Quintana used his poetry and drama for ideological and political ends as no other Spanish poet of the period. His ode to Juan de Padilla, leader of the Castilian *comuneros'* sixteenth-century revolt against Carlos I, the first Hapsburg on the Spanish throne, was a paean to the fatherland's virtues and an indignant denunciation of 'the infamous yoke' that was presently oppressing 'a strong and generous people'; and his subsequent play *Pelayo*, about the eighth-century Visigoth monarch who initiated the 700-year-long Catholic reconquest of Spain from its Muslim occupiers, reminded his reading public of a heroic and glorious fatherland that rejected foreign domination, imposed monarchs and absolutism.
† A sample of thirty-one Sevillian nobles (none of them of the great houses, for sure) averaged one million reales each, without taking account of their entailed estates. (See Álvarez Santaló, 1988–1989, vol. 7, 'Economía y sociedad', pp. 252–254.)

merchants were probably the second wealthiest, although only the top five percent owned assets of more than ten million reales.[40] However, even many of the lesser merchants, as in Valencia, had accumulated 700,000 reales – to earn which a journeyman in the building trade would have had to work 350 years uninterruptedly without spending a real – in little more than a single generation, and in some cases from barely any starting capital.[41]

The richest Cádiz and Sevilla merchants were not inclined to invest in manufacturing ventures. The 'lethargic' uses to which their capital was put pointed to 'an unambitious mentality, a low level of cultural concern and social dynamism. We do not find here the revolutionary bourgeois of other latitudes.'[42] Whether they were aware of it or not – and the indications are that they were not – their refusal to invest in industrial enterprises was a defence of the Old Regime for it obviated the risk of creating new social productive forces which would enter into contradiction with the existing order.[43] And so, once their fortunes were made, they tended to petition the king to be ennobled: self-made wealth was insufficient. They shared the assumptions of the rest of society: ennoblement meant social status.*

The dominance of colonial trade favoured the maritime regions, producing an uneven development in relation to the interior, with the exception of Madrid. This imbalance, however, became of strategic importance during the war: until the French slowly reduced most of the ports, their merchants' capital helped to keep the armed resistance afloat and, though often protesting at the sums of money the patriot authorities demanded of them, they supported the war effort in the hope that the conflict would end soon in order for them to renew colonial commerce. They realized, moreover, that a Bonapartist victory would end their monopolistic control of the trade, opening it to rival French houses. Their objective then was for political stability, peace and good trading conditions, in a reformed Spain independent of alliances which inevitably led to war. In Cádiz, besieged but never conquered, the merchants not only ran patriot government finances for a period but they cashed in their wealth as political leverage during the government's long residence there.

Earlier in the century some merchants in Cataluña, Valencia and the Basque country had taken a step to proto-industrialization and organized 'putting-out' systems. Valencian silk, Viscayan iron, Catalan wool production were organized in this way. But the introduction of cottons opened up new domestic markets by replacing more expensive forms of woollen clothing, especially for the rural population which in the second half of the century was having to spend a greater part of its exiguous income on food; and it was Catalan merchants who took advantage of the demand, launching Cataluña on the path of industrialization.† By the end of the eighteenth century, possibly as many as 100,000

---

* Ennoblement did not necessarily mean becoming a titled noble, but more usually ascending to the nobility's lowest rungs – *hidalgo, ciudadano honrado* (honorable burgess), *caballero* (knight).
† Catalan industrialization stemmed from a particular agrarian and social complex in which large farmers who had won from their señores the virtually perpetual rights to the use of the land, usually more than they themselves could farm, introduced intensive agriculture on their good land and share-cropped their less fertile hillside /*cont'd over*

workers were employed in 3,000 Catalan cotton factories.[44] Of particular social importance was the fact that women – and children – now became industrial workers alongside men. Women's right to work as spinners 'and in all those trades compatible with their decorum and the physical strength of their sex' was recognized and extended to the whole of Spain in 1784.

POOR COMMONERS: THE URBAN LABOURING CLASSES

Three-quarters of the urban lower orders were poor, and at times of economic or agrarian crisis, poverty – if not outright destitution – extended to half the Spanish population.* From the mid-1780s, urban workers' wages or takings lagged far behind inflation: between 1786 and 1800 a Madrid building labourer's wages rose approximately one-fifth; the price of bread, the major staple in the poor's diet, more than doubled in the same period. At the end of the century the unmarried labourer could just manage to remain above absolute impoverishment; the really hard hit were married labourers with two children.[45] Only in Barcelona where the increase of cotton manufacture exceeded that of the population's growth, did wage rises keep rough pace with inflation.

The poor lived in cramped quarters within the cities' old walls. The doubling in size of the urban population under the flood of dispossed landworkers, and new proletarians in Barcelona's case, did not lead to an increase in urban centres' housing: simply twice as many people were crammed into them as at the beginning of the century. In Madrid, an average of thirty-three people lived to a house, a number higher than in Paris after the Napoleonic wars. Most of the poor lodged in narrow, sunless, evil-smelling streets, in a single basement or attic room with little ventilation and light, no sanitation, heating or fireplace. Cooking was done in one corner, on a fire built of bricks, and smoke filled the room where a whole family lived; in basements residual water often ran on the floor, creating an unbreathable foetid atmosphere. Garbage, urine and excrement were thrown out on the street.[46] Madrid was known as one of the filthiest capitals of Europe.

---

cont'd| or scrub land with landless labourers, small peasants and rural artisans, usually to grow vines. Much of the new wine produced was of low quality but was distilled into spirits which soon found a market in the colonies and abroad. Although the señores creamed off a part of the profits, the large peasantry's intensive farming and exploitation of a rural proletariat and smallholders, generated a wealth which 'in the hands of a small nobility, that did not despise profitable speculation, and of an entrepreneurial bourgeoisie', was turned into capital that was invested in 'the most diverse activities from early on'. (Fontana, 1988, p. 90.)

* Impoverishment increased generally in pre-industrial Europe at the end of the eighteenth century; it has been estimated that between forty and fifty percent of the population were at the minimal subsistence level. (Catherine Lis and Hugo Soly, *Poverty and Capitalism in Pre-Industrial Europe*, Hassocks, Sussex, 1971, p. 139, cited by Sherwood, 1988, p. 61. For Spain, see Pedro Carasa Soto, 'La asistencia social en el siglo XVIII español. Estado de la cuestión,' in VV.AA., Madrid, 1990, (1), p. 432.)

ARTISANS, JOURNEYMEN AND APPRENTICES

Among the labouring poor, the specific weight of craftsmen volunteers and recruits at the start of the war was reminiscent of the artisan's importance in the American and French Revolutions. But under Spain's Old Order they, like all manual workers, were treated as pariahs. Stemming from the immoderate Spanish conviction that manual work other than on the land was a degraded and degrading human condition – so pervasive a view that most urban manual workers shared it – artisans adopted a series of stratagems to alleviate their denigrated estate.

In its origins there was nothing peculiarly Spanish in social contempt of 'dishonourable' trades which had been common to most of medieval Europe. The Spanish singularity lay in that this feudal hangover continued with great force as late as the end of the eighteenth century. Deriving its privileges and income from the land, the nobility could not afford to 'dishonour' the land-worker: the villager was kept in place by accepting his role of 'country bumpkin'. But to ensure that urban manual workers kept to 'their' place the dominant culture simply invalidated their occupations in a chain of contemptuous exclusivities that ran right through society.

So deep-seated was this prejudice that enlightened government reformers found it necessary in 1783 to derogate all laws and measures concerning 'ignoble' trades. (Exception was made for professional bullfighters and public executioners since these occupations involved 'corruption of the heart'.[47]) But it took more than a decree to change social attitudes.

Artisans accepted their invalidation as part of the natural order, struggling within it to rise a little in honour, dignity and public esteem. The majority of Madrid masters, for example, owned silver ceremonial swords and wore military-style frockcoats and waistcoats when they appeared in public. One master had a complete (but invented) military uniform. To be respected, status had to be publicly visible: hence the importance of its external symbols. It was not rare, noted a French traveller in the early 1770s, to see 'a simple, fifty-year-old worker in a pink or sky blue taffeta suit'.[48]

But this imitation of their 'betters'' dress was as nothing compared to artisanal aping of noble culture's exclusivity. Excluded from social respect, craftsmen in turn excluded those they felt would bring 'dishonour' to their trade. In the sixteenth and seventeenth centuries their guild regulations had banned mainly 'bad races' – blacks, mulattoes, Moors, Gypsies and Jews. But in the eighteenth century the guilds imposed on their members the demand to prove 'purity of blood'. This meant that guild members had to provide legally acceptable proof that their recent forebears had not been Jewish or Muslim converts to Catholicism – mimicking the legal requirements of access to the first rungs of the nobility.

To be without honour was to be without status; and to be without status was to be without social position. Individual differentiation counted for little: as His Majesty's vassal, the individual was not at the origin of civil society, did not have equal rights and duties, and the concept of subjective consciousness, which

Spanish Romanticism fully developed only from the mid-nineteenth century, was little valued. The individual artisan had a place in society solely as the member of a socially recognized corporation or guild with traditionally accepted (minor) privileges like a place in public ceremonies and religious processions, as often as not in competition with other trades. If the guild failed to achieve such recognition, its members could fear social exclusion. A number of disputes over status ended up in the courts. A farrier, for example, brought a case against a tailor to prevent the latter's son from marrying his granddaughter because a tailor's trade was inferior to his own.[49]

Artisans saw their multiplicity of guilds as a protection against social denigration. Through them the masters regulated production, quality and direct sales to the public; the fact that there were shoemakers but no shoe shops illustrates their control of consumption. One of the guilds' less obvious advantages was their success in guaranteeing that their members' income differentials were kept at tolerable levels. Their takings might be low, rarely sufficient to create substantial savings, but guilds ensured that while none individually could become particularly rich, 'few could sink into a poverty beyond social remission'.[50] Nor did the Spanish artisan forget that not only the French Revolution but many other countries had abolished the guilds.*

Egalitarian impoverishment – the guild-imposed standard – impeded capital accumulation and investment in technological advance even had masters been prepared to contemplate it, which in general they were not. Moreover, the Church was resolutely opposed to the seeking of economic success which it saw as 'pride' and contrary to Christian charity, distancing the soul from God to put it at the service of transitory worldy goods.

Despite their defensive measures great numbers of masters in the more dynamic sectors like silk or cotton manufacture were already proletarianized, working for other masters or merchants as wage labour. And a majority of the others were unable to rise above an elementary level of production, working alone without journeymen or apprentices.†

Over the country as a whole, textiles, footwear and tailoring occupied about half of all artisans. Their productive weakness, already apparent before the war, became doubly evident from the start of the conflict when their large number of volunteers deprived the remainder of the means to provide the Spanish armies in the field with uniforms and shoes in sufficient quantities. Patriot soldiers were constantly reported by their commanders to be barefoot and in rags.

The site of production and reproduction, the family was the master's lynchpin. As a Barcelona artisan's son, José Coroleu, recalled many years later:

* Tuscany in 1770, France (briefly) in 1776, and definitively in 1791, Switzerland in 1776, Austria in 1786, Britain in 1800 by the Combination Act (though the stocking weavers' guild had been abolished in 1753).

† At the national level, there were just under 280,000 master craftsmen and manufacturers, according to the 1797 census which grouped the two categories together, comprising 2.7% of the population. Even so they outnumbered journeymen (91,000) and apprentices (29,754) combined by two-to-one, indicating the high proportion of masters who worked alone.

We lived in a simple, hard-working, frugal society, deeply and fanatically attached to our traditions and accustomed to considering the family as a tribe whose patriarch was venerated. No one observed his faults and all obeyed his orders without second thought . . . I cannot recall that my father ever sharply reprimanded me and yet I trembled before him.[51]

If Madrid masters were anything to go by (and there was no reason to suspose they were not), urban craftsmen were far more likely to be literate than the rural population. At the very lowest guild level, half the individual Madrid members could sign their names, and in most of the capital's guilds the percentage ran from sixty to ninety percent. But their literacy – if indeed they could do more than sign – derived from their occupational needs rather than from a desire for edification.[52] They owned few books and the majority of those that have been identified were religious works. Displaying the same veneration for saints as villagers, they usually had one or more pictures, cheap prints or statues of saints in their shop and home. To be buried in a religious order's habits was as common among them as among villagers.[53]

Apprentices' and journeymen's conditions, usually far removed from those of the masters, were worse. 'There is no more infamous and toilsome slavery [on the Barbary coast] than that which these apprentices experience in Madrid', wrote a well-known playwright, Nicolás Fernández de Moratín, in a 1777 submission.[54] The masters did not care about their apprentices' cleanliness, gave them only an old sack to sleep on in a corner of the shop and often used them for the 'meanest of tasks quite distinct from their trade'; moreover they refused them a place at their table, and beat them. One of the most famous outlaws of the period, Francisco Esteban, became a highwayman rather than take any more of his master's blows.[55]

Significantly, the complex guild ordinances rarely referred to apprentices' or journeymen's conditions of labour. It was left to masters to use apprentices as cheap labour for anything up to ten years – even if the formal apprenticeship term was for only four to six – since the guilds fixed the minimum age for completing the apprenticeship at twenty, paying them with board, lodging and clothing. And, unless he were a master's son, it was unlikely that the apprentice would rise higher than a journeyman.

The latter's relatively low numbers had one significant effect. The guilds lacked the very sharp difference and rivalry between master and worker that distinguished the French; journeymen's clandestine associations and strikes were unknown in Spain. But they and apprentices were volatile groups, more likely than masters to be involved in street disturbances and the anti-French risings of 1808.

VILLAGERS: THEIR LIVES AND LIVELIHOOD*

Throughout the second half of the eighteenth century, villagers' existence grew much harsher than in the first, relatively prosperous half. By the time Carlos IV

* On the use of the term 'villagers' see Foreword, pp. ix–x.

came to the throne in 1789, almost any villager who had in adolescence survived diphtheria, scarlet fever and probably smallpox to reach twenty-five would have also lived through two subsistence crises; eight years of high bread prices; two years of an infant mortality crisis, accompanied by hunger in some regions; and a malaria epidemic (1786–1787) which laid low 875,000 people, of whom 77,000 died, in 1786 alone. This, too, was accompanied by a bad crop year.[56]

Francisco Cabarrús, a notable financier, witnessed villagers dying of starvation and malaria in La Mancha.

> I saw hundreds of its unhappy inhabitants shortly before the harvest running from place to place . . . father and mother covered in rags, livid of face, betraying all the symptoms of poverty, sickness and death, and their children totally naked and extenuated . . . And still before my eyes I seem to see one of these poor people dead at the foot of a tree next to the house where I was staying. [The wife and children] stood by the corpse without tears or any of those expressions of grief that might relieve their feelings; their attitude, their silence told of the horrible calm of desperation.[57]

Death was always imminent – to the villager and the urban lower orders alike. Life expectancy at birth for all Spaniards was no more than 26.8 years (27.3 for males and 26.3 years for females), two years less than in France and about ten years less than in England,[58] and though the chances of living longer increased after adolescence, they also decreased after forty; a rural worker who reached fifty could be considered old.* Village (and urban) parents could expect half of their children to die before the age of fifteen. Infantile mortality accounted for about fifty percent of *all* deaths.[59]

Poverty and malnutrition, if not outright starvation, were largely responsible for villagers succumbing to fatal illnesses. In the second half of the century the rate at which small owners and tenants were forced off the land rose sharply – Castilla la Vieja lost about one-third, and Castilla la Nueva one-fifth of its small producers – and the numbers of landless day labourers, and poverty, increased correspondingly.†[60] By the turn of the century just under one half of Spain's nearly 1,700,000 land working population consisted of landless labourers;‡ a further thirty percent were tenants, and twenty percent owners – many of whom were doubtless smallholders barely earning a self-sufficient existence

Although just over one-third of all villagers were no more than twenty-five years old, there was, understandably, precious little in youth to be joyful about.

---

* While just over one-third of the national population was twenty-five or under, only twenty-eight percent lived to reach more than forty, and just over fifteen percent to reach more than fifty. The twenty-six to forty year age group, at twenty-two percent, made up the remainder, according to the 1797 census.
† This eighteenth century proletarianization of smallholders and tenants was not exclusive to Spain. In France it has been estimated that the proportion of day labourers in the rural population rose from twelve percent at the beginning of the eighteenth century to thirty-three percent in 1789. (Catherine Lis and Hugo Soly, *Poverty and Capitalism in Pre-Industrial Europe*, 1971, p. 139, quoted Sherwood, 1998, p. 61.)
‡ Their numbers increased from north to south. (See chap. 14, pp. 344–5 for the regional proportions; for renters' and smallholders' proportions, see p. 337, fn.)

In the majority of villages, even on the great festive days, there reigned a 'sad silence', observed Jovellanos:

> Only boredom and idleness, it appears, makes some people come out of their houses to wander purposelessly here and there, to the village entrance, to the plaza, the church porch or to lean against a corner, their faces wrapped in their cloaks; and so they sadly spend the hours and entire evenings without enjoyment or pleasure. And if to this is added the aridity and filth of these places, the poverty . . . [and] the sad and silent atmosphere . . . who could not be surprised and saddened by the sight of such a phenomenon?[61]

This 'sad silence' was but a foretaste of 'the horrible calm of desperation' that might, at any moment, strike down the villager.

Most village families consisted of no more than two to three children.* Although sterility generally affected only about ten percent of married couples, many poor families could not support more offspring; infanticide, as in England at the time, was not uncommon.[62] Nor was illegitimacy: somewhere between seven and ten percent of village births overall, though the rate appeared to be declining in the 1790s.†

Villagers worked many hours but few days. That was to say, they worked from sunrise to sundown when they worked, but the work year was frequently interrupted by religious holidays. Not working ('idleness' to the enlightened) was consubstantial to the villagers' life; they worked only because they had to.‡ 'To work was to be poor.' This fact was expressed in their very language. 'Pobres' was the word labourers used about themselves not just because they were poor, but because poverty and work was seen as one and the same thing: one worked of necessity, not for any other reason.[63]

This period also saw the rise of a new type of large farmer, sometimes a nouveau riche villager but more often a wealthy outsider, with the means to rent big estates en bloc from noble landowners or the Church. By subletting the worst lands to small village tenants they were often able to exploit nearly rent-free the estate's best arable. But these new tenant farmers – grain merchants, government contractors, lawyers and nobles' own bailifs among them – did not make an agricultural revolution; instead they tried to turn a profit within the existing system. When it suited their ends, they might make common cause with

---

* In Morón de la Frontera, a large agrarian Andalucian township, the better off averaged from two and a half to three children per family. At the bottom of the social pile, day labourers, shepherds and herdsmen had on average from two and a quarter to two and a half. (Author's calculations from *Padrón vecindario, 1803*, A.M., *Morón de la Frontera, Legajo* 369.)

† The Morón de la Frontera rate among sixteen to twenty-year olds was a modest 4.2% compared to the township's average of 10.6%. Though less marked, the same age group showed a decline over the general average in Igualada, Cataluña. (See Appendix 3, table 3.2.)

‡ Landless labourers worked – when they could find employment – on average (and depending on region) about 120 days a year, or one day in three. Earning a maximum of four reales a day, but more usually two to three, their real wages fell as inflation increased in the 1790s.

the villagers against a noble or ecclesiastical señor, whose 'ancient' rights and prerogatives oppressed the villagers and skimmed off a portion of the large tenants' profits. But in general the new farmers' and villagers' interests were opposed. The former wanted to buy land to exploit; they stood therefore on the side of liberalization which would release land onto the market from the 'dead hand' of Church mortmain or noble entails. While sometimes expressing anger that Church and nobility did not put their lands to better use, the villagers saw only too well they would not benefit from liberalizing measures: higher bread prices, higher lease contracts, lower day wages had been the result of government measures abolishing price controls with the aim of stimulating agrarian development.* Though villagers did not particularly question the existing system of landownership, they might regret, even resent that they did not own the land they worked but they did not claim that they should own it. It was not necessarily this that would guarantee them a living. A villager lived better or worse depending on the extent of the land he could work with security of tenure.

'Apathetic', 'ignorant', 'conservative', 'superstitious' . . . These were the customary stereotypes imposed on the villagers by the hegemonic culture; and yet they were in practice belied in many ways. They could not, for example, account for the vast number of villagers' legal complaints and petitions to one or other authority about rent increases; abrogation of tenants' contracts; nobles' and large tenants' claims over village commons; corn merchants 'who have increased prices three and four times due to the free commerce of grains'; criticisms of the Church as a large landowner – two small villages in Burgos and León refused to pay any money or rent that recalled the villagers' 'miserable condition of slaves of the Church'.[64] Many others refused to pay 'medieval' dues to the nobility, even though the amounts were derisory; and more seriously began to renege on paying tithes.†

In the face of the new conditions they confronted, it was not 'apathy' but an excess of patience that characterized the villagers. Their belief that they would get justice in the end was almost always disappointed; a few crumbs might be thrown their way, but little else, especially when a noble landowner was their adversary. As a Granada scrivener put it, 'the powerful always win the cases brought by a tenant who has been thrown off the land'.[65]

It was a patience, however, tinged with fear: of crop failures and hunger; of not securing a tenancy for want of a pair of oxen or mules, a plough and seed-grain; of being thrown off the land. As a Salamanca small tenant, José Pérez, explained, fear was one of the causes of low agricultural production:

---

* For these liberalization measures see p. xxiii fn.
† As this tax of ten percent *grosso modo* was levied on most agrarian production, without consideration for the outlays of planting and growing the crop, its real cost to the villagers, as a percentage of their surplus, could reach one-third or more; and by allowing no deductions for improvements, it was also a disincentive to invest in increasing agrarian production. The injustice was evident to villagers who saw how little – only one-ninth – their own parish priests received of the total; refusal to pay was an attack on the prelates who took seventy percent but 'it was not an anti-clerical or anti-religious protest'. (Carlos Rodriguez López-Brea, 'La crisis del Antiguo Régimen en el Arzobispado de Toledo. El impago de diezmos (1800–1820)' in VV.AA, 1994 (2), vol. 2, pp. 285–293.)

Because of the unhappiness and dread the worker feels after four years when his lease ends, knowing that the labour he has put in to fertilizing and clearing the land will raise the cost of the new lease, and only the powerful or wealthy farmer will be able to afford it.[66]

There was fear, too, of the Church which, as a large landholder, could give or deny the villagers land to rent; which from the pulpit could threaten them with eternal hellfire; and which, were this insufficient, could condemn them – through the Inquisition – for deviations of religious orthodoxy . . . Fear of many other things, natural and supernatural: of thunderstorms, snakes, menstrual blood, ghosts . . .

From birth to death, villagers lived in a world permeated by the Church: baptism ensured eternal life; their given name, drawn from the calendar of saints, brought heavenly protection in return for homage to and veneration of their eponymous saint. 'The Virgin . . . and the saints were for the villager personages close to them, present in reality; little less than omnipotent, they interceded for those who made a gift-offering – a mass or even a ham – and it was expedient to keep them well-disposed for any daily setback.'[67]

The few young villagers who learned to read,* did so from chapbooks filled with miraculous religious happenings and secular stories, structured as a catechism or sermon, with a religious moral ending. Catholic doctrine was learned by rote at home from archaic catechisms. Most village families told their beads each evening before eating, and at table the bread was blessed; small prints of locally venerated saints, which were commonly displayed, could be had for little outlay.

The major instrument of religious education and control of a still largely illiterate village culture had perforce to be oral. This implement was the sermon – not the pious weekly exhortation addressed to believers, as the word suggests, but a direct intervention in village life, since for the Church all aspects of civil life were immediately appraised by religious standards. 'Sacred, therefore, was the power of the monarch as long as he carried out God's will, sacred the social classes established by God, sacred the belief in the only true religion and those who preached it.'[68] Reading eighteenth-century sermons is like 'being taken back to the medieval world', an historical specialist on the subject has commented.[69]

But as much as Catholic doctrine, the supernatural intruded constantly on villagers' lives, beneficently or evilly, and intercession and protection were needed, for the villagers had little objective defence against natural ills. Their religious practices were a means whereby they sought to dominate nature, deal with the threats of an unpredictable world which was full of sudden fears and shocks, and ensure their personal salvation – and even that of their parish

---

* More young villagers were learning to read and write as the government extended basic education to rural townships. At the beginning of the Napoleonic war, the great majority of those who could sign their names to their enlistment in the Morón de la Frontera district in Andalucía and Igualada in Cataluña were between sixteen and twenty-five years old. (See Appendix 3, table 3.1.)

community.[70] It was hardly surprising then if villagers held a dualistic view of the supernatural where

> God and the devil battled for dominion over the universe, with their courts, their armies, and their vassals in conflicts visible and invisible. There was no space on earth, no moment, no activity personal or collective, that was free of relentless harassment or exempt from the protection of the supernatural. In a terrestial existence subordinated to the other world, there could be no personal autonomy on earth, and physical or natural beings counted for nothing.[71]

The widespread idea that the villagers were characterized by a profound piety is a myth:* they could be aroused to a sudden access of religious fervour, especially by the more rabid of missionary friars' sermons which were deliberately intended to have this effect; but once the preacher had moved on, the fervour almost as rapidly gave way to the necessity of confronting the harshness of everyday life. They might be aroused, as indeed they were, to fight for God, king and country; but once they encountered in the Napoleonic war the realities of military life and their noble commanders' general ineptitude, their fervour to volunteer for the cause not surprisingly waned. Religious passion and piety went only so far.

Villagers in general were modest, patient, God-fearing (though much given to cursing), working out of necessity to earn a poor living, 'idle' for as long as they could be, and not easily roused to action. Had the anti-Napoleonic rising depended on them, rather than on the urban plebeians, it might never have taken place. But similarly, it would never have succeeded had the villagers not taken part.

---

* It was propagated in the nineteenth century by the Church while attempting to stem the loss of some of its earlier influence by appealing to villagers and urban women who had not yet experienced the wave of religious disbelief. (Saavedra, 1994, p. 347.)

Regional population growth rates

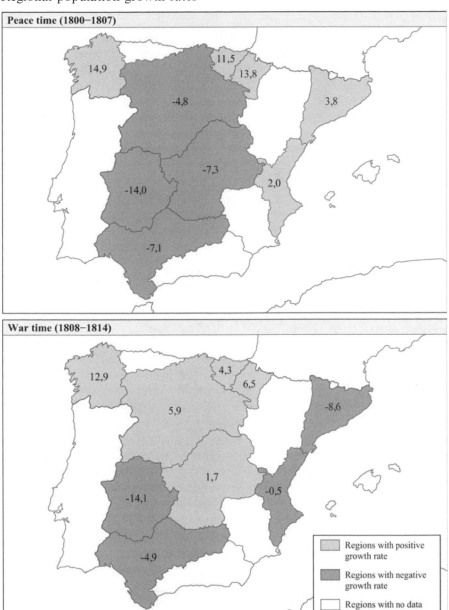

Comparison of the two maps shows the regions which, in demographic terms, suffered more from the prewar famine and yellow fever than from the war itself; and those which suffered the contrary fate (see Appendix 5).

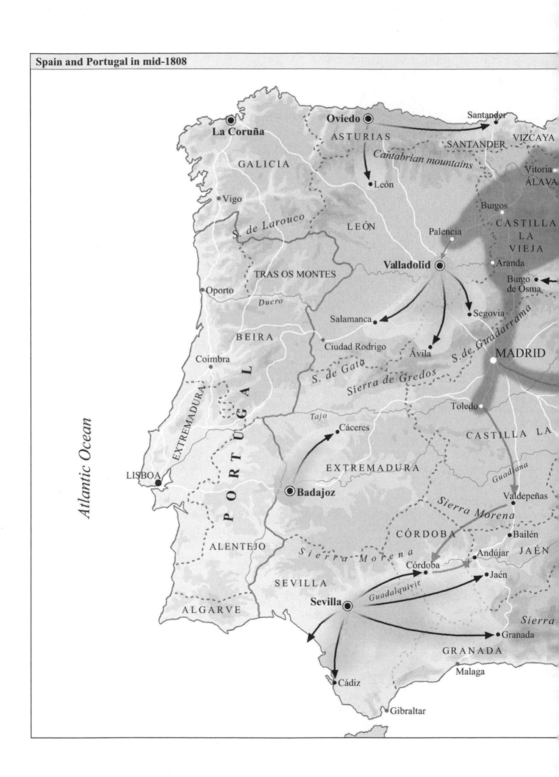

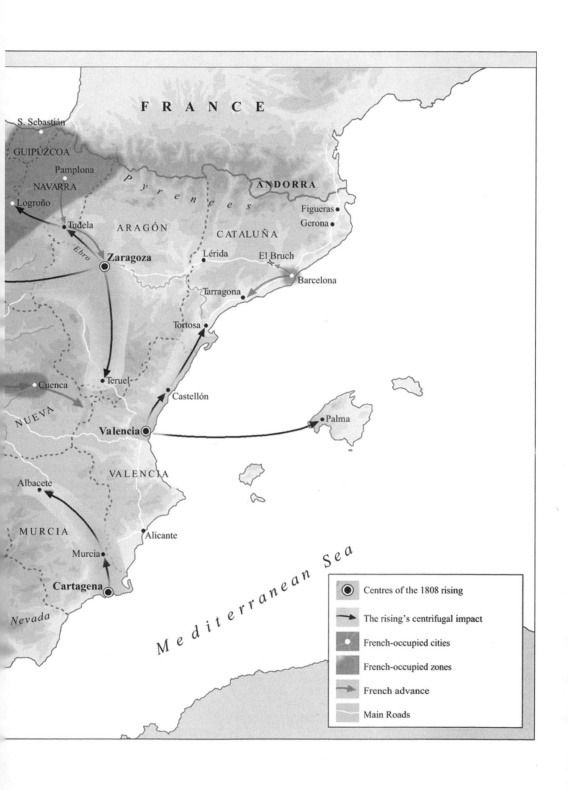

FRANCE

S. Sebastián

GUIPÚZCOA

Pamplona

NAVARRA

Logroño

Tudela

ARAGÓN

Ebro

Zaragoza

Lérida

ANDORRA

Figueras

Gerona

CATALUÑA

El Bruch

Barcelona

Tarragona

Tortosa

Teruel

Castellón

Cuenca

NUEVA

Valencia

Palma

VALENCIA

Albacete

MURCIA

Alicante

Murcia

Cartagena

Nevada

Mediterranean Sea

	Centres of the 1808 rising
	The rising's centrifugal impact
	French-occupied cities
	French-occupied zones
	French advance
	Main Roads

The war's territorial progression

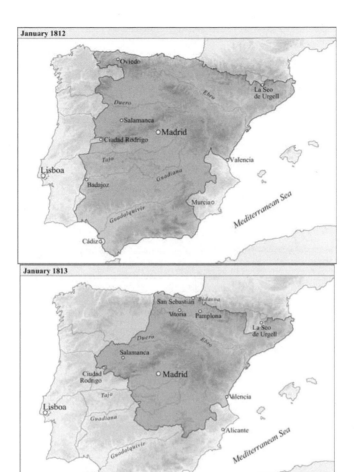

January 1812

Oviedo

La Seo de Urgell

Ebro

Duero

Salamanca

Madrid

Ciudad Rodrigo

Tajo

Valencia

Lisboa

Guadiana

Badajoz

Murcia

Guadalquivir

Mediterranean Sea

Cádiz

January 1813

San Sebastián

Bidasoa

Vitoria

Pamplona

La Seo de Urgell

Duero

Ebro

Salamanca

Ciudad Rodrigo

Madrid

Tajo

Valencia

Lisboa

Guadiana

Alicante

Guadalquivir

Mediterranean Sea

Cádiz

French-occupied territory

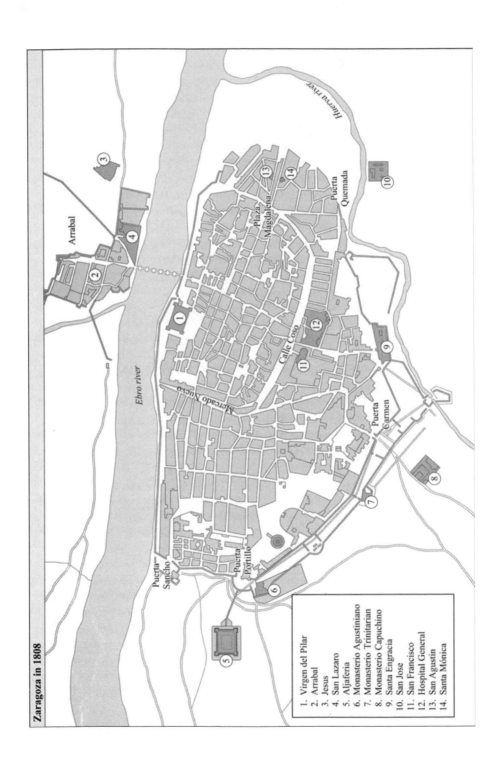

Zaragoza in 1808

Ebro river

Huerva river

Arrabal

Puerta Sancho

Puerta Portillo

Puerta Carmen

Puerta Quemada

Plaza Magdalena

Calle Coso

Mercado Nuevo

1. Virgen del Pilar
2. Arrabal
3. Jesus
4. San Lazaro
5. Aljaferia
6. Monasterio Agustiniano
7. Monasterio Trinitarian
8. Monasterio Capuchino
9. Santa Engracia
10. San Jose
11. San Francisco
12. Hospital General
13. San Agustin
14. Santa Mónica

Gerona in 1808

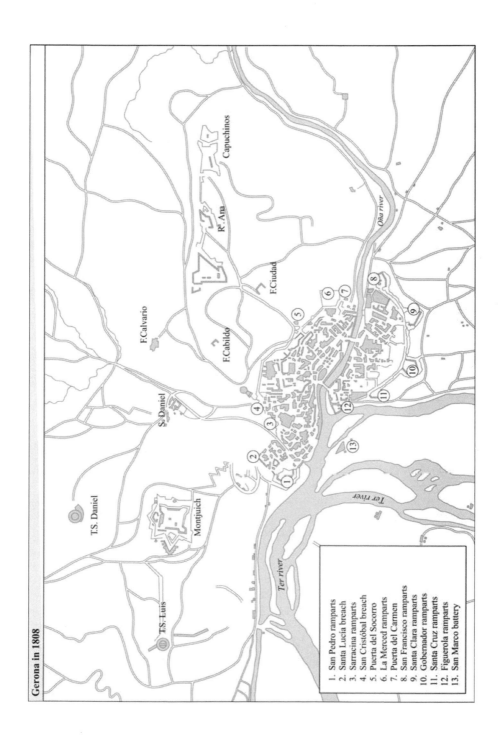

1. San Pedro ramparts
2. Santa Lucia breach
3. Sarracina ramparts
4. San Cristóbal breach
5. Puerta del Socorro
6. La Merced ramparts
7. Puerta del Carmen
8. San Francisco ramparts
9. Santa Clara ramparts
10. Gobernador ramparts
11. Santa Cruz ramparts
12. Figuerola ramparts
13. San Marco battery

Glossary

Money Terms:

Real: the pound sterling was worth 60 reales on the outbreak of war. During the conflict the rate fluctuated, dropping at times to as low as 75 reales to the pound

Peso fuerte (silver dollar in the English of the time): this was worth 15 reales at the start of the war; thus there were 4 dollars to the pound; during the war, the rate against the pound dropped to as low as 5 dollars

Peseta: this Catalan denomination was worth 4 reales

Duro: the equivalant of 20 reales, or 5 pesetas

Land Measure:
Fanega: 0.64 of a hectare, or approximately 1.5 acres

Weight measures:
Fanega: this varied according to grain. For wheat, a fanega equalled about 1.5 bushels.

Pound: the Castilian measure equalled 460 grams

Chronology

1803		Under threat of invasion, Napoleon obliges Spain to pay 6m francs a month for not resuming war
1803-04	Grave subsistence crisis	
1804		Napoleon proclaimed Emperor British naval provocations against Spain
1805	Declares war against Britain; fleet destroyed at battle of Trafalgar	Napoleon's victories at Ulm and Austerlitz; Nelson defeats Franco-Spanish fleets at Trafalgar
1806	Godoy seeks rapprochement with anti-Napoleonic coalition of Prussia, Russia, England & Portugal	Napoleon decrees Continental Blockade against Britain
1807	Escorial affair	
	French troops cross Spain to take Portugal under Treaty of Fontainebleau	Napoleon defeats Russia at Friedland; Treaty of Tilsit
1808 (*Jan–May*)	Napoleon stations 100,000 troops across northern Spain, seizes several fortresses	
	Godoy overthrown by Aranjuez commotion; king abdicates, son and heir Fernando accedes to throne	
	French troops under Murat enter Madrid	
	Madrid popular rising against French (May 2)	
	Napoleon forces Fernando VII's renunciation of throne	

WAR

1808 (*May–June*)	Anti-Napoleonic risings in provinces (May 23-June 4)	Napoleon places his brother, Josef, on Spanish throne
	First Catalan popular victory over French column at El Bruch; civilians attack French military in La Mancha	Napoleon summons Spanish notables to constituent assembly in Bayonne
	Heavy patriot defeat by French at Cabezón, Valladolid	Portuguese anti-Napoleonic risings
	First siege of Zaragoza begins (June 15)	
	Popular defence of Valencia forces French army's retreat from city's gates (June 28)	
(*July–Aug*)	Crushing defeat of patriot armies at Medina de Rioseco (July 14)	
	Andalucian patriot army defeats French at Bailén (July 19)	
	French evacuate Madrid, retire to the Ebro (early Aug)	

First Zaragoza siege raised (Aug 14)
Patriot forces enter Madrid

Wellesley lands with British force in Portugal, defeats French twice; Junot sues for terms
Convention of Cintra (Aug 30)

(Sept–Dec)

Junta Suprema formed
Patriot armies advance to Ebro
Napoleon enters Spain at head of army (Nov 4)
Galician army routed by French at Espinosa de los Monteros
Extremaduran army smashed at Gamonal, Napoleon takes Burgos
Central patriot and Aragonese armies defeated at Tudela
Guerrilla movement begins
Polish lancers and infantry storm Somosierra pass, opening way to Madrid (Nov 30)
Junta Suprema flees to Sevilla (Dec 1–2)
Madrid capitulates (Dec 4)
Napoleon's Chamartín decrees
Junta Suprema issues first guerrilla decree
Catalan army defeated at Cardedeu and Molins del Rey
Napoleon pursues Moore (Dec 20)

Napoleon readies 250,000-strong Grande Armée for offensive in Spain

Moore, at head of British army in Portugal, reaches Salamanca (Nov 13)

Moore moves to cut Napoleon's communications (Dec 10)

Moore orders general retreat (Dec 23)

1809
(winter–spring)

Patriot army defeat at Uclés (Jan 13)
Napoleon abandons pursuit of Moore and Spain, never to return (mid-Jan)
Battle of Corunna, Moore fatally wounded (Jan 16)
La Coruña surrenders
Josef re-enters Madrid (Jan 22)
Popular Galician resistance begins
Zaragoza falls at end of second siege (Feb 21)
Catalan army's third defeat – battle of Valls – in two months (Feb 25)
Vigo besieged and taken by Galician resistance (March 27)
Patriot army routed at Medellín (March 28)

British army embarks from La Coruña (Jan 16–17)

Soult takes Oporto (March 29)

Southern Galicia cleared of French
(mid-April)

Siege of Gerona begins (May 5)

Galician resistance defeats French at Wellesley defeats Soult at Oporto
Campo de Estrella, takes Santiago (May 12)
de Compostela (May 23)

Galician resistance holds off Ney at
Sampaio Bridge (June 7–8)

(*summer*) French withdrawal from Galicia   Napoleon's victory over Austria at
completed (July 3)   Wagram (July 5–6)

Wellesley and Cuesta battle French   Wellesley raised to peerage as Lord
at Talavera (July 27–28)   Wellington

Wellington retires to Spanish–
Portuguese border (Aug)

Patriot army defeat at Almonacid

(*autumn–* Ocaña: patriot army's heaviest
winter)   defeat (Nov 19) opens road to
Andalucía

Gerona falls at end of 7-month   Wellington retires to Portugal (Dec)
siege (Dec 11)

1810   French begin Andalucian invasion;
(*winter–* Junta Suprema flees Sevilla for Isla
spring)   de León (mid-Jan)

Junta surrenders power to regency
(Jan 31)

Sevilla surrenders without struggle
(Feb 1)

Andalucía occupied; region's
guerrilla movement begins

Start of French siege of Cádiz

Oviedo occupied by French and re-   Napoleon creates army of Portugal
occupied by patriots four times   under Masséna

Lérida surrenders after short siege
(May 13)

(*summer–* Ciudad Rodrigo surrenders to
autumn)   Masséna after two-month siege
(July 9)

Patriot Constituent Cortes
assembles at Isla de León (Sept 24)

Goya starts work on *Disasters of*   Masséna's advance on Lisbon
War   halted by Wellington's Torres
Vedras lines (mid-Oct)

1811   Tortosa captured by Suchet after   Masséna begins retreat from
(*winter–* short siege (Jan 2)   Portugal (early Feb)
spring)   French army in Andalucía under
Soult takes Badajoz after 5-week
siege (March 10)

First and second British sieges of
Badajoz fail (March–June)

	Espoz y Mina's Navarrese guerrilleros attack French column at Arlabán pass (May 25)	
(*summer– autumn*)	Tarragona taken by Suchet after two-month siege, followed by fearful sacking (June 29) Five large guerrilla divisions in north officially incorporated as Seventh Army Constituent Cortes decision to abolish only señorial jurisdictions (Aug 6)	
1812 (*winter– spring*)	Valencia capitulates to Suchet (Jan 8) after fortnight's siege British take Ciudad Rodrigo (Jan 19) Famine in Madrid, Sevilla, Cataluña Patriot Cortes proclaims new Constitution in Cádiz (March 19) British storm Badajoz, subject city to fearful sacking (April 6) Wellington begins first incursion into Spanish interior since 1809 (mid-June)	Napoleon withdraws troops from Spain for Russian campaign

Napoleon invades Russia (June) |
| (*summer– autumn*) | Wellington defeats French at battle of Arapiles (Salamanca) (July 22) Josef Bonaparte retires from Madrid to Valencia (early Aug) Wellington enters Madrid (Aug 12) French abandon Andalucía, Cádiz siege raised (Aug 25) Cortes appoints Wellington C-in-C of allied armies (Sept 22) Wellington unsuccessfully besieges Burgos (Sept 23-Oct 18) Threatened by superior French forces, Wellington again retreats to Portugal (Oct–Nov) | Takes Moscow (Aug)

Begins his disastrous retreat (Oct) |
| 1813 (*winter– spring*) | Josef withdraws from Madrid to Valladolid (March) Guerrillas tie down greater part of French Army of the North Wellington begins new campaign in Spain (May) Sea-borne British forces besiege Tarragona, forced by French to re-embark (June 3–13) | Withdraws more troops from Spain, orders Josef to establish HQ at Valladolid (Feb) |

Allied army defeats Josef at Vitoria
(June 21)

(*summer–* Allies reach French frontier at
autumn) Bidasoa river (July 1–12)

Josef crosses into France, never to   Napoleon appoints Soult
return (July 12)   commander of unified army of

Soult attacks through Pyrennean   Spain
passes, held off by allies at two
battles of Sorauren (end July)

French withdraw from Valencia &
Aragón to Cataluña (July)

Allies besiege San Sebastián (July
12–Aug 31)

Soult's attempt to relieve San
Sebastián driven back at battle of
San Marcial (Aug 31)

British troops sack, set fire to and
destroy town

Elections to new Cortes (Sept)

Allies cross the Bidasoa into France   Napoleon defeated by allied
(Oct 7)   coalition at Battle of Four Nations,

French surrender Pamplona (Oct 31)   Leipzig (Oct 16–19)
                                        Treaty of Valençay: Napoleon
                                        releases Fernando VII to return to
                                        Spain (Dec)

1814   Newly elected Cortes convenes in
(*winter–* Madrid (Jan)
spring)   Rejects Treaty of Valençay, decrees
            that Fernando VII on reaching
            Spain swear oath to new
            Constitution (Feb 2)

Fernando crosses into French-   Allied coalition forces enter Paris
occupied Cataluña, disobeys Cortes   (March 31)
decree (March 22)

Provisional government formed

Enters Valencia to scenes of popular   Napoleon abdicates, end of war
rejoicing (April 16)   (April 6)

Fernando abolishes Constitution,
restores absolutism (May 4)

Persecution of liberal deputies
begins in Madrid (May 11)

Fernando VII enters Madrid to
popular acclaim

French garrison of Barcelona
surrenders longest-occupied Spanish
city (May 28)

Goya completes his iconic *Second of
May* and *Third of May* paintings on
the 1808 Madrid rising and its
repression

1

Spain and the French Connection

NAPOLEON'S INVASION OF FRANCE'S ALLY: OCTOBER 1807–MARCH 1808

The heavens had foretold imminent disaster. A comet, visible to the naked eye from Valladolid in the north to Sevilla in the south, had trailed its fiery tail through the western sky in the months of August and September.

> It signalled the death of a king or some powerful person. And cities would be desolated, some said, because of the white and saffron colour of its tail . . .

noted the Sevillan friar, Manuel Giles y Carpio, in his diary.[1]

In the manner of such things, only tortuous human intervention turned the augury into reality. It began with Napoleon's firm resolve to wage total economic war on Britain by blockading her trade with the continent. Portugal alone refused to obey and close her ports to her traditional British ally; this lonely exception, the Emperor decided, must be brought to heel.

On October 18, 1807, nine days before the enabling treaty with Spain was signed, Napoleon pushed a twenty-five-thousand-strong expeditionary force across the Spanish border. Its military objective was to cross Spain and conquer Portugal. The Spanish court raised no objections to the anticipatory troop movement; under the Fontainebleau treaty, Manuel Godoy, Spain's chief minister, royal favourite and head of state in all but name, and the Bourbon monarchy were to share the spoils of conquest in which twenty-five thousand Spanish troops were to participate.

The imperial forces, commanded by General Junot, were the first foreign military the majority of Spaniards west of the Ebro had seen on their soil in living memory. In townships and villages on the long muddy road across the Castilian plain, people gathered to watch the unending march of the 'conquerors of Europe'. Provincial diarists,[2] heirs of an enlightened century, assiduously counted the troops, and noted their regiments' numbers, while the majority gawped at the bright uniforms, the cuirassier's shining breast- and back-plates, the extravagantly attired staff officers. It did not much matter that many of the foot soldiers were Germans, Italians and Swiss,[3] or raw French recruits. This for the spectators was the *Grande Armée*.

The military spectacle temporarily relieved a grim reality. For the past eighteen months, townfolk and villagers had been attempting to rebuild their lives. A catastrophic famine, accompanied by malaria,* had struck central and southern Spain between 1803 and 1805. The dearth had been worsened by the difficulties of moving grain rapidly to where it was most urgently needed because of a deficient road system.[4] Castilla la Vieja was among the worst hit: by 1805 the region had lost seven percent of its mid-1800 population.† Not even in the six bloody years of war that were about to begin would Castilla suffer such a loss.

In 1806 and 1807, crops had been middling good, and the price of bread was dropping again to near half its vastly inflated famine levels. The population began to recover: marriages and births increased at record rates and deaths declined sharply. But of the newly born only half could be expected to reach adulthood. As a popular saying had it, it took two male infants to make a man.

General Junot's troops reached the Portuguese frontier without serious incident: a Burgos student stabbed a French officer,[5] and many petty looters and stragglers – about one hundred, the French claimed – were picked off by Salamanca villagers.[6] The imperial soldiers had yet to learn how to protect themselves against civilians. On November 30, Junot occupied Lisbon. At the last minute the British navy took away the Portuguese royal family and transported them to Brazil.

Napoleon, however, was concerned with more than Portugal. Without waiting to be assured of Junot's position, he dispatched another twenty-five thousand troops into Spain and stationed them across Castilla la Vieja.‡ Soon these were followed by two more corps, totalling sixty thousand men, most of whom were quartered in the Basque country and Navarra. Finally, he ordered fourteen thousand troops across the Catalan frontier to march on Barcelona.

This massive display of military strength was accompanied by guile to secure several major Spanish fortresses: in Pamplona, imperial troops staged a snowball fight with the fortress guards to lure them from their posts, and then rushed the main gate; in Barcelona, an imperial military parade in front of the *ciudadela* swung one of its wings around to seize the entrance and occupy the fortress – a prelude to taking over the city's second fortress on the Montjuich hill. Shortly thereafter, Godoy was forced to permit French troops to occupy San Sebastián and its fortress for lack of troops to defend it.

* Malaria was endemic in Valencia. In 1786–1787 an epidemic had swept as far north as the Cantabrian coast, laying low 875,000 people, of whom 77,000 died in the first year alone. This, too, had been accompanied by a bad crop. (Pérez Moreda, 1980, p. 342.)
† See Appendix 5 for the manner in which natural growth/decline has been calculated.
‡ A secret clause of the Fontainebleau Treaty permitted Napoleon, on receiving the Spanish government's agreement, to send a further forty thousand troops into Spain to reinforce those in Portugal should the English attack; but the Emperor made no attempt to secure Spanish permission before pushing more troops into Spain.

By March 1808, only four months after the first imperial troops had entered Spain en route for Portugal, Napoleon had secured three major peninsular ports – Lisbon, Barcelona and San Sebastián – had occupied four important Spanish fortresses, and had one hundred thousand soldiers on his ally's territory without the government's permission or their certain knowledge of his military objectives. Moreover, he had scattered the Spanish army, twenty-five thousand of its troops to Portugal, and a further sixteen thousand to the Danish islands on the pretext of an imperial invasion of Sweden. On this, his first aggression against a country which was not his aggressor, he had his forces excellently placed in Spain to exert the maximum leverage for whichever of the options he choose to pursue.

*

The Emperor was at the height of his power. He could, it seemed, propose and dispose of nations' destinies and territories at will, create kingdoms, principalities and dukedoms out of their lands, rearrange the map of Europe according to a new 'rationality'. His determination to cause England's economic collapse made the control of coasts, ports and ships vital.[7] For the first time, the Emperor turned his full attention to the Iberian Peninsula and the western Mediterranean. 'Etre maître de la Méditerranée, but principal et constant de ma politique', he pronounced in 1806.[8]

In the immediate term, Portugal had been secured for the continental blockade by General Junot; but there remained Spain: a potentially great naval power with its arsenals and yards at a standstill since the battle of Trafalgar, its long Atlantic and Mediterranean coastline, and a market still closed to French products which could substitute for those lost abroad to Britain's retaliatory economic war and the United States' embargo on trade with the combatants. But Spain was an unsatisfactory ally, a government unreliable in its adherence to the Emperor's cause, with an inefficient economy despite its great colonial resources, and ruled by the last remaining Bourbon on a major European throne.

Napoleon was convinced that if 'disorder and wastage' were put to an end, Spain's navy could recover its former strength. Given that Britain's worsening economic situation due to the Continental System would reduce the effectiveness of her fleet, a rebuilt Spanish navy and the country's colonial resources would be necessary to assist in most of his major aims in the Orient. Subsequently, Napoleon frequently justified his attempted takeover of Spain by his need for a revitalized and enlarged Spanish navy.[9]

With his troops firmly ensconced in his ally's territory, Napoleon had four tactical options before him: he could provoke the Spanish monarchy to follow the example of the Portuguese royal family and flee the country for South America, and thus take over Spain at seemingly no cost – his conquest could then be used to negotiate with England; or he could unite his family and the Spanish dynasty by a marriage between an imperial princess and the heir to the throne, Fernando, as the latter had but recently begged him to do, and thus assure himself direct influence on the country's immediate future. His third option was to take Spain north of the Ebro river – the Basque Country, Navarra, Aragón and Cataluña – and thus, with the southern flanks of the Pyrenees in his hands, he would secure an imperial glacis defended by the great river; the rest of the country could be left to be ruled by a Bourbon, who could be compensated for the loss by a portion of Portugal. Finally, he could force the Bourbons off the throne and replace them by a member of his family to exercise direct control of Spain's destiny.[10]

As to his strategic aims, he kept open various options, which were never put into practice. The unexpected Spanish rising against his covert invasion required massive imperial military intervention that had not entered into his plans.

*

In almost all the occupied areas imperial troops acted like an army of occupation, sacking and requisitioning food which they claimed their Spanish ally was not providing in sufficient quantities or rapidly enough.[11] In some places there was as yet no overt resistance but rather a widespread personal reaction. In Guipúzcoa, the Basque province adjoining the French border and through which the main Madrid–Paris road passed, the incursion of imperial troops was accompanied by a sudden drop in conceptions during the first three months of the year.* Guipúzcoa had suffered harshly from the French revolutionary invasion during the Spanish war against the French Convention of 1793–1795, when its normal death rate had doubled, leading to its greatest population decline of the eighteenth century. Its inhabitants had not forgotten the experience in this renewed French invasion.[12]

But elsewhere, as in neighbouring Navarra, open confrontations and clashes took place between villagers and French soldiery. In Barcelona, there were numerous incidents between Spanish and French troops which led to deaths and wounds.[13] General Duhesme, the French commander, ordered his forces to seize all bell-ropes from the churches to prevent the traditional popular call to arms and self-defence against an aggressor.[14] But the city was too heavily controlled by the French military to permit a rising.

Outside of Barcelona, there was uncertainty and confusion.

Writing to his stepson, a student at Valencia University, Dr Luis Freixas, a town councillor of the southern Catalan township of Villafranca del Penedès, described the atmosphere and the division of opinion between an enlightened reformist like himself and the unlettered commoner. All Catalans had been 'shocked and surprised' by the French troops' occupation of Barcelona, but the 'healthier elements', as he described himself and the educated classes, saw it as a 'precautionary measure to carry out Napoleon's measures'. They did not for a moment envisage 'living under other masters than the Bourbon family'.

> Yet the ordinary people continue to think they are to become subjects of a French prince. . . . It is the clerics who are whipping up these ideas, clearly because their own interests hallucinate and preoccupy them. Imagine the state our good nuns are in,

---

* Conceptions, as used here and subsequently, refer to baptized births backdated nine months. (Author database: *Demography*: Regional monthly births, 1799–1817.)

believing that they are to be sent packing immediately. The friars are in the same state, and the priests fear a formidable reform.

I see everything with serenity and believe that nothing will be as commonly feared. You for your part remain tranquil, as we are at home . . .*

Until early March, when they heard of their 'ally's' occupation of the Spanish strong points, most of the population outside the directly affected areas still believed that Napoleon's troops were intended to reinforce Junot in Portugal, to attack Gibraltar or prevent the British seizing Cádiz. They were assisted in their misbelief by Carlos IV, who was fearful of providing Napoleon with the slightest pretext of aggression, and issued tranquillizing proclamations about the imperial troops' presence; and, for very different reasons, by a faction around the heir to the throne, Fernando, who spread rumours of Napoleon's support of their bitter struggle against Godoy, the Spanish chief minister.

Meanwhile, Madrid life continued apparently as normal: inflation had abated temporarily, pawnshop takings dropped by over a quarter and redemptions increased. The capital's theatres, always a thermometer of public sentiment, did good business; French luxury goods and books were in high demand – Napoleon's France was held in esteem.[15]

Everything changed overnight, however, on the the news of the takeover of the Spanish fortresses and the intelligence from Portugal that Junot's army had not only taken over the country in the Emperor's name after the royal family's flight,† but was also looting its wealth. On the further news that a fifty-thousand-strong French army, under Marshal Murat, was now advancing, slowly but surely, on Madrid, with the stated objective of continuing southwards to Cádiz,[16] fear spread among the capital's inhabitants and beyond into the two Castillas. Marriages dropped sharply, as young betrothed, widows and widowers, postponed or cancelled their weddings throughout the region. There could hardly have been a clearer sign of people's worries about the immediate future than this sudden, widespread change of plan.‡

* Two years later, almost to the day, Luis Freixas was assassinated by imperial soldiers who, on being besieged by Catalan troops, had retreated to the Villafranca barracks, taking with them as hostages a number of local notables, among them Freixas, who had played an outstanding role in defending the local population against the worst imperial excesses. Before surrendering, the French ran Freixas through with their swords. (Benach i Torrents, 1968, pp. 17 and 59–61.)

† On February 1, 1808, Napoleon issued a proclamation declaring that, as the house of Braganza had ceased to rule Portugal, he had taken the country under his protection and it would be governed in its totality and in his name by his army commander, i.e. Junot. Thus Napoleon unilaterally abrogated the Fontainebleau Treaty's provisions on carving up Portugal into distinct realms, of which the southern one was to have gone to Godoy and the northern one to the Spanish Bourbons, and foreclosed one of his options mentioned above. (Junot's proclamation in Toreno, 1838/1916, p. 43.)

‡ In Castilla la Nueva, in which the capital was situated, marriages dropped by 16% and in Castilla la Vieja by 5.5% below their 1800–1817 averages. (Author database: *Demography*: Regional monthly marriages: 1800–1817). After two years of high marriage rates, these would almost certainly have declined sooner or later in 1808. It was the simultaneity of the drop throughout these two large regions that was striking. Even sharper falls of as high as 50% of the average were recorded in Cataluña for six months after the French took Barcelona in February.

In the capital itself, theatre takings dropped abruptly by nearly one-third in the first two weeks of March;[17] the only good news, it seemed, was that Godoy looked sadder than usual on his weekly stay in the capital; the hated favourite's downfall now appeared certain, and the value of the treasury bonds, the *vales reales*, rose accordingly.[18]

THE OLD ORDER IN CRISIS

If not at its nadir, Spain was politically and economically closer to it in early 1808 than at any time in the past three-quarters of a century. The metropolis of the world's greatest empire was to all intents bankrupt. For more than twelve of the last sixteen years, Godoy's Spain had been progressively indebted by war. The economic and demographic progress of the long eighteenth century – the phrase is justified by the fact that agrarian and demographic progress had begun in the last quarter of the seventeenth century – which had seen the population rise from six to eleven million, accompanied by a sizeable increase in agriculture, manufacturing and trade, had come close to ending. Restraints inherent in the Old Regime's landowning structure, dominated by Church and nobility, set serious limits to further agricultural advance. The beginnings of an industrial revolution based on textile manufacturing in Cataluña suffered the loss of its major market, the Spanish New World. Large merchants in the major Spanish ports experienced a massive decline in colonial trade. An inflationary spiral of agrarian prices reduced the labouring classes' meagre purchasing power (even noble and clerical landowners' rents and señorial dues could no longer keep pace with rising wheat prices), and unemployment, especially in the textile industries, rose. Drought and pestilence added to the general distress. In a poor agrarian country, with primitive agricultural techniques as backward as Russia's, and without a developed domestic market, a local crop failure could result in catastrophe: for want of an adequate road system and cheap transport, foreign wheat could not be moved from the ports to inland areas in trouble; nor, in good years, could surplus wheat be transported – except at prohibitive cost compared to imported foreign wheat – from the cereal-growing Castilian plains to the coastal regions, where the eighteenth-century population growth had mainly taken place. Spain thus found itself in a paradoxical situation: Castilla produced surplus wheat and bought mainly smuggled foreign textiles, while Cataluña produced textiles and imported great quantities of wheat. This resulted in a large balance of payments deficit for Spain as a whole. The system could only function as long as colonial trade sustained the deficit.[19]

Although there were temporary respites to the economic setbacks during moments of peace, the colonial trade was the first to suffer in war. War, first on the French Revolution then, in alliance with France, war against Britain, had increased public expenditure over the past decade by between five- and eight-fold.[20] By 1808, annual indebtedness was running at nearly double domestic taxation revenues and the total debt stood at the equivalent of ten years' revenue.[21]

The Old Order's escalating erosion had coincided with Carlos IV's accesssion to the throne on the death of his father, Carlos III, and the outbreak of the

French Revolution only six months later. Foreign and domestic problems, separate and combined, had begun in his reign to challenge the structures on which Bourbon absolutism had rested for the past three-quarters of a century. Though 'well-intentioned and zealous like his father', the new king was 'weak, vapid, and less wise than becomes a sovereign . . . and his pusillanimous spirit came to be dominated by the queen, Maria Luisa', in the words of an enlightened contemporary cleric.[22] A formidable statesman was needed; and if Carlos IV lacked that quality, then he lacked another equally grave: that needed to find and appoint the statesman required.*

SEQUELS OF THE FRENCH REVOLUTION

For several nights the early summer sky over France beyond the Pyrenees was as clear as day, or ablaze in vermilions, gold and blues . . . and always of such variety and clarity that those who witnessed it were amazed. The celestial lights were a manifestation from heaven of the calamities and misfortunes which were to come, and of the martyrs who were to die, in the revolutions

wrote a Catalan posting-house master many years later.[23]

The extraordinary changes brought about by the revolution in Spain's ally, France, resulted in a number of exceptional changes in Spain itself. First, the revolution frightened the enlightened government reformists who, for the past twenty years under Carlos III, had attempted to eliminate inherited 'obstacles' to economic and social advance, without undermining the Old Regime's structures. 'Everything for the people, but without the people', summed up their creed. They believed, for example, that the Church needed reform – the Inquisition, because it concerned itself not only with religious but with state affairs; the religious orders because of the great number of 'unproductive' friars and monks, some of whom displayed a scandalous moral laxity – though, unlike the French *philosophes*, they did not (at least openly) question their Catholic faith. The reformists criticized the nobility for its 'idleness' but believed it had an essential place in society. They thought that the nobility's and Church's entailment of a great part of their landholdings was both a serious obstacle to increased agricultural production, and kept large extents of poorly farmed land from the market – but they did not attack entailment head on. They criticized the artisans' guilds for their monopolistic practices in price-setting and control of production but did not abolish them. Their determination not to bring the edifice crashing around their heads outweighed their reforming zeal. Not suprisingly then, the French Revolution turned them from the path of reform (if they had not already run out of intellectual stamina) because reform in France had set a dangerous precedent.

* Carlos IV's main task was to hunt from nine to twelve and from two to five every day, in all kinds of weather, following his father's example. (Hunting had been proposed to the Spanish Bourbons as a means of avoiding melancholia.) In the evenings he would ask Godoy, 'And what have my vassals been doing today?' As late as 1803 he constantly 'forgot' that the British colonies in America had gained independence, although Spain, as France's ally and enemy of England, had afforded aid to the American revolutionaries.

This change of heart was exemplified by conde Floridablanca, who had led the reformist government for twenty years before the revolution. A scrivener's son, now aged sixty, he was representative of the enlightened commoners or untitled lower nobles who had formed the leading members of the old king's administration, and whom Carlos III had rewarded with titles. His attempt to impose a *cordon sanitaire* to stop the revolutionary 'plague' from entering Spain was more an outcome of panic than a response to any real possibility of the contagion becoming an active epidemic. The country itself was not prepared for revolution, either socially, politically or culturally.*

The differences with France were notable. Put schematically, the Spanish commoner elite and the lower untitled nobility had not been excluded by the upper nobility from political power, as in France; and unlike the French nobility which was unable to extract sufficient economic surplus from its long-lease-holding peasantry and gained this income instead from its control of the state, the Spanish nobility, excluded from the running of the state, ensured its surplus by short-term rents that took advantage of the inflationary demand for land and an oligarchic control of local municipalities.

Absolutism permitted handsome incomes to Spanish colonial traders. The large merchants, of whom there were relatively few in comparison to France and England, had no reason to be hostile to the ruling system, and indeed generally supported it. Whereas the fiscal crisis of the French state was acute, in Spain this was still to come. But perhaps most important of all, there had been no widespread cultural preparation critical of absolutism, as in France; no *sociétés de pensée*, for example, to create a public opinion independent of traditional sources of authority.† In 1780, religious books accounted for only one-tenth of French titles; in Spain the proportion of works of piety, devotion and the lives of saints had shown little or no change throughout the eighteenth century.‡ Nor had the religious rituals of death and burial.[24]

The Enlightenment had never deeply penetrated the labouring classes whose loyalty to Crown, Altar and their traditions remained their overt touchstones. Here again the difference between the two countries was notable: the French

---

* There was only one direct similarity with France: 1788–1789 saw bad grain harvests, and in February–March of the latter year Barcelona was the scene of serious bread riots; there were similar riots in a number of townships in the interior. But these remained localized, did not spread outwards into a wider movement.

† The nearest Spain came to anything like educative discussion societies illustrates the distance from the French example. The purpose of the Economic Societies, the first of which was started in the Basque country in 1765, was to encourage agriculture, industry, commerce, the arts and sciences. Though fundamentally they represented agrarian interests, noble landowners were notable by their absence as were also merchants in the port cities – Barcelona, Cádiz, La Coruña, Bilbao – where no societies were set up. It was the more enlightened clergy and highly enthusiastic commoners who gave them their active support. The Societies' attachment to religion was one of their strongest features. (Anes, 1972, 'Las sociedades de Amigos del País', pp.13–41 and Anes, 1976, pp. 398–400; Herr, 1958, pp. 154–163.)

‡ Madrid was an exception, with more books on the arts and sciences being produced. But in the provincial capitals there was no change. (French figures in Chartier, 1991, p. 71; Spanish proportions in Teófanes Egido, 'La religiosidad de los españoles (siglo XVIII)', in VV.AA., 1990 (1), p. 769.)

literacy rate was double that of Spain where over eighty percent of the population remained illiterate.*

Although the government did everything possible to prevent news of the revolution reaching Spain, it was impossible to stop seditious material being smuggled in. Information was widely spread; but it was a matter of geographical breadth rather than sociological depth. Incendiary posters and anonymous letters citing revolutionary slogans appeared not infrequently in different places.[25] But they were usually isolated cases – the work of a disaffected or hot-headed individual, whose use of revolutionary slogans, one suspects, was most often designed to frighten the local authorities. It was more at the level of the imaginary rather than of ideas that the use of these symbols came to represent a breaking down of values.†

The threat to the life of Louis XVI, the Spanish king's cousin, whom Carlos IV made every effort to save, brought about an extraordinary change in Spain's leadership: the appointment of a twenty-five-year-old former junior Horse Guards' officer, Manuel Godoy, to head the government and try to succeed where two experienced and elderly first ministers – Floridablanca and his successor, conde Aranda – had failed. An unknown recently promoted by the king from the lower nobility to a dukedom and grandee‡ of Spain; a first minister who had not spent a lifetime working his way up through the royal service to reach power; the first royal favourite to rule the country for a century and a half. If nothing else, the change illustrated the problems which the French Revolution had caused among the governing elite. That Godoy was or was not the queen's lover is of no particular historical importance. What is of historical import, however, was that Spaniards of every station in life soon came to believe that he owed his elevation to what they took as a fact; and they despised him and the queen for it, and pitied the cuckolded king. It was the beginning of a popular delegitimization of the reigning sovereign – although not of the monarchy itself – at a critical time for the Old Regime.

As a Spanish historian, Andrés Muriel, wrote in his history of Carlos IV:

> It would have mattered little in the people's eyes that don Manuel Godoy, at twenty-five, had been raised to the dukedom of Alcudia and named chief minister by the

* Forty-seven percent of French men and 27% of French women were literate. (Chartier, 1991, p. 69.) At an estimate, 75% of Spanish men and 90% of women were illiterate. Male literacy solely among the labouring classes – as measured by those who signed their names at the beginning the Napoleonic war to enlistment rolls – ran from 13.5% among agricultural workers in one Andalucian township to 20.6% among urban and rural males in a Catalan town. (See Appendix 3.)

† Elorza, 1989, pp. 102 and 99. This view was confirmed by a French agent, Chantreau, after a secret mission to Cataluña in 1792, who wrote: 'les apôtres de notre révolution seroient très mal reçus' [our revolution's apostles would be very badly received'] (cited in Roura, 1993, p. 136).

‡ Initiated in the early sixteenth century by Carlos I, a grandee was the realm's highest noble distinction after that of infante, which was reserved exclusively for the monarch's children. Although the title was most usually awarded by the sovereign to a duke, persons of lesser or even no title could be raised to grandee and as such were considered the monarch's 'cousin'.

king's free appointment, if they had seen in the favourite superior talents, or knew at least of previous glorious achievements which, in the critical circumstances faced by Spain, could herald important services to the kingdom . . . What hurt Spaniards was the origin of his power, due solely to the queen's passion.[26]

The only earlier 'glorious achievement' known of Godoy was that, as a guards-man, he had fallen from his horse in escorting the then princess María Luisa, and remounted rapidly, which brought him to her attention. His relative good looks could not be ascribed to any previous achievement known to him. In the course of ruling Spain, with one brief intermission, for the next sixteen years, he became – often quite unfairly – the most maligned and hated absolutist chief minister.

Louis XVI's execution shook Spain to its core. Despite last-minute conces-sions to France, Godoy's endeavours to save Louis were unsuccessful. Regicide was the ultimate crime in Spain,* where Crown and Altar were consubstantial with the perceived essence of the country's past and continuing existence.

Alas for you, mad nation who
With your horrendous outrage have
Afflicted heaven, staining the anointed
With blood.[27]

wrote Gaspar Melchor Jovellanos, the personification of Spain's Enlighten-ment. The sympathy with the French Revolution's early attempt to establish a constitutional monarchy – envisaged by the more progressively enlightened as the solution to Spain's absolutism – turned to antipathy; the Terror completed the revulsion.

Finally, as could be expected, the revolution brought forth violent attacks from unreformed clerics and laymen on the Enlightenment which was con-sidered responsible for the 'anarchy' in France. For the more extreme clerics, the revolution was the very incarnation of evil, the work of the 'sinister *philosophes*', and it was monarchy's divine right and fundamental mission to repress such Luciferian work which disturbed the immutable, hierarchical order of society. The Church's help and guidance – and, in Spain, that of the Inquisition – was necessary to this end.[28]

Conservative opposition to enlightened reform had long existed, but the French Revolution gave it a new strength and coherence, joined as it was by the older generation of reformers themselves; albeit temporarily, support for Spain's ancien regime was reinforced.

*

A small number of young writers and poets, however, kept their faith in the need for reform – 'unquiet spirits' like Manuel José Quintana and the clergyman José

* In this respect, it is worth observing that, despite the turbulence of much of Spain's political history since the beginning of the nineteenth through to the first third of the twentieth century, which saw two monarchs exiled and another abdicate the throne in despair of being able to govern, the Spanish have never committed regicide.

Marchena, later to confront each other as the early 'ideologues' on either side of the Spanish political and ideological strife that was part of the Napoleonic war. What marked these progressives* was a belief in liberty and the inherent virtues of the *patria* or fatherland which they saw as having been desecrated by absolutism and the reign of a despot, Godoy. They welcomed the French Revolution's overthrow of the Old Regime and its early attempt to create a constitutional monarchy; supported the Declaration of the Rights of Man; believed in the liberty from oppression, and the freedom of expression, that the revolution had introduced; shared the view that *la patrie* belonged to, and expressed the needs of, the people, and not merely those of an elite. Thus far the French Revolution's political achievements could serve them. But they saw also, in Quintana's words, that the revolution had resulted in 'drowning the Enlightenment; swallowing up the talented; corrupting customs and from the streams of blood and mountains of dead bodies has raised up an insolent and ambitious man to the height of power . . . How could I wish for my country anything of this nature?'[29] In brief, regicide and Jacobin terror in the name of the people had terrorized his generation, while the revolution's ultimate denouement in Napoleon's 'dictatorship' horrified them as a new tyranny – 'a betrayal' of the revolution at its best. The French Revolution was no model they proposed to follow. Even one of the few outright Spanish supporters of the revolution – José Marchena, who took refuge in France and became a Girondin – penned a proclamation to the Spanish in which his most radical proposal was to summon the Old Order's Cortes. He showed himself well aware of the importance of Spain's past institutions and its ardent Catholicism.[30]

In the progressives' view – and this was what was innovative – the Spanish people would have to make the needed reforms in their own way.† Not the uneducated and lowest orders of the people, for sure: democracy was a dangerous illusion that led only to disorder and bloodshed. But when the (respectable) people achieved freedom, the 'fatherland's good became the first law'. The people must effect and carry out this law, as the only guarantee that the 'general will' would prevail.[31] In this sense, then, they could be said to have inverted the earlier enlightened reformers' 'everything for the people, but without the people'. They counted on 'the people' to make the reforms in which they put their faith.

*

What then did the Spanish labouring classes make of the French Revolution? Direct evidence is scanty, but occasional glimpses are afforded through the

* Admittedly anachronistic, I use the word to differentiate those who believed in a constitutional monarchy from others who supported absolutism, albeit slightly reformed.
† I have knowingly homogenized the views of the more progressive poets and writers, views which were influential during the war, in a way that does not do justice to the variety of intellectual argument expresssed in Quintana's *tertulia* (regular literary gatherings). By no means all of those who attended would have shared all of the views put forward here – but it was these that mobilized an articulate minority during the Napoleonic war.

authorities' eyes. In 1791, for example, the governor of Lérida advised the first minister of the innumerable French workers crossing the Pyrenees as usual to seek work in the olive mills of lower Cataluña, parts of Aragón and Valencia. Their conversation could not, in these days, be 'beneficial to the unwary local inhabitants', he reported, because inevitably they talked of

> their new Constitution, their liberty, equality, the lowering by half of the tributes and dues they had paid before, the exemption from taxes, tithes and parochial payments for baptisms, marriages, funerals and other advantages of their new laws. These can leave an impression on the lower people who, without reflecting, compare what they pay here with the apparent benefits they hear of in conversation. I do not presume that the French talk of these things with malicious intent, for they are simple and ignorant people, or that the people of these parts form advantageous ideas of the French revolution; indeed to the contrary the former are generally looked on with scorn because of it.[32]

The governor's report appeared ambiguous: the 'unwary local inhabitants', for whom he feared, almost immediately turned into wary individuals who responded to the revolution with scorn. Scorn for liberty and equality? Or for the fact, as the governor went on to report, that these French countrymen were much favoured by local Spanish mill-owners because they laboured at tasks 'that few of the local inhabitants are prepared to do' and at lower daily wages than a Spaniard? A possible explanation of this ambivalence came in another communication to the minister, this time from the captain general of Cataluña, conde de Lacy, in February, 1792:

> Catalans look with bad feeling on migrant French artisans and journeymen who are willing to work for two *cuartos* less a day . . . and I am taking care to see that this does not lead to blows which would end in no quarter being given.[33]

Throughout the 1780s, there had been large-scale French immigration to Cataluña, attracted by the high wages paid in textile manufacture. But a downturn in manufacturing in 1789 had left many of these without work.[34] What real benefit had the revolution brought them if they could not find jobs in their own country and offered to work for less than a Catalan artisan who, like the Aragonese and Valencian mill-workers and journeymen, was suffering a serious decline in real wages? What meaning had liberty and equality in such circumstances? The scorn for the French Revolution had a perfectly comprehensible basis in the 'bad feeling' which these migrant workers aroused by their labour practices, especially when it is recalled that xenophobia, anti-French sentiment at this time in particular, was easily aroused among the Spanish lower orders – as the serious anti-French riots of 1793 in Valencia demonstrated.

    Possibly there was greater revolutionary effervescence in the large cities like Barcelona and Madrid where '. . . in the taverns . . . and cafés nothing else is heard but talk of battles, revolution, Convention, national representation, liberty, equality: even the whores ask you about Robespierre and Barrere

[sic] . . .'. So wrote P. Estala to Juan Pablo Forner; but as the latter was an enlightened but well-known counter-revolutionary thinker, his correspondent's views may well have been tailored to over-emphasize the revolutionary danger.[35]

The imaginary, which can contain contradictory signs and symbols, is no guarantee of future action; and its twists and turns are difficult to document. Nonetheless, when the Spanish villagers had the freedom to do so, during the anti-Napoleonic struggle, they stopped paying tributes and dues, taxes and tithes; and equality – equality of sacrifice, if nothing more – became one of the most palpable public demands.

WAR AGAINST REVOLUTIONARY FRANCE

Well aware of the cost of war, the two previous first ministers had striven to keep Spain from armed conflict with revolutionary France. Godoy attempted to follow this policy, but after the Convention rejected Spanish interference in trying to save Louis XVI's life and declared war on Spain he responded in kind. On a reduced scale the ensuing war was, in many respects, a precursor of Spain's Napoleonic war.*

The similarity began in the sheer military 'folly' of fighting France – whether Napoleon's armed might in 1808, or revolutionary France in 1793 – which had defeated the Prussians at Valmy and the Austrians at Jemappes the previous autumn, victories that had sent shock waves through the counter-revolutionary powers. And though new to supreme power, Godoy was well aware of his army's weakness and the treasury's poor financial state – both of which would become even more critical by 1808. On each occasion, however, Spain was fortunate in not having immediately to confront battle-hardened French veterans. In 1793 they faced a large but militarily inexperienced Convention force in south-western France and in 1808 mainly raw imperial conscripts in hastily created new regiments. In each case, Spanish arms were crowned with early victories that shortly turned into crushing defeats.

Religious fervour, and initial popular mobilization in defence of 'Religion, King and Country' (the slogan under which the Spanish subsequently rose against Napoleon) were the most visible of similarities between the two wars. Coined by clerical anti-revolutionaries, the slogan combined three elements

---

* The war was both temporally and spatially small-scale compared to the later Napoleonic war. Fighting was basically restricted to Cataluña, the Basque provinces and Navarra, and continued for only a little over two years, whereas the Napoleonic war extended over the whole of Spain, lasted six years, and at its height involved over three hundred thousand imperial troops – seven times more than the maximum deployed during the Convention War. There were many other major differences also: the Convention War did not begin with the French in occupation of Madrid and a large part of the north, there had been no previous dynastic crisis to exploit by the French to eject the Bourbons from the Spanish throne, and it did not directly inspire colonial independence from Spain. (For a comparison of the two wars, see Jean-René Aymes, 'La "Guerra Gran" (1793–1795) como prefiguración de la "Guerra del Francés" (1808–1814)' in Aymes (ed.), 1989, pp. 311–66.)

meaningful to all social orders: religion, the common denominator of all
Spaniards, allied with the monarch, the benevolent secular pastor of his flock,
and the homeland (*patria*) or community to which each individual had a
personal sense of belonging and in which, however tenuously, each had material
interests to defend. For the Church, suitably enough, the trilogy became a
trinitarian unity. 'The homeland, King, even God Himself, form but a single
object and finality', declaimed Friar Juan Izquierdo, doctor of sacred theology,
in a widely reproduced sermon given during the blessing of a battalion's flag in
Barcelona.[36] Or as the best-known missionary preacher of the day, Friar Diego
Josef de Cádiz, put it:

> Every faithful Catholic is obliged to maintain the truth of his religion and faith against
> his enemies, to the point of sacrificing his life in their defence if necessary . . . The
> sanctity of our Catholic religion demands of its professional soldiers . . . that they
> sanctify their hands with the profaners' blood . . . The soldier of Christ kills with
> assurance . . . In death he gains glory, and if he kills it is to the glory of Christ.[37]

The slogan had, however, a deeper significance: it expressed a change in the
definition of warfare from a conflict between states for territorial or dynastic
objectives to a national, ideological war in which the enemy became persona-
lized and anathematized.

The lessons of the French Revolution's summons to the entire French
population to rally to the 'défence de la patrie' against a 'malign' enemy were
most readily turned on their head by Spanish religious counter-revolutionaries.
In their Janus-faced view, *la patrie,* with its revolutionary connotations for the
French, became, as *la patria*, a call to defend a counter-revolutionary homeland,
its laws, customs and traditions, Spain's Old Order, its monarchy and religion.
The Spanish Church was well prepared for this sort of ideological twist, for
waging a crusade against foreign heretics. It was hardly surprising then that the
slogan should re-emerge with even greater strength at the beginning of the
Napoleonic war, just as Diego de Cádiz's booklet again became the catechism of
many volunteer soldiers after the rising against Napoleon in 1808.

The similarities between the two wars did not end there: other more material
elements were shared by both. Spanish army commanders, with few exceptions,
revealed themselves inept; the army itself was undermanned, ill-organized,
badly trained, fed and equipped, and unable to confront sustained and rapid
revolutionary assaults; desertion and sickness became serious problems . . .

During the Convention War, the Church kept up its tireless campaign to
inflame hatred of the 'barbarous' and 'impious' enemy . . . But the conflict
could not be financed by the royal treasury other than by obligatory contributions from the Church and the wealthy and the massive issuing of state bonds,
the *vales reales*, which in consequence depreciated in value, as inflation spiralled
upwards. The sons of township oligarchs managed, thanks to their fathers'
influence, to avoid enlistment which caused resentment among ordinary villagers who were sent to the front; and popular enthusiasm for the 'crusade' waned
notably after the first few months of war fever . . .

Equally, however, the war was the testing ground of self-organization, local resistance and irregular warfare. These were to be among the most striking elements of Spanish popular resistance to Napoleon.

A small Spanish military force rapidly marched over the Catalan border and, taking the exiguous and unprepared Convention troops by surprise, captured the province of Roussillon (whose inhabitants were more Catalan than French and were generally hostile to the French Revolution), and stood before the gates of Perpignan. For the remainder of 1793, the Convention was busy holding back the Spanish; armed French civilians took up guerrilla war as part of the struggle. Angered by this breach in conventional warfare, General Antonio Ricardos, the Spanish commander, issued a proclamation threatening to shoot them out of hand if captured.*

The prime example of self-organization and irregular war was precipitated in 1794, when a French counter-offensive drove the Spanish out of the territories they had occupied in France, and back into Catalonia. Historically, Catalans had been exempt from conscription into the Spanish army; and they retained their hostility to it, having staged a militia revolt in 1773. Their preferred way of defending their country was as 'volunteers' contracted by their municipal authorities.[38] When the French advanced into Cataluña in the autumn, and the Spanish army surrendered Figueras castle, a stronghold on the road between the French frontier and Barcelona, an important element of territorial loyalty was rapidly revealed: the population's readiness to fight by any and all means against an aggressor in its own region. With the Spanish army falling back in disarray, the Catalans, amidst generalized fear that their country was about to be occupied, took their defence into their own hands. Virtually ignoring the central government as they had earlier ignored French revolutionary appeals offering them their independence, a *junta* (assembly) of representatives from all the *corregimientos* (the administrative areas into which Cataluña was divided) met in January 1795 to organize the mobilization of sixteen to twenty thousand volunteers between the ages of sixteen and fifty, and the levying of a general progressive tax on the population for the country's defence. The 'contracted volunteers' were formed into regiments of *miquelets* (militia); and villagers, gathered in local defence groups known as *sometents*,† began irregular warfare on the enemy rearguard. The Convention's reduced forces went on the defensive and the Catalan-reinforced Spanish army secured two victories over them, the last – after peace had been signed but the news had not reached the front – opening the way to a re-occupation of the Cerdagne.

* Roura, 1993, p. 194. That French citizens should be the first to adopt a tactic followed subsequently by Catalan civilians (and eventually by Spaniards generally in the Napoleonic war) revealed the extent to which the French revolutionary wars had 'revolutionized' warfare. That a Spanish general should be the first to threaten armed civilians with execution if captured, as Napoleon's generals in their turn would put into practice in Spain, revealed the extent to which the military generally rejected this civilian intrusion into their professional terrain.
† These had been a traditional Catalan villagers' 'home guard' which the Bourbons had abolished; they were officially re-established by the Spanish army commander, conde de la Unión, in May 1794, because of the Catalans' 'repugnance' to their forces being enrolled in regular army units.

But it was with a lightning attack in July 1794, on Guipúzcoa, the Basque province bordering France, that the decisive French breakthrough came; the Convention's offensive led to panic and disorder in the Spanish army which until then had held a fairly tranquil line. But here the popular reaction appeared initially different. The French advanced almost without meeting resistance and San Sebastián surrendered without a fight on August 4. While Cataluña was just ending a long period of prosperity, the Basque country had, since the mid-eighteenth century, been struggling with a basic structural difficulty: population growth had outstripped the availability of land to support it. This began to destabilize traditional rural society in which the system of small tenants on hereditary leases living on dispersed farmsteads or in small villages and hamlets could no longer be replicated. The social crisis was marked by the appearance of bandits, beggars and vagrants on roads and in villages where previously these were said to be unknown. As the crisis worsened, the landowners who controlled economic, political and social power in the country tried to pass taxation needs – increased by the war – onto their small tenants. The villagers began to confront the landowners. The greatest threat to the latter's power, however, came from Madrid's attempt to impose tighter tax controls when, under the Basque *fueros*, or self-governing rights, the country traditionally contributed its self-raised taxes as a 'gift' to the royal exchequer at the king's request.

Furthermore, the Basque provinces of Vizcaya and Guipúzcoa and also Navarra claimed that the sole duty of their locally-raised and financed forces was to defend their own provinces, outside of which they could not be stationed, or be incorporated into the Spanish army or come under the army commander's orders. Although the Consejo de Castilla rejected this interpretation of their *fueros*,[39] in Vizcaya most villagers agreed that the war beyond their provincial limits did not concern them. In Gauteguiz de Arteaga the youth refused to undergo military training, making 'mocking gestures at the officers whom the authorities had imposed on them, and indicating that they would appoint their own officers to train them'. Although the Church backed the religious crusade against the French revolutionaries, the 'enemies of God', Vizcayans, believing themselves protected by the Spanish army on the frontier and by Guipúzcoa, faced the beginning of the war with relative tranquility.[40]

Nevertheless, after the French breakthrough, when the Spanish army commander, conde de Colomera, sent an urgent request for men to join his force, the Vizcayan authorities prepared to dispatch eight thousand men to Tolosa outside of their borders to reinforce him. This resulted in further village protests. Some said that all were agreed that the war did not affect them, others that they would go to the borders of Vizcaya but not to join Colomera's forces since other villages felt the same. In Sopuerta, the locals, armed with sticks and knives, insulted and threatened the authorities when they were about to hold a ballot to decide who should go to Tolosa, shouting that they would not serve outside Vizcaya.[41] They would be 'better off and freer if the French came to this country and they followed the maxims of its Assembly rather than continue under the (Basque) Constitution'. They shouted insults at the Catholic religion and the state of the kingdom . . . The authorities fled for their lives. In

Guecho, villagers armed with hoes and agrarian implements forced the authorities to give them the lists of those who were to go, tore them up and buried
them. Women, mothers and wives of those who had been selected, were
prominent in the riots. But everywhere the rioters made clear that their protest
was not at serving within Vizcaya but at having to serve beyond its borders.
Finally, as Colomera could not hold Tolosa, the order was countermanded, and
the ringleaders of the protests were arrested and as punishment sent to the
front.

San Sebastián's surrender and the formation of a junta or committee, of a
small group of enlightened individuals prepared to support the French – their
aim being as much to protect the population from reprisals as at outright
collaboration – shocked other Basques. A Bilbaino, probably a merchant,
considered it 'ignominious', a 'villanous affair' for which he claimed the French
had paid twenty million reales. But, as the same writer recorded, it was not until
two weeks after the surrender that the first Vizcayan regiment set out for the
provincial front, the village recruits shouting that to 'avoid betrayal the traitors
must die'.[42]

No sooner had the San Sebastián junta been formed than other local
committees were created to resist the invaders, and they began guerrilla actions.
General Moncey, the French commander, complained that the Basques 'do not
fight ordered battles, [but attack] and escape without leaving a trace, and end up
by killing many of our men without suffering great losses themselves'.[43]
However, the French continued their advance south; after a harsh winter, they
took Vitoria, and, striking into Castilla, Miranda del Ebro. From here, the road
to Madrid was virtually open to them. The time had come to end a war which
had turned out disastrously for the Spanish army and the Old Regime.

Though other, better European armies had also gone down to defeat at the
hands of the French Revolution, the Spanish army had proven itself of poor
fighting worth. Irregular warfare had sprung up on both the Catalan and
Basque fronts and had given the French army a hard time of it; but the guerrillas
could not and would not be victorious on their own. The events of the last days
of the war, however, on both the western and eastern fronts, gave cause for
reflection. Stiffened by large numbers of local recruits and guerrilla reinforcements, the Spanish armies went on the offensive in Navarra and Cataluña. The
conjunction of regular and irregular warfare took its toll on the enemy, and
resulted in last-minute Catalan victories. A twenty-five-year-old general – the
youngest of his rank in the French revolutionary army – noted the Spanish
popular resistance. A land war in Spain was unwinnable, he warned, because of
the national uprising it would precipitate.[44] A decade and a half later, and to his
cost, Napoleon had forgotten his youthful perspicacity.

In seeking peace, Godoy was fortunate: the post-Robespierrean Convention
did not want to get bogged down in a war to overthrow a Bourbon in Spain
when its principal enemy was the far more threatening anti-French monarchical
coalition led by Austria and England. Peace with Spain, moreover, could once
more ensure France of her naval assistance in the struggle against England. By
the treaty of Basel, Spain conceded her half of Santo Domingo to France while

all the Spanish territory, fortresses, armaments, etc, which she had lost in the war were returned.[45]

There was general rejoicing: the treaty's terms were better than those accorded to the other enemies of the revolution.[46] His royal masters rewarded Godoy by naming him Prince of the Peace.

THE OLD ORDER'S ALLIANCE
WITH REVOLUTIONARY FRANCE

Only a year later, in 1796, shortly after the advent of the French Directorate, Spain tied her fortunes once more to France in an unholy alliance of Bourbon absolutism and the new Republicanism. It was a return to Spain's pre-revolution foreign policy in which the French and Spanish Bourbons had been allies against Britain, in the so-called 'Family Compact'. In negotiating an offensive-defensive alliance against Britain with the Directorate, Godoy was less concerned, however, with a return to the past than with playing the foreign affairs card to try to reinforce his domestic position. During the war, several plots against him had been discovered, and though Godoy had foiled them with relative ease, all of them significantly implicated members of the political elite. Without domestic political support, other than from sycophants and the royal couple, Godoy believed that an alliance with France would strengthen his cause. It resulted in the destruction not only of the Spanish fleet,* but of trade with the colonies. At the same time it increased the latter's desire for independence, deepened Spain's internal economic crisis, and accelerated the Old Order's erosion. Although Britain wanted to avoid a conflict with Spain, the latter declared war on England in October 1796.

Colonial trade was immediately affected. After little more than a year of war, Spanish customs revenues had fallen to one-third of their 1792 figure; and the share of these in the state's total revenues had dropped from 28.2 percent to 8.8 percent and would continue to decline even further. Only in the temporary peace after the Treaty of Amiens in 1802 was there a recuperation to fifteen percent.[47] When the war between Spain and Britain was resumed at the end of 1804, the effects on Spain's trade and naval power were even more disastrous. In the year before the resumption of hostilities, 105 merchantmen sailed from Cataluña to the colonies carrying goods worth 76.8 million reales; in 1807 only one Catalan merchantman set out bearing two hundred thousand reales of produce.[48] There were large lay offs in the Catalan textile factories whose major markets were the colonies. In 1797–98 prices increased nearly twice as much as during the Convention War and wages fell in central Spain.[49]

For both the metropolis and the colonies, a further, and equally decisive consequence of the war was the Spanish government's decision to end its

---

* The serious defeat at Cape San Vicente by Jervis and Hood in 1797, and the loss of Trinidad to the British, were the immediate results; to be followed in 1805 by the disaster of Nelson's victory at Trafalgar over the Franco-Spanish fleets in their attempt to break out of the British blockade of Cádiz bay. A defeat as serious, if not more so, as that of the Armada, because thereafter Spain's colonial trade remained without naval defence.

monopoly in colonial trade and open it to neutral shipping – a measure necessary to keep the colonies supplied. In every recent war, even when Britain was not the enemy, this measure had had to be applied, demonstrating Spain's fundamental inability to wage war *and* provision its colonies. The measure became an important impetus to the colonial independence movement, since the colonials derived greater profit from trading with Europe through neutrals than they did under Spain's trade monopoly.*

Godoy himself came to realize that France was using the alliance to her sole advantage and that war with England had been an economically shortsighted error, but his attempts to extricate Spain were met by France with hostile reactions which he lacked the determination to confront.† The experience of the War of the Convention (and even more of the American War of Independence) made it evident that modern warfare was so costly that, without any counterpart, it could strain asunder the seams of societies more prosperous than Spain's. But Godoy continued along this dangerous path, a path which led in the first instance to the state's bankruptcy.

In an attempt to deal with the fiscal crisis, loans were floated abroad, the capital of the Bank of San Carlos, established in 1782 as the national bank, was confiscated,[50] and more state bonds issued. By 1798, the latters' value had dropped by fifty percent. After no more than two years of renewed war against England, the Spanish treasury's situation was so critical that Godoy was forced to take a drastic measure; he ordered Church property sold, a reform that no earlier enlightened reformer had dared to enact. The Church was one of the two pillars of the absolute monarchy, a state within the state, the single wealthiest institution in the kingdom of Castilla.

By 1808, between one-sixth and one-seventh of all Church property not devoted to 'the cure of souls' had been sold to the value of 1,653 million reales. In some regions, like Andalucía, Murcia, Salamanca and Madrid, the proportion reached twenty to twenty-five percent. This measure, which included the

---

* Though the measure was supposed to be only temporary – as during the American War of Independence and Spain's War against the French Convention – the Napoleonic Wars did not permit it to be lifted, despite the Spanish patriot government's attempts to return to the status quo ante.

† In 1798, after the defeat of Cape San Vicente, he sued for a separate peace with Britain, and the Directorate's fierce reaction temporarily cost him his post (Emilio La Parra López, 'Dependencia política española. Los gobiernos de Carlos IV frente al Directorio (1795–1799)', in VV.AA., 1990 (3), pp. 177–190). In the year following the short-lived Peace of Amiens (1802), Godoy, back in power again, proposed to Russia and Prussia an alliance of armed neutrality to maintain a European equilibrium, and though nothing came of it, resisted Napoleon's pressure to rejoin the war against Britain. Napoleon, first consul, demanded that Spain break with Britain or pay a monthly subsidy of six million francs. He threatened to invade Spain if the Spanish government refused to sign a treaty to this effect (The Treaty of Paris, October, 1803). Godoy agreed to the monthly subsidy, although it was beyond the royal exchequer's means to find the money. Finally, late in 1804, as a result of Britain's earlier naval provocations (attacking four Spanish frigates, laden with South American gold, capturing three and sinking one before a declaration of war), Spain declared war on Britain and confirmed her alliance with France. (Lovett, 1965, vol. 1, p. 21; Anes, 1976, p. 429; Izquierdo, 1963, p.87.)

sale of hospitals, asylums, foundling homes, pious foundations, etc., 'caused immense damage to the poor rural classes who were the most in need of help.'[51] But as the amount of debt emitted in state bonds alone reached two thousand million reales, and the bonds' value had dropped by half, the sale of Church property was insufficient to meet state indebtedness. In the king's name, Godoy secured the Pope's agreement for further sales, 'owing to the considerable decrease in the income of my crown because of the wars, shortages, epidemics and other calamities which have afflicted this kingdom', although these sales did not come into full effect before Napoleon's invasion in 1808.

The Church thus bore the brunt of the state's fiscal crisis.[52] As state bonds were now backed by the sale of church property, they seemed to many churchmen similar to the *assignats* of the French Revolution;[53] and the Church's opposition to these measures was in no small part responsible for the downfall of Godoy and his royal master in 1808.[54]

None of the measures solved the treasury's crisis. Even government ministers did not get paid; by 1808 their salaries were the second highest item on the list of outstanding debt.[55] Fiscal pressure forced many municipalities to sell communal lands; as a result townships and villages dominated by noble-appointed oligarchs became 'inveterate enemies of the government'.[56] More accurately, it could be said that all the monied classes had 'lost confidence in the solvency of the crown'.[57] Godoy paid the political price. Hatred of the royal favourite grew in all sectors of the population which suffered, to a greater or lesser degree, the cost of an unpopular war.

2

Preliminaries of War

BOURBON FAMILY SQUALOR: THE ESCORIAL AFFAIR

Napoleon's designs on Spain, and his army's slow but ceaseless advance on Madrid in March 1808, precipitated a crisis at the very heart of the absolutist monarchy. The Emperor continued to keep his plans a tightly held secret. No one, not even Marshal Murat, his brother-in-law and lieutenant general in Spain, knew for certain what Napoleon planned. Although late in the day, only one Spaniard appreciated the full scale of the danger: Godoy. And the awareness brought him his downfall.

To popular jubilation, the royal couple's favourite had been worsted the previous autumn by the heir to the throne, Fernando, whose popularity had soared as a result. An anonymous letter to the king, probably written by Godoy or one of his henchmen, led Carlos IV to search his son's rooms and to the discovery of compromising documents. On October 30 1807, the king proclaimed officially to the nation that Fernando had conspired to usurp the throne, that he was under house arrest, and a number of conspirators had been imprisoned.[1] The twenty-five-year-old heir's conspiracy was in fact a plot to rid the country of Godoy. Fernando's hatred of Godoy went back to his adolescence. Not perhaps surprisingly, as he saw his mother's alleged lover rising in power and noble rank to become a prince, a Spanish title usually reserved only to the throne's heir; and had he remained unaware of the situation, his former clerical preceptor, Juan Escoiquiz, 'an astute, servile, unscrupulous intriguer', would have insinuated the dangers that faced him. But this was probably unnecessary: Fernando had a sufficiently suspicious, cowardly, spiteful and unforgiving nature to need few lessons in revenge. His own mother found him 'sly and cowardly'; and for his first mother-in-law, Queen Carolina of Naples, he was 'stupid, indolent, lying, debased, underhand . . .'[2] Between 1804 and 1806, he had financed a series of scurrilous popular engravings figuring Godoy and his mother, accompanied by salacious rhyming couplets, which he distributed among the aristocracy and its hangers-on. Churchmen and nobles had also contributed satirical, often coarse, verses (occasionally in Latin) to his anti-Godoy campaign.[3]

Fernando feared that Godoy and the queen were planning to deny him the throne on his father's death, which had recently appeared imminent; rumours were rife at court that this was their plan and that Godoy might even be appointed regent.[4] Godoy feared, justly, that when Fernando came to the throne he would be deprived of his supreme power.

Had the affair remained at this personal level nothing much might have come of it. But it assumed wider dimensions because an anti-Godoy court faction found in Fernando the ideal figurehead as future king to plot the favourite's downfall. This faction, the Fernandista 'party', was bent on restoring the nobility's importance in the country's governance from which the Bourbons had excluded it. In foreign affairs, it was purely opportunistic, swinging from support for England to France to oppose Godoy's current predilections. Thus, during the favourite's momentary flirtation with the anti-Napoleonic alliance in 1806, the Fernandistas opted for Napoleon, and subsequently for the marriage of the widowed Fernando to a Bonaparte princess. In pursuit of this aim, Fernando wrote a grovelling letter to Napoleon in October 1807, which also quite explicitly criticized the Spanish government's attitude towards the Emperor. By this date, both Godoy and the Fernandistas were wooing the Emperor.*

Among the papers seized in Fernando's rooms was a decree, the date left blank, appointing his supporter, the duque del Infantado, grandee of Spain, to the post of captain general of Castilla and commander of the forces to overthrow Godoy should the king die; and a long letter, addressed by Fernando to his father, describing the 'perverse' Godoy's aspirations to 'take the Throne and finish with all of us'. It also attacked the favourite's morals, accusing him of bigamy, and worked on the king's fears of the French Revolution. The letter, written by his ex-preceptor and faithfully copied out by Fernando, said one thing that was true: Spaniards had grown cold in their respect for the royal couple, not in themselves but because of 'the pain that the elevation of a monster like Godoy has caused them'.[5]

Opposition to Godoy was by this time practically universal. Apart from the Fernandistas, the court nobility, which had always viewed the royal favourite as an upstart, was joined by regional oligarchs who resented his attempts to increase central control at their expense; the clergy who opposed his sale of Church property; merchants and manufacturers who faced ruin because of his foreign policy; sectors of the liberal professions who experienced the arbitrary appointments of family members, sycophants and flatterers to cherished posts, sometimes accompanied by their own removal to outlying districts; sectors of the enlightened literati who fulminated privately about 'despotism'; and the lower orders in general who suffered from declining wages and increasing prices, and were scandalized by Godoy's moral laxity.

A week after his arrest, Fernando made a full confession, naming all his confederates and admitting to direct correspondence with Napoleon and the

* To demonstrate his understanding with Napoleon, on October 27 1807, Godoy signed the Treaty of Fontainebleau for the joint conquest of Portugal, under which the royal favourite was to receive the southern third of Portugal and to become the Prince of the Algarve.

French ambassador. Once confessed, he wrote an abject letter to his father begging forgiveness which his father granted. His repentance, Fernando wrote, had been proven by his denunciation of the other plotters who had been arrested. Someone somewhere noted this and wrote:

> On my fellows I did peach
> Honour and fame I lost,
> The vile traitor did I beseech,
> And sold my Friends at cost,
> Father, for my sins, forgive me.*

But this perspicacious voice, which understood that Fernando would sell anyone to save his own skin, struck a discordant note among the vast majority of Spaniards who believed that the heir to the throne's tribulations were the result of a plot devised by Godoy and the queen. And when the Consejo de Castilla, constituted as a Supreme Court, found insufficient proof of guilt against the accused, there was further jubilation. Godoy's plot had redounded against him. Although Napoleon was angered by the revelations of Fernando's intrigues with him, the country at large believed that the heir to the throne now enjoyed the Emperor's protection and the latter's popularity rose perceptibly. Carlos IV, meanwhile, also tried to curry favour with Napoleon who became the arbiter of the family squabble and, beyond that, of Spain's destiny. Subsequently, many Spaniards came to see in the Escorial affair, so called after the palace where the royal family was then residing, the detonator of the Napoleonic war.[6]

THE ROYAL FAVOURITE'S OVERTHROW:
THE GRANDEES' REVOLT

In Aranjuez, some thirty kilometres south of Madrid, where the court was residing in March 1808, many people believed that Murat's slow advance on the capital 'was intended to bring pressure to bear on the Spanish royal family to flee the country, following the Portuguese example', as Archbishop Félix Amat, the king's confessor and member of His Majesty's Council wrote at the time.[7]

But the Spanish courtiers' assumptions were incorrect. This option was evidently no longer in Napoleon's mind, for as early as February 21 he had sent urgent orders to his admiral of the fleet bottled up in Cádiz by the British navy since Trafalgar three years earlier, that no Spanish ships should be allowed to leave the port. This was the day after he had appointed Murat as his lieutenant general and head of all French forces in Spain. In chosing his hot-headed and vain brother-in-law, Napoleon probably had in mind a marshal with sufficient ambition to ensure that the royal family did not escape at all.

* Anon, *Papeles de Cathaluña*, 1808, pp. 219 et seq. The queen, talking to Lord Holland in 1814, claimed to have 'shuddered at the unfeeling baseness of his disclosures . . . the treachery . . . more disgusting than any plot of which he could be accused'. (Holland, 1851, p. 86.)

One of Napoleon's private envoys, conte de Tournon, warned his master twice during March of Spanish 'irritation' against the French, and advised him that he should make no 'final decision' on the country's fate until he had judged the situation for himself.

> Spaniards have a noble and generous character, but one which tends towards ferocity and they would not stand being treated as a conquered nation. Once they are reduced to despair they would be capable of the greatest and most valiant revolutions and of the most violent excesses . . . Only [the Emperor's] presence can calm everything . . . The marriage of the Prince of the Asturias [Fernando] with a princess of the Imperial family is still longed for.[8]

Even Murat, who had sent optimistic dispatches on his enthusiastic reception along his march, was forced to recognize that the seizure of Pamplona fortress had caused 'general consternation' and that a possible rising in Navarra might result.[9] But he deceived himself and deceived Napoleon in turn when he informed him that 'Everywhere the people are awaiting Your Majesty and the felicity Your Majesty will bring . . .', unless by this both understood that this felicity depended on the Emperor overthrowing Godoy and granting imperial support and a Bonaparte wife to Fernando.[10] This the latter's supporters firmly believed was Napoleon's aim and they rejoiced openly at the prospect; they, too, deceived themselves and the public. Almost totally isolated, Godoy bent every last effort to persuade the king to move with his family out of the French army's immediate reach to the safety of Sevilla. The arrival in Aranjuez of Izquierdo, the favourite's private agent in Paris, with an imperial memorandum for the king – containing a series of half-truths concerning the reasons for Napoleon's military intervention in Spain and demands on the region north of the Ebro – finally seemed to have concentrated the king's mind.* On March 13, he agreed to Godoy's decision to leave. Meanwhile, a score of grandees of Spain had been hurriedly assembled in Madrid by the conde de Teba (subsequently Montijo) who, in peasant disguise, had ridden posthaste to the capital from Andalucía following the duque del Infantado's instructions to take all possible measures to prevent the royal family's flight. As a Household guardsman who witnessed these and the subsequent events later wrote, the grandees 'agreed to commit their fortunes and their own persons to prevent the flight of the king and queen, and also to annihilate Godoy'.[11]

* The memorandum, of whose precise contents the only proof figures in Godoy's memoirs, claimed among other things that Napoleon had sent troops to Spain because of the threat of English expeditions to the Peninsula, and the violent dissensions among the two Spanish court factions (i.e. Godoyistas and anti-Godoyistas; a third faction, Napoleon added for good measure, favoured a reform of the Spanish monarchy on the lines of the English constitution). The memorandum proposed an exchange of Portugal for the Spanish provinces north of the Ebro – there were 'good historic and political reasons for incorporating them into the French empire' – or at the very least to convert the region into a neutral power as a rampart to protect France from dangers in the Peninsula. (Principe de la Paz, 1956, vol. II, pp. 271–277.)

Despite their various efforts, Godoy's plan remained in effect and was given more urgency by the news that two of Murat's divisions were forced marching on Madrid. The date for departure was finally set: the night of March 17. Teba, now in Aranjuez, was as aware of the date as everyone at the palace. He also knew well how to create one of the conditions by which the grandees' aims could be met.

> Again in Manchego peasant disguise Teba went to all the neighbouring villages, pretending now to be from one place, now from another, to incite loyal Manchegans to join him in preventing the king's flight which, if it took place, would leave them foresaken and defenceless. With these words, he attracted even the old men who came to Aranjuez determined to die rather than permit His Majesty to leave.[12]

Meanwhile, as the guardsman explained, 'the grandees had taken all the places to prevent anyone escaping'. The two to three thousand palace servants and minor functionaries, and their dependents, had a vested interest in the king's remaining. Their pay, in many cases, was several months in arrears and it would be a long time before they saw it if the royal family left. But as another eyewitness, José de Arango, wrote, they were also

> alarmed and worried, like young children who fear their father's absence. They went the rounds of the palace grounds that night [March 16–17], without firearms and without other aim than to obstruct the roads and paths with their bodies, to weaken with their tears and laments the king's resolve to leave.[13]

To prevent any disturbances, Godoy had taken the precaution of ordering the Household cavalry and foot guards from Madrid to Aranjuez. Back in Aranjuez from his village mission, Teba and another grandee, the marqués de Castelar, demanded that the guards officers swear formally not to obey Godoy, and to arrest him.[14] As these officers, all nobles, had no love of Godoy for having allowed the northern fortresses to be taken by the French, and were hostile to the royal family's flight,[15] and since both the grandees were ranking army officers, their task was not difficult. From the night of March 15, guardsmen began to watch for the slightest signs of escape. Inside the palace, the Fernandista faction had a highly powerful ally, the minister of Grace and Justice, the marqués de Caballero, 'perhaps one of the worst among the many bad people at the court of Spain at that time'.[16] He argued forcibly against Godoy's plan and awoke in the king his fears of the riot and revolution that could occur if the royal family attempted to leave. On the 16th the king published a proclamation to his 'beloved vassals' in which, as 'the tender father who loves you', he assured the people of Aranjuez and Madrid that he had no intention of leaving them, as 'some evil intention has made you suppose was necessary'.[17] He again reassured them that the French came as allies and friends.

All the same, the king had lost the people's confidence; despite his promise they believed he would flee. This was the impression of an anonymous Madrid witness – a merchant possibly – writing during the early hours of March 17.[18]

Popular suspicion of royal intentions no doubt made it easier for the nobility with estates around the capital to recruit more villagers – women accompanying the men – to reinforce those already in Aranjuez. To this end 'the gold flowed from Teba's hands, those of one or more other grandees, and a confidential agent of Don Antonio', the king's brother, who sided with his nephew, Fernando.[19]

Another who took the road from the capital to Aranjuez – in a carriage, for sure, not on foot like the villagers – was the French ambassador François de Beauharnais, a 'Fernandista' whose presence among the people – 'sufficiently disguised not to compromise his diplomatic status but not to the extent that he was unrecognizable'[20] – made it appear that the attempt to prevent Godoy's plan had the Emperor's approval. Teba, still in his peasant garb, and now known as 'Tío Pedro', acted as the ringleader of the people on their rounds.

The first anti-Godoy rising at 1 a.m. on March 17 was set off accidentally by the sound of a pistol shot, but the ground had been well-fertilized in advance. In its origins, therefore, the revolt was a traditional ancien regime tumult, in which the nobility or local men of power stirred up and used popular discontent to precipitate a riot against the authorities to serve their own ends. The Aranjuez rising, nonetheless, also combined a number of exceptional factors which gave it an unusual potency: the Spanish army's first direct intervention in influencing the political affairs of state[21] – without the guardsmen's support the rising's success would have been in doubt; alongside this, the unanimity of purpose of conspirators, people and military to prevent the royal family fleeing and to overthrow none other than the 'head of state' – here the people's *active* participation was crucial since the Bourbon regime feared nothing so much as popular revolt; and, by no means least, the national crisis in which the rising occurred and the place at which it occurred: the royal palace, seat of absolutist power.

The sound of the pistol shot electrified the night; a military trumpet sounded the alarm. Suddenly all was confusion, shouts and alarms. Soldiers, villagers, conspirators running, shouting Viva el rey y muera el tirano! (Long live the king, death to the tyrant!). Firebrands blazed in the dark. 'Tío Pedro' on horseback led a party of villagers to Godoy's house, with hundreds of men and women following. The guard refused to fire on them.[22] They broke down the door and swept in like a tidal wave. Godoy's wife, the condesa de Chinchón, who was the royal couple's niece, was found in her underclothes preparing for bed, and carried unharmed by a mob of mainly women to the safety of the royal palace. But Godoy had vanished. The people searched high and low, and then sacked the house, building a bonfire and burning many of Godoy's posessions, though witnesses generally agree that nothing was stolen.*

* In 1809, the condesa de Chinchón claimed that she had lost in the ransacking between five and seven million reales' worth of her best and most valuable diamonds and other jewellery, her China dining set and plates of gold, and more than 637,500 reales in cash. These figures, which give an indication of the great wealth accumulated by Godoy while in power, are contained in the condesa's plea from Puerto de Santa María to the Junta Suprema's Justice minister, Hermida, for financial help 'since I now lack sufficient means to live in decency', March 10, 1809. (AHN, *Estado*, Legajo 72C/228.)

At 5 a.m. a terrified king relieved the missing Godoy of all his official posts. Another disturbance in the palace and outside among the people had followed the sacking of Godoy's house and the latter, reported an artillery officer, Gil de Bernabé, were now

> demanding his head. The Prince [Fernando] had to appear on a palace balcony and tell them that there was a decree which stripped him of his posts. But the people of Aranjuez and Madrid were not content with the decree. They began again to search for [Godoy] while those in the palace continued to plot.[23]

The dismissal, nonetheless, appeared to have had its effect for on the 18th Aranjuez was calm. The royal couple appeared on a palace balcony and were cheered. But, as another acute observer noted, despite the cheers for the king

> nobody thought of obeying his orders concerning the fate of the fallen favourite, when the royal will had solemnly declared [in the dismissal decree] that he should be allowed to retire in peace. Officers, soldiers and villagers continued to look for him to take him prisoner.[24]

Early on Saturday morning, March 19, the first act of the drama ended and the second began when Godoy was found by soldiers in an attic of his own house.*

> The people took him, clubbing him like a Jew, wounding him, shouting that he should be killed, everyone crying out at the same time viva el Rey, muera el Traidor!, and proclaiming the Prince of Asturias [Fernando].[25]
>
> It was an object worthy of compassion to see a man who on Wednesday, March 16, was in command of the entire Monarchy, now defenceless, a prisoner, humiliated. Despite his despondent mien, the people wanted to drink his blood.[26]

As both these anonymous observers related, the mob would no doubt have killed Godoy had the Household cavalry not guarded him and had not Fernando been sent by the king to contain the people. Even so he was lucky to reach the guards' barracks alive. There Fernando saw him again, spared his life and ordered his wounds to be dressed, but told him that he would be judged by the laws of the land. The heir to the throne succeeded in quietening the mob around the barracks which was demanding Godoy's head by assuring them that the prisoner would be tried.

Almost immediately afterwards there occurred one of those fatal mistakes that brought an end to the drama.

---

* Godoy's own version is that, after thirty-six hours, he was driven out of his hiding place by thirst and that a soldier on the stairs whom he approached to get him something to drink raised the alarm. Versions on this theme are contained in two of the early eyewitness accounts quoted here, both of which (*Manifiesto imparcial y exácto*, 1808, p. 13, and *Relato de la caida de Godoy*, 1958, p. 401) also confirm another aspect (which Godoy denied in his Memoirs) and was widely accepted: that Godoy had been hiding inside a rolled-up length of floor matting in the attic with two pistols by his side.

At this very moment [after Fernando's visit] the king ordered a coach, guarded by two hundred royal *carabineros*, to take him [Godoy] to the Granada's Alhambra castle. The people learned of this, and when the coach arrived, they smashed it to pieces, and demanded the prisoner's life. Such was the uproar that, seeing it could not be controlled, the king abdicated the throne in favour of his son . . . King Fernando immediately left the palace on horseback for the guards' barracks to calm the people, and all of them cheered him.*

Not a drop of blood had been spilled in the rising – other than the few of Godoy's wounds; not once had the people or soldiers, who throughout had shouted *Viva el Rey!*, threatened the king – other than by disobeying his wishes concerning Godoy. Not once throughout three difficult days had his councillors or ministers suggested he take any definitive step – other than opposing his flight. A resolute king, determined to keep his crown, would have had little problem in staying in power. But Carlos IV was old, ill, irresolute – and he had seen disgraced the man on whom he had depended for nearly two decades; had seen the army join sides with the people; had seen (and used) his son's popularity and influence with the crowd; and above all he had seen his ally, Napoleon, advancing ever faster on Madrid. He signed his abdication decree with pleasure, it was said;[27] and a few hours later told his confessor, Archbishop Amat:

> Let us speak clearly: Bonaparte is coming and not with good intentions. Fernando will be able better to benefit the nation than I in the circumstances: this is the real reason for my renunciation.[28]

This statesman-like rationalization, for which there were few objective grounds, elevated a primitive fear of the rabble to the high ground of European politics. And so, when a Napoleonic envoy worked on the old king's sudden access of pique at having abdicated 'under duress', he secured a statement from Carlos reclaiming the throne which Murat kept secret to use as imperial policy dictated. But in fact Carlos soon had second thoughts, and his wife and daughter constantly assured Murat that the former king did not wish to resume the throne, but only to be allowed to live peacefully with the queen and Godoy in a climate more suited to his poor health than that of Madrid.†

*

* Gil de Bernabé to Bernardo Iriarte, letter of March 21, 1808 (BL-*Eg* 384/123 &v). In fact, the end was somewhat more complex than Bernabé's summary account suggests. It was not the king, apparently, but Fernando who had ordered Godoy's removal to Granada, under the warrant given him by Carlos IV to take charge of his trial. And several hours earlier the king had begun to talk of abdicating though he did not formalize his decision until after the latest events. (Marti Gilabert, 1972, pp. 181–188.)

† In the rising's immediate aftermath the queen apparently attempted to incite a a second revolt to put her husband back on the throne. Juan Serra y Llored, a high treasury official, writing in 1809, stated that he had refused to help the queen suborn people to proclaim Carlos' return to the throne, and had suffered house arrest as a result, although subsequently he had been freed by Fernando VII. (*Serra Memorial* [abstract] to the Junta Suprema in AHN, *Estado*, Legajo 61N/160.)

And what of the people who, for the first time in modern Spanish history, had participated in dethroning a reigning monarch? To consider them as no more than the nobility's (suborned) pawns is to suppose that bribery alone moved them to act when it was rather that money provided them with the means – their daily subsistence – to be free to act. They had their own reasons for participating, as the witnesses' accounts make clear. 'Alarmed and worried, like young children who fear their father's absence' they would, if the king fled, be left 'foresaken and defenceless'. Men and women, even the old, were prepared to fight and die to prevent this. Paternalistic and patronizing like all the elite in their attitude to the 'simple' villagers and lower urban orders, the witnesses nonetheless were not wrong: the villagers' world remained structured around two constants: Monarch and Church. 'A world without a King, like a world without religion, was a world turned on its head, at the prey of chaos and arbitrary conduct in which the weak and the poor were the principal victims.'[29] The monarch was the paternal father of his vassals, the earthly shepherd of his flock. Without a monarch in place, the people felt 'orphaned', deprived of their terrestial protector, abandoned to their individual fate. The king was the natural source of all justice in this world, as God was in the next; and if the monarchy's injustices starkly contradicted the monarch's justice then it was the king's ministers, advisers or administrators who were to blame. They were acting arbitrarily, being unfaithful to the king's orders. This mystification lay deep in the collective mentality of the Old Regime, part of a long process of cultural conditioning actively pursued by all the instances of power to legitimate the monarchical regime.

Apart from Godoy's plan to deprive them of their king, they also had many more immediate grievances to lay at his door – the costliness of living; the burden of taxes (especially the increased tax on wine); the forced sale of the rural and urban poor's last safety net: the Church's charitable institutions; conscription; the effects of war . . . But above all, his 'shameless, immoral' conduct. However immoral their own conduct, they expected their rulers to be impeccably moral. Moreover, Godoy did little to hide his desire for lasciviousness and lucre; on the latter score, the royal couple more than satisfied him; on the former he seemed well able to look after himself. Apart from the queen, there was his royal wife (the king's niece whom the royal couple had given him in marriage), his attractive Andalucian mistress, and great numbers of female supplicants.* Constantly whipped into a moral fervour by a hostile nobility, the people at large came to blame even natural catastrophes on him: crop failures, hunger, epidemics, earthquakes . . . Village and town poor were only too happy to participate in his downfall.

That said, it was their deep sense of paternal 'abandonment' by their monarch which was was one of the principal causes that moved villagers to take part in

---

* It was openly said that for a placeseeker or official to gain favour it was necessary for the latter to send his wife or young daughter to seek his audience; in 1799 (when Godoy was temporarily out of power) a Ministry of Justice circular forbad officials' wives and daughters from residing at court to curry favour on their husbands' and fathers' behalf.

the Aranjuez tumult, and again to rise in 1808 against Napoleon who sequestered and unseated their new king, Fernando.

*

If there had ever been any doubt that the Aranjuez rebellion was conjugated by the
Fernandista nobility, the events in Madrid confirmed the organized nature of the
revolt. As soon as the news of Godoy's capture was known in the capital on the
afternoon of Saturday, March 19, the houses of Godoy's mother, brother and
sister were sacked and burned, as well as those of a number of his ministers and ex-
ministers. All their furniture, their carriages, horses and mules, silver and jewels
were dragged out on the street and set fire to or killed. But Godoy's own house,
according to Gil de Bernabé, was spared, because the royal coat of arms had been
fixed to its facade – effectively therefore taking it over in the new King's name.

> Despite the rising, on Saturday night there was order, since it seemed that there were
> people in command of the rebels. Viva el Rey, they cried, and death to the Traitor
> sausage-maker,* and whoever wouldn't repeat it, they threw to the ground, shouting
> that people like that should be exterminated. But that night the rebels troubled no one.[30]

In their blind hatred of the royal favourite, a score of Fernandista grandees had
won a greater triumph than they could have hoped for. They expected to reap
the political rewards, and Fernando's appointment of the duque del Infantado
to the presidency of the Consejo de Castilla heralded what seemed like the
beginning of their return to political influence and power. Within a couple of
months, they had thrown their victory away in a humiliating misjudgement of
Napoleon's intentions. In this 'meanwhile' they had further eroded the Old
Order.

A NEW BOURBON KING

Popular jubilation at the news that Spain had a new king began early the
following day in Madrid. The caretaker of the San Fernando Academy arrived
to find an enormous crowd, bearing regimental colours and beating drums,
gathered inside and outside the building. Numbers of people had already
broken the lock on the library door and smashed the bust of Godoy which
stood inside.

> Then they asked for a portrait of our prince the King, saying that they knew there was
> one in the Academy and that if it was not handed over to them they would set fire to
> the building . . .

The caretaker informed them that there was no such portrait in the Academy.
'Let us go', said one. But in the meantime others had taken from the wall the
portrait of the king, and were carrying it off.

* Godoy's popular nickname because he came from Extremadura, a region known for its
sausages.

'In case you are not aware, that is not our prince the King,' I assured them, 'but the King [Carlos] as a youth.' To which they replied, as though giving me a piece of their mind: 'We love the King' and they walked off with the portrait.[31]

Later that same evening, the caretaker saw the Fernandistas sallying forth in procession from Atocha with flags flying and the royal portrait carried under a pallium. Thus their young new king, upon whom the people had set their hopes, was popularly acknowledged and cheered in the youthful image of his unloved father. It made no difference: it represented *the king*.

Scenes of jubilation, the public burning of Godoy's portrait and the tearing down or smashing of busts and plaques took place all over the country. The destruction of these symbols of power – to which most townsfolk had, but the day before, paid reverence as the source of public posts and honours – was often, however, directly or indirectly aimed at unpopular Godoy-appointed authorities. A particularly striking case was Sanlúcar de Barrameda where the rioters demanded the dismissal and imprisonment of the local tax representative and provincial intendente. While the people were smashing busts and portraits of the royal favourite and devastating the botanical garden – one of Godoy's most prized endeavours, where American, African and Asian plants and trees, among them cinnamon, cocoa, and bananas, were being acclimatized for planting on the Mediterranean coast – a representation was submitted to the town hall demonstrating 'the many favours' Godoy had done for the town and giving thanks for them.[32]*

In Valladolid, the municipal council showed some reluctance in delivering up to the people the full-length official portrait of Godoy hanging in the town hall, until the threat of a tumult made them change their minds.[33] The people then dragged the portrait to the centre of the main square, and breaking it, built a bonfire and burned the pieces, cursing Godoy as a traitor. Others went to the royal palace, to pull out the triumphal carriage on which the portrait had originally been paraded through the streets. They were watched by many, including an attorney of the Chancillería, Francisco Gallard.

Pulled by the people, it was taken to the Plaza Mayor, amidst taunts and ignominy, pelted by stones, stalks and lumps of mud. They put a large chamberpot full of filth in it, and two wretched, dirty, black urchins, with brushes, on either side, and in front a man on horseback who shouted, viva el Rey y muera el traidor. They reached the place in the square where the gallows are raised, and there they burned the carriage, taking the ashes to the river, saying that of so infamous a man not the least relic should be allowed to remain.[34]

* More than a year later, during the Napoleonic war, the priest of Sanlúcar's principal church felt obliged to make a public self-criticism of his esteem for the benefits Godoy had brought to the township: thanks to the favourite the port had been given the right to trade with America; fluvial transport of national and foreign agricultural produce on the Guadalquivir had been liberalized; a new mole built in Sanlúcar, canals cut and a royal road built to connect the township with Jerez. The priest's self-criticism was made at a church ceremony celebrating Fernando VII's birthday on October 14 1809 (AHN, *Estado*, Legajo 13/2/8).

This reversed, carnivalesque repetition of the portrait's inaugural procession was repeated to some extent in Salamanca. After stoning the medallion of Godoy, which the military governor, the marqués de Zayas, had had errected with 'great pomp and majesty' only eighteen months earlier, Salamanca university students obliged him to send for a stonecutter to efface it. They then made the governor, who it would seem was their main target of attack, repeat the festivities he had organized when he inaugurated the medallion.

> This was the biggest affront a man could receive, to make him efface what he had had errected and accompany it with the same festivities. It is true that the general rejoicing at the obliteration of the medallion was greater than for its erection . . . But oh! The inconstancy of things human![35]

So wrote Joaquín Zaonero, an hidalgo rentista who lived in the town.

*

Abased and abused, Godoy had been brought down for pursuing the correct policy; even some of his bitterest enemies came to recognize this. The move to Andalucía, where the Spanish armies could be assembled without difficulty, and the king could address his people openly on Napoleon's intentions, was

> the only prudent measure in the circumstances, as events have shown; but because it was proposed by the Prince of the Peace, it found not a single supporter.
>
> An expedient and wise [measure] . . . In proposing the move, Godoy acted correctly and in this aspect posterity cannot censure his conduct.[36]

These were both the immediate and the mature reflections of two anti-Godoyista participants in the coming war: a high-placed government official at the time, José de Arango, and conde Toreno, who years later wrote the classic Spanish history of the war. Although Godoy's foreign policy had been driven as much by personal ambition as reasons of state, his domestic policy had followed the enlightened reformers' line and, completing some of their uncompleted tasks, had also initiated others. His reign saw the founding of the Royal College of Medicine, the Astronomical Observatory, the Veterinary School, the extension of primary education in the countryside, and a nationwide campaign to vaccinate children against smallpox.[37] Many of these reforms had little time to become operative. In questions of censorship, he was fairly broad-minded, permitting the first Spanish translation of Adam Smith's *Wealth of Nations*, which had previously been banned by the Inquisition.[38]

But he alienated all reformists, old and young, by incarcerating (or at the very best, accepting the incarceration of) Gaspar de Jovellanos, the embodiment of Spanish enlightenment, for seven years in the Palma de Mallorca fortress. Although an absolute ruler, it was his weaknesses, his hesitancies, which most characterized him. In the era of Napoleon and Talleyrand, Metternich and Pitt, he was little more than a dwarf amongst giants.

POPULAR HOPES IN THE NEW MONARCH

From the start of the new king's reign his noble 'Fernandista' councillors proved themselves singularly inept, trusting unduly in Napoleon's support of their protégé. The tactical advantage to be gained by Fernando's entry into Madrid before Marshal Murat and his troops escaped them. The new king would wait until the capital was calm, an official announcement said, revealing the Old Regime's terror of popular mobilizations.[39] To reach the capital from nearby Aranjuez, Fernando had barely to bestir himself, while Murat had to force march his men from Castilla la Vieja. At the head of a cortège of brilliantly attired officers and a detachment of the Imperial Guard, he beat the new king to it by nearly twenty-four hours. For sure, there was little popular acclaim for him: apart from the Imperial Guard and the cavalry, the French troops did not impress the local population. 'There are hardly any old enough to have beards, they are all youths of sixteen or so.'[40] Few Madrileños, moreover, answered the local authorities' call for bedding for the troops, despite the promise to pay for it and return it later.[41]

Popular acclaim was reserved for Fernando VII who entered Madrid on horseback on March 24 without military escort and to a rapturous welcome. An immense crowd pressed around him and, cheering and shouting for joy, raised him and his horse in their arms and carried them through the streets, recalled a young witness.[42] 'The king said he wanted no more soldiers than the hearts of his vassals', wrote another onlooker, and this he certainly achieved.[43] Knowing that his support depended on the people as much as on the nobility, he ordered his first minister to prepare plans to make more cultivable land available from the royal estates and to bring water to Madrid, but surprisingly did not abolish Godoy's much-hated takeover of the clergy's beneficent property or alleviate taxes on the rural world.* In fact, his major reforms consisted in appointing anti-Godoyista ministers, releasing Jovellanos from prison, and permitting other members of the political elite, whom Godoy had banished from court, to return. The new reign raised great popular hopes – but of what? In the first instance, a negative hope: Spaniards did *not* want a return to Godoy's 'arbitrary despotism' or even the 'enlightened despotism' of his predecessor, Floridablanca. As an enlightened contemporary cleric, Joaquín Lorenzo Villanueva, wrote:

> Unlike the French in their revolution, the Spanish did not want to change their original system of government, to convert their monarchy into a republic. They were happy to be ruled by a king . . . who was faithful to his oath to observe the fundamental laws . . . to ensure that in no way would the rights of all subjects, and even less so those of the nation, be predjudiced. All Spaniards were agreed on the re-establishment of the moderate monarchy.[44]

* The suspension of the sale of ecclesiastical property, and lightening the tax burden on the rural community, especially the detested special tax on wine, were measures taken by local juntas after the anti-Napoleonic risings of 1808 or by the Junta Suprema, the new central government which emerged in the autumn of the same year. (See Fontana and Garrabou, 1986, pp. 16–17.)

'Nobody is opposed to reforms', an informant of the French consul in Cádiz wrote. A 'great reduction' in the number of royal tax administrators and excisemen in favour of free domestic trade would be generally welcomed; so too, would the abolition of the *millones* (a tax on wine, vinegar, olive oil, meat, soap and tallow candles), and 'the suppression of tithes and feudal dues'. A system which assured that the state serviced its debt, including the *vales reales*, or state bonds which could be used as paper money, would be 'of the major importance' and should be accompanied by the creation of a commission of intelligent merchants, former treasury administratives, state cashiers and court individuals, etc., to agree on the means of achieving 'this great enterprise'. 'If the merchants and traders of Madrid, Cádiz, Sevilla, Barcelona and Bilbao were summoned to form a pecuniary council, I do not believe that anyone would regret it.' As to the legal system, the informant wrote that 'I do not doubt that a new legal code would be accepted in place of the existing laws because of the despicable corruptness which permits their manipulation.'[45]

Although these prescriptions must be treated with caution, given their source, they were more than likely a fair description of some of the grievances of merchants, farmers and to some extent the rural poor, in western Andalucía, if not elsewhere. Fernando VII's government included reform-minded ex-ministers or high administrators whom the former favourite had dismissed or who had personal or political reasons for desiring Godoy's downfall. Given the chance, under Fernando VII, they would presumably have attempted to continue their enlightened predecessors' gradualist reforms without undermining the Old Regime. But within eight weeks of Fernando's assuming the throne, Napoleon had dethroned him and his father and put his own brother, Josef, in their place. Force majeure – and the apparently favourable opportunity of reforming Spain under a Bonaparte regime – outweighed loyalty to the Bourbons; many of Fernando's ministers – Jovellanos was a major exception – struck their colours and collaborated with Josef, the new king.

MADRID: THE PEOPLE'S STREET WAR
AGAINST THE FRENCH MILITARY

As a foretaste of things to come, three French soldiers were admitted to hospital with wounds received in the streets during Fernando's triumphal entry into Madrid; and a few days later there was a near battle between the people and French troops in the Plazuela de la Cebada.[46]

The French troops had barely entered Madrid when

> they began to put on imperial and señorial airs as if they were already the sovereign power in the capital. The people, who are all eyes and ears and see and hear everything, started to look without confidence on the (military) movements which had all the appearances of being hostile, and doubted the friendship and alliance of their guests,

noted an enlightened friar, Vicente Martínez Colomer.[47]

The authorities' repeated demands for supplies for the French troops, to be paid for at — and even above – market prices, found few takers. Madrid theatre admissions, that thermometer of the feelings of the capital's inhabitants, fell to only thirty percent of their previous quarter's takings.[48]

The nervousness was grounded in reality. From the first Murat refused to recognize Fernando VII. The French ambassador, François de Beauharnais, who had been an ardent Fernandista during the Aranjuez rising, now turned his back on the new king. Aranjuez had definitively determined Napoleon to be rid of the Bourbons. Although in the first days of his reign Fernando had written to the Emperor to assure him that he would pursue 'all possible means to draw tighter the bonds of friendship and close alliance which happily exist between Spain and the French empire',[49] Napoleon did not want on the Spanish throne a new, young and popular Bourbon, who owed nothing to him for his accession to the monarchy. He immediately ordered the French press to launch a campaign claiming that Fernando VII had come by the crown through unworthy intrigues and that the throne was in consequence vacant.[50] The Aranjuez rising might well be called an 'unworthy intrigue'. But Napoleon's subsequent plotting to put his brother on the Spanish throne can be called – in his own words – little less than 'cynical, immoral trickery'.* Keeping even Murat – who himself had ambitions to the throne of Spain – in the 'mysterious obscurity' of his intentions, the Emperor dispatched to Madrid his henchman, General Savary, an army 'policeman' of unsavoury reputation, to entice Fernando with false promises to meet him in Burgos on his much-bruited visit to Spain which he had no intention of making. In an audience Savary swore to the king that Napoleon would recognize him as soon as they met, and that the Emperor would be pleased and flattered if Fernando VII set out to receive him. Savary, in fact, was under orders to bring Fernando to Napoleon in Bayonne, the last main town in France on the Paris-Madrid road, where the Emperor had expressly established his headquarters, and to hold him there until he had renounced his rights to the throne in return for compensation in Italy – for example, the kingdom of Etruria.† If the king refused to make the trip, Carlos IV's protest at his 'forced' abdication and the declaration that he was resuming the throne – the statement he had made in his pique to a French envoy and which Murat had kept secret‡ – was to be made public, and his son declared a rebel. The Emperor's need was to 'regenerate' Spain and establish closer relations with France by changing the dynasty.[51]

While it was evident to everyone in those critical days that the solution to the dynastical and political crisis lay in Napoleon's hands, not even the most sceptical of Fernando's councillors could believe that Savary had been sent deliberately by the Emperor to deceive the new king and to usurp the throne.[52] But this was indeed Napoleon's plan: to lure the whole royal family to Bayonne on the pretext of resolving the Spanish succession and to secure their abdications in

* See p. 55.
† One of Napoleon's new Italian kingdoms, covering Tuscany, which he created for the Duke of Parma, Carlos IV's son in law, in 1801. On the Etrurian king's death, Napoleon ejected the queen, who returned to Spain, and took over the kingdom.
‡ See p. 34.

favour of his brother. By their 'voluntary' removal to France he hoped to avoid their becoming the focus of armed resistance in Spain. In the extreme that Fernando refused to cross the French border of his own will he was to be arrested and brought by force. Despite a few days' hesitation in Vitoria, where many advised the king not to proceed further and even to flee in disguise, and despite Fernando having received a letter from the Emperor which should have alerted him and his councillors to Napoleon's views of the new king – an heir to the throne who communicated with a foreign power, as Fernando had done in writing to him before the Escorial affair, was acting 'criminally', Napoleon wrote, adding: 'It is very dangerous for kings to accustom their people to shed blood in taking justice into their own hands. I pray that you will never experience this one day . . . the people are always happy to avenge the tributes which they have paid us . . .'[53] – nonetheless, Fernando allowed himself again to be persuaded by Savary that the Emperor had been delayed by affairs of state and was waiting in Bayonne to confirm him in his throne. On April 20, ten days after setting out to meet Napoleon in Burgos, Fernando crossed the Bidasoa into France. He was met by his younger brother, Carlos, and three grandees, whom he had sent ahead. They broke the news: Napoleon had decided to end Bourbon rule in Spain. It was too late to turn back: Fernando was now in fact Napoleon's prisoner – as in effect he had been since the day he relied on the Emperor to validate his reign.

The Napoleonic 'card', which the 'Fernandistas' had played for so long, had turned against them. In their deployment of 'reasons of state' they had again proven themselves singularly inept. Many of the common folk, like those in Vitoria who cut the traces of the king's carriage to try to prevent him leaving for France, knew and cared little about reasons of state: they sensed the danger and responded in the only way they knew how.

While, in Bayonne, the Emperor was resolving Spain's dynastical succession, in Madrid Murat was acting as the master of direct politico-military domination. French forces confiscated shipments of weapons for Spanish troops;[54] and orders to keep the peace, not to insult French forces and not to circulate handbills and lampoons against the French flowed constantly from the government junta* which Fernando had left behind to deal with urgent state matters, but with no other instructions than to keep the peace with the French. These orders were a constant reminder to the population of the occupation troops' intensifying unpopularity in the capital.

An affray between a French and Spanish soldier on April 1 'caused a general commotion among the people who ran shouting "a rising! a rising!" which could have had serious consequences had calm not been restored by the duque del Infantado, Negrete [Spanish military commandant of Madrid] and French generals'.[55] Simultaneously, a rumour was put about that the French forces were seizing food supplies bound for Madrid and arresting suppliers with the aim of creating shortages in the capital and raising the price of foodstuffs, which

* The word's sinister ring in English, where it is popularly associated with a *military* junta, is not replicated in Spanish where the word is used for all sorts of special committees or councils, from a 'junta municipal' to consider a village budget, to a state junta appointed to decide on singular matters

made a considerable impact on the population, always alert to the possibilities of food shortages, especially bread, since the disastrous famine year only four years earlier.[56] (The fact was rather that the need to supply Murat's large force in a city where the bulk of all food had to be transported from considerable distances, meant the certainty of 'shortages and rising prices', as later the governing junta pointed out.) At that moment there was no good reason for the French high command to increase popular tension when everything depended on securing Fernando's departure to meet Napoleon.

Throughout the month, however, there were increasing complaints to the authorities about the 'outrageous' conduct of French officers who, among other things, were said to have committed an 'enormous number' of thefts in the wealthy houses where they were billetted. An anonymous diarist, who was politically favourable to the French cause, wrote that 'these houses have been sacked as though Madrid were a conquered city', reporting at the same time on an edict in Spanish and French of April 26 threatening punishment of anyone who bought stolen furniture, clothing and jewellery.[57]

Ready to take offence at any breach of local custom, the population was irritated by the French soldiers' lack of respect for Spanish women – a French soldier was killed on April 18 on the Toledo Bridge when he tried to kiss a Madrileña, and several of his companions wounded.[58] The troops' religious irreverence – they did not take off their hats or caps on entering churches to the sound of military music and beating of drums – and their demonstration of armed strength displayed in frequent military parades, as a young Madrileño at the time recalled, were further serious irritants.[59] But the inhabitants were even more angered by Murat's refusal to recognize Fernando as their king and his patent support for Carlos IV, whom rumour had it he wished to restore to the throne, as well as by his persistent attempts to have Godoy freed from prison. 'The nation appears calm, but . . . it is electric, it will need only a spark to produce some event', wrote the French ambassador to his minister on April 7. And a French army officer who travelled from Madrid to Badajoz warned that the Spanish were demonstrating a 'strong resolution to resist'.[60]

Tension rose even higher after Fernando left the capital for Burgos. On April 13, the Wednesday before Easter, the parish priest of Carabanchel de Arriba, Andrés López, killed a French captain billeted on him. The priest went into hiding and the French burnt his house to the ground. The following day, the fear of a generalized outbreak of violence caused the authorities to order the churches to be closed at night – an unprecedented act in the middle of Holy Week. (It was reported privately that the queen had paid vagrants to go about on Holy Thursday and Good Friday proclaiming Carlos IV as king.*) A more potent rumour, initiated apparently by a friar of San Gil, said that 'a great riot,

---

* This runs against the evidence of the queen's frequent pleas to Murat to allow the royal couple and Godoy to retire to some warm place for the king to recover his health; yet the rumour was rife at the time (see, for example, Anon, *Diario de lo ocurrido*, 1808, entry for April 17; Vicente Martínez Colomer, *El filósofo en su quinta*, Valencia, 1808, p. 26; the Easter report in *Noticias*, MS., undated, unsigned, but most probably written in Madrid around April 20, BL-*Eg* 385/40–41v).

prepared by paid people', was planned for April 14, Holy Thursday night.[61] There was possibly more than wishful thinking in the latter rumour since there was documented evidence to show that attempts to stage risings in April in Madrid, Valencia and Pamplona were made, though in the event none occurred:[62] it was the friar's account which led to the closing of the churches.

At all hours of the day, the capital's streets were patrolled by groups of fifteen to twenty city fathers, led by a magistrate, to 'prevent the people from committing an outrage'. The patrols, reported the writer, also had another objective: 'To show the French troops that we are neither negligent nor trusting of them. . . . We have seen so many and such extraordinary things that nothing should surprise us any longer.'[63] In a move typical of the Old Order under popular stress, a government ordinance made all parents and employers responsible for ensuring that their sons and daughters, domestic servants, and employees kept out of trouble, and if they did not obey, they should be reported to the justices. Masters were to report by name and address any journeyman or apprentice who did not come to work daily.[64] In a French attempt to reduce tension, the imperial military command in mid-April moved a division out of Madrid.[65] But none of these measures had any real effect because an undeclared war, fought with cold steel, was already being waged in the streets; and the French troops were its victims. How many were assassinated or died of their wounds is open to the interpretation of confusing hospital records.* Their woundings and murders were not the response to similar French outrages – though drunken French officers did kill a peace-abiding merchant on April 26 – but stemmed rather from anger and desperation after Fernando VII's departure.[66] The most feared by the French, and the most skilled with the blade, were the *chisperos* – the tradesmen and workers of the popular neighbourhoods, 'the legitimate people (men and women) of Madrid', in the words of José de Arango:

> And although they usually wounded more with their sharp tongues and piquant wit than with the blunt knives they used for cutting their wads of Brazilian tobacco, Murat was fearful of them . . .†

In reality, however, Murat was more scornful than fearing of the undisciplined mob. Napoleon had demonstrated in Egypt and Italy that a whiff of grapeshot

---

* A French historian, Claude Martin, has written that of the 174 French soldiers who died in the Madrid General Hospital between March 23, the day of Murat's entry to the capital, and May 1, most of them were victims of assassination attempts. A Spanish historian, Emilio de Diego, puts the number as, 'at the least', 42 soldiers admitted to hospital in the second half of April alone with wounds from which some of them died. (Claude Martin, *José Napoleón I. 'Rey intruso' de España*, Madrid, 1969, p. 98, cited Morange, 1989, p. 29, fn. 38; Diego, 1992, p. 252.)

† The name *chispero* meant blacksmith, but it had been extended to a large part of Madrid's lower orders, especially those who differentiated themselves by their showy, ornamented dress and arrogant, wittily uninhibited attitudes and speech. They were also known as *manolo(a)s*, or *majo(a)s,* and they figure in many Goya paintings. However, the description of this particular sub-culture as representing the 'legitimate' Madrileños, unless by that is meant their hostility to the dominant French influence in the capital and at court, must be taken as a piece of patriotic, anti-Napoleonic fervour. /cont'd over

was sufficient to deal the rebellious natives a sharp and salutary lesson in the superiority of French armed strength. There they had not risen their heads in revolt again. In Burgos French troops fired on a menacing mob, wounding several people. On April 26 Napoleon wrote to Murat: 'It is time to show the necessary energy. I suppose you will not spare the *canaille* of Madrid if they make a move, and that immediately afterward you will them have disarmed.' To which Murat replied, on May 1, that he was ready to give any rebel 'a good lesson', while recognizing that news from Bayonne was causing great restlessness.

There can be little doubt that the Fernandistas strove to keep the Madrileños' desperation on the boil – but just short of boiling over – with anti-French rumours and propaganda. They could play on the people's latent xenophobia, and most notably the *chisperos*' anti-French sentiments.

While the king on his peregrination northwards to meet Napoleon continued to issue placatory orders to respect the French troops in Madrid, nothing, in the staunch Fernandistas' views, would be more fatal than if these were strictly obeyed and the inhabitants lapsed into passive acceptance of French military rule. On the other hand, a rising would jeopardize Fernando's cause, giving the French the pretext they needed to overthrow him. What was required then was the threat, but not the actuality, of a rising to prove to Napoleon that the king had wide popular support which would not passively condone anything but the Emperor's confirmation of his right to the throne. Thus the government junta wrote to Fernando on April 18 in Vitoria on the need to conserve 'the people's spirit at the climax of vigor and energy in which it now finds itself'. Once the king's departure from Vitoria to France was made officially known, many Fernandistas, however, gave him up for lost: his fate was only too clear in their eyes. For once, French and Spanish participants in the events broadly agreed on this generalized feeling, though significantly disagreeing on its future significance. On April 21, Murat wrote to Napoleon that Fernando had lost much of his credit with the people who were whispering: 'C'est être par trop bête de ne pas voir le piège . . .' ('It is the greatest stupidity not to see the trap that has been set [for Fernando] . . .'). Antonio Alcalá Galiano commented that if no one thought of being able to save the king, very few were willing to subject themselves to the crown's French usurper.[67] The Spaniard, writing with hindsight, was of course correct: only ten days after Murat's letter came the Madrid anti-French rising of May 2. Giving up their king for lost by no means signified that the common people had abandoned their monarch. As one diarist recorded:

> The sad and melancholic say that as soon as Napoleon has all the royal family and Godoy in his power, he will unmask himself, and embroil us in a civil war. The opposing Party continues joyfully to expect the satisfactory outcome that has been

cont'd/ (It should be borne in mind that Arango's younger brother, Rafael, was one of the small number of army officers who participated in the Madrid May 2 rising against the French.) The more usual 'enlightened' manner of considering this sub-culture was as 'vulgar brutes . . . crude *majos* . . . dirty *chisperos*'. (See León de Arroyal's *Oración apologética en defensa del estado floreciente de España*, commonly known as 'Pan y toros' in Elorza, Antonio (ed.), 1971, p. 23.)

announced. There are reasons for reflection and reconciliation between these extremes.[68]

Rumour, always a powerful influence in times of crisis and doubly so in a society where few were literate, kept the lower orders on a knife edge of optimism and angry desperation during most of the second half of April. Rumour could be invented on the spot or fed by those in positions of power through their retainers who moved with ease among the people, or by royal guardsmen in or out of uniform, mingling with the crowd in their off-duty hours. Given their awareness of the decisive role they had played in the Aranjuez rising and Fernando's accession to the throne, the guards were not prepared to sacrifice their achievement to Napoleon's or to the French military's plans. Murat was under no doubt that they were spreading anti-French sentiment among Madrid's labouring poor, for he constantly instructed the governing junta to post the guards out of Madrid for that very reason. Rumour was fuelled also in clerics' sermons and by friars, who feared that they had everything to lose under a Bonapartist regime.

But rumour was not the only manipulated news. The royal bulletins from Bayonne were almost invariably 'optimistic', raising new hopes of a satisfactory outcome to the talks. Napoleon ensured this: all Spanish dispatches from France were 'censored', and much fabulation went into their writing to tranquilize domestic opinion. Caught up in this web of disinformation, to use an anachronistic phrase, it was little wonder that the population's spirits rose and fell almost by the hour.

Another weapon used in this propaganda war, the pasquinade or satirical lampoon, revealed that despite their customary respect for authority, Madrileños had condemned to indifference the governing junta. At noon on April 23, the city police affixed an edict in the Puerta del Sol forbidding the posting in public places of pasquinades. With the police barely out of sight, a man of some apparent standing stuck a poster across the edict:

> By pragmatic sanction
> It is hereby proclaimed
> In the public's criterion
> The bollock to name
> 'Napoleon'
> And for the same reason
> A law shall decree
> And in the Gaceta be placed
> In a section apart
> That the latrine be called
> 'Bonaparte'*

* Pérez de Guzmán, 1908, p. 283, fn. 3. My translation is rather free: the original Spanish reads: 'Por pragmática sanción / Se ha mandado publicar / El que el vaso de cojón / Se llama "Napoleón". / Y por la misma razón / En una ley se decreta / Que se ponga en la Gaceta, /En un capítulo aparte, / Que se llame "Buonaparte" / La parte de la secreta.' (The 'secreta' was the common name for latrine.)

This scatological lampoon, obviously written to appeal to the unlettered to hear, memorize and repeat, was presumably the work of a Fernandista stirring up the crowd. There were *frondeurs* aplenty always ready to keep the inhabitants on an emotional edge with posters and fresh rumour. The strength of the latter was brought home by an incident which caused a considerable popular impact.

On the morning of April 25, Antonio Pérez, a 47-year-old cacao-seed grinder went out to buy a clasp knife. Like many other Madrid tradesmen, he was not a Madrileño by birth, but a Galician from the village of Coba de Ornia. On the scant evidence available, he had been in the capital for about nine years. With his newly acquired weapon, Pérez went to the Plazuela de Antón Martín, and stabbed in the lower abdomen the first French soldier he came across, Captain Josef Luci. Then spying three more French soldiers in the patisserie in the square, he entered and stabbed two of them, a soldier in the stomach and a drummer in the hand. The captain and the soldier died two days later of their wounds. Rapidly arrested and admitting to being the author of the stabbings, Pérez confessed that he had bought the knife with the express aim of killing all the Frenchmen who crossed his path, convinced as he was that 'they had come with bad ideas against the Spanish'. On being asked by the court if the French soldiers had done him any personal harm, he replied 'No'. His motives, he said, were that the 'French rogues had come to sack the temples of the one and only true God, and to rob him of the fruit of his labours'.* He had done what he believed any right-thinking man should do, but had been mistaken, finding himself alone in the streets. In self-defence, he pleaded that he had acted in an access of 'frenzy or fury'.† A rumour had claimed two more lives.

Another prior event may also have caused Perez's fury, for it enraged the majority of Madrileños – and the rest of the country. On April 21, Murat's troops released Godoy from prison:

Today 22

The saddest and most fateful day that Madrid has known since it became Madrid . . .
The people here are in a tyrannical mood beyond belief. To see their faces so pale one would believe they had just risen from their sick-bed. A stream of ranting against all and sundry issues from their fiendish mouths . . .[69]

Such emotive language in the habitually restrained, personally inexpressive writing of the times is as clear an indication of the feelings which overwhelmed this unknown letter-writer as those he was describing.

* This is a reference to an earlier rumour that the French were about to impose an obligatory financial levy on labouring people as they had done in Portugal.
† The quoted phrases are from the report of Pérez's second trial (AGS, *Papeles del Gobierno Intruso, Gracia y Justicia*, Legajo 1090, n.n.) and from J. de A. (José de Arango), *Manifiesto imparcial y exacto*, p. 25, who in reporting the incident, raises Pérez to the stature of an ancient Greek or Roman hero, an indication of the height of anti-French passion that could affect an otherwise fairly sober crown official.

No sooner had Fernando crossed into France than Murat had felt safe in
ordering Godoy's release – 'une affaire extremement délicate qui blesse
l'orgueil national' ('an extremely delicate affair which offends national
pride') as he wrote to Napoleon on April 15,[70] and the official announcement of which was delayed for a further two days in case a mob attacked the
palace in Chamartín where Godoy was being held. The former royal
favourite's freedom from incarceration was the turning-point for Madrileños. Godoy, whom they so roundly hated, on whom they had cast the blame
for all of Spain's and of all their own woes, whose culpable consent had, in
their view, allowed the French to invade the country and take over its
fortresses – this scapegoat on whom their vengeful passions were concentrated, was to go untried and in peace due to French military might. More
than any other so far, this intervention in Spain's affairs was felt as a
betrayal of the people and of Fernando. It was hardly to be wondered that 'a
sense of anger and panic overtook the people'.[71] They turned their hatred of
Godoy on to his saviour, Napoleon.

The situation was coming too close to boiling over. On the same day, in fact –
but of course unknown to Madrid – the first minister, Cevallos, wrote to the
governing junta from Bayonne to 'redouble its precautions to ensure public
tranquility because the least attempt at insurrection would endanger the king's
safety and that of the people themselves.'[72] Good news was needed, and good
news came just as required the following day. To the crowd milling in the Plaza
del Sol in front of the post office waiting for correspondence from Bayonne, an
official Spanish report from France (censored, of course, by Napoleon's
functionaries) brought 'joy and relief.' Napoleon and Fernando had reached
agreement, the anonymous correspondent reported. Fernando VII had been
recognized as king – and had also been appointed regent of Portugal – and
would make peace with England. The king would be given the hand of a
princess of France. French troops would be gradually withdrawn, beginning in
May, and Spanish fortresses returned to Spain. Napoleon would excuse Spain's
three-year debt to France and end the monthly subsidy payments. Godoy was to
be expelled from Spain and handed over to France where he would be tried. The
following noon at his daily military parade, the writer added, Murat was to
proclaim Fernando King of Spain. Popular jubilation at such news was
exemplified by:

> the people running through the streets for sheer joy and the greengrocers in the Plaza
> Mayor throwing their fruit and vegetables into the air out of delight; in this way the
> people went from the extreme of despondency to the extreme of rejoicing, pleasure
> and happiness . . .[73]

On all points the report was pure illusion. Designed to calm spirits, the fact that
it was so readily believed demonstrated Spaniards' precise hopes at that
moment. But when the government junta did not publish a much-awaited
communiqué confirming the news, Madrileños were again thrust into despair
and anguish.

To a rationalist attempting to steer a course between rumour and fact, like the earlier anonymous diarist cited, rumour reached such heights that over the coming days he withdrew from several gatherings of distinguished individuals

> because all were like savage animals facing extinction. The least they predict is that the stars are about to fall from the heavens, and the sun split open like a pomegranate . . . Others are making their wills and disposing of their possessions, from which, unluckily, I shall receive nothing.[74]

The propaganda war took a new turn with Murat's attempt to take control of a printing press. Napoleon was very well aware that the war of the pen was an important weapon of combat. 'Pay especial heed to everything concerning the printing presses', he ordered Murat in mid-April.[75]

In order to achieve his aims, the Emperor had meanwhile determined that he needed a 'legitimate' reigning monarch to abdicate the throne, and was adamant that Carlos IV resume his former crown. Carlos' renunciation of his abdication was to be made public. The Madrid printer whom Murat's officers had ordered on April 20 to print it refused unless specifically ordered by the Consejo de Castilla to do so. There was a near riot when the people learned what was – or what was rumoured to be – up: for one rumour had it that the officers had ordered the printer to set in type a proclamation including the phrase: *Viva Carlos IV! Viva Godoy! Muera Murat!* (Long live Carlos IV, Long live Godoy, Death to Murat) – an incendiary provocation; while another claimed that the French were to sack all churches and impose a forced financial levy on the people. But the actual fact – the possibility of Carlos' return to the throne – was sufficient to bring out the mob the following day in the streets of Toledo when a French officer, who had arrived to seek billets, proffered 'with a lack of prudence and good sense' certain comments on the current situation which enraged the people. They responded by sacking and burning the houses of some of the former king's supporters and authorities who had collaborated with the officer.[76] Murat was obliged by the incident to set up a press in his residence, from which issued the first pro-Bonapartist pamphlets in Spanish. José Marchena, who had returned as Murat's secretary from France where he had fled in 1792 under threat from the Inquisition for his anti-clerical opinions, published what was probably the first of these in the guise of a retired Spanish army officer's letter to a friend. In France, Marchena, an exceptionally intelligent and well-read cleric, had become a Girondist supporter, been imprisoned by Robespierre, and finally welcomed Napoleon's reign as the culmination of the French Revolution. Adopting the pose of a patriotic Spanish officer who had fought against the French in the War of the Convention, and who was deeply concerned for the fate of the Spanish monarchy after the Escorial and Aranjuez affairs, his pamphlet displayed notable political realism in its attempt to convince educated Spaniards to accept that the feuding Bourbons had discredited the crown, becoming 'mere instruments' of 'criminal intrigues' which had led at Aranjuez to the 'beginnings of a revolution' (understood here as the people's irruption in political life). Only a 'great arbiter' – Napoleon – could re-establish a monarchy capable of restoring Spain to its past grandeur and dispelling the threat of revolution.[77] The pamphlet was cleverly aimed at both the middle levels of polite society and the political elite.

Its publication just before the May 2 rising in Madrid irritated or incensed the reading public, depending on their political passions – for the time being at least. In the propaganda war, the French occupiers were outmatched by Madrid rumour and hearsay, since much of it concerning Spain's fate was closer to the truth (indicating its high-placed origin) than the fabricated Bayonne communiqués.

On April 30, our diarist reported, offhandedly, a new and disturbing rumour:

> Since last Thursday (April 28), it has been put about that on May 2 next, coinciding with [Carlos IV's] appointment of the Gran Duque [Murat] as his Regent in Spain, a popular commotion is to be feared. Alarmed by this, a number of families left Madrid today. On the said day, the Queen of Etruria [Fernando VII's sister] and her children are to leave the capital for Bayonne.[78]

This warning of a possible rising did not make clear whether the event was being 'planned' or was simply 'feared'. The date – April 28 – coincided, however, with the governing junta's first fears of a popular rising, and presumably the rumour originated with some junta member. And it was obviously taken seriously enough by some to flee for safety.

BAYONNE: NAPOLEON DETHRONES THE BOURBONS

At the same time as ordering Godoy's release, Murat gave up all plans of persuading Carlos to return to the throne, and prepared the royal couple's dispatch to France. Once Godoy was free to accompany them, so he believed, they were certain to fall in with Napoleon's plans.

Over two weeks of forceful negotiation in Bayonne, the Emperor achieved his aims. For the first week, Fernando's councillors, who had made so many mistakes, resisted Napoleon's abdication ultimatum, which was accompanied by 'threats made in so imperious and unheard of tones that they cannot be transcribed to paper'.[79] The Spanish prime minister, Cevallos, told the French foreign minister, Champagny, that Fernando 'could not and should not renounce his throne in favour of another dynasty, because to do so would be to break faith with his vassals and his own reputation'. Nor could he 'consent to another dynasty reigning because only the Spanish nation, by virtue of its original rights, could elect another family to the throne once the present ruling family ended its reign'.[80]

In stating the latter point, the prime minister was the first to put forward against the Emperor's pretensions the ideological argument which, in differing modalities, informed and justified the patriotic coalition of progressives, moderate and absolutist monarchists in their resistance to Napoleon during the war. It was a myth generated by a particular (and religious) vision of natural law* which supposed that in the formation of human society, individuals had relinquished all or part of their natural freedom in exchange for the protection and benefits that would accrue to them from living conjointly in society under an elected king. This portmanteau 'compact' allowed for many interpretations including, somewhat surprisingly, absolutism: the people's initial election was a once and for all choice, a 'pact of subjection' to a king whose only obligation was to maintain intact his royal 'prerogatives'. The vassal's duty was to obey.[81]

But the compact also implied the existence of a 'fundamental law' which bound rulers and ruled 'so that nothing is judged to be done justly if anything is done contrary to that primary law'.[82] Any violation of the fundamental law was null and void. This opened the door to a conclusion diametrically opposed to that of absolutism: in the case of such violations, society had the right to establish a new compact to determine the form of monarchy it wished to live under. In this interpretation, then, the mythical notion of the compact would during the war strike at the heart of absolutism, opening the way to 'national sovereignty' and a constitutional monarchy, as the Cádiz constituent assembly of 1810 to 1812 demonstrated.

If Fernando's ineffable former preceptor and cleric, Juan Escoiquiz, was to be believed, he was the first of the Spanish royal party to be informed directly by Napoleon of his reasons for demanding that the Bourbons abdicate the throne.

> My empire's interests demand that the House of Bourbon, which is my implacable enemy, does not henceforth reign in Madrid. It is also in your nation's interests because the last kings of this dynasty have done Spain nothing but harm.[83]

Napoleon returned many times to his conviction that Carlos IV's abdication during the Aranjuez tumult, when his guards had mutinied, could not be anything but a renunciation under force and therefore illegitimate. To Escoiquiz's long-winded denial of the allegation, the Emperor replied: 'Say what you will, Canon, I stick to my maxim. . . . Moreover, my House and Empire require that the Bourbons no longer reign in Madrid.'

> Whereupon his Imperial Majesty good humouredly took hold of my ear and jokingly tweaked it, adding, 'even if you were right, Canon, I repeat: Ma la política'.[84]

The ear tweaking, one of Napoleon's notorious personal proclivities, was shortly thereafter repeated with somewhat greater force when Escoiquiz still refused to agree with the Emperor's propositions.

In a more serious vein, Napoleon justified his political reasoning in a report to

---

* 'Natural law' had its origins in ancient Greece, had been codified by the Romans, and re-emerged in Europe in the seventeenth century. It supposed that there were 'eternal immutable principles of morality that stand as critics of positive [i.e. man-made] law'. Although it had been demolished as a myth by Voltaire and others since the mid-eighteenth century, it continued to enjoy great influence in Spain where the 'eternal principles' were credited to God. (Gay, 1977, p. 457; Herr, 1958, pp. 176–179.)

the Spanish purportedly by his foreign minister, Champagny (but to all intents and purposes the Emperor's own work), which maintained that the Empire's security depended on good relations with Spain, whose forces and resources must be increased, in order to oblige England to sue for peace. Napoleon considered it impossible to return Carlos IV to the throne against national opinion or Fernando VII who, supported by England, had risen against his father; but nor could he leave Spain submerged in anarchy and in England's hands. Spain had descended into decadence and it was necessary to regenerate her. Policy advised it, justice authorized it, the recent Bourbon troubles proved the necessity of putting a prince of the imperial family on the throne.[85]

The Spanish played for time, asking for everything in writing. But time was not on their side. The arrival of the old king and queen on April 30 changed the scenario totally.

In Madrid, meanwhile, the governing junta, composed of a number of ministers, failed to resist Murat's orders and set an example of leadership. Effectively the only sovereign power in Spain once the king was in France, it acted as though hamstrung by the limited remit Fernando had given it before his departure and its respect for superior French military strength. Although informed on the night of April 28 that Fernando's councillors were resisting Napoleon's abdication ultimatum, arguing that if Napoleon considered that Carlos IV had abdicated 'under duress', Fernando's abdication would be even more 'forced', since it would take place in a state of un-freedom and removal from his vassals 'by means that everyone is aware of and that will horrify and outrage all Europe',[86] the Junta took no action in the capital to reinforce this resistance. No doubt its legalistically minded members were more concerned than Murat by the possibility of a popular rising which would jeopardize the king's (and their own) future. Given that they acted almost only on orders from the king – had they received his instructions to declare war they would have surely, though unenthusiastically, executed them – their task was made more difficult because open communication with the king's party in Bayonne had been cut off by the Emperor's police who seized all correspondence between them.

Nonetheless, by the night of May 1–2, the junta – now amplified to include the governors, deans and two ministers of each of the realm's supreme councils – had been driven by the critical situation in the capital to initiate a discussion on the question of declaring war. At that moment an emissary arrived from Bayonne with a message that the junta should do everything in its power to 'conserve peace and harmony with the French'. This put an end to the dicussion. Instead, the junta decided to send Fernando a verbal message placing four questions before him; the message's bearers reached Bayonne on May 4.[87]

The questions were these: 1. Would the king authorize the creation of a substitute junta, whose members he should name, and which would be free to move out of French reach if the need arose? 2. Was it the king's wish for hostilities to be opened against the French, and if so how and when should they begin? 3. Should the frontier posts be immediately ordered closed to prevent more French troops entering the country? 4. Did the king consider it opportune to convoke the Cortes?[88]

The day after receiving the questions, Fernando wrote out in his own hand two decrees. In the first, he stated that as he was 'without liberty and in consequence disabled from taking any measure to save his Person or the

Monarchy', he authorized the junta to remove itself to an appropriate place and to exercise all the functions of sovereignty in his name. In other words to act as a regency. Hostilities should begin as soon as, by 'an act of violence', he was interned in France, whereupon the junta should take whatever measures it considered appropriate to prevent the entry of further French troops. In the second decree he expressed his wish that the Cortes be summoned to whatever place seemed the most expeditious, and that for the moment the Cortes should confine itself exclusively to raising the money necessary for the kingdom's defence.*

By the time the decrees reached Madrid they had been superseded by the official news of Fernando's abdication. These decrees were never presented to the amplified governing junta, according to Bernardo Iriarte, a member for the Consejo de las Indias, who maintained that Miguel Azanza, Fernando's treasury minister at the time and shortly to be a minister of King Josef Bonaparte, had kept them secret.† In the immediate, this mattered little. But in the medium term of the war, fought by the patriots in the name of Fernando, the decrees, had they been widely known, could have conditioned several political choices: the creation of a regency, the summoning of the Cortes, albeit in a limited role, indeed the very declaration of hostilities against Napoleon, which could have cut the ground from under the feet of those, especially his former ministers, who collaborated with the Bonaparte regime.

In Bayonne, the day after the old royal couple's arrival on April 30, Napoleon manoeuvred Carlos into stating that Fernando should return the crown to him, and informed the latter's councillors accordingly. Although previously they had refused Napoleon's dogma that Carlos had abdicated 'under duress', they now accepted with alacrity on three conditions which Fernando set out in a letter to his father: he was prepared to renounce the throne, but only in Madrid, and before the Cortes or an assembly of notables, and that if Carlos did not want to rule, Fernando would do so as his designated lieutenant. The conditions were obviously dictated by the desire to release Fernando from Napoleon's immediate grasp and by the certain knowledge that any representative Spanish body would refuse his handing the throne back.

Within fifteen minutes of Fernando's dispatching the letter, it had been delivered by the French police to Napoleon's hands, and he was reading it to Carlos. The Emperor offered to draft a reply which, with a Cartesian logic that Carlos could never have mastered, surveyed events since the Escorial affair, and

---

* The Cortes, a medieval institution originally confined to prelates and upper nobility, was the nearest equivalent to a parliament that Spain enjoyed, but which the absolutist monarchy barely ever summoned. During the earlier seven-hundred year Catholic reconquest of Muslim Spain, the importance to the struggle of existing or newly founded municipalities made imperative the representation of the third estate. But from the close of the fifteenth century and the reconquest's end, with power increasingly concentrated in the monarch's hands, the Cortes' suffered a corresponding loss of power, consummated finally by absolutism. At a moment of extreme crisis without its king in place, the Cortes remained, however, the only representative national body which could take measures fundamental to Spain's independence from foreign domination.

indignantly rejected Fernando's offer. By now Carlos IV was dominated exclusively by hatred of his son who had 'usurped' his throne.[89]

Three days later, on May 4, Fernando repeated his offer. That evening he received the verbal questions sent by the governing junta in Madrid; the following morning, May 5, he wrote out his two decrees – the last of his first reign. That afternoon, Napoleon received word of a popular anti-French rising in Madrid three days earlier. Infuriated, the Emperor went to the appartments of the ex-king and queen. Fernando and his brother, Carlos, were summoned to their presence, and their father told his oldest son that he was responsible for the bloodshed and that if he did not give up his rights to the throne he and his retinue would be considered traitors. Napoleon is supposed to have added: 'Prince, you must choose between cession and death', and to have told him that he had until midnight to renounce the throne in favour of his father, and to inform Madrid of the fact. 'With an almost imperceptible nod of his head, Fernando withdrew.' Alone with the old royal couple, Napoleon had little difficulty in persuading Carlos, who had indicated his wish to renounce the throne, to abdicate in his favour 'as the only person who in the state of things prevailing can reestablish order'.[90] But Fernando and his councillors were unaware of this.

Having conceded ground since the arrival of his parents, Fernando now collapsed. He was not made of the stuff of patriotic martyrdom. Moreover, he had just dispatched a decree effectively declaring war on Napoleon, which the French police might easily seize. Whether Napoleon actually threatened him with death or not is immaterial: Fernando knew that the Bourbon duc d'Enghien had been abducted and shot on the Emperor's orders. The following day, May 6, Fernando renounced the throne in his father's favour; and the latter, after confirming Murat as his lieutenant general in Spain (Murat had packed don Antonio, Fernando's uncle and president of the governing junta, off to France on May 3 and taken over his presidency), handed his throne over to Napoleon.

But Fernando went even further. Abandoned by his councillors, he subsequently renounced his rights as heir to the throne. And on May 12, he, his brother Carlos and his uncle Antonio issued a proclamation in Bordeaux absolving Spaniards of 'all obligations' to them. The three then continued on to their internment at Talleyrand's country estate at Valençay where the young ex-king spent the war years grovelling before Napoleon, going so far as to congratulate him on placing his brother on the throne of Spain. Fernando thus became the first *afrancesado* – the name given to collaborators with the Bonaparte regime by the anti-Napoleonic patriots who had risen in *his* name and in defence of *his* throne.

Courage and dignity in the morning; cowardice and vileness in the afternoon. Fernando was dominated by events. His shifty character, lacking in all decorum, allowed him to humble himself before events in the hope of better times without any sense of humiliation to outrage his feelings. He had a plebeian soul which accounted for his popularity.[91]

Thanks to Bourbon turpitude, Napoleon won the Spanish throne easily. But he would live to regret it. On St Helena, he confessed that the resulting 'accursed Spanish war was the primary cause of my misfortunes'[92] – 'I started this affair very badly, I confess; the immorality of it was only too patent, the injustice too cynical, and it was a very vile trick because I have fallen victim to it myself.'[93]

3

The First Shots of War

THE MADRID RISING, MAY 2–3

On Monday, May 2, for a matter of hours, the people of Madrid rose against the French. After heavy fighting they were defeated by a combination of their own authorities and greatly superior French forces; and finally they were repressed with brutal savagery by Murat. The outcome, common sense assured, was foretold: the balance of opposing forces was too heavily weighted against the insurrection's success. But common sense is not the stuff of which such risings are made.

In the event which precipitated it, and the social groupings which participated in it, the insurrection was typical of the national rising which still lay in an uncertain future. But in other aspects it was totally atypical: it took place under direct French military occupation and had immediately to confront French military might, something which occurred in none of the major insurrectionary cities subsequently. As the culmination of a month-long agitation against the French army in the capital, the labouring poor rose, and though rapidly joined by a sizeable number of members of other social groupings, the former remained (along with Spanish military) the principal protagonists. Without evidence of prior planning or leadership and without money flowing, theirs was in this sense closer to a spontaneous rising than many of the later provincial insurrections which were planned by Fernandista supporters who used, and frequently 'remunerated', the lower orders, as in the earlier Aranjuez rising, as an intimidatory street force. Finally, while the Madrid rising could justly be called the first shots of the Napoleonic war, it was not the 'spark' which immediately set off the conflagration in the rest of Spain.

The undeclared war which, for the past month, had been fought against the French in the capital's streets might have exploded into open warfare earlier or later or perhaps never at all. Why then did it happen on this particular day? An event, already familiar from the Aranjuez rising, and shortly to be seen again in the wider anti-Napoleonic risings, occurred on that Monday in Madrid: the threat to the people of losing their last remaining link to *their* monarch.

Running like a mobilizing thread through all of these risings was the fear, solidly embedded in popular consciousness, of living in a world without their king. In Aranjuez, it had been the planned departure of their then king, Carlos IV, which had aroused the villagers' fear – cleverly exploited by the anti-Godoy nobility. In Madrid on May 2, it was the forced departure to France of the last direct heir to Fernando's throne remaining in Spain; and within the month it was the definitive news of the loss of the Spanish throne to Napoleon which aroused popular urban anger and support for a handful of anti-Napoleonic patriots to launch risings and effectively to begin the war against the French. Moreover, if the king's departure from Aranjuez had been an outrage of Godoy's, these last two outrages were the French Emperor's work in order to conquer and subdue Spain, leaving the people 'orphaned' and abandoned to their fate. The people's passionate hatred for Godoy was now transferred to Napoleon or more immediately to his lieutenant general in Spain, Murat.

This thread of abandonment by their king was woven into a fabric of other fears, passions, anxieties, resentments and hopes, as was seen during the Aranjuez rising. But within this fabric a new warp had also recently been woven: the knowledge, since Aranjuez, that the people, by their joint action, could definitively affect the affairs of state.

On May 1, a large crowd in the Puerta del Sol had waited since early morning in front of the post office for the latest official Spanish communiqué from Bayonne – which did not arrive, stirring up new conjectures and exacerbating old fears. The crowd booed and hissed Murat on his way through the square, and wildly cheered don Antonio, Fernando's uncle and president of the governing junta, as his old and unstylish carriage drove past. Only at 10 p.m., under a shower of rain, had the waiting crowd dispersed, still without news from Bayonne.

For the past four days, Murat had been pressuring the junta to dispatch to Bayonne Fernando's two siblings still remaining in Madrid: Luisa, the ex-queen of Etruria, whose husband had been enthroned and she, his widow, dethroned by Napoleon, and the fourteen-year-old infante (prince) Francisco de Paula, the youngest of the royal children. On May 1, the junta had finally agreed to the young prince leaving the following day: as a gesture to the junta's fear that the royal departure would lead to rioting, Murat agreed that it should take place after dark on May 2. The news of the impending departures, spread by court officials and palace servants, became known. On the same day, moreover, the first of the French-inspired Spanish pamphlets of the propaganda war appeared from Murat's press, which attempted to persuade Spaniards to abandon the decrepit Bourbon monarchy and accept a new Napoleonic crowned head. It was clear from this that Napoleon was intent on taking over the throne. Fearing the worst, the junta ordered the three-thousand-odd Spanish troops in the capital to be confined to barracks and deprived of munitions.

From an early hour on May 2, the street sellers were chanting their wares as usual, reassuring a visitor to the capital that everything was normal;[1] it was 'St Monday' – the day of the week when, as in other west European countries, those manual workers who could afford to do so (and many who couldn't), took the day off. More artisans and the like were able, therefore, to gather in public places than on a normal work day. The Puerta del Sol was again crowded with people waiting for the long-delayed bulletin from Bayonne. Only a handful had gathered outside the palace gates. By 8.30 a.m., Luisa was on her way. She was not popular, being considered almost a foreigner, and had remained close to her discredited parents, Carlos IV and María Luisa, on whose behalf she had corresponded frequently with Murat. No one attempted to prevent her departure. A second carriage still waited, its driver and postilion already in place.

The immediate events following on Luisa's departure were confused. Different accounts and participants' reports almost inevitably varied; but the significant aspect was that all led to the same conclusion, expressed in an old woman's cry, 'They are taking them away from us!'

'Treachery!' cried a man who had suddenly appeared, 'they have taken our king and now they are taking the whole royal family to France! Treachery! . . . Death to the French!'

A former royal locksmith and Fernandista confidential agent, José Blas Molina Soriano, had seen Luisa's coach driving through the streets, and had run to the palace where he found another royal coach waiting; immediately he had enquired of the coachmen who they were waiting for. On his worst fears being confirmed he launched the cry to the sixty or seventy people gathered outside. He then ran into the palace, followed by the people, shouting, 'the prince must not leave . . . .' By chance, they encountered the tearful prince who, to their acclaim, promised to appear on a palace balcony if they returned outside. This they did and the prince duly appeared, bowing his head several times in acknowledgement to the crowd which had now increased to about two hundred.[2] An Asturian-born inn porter, José Muñiz Cueto, who was outside the palace early in the morning, independently confirmed Soriano's story, but added, as other witnesses also claimed, that a court official had appeared on a palace balcony and shouted to the crowd: 'Vassals! To arms! They are taking the prince!'[3]

The confidential agent, Soriano, a man of humble origin who understood the popular mentality, played the role of 'agitator' to perfection, an essential role as would be seen in the later provincial risings. He claimed subsequently to have been acting independently, yet his vigilance of the movement of the royal carriages and his easy access to the royal palace suggested that he was well known there and was informed of the junta's fear that Murat might try forcibly to smuggle the prince out of Madrid. If he was in reality acting on the junta's behalf, it was, however, as a spy, not as a popular agitator, since the junta was trying at all costs to maintain public calm.

Another person at court had no doubt as to the rising's origin: 'There is a great rising', a lady of the court cried to the naval engineer and poet, José Mor de Fuentes, as was making his way to the palace at about 10 a.m. 'A rising, why?' 'Because the French want to take the prince.'[4]

Rapidly informed of a crowd gathering outside the palace, Murat dispatched a general and another officer to discover the cause; seeing them riding in and believing that the officers had come to take off the prince, the crowd turned on them and they unsheathed their swords. The situation was momentarily defused by a Spanish guards officer who protected the French general, and by the arrival of a small party of French soldiers who escorted the two officers back to Murat's residence. Almost immediately, French cannon were wheeled to the edge of the palace square and fired into the crowd which, leaving the dead and wounded behind, fled through the city, crying out the news.

Hearing the cannon fire, a Galician hidalgo, Joaquin Terreiro Montenegro, made for the Plaza de Santo Domingo near the palace. 'Seeing the people sadly defenceless in the face of the enemy', he 'exhorted them to take arms'. To a judge of the Madrid court, Francisco Cano Manuel, who was there at the head of a police patrol, and to the commander of the palace guard picket, he made the same proposal. 'The latter replied that he was without a single cartridge, the judge that he lacked all support, and the people that they had been refused arms at the depot.' Terreiro, jurisdictional lord of 'a number of places in the Kingdom of Galicia', told them that if they were determined 'they should demand arms again and again. But it was all in vain . . . .'*

However, elsewhere in the city armed French troops were attacked wherever they were met – the unarmed usually being left to go free – by Madrileños using any weapons they could lay their hands on at first: clasp knives, clubs, cutting tools, and a few blunderbusses, shotguns and pistols. Barely an hour had passed since the French cannonade had precipitated the insurrection.

'To arms! To arms!', a Sevillian priest, living not far from the palace, heard rushing people shout from the street. The Rev. José María Blanco went out to see what was happening:

> I had just arrived at an opening named Plazuela de Santo Domingo, the meeting point of four large streets, one of which leads to the palace, when, hearing the sound of a French drum in that direction I stopped with a considerable number of decent and quiet people whom curiosity kept rivetted to the spot. Though a strong piquet of infantry was fast advancing upon us, we could not imagine that we stood in any kind of danger. Under this mistaken notion we awaited their approach; but, seeing the soldiers halt and prepare their arms, we began instantly to disperse. A discharge of musketry followed in a few moments, and a man fell at the entrance of the street, through which I was, with a great throng, retreating from the fire. The fear of an indiscriminate massacre arose so naturally from this unprovoked assault, that every one tried to look for safety . . . I hastened on towards my house, and having shut the front door, could think of no better expedient, in the confused state of my mind, than to make ball cartridges for a fowling piece which I kept.[5]

The overwhelmingly plebeian nature of the rising was evinced in the much-quoted experience of Antonio Alcalá Galiano, nineteen-year-old son of a naval commander killed at Trafalgar and scion of an elite family of government

---

* Terreiro, who later fought the French in Galicia, passed over the fact that he was evidently not disposed to lead the Madrileños in their demand for arms. Instead, he spent the rest of the day with the judge 'witnessing with despair the sad catastrophe'. (AHN, *Estado*, Legajo 77C/166–168, Terreiro Memorial to Junta Suprema, 1809.)

administrators, who on taking to the streets was rejected by a group of young working men for his youth and evident social status. 'You're no good for anything', one of them told him. His reaction was to believe that he had as much to fear from the plebs as he had from the French, and he went home to wait 'until decent and sensible folk joined the rising'.[6] In fact he was mistaken: considerable numbers of 'decent' people had joined the rising from the start, and the Rev. Blanco recalled one of them, a 'well-dressed man', who went down the street calling loudly on the male inhabitants to make for an old arms depot. But he made no impression on Blanco's part of the town.[7]

The fighting lasted until three in the afternoon. Murat had laid his plans well; his troops occupied the dominating heights around the capital, he had ordered artillery into the Retiro, and his cantonments had been well chosen to allow his soldiers to advance rapidly into the city's centre from all directions. With thirty thousand troops under his command, he expected to be able to control any unforeseen situation. A month earlier, he had been concerned that the organizers of the Aranjuez rising were plotting a popular revolt in Madrid; and at the time of General Savary's arrival in the capital to 'persuade' Fernando to go north to meet Napoleon, Murat was evidently considering arresting the duque del Infantado, Escoiquiz and other Aranjuez plotters.[8] It was known that the two principal Fernandista nobles who initiated the Aranjuez rising – Infantado and conde de Teba, now conde de Montijo – met in Madrid; but nothing was known about the outcome of their talks. However, there was no doubt – for the documentary evidence existed – that a plot to precipitate a widespread rising, including Madrid, had been planned for April. In the Spanish capital two 'well-dressed individuals' offered large sums to whomever could assemble three to four hundred armed men. A wig comber informed the authorities that a shoemaker and a rag picker who had been approached had rejected the offer, and nothing more was heard of this plot, which the Spanish authorities presumably managed to abort. Nonetheless, three merchant brothers and purveyors to the Valencia city hall, of a certain standing and wealth, and who subsequently were the major conspirators behind their city's participation in the nationwide rising had, from shortly after the Aranjuez insurrection, raised their own private 'army' of five hundred paid men to support Fernando VII's cause and to begin a popular anti-Napoleonic rising in late April. One of the brothers later wrote that an unidentified relative who had taken a leading part in the Aranjuez mutiny and was close to Fernando had asked them to organize a 'popular commotion' demanding that the French leave Spain. A special agent was also sent from Madrid at about the same time to prepare a rising in Pamplona. None of these risings took place, probably because the Madrid attempt had failed.[9] Finally, artillery Captain Pedro Velarde's outline of a plan for a nationwide military resistance was also documented; but it did not include a civilian rising in Madrid whose chances of success he, as an experienced military officer, must have certainly doubted, though he died in its defence once it had started.

When the fighting began, columns of French soldiers converged on the centre from barracks and cantonments around the capital. But they met stiff opposition and suffered losses in their advance. In the course of the morning, considerable numbers of Madrileños armed themselves: from the artillery park, where they clamoured outside the closed gates until these were opened and arms were distributed; from the guards barracks;[10] from the town hall guard;[11] but also from individuals – an armourer claimed to have armed more than eighty people that morning.[12] Others threw arms down from their balconies (as well as heavy objects onto French soldiers' heads, one of which killed an officer), and nobles armed their retainers and released them to fight.[13]

Shortly after 11 a.m. the French cavalry – the mamelukes, Imperial Guard chasseurs, Polish lancers and dragoons – charged the crowd in the Puerta del Sol. The *chisperos* leapt onto the horses' haunches and knifed their riders, or stabbed the horses in the belly to unseat the cavalrymen. It turned into a bloody hand-to-hand conflict; the chasseurs' colonel had two horses killed under him in charges across the square, twenty of his men were put out of action, and he himself was slightly injured.[14] The wounding of the *chispero* Antonio López Regidor bore witness to the close quarters of the fighting: he was struck in the chest at point-blank range by a pistol shot as he knifed a mameluke from the hindquarters of his horse. . . . To reduce the *chisperos*, who also quickly learned to take advantage of the cover of buildings, the French had, after two hours of fighting, to bring up cannon and sweep the square with grapeshot.*

In the wards and kitchens of the General Hospital in the Calle Atocha fighting suddenly broke out when French troops entered the building; kitchen lads, male nurses, hospital assistants and other employees, who armed themselves with kitchen knives and other instruments, rushed to the defence and there were wounded on both sides. The French called for reinforcements and these took seven of the hospital workers captive, none of whom was ever again seen alive. The same fate awaited a number of building workers who threw their buckets and tools at the French from the scaffolding of the new Santiago church which they were building, causing casualties among the Polish cavalry.

The sound of musket fire spreading through the city brought out more volunteers. More than fifty prisoners in the city prison offered to fight, giving their word of honour to return afterwards; one of them was killed and another wounded – but only one did not keep his word to go back to gaol.[15] More typical, however, of the type of combatant who responded to the sound of fighting in the streets was a twenty-three-year-old Valencian journeyman, Francisco Matas, who, on hearing 'the heroic efforts beginning to be made by the city's inhabitants', knew he had 'to share their glory with them. And though only a poor journeyman . . . [I] left my master's shop and ran amidst the confusion and danger in the streets to the artillery park which troops and civilians were defending with great heroism.' There, when his master, a hatter, Francisco Labal, went to take him his food, he found Matas serving one of the cannons and firing other arms with 'great ardour and courage'.[16]

It was not only journeymen but masters who rose, though it is probable that

---

* Thanks to Goya's famous painting *El Dos de Mayo*, the fighting in the Puerta del Sol has become emblematic of the rising. (On Goya, see chap. 19.)

there were as many of the former as of the latter.* One such master was the forty-two-year-old embroiderer, Agustín Pérez de Hiriás, who stemmed originally from Mier, 'in the mountains of Santander'.

> I went out into the street exalted by feelings of patriotism. I had a blunderbuss and a sword, and other patriots joined me.† After firing at the enemy a few times, we reached the Calle de Alcalá. There the French unleashed a fusillade and I was hit in the chest by a musket ball and, bathed in blood, was left for dead. Some neighbours carried me back to my house in the Calle de Mira el Rio, without any hope of living.

He was fortunate enough to be treated at home by the hospital's chief assistant who extracted the ball and various breastbones, and after nine months of treatment he miraculously survived. But he was left with an asthmatic affliction that had made it impossible to practice his trade, 'and moreover with the misfortune of a wife who went mad at the fright of seeing me brought home nearly dead . . .'.[17]

The neighbours, who had also been resisting the French advance in the Calle Alcalá, where some of the bitterest street fighting took place, were all men in their forties and fifties but of mixed occupations. They carried Pérez home 'through back streets and at considerable danger to their lives' lest they encounter a French patrol, having taken the precaution of throwing the master embroiderer's arms into a doorway. Among them was another master embroiderer and a tavern keeper, both of about Pérez's age; a forty-eight-year-old excise and revenue man; and a 'worker' (without further specification) who was fifty-two.

The combatants often fought in groups formed by affinity or friendship which had gathered around the best-armed or the most authoritative amongst them. Of the fifteen identifiable groups, eight were led by civilians, four of them of the educated elite, five by military men, and two of unknown leadership.‡ Two of the civilian-led groups were formed in public drinking places; and another was made up of the conde de Altamira's and the Portuguese ambassador's retainers.[18]

Early in the rising, at about the time the Galician hidalgo was exhorting the people to arm themselves, Mor de Fuentes encountered in the streets close to the palace 'a tall, well-built, twenty-five to thirty-year-old woman waving a white handkerchief and crying discomposedly, Arms! Arms'![19] At the Puerta de Toledo, not far distant, the *manolas* of the surrounding plebeian neighbourhoods had massed in a tactically intelligent attempt to prevent French

* Only ten journeymen were listed as such in the combatant rolls, but the young ages of many of those who were classified simply by trade suggested that they were in fact journeymen – unless their fathers were masters, giving them privileged access to becoming at an early age masters themselves.

† His anachronistic use of the word 'patriot' is explicable by the fact that his testimony, like all those quoted, was written after the war when the word had come into widespread usage in the sense used here which was not the case in 1808.

‡ Among these leaders were an Asturian-born student, a silversmith, an inn-keeper, an architect, the royal family's doctor, a priest, and a couple of inn porters.

cuirassiers from entering the capital from their cantonment in Carabanchel. The women gathered at the Toledo gate dragged whatever they could lay hands on into the street to form barriers to the oncoming cavalry, dismounted a few cavalrymen, stabbing their horses, before being ridden down by the mass of horsemen. As one of the young women, Benita Sandoval y Sánchez, escaped into a nearby house, she was seen and followed: French cuirassiers on foot riddled her body with bullets as she tried to hide amidst clothes and furniture.[20] Of the two neighbourhoods which suffered the highest number of casualties in the rising, the area around the Puerta de Toledo was one.[21]

Irrespective of social status, women played a notable role in the fighting. They ranged from adolescents to sixty-year-olds – the mean age of those killed was thirty-four. Thus half of their numbers were, in terms of contemporary life expectancy, already middle-aged or elderly. Their high casualty rate – eleven percent of the total inflicted although their proportion of the combatants was only just over seven percent[22] – can only be explained by their bravery. For example, a twenty-year-old, Ramona Esquilino, and her mother rushed out unarmed into the street on hearing the French advance on the artillery park. Ramona seized a French officer's sword from his hand and laid about her, wounding the officer. Within minutes, French soldiers had felled mother and daughter and left them, apparently lifeless, in the street. Amazingly both survived.[23]

Considerable numbers of civilians who had escaped the cannonade at the royal palace and the fighting in the Puerta del Sol made their way by back streets to the artillery park where they hoped to find arms. It was there that some of the final and most desperate fighting of the day took place.

The park, then on the capital's perimeter in the original *chispero* quarter of Maravillas, was indefensible; neither its emplacement in the grounds of an old ducal palace nor the wall which enclosed it had been planned for defence. It lay between two major access streets to the capital's centre, la calle Ancha de San Bernardo and Fuencarral, and its perimeter was bounded on two sides by smaller streets. The stores contained a considerable quantity of arms and munitions – but the storeman who held the key failed to report for duty. At the start of the rising, only sixteen Spanish artillerymen were on duty, outnumbered five to one by a French contingent which Murat had posted there. A junior officer, Lieutenant Rafael Arango, had been ordered to the artillery park that morning with the official order confining all Spanish troops to barracks; and it was not until the situation became critical that Captain Luís Daoíz, a forty-one-year-old Sevillano, and the park's commandant, was dispatched to take command, bringing with him a repetition of the official order. A reflective officer, Daoíz appeared to be weighing up, Arango recalled, his duty to obey orders or to come out in support of the rising.[24] While outside the closed main gate increasing numbers of people were clamouring for arms, and inside a few artillery and infantry officers waited, Daoíz paced the parade ground in reflection . . .

Like many others that day, it was the sound of combat in the streets that brought Captain Pedro Velarde, aged twenty-eight, from Muriedas, Santander, rushing from his desk job to the park. Realizing that French artillerymen outnumbered the Spanish, he made first for an infantry barracks close by and, together with Captain Andrés Rovira y Valldocera, a Catalan infantry officer on leave from Cuba who led a civilian group, persuaded the commanding officer to let him have one company of 40 officers and men, commanded by a captain, to contain the civilians trying to break down the park gates in their demand for arms. It was his first ruse; his second, once inside the park, was to secure the French artillery contingent's acceptance of protective imprisonment rather than face slaughter at the hands of the mob clamouring at the gate. Meanwhile, Daoíz suddenly drew his sword and ordered the gates opened.

The people poured in, were armed with the weapons laid down by the French contingent and from the park's armoury, and poured out again to fight in the streets. Many preferred edged weapons to muskets which they did not know how to use. Even as they went to their almost certain death, the people's instinct was right; the enemy had to be harried in familiar streets and alleys unknown to him. The strategy of static defence of an indefensible place could only attract the concentrated fire-power of superior French arms. Even though disciplined military presence strengthened the people's fighting capacity in the park, unless the defenders could hold out until the following day at the very least, the park's defence would do nothing to support existing foci of insurrectionist combatants or to inspire continuing popular resistance throughout the city.

At first, cannon fire and disciplined military action in combination with unskilled civilian daring – Velarde had managed to retain some of the armed people for the park's defence – repulsed two French attacks; but the cannon, which had had to be brought out into the park's flanking streets, were exposed to enemy fire, and for want of grapeshot were less effective in close-quarter fighting than they might have been. It remained one of the mysteries of the day why the artillerymen did not break down the storeroom door to secure at least the grapeshot which they knew was kept there and which they desperately needed to sweep the streets of their attackers. Instead, they fired only ball.

Civilians acted as the park's advance guard. After the war, the captain who commanded the small infantry detachment in the park during its defence testified that he had seen a young girl carrying musket cartridges under fire to her aged father and his companions who were firing on the French from beyond the park's wall. Suddenly struck by a musket ball in the breast, she dropped to the ground dead. Her father saw her die, but continued at his post. Feeling for the old man's grief, the captain ordered him three times to leave his post before he agreed to do so, having run out of powder. He came and knelt by his daughter's body, kissed her face, and lifted her up tenderly to carry her home in a nearby street. Subsequently the dead girl was identified as fifteen-year-old Manuela Malasaña.

But in 1816, Manuela's only surviving relative, her aunt, gave a far more horrifying account of her death. She was returning home from her job as an embroiderer, carrying as was customary her scissors attached to her waist when she was stopped by French soldiers who searched her. On finding the scissors, an aggressive weapon, she was shot out of hand by the soldiers close to the artillery park gates.[25]* The young girl who was killed under fire bringing her father munitions remained an anonymous heroine.

In the midst of the fighting, a forty-two-year-old mother of five, Clara del Rey, another long-unacknowledged heroine of the park, was killed serving the cannons as she had throughout; living close by the park, at the first sounds of the rising, she had roused her three sons and her husband to 'help the heroic Spanish artillery-men'. Like so many of the Madrid labouring poor, she and her husband were originally villagers – from Villalón de Campos, Valladolid in their case – who had abandoned their smallholding to migrate to the capital, probably during the great dearth of 1804. Her oldest son, Juan, the only one of the family whose trade is known, was a nineteen-year-old bricklayer who, to avenge his mother, joined the patriot army and fought throughout the war.[26]

The number of fathers and sons, mothers and daughters who fought along-side each other was remarkable. Almost inevitably, one or other of the family was killed: in one instance, a father and son faced a French firing squad together. The death of a parent often led to a surviving son swearing vengeance and joining the army. Three bereaved sons wreaked a different form of revenge: they began guerrilla actions, and one of them, from the village of Miraflores de la Sierra, whose father had died fighting alongside him in the Madrid streets, became a guerrilla leader.[27]

In the few hours that the park's defence lasted, seven women were known to have been killed or to have suffered fatal wounds, and at least another two were wounded.[28] Like many of the women who died fighting, Clara del Rey was given a pauper's burial. The Maravillas quarter, where the park was located, was the scene of the rising's greatest number of casualties.[29]

A considerable number of non-combatant women also died when they went out onto their balconies to watch the fighting, or from musket balls fired through their windows. But women suffered, too, the effects of their husband's near or actual deaths, as was seen in the master embroiderer's case. Another wife, soon to give birth, went mad and jumped to her death from the second floor of her house. Four women whose husbands were killed died of the shock almost immediately, while the sister of another man shot out of hand was literally struck dumb and remained so. (These cases were not gender exclusive: the brother of a non-combatant lawyer who was also shot out of hand ended his days in a lunatic asylum; while the father of one of those executed died of shock.[30])

Angered at his troops having been twice repulsed, Murat gathered a force strong enough to attack the park on all sides and placed its command under a trusted general. The end was not long in coming. Ammunition and powder were running low. The defending artillerymen were killed at their cannons exposed in the streets, a musket ball struck Captain Velarde in the heart, and Captain Daoíz was wounded in the foot. The defence crumbled. As he approached the silent cannon on which Daoíz was holding himself erect, the French general had bitter

* In public consciousness, however, she remained the young woman the captain had seen, and though her role as a national heroine has always been subsidiary to that of Daoíz and Velarde, in 1879 a street close by the former Park was named after her, and today the whole neighbourhood is known by her name.

words for the captain, who took his sword to him, only to be bayonetted in the back by a vigilant French guardsman, a wound from which he died a few hours later. Both Velarde and Daoíz, the commanders of the defence, found subsequent fame as Spanish national heroes.

A short time later, all fighting, if not the bloodshed, was brought to an end. O'Farril and Azanza, War and Treasury ministers respectively, and members of the governing junta, persuaded Murat that the rising was not a conspiracy and that they could bring it to an end if his troops stopped firing and a French ranking officer accompanied Spanish civilian and military authorities into the streets in a call to end resistance and declare an amnesty. This they did. But as the fighting ended, the French repression began. Most of those captured with arms in hand were summarily tried by a drumhead military commision, and those caught with concealed 'weapons' (among them shearing clippers, scissors, sack sewing needles and other 'offensive' tools of their trade) were shot out of hand.

Only one thing appeared likely to save someone: the ability to speak French. Esteban Sorrolla who had been captured after fighting in the Puerta del Sol was taken with others to be shot; speaking French to his guard he managed to awaken his pity and was allowed to escape.[31] Celestino Espinosa, a French-speaking scrivener attached to the street patrol of a member of the Madrid court, had managed to save one man's life during the fighting by crying loudly in French to the officer who was on the point of executing him on the spot for stabbing a French soldier, that it was 'dishonourable' to shoot a man without trial, and he should be turned over to the court member. Espinosa promised to act as guardian for the fugitive, whom he turned loose. The scrivener himself escaped only with great difficulty after this act and again largely because he spoke French.[32]

As frequently occurred in mass executions, one or two individuals escaped by luck, cool-headedness or both. Juan Suárez, who had fought in the artillery park, was already kneeling waiting to be shot on the Montaña del Príncipe Pío when he succeeded in freeing himself from the rope that bound the victims' wrists, and, throwing himself down before the fusillade, rolled and then ran down the hill, hotly pursued by French troops who inflicted several sword wounds before he managed to leap over a wall and vanish into the safety of the church of San Antonio de la Florida.[33] Another man, don Cosme Martínez del Corral, an ex-artilleryman who fought in the Puerta del Sol and later in the park, was found to be still alive after being 'executed' with others in the patio of the Buen Suceso Hospital. Taken into the hospital, he slowly recovered.[34]

At least eighty-six men – one in seven of the identified combatants – and thirteen non-combatants, including two women, met their deaths in front of firing squads.*

---

* See Appendix 1, table. In fact the numbers were higher. Parish records indicate that at least a further nineteen unidentified individuals were shot on the Montaña del Príncipe Pío; and it is possible that sixteen more unidentified people were shot in El Prado where the identified numbered thirty-two. Nine cartloads of bodies were collected from there to be buried. (See also Nicolas Horta Rodríguez, 'Represión en Madrid, mayo de 1808', in *Revista Historia Militar*, no. 38, Madrid 1975, pp. 49–75.)

In the early hours of the afternoon, there reigned a sad peace in Madrid, accompanied by terror and rage . . . And when darkness fell, the silence and solitude was rent by the sound of musket volleys and shots which continued until dawn . . . In the morning came the news of the gravity of the atrocities . . .

recalled Antonio Alcalá Galiano many years later.[35]

This brutal revenge – 'the blackest, perhaps, which has stained the French name during their whole career of conquest'[36] – shocked 'decent and sensible' Madrileños who had taken no part in the rising, or who had even secretly condemned it. The French military had failed their word when they agreed to bring the fighting to an end. The repression's major burden fell on the labouring poor: craftsmen and journeymen, tradesmen, labourers, servants, waiters, porters, muleteers, carters . . . These had formed one-third of the combatants, and made up over half of the known executed. Artisans were hard hit: as a proportion of those executed, they lost twice as many to the firing squads as they had contributed proportionately to the insurrection. Royal servants met an even harsher fate: they suffered a proportional execution rate of two and a half times their combat strength.

The middling to upper commoners – liberal professions, gentlemen, administratives and clergy – were not spared either, though their percentage of executed was only slightly higher than their proportion of combatants. However, within this group, the liberal professionals paid a heavier price than the others: their percentage of the executed was one and a half points higher. Whether by design or chance (and the figures would suggest the former) the French military struck – and struck hard – at their major enemies, sparing only the Spanish military. They evidently had no desire to alienate a national organization with the means to extend armed risings to other parts of the country;* and Murat in consequence accepted the junta's pleas not to extend the repression to the artillery park's surviving military defenders, now prisoners.

A number of civilians, like Francisco Matas, the Valencian hatter's journeyman who, on hearing the sound of fighting in the streets, had run to the park, and had subsequently been wounded and taken prisoner there, owed their lives to the junta's intervention and Murat's concession. As Matas relates:

At ten at night the few prisoners, including myself who had a slight wound in the thigh, were marched with the utmost brutality from the park under guard to the village of Chamartin where we were held until the following day, May 3. Then we were brought back to Madrid and taken to the Montaña de Monte Pío where I thought we would be shot as so many other victims had already been; but then they took us to the Puerta de Recoletos, and finally locked us up in the basement of the Geronimos friary.

The following day they were taken out and marched under guard through Madrid's major streets,

* Nonetheless, two companies of sappers deserted from their cantonments in Alcalá de Henares to be out of French reach – the first organized Spanish military units to vote with their feet against the French.

an act they believed was ignominious, as though we were to be ashamed of having taken up arms against the French. Then they made us sign a deceptive and fanatical statement before freeing us . . . During those two and a half days we were beaten and insulted constantly and given no food . . . Divine Providence spared us in the end.[37]

But many of the dominant elite no longer had much faith in Divine Providence and they fled the capital, Antonio Galiano's uncle, a judge of the Madrid court, among them. The many regional dignitaries who had come to Madrid to kiss the hand of their new monarch and had remained, returned home. There was no lack of authoritative personages to spread the news of the May 2 insurrection through the provinces, although private correspondence sent by the efficient and rapid crown mail services, and the latter's carriers, were often the first to relate it.

In an Order of the Day to his soldiers on May 2 and in a proclamation to Spaniards on the same day,[38] Murat attempted to drive a wedge between the 'good Spaniards' who must deplore the rising and the capital's 'rabble' who had been aroused by 'villainous agitators' and 'our common enemy', the English. His tactic was to no effect; the repression, if not the rising, had seen to that. As usual the Madrileños' real mood could be gauged with some precision by theatre attendance. In an attempt to placate the capital's population, Murat ordered the theatre company 'forthwith' to put on plays every day of the week. 'For several months the theatre-going public declined to such an incredible degree' that, 'with no financial help forthcoming from the government, the players ran up a debt of more than one hundred thousand reales with the Treasury'.[39]

Murat was triumphant at his victory. 'Yesterday's affair delivers Spain to the Emperor', he is alleged to have told O'Farril, on May 3. 'You should say that it places Spain beyond his reach forever', O'Farril is said to have retorted.[40] Apocryphal or not, O'Farril's response was correct.

In one aspect, Murat's triumphalism was vindicated, however. The Madrid population did not again collectively raise its head against the French occupation. Indeed, once Josef Bonaparte was established on his throne in Madrid, and began to court the labouring classes with free entertainments, bullfights, and distributions of bread and money, the *chisperos* settled down to enjoying themselves, at least until the bread ran out in the famine of 1812.

*

Who were the people who rose? Individuals in low-paid 'petty service' jobs – servants and inn porters mainly, but with a large sprinkling of coachmen, hospital attendants, water carriers, small traders and the like – formed the largest single civilian group. Close behind them were artisans, journeymen and apprentices. Together these two groups made up thirty percent of the identified combatants.* Among the artisans, shoemakers and cobblers, tailors and

---

* Hitherto, occupational analysis has included nearly one-fifth of accidental casualties or those executed without having fought, distorting the combatants' occupational and gender data. The figures in Appendix 1, table attempt to correct this by segregating combatants, whose numbers have been expanded by further research, from non-combatants.

building workers – as might be expected of a capital devoted to sustaining courtiers and government officials – were the foremost trades, representing one-fifth of the insurrectionist tradesmen. In all, thirty trades were represented – about half of those then existing in the capital.

The next largest group, representing nearly fifteen percent of the combatants, is the one that the least is known about: those whose trades or professions, and frequently even their places of origin, are unspecified. Leaving aside the prisoners, whose effectiveness in the combat, judging by their casualty rate, was practically nil, women made up the next largest plebeian grouping (six percent). A relatively small number of labourers and agrarian workers completed the manual labouring contingent. Including women (an assertion based almost exclusively on the humble quarters where they lived since the documents barely ever referred to their jobs), plebeian combatants made up forty percent of the total.* Their social composition was not unlike that of the Parisian revolutionary *menu peuple*.

Although less numerous, the fourth largest civilian grouping was composed of liberal professionals, gentlemen,† administratives, clergymen and ladies at just under thirteen percent of the total. Of these, liberal professionals – doctors, surgeons, professors, teachers, architects, notaries, scriveners, musicians and painters – represented over one-third, with gentlemen forming another third. This educated commoner stratum was more numerous than contemporaries or historians have generally allowed, and played a significant, albeit not a leadership, role. Though perhaps not as emotionally motivated as the plebeians by the last of the royal family's removal to France,‡ they patently felt that a Napoleonic takeover of Spain, engineered by trickery, threatened their interests: their aim to have a voice in the reforms which they knew only too well the country needed, and which they expected of the Fernandista regime, coupled with the fear of a return to the 'despotism' of the past under another – Napoleonic – name; the loss, in short, of the country's freedom. After nearly thirteen years of war as France's ally, and at considerable financial and naval cost to Spain (for which they blamed Godoy), they were not prepared to see their country surrendered to any foreign power.

Somewhat surprisingly, given that they were officially confined to barracks, the military made up fourteen percent of the combatants, not far short of the number of artisans. The soldiers, most of them individuals of regiments not stationed in Madrid, were led by junior officers, especially of the elite artillery corps. Like many of their rank, the latter had admired Napoleon, an artillery-man, for his military genius, until his 'treacherous' takeover of Spanish army fortresses. Their admiration turned to hatred of the invader, and it was then that Captain Velarde began to plot a national military rising against the French.

* Of the women identified as combatants, just under one woman in five was a *doña*, indicating a higher social status than that of the working women. For want of a better word I have called the former ladies. They made up 1.3% of all combatants.

† *Dons* without known occupations.

‡ A small number of these liberal professionals were court physicians, scriveners and professors, and may therefore have been demonstrating their personal loyalty to the monarchy.

Royal personnel and revenue men comprised a further 5.4 percent. Adding to these the military, and the middling to upper commoner classes, these non-plebeians represented one-third of the known combatants. (Many of the soldiers and royal personnel were obviously of plebeian extraction, but they are included in their respective professions.)

Identified villagers from outside Madrid, whose remaining presence in the capital after Sunday, May 1, has – in the traditional historiography of the rising – been said to have constituted an important insurrectionary force, totalled three percent of the known combatants; but it may well be that among those of unknown trades and places of origin there were many villagers whose identities could not be established after their death.*

Numerically, the clergy took little part, their representation being the second equal lowest above beggars; but their few numbers, five in all, should not allow one to overlook their importance in mobilizing and enthusing the combatants in the struggle. One of them indeed led a group in the streets. All were ordained priests. Surprisingly no members of religious orders appear to have risen, even though one of the priests was a monastery chaplain.

There were also significant absences in the combatant rolls. The titled nobility and large merchants did not appear. These privileged strata temporized; like Alcalá Galiano, they saw the rising as an exclusively 'plebeian' outburst and almost certainly doomed, while they might yet have to defend their real interests more effectively under a Napoleonic king. Only one grandee, a military officer, was known to have risen: an infantry captain, he raised a group of soldiers and civilians which fought in the Puerta de Toledo; and another four officers who led groups would almost certainly have been hidalgos (untitled nobility). In order to keep one foot in each camp, the aristocracy participated by proxy, sending their servants out to do battle – and the latter suffered the consequences: one in four of the service contingent killed in combat or executed was a noble's servant.

Ranging from adolescents to seventy-year-olds, the majority of the combatants killed or executed were twenty to forty-year-olds. The widespread nature of the rising can be judged by the fact that the combatants came from forty-five of the capital's sixty-four neighbourhoods.[41] But the rising's physical spread should not be confused with its demographic extent: as far as can be calculated, less than one percent of the Madrid population took part; and the proportion of combatant tradesmen and service personnel, for instance, barely exceeded 0.5% of their respective occupations.† Most remarkable in this respect was the relatively high proportion of liberal professionals: just under one percent of their occupational stratum, the highest of any civilian grouping.

* For further discussion of this, see Appendix 1, 'Villagers'.
† These proportions should not surprise us: the storming of the Bastille cost ninety-eighty civilian dead and seventy-three wounded out of a Parisian population of 547,000. Even the seven to eight thousand citzens who earlier on the same day staged the spectacular raid on the Hotel des Invalides in search of arms, represented no more than 1.5% of the population. George Rudé, *Revolutionary Europe, 1783–1815*, London, 1985, pp. 96–97.

Though with some significant permutations among them, the major group-ings of the Madrid rising – the labouring poor, petty services, women, military and professional classes – would be among the participants in the provincial risings later in the month. There, artisans were more important than petty services, and middle-level merchants as important as the professional classes; a new group, students, almost absent from the Madrid rising, entered on the scene in some places, while royal servants, excisemen, gentlemen and ladies were unrepresented.

In the records of many combatants it is said that they acted out of 'patriotic exaltation', an anachronistic expression at the time of their action. But the scriveners and the like who crafted their testimonies after the war knew the formulaic expressions made current during the conflict which would bring their clients the honours they sought. What really mobilized them on the day? King and Religion, for sure. But more than that, a hatred of the invader – a rage against these foreign troops advancing through their neighbourhoods to kill their fellow women and men who had risen to assert their right to live in their customary ways, unsubjected to any alien power. In this the women no doubt differed little from their menfolk; but they threw themselves, unarmed and unhesitatingly, into a combat of which they had no experience, and paid a heavy price for their incredible courage.

In rising against French domination, the Madrid struggle was thus for *freedom*, a concept which at that moment asserted Spaniards' right to be ruled by the monarch they had elevated to the throne with the hope of instituting reforms which would correct what the detested Godoy had refused them; and the right to continue to live in the way they chose. (It was not individual freedoms, it should be added, since such concepts were barely conceivable to the majority under the Old Regime.) Spain was an old and proud nation that had suffered no major foreign invasions since finally defeating the Muslims five centuries earlier in a reconquest that in itself had lasted seven hundred years.* Nowhere else in continental Europe had Napoleon attempted to overthrow his major enemies' monarchs: the houses of Austria, Prussia and Russia. But he was prepared to do so to an ally, Spain, which had been relatively faithful to its alliance, though at high cost for the privilege. To shake themselves free of this alliance, instituted by Godoy, and the Bonapartist intervention which had resulted from it, was to become the cherished aim of a great number of Spaniards. They did not need, indeed resented, Napoleon's efforts to reform their country under his brother Josef's rule. The cries of *Viva Fernando VII!* in the Madrid streets during the rising expressed a popular desire for their king's return, announcing the concept of the 'desired' Fernando, which became one of the rallying cries – and, from a later perspective, greatest mystifications – of the coming struggle.

* In the War of the Spanish Succession (1701–14) foreign armies crisscrossed the country, even briefly seizing Madrid, but without occupying a large extent of national territory; in the Spanish historical psyche (outside of Cataluña) this war bears little comparison to either the Muslim or Napoleonic invasions which are considered for-mative historical experiences.

TWO MISSIVES AND A CONSTITUTENT ASSEMBLY:
MÓSTOLES, ORENSE AND BAYONNE

People fleeing the capital and the French repression after the May 2 insurrection reached nearby townships and villages with the news on the same afternoon. One of these was Móstoles to the southwest of Madrid. A high official of the Council of War and secretary of the naval ministry, Juan Pérez Villamil, owned a house there and was in residence at the time. A convinced Fernandista absolutist, Villamil verified the first fugitives' reports from an acquaintance he recognized among those who were fleeing, and then informed the local justice. The latter ordered the church bells rung to summon councillors and local inhabitants to an urgent meeting. On being informed of the news from Madrid, many locals spoke in favour of gathering to march on Madrid; but persuaded of the futility of this course of action – what could they do alone at this stage of events? – the gathering agreed to issue a proclamation calling on Spaniards to 'arm themselves against the perfidious enemy' and be 'prepared to die for king and country' by coming to the aid of Madrid. 'No force can prevail against the brave and the loyal like the Spanish.'

The proclamation was in all probability largely written by Villamil; to the octogenerian justice of Móstoles, Andrés Torrejón, an honest farmer of no great learning, goes the credit of putting his name to a 'seditious' document only a short march away from the French encampments. In its insistence on French 'perfidy' (a term usually reserved for the English), its call to defend 'King and Country' (religion is curiously absent), and the notion that the Spanish characteristics of bravery and loyalty to their prisoner-monarch were sufficient to overcome all obstacles, the proclamation is premonitory of the many that would shortly flood the regions unoccupied by the French. But its major significance is that it was issued at all: unauthorized by – and therefore in defiance of – the competent authorities who held a monopoly on making pronouncements to the country, it was a privately originated declaration of war. It was not irrelevant that a high government official took this step: it showed that the constituted authorities, the governing junta and the Consejo de Castilla, were discredited, had lost their legitimacy – among many of his class certainly – because they had temporized too long and too uncritically with the French occupation forces. That Villamil believed local authorities, most of them government-appointed, would act on the orders of a small and unknown township justice is surprising; but he judged the state of the country well.

The practical effects of the proclamation were limited to towns and villages along the Madrid road to Andalucía via Extremadura. Having been entrusted to a single Andalucian courier who was fleeing Madrid by this road, this was hardly surprising. In Talavera de la Reina, Trujillo and Mérida general mobilizations were ordered. In Talavera, the first main town the courier reached, it was the acting corregidor who summoned the inhabitants to hear the news and gave orders for the regiments quartered there to prepare to move on Madrid, accompanied by all local inhabitants who wished to enlist to defend 'King and Country'. At the same time he dispatched the proclamation with his own orders to all the villages of his jurisdiction, calling for more volunteers and for the wealthy to pay their subsistence.[42]

On receiving the news in Trujillo not a moment was lost in deciding

> to die in defence of the grief-stricken Madrileños and to avenge the Outrages committed by our disguised enemies. A Junta of the three estates was immediately summoned by the Corregidor to enlist all men capable of bearing arms in the City and the eighty-two villages of its jurisdiction and with them all horses, money and provisions to march on Madrid under the command of senior and junior army officers whom the captain general of the Province was summoned posthaste to provide.[43]

Enlisted men from the whole jurisdiction had begun to reach the city on the morning of May 6 when a government order, 'distorting the horrible scenes of May 2 and imposing calm and harmony with the perfidious French', was received by the authorities, and the mobilization was called off.

In Mérida, nearly 400 kilometres from Madrid, the corregidor ordered the village justices to recruit men and, as 'loyal Spaniards', to expedite all necessary measures to 'aid the capital and its inhabitants in the briefest time possible. . . in order that they may triumph over this unprecedented iniquity so that its authors learn that we are true Spaniards'.[44]

More significantly, in Badajoz, General Francisco Solano, one of Spain's ablest military commanders, convinced the captain general to issue a joint proclamation against the French on May 5. This called on Spaniards to take up arms to avenge the bloodshed in Madrid and recover the monarch held prisoner in Bayonne.[45] But Solano's messages to military leaders in Sevilla and elsewhere, and to the War minister, O'Farril, in Madrid, calling for all out military resistance, received no answer. Believing himself without support, Solano obeyed Murat's orders to take up his duties as captain general of Andalucía and governor of Cádiz – where a month later he was assassinated for refusing unequivocally to support the rising.

After riding for twenty-four hours the courier fleeing Madrid fell ill with fatigue, but the practice of one local justice urgently forwarding messages to the next worked admirably. Within seventy-two hours the Móstoles proclamation – which had in each of the cities, towns and villages to be copied and the justice to add his notes on where he had received it and from and to whom he was dispatching it, as well as the measures he was taking – travelled 550 kilometres to reach Andalucía just inside the provincial limits of Huelva. Napoleon's courier travelled no faster: the Emperor in Bayonne, at approximately the same distance from Madrid, received the news of the Madrid rising at about the same time.*

This brief mobilization against the French, which was brought to an end by the governing junta's urgent orders issued by the Consejo de Castilla, took place

---

* For unknown reasons, the forwarding system broke down in Cumbres de San Bartolomé, the first Andalucian village the proclamation reached on the evening of May 5. However, the news of the Madrid rising was also received in Llerena, Extremadura, on the same day, and it was probably from there that the proclamation reached Sevilla on May 6. (AHN *Estado*, Legajo 2A/n.n., Oct. 6, 1808.)

in a region sensitive to the effects of the French occupation of neighbouring Portugal, and which had had to live with, and now live down, the shame wrought on the country by its native son, Godoy. To the extent of accepting the orders of an obscure local justice, the highest local authorities were obviously predisposed to act since in each case the mobilization was ordered – and equally countermanded – by them. Two took the responsibility on their own shoulders; a third, in Trujillo, instituted what would shortly become a major form of governance: a local junta, composed in this case of members of all three estates. These authorities were in all cases dutifully obeyed in the manner the Old Regime expected of its subjects.

> . . . when the Alcalde of Mostole [sic] demanded aid on May 2, the justice mobilized all the neighbourhood and the inhabitants would have marched to Madrid, had it not been that Superior orders determined the contrary . . .

wrote the justice of the small village of El Cerro some months later.[46]

In contradistinction, when the proclamation reached Jerez de los Caballeros, an Extremaduran township of some 7,000 inhabitants, where landless labourers and small tenant farmers had revolted against landlords' enclosures of municipal lands only eight years earlier, a local priest had little success in raising the townsfolk. An hidalgo 'inflamed by true love of the patria', the Rev. Sanabría Solís had, from the time when 'the French Emperor's perfidious intentions to usurp the Spanish crown became clear', begun to look for ways in which his small contribution' could be employed to free his country 'from the threat of slavery'. At that very moment the Móstoles proclamation reached his hands:

> What Spaniard could remain unmoved by those inhuman atrocities and perfidious-ness? Justly angered, I threw myself into the street, despite the early dawn hour, to seek out the military commandant and beg of him the loan of a horse in order to proclaim Fernando as king throughout the whole town and to rouse the inhabitants to fight against France. But my wishes could not be realized at that time. Some people of repute did not agree with my manner of acting.[47]

The moment of activist anti-French priests had not yet arrived. But Sanabría did not allow this to deter him. Some days later, on the news that Fernando had renounced his throne, he was again in the streets, wearing the red sash of San Sebastián and carrying the standard of the Purísima Concepción 'to demon-strate that under the Patron of Spain's protection I was prepared to shed my blood like the Holy Martyr in defence of my country and its just cause'.

> I proclaimed openly that the abdication was a fraudulent deception and that Fernando VII was incapable of handing over his nation to the odious France. A transhumant sheep-master was holding the abdication document in his hand. Eyes burning with rage, I seized it from him and tore it up. Nothing could now stop my zeal. Without concern for my life or the dangers that surrounded me, I rode through the streets proclaiming Fernando as our true king, arousing the people with vigorous

exhortations to take up arms. Not content with this, I scattered among the people all the money I carried to show them my extraordinary joy.[48]

Neither priestly largesse, a saint's standard nor vibrant harangues resulted in greater success on this second venture than on the first, for the priest did not succeed in rallying the people to his cause.* Here as elsewhere, the rural townships were not prepared to move until they had seen their region's capital rise. The absence in the priest's harangues of any appeal to the people's religious feelings was also striking. Possibly, he believed that the religious regalia he outfitted himself with was sufficient; or that religion was so consubstantial with monarchy that it seemed irrelevant to single it out.

When the Móstoles proclamation reached Sevilla on May 6, popular unrest broke out almost immediately. Two days later, the chief civil authority in the city, the asistente of Sevilla† and intendente of the four Andalucian kingdoms, Vicente Hore, raised the royal standard in a town hall meeting, ordered a voluntary enlistment, and sent orders to Córdoba, Jaén and Granada to contribute men and aid to the force being raised in Sevilla. His hand – he was a Godoy favourite – had in no little part been forced by the popular agitation; but his proposals were received 'with public acclamation since these were the measures the people desired'.[49]

Shortly, however, the orders from Madrid 'deforming the events of May 2' were received in Sevilla, as elsewhere, strictly forbidding any mobilization. Vincente Hore then began to calm the people,

> but not to dishearten them. I was zealous in ensuring the prevention of disorders resulting from the popular convulsions; but not in a manner to destroy the enthusiasm and love for King and Country which the people had demonstrated. On the contrary, I exhorted them publicly to preserve this for the opportune moment . . .[50]

The imminent national rising would have taken place without a proclamation signed by a mere local justice under the auspices of a high government official. What the Móstoles document showed – in a relatively narrow strip of the country which included, however, its fourth largest city, Sevilla – was the conviction among a part of the ruling elite that the loss of the king, in whom they had placed their hopes for reform, was equivalent to the loss of the fatherland's future well-being, a feeling shared by the larger urban populations. Napoleon's domination must be resisted at all cost, their king returned to them. In the countryside, however, villagers responded dutifully to their local authorities as was expected of them, and ignored fervent Fernandista agitation, even

---

* Jerez de los Caballeros, close to the Portuguese border and easy escape, was not subsequently known for its great dedication to the patriot war. A member of the Extremadura junta, commissioned in 1809 to raise the Badajoz villagers, reported to the Junta Suprema that 'observing the indolence in enlisting the young of Jerez and its neighbouring valleys, the enlisted men of other places also disperse'. (AHN, *Estado*, Legajo 67A/153, n.d. but probably June, 1809.)
† Asistente was the name given in Sevilla to the intendente.

from the mouth of their local priest, a powerful figure in the landscape of their lives.

BAYONNE: NAPOLEON'S CONSTITUTION FOR SPAIN

Having achieved his immediate aim of displacing the Spanish Bourbon monarchy, on May 10 Napoleon informed his brother, Josef, King of Naples, that he had made him King of Spain; two days earlier, the Emperor had ordered Murat to apprise the Consejo de Castilla to request Josef as the new sovereign, but he did not wait for an answer before appointing his brother.[51] Two weeks later Napoleon issued a proclamation to Spain in which he announced grandiloquently that the Spanish nation was 'perishing' and that he would remedy its ills. 'I want your last descendants to remember me and say: He is the regenerator of our *patria*', he concluded.[52] Napoleon in fact plannned to rebuild the Spanish navy as quickly as possible, to solve the country's financial crisis and to 'make the colonies safe from British influence, to prevent them from separating from the metropolis, and to open them up to French trade'.[53] He ordered ships prepared to sail to various parts of South America to give effect to his plan.

As part of the country's 'regeneration' process, the Emperor hastily drew up a draft constitution, and summoned an assembly of 150 Spanish notables of the three estates to approve it in Bayonne. Although the majority of these were nobles and prelates, some were to be elected by the town councils of major cities of the realm. The elections were about to be held or were in the process of taking place when the nationwide risings occurred. The widespread knowledge of the elections was a factor in precipitating the insurrections.

The Bishop of Orense, Galicia, was one of those summoned to attend the Bayonne meeting. Pedro Quevedo y Quintano was an Extremaduran by birth, and seventy-three years old. An absolutist, his letter to the Madrid governing junta refusing the summons became a well-known statement of an ideological posture which, while adopting predictable hostility to the Emperor's procedures, expressed views that were widely held by many patriot commoners at the time. Diplomatic and formal in style, he confronted head-on Napoleon's 'regenerationist' rhetoric of curing Spain's ills and 'substitutionist' policy of 'improving the nation's and monarchy's destiny':

> Has the Nation approved, has it given its firm authority for this? Is it prepared to submit to awaiting its cure by these means? . . . The renouncements [of the throne], on which all authority depends, have made the entire Nation suspicious . . . and require, for the Spanish Kingdom's satisfaction at least, that they be ratified . . . so that, exercising its independence and sovereign responsibility, the Nation may recognize as its legitimate King whomever nationality, rights and circumstances may call to the throne.[54]

The bishop was no doubt well aware that Fernando VII had proposed in Bayonne that Napoleon allow him to return to Spain to offer his abdication before the kingdom's Cortes; and that the latter would almost certainly reject the offer. In this sense, his letter was no more than a veiled attempt to secure Fernando's return to the throne – and if that proved impossible, a Bourbon successor at the least. But at the same time he enunciated the nation's *independent* and *sovereign* right to recognize as monarch the person it considered best suited for the position. A convinced absolutist was therefore among the first to express publicly to Napoleon the doctrine of the Spanish nation's right to choose its sovereign.

That said, it is necessary to enter two caveats. In the first place, when the bishop spoke of the 'nation' he did not distinguish between it and the 'kingdom of Spain'; in other words, he was not speaking of popular national sovereignty, but of a sovereignty restricted to those who had the right of representation in the kingdom's Cortes – historically certain towns which had been granted the privilege in the past. Secondly, implicit in his absolutist posture, was the argument that once the 'nation' had chosen its ruler, it had no right to reject him (or her). If the Spanish people rose to defend Fernando as the country's sovereign, no one might question his right to absolute monarchy. On the one hand then, the absolutists could not deny that the nation was independent and sovereign in its right to select its monarch, but on the other they denied that this choice was revocable or that the monarch could in any manner be restricted in the exercise of his divine rights. It was on these arguments that the great patriotic debate – and the bitter gulf between absolutists and progressives – opened up during the war: 'national sovereignty' versus 'popular sovereignty'.

The bishop had still another point to make:

> At the same time as it is offered its happiness, the nation believes itself enchained, enslaved. More than artifice, this is a work of violence: a numerous army which was admitted to Spain as a friendly ally, or as the result of indiscretion and timidity, or perhaps of vile treachery, serves as an authority which it is difficult to envisage as legitimate.

There could be no doubt that every patriot shared this view. Imperial military force had become the basis of an illegitimate authority. Napoleon's nomination of his brother to the throne might attempt to create a new, civilian legitimacy, but in the last resort the new monarchy was always dependent on the imperial army to sustain itself.

In conclusion, wrote the bishop, an assembly called outside Spain could not be free to decide on a new constitution. Tumults could be feared in the kingdom and if these led to foreign troops being offered or asked for to fight the French on Spanish soil, 'what desolation, what more lamentable scene can be imagined? The Emperor's compassion, love and solicitude [for Spain] may cause her the worst of disasters rather than cure her of her ills.'

The bishop's prescience was considerable. Not only did he foresee that Napoleon's policy would drag Spain into Britain's war with France, but that this would result in a war of Spaniard against Spaniard, anti-Napoleonic resister against Bonaparte supporter.

The bishop alleged that his age prevented him from attending the Bayonne assembly, a thin excuse, for it did not exclude his subsequent – and highly controversial – participation on the patriot side. Many other members of the elite also refused to attend, on the then common excuse of their 'ailments', or on receiving threatening anonymous letters[55] – or even turning back once on the road to Bayonne. The Galician hidalgo, Joaquín Terreiro Montenegro, who had witnessed the May 2 events in Madrid, was one of the latter. Apprised while still in Madrid at the beginning of June that he had been appointed to attend the assembly, he tried to evade the commission, but was threatened by the French if he did not attend. He set out on the road, having shortly before learned that his native region had risen against the French. On reaching Valladolid, which had also risen, he encountered people fleeing the city; General Cuesta had just led an army of civilian volunteers and patriot regulars to a crushing defeat by the French military at Cabezón. Retracing his route, Terreiro retreated to the township of Olmedo where he encountered six other deputies to the assembly, among them the conde de Altamira, a convinced Fernandista and one of the richest nobles in Spain. As Terreiro later wrote:

> With great art, the conde sounded out the deputies' opinions. The present writer was the only one to respond openly with the words: 'My decision is taken. Galicia has raised her head, my homeland's fate is mine.'*

Altamira and he were the only two to elude local surveillance, and Terreiro set off for Benavente, the township to which General Cuesta had retreated. In the latter's presence he tore up the deputy's papers to the Bayonne assembly and the French passport with which he had been issued; and in their place was given a Spanish passport with which he reported to the junta of La Coruña, and subsequently to that of Santiago, where he handed over the fifteen thousand reales he had withdrawn for the journey to Bayonne.

Of the 150 deputies from the three estates due to attend the Assembly only sixty-five, mainly from areas controlled by the French military, initially attended. Even this number was reached only by nominating a score of new deputies, a process that Murat, the governing junta in Madrid and Napoleon himself continued until by the assembly's end the total reached ninety-one.† The rest of the country was already in the throes of a general anti-Napoleonic insurrection.

Napoleon's draft constitution envisaged a number of profound reforms: religious reform, including the Inquisition's abolition; the creation of a unified

---

* Terreiro was not alone in turning back; the Granada deputy took the same course, while Antonio Valdés, a former Navy minister, fled his native Burgos for Placencia rather than attend. (AHN, *Estado*, Legajo 77C/166. Terreiro memorial to Junta Suprema, February 8, 1809; Toreno, 1838/1916, p. 83.)
† The clerical estate, due to send fifty deputies, the highest single contingent, and one third of the total, showed the largest single decline with only seventeen clergy attending. The nobility sent thirteen of its thirty members, although the grandees were exceptional in that nine of their ten allotted members attended. Commerce (which included ennobled commoners) sent only half of their fourteen due, while all but one of the third estate's eight members were present. Only the high councils of state finally exceeded their quota with seventeen deputies instead of their allotted twelve. (Artola, 1968, table, p. 74.)

national tax system; the ending of all noble and corporative privileges and the introduction of the Napoleonic code. All of these vanished in the face of stubborn Spanish resistance, usually in the form of legal-historical objections. ('Vous êtes des bêtes', Napoleon wrote on the Consejo de Castilla's representative's submission.[56]) Nonetheless, on July 7, Spain received its first written 'Constitution' – a debatable status within constitutional theory which maintains that a Constitution can only be drawn up by a sovereign assembly on national soil, and that Bayonne was rather a charter graciously granted by a foreign monarch.[57] Whatever its formal status, it was mild medicine for the country's regeneration. As finally approved, there was no religious reform – indeed, Catholicism was granted the status of the only religion to be permitted in Spain and her colonies – and even the Inquisition survived unscathed.* But at the same time it virtually sealed the fate of the Old Regime.

An amalgam of the Bonapartist constitutions created for France, the Bayonne statute represented the culmination of Spain's eighteenth-century reform movement. It put a king, whose powers were not specificially limited other than by his swearing to observe the Constitution, at the head of state and government. But, if not explicitly then implicitly, he was no longer a king by divine right: the new monarchy's 'fundamental law', as the statute's preamble stated, was a pact between the people and their king, the king and his people, in which the sovereign swore to preserve Spain's territorial integrity and independence, individual liberty and property. And men of property were given a measure of representation in a Cortes which, although without legislative power, allowed them to debate and approve ministerial bills, especially the triennial state budget, and to consider ministerial misdeeds. These arrangements were a considerable advance on the previous absolutism.

Most significantly, the statute made a number of important judicial, commercial and financial reforms. The judiciary became independent of the administration, thereby losing its former overlapping feudal role of government administration and justice;† *habeas corpus* was introduced, torture banned, arbitrary arrest and imprisonment made punishable by law. An individual's house was inviolable and could be entered only by day and with adequate legal authority. A single civil and criminal code would apply to all of Spain and its colonies; the previous privileged laws for nobility and clergy were abolished as were señorial-appointed justices. Similarly a single commercial code would apply. Freedom of trade, industry and commerce was guaranteed; all internal customs were abolished, as were commercial privileges, and the colonies were granted equal trade rights with the metropolis. All special tax privileges were abolished, and taxation would apply equally to all those liable to pay. Entail, which had caused so much anguish to the Spanish reformers, was effectively restricted.‡

---

* The Inquisitor, Raimundo Ettenhard, submitted that the Holy Tribunal was necessary to 'maintain the unity of the Catholic religion which the Constitution prescribes . . . [and] the respect due to the kings and constituted authorities.' But he admitted that the Inquisition's tribunals needed reform, a notion of reform which was evidently sufficient to save the Inquisition. (AGS, *Papeles del Gobierno Intruso, Gracia y Justicia*, Legajo 1184, n.n.)
† See Prologue, pp. xi–xiii on these dual roles.
‡ On entailments and señorial jurisdictions, see prologue, pp. xviii–xix.

While the existing nobility was preserved, a noble condition could no longer be demanded for civilian posts or for the army and navy. 'Service and talent will be the only criterion for promotion.' Freedom of the press would be introduced two years after the new Constitution came fully into effect which, to give time for enabling legislation (and probably as a Spanish delaying tactic) would be only after five years.[58]

The war saw to it that the Bayonne statute was never fully put into effect, and during the conflict it was only partially applied in some Bonapartist-controlled regions. In the patriots' eyes it was a constitution imposed by the Emperor and validated by an unrepresentative assembly on foreign soil. They did not need 'regenerating' by a foreign power, even by the most powerful of Emperors. They knew the reforms the country needed, and they, as Spaniards, were more than capable of instituting them.

And yet in more propitious circumstances, the statute would have constituted a good transitional programme for modernizing Spain. Gradualist, moderate, careful not to offend religious or regional sensibilities,* leaving in place a powerful sovereign, offering improved conditions for industry and commerce, making a cautious start to freeing land for the market, reforming an antiquated judicial system, attacking noble privileges but leaving the nobility in control of their most valuable asset, their land – such a constitution, if originated in and adopted by a Spanish constitutional assembly, would have won acceptance from the majority of the enlightened elite. It would no doubt have been attacked by absolutists as undermining the divine right of kings, or for failing to give the nobility a special role in the affairs of state, and by the more extreme progressives as being an authoritarian rather than a fully constitutional monarchy; but both would have found it difficult to mobilize large sectors of society in their support. One of the most lucid and enlightened contemporary Spanish observers of the moment, the Rev. José María Blanco (better known later as Blanco White), who admitted that from an early age he had 'ceased to admire Spain as a political entity, miserably oppressed by government and Church, as it was', put it many years later like this:

> I was convinced that if the people remained tranquil under the form of government to which they were accustomed while the country rid itself of a dynasty from which it was no longer possible to expect any improvements, the political humiliation of accepting a new king from Napoleon's hands would be amply compensated for by future rewards . . . Many of the most enlightened and honest Spaniards had placed themselves on José Bonaparte's side. [The] new Constitutional framework, despite the arbitrary manner of its imposition, contained an explicit declaration of the nation's right to be governed by its own consent, and not by the king's absolute will . . .[59]

---

* The Basque representative, for example, supported by his Catalan and Navarrese colleagues, defended Basque self-governing rights (*fueros*) and persuaded the assembly to postpone final decision until the newly created Cortes met for the first time. As this never happened the matter was never constitutionally resolved; the solution came by Napoleon's intervention during the war which effectively abolished Basque rights. (Rubio Pobes, 1996, pp. 129–134 gives a good account of the Basque case).

This retrospective view overlooked some timely contemporary issues, however. What national state, however decrepit, could willingly submit to foreign invasion and domination? And let alone by an enemy but by an ally? To the imposition of a new king from abroad? To the infliction of foreign 'regeneration' and 'felicity'? To manipulation by subterfuge and chicanery?

> To pretend friendship the better to plunge a dagger in the breast; to remove her troops, the better to sacrifice and reduce Spain to the last extremity and, as she lay dying, to suffocate her between his [Napoleon's] nails; to take over without effort her forts, war materiel and munitions prepared for her defence and to use them to sow death and desolation; to come with promises and the intention of carrying out none; to take our sovereign from us with violence, treachery and felony. Who before has ever done this? No one except the French.[60]

The labouring classes, the majority of the country's working population, could expect nothing from the Napoleonic Constitution. Indeed, they did not wait to discover their 'constitutional' fate. Under the leadership of Fernando's supporters, the urban poor rose in passionate anti-Napoleonic fury a month or more before the statute was formally approved. Existing authorities who favoured, or fell under suspicion of favouring, the Bonaparte regime were replaced and sometimes killed. New governing bodies came to power. In Sevilla this body put it simply: 'It is an act of rebellion for an independent Nation to obey a foreign Prince.'[61] Or, as another anonymous writer stated in an essay entitled *Spain's Happiness*:

> Spaniards are recovering their strength: they have almost miraculously revived, and are determined to finish off all their enemies . . . The nation has resuscitated itself, and will without doubt achieve its complete regeneration and happiness. Unexpectedly Napoleon is going to realize what he promised; but he shall not carry it out.[62]

4

Declaration of War: The National Rising

What blessings Napoleon would have reaped if Fernando had remained to rule, even though the French had governed! The country would have accepted any new government, forgetting Godoy, and celebrated the old King's exile. (Cádiz French Consul's informant)[1]

More than three weeks passed between the Madrid insurrection and the first provincial risings.* During this time, a majority of local notables hesitated doubtfully on the course (if any) to take, while many existing authorities, who knew of the abdications well before they were officially announced, considered a rising a folly to be prevented at all costs and worked actively to that end. Intendente Xavier Aspiroz of Valencia, for example, told a meeting of elected huerta leaders to remain calm. What did it matter whether Josef, Peter or Francis were king? What was important was that the taxes on commoners be removed so that the farmers might live easier.[2] The Bourbons were 'ridiculous dimwits who had ruined themselves with their family rivalries and we should not ruin ourselves because of them', he told another meeting, urging those in attendance to convince 'the people to accept as king whomever the Emperor Napoleon decided should rule over Spain'.[3]†

The fact that officials like Aspiroz almost invariably owed their positions to Godoy only brought them into further disrepute with the Fernandistas‡ who, equating Godoy with Napoleonic treachery and despotic French domination,

---

* A rising, in this context, is to be understood as an insurrectionary movement leading to the formation of a regional government junta.

† Aspiroz was finally relieved of his post in March 1809, and investigated in Sevilla on his 'patriotic conduct' by a Junta Suprema appointed judge. The latter refused to take into account Aspiroz's actions prior to the rising since 'all the authorities vacillated, and not without serious reason, and as a result his [Aspiroz's] opinions in those anguished moments have not been examined in this case'. To the Junta Suprema's fury, the judge found him not guilty of all other charges whereupon the Junta ordered three judges to interrogate him. They recommended that he be suspended from his position as intendente until their hearings were completed. (AHN, *Estado*, Legajo 45¹/142, 144, 174, 180, 185, March 1809–Jan 1810)

‡ I use the term generically to describe all those who supported Fernando's cause in the period prior to the insurrections. They were therefore both anti-Godoyista and anti-Napoleonic.

envisaged the need to supplant them in an eventual rising. In this sense, the risings were dual-headed: on the one hand a continuation of the confrontations between the Fernandistas and Godoy which had culminated, but not ideologically ended, in the Aranjuez tumult in March, only two months earlier; on the other, against the Napoleonic occupation of the country. The Fernandistas also required time to ensure that they could precipitate and control the desired insurrection to prevent it from turning into a dangerously uncontrollable popular outburst. Finally, the main condition for which the lower orders would rise had not yet been met: the definitive and absolute certainty that they had lost their new king. They retained to the last their illusions of Fernando's return to the crown.

The conspirators left few accounts of their activities during these three weeks in the eight cities and towns which were the foci of the risings. It suited all persuasions of Fernandistas after the risings to maintain that the 'people' had spontaneously risen against the hated Godoyistas and Napoleon in order to validate the power they seized 'in the people's name' during the insurrections. In rising, they proclaimed, the 'people' had reasserted their right to the sovereignty with which the enforced absence of their monarch in France endowed them and had graciously bestowed this sovereignty on the local juntas of notables which sprang up everywhere. These myths, most especially of the risings' spontaneity which the Fernandistas ardently fostered, have remained alive for the last two hundred years in the Spanish imagination of these historical events.

With the exception of Cataluña, the main risings were an exclusively urban-originated affair, the majority on the mainland's periphery. The eight cities in which the principal risings took place – in the sense that these were the major foci from which the insurrections spread outwards: Oviedo, Valencia, Zaragoza, Sevilla, La Coruña, Badajoz, Valladolid and Cartagena – varied in size from about twelve to twenty-three thousand inhabitants (Badajoz, Oviedo, Cartagena, Valladolid) to forty thousand (Zaragoza) and eighty thousand (Sevilla, Valencia). The risings were not thus dependent on the size of the towns – indeed, cities like Granada, Málaga and Cádiz, with populations of fifty thousand or more, and regional or provincial capitals like Murcia (fourteen thousand) and Santiago de Compostela (twenty thousand), did not rise until other towns in their provinces or region had led the way, although only a day or two separated them. The significant factor was that, almost without exception, the major risings took place in the most important regional towns that were the seats of captain generals and audiencias.*

None of the insurrectionary towns was occupied by French forces which, with the exception of Valladolid, were several days' march distant. (French columns were – or were feared to be – marching on Sevilla and Zaragoza, however.) None, therefore, had immediately to confront the Napoleonic occupation forces, as had the people of Madrid on May 2. Had they had to do so, the results might have been similar to those in the Spanish capital.

* The captain general was not only the supreme military but also the politico-administrative authority of the region. The audiencia was a high court, but its judges exercised as well a great number of administrative functions. (See Prologue p. xii.)

In Cataluña, on the other hand, the risings were widely disseminated in townships throughout the region. Under French military occupation, the capital, Barcelona, did not rise, leaving pride of place to Lérida. But it cannot be said that the latter's insurrection conditioned to anything like the same degree the subsequent risings in the region, as was the case with the major cities in the rest of Spain.*

The insurrections in some towns but not others can only be explained by the determined planning of local Fernandistas to raise their inhabitants and the degree of prior popular agitation. These factors were not independent one of the other; and the attitude of the army, active in support or studiously passive, was vital to both. Moreover, gratifications, or subornations, were not uncommon, in the Old Order's manner of organizing commotions.

Popular agitation may to some extent be attributed to a generalized malaise due to the bad economic conditions, especially for artisans, or specific conditions like that of Cartagena, where the Spanish Mediterranean fleet's major arsenal had been at a virtual standstill since the Trafalgar defeat.† But the crowd's motivations were multi-layered and complex. One general aspect of these must be taken into account. In a traditional society, where everything was apparently regulated from above by laws, decrees and custom, nothing was a greater destabilizing factor than *political* uncertainty. To be 'unsure of the future', 'not to know what to expect', represented a rupture with the Old Order's 'monolithic mental and operative system'.[4]

At a more prosaic level, the popular classes were deeply affected by a persistent rumour that swept the country from the moment of the French army's invasion: it had brought in its baggage train thousands of manacles to seize the young and force them into Napoleon's army in the north of Europe. While the rumour was unfounded, the dread of conscription into the Emperor's army was one of the most powerful fears that mobilized the lower orders. Aware of the rumour's potency, and before setting a foot in Spain, the new French king issued a proclamation denying that Spaniards would be conscripted into the Napoleonic army; but it made no difference.

A fundamental distinction between the different risings lay in the balance of military to civilians. In almost all the insurrectionary cities, a few junior military officers were among the conspirators; but in garrison towns like Cartagena, La Coruña and Badajoz, the military (or naval) forces assumed a particular importance, as their relative weight on the post-rising juntas showed. In the others, civilians, though usually able to count on the support of at least part of the local military, were pre-eminent. No military forces rallied to repress the main risings.

Of the major risings, three – Oviedo, Valencia and Zaragoza, none of them with important garrisons – were civilian led and organized; four, where the presence of garrisons was marked – Sevilla, La Coruña, Badajoz and Valladolid

---

* An account of the special Catalan situation will be found in the next chapter.
† In El Ferrol, the Atlantic fleet's arsenal, where the artisans were suffering equally, the fleet commander's opposition to the rising detained its course for a few days, indicating the importance of the armed force's active or passive support for the insurrection.

– were civilian–military affairs; and one – Cartagena, the great Mediterranean naval base – was a garrison-organized insurrection.

THE CIVILIAN RISINGS: OVIEDO, VALENCIA, ZARAGOZA

Prior planning, hostility to the authorities who temporized with the French, the Fernandista need to prevent the risings from getting out of hand, popular agitators, and the people's seizure of arms, were in differing degrees essential to almost all the civilian-led risings. Oviedo, the capital of Asturias, was a prime example of planning. A group of Fernandista commoner elite who 'formed a real revolutionary committee' organized the coup on the night of Tuesday, May 24, and the formation of a supreme junta early the following day,[5] after nearly two weeks of popular commotion. Among this group of Fernandistas were the senior Oviedo judge, two government officials, the Oviedo arms factory purveyor, the local postal service head, an artillery commissioner, a military officer, two cathedral canons and a number of private individuals; only one titled noble joined the group.* The decision to stage the coup on the night of May 24–25 was quite deliberate; the group's determination to control events equally evident in that the conspirators had earlier joined with the old authorities to pacify the crowd for fear of a popular rising. In Valencia, which rose a day earlier but only formed its junta two days later, the same preoccupation was patent. Two agitators, armed with plentiful money, raised the crowd and ensured that it remained orderly.

In all of these risings, the existing authorities – as a rule represented by captains general and audiencia magistrates – tried to quell the revolt and were the insurrectionists' first enemy. In Oviedo, for example, where a fortnight separated the start of popular commotions, which even the Fernandistas wanted controlled, and the actual 'controlled' insurrection, the news on May 9 of the Madrid May 2 rising and subsequent repression, saw an indignant crowd shouting 'To arms! Death to the French! Revenge for our people vilely assassinated!', and setting off for the audiencia to demand the orders the authorities had received from Madrid. The magistrates stalled, and the people, who included a large number of vociferous women, threatened to break down the doors. Amidst utter confusion, the principality's procurator general, a known Fernandista, demanded the orders in the name of the people who were to be praised for their understanding that 'the monarchy and the nation's freedom and independence are endangered'. Still the magistrates havered. Seeing the orders in one of the chief secretary's coat pockets, the procurator took them and showed them to the crowd, saying that he would read them aloud in the Campo de San Francisco; and there having done so,† he tore them up. He

* He was José María Queipo de Llano, vizconde de Matarrosa and the future conde de Torreno, author of one of the classic histories of the war. (Carantoña Álvarez, pp. 76–77, and Álvarez Valdés, 1889/1989, p. 39.)
† They consisted essentially of an order from the Madrid governing junta to the audiencia to take all measures to ensure that no repetition of the May 2 rising took place in their territory, and Murat's Order of the Day to his troops on May 2, announcing the severe repressive measures he had ordered. (Álvarez Valdés, 1889/1988, Appendix 4, pp. 259–262.)

then told the people to remain orderly, respect the constituted authorities and not to insult, directly or indirectly, anyone. He formed the armed into street patrols and ordered their leaders to inform him immediately of any incidents.[6]

The commotion was as 'spontaneous' as they come – and therein lay its danger for Fernandistas and local authorities, who equally feared popular mobilization and the 'inevitable descent into anarchy' that this entailed in their eyes. This was shown a few hours after the disturbances when a special session of the Junta General of Asturias,* which had begun its triennial sessions in Oviedo on May 1, unanimously recognized that the people's 'noble enthusiasm' to preserve the monarchy and ensure the country's defence was not ill-judged,

> as long as the people maintained and acted without resort to commotions but at the orders of the legitimate authorities and the people's natural representatives . . .[7]

But the Oviedo audiencia did not admit defeat. It ordered that further Junta meetings be postponed until July, that the university be closed, and all arms seized during the commotion by the armourers from the arms factory be handed in. Incensed by these measures, the crowd was pacified only by respected Fernandistas' assurances that another opportunity to achieve their aims would soon arise.

*

In Zaragoza and Valencia, the other two civilian-led risings, where prior commotions had been less marked, more threatening procedures had eventually to be taken against the old authorities during the insurrection itself. Moreover, in neither of these two cities was the rising as meticulously planned as in Oviedo. In both, it was not until the arrival of the *Gazeta de Madrid* officially announcing the Bourbon abdications, that the people rose.

Amongst the crowd that Monday morning, May 23, in the Plaza de la Compañía, where Valencians normally gathered to read the latest Madrid news – the newspapers could be bought or hired and read aloud for the benefit of the illiterate – was a smallholder and his companion from the *huerta*, the rich, irrigated land around the city. As the full import of the news was silently taken in, a sudden, solitary cry was heard: *Viva Fernando VII!*

The smallholder, Francisco Lluesma, and his companion, Vicente Rausell (whose profession is unknown but who as likely as not was also a smallholder) had come well prepared for such a moment; money in their pockets and a

* The Junta General represented the principality's historic form of self-government which, despite centralism, still retained certain rights. The Junta elected a standing commission and a procurator general for three years to run affairs between the general Junta meetings. But, as everywhere, the audiencia had far greater powers than the Junta. (Carantoña Álvarez, 1984, pp. 44–45.)

Fernandista standard ready to be unfurled. Inspired by their 'patriotic zeal' and 'without thought for the dangers and risks involved' they had thereupon immediately

> inflamed the good vassals' spirits to ensure that they proclaimed Fernando VII as their legitimate king . . . Both distributed largesse from their own pockets to the needy and poor who had gathered in order to prevent pillage and disorders, a purpose they indeed achieved at that critical moment.[8]

Three merchant brothers and purveyors to the town hall, of a certain standing and wealth in Valencia, were known to be the major conspirators behind the rising. Vicente, Manuel and Mariano Bertrán de Lis had, from shortly after the Aranjuez insurrection, raised their own private 'army' of five hundred paid men, mostly huerta smallholders, to support Fernando VII's cause and to begin a popular anti-Napoleonic rising in late April. That rising had not taken place, but their private militia was still in existence. Moreover, they had a couple of city councillors, a lawyer, a doctor and an army captain from the small garrison of six hundred-odd soldiers, in their group of progressive Fernandistas.

There could be little doubt that the smallholder and his friend, who went unnoticed for nearly two centuries by local historians and chroniclers, were trusted members of the Bertrán private army who had been posted among the crowd that morning to ensure both a popular rising and to control it. The crowd, thus inspired (or paid) to stage an 'orderly rising', tore up the *Gazeta de Madrid* and the official paper in the duque de Berg's (Murat's) name, and set off for the captain general's palace on the far side of the Turia river. There, this dignitary, the conde de la Conquista, appeared on a balcony and told them to trust to the constituted authorities to take the necessary action, and called on them to disperse quietly to their homes. The crowd turned back without protest; but it did not obey orders to return home. Very shortly, it discovered carts laden with tax-revenue money about to leave for Madrid, seized them and dragged them to a trusted noble's mansion. Amidst the crowd's clamours and shouts that more money had been sent the previous day and on the need to secure its return, a Franciscan friar, Juan Rico, who happened to be visiting the noble, the conde de Cervelló, asked to be heard:

> Señores: The people is a monster unless it permits itself to be governed by one person whom all the remainder obey. Without that everything will be disorder and confusion . . . Remember, with clamours and shouts we shall not defeat the French, but only with arms and armies and a good government to lead us. And all of these we are presently lacking . . . If we know how to lead ourselves, we shall triumph.[9]

The demand for a leader was immediately accepted by the crowd which, evidently convinced of its own 'monstrosity', elevated Rico to the leadership.

At the head of the crowd, the new people's tribune set off for the audiencia where the local authorities were meeting. He and another Franciscan entered the council chamber. After informing the authorities that the Valencian people accepted no other king than their 'beloved Fernando VII', Rico launched into a long tirade on Godoy which ended finally with the people's demands: declaration of war on Napoleon, a general enlistment and arming of the people, and their favoured noble's appointment to train and lead the recruits. When his harangue was countered by the captain general, Rico retaliated: 'There are forty thousand people outside waiting for your reply. It is my duty to inform them of your way of thinking and your replies to my glorious demands.' Whereupon, according to the friar, the gathered dignitaries panicked, fearful of being slaughtered by the crowd, and granted the demands, including that of issuing the enlistment edict in the name of Fernando VII.[10]

*

The Zaragoza rising on the morning of Tuesday, May 24 – precipitated, as in Valencia, by the arrival of the *Gazeta de Madrid* following on earlier information that a column of French troops was marching on the city[11] – was exceptional in originating amongst an urban-based group of medium-sized vineyard owners and agrarian foremen.[12] As elsewhere, the news of Madrid's May 2 rising and the French repression had resulted in popular anger. The vineyard owners, who worked their own land, and the agricultural foremen, included two men, Mariano Cerezo and Jorge Ibor,* who were said to have 'a great ascendancy' over their fellow parishioners, and collaborated closely together. They began in one of the traditional ways of articulating public discontent: the lampoon or satire posted overnight in prominent places. But having taken their agitation so far, they felt inadequate to the task of leading a rising, and went in search of a reputable and respected local leader.† In each case they were turned down on the pretext that 'the authorities' intervention was indispensable', and things must be done 'in an orderly manner'.[13] As they subsequently wrote, their

> spirits flagged at discovering that no leader, amongst the many who existed, could be found to take on this arduous task . . . Those who should have been prepared to shoulder this great work were seduced by their base interests, promising themselves greater prizes at the cost of enslaving their fatherland . . .[14]

* Cerezo owned about seven and a half hectares; the bulk of it vineyards. Ibor, better known as 'Tío Jorge' or 'Cuello Corto', does not figure as a landholder in the Zaragoza property register of 1807. (Antonio Peiró Arroyo, *Las Cortes Aragonesas de 1808*, Zaragoza, 1985, p. 107, fn. 90.) Possibly he was an agricultural foreman which would explain why the city's chronicler, Alcaide Ibieca, referred to the group as composed of vineyard owners and foremen.
† Two of the men approached, and who turned down the conspirators, later became ministers of the patriots' Junta Suprema: Antonio Cornel, minister of war, and Benito Hermida, minister of grace and justice.

When the revolt broke out without an apparent leader, a surgeon's assistant was the first to afix the red Bourbon cockade to his hat and was rapidly imitated by others. As the city's chronicler put it, 'the people who had been observing the movement saw that this was a moment favourable to a rupture'.[15] The crowd, presumably incited by these observers, made for the palace of Captain General Guillelmi, as it had in Valencia. But here, unlike Valencia, there were obviously some – the surgeon's assistant, Carlos González, among them – willing to take the lead, and immediately demand arms. The captain general tried to pacify them, to no effect. Fearing for his life, two brothers, both commanders of paramilitary forces, proposed that the crowd follow them to the Aljaferia castle, outside the city walls, where a good number of arms and artillery pieces were stored. Surrounded by a multitude, shouting 'Arms! Arms!', the brothers and Guillelmi reached the castle, and members of the crowd followed them in. Again the captain general tried to calm them, saying it was useless to hand over arms to people who did not know how to handle them, and he would assent only to arming military men,[16] whereupon the two brothers accepted responsibility for the arms.[17] Shortly afterwards, Guillelmi resigned his post in favour of his second-in-command.

The people found twenty-five thousand muskets and eighty pieces of cannon in the castle. After arming themselves, they loaded muskets onto carts and dispatched them to the elected heads of each neighbourhood for distribution.

In the afternoon, armed civilians issued an edict to the town crier which called on all Spaniards to arm themselves at the castle or face the threat of death.[18] By evening, five thousand muskets had been distributed; the night passed without serious incident.

*

Meanwhile in Oviedo, shortly before midnight of Tuesday, May 24, the rising began. Undaunted by the earlier news that Murat, now president of the Madrid governing junta, had ordered Spanish troops to march forthwith on Oviedo and had appointed two new and 'reliable' Spaniards to the head of the principality's military and civil government, or that the Asturian envoys dispatched by the Junta General to León and Santander, an action taken after the May 9 commotion, to inform these neighbouring provincial capitals of the Oviedo events, had reported negatively on their reception, the Fernandistas had continued their plotting. Although reinforced by the newly elected procurator general, Antonio Florez Estrada, a leading political economist who had twice been exiled under the Old Regime for his advanced ideas on a constitutional monarchy, the Asturian insurrectionists seemed to be standing alone. On May 20 they sent three members into the countryside to rally support amongst the villagers. The rural world was easier to control than the urban. Each villager prepared to take part in the rising was offered four reales a day. Serious commotions nonetheless broke out in Oviedo on the nights of May 22 and 23 which the Fernandistas managed to prevent from exploding into insurrections.[19]

The date of the Asturian rising was conditioned by two factors. On May 21 orders from Murat were received to execute fifty-eight named individuals who had attended the May 9 Junta General meeting which had unanimously approved the 'people's noble enthusiasm'. (The order was addressed to the newly appointed military commandant, La Llave, who had not yet arrived. The existing commandant did not dare open the sealed document, whereupon Florez Estrada took it from his desk and broke the seal. Both men were shocked to read the order.[20]) Two days later another order arrived, which summoned the local authorities to elect deputies to the Bayonne constitutional assembly. It was to pre-empt this and the newly arrived military commandant carrying out Murat's execution orders that the insurrection was planned for the following midnight.

By this time the conspirators had assembled four thousand villagers on the city's outskirts. The arms factory was seized with the artillery commissioner's complicity and the help of some artillery officers and workers; and the villagers were armed. A column of these made for the new military commandant's quarters: its Fernandista leader, disguised as a villager, handed the commandant a letter from Oviedo's senior judge which, 'in the people's name', called on him to summon within the hour a junta of the individuals listed in the letter. The lower orders found no place among them. Seeing the square outside full of armed men discretion overcame valour, and the commandant agreed. Thus the junta of Asturias came into being. At about the same time two men, their faces covered by cloaks, knocked on the cathedral sacristan's door and demanded the keys. At midnight exactly, to the flare of fireworks, the cathedral bells began to ring, accompanied by those of all the city's churches, summoning the inhabitants to join the rising. They gathered in the main square and 'broke out in shouts of *Viva el Rey!* and in favour of national independence', wrote an eyewitness, Ramón Álvarez Valdés, many years later.*

The Oviedo rising's repercussions were considerable. Two of the new junta's representatives were hastily sent aboard a privateer to England, Spain's traditional enemy, to call for aid in the Asturians' apparently solitary struggle against Napoleon. Thus it was that Britain's direct military intervention in the Peninsula began.†

*

In Zaragoza, the people's insurrection finally found the leader it had been looking for. Royal guards officer José de Palafox, aged thirty-three, member of a prestigious local noble family, was a well-known Fernandista who had been involved in both the Escorial and Aranjuez affairs; after the latter he had been charged by Fernando VII with Godoy's custody. Once the royal favourite had been released to the French, Palafox had been ordered by his military superior to the French frontier at Irún, with three other young guards officers, to attempt to communicate with Fernando VII, and possibly organize the king's escape. Napoleon's police discovered them, and they fled in disguise at night, hotly

* Álvarez Valdés, 1889/1998, p. 65. The expression 'national independence' was certainly an anachronism, since the term became current only later.
† See Chapter 5, pp. 131–2.

pursued by French gendarmes. Still disguised, Palafox reached a relative's home a couple of hours' ride from the city where he remained in hiding.

Learning of Palafox's presence, the insurrectionists set out to find him. Did they know that the brigadier they were about to charge with the supreme command of Aragón's defence had never, in his seventeen years in the army, been involved in a hostile military skirmish, let alone a battle?[21] Probably not. But it was not this that mattered. They knew that he was an impassioned Fernandista – so impassioned, indeed, that he was (and for long remained) totally blind to Fernando VII's defects – and the son of a leading local noble. Loyalty to the cause, fear of turncoats and betrayal, rather than military expertise, was uppermost in the their minds. Evidently unaware of the previous day's rising, Palafox was fearful, on seeing a band of armed men approaching, of being arrested. Instead, the vine-growers offered this 'magnanimous hero' the leadership of Aragón's defence, and

> led him in triumph to his palace [where] the people received him with the greatest of joy, and repeated acclamations. They appointed him their Governor, their Leader, their Father and Protector.[22]

Palafox wanted no revolutionary rupture, no uncontrolled plebeian outburst. In no other city had the lower ranks *on their own* come to seize such power, even if this was not their original intent. He was well aware, as he later wrote, that

> the insurrection had not sprung from a single talent who could lead it, arouse, temper or stop it at will: it was a volcano which could have devoured and destroyed by its strength the finer elements of its honorable objectives.[23]

Like the conspirators before him, Palafox wanted his actions legitimated by a higher authority, and asked that the *Real Acuerdo** meet the following morning. Appearing before the assembled dignitaries, Palafox energetically defended the people's 'spontaneous determination to seek revenge for the outrages committed in Bayonne against their king', but refused their offer of leadership which only the highest royal authority could confer on him.†

The magistrates began to debate the situation. The large crowd gathered in the Plaza de la Seo outside the building grew impatient. Soon there were sharp knocks on the chamber door. The porter informed the assembly that the people wanted to enter, and the magistrates panicked, 'convinced that they were about to perish'; by his own account Palafox had to calm them with the words that they had 'nothing to fear from a people loyal to their king and meek when they

---

* The meeting of the audiencia members presided over by the captain general which formed the highest authority of all cities in which these two existed.

† To be sure, both the Valencian and Asturian insurrections had also appointed their own military chiefs, but in Valencia they had not displaced the existing captain general, and in the latter they had forced the decision on the Junta General, not on the audiencia magistrates. Both of those chosen were reluctant candidates, fearing the personal consequences that might ensue.

know they are being led on the path of reason'. And it was he who suggested that two or three of its representatives be permitted to address the meeting. Momentarily recovering their composure, the magistrates returned to their seats and did as he bade.

Within moments three 'determined and respectably attired young men' entered the chamber. They were University of Zaragoza doctoral graduates, and thus most likely university teachers.[24] After seeking the president's permission to speak, they said, as Palafox later recalled, that the people of Zaragoza had sworn to be faithful to Fernando VII:

> We shall fulfil our oath . . . The people are armed . . . They only have confidence in those they have chosen. Do not waste more time, señores. Either Sr. Palafox will be our leader and captain general or all these heads (the three pointing with their hands at the magistrates) will roll in a moment.

Once again, the threat of armed force won the day. Terrified, the magistrates prostrated themselves at Palafox's feet and implored him as their 'liberator' to take command, to save king and country at this hour of danger. Stressing that he was not usurping power, Palafox accepted in the name of Fernando VII and the Aragonese people. Then turning to the people's representatives, he added:

> Let this be the last popular commotion . . . I shall march hand-in-hand with the law on the path of duty, religion and honour. Whoever does not follow this path will find an enemy in me . . . But I need public tranquility until I have determined the course the kingdom of Aragón must take . . .[25]

The following day, Palafox decided that course. Aragón was to be governed under military law, private property was to be respected, and armed *centurias* formed to maintain order. With these measures he 'cut off at its roots, or at least suspended, the troublesome effects and complications of differing opinions', he subsequently wrote. In short, Palafox had doused the 'volcano' and taken personal power, thanks to the insurrectionist people who had voluntarily surrendered it to him.

*

The matter of arming the people was vital to the Fernandistas' enterprise. On the first night of the Valencia rising, while the captain general sent a clandestine letter to Murat in Madrid asking for troops to restore order,[26] the Bertrán de Lis faction determined to storm the following morning the Ciudadela, a Bourbon fortress designed not for the city's defence but for its inhabitants' submission and which contained arms, and to set up a junta to govern Valencia during the enforced absence of Fernando VII.[27] Friar Rico suggested that an attempt be made to take the fortress peaceably, and supported by Bertrán's private army and scores of smallholders, he finally succeeded in getting the captain general to allow a small number of people into the Ciudadela to determine the arms it contained. Behind the designated persons the crowd poured through the fortress gates; the armoury door was smashed open, with the complicity of a captain on guard duty, and the people seized arms.

The Bertrán faction was now in near total control of the city. Writing several years later Friar Rico described the rising as initiated by

> a short number of the most impoverished and wretched plebeians . . . [who] dared to oppose [Napoleon's] colossal power and declared him to be the most execrable monster of the human species . . . There was not a decent person to be seen amongst them . . . What more ignominious and humiliating affront to the European tyrant's pride than this beginning to his destruction in Spain.[28]

The smallholder and his companion, who had ensured the initial rising's orderliness and had entered the Ciudadela with the permitted few, put their own gloss on the matter, writing that they 'confessed without shame' that

> their [social] sphere and birth is far distant from those classes which believe themselves honourable. In those dangerous circumstances, however, they manifested an honour of greater merit for having so few examples to imitate in their own families.[29]

These two smallholders thus revindicated the honour which plebeians were denied by the nobility, and at the same time cast doubt on the nobility's inherent right to honour – not without reason, for no titled noble, other than the reluctant conde de Cervelló, whom the insurrectionists named their military leader, had taken any part in the rising.

The Valencia rising was significant not only for taking place in a large city but because its impact spread into southern Cataluña, the Balearics and southwards to Alicante, thus creating a lynchpin for the insurrectionary powers which would shortly control the Spanish Mediterranean coast from north of Tarragona to south of Cartagena, as well as the strategic Balearic islands. Only a few days later the Sevillan rising extended this southern thrust to the limits of Gibraltar and by the end of May to the great trading port of Cádiz and along the Atlantic coast to the confines of Portugal; while the Oviedo rising would spread outwards along the Cantabrian coast from Santander to Galicia and into Castilla la Vieja; and the Zaragoza insurrection – one of the two (Valladolid was the other) which did not take place on the country's periphery – exercised a decisive influence on the rising in the adjoining Catalan province of Lérida.

THE CIVIL–MILITARY RISINGS:
SEVILLA, LA CORUÑA, BADAJOZ, VALLADOLID

Apart from the fact that the civilian conspirators succeeded in mobilizing considerable numbers of the local garrison, these insurrections differed little from the civilian-led risings. However, the Sevilla revolt on the evening of May 26, which continued throughout the night, was a seismic event, for its shock waves produced secondary quakes throughout Andalucía and were felt as far away as Extremadura. In the following days, insurrections broke out in Cádiz, Córdoba, Granada,

Jaén, Málaga and the Extremaduran frontier city fortress of Badajoz, controlling access to and from the southern reaches of Portugal. No other insurrection to date had affected such a wide territory – effectively the whole of southwestern Spain – or such a large population. Of even greater importance, the only Spanish army still left intact – nearly seven thousand men under General Castaños stationed in front of Gibraltar – placed itself at the Sevilla junta's orders.* This gave the latter a military strength which, with the exception of La Coruña, no other junta enjoyed. Moreover, the Sevilla insurrection could count on an immediate and important strategic success: the remains of the French fleet, immobilized in Cádiz since Trafalgar, was bombarded into submission on June 14.†

As in the civilian-led risings, various plotters were at work, all of them virulent anti-Godoyistas: among them a merchant of contraband goods, Nicolás Tap y Nuñez Redón;[30] a friar, Father Manuel Gil; and a noble, conde de Tilly. A recently arrived cavalry captain also claimed to have agitated among the military. As in Oviedo they knew that the inhabitants were well-disposed to a rising. On receiving the news of the May 2 Madrid insurrection four days after the events, the popular ferment had been so great that the Sevilla authorities had been obliged to stage in due form a public oath-taking to Fernando VII as their sovereign. To the beat of a drum, a portait of Napoleon was carried through the streets upside down on a pole covered in black cloth; and a voluntary enlistment called.[31] Though pushed to the extreme, the authorities managed to restore and maintain a tenuous public order until the evening of Thursday, May 26.

It was then that the rumour began to circulate that a French column under General Dupont had reached Andújar, a short march from Córdoba, on its officially announced sortie to Cádiz to relieve the blockaded French fleet, and which was due to pass through Sevilla en route.‡ The rumoured proximity of French troops helped to arouse the Sevillian population.

The risings in La Coruña and Badajoz owed less to planning than to prior agitation, and the authorities' failure, on May 30, to honour Fernando's feast day. This was traditionally celebrated – in honour of Fernando III, the canonized thirteenth-century king who had taken Córdoba and Sevilla from the Muslims – by a cannon salute and the royal flag raised on battlements and castles. In 1808 the ceremony took on a new significance as a visible indication of whether the authorities' allegiance lay with Fernando VII or with the French-dominated regime in Madrid. Failure to observe tradition aroused the people's anger and afforded the opportunity (or the pretext) to begin an insurrectionary movement.

La Coruña's authorities had been successful in keeping down any previous

---

* Castaños, who appeared to accept Madrid's orders, established secret contact with Gibraltar's British governor-general Sir Hew Dalrymple to ensure himself of English aid if the French army entered Andalucía. (Lovett, 1965, pp. 153–54.)
† The newly-formed Cádiz junta had previously signed an armistice (in effect a peace treaty) with Lord Collingwood, commander of the British fleet.
‡ By May 26, in fact, Dupont had reached only Manzanares in La Mancha, having delayed his departure from the environs of Toledo while awaiting fresh orders from the Emperor. (García-Noblejas, 1982, pp. 28–29.)

unrest – using displays of force, where necessary. But the news of the Madrid May 2 events and the almost concurrent arrival on May 10 of a French staff officer to report on the 'state of Galicia's public tranquility', which had been interpreted by locals as spying on the city's defences, arsenals and military preparedness, had excited their spirits;[32] and agitation among military officers, especially those of the Regiment of Navarra, incensed by the French seizure of the Pamplona fortress, had been intense.

*

In Sevilla, May 26, although unconnected with Fernando's saint's day, was a date propitious for a rising – indeed it had probably been chosen deliberately, being a public holiday when the people were in the streets.[33] As Friar Giles y Carpio recorded in his diary:

> On May 26, the day of Our Lord Jesus Christ's Ascension, it being five of the clock in the afternoon, a revolt or insurrection began amongst a multitude of people in the Plaza de San Francisco. The people made for the house of Sr. Saavedra, lieutenant captain general, to ask for arms, but they did not find him at home. They then went to the artillery depot to seek arms but it was shut.

After going to another lieutenant captain general's house without finding him at home, they returned to the square and then set off in search of the asistente.

> And they found him, and they told him to send an order to the military commandant to hand out arms to all . . . to defend the city against the French canaille. This he did. It was the people, accompanied by troops, who were the cause of this rising.[34]

Acting apparently outside of the main Fernandista conspiratorial group, the merchant and known smuggler Tap y Nuñez and a couple of accomplices raised a cavalry squadron by liberal use of money.* The sound of soldiers in the streets rallied the people who had risen earlier and who now joined what was becoming a 'revolution'. Accompanied by troops and a growing crowd, Tap's associate, Antonio Esquibel, hastened to the artillery park, where the commandant handed over the keys without ado and retired. Esquibel claimed to have found twenty-six thousand muskets and a considerable number of light artillery pieces among much other war materiel. Having armed his civilian followers, he made

---

* In his *Apuntes para la historia de España*, written under the pseudonym Mirtilo Securitano, Tap y Nuñez Redón, left a long and circumstantial account of his and two acquaintances' role in organizing a part of the rising which was discredited as soon as it was published in 1811, and has largely remained so ever since. The book can be criticized on many scores, not least its megalomanic insistence that the author alone was responsible for raising the city; yet a city councillor and member of the junta which arose from the insurrection, Col. José Checa y Xijon, gave Tap full credit for his role: '. . . the revolution [was] led by D. Nicolas Tap y Nuñez and others with good judgement and prudence, without bloodshed or disorder and at much risk and considerable work on Tap's part,' he noted in his diary, significantly not attributing sole authorship of the events to the merchant. (Checa y Xijon, 1808, p. 12.)

the rounds of the nobility, farmers, bakers and innkeepers to demand mules to draw the artillery from the depot to strategic positions in the city streets.[35]

To control his supporters Tap had to regale them with wine.

> But then he heard the owner of a drinking place complain that an insolent man had fled without paying for what he had drunk, saying: 'The Revolution will pay . . .' After settling the small amount owed, Tap selected a number of men and ordered them to find the man and execute him on the spot and to arrest any others who committed the same fault. 'From one single grain grows an ear of wheat,' he commented.[36]

Tap's accomplice, Esquibel, with less money than Tap but much willingness to spend it on the cause, 'gathered together, thanks to gifts and money, a multitude of troops and civilians to stage the rising', wrote his wife later.[37] Popular insurrections did not come cheap.

At 7 a.m. the audiencia magistrates called a meeting for a hour later, at the town hall, of all the authorities and influential individuals with sway over the people: outside the hall were gathered a mass of Tap's insurrectionists. A new governing junta which Tap claimed a leading role in forming emerged from the meeting, though he did not ask for, or receive, a place on it. But his pretentions to influence and power, as the leader of a strong armed force, soon came to nought after agreeing with the junta to remove his forces from the city. The junta did not acknowledge his first dispatch announcing that he was encamped with his men beyond the city walls; his troops were quickly reclaimed by their commanders, and the civilians either enlisted or melted away, leaving him without his 'popular army', as he had earlier titled it. He was faithful, however, to the new junta he claimed to have helped create, and informed it of popular demands – a more rapid way of enlisting men, for example – which the junta acted on. But when he warned the junta of having received an approach to lead a plot to force out three of its members, conde de Tilly among them, his fate was sealed. Ten days after the insurrection he and his comrade-in-arms, Esquibel, were thrown into solitary confinement in Cádiz castle dungeons by a Sevillan junta which feared, or was angered by, his intrusion – on the people's behalf – into their august affairs carried on in the name of the newly-asserted people's sovereignty.[38]

In Zaragoza, the insurrection's leaders had surrendered armed power voluntarily. In Sevilla it was taken from them by their leader's ingenuous illusions of power.

*

Like May 26, San Fernando's feast day on May 30, a Monday, was also a public holiday – an opportune time, as Sevilla had shown, to gather the people in the streets. In La Coruña, a popularly respected master-saddler, Sinforiano López y Aliá, had been given 'all the money thought necessary to be distributed as and when he wanted to ensure that San Fernando's day did not pass without the mine exploding', subsequently wrote Cristóbal Conde García, confessor to Archbishop Múzquiz of Santiago de Compostela.[39]

The saddler, who, since the news of the May 2 events in his home city of Madrid, had been 'working to achieve a rising against the old [Godoy] government and Napoleon's tyranny'[40] would live up to the expectations placed in him. 'He was an ardent man, endowed with popular verbosity, loved by the crowd and who led the people at will.'[41] At 10 a.m. on the feast day, López headed a crowd, including many women and children, to the captain general's residence with shouts of *Viva Fernando VII!* and *Death to Murat!* The military guard did nothing to stop the children, many with banderoles fixed to sticks, from running amongst them. Encouraged by the troops' inaction, the adults began to crowd round the door, to stone the windows and demand the captain general's head. The military governor of Coruña, Major General Antonio de Alcedo, and other high-ranking officers, were within paying their respects to Captain General Filangieri, who had been newly appointed to his post. Seeing that the tumult was increasing, Alcedo proposed that someone should go out to address the crowd, but of the many officers and nobles there none responded. He decided to go himself. With no little difficulty and at some risk he moved into the crowd and shouted that three or four persons should step forward to treat with him. This they did, demanding, according to Alcedo, that

the flag be flown . . . and a cannon salute fired. Immediately I issued orders for this to be done. Then they demanded that the people be armed, and to hand over the persons of Filangieri and Biedma [the previous captain general]. I refused to accept this, and I told them I had only sufficient arms to defend the city and that I would give them out, but not to women and young girls. They could be sure, I said, that they would always find me at their head even at the cost of my life, and that the generals were the king's loyal vassals . . . Convinced, they began to break out in cheers for the governor.[42]

Alcedo returned to the captain general's residence where to his great surprise he found himself alone. Filangieri and all his guests had escaped across the garden at the back and into the nearby secret door of a friary. Then, as Alcedo relates,

the people again became infuriated by the news that on Murat's orders muskets were being embarked on a warship at El Ferrol for America. They invaded the residence and smashed all the glass, tore the paper from the walls, broke to pieces all the furniture and made off with many things. From there they went to the artillery park where they seized all the arms. I assured them that the muskets being embarked for America would be unloaded and that the Regiment of Navarra would be ordered to return from El Ferrol; tired at last and heeding my persuasions, they quietened down.[43]

Despite the military governor's admonitions, it was not only men of all ages but women and children who armed themselves from the store of forty thousand muskets. 'And those who seemed dubious about arming themselves were obliged to do so by the women.'[44]

A blacksmith, one Francisco Conde, now launched a rumour that manacles were being readied on the French consul's orders to take conscripts off as captives to France. This caused a new disturbance, which was only subdued when Sinforiano López, the saddler, led the people out in a procession carrying a portrait of Fernando VII, and to the usual *vivas!* and huzzas.

The following day, all the Coruña authorities met in a provisional general junta to resolve what to do about the commotion which had 'inconvenienced the authorities' and led to a 'critical situation'. With 'the armed and riotous people outside the audiencia building', the junta noted that

> the people continued to remain firm in their ideas . . . that it was in the Nation's best interests to defend the Fatherland, Religion and Liberty which the French wanted to violate and that they were prepared to die and to kill whomever opposed them.[45]

The junta's statement was signed by General Biedma who, along with Filangieri,* had earlier sworn loyalty to Fernando VII. The old authorities, when they turned coat, were not always easy to sweep aside.

Nonetheless, as a result of the risings in La Coruña and a day later in the capital, Santiago, Galicia as a whole, with its deep sea ports dominating the Atlantic to the west, with its borders adjoining Asturias and Castilla la Vieja to the northeast and east, and with Portugal to the south, was ensured for the Fernandista cause.

*

The rising in Badajoz, the Extremaduran fortress city astride the Portuguese border, commanding the southwestern approaches to Spain's neighbour, appeared to be the only leaderless civilian–military insurrection – at least as far as the inadequate records go – and one of the most violent. On May 23, there had been a riot; no source stated the reason, but it can be surmised that the cause, as elsewhere on that date, was the arrival of the *Gazeta de Madrid* with the news of the Bourbon abdications. The authorities had not been able to contain the rioters without calling on the clergy. The archbishop, at the head of the cathedral chapter, had sallied forth at the authorities' request and, passing from street to street, had calmed the people, exhorting them to maintain 'peace and tranquility'.[46] (The clergy's Godly authority was the Old Order's 'shock absorber' at times of social crisis – the secular powers lacking any *natural* authority over the people and unable to turn to a reliable repressive force since the army, though summonable, was generally unwilling to be used as a domestic police force.) The Fernandista conspirators, who included the governor's second-in-command, the intendente, Martín de Garay, and the treasurer of the Spanish army in Portugal, Félix Ovalle, were planning a provincial rising on June 3 or 4; but as it turned out events overtook them.[47]

---

* Filangieri's fortune did not last long: he was assassinated by drunken troops of the Regiment of Navarra under his command in Villafranca del Vierzo on June 20, 1808 – the last captain general to die as a result of the rising. To the end he remained distrusted, and, just before his death, had been relieved of his command as head of one of the two Galician patriot corps.

On the morning of Fernando's feast day, the royal standard was not flying; nor had there been a cannon salute.* Informed by the governor's second-in-command that the people were demanding that the feast day be celebrated according to custom, the captain general, Conde Torre del Fresno, appeared on his balcony and informed the crowd that he was giving orders for its demands to be met.[48] He then told an assembly of the town's leading authorities of the Sevilla rising; barely had he the time to state his support for the Fernandista cause and call on others to state their views when the sound of cannon fire broke out, accompanied by much shouting.[49] Enraged by the failure to fly the royal standard, a crowd had gathered on the city walls and reprehended the artillerymen for not firing a salute. A woman, María Cambrero, is credited with having seized a linstock from one of the soldiers and set fire to a cannon, whereupon the artillerymen followed suit.[50]

The crowd, meanwhile, made for the captain general's quarters. Voices spoke up angrily against Torre del Fresno for not making public the news of the Sevilla rising and declaring his support for it. Crying, 'Death to the traitors!' 'Long live our king, Fernando VII!', they stopped at the gates of a cavalry barracks, and called on officers and men to join them. When the officers replied that they could move only on their superiors' orders, the crowd brushed aside the sentries and rode roughshod over the officers; thereupon the other ranks joined them.[51] As in Sevilla, the garrison cavalrymen identified with the mutinous people whose cause they perceived as their own. They were soon joined by individual artillerymen and sappers.

Blazquez Prieto, an ecclesiastical judge, and a town councillor whom the captain general's assembly had appointed to pacify the people, made for the plaza Real where they had been informed a crowd had gathered. There the judge found 'a large number of men and women, none of whom, because of their station in life, I recall recognizing'.

> Their cries of *Viva la Religión! Viva el Rey!* Death to the traitors! and similar things was indescribable. The men were mutinous, but the women appeared no less than raging Furies . . . The task [of calming such a crowd], under the burning sun was hard; but after an hour and a half it was beginning to bear fruit when a small column of soldiers, wearing their barracks uniforms – some armed with musket and bayonet, others with only a musket or sword – accompanied by drummers and regimental flags, advanced in quick step, followed by many of the crowd whom I and my companion had just calmed.[52]

Shortly, it became known that a French courier had arrived in the town. This set alight new rumours: the captain general was preparing to hand over Badajoz to General Kellerman, commander of a French occupation division a short distance across the border in Portugal. The people invaded the captain general's

---

* In fact, the Badajoz custom, 'since time immemorial', had been to fire the first salvo one hour before sunset, the second half an hour later and the third at sunset. (*Declaración del Coronel D. Diego de Toro*, Feb 16, 1816, Appendix no. 9, Gómez Villafranca, 1908, p. 10.) The population must have been aware of this.

quarters; he escaped by a secret door and made for one of the city's gates, La puerta Palmas.[53] But the mob traced his steps and he was forced to take refuge in the gate's guardroom. A number of garrison officers hurried to the scene to try to contain the infuriated crowd of 'young women, soldiers and civilians' who were demanding his head. To no more avail than Torre del Fresno's last-minute plea of his patriotic sentiments and readiness to relinquish his command. Hardly had he finished speaking than he was run through the back by a soldier's iron-tipped stave.[54] The mob dragged his body through the streets and dumped it at the door of his quarters.

Little less than three weeks earlier the captain general had been the city's hero. His proclamation calling on the population to arms in defence of Madrid's May 2 rising had led to his acclaim. With the exception of General Solano, the real force behind the proclamation, no other top-ranking military commander had come out in support. Dismayed by the experience, Torre del Fresno and Solano, captain general of Andalucía, delayed in giving their immediate support to the rising; and both met the same fate at the hands of their own troops.

The assassination brought the Badajoz commotion to an end. That evening, a junta was formed, nearly two-thirds of whose members were army officers. This proportion was only exceeded on the junta which arose from the most military of all the insurrections, Cartagena. Though justified by the two towns' military and naval importance, their juntas demonstrated the military's willingness to intervene directly in their country's political affairs.*

*

Astride the main line of communications between France and Portugal, Valladolid was a crucial strategic city in Napoleon's plans. There the Spanish military were 'the motor of the people's insurrection', Hilarión Sancho, a well-placed eyewitness, confided in his diary of 1808.[55] In this case it was the Household Guards who had accompanied Fernando VII to the French border on his fatal passage to Bayonne to meet Napoleon and who, on their return, had been ordered to remain in the Castilian capital.

However, they confronted a formidable military opponent in the captain general of Castilla la Vieja, General Cuesta, who had been appointed to the post shortly before by Fernando VII, and was as opposed to a rising as the majority of the old authorities. He did everything he could to stifle it, issuing a proclamation on May 21 calling for public tranquility throughout the region of his command. The population should remain 'quiet and prudent'.[56]

A week later, on May 29, he wrote in a letter to the León town hall, which fell in his territory, to advise the town councillors that he accepted the Bourbon renunciations of the Spanish throne 'under the pact recognizing our independence and that Spain will not be dismembered [i.e. not have part of its territory annexed to France]'. This, he argued, was in the nation's best interests, aware as he was that 'all sensible Spaniards and lovers of their fatherland' shared his views.

* See Chapter 5, p.147.

However, there are many amongst the vulgar who are incapable of reasoning and who, I must suppose, are unfortunately seduced by some malevolent and rebellious men . . . who allow themselves to be swept blindly into an insurrection . . . But who would lead us in such an event? . . . Do they do not take into account that their own leaders would come to dispute the supreme leadership, and take us into civil war?[57]

Cuesta's opinions were no worse – and certainly no better – than those of the majority of the old authorities. Only four days later, however, he found himself at the head of the insurrection which finally broke out at three o'clock on the afternoon of Tuesday, May 31:

a crowd of all classes of persons went to the Plaza Mayor and in front of the town hall began to shout *Viva Fernando VII! Death to the country's traitors!* They demanded a general obligatory enlistment without distinction of estates to defend the homeland, the issuing of all arms in the city, and the appointment of a leader whom they could obey. The city councillors, who were in meeting, agreed, and the four thousand people who had gathered went to the captain general's residence and repeated their demands.[58]

Cuesta refused to do more than issue the two hundred and fifty muskets the French army had left behind on its march to Portugal the previous year. Even so, the people were roused to action, placing guards at the royal gates, the town hall entrances and the captain general's residence.

They seized various carts without waybills loaded with cotton and arms en route for Madrid, and merchandise of people they considered suspect, allowing no one to leave or enter the city unless their good conduct was accredited. Those coming from outside they questioned. They detained postal couriers and took them to the town hall to declare the purpose of their arrival.[59]

Though they hid their traces well, some influential people were behind the demonstration; but of only one individual – and then not a socially high-placed person – was there any precise information. This was a butcher who had made a small fortune as a purveyor of meat to the city, one Pedro García known locally as Perín. At the time of the insurrection he was 'one of the persons who distinguished himself most in favour of fatherland and nation'.* The presence of a well-to-do city purveyor was not surprising: these were generally well connected to town hall authorities responsible for ensuring the city's food supplies and enjoyed an influence beyond their ordinary status. The Valencia purveyors, Bertrán de Lis, were the main organizers, it will be recalled, of the rising in the Levante capital.

On the following day, June 1, the crowd, once again of 'all classes of persons', demanded of Cuesta that he order a general enlistment, and appoint a leader; he

---

* As the anonymous diarist quoted above carefully noted, the butcher was only 'one of the influential people involved'. If, as is believed, the diary's author was a Valladolid Appeal Court attorney then he was in a privileged position to know who the others were, though he gave no information about them. (See Anon, *Noticia de casos particulares ocurridos en la ciudad de Valladolid*, 1886/1989, p. 250.)

agreed only to the enlistment of volunteers – the authorities' general ruse to control a dangerous situation – and that these should return to their homes. Believing that they were being taken in, the crowd grew infuriated and made for the Inquisition's tribunal where they asked for and received the standard of the Faith which was carried through the streets by three priests to the people's huzzas of '*Viva la Fé!*' ['Long live the Holy Faith!'], 'Religion, King Fernando and the Fatherland', and to the sound of church bells ringing out the alarm.[60] Under the pressure, Cuesta began to shift ground and ordered a general enlistment.

The people remained suspicious, however, and when on June 2 an edict was published calling for tranquility and on everyone to return to their homes, the insurrection took a more direct course: men brought out their firearms and attached royal cockades to their hats, as did many women, and the criminal courts released all their prisoners.[61] The people felt the authorities were deceiving them. To concentrate theirs and especially Cuesta's mind they erected the gallows in the main square to the cry of 'traitors', and shouted threats to make gallows birds of the authorities if they continued to dupe the people 'by turning everything into a delusion'.[62]

The gibbets had the desired effect. Cuesta gave in. The proclamation of Fernando VII as king of Spain and the Indies was rapidly organized, with the town councillors on horseback leading the way, followed by the Household troop and a cavalry battalion. Behind them marched the insurrectionists and a company of merchants, 'richly dressed in new uniforms'; an empty carriage and a coach symbolically brought up the rear. Under a canopy on the High Court's main balcony, Cuesta and the Court's magistrates solemnly proclaimed Fernando as king and the procession returned to the town hall where the royal standard was hung from a balcony.[63]

Reluctant to the end, however, to concede power, Cuesta allowed an Armaments and Defence Junta to be formed but limited its attributes strictly to military affairs. He permitted similar juntas in only those cities of his territory which had intendentes.[64]

By the evening of the insurrection 1500 people had been armed. Commissioners were sent out to surrounding villagers and shortly two thousand or more villagers had come in and were despatched up the road to Palencia from where the immediate French threat was expected.[65] On June 9 Cuesta led all the regular troops at his disposal and an enthusiastic but untrained and undisciplined rabble of armed civilians out to meet the French army; in a pitched battle at Cabezón three days later he lost the bulk of his force. Inexplicably, he drew up the greater part of his men with their back to the river Pisuerga instead of using the river as a natural protection. Many of his soldiers drowned trying to escape the French forces.* It was the first setback for Spain's patriot forces which in Cataluña, La Mancha and Valencia were almost simultaneously winning their first victories over Napoleon's generals.

---

* 'There were many who attributed his strange conduct to treachery or to revenge for having been forced to compromise himself in the rising.' In other later battles, though exposing himself to considerable personal danger, 'his troop dispositions were equally misguided, proving that he had not acted out of bad faith [at Cabezón] but through lack of strategic knowledge'. The comment is Toreno's, 1838/1916, p. 90.

Nonetheless, General Cuesta was the only captain general of the main risings to retain his post without suffering the humiliation of the insurrection electing another general to lead it or of being dismissed, let alone of losing his life. A staunch traditional monarchist, and one of the few surviving generals capable of commanding an army in the field, he would live to lead patriot arms to their only near victories in the disastrous year of 1809.

AN ARMED-FORCES RISING

The Cartagena insurrection was planned by naval and military officers who, like most of officialdom throughout the country, had known of the royal abdications for a good week or more before the *Gazeta de Madrid* published the official confirmation.[66] The second senior naval officer, Lieutenant General Baltasar Hidalgo de Cisneros,* his adjutant and the colonel of the infantry regiment garrisoning the town, all known anti-Godoyistas, were the masterminds.[67]

An enormous crowd was awaiting the *Gazeta*'s distribution outside the post office and broke into huzzas for Fernando VII and shouts of 'Death to the French!' when the news was read out. Immediately cockades were distributed – evidence of some prior organization – and the crowd made for the arsenal, where artillery and naval officers handed out arms and munitions; and the six thousand garrison troops (out of a civilian population of seventeen thousand) immediately sided with the insurrection, giving it an experienced armed force which made it practically invincible locally.[68]

The newly armed, who included the dockyard and arsenal's craftsmen, immediately began to make their power felt, but without any apparent thought of taking power themselves. Instead, they rounded up the captain general, the governor, and municipal authorities, often under threat of armed force, and made them report to the town hall; there they obliged these authorities to declare publicly for Fernando. They had little choice if they did not want to see the situation turn dangerous. Once the ceremony had been performed, to the usual huzzas for Fernando, the crowd invaded the council chamber and determinedly demanded that couriers be sent immediately to the captain generals of Granada and Valencia, and the corregidor of Murcia, the provincial capital, informing them of the rising and asking them to report on their cities' situation. The authorities agreed. Meanwhile, other armed people were fetching all the military and naval commanders of the garrison, the city's chief magistrate and the postal administrator. When all of these were present, they effectively formed a general junta. But on several accounts it was a very exceptional junta in comparison to those of other risings. In the first place it was almost totally composed of military and naval officers – seventeen out of a total of nineteen members – and not a single cleric amongst them, a situation shared only with Oviedo. Whether the conspirators had instructed trusted insurgents to round up all the authorities was unknown. If they had not done so, then the junta had

---

* Apart from admiral and one or two lower ranks, the navy shared with the army its officer titles.

been created *de facto* by the people – rather than as was usual by the Fernandista leaders. Furthermore, it was by no means yet freed of dependence on the armed crowd. So tumultous was the populace in its demands and petitions that the junta could not quieten them. One demand was insistently repeated, however: that Cartagena's captain general, Francisco de Borja, rescind the orders he had received from Madrid the day before to dispatch the Spanish Mediterranean fleet from Mahon in Menorca to the French port of Toulon. (Many of the insurgents had relatives aboard.) His agreement calmed the crowd and they accepted the junta's proposal that two of its members act as the people's spokesmen, and the remainder vacate the chamber. The junta then got down to the business of planning the town's defence and calling volunteers to the colours, who were to be armed and trained by the garrison. At 4 a.m. it suspended its session until the following morning.

Gathered again at 9 a.m., the junta was about to consider the urgent measures to be taken when the postal administrator hurried in. A great crowd had gathered in front of the post office and was refusing to allow the ordinary mail to leave, even threatening to burn the mailbag. The junta sent two of its members to try to calm the crowd, in vain. The people believed that dispatches to inform Murat of the rising were being sent to Madrid. Suddenly the two junta members were surrounded by a furious mob brandishing the mailbag and shouting that all mail must be checked, and letters for Madrid removed. The crowd acted with the same instinct that moved the people in all the risings: traitors to their cause among the old authorities or educated people would use the mails to betray them. Proven correct in more than one case, the precautionary instinct was justifiable; and yet it was hard not to believe that the unlettereds' fear of the educated's command of an idiom alien to them – 'a mess of fishhooks' on paper which they did not understand – was also at work in these instances.

The demand to censor the mail was just the beginning; immediately shouts were heard demanding that the captain general (a known Godoyista), the governor and the engineers' commander be removed from their posts because they were French sympathizers. The tumult now rose to a new height; the two junta members could not make themselves heard. When finally they secured the crowd's attention, they told them to elect a person to speak in their name. This the people rapidly did, their choice falling on the magistrate's senior bailiff. The latter informed the full junta of their demands: the dismissal of the three senior officers, and the appointment of the infantry colonel, marqués de Camarena la Real, as governor and General Hidalgo Cisneros as captain general. While the three 'deposed' officials left the meeting in high dudgeon at the accusations against them, the two new appointees were sworn into office. This was a totally irregular procedure; but both officers accepted their appointments without a qualm, revealing thereby their readiness to overthrow the former authorities. And here again the crowd acted as it did in many of the risings, choosing a new military leader in whose loyalty to the cause it believed it could trust. A new junta was also formed which brought in new members, among them two who were to represent the people. Significantly, the armed plebeians did not elect their representatives from among their own ranks but from those of their 'betters': an artillery colonel, the military governor's second-in-command, and the bailiff already mentioned. As in Zaragoza, the commonality lacked the confidence to command, let alone take advantage of, the new situation. It was trained to accept that it was not part of the 'political nation' – those whose right it was to govern.

The touchstone of loyalty and patriotism was anti-Godoyism; and replacing or eliminating known Godoyistas was considered the insurrection's first task. One further event graphically illustrated this and the army's position. Fearing for his life, de Borja, the former captain general, requested, and received from the junta, an armed guard on his residence. Aroused by news of both French army slayings and patriot assassinations of suspected 'traitors' in other insurrectionary cities, an armed mob, including many arsenal workers, made for de Borja's residence on June 10. The guard abandoned its post, de Borja was seized and taken to the arsenal where a gallows had been erected. The military officer on guard duty at the entrance ordered his men to shut the gates to prevent the mob entering, but made no attempt to rescue his former superior who was stabbed to death on the spot.[69] He was but one of the four captain generals assassinated as a result of the risings: in each case, the military made little or no real attempt to save them, never calling out the troops to protect their superior officer.

Finally, as elsewhere, the rising spread outwards beyond the city gates. On receiving the news, Murcia, the provincial capital, rose the following day, forming a supreme junta for the whole region. The rising thus spread throughout the kingdom of Murcia which covered at the time a large territory reaching north to Albacete in La Mancha and to the southern borders of Cuenca, westwards to the limits of Granada and Jaén, and eastwards into parts of what are today Alicante.

By mid-June, the major urban insurrections had spread to the whole of Spain, with the exception of those areas directly occupied by the French: the Basque country, Navarra and La Rioja, with a long thin tongue of territory stretching south through Burgos and Madrid to the Tajo river; in Catalonia, solely the occupied capital, Barcelona, had not risen. The juntas of Galicia, Sevilla and Valencia had joined Asturias in asking England for aid in arms and money.

The Spanish insurrections were both influential on, and supported by, similar risings in Portugal. The Galician junta had sent emissaries to the Spanish army regiments stationed in Oporto, as part of the Fontainebleau treaty agreement, calling on them to desert their post and join the Galician insurrection. On June 6, they did so. Five days later, the northern province of Tras Os Montes, bordering on southern Galicia, rose, followed soon afterwards by the whole of northern Portugal. It was not many days before the Portuguese insurrection spread southwards into the Alentejo and Algarve. On June 16, the southernmost town of Faro rose. General Junot, the French commander and governor of Portugal, found himself in Lisbon surrounded by an insurrectionary countryside.

*

Predictably, the risings were heralded by strange natural phenomena. In Zaragoza, a cloud was said to have formed in the shape of a palm tree over the chapel of the Virgen del Pilar, one of Spain's two patron saints, and a palm branch over Valladolid's plaza Mayor two weeks later.* In a sense the urban lower ranks' insurrectionary passion was a response to the dispassionate reasoning of their earlier enlightened reformers, many of whom nailed their colours to the new Bonapartist mast. In other words, the insurrection was the common people's Baroque victory over the Enlightenment. A counter-revolutionary insurrection: was this another Vendée? In part, yes – and the comparison did not escape some Spanish participants;[70] defence of king and religion were common to both. And one social stratum, the artisanate, was prominent in both. But the dissimilarities were greater than the similarities. In contrast to the largely peasant counter-revolutionary mobilization of 1793–1796 in one part of western France,[71] the Spanish insurrection was *urban* in its origins and *national* in its scope. Though both risings were directed against the 'usurpers' of the absolutist monarchy, the French reaction was against its own revolution, while the Spanish insurrection was directed against a royal favourite and his administration, which had begun the process of temporizing with an ally's invasion, and the abduction of their king whom the people had been instrumental in putting on the throne. If in the first place the Spanish insurrectionists sought to replace the authorities whom they suspected of pro-French sympathies, in the longer term they were prepared to fight the greatest continental power not only in defence of their king and religion but also for the *patria*, the 'fatherland' in differing senses of the word: in the geographically national sense, but more often in the geographically restricted sense, the regional or literal homeland (the villagers' habitat or *patria chica*). In both these meanings, the word contained social and moral connotations: the identification with monarchy and religion, familiar customs and traditions, and a sense of continuity over sudden and radical change, generally feared to herald conditions prejudicial to the labouring classes' interests.† Popular insistence on ensuring a general enlistment, almost always 'without exception of classes', meaning that nobility and clergy were not exempt, demonstrated their readiness to fight, but only on the basis of equality of sacrifice.

Underlying the lower orders' trust in new authorities was the notion that only a change at the top could bring the reforms they had hoped for from their new king's reign. The Old Regime mentality of reform from above remained deeply embedded.‡ In a deferential distrust of their own capabilities, the urban – and subsequently village – poor insisted on finding and entrusting politico-military leadership to new 'leaders' among the educated classes. Their trust was generally betrayed; the new leaders were no more interested in their fate – other than as servile cannon fodder – than the old.

* The time-lag between the two events, on May 17 and June 2 respectively, suggests the possibility that a traveller from Zaragoza who had heard of the phenomenon in the Aragonese capital reported it in Valladolid, which was not to be outdone in matters of religiosity.
† See also reflections on the word 'patria' in Chapter 1, p. 20.
‡ The notion that a *political* revolution would solve all *social* ills was common enough at the time, at least in the Anglo-Saxon world. From Tom Paine to the Chartists, the idea was the radical response to the existing status quo.

THE CATALAN INSURRECTION

From today's perspective of Cataluña as an historically distinct and different country from the rest of Spain, the question of why the Catalans were prepared to defend the Spanish Bourbon monarchy, which had deprived them a century earlier of their cherished self-governing rights, was paradoxical. And yet not only did they rise and fight, their resistance was longer, more bitter and more costly in lives and property than in almost any other part of Spain. No sooner had they risen, indeed, than their civilian 'home guard', the *sometent*, with some military help, battled and defeated a Napoleonic force.

Lérida, the Catalan provincial capital closest to Aragón, was the first to rise on May 28, four days after Zaragoza. News of the latter's insurrection was highly influential: popular pressure, demanding that the authorities declare openly that they 'followed the Spanish party, as the people demanded',[72] resulted in the creation of a profoundly conservative junta, which included members of the three estates under the bishop's presidency; the junta immediately declared its preparedness to join the Aragonese in their struggle, and dispatched emissaries to Tarragona, Tortosa, Vich and Manresa to foment risings.

On June 1, General Duhesme, the French military commander, issued a proclamation threatening to shoot out of hand any Catalan found carrying arms and munitions, and to deprive any township, small or large, of its rights if 'it dared to rise'. Should French blood be shed in any of them, the township would be burned to the ground and its authorities tried as criminals.[73]

Two local insurrections illustrated the similarities and differences between Cataluña and what had occurred in the rest of Spain. Manresa and Igualada were textile-working towns of between six and eight thousand inhabitants about one hundred kilometres north west of Barcelona. Unemployment in both was extraordinarily high. In Manresa until recently four hundred master artisans had employed over two thousand journeymen in the production of silk and other textiles. But by early 1808, most of the manufacturing had ground to a halt because of the decline in colonial trade, reducing the journeymen to public beggars. Despite the creation of a 'Charity Junta' with the aim of finding work and food for the unemployed,[74] the mass of out-of-work small masters and journeymen resented being reduced to road workers, clearing tracks from the town and improving the Manresa to Barcelona highway. Impotent rage at their work situation sharpened their will to rise against a threatened and feared French military domination.

Enraged by Duhesme's proclamation, Manresa inhabitants on the following day – market day – publicly burned in the township's main square all official paper stamped with the duque de Berg's (Murat's) name to the usual huzzas of *Viva la Religión! Viva Fernando! Viva la Patria!* Local Fernandista notables took over, defying the governor who had issued an order for all inhabitants to return to their homes and await further orders, although resorting to the usual stratagem of agreeing to volunteers joining up. The immediate appearance

on a balcony overlooking the square of two parish priests, wearing Spanish
Bourbon cockades, was indicative of the authorities' fear that the burning might
lead to much graver events.[75] The clergy could well be needed to contain the
people's ardour.

The Fernandista elite met rapidly and agreed on the need to set up a junta.
But they were careful to enlist the guilds in their enterprise, trusting in them to
control the lower ranks, and calling on them to hold immediate elections to
appoint their delegates. The Fernandistas were not mistaken. The general tenor
of the guild leaders' sentiments can be judged by one guild's unanimously voiced
decision to 'obey our king, Fernando VII . . .' and to join together with the
other guilds to establish a junta to govern during his absence. Their main
demand was to

> defend the town, the Principality [of Cataluña] and the whole Kingdom [of Spain]
> from the hostilities and violences which the Emperor may attempt or carry out. The
> guild's will [is] solely to defend Religion, King and Country.[76]

That same evening Manresa's leading notables and authorities complied. Apart
from the governor and town councillors, the defence junta included some of
these public figures, as well as priors, canons and other ecclesiastics, and the
guild representatives. The junta sent out members to the villages in its district
and to townships beyond, informing them of the events and calling on them to
raise their local 'home guard' or sometent. Though within the month this
conservative junta was in serious trouble from some of the Manresa populace
who assassinated the governor and three gaoled resident Frenchmen, and tried
to take over the junta in the common people's name, it acted with dispatch in
terms of the town's defence.

After many days of popular agitation, Igualada rose on June 4. Its 950 textile
workers were suffering the same economic conditions as in Manresa. The town
also had over five hundred landless agricultural day labourers among its
working population. The rising was led by Antonio Franch, a well-to-do
merchant in his thirties who had recently inherited a 'respectable patrimony'
from his deceased father and subsequently became a noted guerrilla leader in the
region;[77] and Joseph d'Olzinellas, another man of wealth.

From the last days of May, the Igualada townsfolk had begun to agitate and
the authorities had had their work cut out to contain them. On June 3, the town
councillors' minds had been concentrated by the people's armed appearance in
front of the council chamber, waving a paper – either Duhesme's decree of June
1 or the officially stamped paper in the duque de Berg's name, to which
apparently they set fire, as in Manresa – and by their threats of more drastic
action if their will was not met.

> The people have demanded and forced us into providing them with the means of
> defence. The town council has no arms to distribute, but it is said that in Villafranca
> there are more than sufficient to lend us for this purpose.[78]

All the while, for three days and nights, the town's main church bell tolled unceasingly in the traditional summons to the sometent. A cobbler, his youngest son and a neighbour, a fuller by trade, had shut themselves in the tower with sufficient food to keep the bell ringing for as long as was needed to awaken the authorities to the people's demands.[79]

On the same day that Franch and another man set out for Villafranca del Penedès, the district's main town, to seek arms, even more startling events occurred. On June 4, two columns of French troops marched, on Napoleon's orders, from Barcelona, the first such expeditionary forces to venture out of the occupied capital to western Cataluña. One column, under General Chabran, made for Tarragona and was to continue southwards to Valencia to join a force under Marshal Moncey which was advancing from Madrid on the Levant capital; the second, under the Austrian General Schwartz, and composed of four thousand Neapolitan conscripts and Swiss troops and two cannon, was to march to Lérida up the Barcelona to Madrid royal highway, on which Igualada lay, and then on to Zaragoza to unite with a French force assembling before the Aragonese capital. Napoleon's strategic plan, brilliantly conceived on paper from a Parisian distance, but abstract as was often the case when its results were translated into actions in Spain, was now thrown out of joint by the Catalan risings – and decisively defeated in the first sometent resistance at the battle of the Bruch pass on the royal road.

Barcelona patriots sent news of the French forces' departure and destinations, which was received in both townships on June 5. Once across the Bruch pass, the imperial troops would be only a short distance from Igualada; and if they made a thirty-kilometre detour from the top of the pass, they could march on Manresa.* In both townships there was an immediate and instinctive reaction: to defend the pass which had seen other decisive battles in the past. Heavy rain which held up the imperial column on June 5 in Martorell came as a stroke of luck to the Manresa and Igualada sometent, giving them more time to take up positions on the six hundred metre high pass. As a backdrop reared the columnar grey rock of the Montserrat mountains amidst which stood the famous monastery of the same name. On the last part of the climb, the road curved in a wide arc forming, as it were, the perimeter of a vast amphitheatre. On the left the land dropped precipitously; on the right, there was a pine wood and great boulders to shelter the sometent in their traditional village white wide-kneed breeches and red bonnets. The defenders felled a large number of the trees to lay across the highway and dug a wide trench in it to obstruct the enemy's advance.

The Manresa sometent was led by a local retail merchant's son, Francisco Riera, a great number of the volunteers being almost certainly young artisans and journeymen, for the two religious banners under which they fought were those of their Brotherhoods, the town's most numerous and flourishing at the

---

* In fact Schwartz' orders, though unknown to the patriots at the time, were to march on Manresa, destroy its gunpowder manufactories, cart to Barcelona its existing powder supplies, and impose a massive fine on the population to pay for the column's continuing advance. (The order in Sarrat i Arbòs, 1922, pp. 32–33.)

time.[80] The junta had managed to acquire several stand of muskets; powder, manufactured in Manresa, was plentiful; but there was a shortage of ball, and the lead with which to make it. The town's blacksmiths were set to work to produce horseshoe nails until it was discovered that these damaged the muskets after four or five shots. Instead, they turned to producing cylindrical iron ball, which was rapidly proven to be more effective than lead against the French cuirassiers' breast and back plates.[81] The wealthy – for the poor had none – contributed their iron curtain rails to the cause.

The Igualada contingent, which was initially organized by clerics and guild leaders, included a number of foreign mercenary soldiers and officers* – the Spanish army included several regiments of Swiss and Walloon troops – and almost certainly a handful of women: four pairs of women's *espadrilles* figure among those which the town council bought to shoe its combatants. It also purchased ninety shotguns from a local armourer: Igualada was known for its gunsmiths.[82] Despite the arms which both towns obtained, many of the some-tent set off with no more than the rudimentary sharp-edged weapons they had fashioned.

Divided into squads and marshalled by a conch bugle, these men, as they later showed when they went to the relief of Zaragoza, liked best to fight hand-to-hand with long knives.† Not all the local volunteers, however, were raw recruits; a number had fought in the War of the Convention. One of these subsequently confided:

> I had been with my battalion in almost all the battles of the 1793 campaign, but I was never as frightened as I was at the Bruch pass. The disorder of the men – one with a musket, another with a carbine, pistol or sword – men with mattocks and sickles and even long poles with bayonets tied to the end. What sort of a force was this to hold off the French division we were facing! But the enemy fled, I don't know why.[83]

Despite this former soldier's dismay, military men played a far more important part in the battle than subsequent myth allowed. A lieutenant of the Swiss mercenary Wimpffen regiment which sided from the start with the rising; a retired lieutenant colonel living in Igualada; and a major and a captain who had escaped from Barcelona were among those who in fact led the battle. The officers and mercenary troops gave the sometent the organization and discipline they needed; the sometent the popular enthusiasm which ensured that the soldiers continued to fight.[84] Nonetheless, each sometent fought under its own leader, and under its own religious flag – appropriately enough, the purple Igualada banner bore the words, *Holy Lord, Help Us*. Equally striking was that no source provided even a rudimentary estimate of the defenders' total numbers or of their casualties.

---

* Twenty-five royal Walloon guards, who had escaped from the Barcelona garrison, and an unspecified number of Swiss troops from the Wimpffen Regiment, which had a detachment stationed in Igualada. (Carner, 1963 (1), p. 19 fn. 5.)
† See Chapter 6, p. 171.

However, a considerable number of sometent from the two towns and surrounding villages – including one group under its parish priest, and a group of students, the 'Company of St Thomas Aquinas', from as far off as Vich[85] – were occupying the pass and its approaches when General Schwartz began his ascent. Expecting no resistance – since he had encountered none so far – the general advanced up the highway without particular precaution, sending out no light infantry to reconnoitre the terrain. When his vanguard, which included a detachment of cuirassiers, came under withering fire from behind trees and rocks, and recoiled, he was surprised; but though only a minor Napoleonic general, he was not long in counter-attacking. Reorganizing his forces, infantry companies, supported by cavalry, charged up the highway and threw back the defenders to the top of the pass. Here, the sometent held out in an abandoned hospice, Can Masana, at the junction of the road to Manresa; but the imperial forces dislodged them and they were beginning to retreat along the two roads towards Manresa and Igualada when, incomprehensibly, General Schwartz failed to press home his advantage;[86] perhaps he was unsure which of the two groups to pursue. At this moment, providentially, new sometent forces arrived. Fresh to battle, they threw themselves into attack, carrying with them the original defenders: so impetuous was their charge that they drove the imperial troops from the hospice, and, pursuing them hotly, sent them retreating to the top of the highway. At this point, they were met by the concentrated fire of the sometent led by Antonio Franch, who had hastened to the pass with fresh volunteers on returning from his unsuccessful mission to Villafranca del Penadès. The imperials fled down the highway to rejoin the column's main body whom they infected with their panic, while the sometent, shouting *Victoria! Victoria!*, closed in on it. It was mid-evening and the fighting had lasted several hours.

Harassed on all sides, Schwartz formed his men into squares and they defended themselves ably. With night approaching, however, the general could no longer hope to cross the pass in safety; or even to remain in his present position, exposed to the swarm of sometent fire. Withdrawal along the road he had come on was the only option. Yet even as his buglers sounded the retreat, he tried one more tactic: his troops staged a last and desperate attack which the sometent threw back. Thereafter Schwartz began his retreat in earnest, a nightmarish march harried by the sometent on his heels and flanks throughout the long night. He lost one of his two cannon and carts bearing equipment – after the parish priest and others of the small village of Abrera had set a slow fire to the wood pylons of their bridge which collapsed under the imperial forces' weight – and finally reached Martorell at seven the following morning. The local sometent there might have dealt the weary and hungry column a serious blow; but forewarned of Schwartz's retreat the villagers, who had the previous afternoon killed some imperial soldiers guarding carts with additional supplies for the column, feared revenge and sought refuge outside the village. The imperial column passed through and continued to San Feliu de Llobregat, in the shadow of the French occupation forces in Barcelona. The sometent harried them as far as Molins del Rey, and remained in the latter's vicinity to prevent

more French troops from advancing on their towns and villages.[87] Three
hundred and eighty five imperial soldiers – ten percent of the column – were
killed or wounded, it was claimed.[88]

Even had he conquered the Bruch pass, General Schwartz would have had to
return to Barcelona. General Duhesme, the overall French commander, had
realized that risings in Gerona, Figueras and other places on the highway between
the Catalan capital and the French frontier threatened his lines of communication
with France. Not to lose direct and unimpeded contact with France was obviously
more important than ventures into western Cataluña and beyond. Barely had the
second French column under General Chabran reached Tarragona than Duhesme
ordered it to return to Barcelona. Nonetheless, while setting his sights on Gerona,
Duhesme could not overlook the humiliation of the Bruch defeat. To teach the
'brigands' a lesson, he ordered Chabran to take the pass with a column of five
thousand men and several artillery pieces a week after Schwarz' defeat. Again the
local sometent rallied; and this time they were joined by Spanish military forces –
mainly a Swiss mercenary regiment of five hundred men outfitted as villagers[89] –
who gave them a trained backbone; equally important, they had four cannon served
by regulars. The outcome was a second victory for the Catalan forces, who sent
Chabran retreating back to his base with 450 casualties, and the loss of a regimental
eagle. This double victory – plus Duhesme's defeated attempt in the face of the
population's resistance to take Gerona on June 20 with eight thousand troops but
insufficient artillery, and his subsequent withdrawal to Barcelona – seemed to
augur a great future for the Catalan popular struggle.

From the start the risings in Cataluña had been more widespread than those
in the rest of Spain. Popular disturbances in Barcelona at the end of May led to
no more, because the considerable number of French troops in the Catalan
capital made a rising there impossible. In consequence, the Catalan insurrection
in the last days of May and the first week of June was more territorially
dispersed than elsewhere. The Catalan *region* rose rather than spreading outwards from an insurrection in a major city within it. This resulted in a dispersion
of local powers which was shortly overcome by their incorporation into a
central organization or regional junta.

But there were also other significant differences. The organized labouring
classes, through their guilds, took a more active role than elsewhere in inciting
or inflecting the insurrection, recalling their traditional role in civic affairs.* In
Gerona, for example, it was four master craftsmen, in the name of their guilds,
who called for a rising. After hearing the previous day that Figueras, close to the
French border, had revolted, a saddler and harness maker, a corder, potter and
carpenter, demanded on June 5 that a town-council meeting be called immediately to hear the workers' determination to defend their town against the
French. And although, as was seen in Manresa, the guilds were conservative –
usually in the sense of attempting to protect the artisans' position within the Old

* Prior to the War of Succession at the beginning of the eighteenth century, the guilds
had formed part of Catalan self-government. The Bourbon victors annulled Catalan self-
governing rights because the Crown of Aragón had allied itself with the Hapsburg
pretender to the throne who was backed by England.

Regime – their participation opened a political space for guild representation in a number of local juntas. This and the sometents' determined resistance made the Catalan insurrection in general more truly 'popular' than in the rest of the country. Amongst the Fernandistas who did play a role, local merchants were far more important than elsewhere.*

While in much of Cataluña the general features of the Spanish insurrections remained true, the exceptions to the rule demonstrated in part the Catalan region's particular social character. The prior existence of an armed local self-defence organization, through which villagers and townships' inhabitants could forcibly express their social needs and demands, was a case in point. Resuscitated during the war against the Convention, the sometent now frequently became the vehicle for anti-feudal agitation, which had been rife prior to the rising, and which became part and parcel of a number of local insurrections. Although the popular hatred of those in authority who were thought to be pro-French was as profound as elsewhere, the hatred did not stop at these people but included señorial tax-farmers, tithe collectors, usurers, scriveners and others who directly extorted the population. The risings in such places were not so much due then to local Fernandistas as to the labouring classes who took the initiative of carrying them through.

Cataluña, furthermore, demonstrated a sense of unified command which it would take the rest of Spain several months still to realize. Only a week after its formation, the Manresa junta proposed the creation of a superior Catalan junta to take charge of the regional resistance. The Lérida junta had come to a similar conclusion, and issued, a day after Manresa, a circular to all those townships which it believed free of French military occupation, to form a general Catalan junta. Stressing the need for the greatest unity, it called on all districts not subjected to French force to send 'the most enlightened delegate possible' to ensure 'the fatherland's glorious defence'.[90] The call met with an immediate response. On June 18, the supreme Catalan junta was created in Lérida, although only twelve deputies had arrived with their respective juntas' credentials.

However conservative it turned out to be, the regional junta's creation was highly necessary in terms of Cataluña's defence. In the most difficult conditions of a constant French military presence – the junta changed its place of residence twenty-two times in the first four and a half years of the war[91] – it remained in existence throughout, even in the darkest days when it seemed that Catalan resistance must come to an end.

*

The Catalan paradox was less paradoxical than at first sight appeared. There can be no doubt that in 1808 and throughout the war the principality's

---

* For a start there were more of them in the manufacturing townships, and they were obviously aware, as were all merchants, that French – or any foreign domination, particularly British – could jeopardize Spain's (and thus their) monopoly of the colonial trade. But Catalan merchants had another reason for rejecting French domination: Napoleon had demanded that Spain open its markets to French textiles which, if it occurred, could only harm their own domestic trade.

inhabitants felt themselves Catalans above all – as will be seen on more than one occasion in the course of the struggle – but simultaneously this did not prevent them from feeling part of the Spanish monarchy: a large part of their prosperity had derived (as part of the monarchy) from the colonial trade in textiles and spirits, and there were few who were not aware of this, since the decline in colonial commerce after the Trafalgar disaster, which left Spanish exports without naval protection, had reduced their profits or even, more dramatically, left them without work. Moreover, the Spanish interior was itself part of the Catalan domestic market for textiles, particularly woollen goods. Like most people in the rest of Spain, Catalans had hoped that Fernando VII's reign would bring in its train renewed prosperity, especially to their burgeoning textile-based industrial revolution, the first in Spain. This view, however, was insufficient to explain their resistance to Napoleon's designs.

The Catalans had not yet turned their sense of a distinct identity into a political project. This would take another three-quarters of a century. In the Convention war only fifteen years previously, seemingly aghast like most Spaniards at the French Revolution's regicide, they had fought alongside the rest of Spain – indeed, had been forced by the Spanish state's weakness to organize their own war – against the revolution which threatened their country. It was their *homeland* which they were defending from a foreign invader. They had ignored French revolutionary siren calls for Catalan independence. Generally respectful of the established religion, and of their priests, the population appeared to have accepted the latter's slogan of religion, king and fatherland as the banner under which to fight the revolution.

Now, in 1808, they confronted a second, and even more dangerous, French invasion of *their* country. By guile, Napoleon had advanced further than the French revolutionaries of 1793–1795, seizing their capital, Barcelona, and their fortresses and citadels. The lower orders, who had always suspected French military intentions, were as outraged by Napoleon's treachery as the inhabitants of regions as yet unaffected by the French invasion. And the Catalan anti-Napoleonic propertied and lettered classes were united by a sense of their historic past. This stratum of society 'scrupulously respected the hierarchical edifice of existing Catalan society . . . rejecting the introduction of any innovations which lacked historical foundation . . . and aspiring to recover their freedoms which had been suppressed a century earlier'.[92]

As the Catalan social and landed 'hierarchical edifice' rested on much the same principles as in the rest of Spain,* these men had no difficulty in identifying their general interests with those which were being defended elsewhere: the Old Regime's socio-economic status quo. If anything, the Catalan junta was even more conservative than others, 'sacrificing on many occasions questions of principle and desirable and useful reforms to safeguard the established order' and 'remaining always faithful to the [Spanish] common cause'.[93]

---

* A señorial system which, even if some of its forms were different – i.e. virtual lifetime and inheritable tenancies – represented essentially the same feudal domination by landowners who increased dues and other tributes to make good the lack of rental income.

In 1808, then, Catalan sentiment was not experienced as dividing the country from the patriot cause; the ruling elite, by a combination of repression and appeals to Catalan 'patriotism' saw to that. As a result, no region was more loyal to the Spanish anti-Napoleonic war. And when there were doubts about this, they as often came from Castilians as from Catalans.

*

The Bruch battles were signal victories, for sure. But of the multiple myths the victories engendered,* one was particularly double-edged: Catalan volunteers, with the most rudimentary of arms had, under the Almighty's protection, conquered by their bravery the victors of Austerlitz, Jena and Friedland. The *Grande Armée*, in other words. Nothing was further from the truth. The *Grande Armée* had not yet made its appearance in Spain. At the first battle of El Bruch, the imperial troops were raw Neapolitan conscripts and Swiss; Schwartz was a minor general, whose biographical details do not figure in the majority of Napoleonic sourcebooks, and whose major claim to fame was probably his defeat at El Bruch. And the remainder of the imperial army was mainly made up of raw French recruits. But the myth brought a confidence which both inspired resistance and led to despondency when the imperial armies began to impose their will.

Another, though more harmless myth, was that the first battle of El Bruch was the patriots' first armed civilian resistance to a French army column – when on the very same day, June 6, the inhabitants of Valdepeñas in La Mancha, and the villagers of Santa Cruz de Mudela, sixty kilometres to the south, were successfully fighting the tail of General Dupont's column marching on Andalucía. And this without the sometent tradition or the advantages of terrain which the Catalan volunteers enjoyed. In Valdepeñas, with a population of about twelve thousand, the inhabitants rose to prevent six hundred fresh cavalry en route to join Dupont's column from entering their town, strewing the main street with nails, sharp irons and ropes hidden under sand to bring down the horses. As the vanguard cavalrymen fell, they were shot, and hit with stones, bricks and boiling water, suffering considerable casualties. The commanding French general attacked the town from the side streets, setting fire to eighty or more houses as he went and massacring many of their inhabitants. Finally, the local authorities and the general agreed a truce; but, having learned their lesson, the French retreated northwards in the direction opposite to which they were marching.[94] In Santa Cruz, where Dupont had left a detachment of four hundred soldiers to guard food supplies he had stored there, the parish priest subsequently claimed that one hundred French had been killed and the same number of prisoners taken, along with one hundred and fifty supply carts.[95]

---

* The most persistent and innocuous myth of the first Bruch battle is that a sometent drummer-lad beating out military tattoos led the imperial forces to believe that regular Spanish infantry was about to attack them, and caused their flight. The fact that the lad joined the struggle only three hours before the imperials' final retreat undermines the myth. However, another drummer and an ex-cavalry bugler were also among the sometent. If any of these might have deceived the French it was most likely to have been the latter.

THE VILLAGERS' RISING

The Catalan township and village risings put in sharp relief an important element of the rest of the Spanish risings. These, as has been seen, were initially and exclusively confined to major towns and cities. The urban population's anger, defiance and desire for vengeance would, however, have remained a minority affair – and would almost certainly have been put down by the French – had the villagers not joined it, transforming it into a majority nationwide insurrection. As in Cataluña, this made it physically impossible for the French military to occupy the entire country: they could control the principal towns, but not simultaneously all of the 6,500 townships, villages and hamlets disseminated over the face of Spain.[96] The Napoleonic army marched fast, and was usually on the move, but it did not have the technological means to engage in distant surprise attacks. Patriot spies, whether through loose tavern talk or direct observation, were usually able to discover where a column was marching to. Even at the height of Napoleon's military intervention from October 1808 to October 1812, when three hundred thousand imperial troops or more were stationed in Spain, they could not totally control even the northern part of the country.[97]

Villagers' participation in the resistance to Napoleon was therefore a crucial element of the patriotic struggle. In effect, as the majority of the population, it was they who had to bear the brunt of the fighting, the brunt of exactions, intimidations and terror to extract the one element essential to both sides which only they could provide: food supplies. The control of the latter became one of the strategic elements in the war: much of the ensuing patriot guerrilla struggle revolved around them. With the exception of places on the imperial army's direct line of march, as was the case of Valdepénas in the Mancha (see above), or close to urban insurrectionary centres, villages and rural townships did not generally rise until they were incited by envoys from the capital and ordered to form juntas or had news of the capital's rising. This in itself was hardly surprising: a single village rising made little but dangerous sense to even the most ardent Fernandista. All the same, it may be wondered whether villagers would have risen at all had it not been for the example they were set by the urban centres. Indeed at least one village found the latter's example sufficient reason not to rise: the local authorities of Pedroches de Córdoba wrote to the Consejo de Castilla that they refused to comply with the the the Sevilla junta's appeal to revolt and call a general enlistment, collect arms and munitions, gather funds from persons of law and order; they would only obey the previous orders received from Murat via the Consejo:

> This village is tranquil. The revolution which has begun in Sevilla and Córdoba, and this village's invasion by tumultuous troops, leaves us defenceless, without means to resist. We can only flee, be devastated or suffer death rather than be disloyal to [Murat's] sacred orders . . .[98]

However, after the Córdoba junta's formation and its formal declaration that the Bayonne royal abdications were annulled, the Pedroches authorities changed their minds and adhered to the patriot cause.[99]

Such a case was exceptional. But villagers' impassivity in the face of events was notewothy. In Jerez de los Caballeros, Extremadura, at the news both of the May 2 Madrid events and Fernando VII's subsequent forced abdication, the local priest tried in vain twice to arouse the villagers to action, even to the point of scattering money at their feet.* A random sample of the reaction of other villages and rural townships illuminated their uncertainty about the wisdom of rising, though it must be observed that the reports came from Fernandistas determined to prove their own patriotism and loyalty.

Fortuna, an isolated township of some 4,500 inhabitants about thirty kilometres north-east of Murcia, existed largely on self-subsistence agriculture. The provincial capital, under the impact of the Cartagena rising of May 23, had itself risen the following day and set up a junta on May 25. Three days later the Fortuna justice wrote to the Murcia junta that the inhabitants had had to 'suffer in silence',

> until last night when the storm broke with a fury that all the town's respectable people could hardly contain. It still continues but with welcome signs that it will shortly be directed . . . to that indispensable fire of valiant self-sacrifice to the last breath.[100]

If Fortuna villagers had 'suffered in silence', the relatively isolated town of Villanueva de la Serena, about thirty kilometres from the Madrid–Mérida highway in Extremadura, had not 'moved' until in the first days of June a cavalry captain dispatched by the Sevilla junta reached the town with the 'laudable aim of raising the people against the common enemy'. This was all the more remarkable because, on receiving the news of the Madrid May 2 rising, the township had ordered a general enlistment of men and arms in its district to go to the capital's aid. The town's inhabitants swore not to obey any of Murat's orders. All of this Villanueva had done on its own initiative, 'without receiving any superior orders'. In May, then, it seemed as though the town's district 'desired nothing more than to break with the French'.[101] Although the Extremaduran capital, Badajoz, rose on May 30, Villanueva remained passive until the Sevillan emissary aroused them, and the authorities, in his presence, swore allegiance to Fernando VII. On June 5, in response to a request from the newly installed Badajoz junta to send all available horses – possibly the first communication Villanueva had received from it – the town assembled in three hours sixty-one horses and riders who were sent off to the regional capital.[102]

Of another isolated Extremaduran village the Rev. José Blanco left an indelible account. He had escaped from Madrid in mid-June with a friend in a mule-drawn wagon to return to his native Sevilla to take part in the patriot cause, and had reached Almaráz, which was famous only for its bridge which spanned the river Tajo. Here he was informed by the local magistrate of what had happened when the village rose. The inhabitants, armed with whatever

* See Chapter 3, pp. 74–5.

weapons they had been able to collect, including sickles, pickaxes and similar farming implements, had gathered in front of his house. He came out to meet them and asked what they wanted.

> 'We wish, Sir, to kill somebody,' said the spokesman of the insurgents. 'Someone has been killed in Truxillo; one or two at Badajoz, another at Merida, and we will not be left behind our neighbours. Sir, we will kill a traitor.' As this commodity could not be procured in the village, it was fortunate for us that we did not make our appearance at a time when the good people of Almaraz might have made us a substitute on whom to display their loyalty.[103]

The outlandish reasons for this village's rising confirmed the emulatory nature – in this case only for the worst of reasons – of many villagers' willingness to participate in and support the urban insurrection. There was nothing here (if Blanco's report was to be believed) of rising for religion, king and fatherland.

To return to the Mediterranean coast, Orihuela, in southern Alicante, was exceptional in being the first to rise in the province. Closer to Murcia than to the city of Alicante, news of the Cartagena insurrection reached Orihuela on May 24.[104] An economically declining agrarian town of about five thousand inhabitants with a high percentage of hidalgos and clerics, impoverished artisans, smallholders who had been reduced to renters or landless day labourers and beggars, and where an old landed oligarchy was bitterly engaged in fighting off the attempts of nouveau riche farmers to take political control, Orihuela could fairly be said to be suffering the Old Regime's social crisis.[105] Even one of its past splendours, the university, had been closed down. In the words of one of the local town hall's penmen, the inhabitants' 'faces gave clear proof of the real feelings which had taken hold of their hearts. They were like lambs which have lost their mothers, like lions which feel themselves maltreated.'

Unable to resist the authorities' apparent acceptance of Napoleon's takeover, the people's silence was at last broken by news of their king's abdication, and on the afternoon of May 24 they issued a proclamation claiming their sovereign, 'with a barely contained desire for vengeance on the usurpers and in defence of religion and the fatherland . . .'

> Our decision to take up arms was ratified by a growing number of inhabitants, although some of those engaged on their agricultural tasks were, in accord with the orders given, excused from doing so.[106]

The most notable element in these various local reports was the townships' original silence and lethargy in front of the extraordinary events which were shaking Spain. Whether or not these towns' inhabitants were silent because they were repressing a rage that only their faces mutely expressed it is impossible to know; but if it were so they were not prepared, before their own capitals had given them the lead, to act on their anger, as did the Catalan inhabitants of similar-sized towns. But then, the latter included large numbers of artisans and unemployed workers who were facing an immediate French military threat, something that none of the almost totally rural or coastal towns' inhabitants cited here had yet to confront.

There was, however one very good material reason why the rural population remained silent and not easily distracted from their daily concerns: in the fields stood the best wheat crop of the first eight years of the new century. Here was relief at last from the dearth of 1803–05. This bounty had to be harvested and the grain brought safely in. Neither the smallholder nor landowner, neither the small renter nor farmer, was prepared to see this crop jeopardized by a war which would inevitably leave the countryside short of hands; it was to this without doubt that the Orihuela statement referred in 'excusing' those engaged on agricultural tasks from publicly affirming their patriotism.*

In conclusion, it was highly doubtful that the countryside would have risen when it did had it not been for the urban population's action. That the latter's insurrection was supported by the rural – basically for the same three reasons: religion, king and fatherland – saved the passionate urban response from isolation and almost certain destruction.

THE RISINGS' POPULAR OPPONENTS

The Pedroches de Córdoba situation illustrated one often-overlooked aspect of the rising: the insurrection was not as unanimously supported as is still sometimes put about. In a couple of Aragón townships, for example, dissidence was openly expressed. In Borja, Major General Eugenio Navarro, who had turned down the command offered to him by the original Zaragoza conspirators, criticized at a town council meeting what had taken place in the Aragonese capital 'and spoke long in his attempt to dissuade attendance at the Aragonese Cortes' summoned by Palafox. Other military men appeared to share his view. The local authorities viewed the rising 'with small honour and coldness', reported a Dominican friar who argued in its favour at the meeting.[107]

In Mallén, seven of the township's more distinguished inhabitants gathered each afternoon on benches in the main square and spoke openly of the fact that 'they would be happy to live under the Napoleonic code' and that it was 'foolishness for Zaragoza and other provincial capitals to rise, that they should remain tranquil and obey the Grand Duke of Ber [sic], and a thousand other expressions against Spain and the patria'. The effect, wrote an informant, was to 'cool down the inhabitants' ardour to take arms against the French'.[108]

Some individuals were even more violent about their beliefs. In the small Catalan village of Conques, near Tremp, Juan Castejón, 'a man of very bad conduct', spoke out openly in Napoleon's favour and uttered 'outrageous'

---

* A pertinent confirmation was afforded by the captain general of Andalucía's call on the Cádiz populace *not* to rise. He argued that, after England – an 'enemy of insatiable lust for lucre which threatens our coasts' – the good harvest was the second 'gravest disadvantage' to a rising. '*After many a poor crop, Providence has sent us an abundant harvest, which will meet all our needs. Should, we now leave it, abandon it entirely, by calling to arms all the robust young men who are needed to harvest it?*' (Stress added: General Solano's May 18 edict in full in Mirtilo Sicuritano, 1814, pp. 206–12.)

expressions against Fernando. He said he hoped the French would take all of Spain.

> He is a man without religion, the proof of which is his saying that religion and clergy are unnecessary, prejudicial to Spain. He has terrified the people by telling them their cause cannot win . . . threatened many villagers with a loaded fowling piece, and insulted them . . . His son, who is barely twelve, is no better. He threatened to hit the senior town councillor, broke María Pla Casada's head, and pointed a pistol at Buenaventura Puig. (Letter from the Conques senior councillor, Pedro Cudés and two others to junta superior de Cataluña, November 16, 1808).

These few dissident voices could not be considered conclusive evidence of widespread disaffection with the insurrection in the moments immediately afterwards. But they were a reminder that it existed in townships and villages across the land. And when it was recalled that most of the old authorities were similarly inclined, even if they joined the patriotic cause once declared, and that many more people no doubt kept their opinions to themselves, secret dissidence in the insurrectionary zones may have been greater than is generally thought. Many may have found themselves in Rev. Blanco's position:

> I knew only too well my country's moral and intellectual situation to feel optimistic about the popular insurrection's favourable outcome . . . I never for a moment doubted the justice of the national cause, nor justified the form in which Napoleon changed the Spanish dynasty. The only thing I doubted was the usefulness of a popular rising. But since the rising had taken place I was prepared to defend the Spanish cause against France at whatever risk to myself.[109]

INSURRECTIONARY REPRESSION

With the exception of Valencia, the insurrection was not excessively bloody.* Some fifty Spaniards – corregidores, senior military officers, functionaries, local magistrates and entrepreneurs among them – were known to have been assassinated, either for refusing to join the rising, as Godoy appointees and sympathisers, or for reasons of social vengeance. But there were certainly more whose violent deaths have gone unrecorded or not been discovered†

Although attention is usually focused on the four captain generals killed, it was the local corregidores (or governors, as they were called in the old Catalo-Aragonese kingdom where they were invariably military officers) who were the single largest category of victims, just under one-quarter of the total. Representatives of central power (and almost inevitably appointed under the Godoy regime), these were the major targets of popular hatred. And half of those assassinated were in Cataluña, Valencia and Aragón.

* The Valencia case is described in Chapter 6.
† For example, Rev. Blanco, on his escape from Madrid to Sevilla in mid-June, gave the impression that the assassinations in Extremadura were widespread. (Blanco White, 1822, pp. 430–31.)

Excluding French deaths in Valencia, Cataluña was the hardest hit region with more than one-third of the total assassinations, double the number of the next most numerous region, Castilla la Vieja.* Social vengeance was also highest in Cataluña. The victory over the Napoleonic army at the Bruch pass emboldened the sometent who, apart from a scattered military, were the only existing armed force. They took advantage of this to impose a 'sacrifice to justice and to the faith', as they themselves called it.[110]

EPISODES: CATALAN POPULAR SOCIAL REVENGE

Early on June 8, two days after the first Bruch victory, eight hundred armed sometent invaded Villafranca del Penedès with the intention of killing a number of its prominent inhabitants. The administrative centre of the district in which Igualada lay, Villafranca had been tardy in rising. The suspicions of the sometent who had fought at El Bruch, many of whom came from Igualada, were aroused by rumours that the local authorities had afforded General Chabran and his French expeditionary column a cordial welcome on their overnight halt in Villafranca as they marched on Tarragona, and had even sworn allegiance to the French cause. This motive for what was about to happen would in itself have been sufficient; but the hostility which traditionally existed between nearby towns and villages bedevilled the relations between Igualada and Villafranca, the district's two major townships. The rumours about Villafranca's reception of the French general were, in fact, false. But the sometent attack provided a forceful idea of the destruction of life and property they were prepared to wreak for social vengeance.

On hearing that the sometent were gathered outside of the town, the governor called on the commander of the Spanish Guards battalion stationed in the town to bring out his troops to maintain order. He categorically refused as did other officers. Dr Lluís Freixas, a local town councillor, whose reassuring letters three months before to his student stepson about the French invasion, was reproduced earlier was with the governor at the time. Freixas insisted that the latter go into hiding in the friary where the guards were quartered. He replied that he must first pass by his house, but would return to follow Freixas's advice.

> No sooner had I turned the corner by the confectioner Gras' house than I found myself surrounded by a disorderly mob shouting savagely, firing their arms continually, and uttering horrible death threats. All the inhabitants, the strong and the weak alike, were terrified. I asked to speak to the sometents' leader to see if I could come to some agreement, but none of them paid attention to anything but exciting horror in all and sundry . . . They pointed their shotguns at me, forcing me to leave.[111]

* These comparative figures should be taken with some caution; they may reflect only the fact that Catalan local historical research is more developed than in most other regions, thus more assassinations may have been discovered there than elsewhere.

One group made for the governor's house. They broke down the doors and, finding his wife in the garden, shot her dead where she sat with her two lapdogs. Then they sacked the house, lit a great fire in the street outside and burned everything: clothes, jewels, furniture and all the governor's papers. 'And what they didn't burn they stole.'

> Then they made for the house of [his secretary] Garrigó. They maltreated him and then killed him. They burnt all his belongings, even the clothes from his corpse on which they inflicted a thousand sword cuts. Then they threw his naked corpse into the flames.

They found the governor in a lady's house and the leaders seized him and shot him immediately in the street. After that they went to the magistrate's home but he had hidden under vine prunings or wheat sheaves in the next door granary. They burnt all his possessions. That same night, he escaped, disguised as a Trinitarian friar, but after various mishaps they found him close to Monistrol de Noya (a village about fifteen kilometres distant) still dressed as a friar, and shot him, too.

The sometent went after eleven other men. Three of them were tax farmers of the special impost, imposed by Godoy in 1805,* one of them a merchant, another a saddler and harness maker. A fourth man was the attorney in charge of this impost who was at the heart of 'all those disreputable troubles'.[112] Two other attorneys and the town hall scrivener were also hunted down. (The others' occupations were not noted.) All of them managed to escape with their lives if not their possessions which were burnt, with the exception of a couple of the pursued who saw to it that the sometent were paid large sums of money. The massacre might thus have been very much greater but for these eleven men's escape. Even so, the violence had one final touch that confirmed its underlying motives. Many local men joined the sometent, wrote Freixas, and they forced their way into the town hall and broke open the room where the land registry papers were stored and destroyed them all.

However, the attack also had its patriotic side. Under threat of death, the sometent obliged all inhabitants immediately to put on red cockades; and ordered all mule owners to bring their animals to the Rambla where, it could be be assumed, many of the mules were expropriated for the sometents' war aims. Throughout the whole of the day the church bells never stopped sounding the alarm. Finally late in the evening, Freixas succeeded in getting the sometent captains to meet him and come to an agreement whereby peace was restored for the night. The sometent were given – or took – all the meat, wine, rice, dried

---

* This impost of 3.3% collected for the Royal Treasury was on agricultural products which had previously been free of tax, such as charcoal, firewood, vegetables, pumpkins and the like.

cod and other provisions held in the shops or private houses to satisfy their stomachs. Meanwhile Freixas spent the night giving orders and arranging for two cannon to be sent from Sitges to defend the town against Chabran's return which the town councillor judged, correctly, was inevitable after General Schwartz's defeat at the Bruch.

Scenes of such violence, it must be said, were quite exceptional.* The explanation may perhaps lie in the diary of a well-to-do farmer living close by. Isidre Mata del Racó i Mir recorded that the sometent were led by a theology student, a 'slightly hunchbacked learned little lad from Barcelona', Joseph Marimon by name. Ordained only in the first four minor orders of the priesthood,† he was the son of an elementary schoolteacher. 'When this land was quiet again and there was a government, the said Marimon was tried for having seized the governor . . . but because he was of the minor priesthood he was sentenced only to banishment in Tarragona for eight years.'[113]

In some regions, most notably Asturias, the rising was bloodless – though only by a hair's breadth. Three ranking military officers, who had been ordered by Murat to put down the Oviedo insurrection, and two notable civilian emissaries dispatched for the same purpose, were seized by a crowd of raw recruits, tied to trees in the Campo de San Francisco outside the city walls and were about to be shot when a cathedral canon, with the host in his hands, managed in extremis to save their lives.[114] The total number of French victims outside of Valencia was far lower than those of Spaniards: only eighteen were recorded killed, twelve of whom were hospitalized French soldiers massacred in a particularly brutal incident in Manzanares.[115] The local juntas' rapid incarceration of French residents to protect them, and the intervention of priests carrying 'that powerful charm',[116] the consecrated host, saved a great number of their lives. In Jerez de la Frontera, for example, the local priest bearing the host brought to a temporary halt the threatened massacre of French merchants and their families which was finally ended by the expedient of letting loose a number of fighting bulls to run through the streets to distract the mob from their murderous intent.[117]

* They are reminiscent rather of the early days of the revolution at the start of the Spanish Civil War in 1936.
† Known as 'clérigos de menores' ('clerics of minor orders'), these had taken only the first four of the seven orders necessary to become a priest, of which the last three, including the vow of celibacy, were the most important. The number of these minor clerics was considerable, indicating religious or material doubts about their destiny as fully-fledged priests.

5

New Self-Government: The Juntas

THE MILITARY, CLERGY AND TITLED NOBILITY IN THE SEAT OF POWER

With apparently surprising unanimity, all the major insurrections resulted in the immediate creation of juntas. Yet it was only superficially surprising that this should be so, for in the new situation created by the risings, a new form of government independent of French-controlled Madrid had to be found; and the junta was an historically accepted institutional response to resolve matters of urgency, whether at local or state level. The insurrection's organizers and leaders were filling a local power vacuum which their rising had created; and local township juntas sprang up throughout the insurrectional zone.

The similarity of the juntas' early proclamations was perhaps more surprising. The events of the last four months, however, had been so dramatic that reminders of Godoy's despotism, Napoleon's perfidious betrayal, the forced and illegal abdication of their new young king, and the threatened French despotism inevitably filled many pages. As a proclamation of the Orihuela junta had it:

> Valiant Spaniards, the Fatherland's independence, its institutions, the sacred religion we profess and the preservation of our king, lives and property call us imperiously to arms. . . . A traitor to the country [Godoy] has placed us before the harsh choice of being subjugated by a perfidious ally or of taking up arms in defence of our independence and rights. What Spaniard can doubt the side he should take? None surely.[1]

Exhortations to take up arms, the war's justification – which now included the preservation of lives and property – the need for union, the defence of the fatherland, the call to God and the appeal to the rich to demonstrate their patriotism were further themes pursued by many juntas' proclamations:

> To Arms! To Arms! . . . Victory or death! . . . Is it not better to die arms in hand on the field of honour defending our unhappy Monarch, our homes, our sons and wives

than to die a vile and ignominious slave's death? . . . Do you want fetters on your feet and manacles on your hands? To be taken off forcibly to remote climes beyond the Pyrenees? . . . Let us invoke the God of the Armies . . . For our cause is just and God will lead and support us . . . We fight in defence of Religion, the Fatherland, our Laws and King . . . A people resolute and united, is never defeated . . . Landowners, merchants, the wealthy, show your generosity by contributing liberally to the homeland's common needs . . . War is a lesser evil than peace, only this terrible means can save us . . .[2]

Two new words, had begun to enter patriot language: *Independence* and *Revolution*. Alongside the earlier 'freedom' or 'liberty' and sometimes replacing them, the first word signified independence *from* any foreign domination, Napoleon's in particular, and Spain's secondary role in the long prior French connection, though it would also apply to Spain's new ally, Britain. But depending on context it also meant independence from the 'despotism' of a royal favourite, first minister or government. As a result, it took on an additional meaning: independence . . . not just *from*, but *to* put in place the necessary reforms to prevent any such recurrence and, in the progressives' minds, to create a new constitutional monarchy.

The significance of the word 'revolution' was if anything more complex, since all and sundry came to use it, giving to it their particular shades of meaning. As a catchword, 'our Glorious Revolution', for example, could be interpreted as each wished. For the absolutists, revolution maintained its original sense, a complete turn of the celestial sphere to its original starting point:[3] as the heavens turned in their orbit, things changed so that everything might finally remain unchanged, with the sole exception of disbarring 'despotism' for ever. But to the progressives it signified a political (but not social) revolution: an institutional rupture with Bourbon centralism and its organs of power, and their replacement by new forms of government.*

The rupture with the Old Regime's institutions was a fact. In the insurrectionary zone, only four of the eight captain generals, the most important regional authority, remained in place, indeed alive, after June. And these had lost most of their former power to the juntas. The highest body in the land, the Consejo de Castilla, had been delegitimized because it had temporized with the French. Other leading institutions – the audiencias and intendentes, for example – continued to exist but their *de facto* role was shortly reduced: the rupture went deep but it was not a revolutionary break.

Apart from the need to fill the power vacuum, the rapidity with which the juntas were created responded to the Fernandistas' need to be seen to be

---

* It seems doubtful that the words 'Independence' and 'Revolution' were taken over from the American War of Independence. Compared to her ally France, Spain's intervention in that war, and its impact on the country, had been minimal; moreover a Republic was not generally envisaged as a solution to Spain's problems. In any event, what was missing in the Spanish case was an equivalent of the American Declaration of Independence which stated to what political ends the Independence that had resulted from the Revolution was aimed at.

forming 'patriotic' local governments satisfactory to the people in order to ensure the existing social order's continuing stability and to put an end to any further street commotions that might threaten it. To reinforce the fact that the risings had not changed, and would not change, the social status quo, many of the more important juntas selected their members as representatives of the Old Regime's three estates (expanded to include the military, and sometimes various classes of commoners, as in Valencia's case). Needless to say, the juntas' members were, with only one known exception, appointed, not elected; the need for speed made any other procedure unviable, the leaders claimed.

The major juntas then were the direct outcome of the risings, but they were not a direct emanation of these. That is to say, they did not generally spring from or – even less – represent the insurrectionists in the streets, and if they made a gesture towards doing so, it was only tangentially and in minority form. This disjuncture between rising and junta was determined by the insurrections themselves, in which the people had either yielded leadership of their movement to their Fernandista social superiors or the latter had to all intents and purposes controlled the rising from the start.

Having succeeded in displacing if not overthrowing the old authorities, the Fernandista leaders however lacked the conviction of their own political weight to govern local and regional affairs. They needed, they felt, a good dosage of the old authorities in the juntas for these to command their regions' respect. It made no difference that these authorities had until yesterday obeyed Madrid's orders and done their utmost to prevent the rising: their titles were known and respected and would ensure that the juntas were obeyed. All the juntas considered the presence of local royal officials and municipal councillors indispensable – to such an extent, indeed, that these on average together formed the largest single block – forty percent – of members of the first juntas created.*

Two other social groupings, new not to the exercise of power, but to the direct tasks of government, were also important in reinforcing the juntas' authority: the military and the clergy. The military overall occupied nearly one-fifth of the first junta seats; and their presence was even higher in garrison towns where they had participated in the rising. They were obviously necessary to plan their region's defence against the imminent French attacks which the juntas feared – rarely did they imagine being able to go on the offensive to pre-empt the attack – and in non-garrison towns junta members were often military engineers and fortification experts.

The clergy's share of junta seats was the highest after municipal and provincial government representatives, nearly a quarter of the total number on average. They included the whole gamut of the Church hierarchy, from archbishops to parish priests who, unlike the religious orders, had in general adopted a vacillating attitude towards the change of monarchy. It was rather the religious orders which were violently opposed to the Bonaparte regime, as they

---

* For a detailed examination of 29 of the first juntas' nearly six hundred members in a comparative regional context, see Appendix 2, Table 2.1. I am grateful to Richard Hocquellet for allowing me to consult his doctoral thesis on the juntas from which much of this information is derived.

had been to the French Revolution, for the friars foresaw their own demise under a Napoleonic monarchy; the abolition of their friaries was equivalent in their minds to the demise of religion in Spain, and so to the demise of Spain *tout court*. However, it was not they who formed a clear majority of the clerical representatives, but canons who occupied a high rank in the traditional urban hierarchy of authority.

Finally, the juntas co-opted about ten percent of their number from local elites, almost exclusively from the upper and lower nobility. Nearly half of these were grandees and titled nobility. The top ranks of nobles thus made a return to power from which half a century of absolutist Bourbon reformism had virtually excluded them by turning them into court functionaries.

Those absent from the juntas were equally significant. Merchants, for example, formed a paltry two percent overall; on average, the labouring classes fared slightly better – nineteen members, compared to the merchants' thirteen, out of a total of 597 – but this was mainly due to their relatively high participation in Catalan and Valencian juntas.

SUPREME AUTHORITY:
THE ASSUMPTION OF POPULAR SOVEREIGNTY

Very shortly, if not immediately, the juntas took to themselves the title of 'supreme' in their regions (with the exception of Sevilla which, voluntaristically, declared itself supreme over all of Spain and the Indies), and assumed sovereign powers. They justified the latter on two overlapping political scores. In the first place, their 'legitimate' king's (and his family's) forced and thus illegal abdication, and the juntas' readiness to fight to restore Fernando VII to his throne, allowed them to assume a delegated sovereignty in the king's name until he should return. This, however, was the lesser of the two political justifications. The major reason, with its historical roots in the widely accepted theory of the 'social pact'* was that, deprived of a ruling monarch, sovereignty devolved on the people; and by rising, the people had demonstrated their sovereign will, which, subsequently, they had bestowed on the juntas. The effects of this legalistic sleight of hand depended on the interpretation given to the word sovereignty: in the absolutist view, which predominated despite the political rupture, the people had risen for Fernando VII, and the juntas' sovereignty was no more than temporary until the king should be restored to his throne.† In the minority progressive view, the risings had instituted a popular sovereignty (that's to say, the sovereignty of those with property qualifications) subject only unto itself and the need for a constitution.

In either case, Spain was again split into its constituent kingdoms and regions, each of them autonomous and sovereign. It was not now the state, but the individual juntas which declared war on Napoleon, negotiated treaties with Britain, raised armies, took over state and municipal funds and communal

* See Chapter 2, p. 51.
† See, for example, the Bishop of Orense's letter refusing to participate in Napoleon's constitutional congress in Bayonne, cited in Chapter 3, pp. 76–7.

property to attempt to finance their war effort, and expropriated French-owned property. Always short of money, the juntas tried to make good the remainder with new taxes, forced loans, donations – and some of them with British subsidies. But this is not to say that the juntas lived in splendid regional isolation. On the contrary, once the insurrection's nationwide nature became known, they corresponded with enthusiastic frequency, passing on proclamations, reports, letters, and edicts from other juntas as well as their own. All the maritime regions from the Cantabrian coast (Asturias and Galicia in the van) to Andalucía, Levante and Cataluña immediately understood the need of communicating the news of their rising to Britain through any means that came to hand: sending deputations to London, contacting patrolling British naval vessels, approaching privateers to take their messages to British commanders, dispatching emissaries to the British military authorities in Gibraltar. They sought, and signed, armistices and peace treaties, and asked for money and arms to support their war effort. The Spanish adage, 'War with every land – but peace with England' was being put into effect.*

THE JUNTAS' WAR EFFORT: A STATE OR NATIONAL WAR?

Against whom and for what aims were the juntas preparing to wage war? A question, surely, which admitted of only one answer. In fact, however, the answer to the question was not as obvious as it appeared. Only two days after the rising, the Sevilla junta published a long proclamation in which it rehearsed all the usual arguments against Napoleon's 'perfidious' actions. It then continued:

> There is no revolution in Spain. Nor do we declare war on anyone. Our sole objective is to defend what we hold most sacred and of which [Napoleon], under the pretext of an alliance and friendship, has attempted to deprive us. It is to be feared that unless we fight, he will strip us totally of our laws, monarchs and religion.[4]

The strategy behind the statement's somewhat diffuse logic was actually fairly simple. By *not* declaring war, by claiming that *no* revolution had taken place, it furnished Napoleon with no new grounds for further intervention in Spanish affairs. At the same time the proclamation, and the juntas' mass enlistment, showed the Emperor that the Spanish were *prepared* to fight to defend their 'sacred rights' if he continued to pursue his present policies. It was the *threat of war* and *the dangers* of such a course that was aimed at deterring Napoleon. All of Europe, moreover, would come to Spain's aid, especially those nations

---

* This saying must be understood in its particular context. An alliance with France automatically meant war with England. As long as the latter was Spain's major enemy, the British navy could – and had – cut off communications between the metropolis and South America, doing great damage to Spanish colonial trade. Spain's 1808 insurrectional rupture with France and alliance with Britain meant the possibility of Spain's renewing this trade, but it did not mean that Spaniards were any the less suspicious of British intentions in South America. (Vilar, 1982, p. 175.)

suffering under Napoleon's 'harsh Empire' and who saw the possibility of recovering their freedom, the proclamation insisted. Finally, the French people themselves would reject the 'infamy' of becoming the instrument 'of such horrible perfidy', or of shedding blood 'for so vile a cause'. To those who might reasonably doubt the possibility of defeating French military power in the field – the majority of junta members most probably – such a policy made sense. The statement's purpose was an attempt to achieve the insurrection's aims without having to go to war, but it was also an illusory strategy, based on the idealistic conviction that Spain's cause was as 'just' in the eyes of all nations as it was in God's sight.*

A war against Napoleon was a different matter to a war against the French people. The former implied a war of state against state (in as far as a junta could claim now to represent the state), an eighteenth-century-style war in which high dynastic, territorial and diplomatic interests were at stake and which did not involve the people other than as conscripts. The second option, of nation against nation, the Spanish against the French people, meant the type of people's war which the French Revolution had introduced. The juntas had little or no desire to engage in the latter: its outcome might result in an 'uncontrollable' revolution of the sort they most feared. While the hope persisted that the French people would reject the Emperor's 'perfidious' policies, it could only be counterproductive to antagonize the former by declaring war on them. 'It is not a war of nation against nation. Our concern is only to protect ourselves from a tyrant's oppression', declared the Catalan junta of Vich on June 11.[5] The Galician junta went further. Only a few days after requiring that all French persons in Galicia swear fealty to Fernando VII and confiscating all property belonging to those who remained 'Napoleon's vassals' – common enough junta measures – the junta quite uniquely rescinded all confiscations. 'The war is against Napoleon, not against the French people', the proclamation stated.[6] 'The enlightened and generous French' had not participated in the 'abominable and deceitful breach of faith committed by their tyrant'.[7]

Barely a week after Sevilla's original proclamation stating that there was 'no revolution', and that it was declaring war on no one, the junta changed tack and, in the name of Fernando VII and the Spanish nation, which it claimed to represent, declared war by land and sea. On whom?

The Emperor Napoleon I, and on France while the latter remains under his domination and tyrannical yoke. We order all Spaniards to act in consequence and to do them all possible damage, according to the rules of War . . . We shall, moreover, not lay down our arms until the Emperor Napoleon I restores our King Fernando VII and all the remaining Royal Family to Spain, respects the Nation's

* 'The cause we defend is just, God supports and leads it, our enemy will be destroyed.' (Cartagena proclamation, n.d., in Delgado, 1979, p. 43). 'Our cause is just . . . Heaven has declared in our favour; the most portentous triumph will gloriously crown our endeavours.' (Lérida junta proclamation, n.d. in *Demostración de la lealtad*, 1808, vol. 1, pp. 170–172.)

sacred rights which he has violated, its freedom, territorial integrity and independence.[8]

What had caused the junta's change? In the intervening week, Sevilla had received news of other juntas arming and preparing for war.* Furthermore, General Dupont's expeditionary column, marching from Madrid to Cádiz, was threatening Córdoba; and the junta had learned that another, smaller French-led column due to join him from Portugal had been ordered to fall on Sevilla.[9] In these circumstances the earlier strategy was of dubious value, and a more vigorous junta statement was evidently called for.

The Sevilla declaration coincided to the day with the first civilian victories over the imperial military at the Bruch pass in Catalonia and in La Mancha. In the Puerto del Rey pass in the Sierra Morena, the access route from Castilla la Nueva to Andalucía, five thousand Andalucians had gathered under the leadership of a local township justice, who had raised the force at his own expense, to cut off Dupont's supplies travelling down the main road from Madrid. The number of men was no doubt exaggerated. But on June 7 there were sufficient to capture a supply train, killing a general, his aide-de-camp, and a colonel, and taking thirty-four prisoners. The rest of the escort was put to flight.[10] A people's war, outside of direct military command, was already a fact; but it would always remain for the new authorities a disputable fact as they tried, and generally succeeded, to bring it under control.

But on one aspect of the conflict all could agree: it was a defensive war. If Napoleon restored Fernando VII to the throne – renouncing his brother as the new monarch – withdrew his troops from Spain, relinquished the right to intervene in the country's domestic affairs and left reform of the country to Spaniards well aware of its need, there would be no cause to fight. In other words, Spanish resistance was aimed at restoring the country's situation to a moment prior to Napoleon's intervention in its affairs.

These aims limited to Spain alone were not usually understood by Britain, Spain's new ally in the anti-Napoleonic conflict. Britain was involved in a struggle with France for world hegemony, and Napoleon's overthrow was essential to this. Patriot Spain was concerned in ridding itself of the Bonapartist regime which the Emperor had imposed; what happened to Napoleon once this objective had been achieved was of far less concern to it. These different objectives led to many of the misunderstandings between the new allies.

The one Spanish objective – the important exception unmentioned in most of the early manifestos – which did bear on global interests rather than the merely domestic, was defence of the South American colonies and of Spain's monopolistic trading rights with them. The more perspicacious patriots were fearful of both the Emperor's and Britain's intentions on this score, for both pressured Spain to open its colonies' ports to their trade.

---

* The Asturian junta had also in its first session on May 25 formally declared war on 'Napoleon, Emperor of the French, and on all his allies' (Álvarez Valdés, 1889/1988, p. 74, and appendix 10, Article 8, p. 274).

We do not believe that [Bonaparte] is unaware that if he persists in his plans, the absolute loss of our's and all Europe's patrimony in the Americas will be inevitable. New, different dynasties will arise [in the colonies] which will become formidable and independent of their former metropolitan powers. Britain will acquire a preponderance over them that it has never previously enjoyed.[11]

The anonymous writer's perceptions were correct. To counter Napoleon's growing hold over Spain in the first half of 1808, and his feared control over her vast Empire, Britain planned to break Spain's colonial power by fostering and aiding independence movements in her colonies.[12] Britain's last-minute evacuation to Brazil of Portugal's regent in 1807 was already bringing her considerable advantages in the right of direct trade with Brazil when the regent threw open his ports to ships of friendly nations. In short, Napoleon's direct intervention in Spain was inciting Britain's direct intervention in her colonies; Spain had nothing to gain and everything to lose from either of the world rivals' policies. The Spanish insurrections, however, changed the scenario. In place of the Spanish colonies, Britain's immediate intervention would now take place in metropolitan Spain and, to an even greater extent, in Portugal.

THE JUNTAS AND BRITISH AID

The maritime juntas closest to Britain or Gibraltar – Asturias, Galicia and Sevilla – were those whose deputies reached London the earliest. The two Asturian deputies set sail on a British privateer on May 30. When they reached the Admiralty on June 6, astonished officials had to search a map for Asturias's location; but a few days later the deputies had secured the British government's agreement to provide financial and military assistance to the region. In the meantime they were wildly applauded and feted wherever they made public appearances. Soon Britain had signed similar agreements with two other insurgent provinces, others following on later.[13]

The early birds caught the worm. All the envoys asked for at least five million Spanish dollars* (about £1m) for each of their regions. Foreign Secretary Canning told them Britain would send 'as much specie and arms as she could spare'. Before the end of summer Britain had provided £1,100,000 (about sixty-six million reales)† in what, formally, were loans to be repaid after the war, to

---

* The dollar was worth fifteen reales. At the start of the war the £ sterling's value varied between four to five dollars (sixty to seventy-five reales). (Sherwig, 1969, p. 198 fn. 41.) Until Pitt's death in 1806, Britain had relied on large European trade credits to subsidize foreign troops (at £12.10s a head armed and in the field) to do its continental land fighting. Napoleon's Continental system, however, put an end to the trade credits as a source of subsidy, obliging Britain to rely heavily on the export of specie to implement its foreign military aid. Because of this difficulty, Britain adopted the policy of sending arms and supplies rather than money. (Sherwig, 1969 pp. 182 and 198.)

† To set this figure in context, the Valencia junta spent about sixty-seven million reales to maintain an army of some thirty thousand during the first year of the war, and a further 2.5m reales for the navy. (*Manifiesto que hace la Junta Superior de Valencia*, 1809, Appendix 15. I have deducted funds received from the Junta Suprema and passed on to other armies.)

five major juntas; and by November, 1808, had sent one hundred and sixty thousand muskets with another thirty to forty thousand to follow within a month.[14] Although this was considerably less monetary aid than the juntas had asked for, in their precarious financial state it helped to resolve the most immediately pressing problem of raising and paying armies for those fortunate enough to have secured it.

But the windfall did not seem to persuade the recipient juntas to help out other less fortunate regions. The Galician junta, for example, which received about forty percent – twenty-six million reales[15] – of the British total, rejected pleas for financial help from its Castilian and Leonese companions on the united junta they had formed, and from Ciudad Rodrigo and Cataluña.[16] As the Galician army advanced eastwards into León, it thought nothing of ordering the justice of the township of La Robla to provide the united junta with one and a half million reales. It received a tart reply:

> Neither in a single year nor in one hundred years does this township in my charge produce one and a half million reales. At most it produces two to three thousand reales a month. Your request leaves me astonished.[17]

Despite the aid received, the Galician junta maintained in November 1808 that it was broke, and the archbishop of Santiago provided one million reales to keep its army in the field.[18] A lot of money appeared in the meantime to have disappeared; it was not perhaps surprising that four respected members of the junta's treasury committee, including one of the representatives the junta had sent to Britain in search of aid, resigned in October.[19]

Other juntas, Sevilla in particular, were no less blameless in their financial conduct. But whatever they did with the money, and even if they had received none, the juntas had established one important principle: British finance, arms, uniforms and supplies had been secured without the threat of British soldiers on their soil. They had no wish to see another foreign army in Spain: they had sufficient men (theoretically) to fight the war. All they needed was money and equipment to keep them in the field. The juntas had one other immediate request of the British: that they secure the return to Spain of the nearly fifteen-thousand-strong Spanish force, under the command of marqués de la Romana, which Napoleon had demanded of Godoy and had stationed first in north Germany and subsequently in Denmark. The force included some of Spain's best troops who would be invaluable to the patriot cause. This resulted in one of the most bizarre – and ultimately successful – events of the early days of the war.

EPISODES: RESCUING ROMANA[20]

The idea of relieving Napoleon of the Spanish force had occurred to Britain before the start of the Peninsular War; but British agents had failed in their attempts. It now fell to a Scottish monk and a Catalan sub-lieutenant to make good the earlier lack of success. Of necessity, the first objective was to enter into contact with Romana and apprise him of Britain's readiness to evacuate his troops. The Spanish force had been intentionally deprived by their supreme commander, Marshal Bernadotte, of all anti-Napoleonic news from their homeland, and obliged to swear an oath to Josef Bonaparte as their new king. Like many of his military contemporaries in Spain, Romana was a general not readily prepared to burn his boats in defiance of higher authority, especially when the latter was Napoleon. But a great number of his junior officers were less cautious; and even Romana made the oath to Napoleon's brother as king of Spain contingent on his country's 'unanimous consent' to the dynastical change. In a number of the Spanish regiments there had been disturbances over the oath-taking.

On June 4, two days before the Asturian deputies reached London, the Rev. James Robertson set out on his secret mission. Robertson was an ordained priest and Benedictine monk of a Scottish abbey in Ratisbon, Germany, who had some years earlier returned to Britain. Sir Arthur Wellesley, then chief secretary to the Lord Lieutenant of Ireland, had embarked him, a fluent German-speaker, on this clandestine commission. The monk had accepted with alacrity. 'I feel the deepest interest in the cause of his [Romana's] country, because I view it not only as the cause of an oppressed people but as the cause of religion.'

The Foreign Office instructions Robertson was to convey to Romana were that British transports would carry him and his troops to any place or country he should choose. 'We ask nothing in return: we do not require that they should fight for us . . . we offer to carry them free of cost to South America, to Minorca, to Canada, to England, or to Spain, at their option.'

In the meanwhile, the Sevilla junta had sent a naval lieutenant, Rafael Lobo, to London to help organize the attempt to rescue Romana and his forces, and the various junta deputies who had reached Britain had united their efforts to the same end.

But at that moment no one had a clear idea of where Romana's troops were. They had been guarding the north German Weser and Elbe river approaches from the English, but, under pretext of invading Sweden, Napoleon had ordered them posted to the Danish islands, a move northwards to isolated stations at the moment that the Emperor was planning to depose the Spanish Bourbons. Robertson set off without any assurance of where to find Romana.

Put ashore in Heligoland, the monk encountered considerable difficulties in reaching the German coast. No traveller by road in any part of continental Europe could at the time expect to reach his destination without official harassment if not armed with a passport – a document which confirmed the traveller's identity, point of departure and arrival and the purpose of the voyage. Robertson lacked the primary necessity: a German identity. This he fabricated by adopting the name of a German acquaintance, and writing to the parish priest of the latter's birthplace who readily provided him with a copy of his baptismal certificate.

All this took but a few days, testimony to postal and priestly efficiency. Robertson, however, had still to ascertain where Romana's forces were stationed. On presenting a letter of credit to a highly respectable Hamburg merchant, the monk asked him outright. The merchant guessed why he asked. '"What, do you suppose you can outwit Bonaparte? Let me tell you he is too many for you." "We can never know unless we try," I answered. "Try! That has been sufficiently tried already. I know of three or four who have attempted to reach the army: they and their papers were seized, and I need not allude to their fate."'

Nevertheless, the merchant let drop that Romana was at Nyborg, on the Danish island of Fünen, 'a long way from here'. Electing a circuitous route to confound the Napoleonic police, the monk reached Nyborg by a combination of post-chaises and hired boats without serious incident. He took lodgings at the hotel where Romana and his staff resided; and on the morning after his arrival he sent the Spanish commander a note in French to the effect that 'a foreign merchant desired to have the honour of a private interview with his Excellency . . . in order to present to him samples of some articles he dealt in'. Before leaving Lübeck, Robertson had bought a small quantity of the best Havana cigars and a few pounds of chocolate to represent himself as a merchant. Almost immediately, he received a favourable reply, and found himself in Romana's presence, where he set about verbally establishing his credentials for, as he assured the general, he brought no papers of any kind that could compromise the Spanish commander or himself.

> Señor, you see before you a stranger who comes to put his life in your hands. I am a Catholic priest, chosen, perhaps partly on that account for the mission I am about to explain, as it was imagined that a Spaniard might be disposed to put confidence in the word of a Catholic clergyman. I am directed to your Excellency by the English Government . . .[21]

Romana, dwarf-like in stature but with a certain dignity, listened silently to Robertson's further credentials, and the message he brought. Romana remained silent. The monk trembled for his own safety. 'Is he, thought I, so weak that he shrinks from any show of difficulty? – then he may be wicked enough to sell my life to Bonaparte, merely to give him a proof of his fidelity.' Romana finally reassured him that he had nothing to fear; but continued to question him so closely that Robertson was little relieved. Nonetheless, taking courage in his hands, he said: '"Well then, General, may I beg the favour of an answer to my principal?"' '"An answer – what now? Surely you will not depart immediately!" "Certainly not, my Lord; though I came at the peril of my life, and remain at the same risk, I shall not take my departure today." "Then we shall meet again?" "Whenever your Excellency pleases."'[22]

The monk had not long to wait. After sauntering through the town as if on a business mission, he returned to the hotel to receive a message bidding the 'man with cigars' to attend on the Spanish commander. On re-entering Romana's cabinet, the monk said: '"I presume, General, I shall now have the honour of your reply?" "Sir," said he, "before I decide on your proposition, let me observe that we are utterly ignorant of what is going on in Spain. For a whole year, not one letter has been suffered to reach us." '

Robertson informed him of the Asturian and Galician risings.* ' "Asturias already has a deputation arrived in London to solicit aid and protection of our Government. The names of the Deputies are . . ." "How!" interrupted the Marquis, "these are men I know well; men of the highest influence in the country . . . But what can I do, situated as I am at present? My troops are dispersed through all the provinces and islands of Denmark . . ." "Well, Señor, if you cannot rescue all, rescue at least what portion of your force you can." "Alas! To what purpose?" answered Romana; "what can we – what can Spain do against France?"[23]

Romana refused to help the monk effect his escape; and his mission unsatisfactorily ended, Robertson took his leave and set out for the shore where, under the pretence of collecting shells and pebbles, he occasionally waved a white handkerchief to attract a British man-of-war cruising in the Belt. But it was a Danish guard's attention that he first attracted, and Robertson found himself under arrest. It took him no little ingenuity to secure his freedom.

The misadventure was a stroke of fortune, however, for on his return to the hotel he encountered Romana ascending the stairs with some of his officers. ' "Come to me – tomorrow morning – eight o'clock", the marqués half whispered over the banister in broken English . . .' At the agreed time the monk again entered his cabinet to be informed that the Spanish commander, having consulted with those of his officers in whom he placed unreserved confidence, 'had finally determined to accept the proposal of the English Government, and would immediately proceed to take his measures.' Thanking Robertson for his valuable service, he advised him to depart rapidly so as not to excite suspicion and regretted that it was not in his power to place him out of danger. Little did either man know that the monk would find no means of escape from the continent until long after Romana and his force had been returned to Spain, and even then only hotly pursued by French hussars.†

---

* This news Robertson received when in Hamburg from the British agent in Heligoland. (Robertson, 1863, p. 46.)

† Seeking means to escape, Robertson remained for a time outside Hamburg where he learned of Romana's flight. On finding it impossible to flee via the north German coast, Robertson decided to travel south, spending some time at his former convent at Ratisbon, before going to Linz and Vienna. However, when Austria declared war on Napoleon in early 1809, the monk decided, now that it was again peaceful in the north, to return there in the hope of finding an escape route to Britain. On reaching Dresden, which had just been captured by the French, his real identity became known to the police. Fleeing immediately on secondary routes whenever he could, he posted without stop via Berlin to Hamburg. Only later did he learn that, by a number of strokes of fortune, he had narrowly escaped his French hussar pursuers. But once safe in Hamburg, he had little difficulty in taking ship to Heligoland and returning to London. Although his account gives no precise date for his return, it was certainly not before the late spring of 1809, in other words a good nine months after he had set out.

Romana's sudden decisiveness sprang from a Catalan sub-lieutenant's actions rather than from the monk's persuasiveness. Lieutenant Juan Antonio Fabregue,* of the first battalion of Catalan volunteers, which formed part of Romana's force, was returning with official dispatches from Copenhagen to his post on the island of Langeland when, on close examination of the shore, he discovered a small fishermen's boat, and impetuously offered its owners a fair sum to be taken direct by sea to his station. About four leagues out in the Belt he had observed three English warships anchored; and once underway, 'in an access of patriotism, and without a second thought', he drew his sword and ordered the two fishermen to take him to the ships. A Spanish soldier accompanying him was so surprised and terrified by the order that he tried to jump into the water. One of the fishermen caught hold of the soldier's musket, while the other also prepared to resist.

> I saw now that I was in real difficulties, and I determined to kill them rather than return to land, from where my action had been observed and I was doomed. The sailors realized I was determined to sell my life dearly. A fortunate sword thrust knocked the musket from the sailor's hands. I do not know how, but I made them row towards the English ships, a white handkerchief fixed to the mast . . .[24]

The British sent out a boat to take the sub-lieutenant aboard, and he was soon transferred to the naval commander's ship. To his surprise and joy he was shown letters and dispatches for Romana which the British had no way of conveying to the general. He was asked if he would take them ashore. Though a known deserter, he volunteered and was landed by night from an English cutter on the coast of Langeland. He made his way to his commandant and from there, in disguise, to General Romana. As he later wrote:

> Everyone was amazed by the news. I myself did not know what was happening to me. The dispatches were all directed towards the objective that Romana save the division and return with it to Spain, because the present circumstances demanded it. Orders were issued to assemble the troops, and to the English to gather their ships.

Romana entered into secret negotiations with Rear Admiral Keats, the British second-in-command, on the means of taking his troops off and returning them to Spain. Meanwhile his forces on Langeland took over the island and, on August 9, the Spanish commander seized Nyborg which became the main concentration point. Four days later, nine thousand troops were evacuated by sea to Gothenburg where they awaited the British transports that would return them to Spain. Some

---

* His surname was given as such in the *Gazeta Ministerial de Sevilla*, although it was almost certainly Fábregues (as written by Toreno, 1838/1916, p. 126).

five thousand Spanish troops were left stranded, captured by French forces to whom Romana's second-in-command, Juan de Kindelan, had betrayed his superior's plans. Surrounded by a large enemy force, one Spanish cavalry captain shot himself rather than surrender.[25]

THE JUNTA ARMIES' SOCIAL COMPOSITION: VOLUNTEERS AND ENLISTED MEN

The regional juntas immediately summoned all men between the ages of sixteen and forty-five to enlist. It was a measure initially taken as much to get the insurrectionary crowd off the streets and under military discipline as to increase the existing army's strength; yet, when it came to the latter, popular enthusiasm for the cause was such that more than sufficient recruits enlisted to make good the heavily depleted strengths of most regiments, and enough men still remained to create new volunteer regiments.

One of those who volunteered was Francisco Guervos, a young Granada cathedral violinist. Little over eighteen months earlier, when he was conscripted to serve ten years in the pre-war army, he had paid a substitute to take his place; but as soon as war was declared, Guervos had not doubted a moment about joining the colours.

> I desired only to sacrifice my peace and quiet, my interests, and what is more my life, as any man must who loves his country and freedom. And the principles of religion which have been engraved on my heart similarly induced me to volunteer.[26]*

It was the only time in the war when volunteers flooded into the army in great numbers. Where did they come from? Young educated men like Guervos were obviously a minority in a country where seventy percent of the people were engaged on the land. It stood to reason that the majority of recruits must be villagers. And since day labourers and smallholders together formed the predominant rural population, they could be expected to have provided the greater part of those who enlisted. But the extremely rare enlistment rolls which record trades, occupations and professions, albeit only partially, reveal that this was not so. Two such rolls from Morón de la Frontera in western Andalucía and Igualada in Cataluña reveal that artisans who made up little more than four percent of Spain's active population, enrolled in equal numbers to agrarian workers. A third such roll from the city port of Alicante shows artisans providing the same number of men as service workers, the two largest groups to enlist. In all, over 2,000 recruits were recorded in the three rolls which were the only examples of their kind brought to light in the research for this book.†

* Guervos, who rose to captain, lived just long enough to see the final victory. War wounds and the hardships he suffered as a prisoner of war, claimed his life in 1815 when he was still in his twenties.

† Enlistment rolls generally record only names, place of residence and marital status of the labouring classes, patently revealing the Old Order's disdain of manual workers and their jobs. Those of higher social status – indicated by the title 'don' – more often than not are recorded also by profession.

Morón de la Frontera was an important town of some ten thousand inhabitants, the administrative centre of a large agrarian district sixty-five kilometres south-east of Sevilla. Here, between May 30 and June 13, 1808, 772 men were enrolled, of whom just under half were volunteers.[27]

The enlistment itself took a dramatic form. On Monday, May 30, Morón found itself invaded by nearly ninety men who had walked from the small, isolated village of Puerto Serrano, thirty-five kilometres to the south, and who clamoured to volunteer. The Morón authorities had taken no steps at that point to begin an enrolment, but their hand was forced by the new arrivals, nearly half of whom were aged between sixteen and twenty. That day, only one man from Morón – job and age unstated – volunteered. On the Tuesday, an even larger group arrived from Puerto Serrano. By the end of the day 194 men had volunteered and twenty-five had enlisted, all but eighteen of them from Puerto Serrano. The proportion of sixteen to twenty-year-olds had risen to little short of sixty percent.

On Wednesday, June 1, the last large contingent from Puerto Serrano arrived: seventy men, all but half a dozen of them volunteers. On this day the Morón inhabitants began to stir: twenty men volunteered and six enlisted. However, this was small beer compared to the effort made by Puerto Serrano: in three days this village of about one thousand inhabitants – one tenth of Morón's size – had enrolled 311 men, only one less than those eventually enlisted by Morón township. Moreover, the overwhelming majority of the Puerto Serrano men were volunteers, almost all of them between sixteen and twenty-five years old.

Who were these men? Regrettably, the Morón scribes, as was official custom at the time in regard to the lower orders, did not generally think fit to note their trades, recording those of only thirty-nine of the Puerto Serrano volunteers and ten of their enlisted. Taking both categories together, there were twenty-six day labourers and four smallholders, who outnumbered the remainder by thirty to nineteen. On this very small sample, the supposition that day labourers and smallholders formed the majority of volunteers and enlisted men appeared to be borne out. And in the Morón district as whole (as opposed to the township alone) land workers slightly outnumbered artisans.

The Morón township enrolment of 312 recruits was less inexplicably dramatic, but more socially instructive, since 182 had their trades or professions listed, seventy percent of all those in this category.[28]

Here, artisans, who formed just over ten percent of the inhabitants, provided half the recruits. Day labourers, who formed nearly half the population, provided just over ten percent of the enlisted. Only one Morón man in just under seven volunteered – compared to Puerto Serrano's five volunteers for each enlisted man. Not a single Morón landowner's name appeared among those whose professions were recorded; and only seven master craftsmen. It was their journeymen or occasional apprentice who answered the call. Again, as in Madrid during the May 2 events, journeymen shoemakers, cobblers and bricklayers formed the majority, followed by barbers and carpenters.

Why were craftsmen the largest group to enlist? The answer in part depended on another question: why were day labourers so remiss in joining up? For had they enlisted in anything like their proportion of the population, they would have largely outnumbered the craftsmen. The answer to the latter lay without doubt in the excellent harvest standing in the fields. The landowners pressed them not to answer the call, fearing that the first good wheat crop of the century would remain unreaped in the fields. And probably the labourers themselves saw the opportunity of finally securing a better day wage – or at least more day wages – by staying to reap, gather and thresh the good crop.

No other social group outdid the craftsmen in producing five times the number of recruits compared to their population percentage. Journeymen were evidently anxious about the future. While masters would always be needed, the journeymen had no certainty of becoming a master within the restrictive guild system which the latter manipulated to their own ends; and if the guilds were abolished, as seemed likely under the new Bonaparte king, the journeymen would be left to sink or swim, and most likely the former, in a world that no longer offered them any protection. In other words, they were fighting against sinking to the lowest depths of proletarianization.

However, one sector of the agrarian world enlisted in almost the same proportions to their numbers in the population as the craftsmen: tenant farmers – the *labradores*.* These were local men with the knowledge and means to farm considerable areas of land, which they rented from the nobility or large landowners. The inflationary spiral of agrarian prices, however, was bringing in new labradores – often not men of the land at all – who were prepared to pay higher rents in order to make a quick return on their investment, relegating the old labrador class to unemployment and a decline in social status. Like the journeymen, though at another level, the old type of labrador confronted the same dilemma, and saw their future as fighting to preserve the past; the new labrador as fighting to become the owner of the land.

The question of fervour to fight can be resolved without recourse to simplistic or rhetorical assertions, as has usually been the case in Spain for the last two centuries. The enrolment demonstrated quite clearly that very few recruits sought at that moment to escape army service as they had done pre-war and would again do later in the war. Both the Puerto Serrano and Morón contingents displayed surprisingly few infirmities or physical defects which would prevent them from serving. Less than twenty infirm men in all compared to the three to four and a half times that number proportionately in some pre-war enlistments. Hernias had been the most common rural affliction adduced to escape military service in the past; there was not a single case among the Morón enrolled, and only two among the Puerto Serrano recruits. (Poor eyesight, deafness, lameness, loss of an arm, heart trouble, and one case of epilepsy – that was the total range of infirmities.)

Confirming this change were other, equally striking, figures. Only twenty-six men from Morón and Puerto Serrano claimed that they were the sole support of an aged or widowed parent, a cause for not serving which previously had

* Their enlistment rate was four times higher than their proportion of the population.

outnumbered physical infirmities. Those using this excuse in the Morón enrolment fell to one-quarter of the usual pre-war rate. Puerto Serrano's quasi-messianic mass enrolment, if not patently duplicated by the Morón men, was certainly replicated in their attitudes and actions.

Whatever their trade or employment, it was the sixteen to twenty-five year-olds who dominated in the district enrolment. They made up eighty percent of the volunteers – the sixteen to twenties alone accounted for just over fifty-six percent of the total – and one-third of the enlisted; of the latter, however, the older men between twenty-six and forty-five formed half, no doubt because many were married with children and expected to be exempt; bachelors and widowers without children were always the first to be conscripted.

A Catalan comparison – Igualada volunteers' enrolment from May to the beginning of October – illustrated similarities and differences with Andalucía.[29] After an initial enrolment of some three hundred men, of which no record remained – and was perhaps never kept – the Igualada volunteers were almost equally divided between land workers and craftsmen, with a scattering of other trades or professions. Four out of five were twenty-five years or less of age; one in two was between sixteen and twenty. These proportions were identical to those of Morón district; but there the similarity ended for, like the rest of the volunteers, the two youngest age groups represented an equal division between agrarian and artisanal occupations, with a handful of students in a very distant third place.

Though chronologically the first, the last of the three enrolments which recorded trades and profesions took place in Alicante, the Valencia region's major port, on May 29, 1808 when seven hundred and five volunteers joined up.[30] The roll again showed the weight of artisanal representation, though here it was shared with men in various types of service employment rather than with agrarian workers. Bricklayers, shoemakers and cobblers were, as so often, at the head of the artisans, closely followed by ropemakers, as might be expected of a port.*

As the only urban roll, it reflected a far wider occupational spectrum than the others. Royal and municipal employees, domestic servants, a rather large land transport sector, and for the first time in the three rolls, members of the privileged classes, including five nobles, an estate-owner, and a priest. In the service sector, which matched that of the artisans in size, there were merchants, agents, brokers, dealers, retailers and salesmen, as well as shopkeepers and their assistants. And following them, tavern-keepers, bakers and breadsellers, water carriers and cacao grinders, a wig dresser, a butcher, three blood-letters and a couple of surgeons.

For a port, however, there was an absence as striking as that of the Morón day labourers: the lack of maritime volunteers. A fisherman, a couple of sailors and five galley owners were the only seafaring men enrolled, just about the least numerous group of all. Presumably, pressures similar to those of the

---

* However, one hundred and eighty-four volunteers were simply listed as 'workers', which in the unspecific vocabulary of the time could mean any number of things, and two hundred and fifteen had no stated trades or professions.

Andalucian township were exercised by the large wholesale merchants to ensure that, in the new and seemingly profitable situation where the British navy would no longer hinder their exports to the colonies, lack of crews to man the ships would not prevent their goods reaching their destination.

None of the three enrolment centres – Igualada, with its relatively advanced farming and the beginning of a cotton-based industrialization; Morón, a large Andalucian township dependent on a relatively backward señorial and latifundista agriculture; or Alicante, a small town but nonetheless a major Levant port – could be considered typical of Spain at large. Nonetheless, it was striking that, for varying reasons, the apprentice, the journeyman under twenty or the artisan in his thirties made up in one or other of them almost half of the original volunteers and enlisted of three of the new junta armies. This was not what might initially have been expected from the majority social composition of Spain at the time. But it was not atypical of the age: apprentices, journeymen and artisans had played important roles in the American and French revolutionary armies; and now they were to do so again in a nationwide struggle against what they saw as the threat of domination by a foreign power. Less surprisingly, they were joined by agrarian workers – who overall matched the artisanal sector's numbers more or less exactly. In Alicante, predictably, the agrarian workers were replaced by service workers who made up the other half. According to these three enrolments, the new armies' composition was an almost equal mix of the artisanal and agrarian in the township recruits, and of artisans and service workers enrolled in the towns.

The almost exact coincidence of the proportions of the predominant volunteers' age groups* from two widely separated areas – Andalucía and Cataluña – left little reason for doubt: whatever their trades or employment, the majority of the volunteers were between sixteen and twenty-five, with the bulk of them not yet turned twenty. Spanish labouring youth had turned out en masse to fight Napoleon.

INCITING ENEMY DESERTION:
THE JUNTAS' PROPAGANDA WAR

Apart from their major tasks of simultaneously consolidating themselves in power, raising armies, and seeking the means to finance them, some juntas proved themselves singularly adept at pursuing a propaganda war. Sevilla was among those at the forefront, one of the first to call on Napoleon's French and foreign troops to desert† and, like many other juntas, made considerable play of the insistent popular rumour that the Bonapartist regime would forcibly conscript young Spaniards into Napoleon's armies.

---

* The Alicante roll did not include ages.
† Desertion, it should be recalled, was common to all European armies of the times, and desertion to the enemy not infrequent to avoid the far greater rigours of being taken prisoner of war, or even to secure warm clothing or a new uniform. Though during the war it was strictly punishable by death, the Spanish army preferred to reincorporate a deserter rather than to lose a soldier.

Frenchmen: You have been forced to shed your's and your sons' blood to enslave Europe for a non-French family which reigns in various European nations in your name but not in France's interests . . .

Italians, Germans, Poles, Swiss and all the others who form the so-called French army: why do you fight for your oppressor who has deprived you of all that you hold most sacred? For him who has forced you from your homes, depriving you of your wordly goods, your wives and children, your fatherlands which he had previously enslaved? Your ally and generous friend, the Spanish Nation, invites you to desert the flag that is enslaving nations and to enlist under ours that has been unfurled for the most just cause the world has known. [31]

Attempting to drive a wedge down the fault-line of national sentiment was innovative but insufficient, the junta realized, and it went on to offer all deserters the same reward: when the war ended victoriously for the Spanish cause, as was to be hoped, they would receive land to cultivate and live peacefully for the rest of their lives 'in the midst of a nation which loves and respects you'.

The proclamation brought some immediate results from General Dupont's expeditionary force encamped around Córdoba which, though undefended, it had just seized and sacked in tremendous manner. Many more potential deserters, the Sevilla junta had learned, were fearful of changing sides lest they be assassinated, given 'the people's professed hatred of all Frenchmen, and other foreigners, who do not clearly speak our language'; and the junta was forced to remind these people that they must treat deserters with every consideration for not only did the latter diminish the enemy's strength and increase their own, but deserters could provide invaluable information on the enemy army's movements.[32]

The example set by the Sevilla junta was soon followed by Asturias[33] and subsequently developed in greater and more extensive detail by the Junta Suprema, the central government formed by the regional juntas in the autumn of 1808. Proclaiming that one of the most powerful ways of making war was to 'debilitate the enemy without loss, indeed even increasing our own forces in the process', the Suprema issued a proclamation in four languages to the 'Germans, Poles, Dutch, Swiss and Italians' serving in the Napoleonic armies calling on them to desert. Each soldier who crossed the lines would be paid two hundred reales, and three hundred if he brought his musket. Cavalrymen would be paid extra for their horses. Once again it warned Spaniards to 'protect and welcome' all deserters.[34] Finally, the Suprema published a second proclamation, now in five languages (Spanish, Italian, French, German and Latin – the latter in the hope that, lacking a Polish translator, Catholic Poles would be able to decipher it), stressing the Napoleonic armies' defeats in Portugal at the hands of the British, and the fact that Austria, Russia and Turkey had declared against France.

If you continue to serve under Napoleon's banner you will die as hated as the French who brought you here to fight Spaniards who were and are your friends . . . Already thousands of your men have joined our armies and find in them a friendly welcome and a reward for adhering to our cause.[35]

Within the nine months from the Sevilla junta's proclamation to the last of the Junta Suprema, there had been a notable change in approach. No direct appeal was any longer made to French soldiers to desert, only to the non-French serving in the Napoleonic army. The latter were obviously the weak link, the most likely deserters on whom all attention had to be focused. The French as a nation, rather than the 'tyrant' Napoleon who had earlier to be distinguished from the French people, had become the enemy. The 'national wedge' was no longer used; national languages replaced it. Deserters were no longer offered some idyllic and distant recompense, but an immediate financial reward. The war was no longer painted in terms of the justice of the Spanish cause (though the Suprema did not doubt it) but in terms of emphasizing the dangers of continuing to serve Napoleon, whose army had suffered defeat. The Emperor was no longer invincible: international alliances against him were again being formed. The Spanish war in this sense had become internationalized, less an idealistic struggle than a life or death conflict dependent no longer solely on its own strengths but on factors external to it.

The Junta Suprema's claim that 'thousands' had deserted was a propagandistic effect; but there could be no doubt that from 1809, one of the harshest years of the war, a growing number of non-French in the Napoleonic army in Spain began to desert.* Some of those who deserted – but only a few – joined the Spanish guerrilla. Forty Russian deserters were recruited by Brigadier Mariano de Renovales in his initially successful resistance movement in the Navarese Roncal and Ansó valleys during the spring and summer of 1809. What their immediate past had been, where they had been taken prisoner by Napoleon – one can suppose at Austerlitz or Friedland – or why they had joined the French army, Renovales did not relate. He had gathered them together 'from the many who had deserted the enemy army'. He was full of praise for their bravery. 'Their fidelity to our cause and the valour with which they fought was inexplicable', he wrote.[36]

POPULAR DISAFFECTION WITH THE JUNTAS

Despite their ardent patriotic proclamations, the juntas did not arouse great popular fervour. Their war measures, particularly new taxes, were inevitably responsible in part. For the first few months, the wealthy (often redeeming their past passivity or overt hostility to the rising) contributed liberally. As an institution, the Church was a large donor: in Galicia, for example, it contributed

---

* By 1810, however, the Junta Suprema's figure did bear more than a little resemblance to reality. So great was the influx of deserters processed through Gibraltar that double foolscap description forms were specially printed to deal with the numbers. On one day alone, Sept 27, 1810, over fifteen hundred deserters passed through the receiving depot, which ran out of printed forms. (Robert W. Gould, *Mercenaries of the Napoleonic Wars*, Brighton, 1955, pp. 5–6.)

six and a half million reales in the first six months of the war.[37] But donations came from all sectors of society. In Extremadura, one of Spain's poorest regions, more than two and a half million reales were contributed between June and the end of December, 1808, by townships, ecclesiastical institutions and most notably by individuals.[38] But these donations soon dropped off: the cost of maintaining the war effort affected the latter's pockets too directly, and they were unwilling to finance it from their private wealth, some of which had suffered losses because it originated in the Bonapartist-controlled zone.

Not surprisingly, the labouring classes were frequently dissatisfied with their lack of representation on the juntas, and the manner in which the latter, 'to avoid the convulsions of a nascent liberty', as the *Gazeta de Valencia* put it, were exercising their power.

In Alicante, for example, where after co-opting a few local notables, the entire municipal council had turned itself into the junta, the populace protested at its lack of representation and obliged the junta to accept two clergymen to speak and vote on its behalf. This was not an uncommon choice: the clergy enjoyed status and was literate, and among them there were always a few priests well-known and trusted for their generosity to the urban poor. In this case, however, it was insufficient. The following day, June 13, a crowd gathered in the junta's anteroom and 'imperiously' demanded, on their behalf, that one of the junta members be relieved of his post immediately. *Fuera! Fuera!* (Out! Out!) the crowd shouted. The junta agreed to his suspension while it investigated the member's case. The people showed that they had a long memory. In 1802, this junta member, Ignacio Spering, had been accused of favouring merchants, at the inhabitants' cost, in supplying the town with foodstuffs.[39]

The crowd then demanded that the young single enlisted men who still remained in Alicante be ordered to march immediately to Almansa where the southern Valencia and Murcia conscripts and volunteers were gathering. The junta issued the necessary edict. Evidently encouraged by its success, the crowd gave two junta members a hard time when they went the next day to collect the mail just received from Madrid and France. Believing that they were deliberately being kept in ignorance of important and adverse news, the people began to riot in front of the post office, demanding that the mail be opened and read aloud. The junta members' indecision only increased the tension. 'Let real Spaniards collect the mail!' the cry was raised. Finally, one of the members took the packet of letters from Madrid and France, which numbered very few, and read them out.[40] Such scenes were still continuing as late as July 4 when a crowd, 'creating the greatest of disorder and threatening the lives of junta members', demanded that official mail received by the junta be made publicly known.[41]

These protests were a minor affair compared to the events in Manresa, which had been among the first Catalan towns to rise, and where the junta's unpopularity extended to more than the lower orders. Additional taxes to pay for the war effort had led many of the wealthy to leave the town for neighbouring places where they were out of harm's way. 'The rich leave the hardships to the poor', the people responded, and rioted. The junta managed to restore order by assuring the rioters that it would expropriate many of the wealthy's valuables to meet its war needs; but, as the days passed and the junta did not fulfil its promise, tension again rose. An earlier edict had ordered all arms to be handed in, and offered a reward to informers who gave the names of those who did not comply. The disarming had angered the inhabitants; if nothing else they found themselves defenceless against a surprise French attack.

Voices began to be heard accusing the junta of betraying the people's trust. On July 3, thirteen men armed with swords assaulted the gaol, killing three prisoners, one a Frenchman, and another a man being held on suspicion of spying for the French. They then went to the governor's house, forced open the doors and assassinated him in cold blood. 'Preparing to take the lives of more inhabitants, they were intimidated by a large funeral procession, with a great cross at its head, which the priests had wisely and opportunely decided to hold'.[42] So intimidated, indeed, that it was said they joined the procession with their assassin's arms.

On the following day, at a special meeting of the guilds' leaders called by the rebels, one of the latter read out a paper containing a number of demands, among them that the previous day's assassins be pardoned, that the people seize all tithes and the junta be reformed. At the end of his peroration, the speaker said, 'Mana lo Poble baix': 'the plebeians must be in charge', and gave the names of those, including himself, who must become junta members.[43]

Meanwhile, the tumult continued, apparently raised by one of those shortly to be arrested for the assassinations, causing one more death and two seriously wounded. Public order was restored, albeit temporarily, by Francisco Riera, a local retail merchant's son, who had led a Manresa sometent at the victory of the Bruch pass. He arrested three of the main suspects, and at the same time reformed the junta, on which eighteen laymen and eight clerics were now to sit. By ensuring the exclusion of two former members, both of them town councillors, the populace had won a minor victory at the expense of considerable bloodshed.[44]

But as late as September 1808 there were serious fears of another popular revolt. Commenting on the earlier events, the Manresa magistrates wrote that they had been the work of a 'few persons who, with artful guile, spread the fire of sedition amongst the lowest of the plebs, and deluded and inflamed them to execute the greatest of assassinations'. Anonymous letters, which in the past had been the precursors of disaster, were again being received by the magistrates . . .[45]

The implication was clear. Behind the rebellious plebs stood others of higher social status – 'enterprising revolutionary people' – who manipulated, or paid, the lowest of the low to achieve their aim of replacing the junta by a popular town government.[46] Was this anything but the elite's manner of understanding (or misunderstanding) the lower ranks, who in their eyes were incapable of acting autonomously, and could only be led or manipulated by people of higher social status? The question was impossible to answer conclusively in this instance, though it was suspected, on the evidence of the earlier risings, that agitators – though not necessarily men of higher rank – had been at work.

To many other townsmen and villagers liberty and popular 'sovereignty' evidently meant something other than government by the juntas: '*Carajo*! Now there is no king, we're all one and the same . . .', 'There's no justice of the peace to order us about any longer . . .', were the sort of comments heard in Aragón.[47] In Cataluña, the protest took a more direct form: 'We have no king, therefore we won't pay', the inhabitants of Falset told the tax collectors. 'The poor . . . who have been skinned all our lives . . . say that the rich who have money should pay', added the villagers of Cunit. 'Now there's no justice of the peace, or king or God, we're all equal', some Martorell inhabitants told the local justice who reported these comments to the commander of the Catalan army on July 19, 1808, in shocked disapproval.[48] Not unexpectedly. The disregard for king and fatherland might perhaps be excused – but the denial of God? What had become of fighting for religion, king and country if some individuals thought like this? For these people, social equality had become the insurrections' and war's rationale. Certainly only a minority dared openly express such views, but their attitude to the sacrifices demanded by the war became widespread.

Social protest, as will be seen in a later chapter, did not stop there. It was clear, however, that many of the lower ranks were not unduly impressed by the juntas' pretensions to sovereignty. Either there was a king who ruled or there was not, and the juntas, whatever they proclaimed, were not an annointed king. In Valencia, the people's opposition to their junta led to the most violent reaction to be witnessed in the Spanish peninsula.

VALENCIA: THE JUNE 5–6 MASSACRES

Two days after the initial Valencia rising, the Franciscan friar, Juan Rico, whom the insurrectionaries had elevated to the role of their tribune, and a lawyer of the Bertrán de Lis faction, presented a list of junta candidates to an ad hoc meeting of the old authorities. Prior to this, Vicente Bertán de Lis, one of the insurrection's major planners, had sought out intendente Aspiroz, who had opposed the rising with all his strength, and insisted that he attend the meeting and form part of the proposed junta. Bertrán de Lis was quite clear on the need for the latter to be made up of 'notables of all the classes, together with the [existing] authorities and the captain general'. He gave three reasons to support his argument:

> Our [the insurrectionary leaders'] sole value to the people today is that we represent their feelings; but if we alone govern, at the first setback the people will drag us through the streets, ride roughshod over us. No one knows us in the province and even less so in Spain. It is important that the country sees that there is no opposition to the rising in order to encourage the other provinces to do the same . . . And in the junta we will govern in the authorities' name.[49]

At that moment, the Valencian insurrectionaries had no idea that other provinces had risen; they could not even be sure that their own province would follow their lead. Thus the idea of presenting a 'united front' to the country had its logic; but underneath it lay another: non-members of the political elite, *the unknown*, could not be seen to govern. Institutional authority was sacrosanct, even if those who filled its posts had done their level best to quash the rising. But this was now to the insurrectionists' advantage. As a result of the old authorities' previous hostility, they had fallen hostages to the rising's success: their positions, even their lives, depended on it. So, Bertrán de Lis could argue, his group of reformers would govern in the authorities' shadow. The argument had only one flaw: the group could govern only as long as it controlled armed power in the streets.

As finally formed, the fifty-member junta included all the old authorities. The urban population and the huerta smallholders were highly discontented. Rico himself recalled how the people 'remained . . . in a perpetual state of commotion, distrusting the old authorities'. A riotous crowd frequently approached to the very chamber where the junta was meeting.

> The people's distrust and suspicion that they were not being led in good faith and with a sincere desire to defend and save the country, grew daily stronger, and their tumultous conduct became so frequent . . . that not even the junta's most active and energetic measures could contain them.[50]

Only two days after the junta's creation, one of the nobles appointed as a member was assassinated. Here again the people demonstrated their long memory. At the start of the rising, barón de Albalat, who had commanded the militia during the 1801 anti-militia revolt, when he had ordered his troops to fire on the crowd, killing three men, had fled for his life. But on hearing that he had been appointed to the junta, he returned to the city believing himself safe. He was seized by the crowd and brutally murdered, his head cut off and stuck on a pike which was paraded round the city.[51]

Meanwhile, in the Ciudadela, the city's fortress seized by the insurrectionaries on the second day of the rising, infantry captain González Moreno, one of the rising's original plotters, commanded a sizeable force of armed smallholders, and had titled himself *Comandante del pueblo soberano* (the sovereign people's commander)[52] or, in another version, *Comandante del pueblo armado en defensa de sus altares, Patria y Rei* (the armed people's commandant in defence of their religion, fatherland and king).[53] The *comandante* was almost certainly dubious about the loyalty of many members of the new Valencia junta and was prepared, it was said, to hold out in the Ciudadela against the junta if need be.[54] And his smallholders' force would have followed him. (If the allegation was true, the captain became one of the first of a number of army officers prepared to intervene, as non-junta members, directly in the new political situation.)

Despite this putative display of strength, the weakness of the Bertrán de Lis' political stance became rapidly evident. The old authorities on the junta effortlessly removed three of the original insurrectionists from the city by promoting the *comandante* to colonel (to command its freshly raised division at its outpost along the Ebro) and the two younger Bertrán de Lis brothers to captains in the same force. Almost simultaneously, the junta decided to imprison all French residents for their own safety in the Ciudadela which, with the *comandante*'s and his men's departure, was now ungarrisoned.

Apart from their distrust of the junta, fear of a French attack on the city kept the remaining smallholders in a state of high tension, as did the threat of the 'internal' enemy – the imprisoned French residents. To find themselves the major armed force in the city added to their frenzied determination to act. But, it should be noted, their determination did not run to demanding seats on a reformed junta, but rather to expelling the 'traitors' from it or to abolishing the new government body altogether.

Into this conflictive situation, an ultramontane cleric suddenly catapulted himself. Baltasar Calvo, a forty-five-year-old Valencian-born canon, well-known for his 'violent character' and anti-reformist ideas[55] which had resulted in his explusion from the Spanish capital, reached Valencia. After failing in his aim to be nominated to the newly-formed junta – friar Rico turned him down flat – he looked for, and found in the smallholders, the means of overthrowing the junta and establishing a new one under his leadership. But equally – indeed perhaps more so – the smallholders found in his violent anti-French demagogy and determination to 'clean out the junta's traitors' and deal it a deathblow the perfect means of achieving their aims. On the afternoon of June 5, the smallholders surrounded the Ciudadela shouting:

> There are traitors in the junta: we have been sold out! Their treachery has left the Ciudadela unguarded and in the Frenchmen's power! Death to all of them, and an end to the junta![56]

Within a few hours, under cover of darkness, the mob began to massacre the French. As the victims' screams were heard, all the city's religious orders hastened to the fortress; but even two consecrated hosts, a venerated crucifix and the friars' reasoned pleas could not end the slaughter.[57] Friar Rico was twice turned away at the Ciudadela's gates by sympathetic smallholders who were concerned to save his life which would have been endangered had he entered the fortress. The assassins were encouraged and protected by another religious authority – canon Calvo.

They murdered two hundred French that night. Some 140 survived until morning. Friars came early to take the living to safety in the Torres de Quart, one of the tower gates that protected the city. The assassins were waiting for them by the newly-built bullring. There they put all of them to death and then went in search of French hiding in the city. Only a dozen or so were said to have survived.*

That same morning, June 6, Calvo entrenched himself in the Ciudadela. He ordered its cannons to be loaded and aimed towards the city. Then he sent an

---

* Ardit, 1977, pp. 130–131. Some French were also killed in neighbouring Sagunto; but far worse happened in Segorbe and Jérica, the latter Calvo's birthplace. In the former, Calvo's nephew oversaw the slaying of thirty-six French after a mob assaulted the local prison. They then attempted to kill the township's governor, which Dominican friars managed to prevent only by giving the assassins money. (Ardit, 1977, p. 133.)

order to the captain general to resign his post, and to the intendente and postal administrator to send him money and current correspondence. The latter two complied, but the captain general refused. Calvo ordered him to report to the Ciudadela with the junta. This, with some junta members, he did. Calvo publicly dismissed him and abolished the junta. He told two members (one of them the Bertrán de Lis group's junta secretary) that the junta had made many 'errors'. The way to correct them was to rid it of 'the traitors' in its midst; but as the junta itself was 'incapable of saving the kingdom [of Valencia] it was necessary to create a new one with far fewer, but recognized patriots, as members'.[58] The existing junta was powerless; at that moment Calvo enjoyed wide popular support and the armed smallholders and assassins of the French dominated the city streets. The junta had no armed force it could immediately call on to put down the revolt.

Had Calvo been anything but a fanatical cleric who believed that his writ was God's, he could have organized his forces to achieve his aims. Instead, he allowed Bertrán de Lis and friar Rico time to gather their forces. Ingenuously, the following day, Calvo attended on its own terrain a meeting of the junta he had abolished. By this time, the bloodlust of the massacres had been sated; Calvo's supporters believed they had done what was necessary and that he had abolished the junta they abhorred. Bertrán de Lis had the junta chamber surrounded by men in his pay. Once the junta had gathered, Bertrán de Lis or Rico – both claimed the credit – launched their accusations to the canon's face. Thus encouraged, other junta members joined in. Isolated, Calvo was easily picked off. Bertrán de Lis called in his two trusty smallholders, Francisco Lluesma and Vicente Rausell, to arrest him and put him aboard a frigate which that evening sailed for Mallorca.[59]

Calvo was brought back to Valencia, tried and executed in the Inquisition's prison at dawn on July 4, and his body publicly displayed in the plaza de Santo Domingo. The junta created a tribunal of public safety, the first (but by no means the last) of its kind on the patriot side. Three of the existing audiencia magistrates sat on the tribunal which wreaked a formidable vengeance on those accused of taking part in the massacres: twenty-four smallholders and three urban labouring men were executed for the Valencia slaughter and a further twenty-three for the massacre of the French in Segorbe. Apart from these another eighteen were executed for the assassination of the Ayora governor, his two maidservants and another man during the rising. In all then, sixty-eight people. The royal road to Madrid, beside which the executed were buried in shallow graves, became virtually impassable owing to the stench of rotting corpses.[60]

CONTROLLING THE PEOPLE

The French massacres reinforced the power of the old authorities on the Valencian junta. Unjustly, the latter held the Bertrán de Lis progressives responsible for the slaughter. It was this sort of terror that, from the start, all the juntas were determined to avoid. The crowd had played its necessary part in the insurrections, but now it must subside again into its customary sub-servient and passive role. Even the majority of progressives would have agreed, heirs as they were to the eighteenth-century absolutist reformers who had feared nothing more than popular risings. As a result of the massacre, on July 21, two months after the rising, the Valencia junta ordered the gallows raised and the garrotte publicly displayed throughout its region, because of the 'threat to public tranquility in all places'.*

Almost unanimously, the juntas' first proclamations included the demand to restore public order, threatening strong measures against any who disobeyed. The Sevilla junta stated that

> cavalry and infantry patrols will prevent any public gatherings, which only serve to foment false and prejudicial ideas, instead of obeying the orders of those in command to enlist and organize for the defence of the fatherland . . . Cafés, taverns, wine shops, billiard rooms and all other places of public entertainment will without exception close at the evening church bell to prayers for souls in purgatory. Any infringement of this order will be punished in proportion to the offence.[61]

Ten days later, surprised that there were still some 'evil people who disturb the social order . . . and foment sedition which only causes irremediable harm', the Sevilla junta found itself obliged to repeat its original proscriptions in even stronger language. It would severely punish

> all persons who, in whatever manner, oppose or obstruct [the junta's] just plans. In consequence it forbids any gatherings, meetings or secret conventicles which, by an orderly government, must always be seen as suspicious. People are forbidden to go in armed groups through the streets . . . or to join together to search rooming houses, treating their occupants as criminals.[62]

The Cartagena junta had also to repeat its orders for public tranquility. It had immediately ordered all beggars out of town, but strictly forbade anyone else of whatever class or age, other than women with young children, to leave without its express permission. It set up a police junta, and warned parents, master craftsmen and householders that they would be held responsible for the obedience to its orders of their children, apprentices and servants.† It assured the inhabitants that the junta had 'sworn on its honour to defend your just desires' and in consequence 'your contribution must be a real and effective subordination' to the new authorities.[63] Evidently, these counsels were insuffi-cient, for the junta rapidly issued an edict which, incidentally, provided a new image of the popular protest. The junta had

---

* On August 15, 1809, Alicante asked permission of the Valencia junta to remove the gallows and garrotte because 'the reasons for their public display are no longer applicable', adding that they were blocking traffic in the streets. The Valencia junta replied that they could be removed 'as long as the purpose for which they were raised is not forgotten' (AM de Alicante, *Cartas recibidas*, vol. 59,n.n).
† This was an order common to the Old Regime.

observed with surprise and sorrow that women who, by reason of their sex, should withdraw from popular street agitations into their houses, have gathered in great numbers, either out of a spirit of curiosity or for other less obvious reasons, increasing street disorders with their agitated and even perhaps irritating voices . . . They are warned in future to abstain from such disorders, leaving it to the true and good patricians to settle in calm their real interests and needs. If the contrary occurs, these same men who, by the dignity of their sex, must sustain this task, will be the first to give notice of the women in question who shall be punished as they deserve. The same holds for young lads who . . . have been acting similarly.[64]

Like the Sevilla edict, Cartagena displayed the clear notion that the people existed to obey their social betters. But in one aspect, the Cartagena edict exceeded the norm: its concept of the true and good patricians whose natural right to govern was reinforced by their *maleness*, was no doubt what many felt but would not in the circumstances have cared to commit to an official paper.*

Nor, of course, was the defence of property forgotten in the juntas' strictures:

Respect property; observe the greatest discipline; obey exactly your appointed leaders; bury resentments which ignorance or mistaken understanding have aroused in you; united as one body, and raising our prayers to the God of the Armies . . . you can be assured that shortly you will see your liberty restored.

stated the Vich junta in Cataluña on June 11, 1808.[65]

To keep the people under control, a number of juntas (for example, León, Segovia and Tarragona) had no hesitation in declaring their inhabitants subject to military justice. The Catalan junta went a step further. On June 22, only days after its creation, the junta set up criminal tribunals functioning under military law in all the French unoccupied zone. These courts could pass sentence without reference to higher authority. At the same time the junta ordered a cavalry squadron, under an army officer, to be formed in each district to patrol those villages which had undergone – or were thought likely to undergo – disturbances and troubles.[66] It was not long before most of the major juntas throughout Spain had appointed police commissioners or juntas – an unpopular innovation, even to some of the municipal councils whose traditional policing duties were thereby ignored – and had formed volunteer militia companies under the command of nobles and honorable burgesses to maintain law and order. The urban lower classes saw these as a standing force to police them on behalf of the new authorities; resentment at this measure was one of the causes of the riots which swept a number of towns at the beginning of 1809.†

From La Coruña to Cádiz the newly formed juntas made determined efforts to recuperate the arms the people had seized during the insurrection. Although

---

* Whether the Cartagena patricians' ire finally fell on any particular women the records do not relate.

† See Chapter 10, pp. 234 et seq.

no one could be sure of their exact number, the pre-rising musket inventories in four of the major insurrectionary towns' arsenals alone stood at 143,500, more than sufficient to arm a large army,[67] though of course the arms stocks were in widely separated parts of the country. Many of those who had seized arms would have joined the colours with them as each junta immediately began to form its own army; and most of the population was unfamiliar with the use of muskets and would have seized small arms instead. Nonetheless, there were evidently sufficient arms in the rearguard during the weeks after the rising seriously to concern the juntas.[68]

Not all the juntas' initial measures were directly repressive: they also took some steps to appease the labouring poor. They abolished Godoy's hated war taxes, especially on wine, and rescinded further disentailment of religious property introduced by the former royal favourite which, affecting the Church's charitable institutions, had left the poor without one of their last resources for staying alive in times of extreme poverty. Moreover, in Sevilla's case, the junta instituted a special tax on large landowners' income to help finance the war. This, as the junta stated, demonstrated its determination

> to distribute the cost of maintaining an army in the most equitable manner possible. Taking into account the advantage to Andalucian grandees and other landowners of preserving their property, the junta has decreed that, over and above their ordinary taxes, they shall pay ten percent of the cash incomes which their estates produce.[69]

The measure, taken by a junta which had co-opted the second highest number of titled nobles after Valencia, suggested that the great Andalucian landowners were prepared to make a gesture to the villagers to try to avoid trouble on their vast estates. In the last resort the special tax was easier to evade – if in fact it was ever imposed – than the fate which awaited the poor: conscription and death in their country's defence.

The popular ferment continued for several months, and when it subsided it was only temporarily. But it would be mistaken to conclude that, in present-day terms, it had a revolutionary content or that it was necessarily as threatening to the authorities as they usually painted it. The latter's tolerance level of any popular protest was exceedingly low, almost to the point of paranoia. Any 'gatherings, meetings or secret conventicles' they saw immediately as 'suspicious', aimed at disobeying their orders. The lower classes, it was true, were often disposed to take justice into their own hands if they felt the authorities were untrustworthy. But rarely were they seeking to overthrow the new authorities. They wanted to be sure that junta members were truly loyal to the cause, and sometimes demanded a minimal junta representation, though not by individuals of their own lowly standing. They wanted to be informed of all events, favourable or unfavourable; and they wanted a social equality of sacrifice in the war effort. This could not be termed 'suspicious' except by those who rejected totally the idea of the popular classes' right to have any say in the conduct of affairs.

   The Alicante protests had achieved some of their demands. But the common people staged one further protest against their junta which revealed in caricature another aspect of their Old Regime mentality. When the junta appointed some non-nobles to command urban volunteer militia companies in which the lower orders served as the rank and file, the latter rebelled. They demanded that their commanders be nobles as the Valencia junta had ordered; and the Alicante junta again was forced to accept their demand.[70]

6

Early Victories and Defeats: Lessons of the Popular War

STRATEGIES OF WAR

From the moment of war, military men and civilian polemicists speculated on how such a conflict must be fought. Somewhat ironically, one of the first into the field with a published consideration of the question was a Bonapartist polemicist who argued that, to stand any chance of resisting, the anti-Napoleonic forces would have to adopt

> a defensive system in which the climate, the hidden animosity of the civilian population, shortages, sickness and desertion slowly consume the aggressor and finally hand him over, deeply weakened, to a battle-hardened army of equal or greater numbers to deal the fatal blow.[1]

Such a resistance, the polemecist continued, required the full resources of the state, a supreme commander armed with all the authority of the law, and the unanimity of the entire population. Even if reinforced by foreign troops assembled as a result of new foreign alliances, the author plainly doubted that final victory was possible. But even if it came about, 'would the victory compensate for the cost of the sacrifices that had had to be made?' In his polemic against those who had chosen war, his answer was a decisive 'no'.

The Sevilla junta weighed in thereafter with a paper entitled *Pre-emptions*. It warned that the first matter on which Spaniards must be convinced was to avoid full-scale battles.

> We must practise guerrilla war, of harassment, of wearing down the enemy by cutting off his access to supplies, of destroying bridges, cutting roads . . . attacking the enemy on his flanks and rear, and not permitting him a moment's rest . . . Spain's situation, with its many mountains and defiles, rivers and watercourses, and the Provinces' geographical situation, makes it possible to wage such a war with happy results.[2]

The anonymous author was aware, moreover, that the sacrifices such a war entailed required the prospect of political and social improvements. The nation must be persuaded that when once again free, and Fernando VII had been restored to his throne, the Cortes would be convoked 'to correct abuses and enact the laws which the times and experience dictate for the public good and felicity'.

A number of Spanish army officers agreed with the military reasoning behind this guerrilla strategy. But the great majority shared the traditional view that war was solely a military affair, as did Napoleon himself. Moreover, the military victor of Austria, Prussia and Russia believed that he would not find the local Spanish armies, reinforced by a great number of raw recruits, much of a problem. As it turned out, this view was initially proven wrong; Napoleon was either badly informed or self-deluded about the extent of the risings and considered them an isolated series of 'police' problems which could be punitively dealt with by small military columns. In character, the Emperor adopted an early nineteenth-century imperialist solution to the Spanish risings. Backed by resolute civilians, the regions were able to make the most of Napoleon's military error and succeeded on three further occasions in throwing off the imperial columns, as they had at the Bruch pass in Cataluña.

Before they did so, however, they learned two sharp lessons. The first was that hastily raised and untrained civilian levies were easily defeated in open battle by French cavalry and infantry charges. General Cuesta's defeat by imperial forces at Cabezón in the first days of the Valladolid rising had amply demonstrated this; three routs in Aragón and another at the Alcolea bridge where Cordoban patriot forces were rapidly dispersed by Dupont's column advancing into Andalucía, confirmed it.

The second lesson was that patriot regional field commanders' disputes and rivalries – let alone their tactical follies – bedevilled their armies' success in open battle, a fact which Marshal Bessières exploited to the full in his crushing defeat of the Galician and Castilian forces, under Blake and Cuesta, at Medina del Rio Seco on July 14.* Though the patriot defeat was shortly redeemed by victory in Andalucía, the Medina defeat relieved the threat in Castilla la Vieja of attack on the imperial lines of communication to France. The Emperor's choice of Spain's new king, his brother Josef, could now proceed with relative tranquility towards his unknown capital, Madrid.

The obverse of these lessons was that the inhabitants fought with a tenacity and courage unprecedented in the previous century to defend their own cities and repulse French attacks on Zaragoza and Valencia; and a unified Andalucian army command of mainly regular troops won a startling victory in open battle over Dupont's column at Bailén on July 19. These three Spanish victories, especially the Bailén triumph, changed the course of events in the early part of the war.

---

* Like many Spanish army officers from the era when Irish Catholics were not permitted to join the British army and served Spain instead, Blake was of Irish descent. A colonel of a regiment stationed in Galicia at the start of the war, the Galician junta promoted him to general and the command of its army to replace the assassinated captain general Filangieri.

THE PEOPLE'S DEFENCE OF ZARAGOZA

On Wednesday, June 15, General Lefebvre Desnouettes appeared before the Aragonese capital at the head of a small column of 3,500 infantry, 1,000 cavalry and a single artillery battery.[3] At the same time, the popular hero, Brigadier José Palafox, whom the insurrectionists had elected as their supreme civilian and military leader, quietly slipped out of Zaragoza. In open battle, Lefebvre had just twice devastatingly defeated the Aragonese levies in their attempt to halt his advance on the city, the French cavalry riding down and slaughtering village and urban conscripts. Convinced that the capital could not be defended, Palafox left, he said, because of the French government's 'lively desire to sate [its vengeance] on my head', and to find reinforcements to continue the struggle.[4]

Zaragoza dominated one of Napoleon's two lines of communication, which the Emperor always chose with care and zealously protected. Having established his operational base in southwestern France, his major line ran along the main Spanish road from the border diagonally south and westwards to Burgos and Valladolid, each of which provided a direct route southwards to Madrid, and continued from Valladolid through Salamanca and Ciudad Rodrigo to the Portuguese border.* Traversing this major line just to the south of the Basque country another diagonal cut across Spain from northwest to southeast: the Ebro valley. Though Napoleon judged this of lesser importance than the first, the river linked the Basque country, Navarra and Aragón to southern Cataluña. Zaragoza dominated the Ebro diagonal, and thus could not be left in the insurrectionaries' hands. He detached Lefebvre's column from Pamplona to take the city in what he imagined was no more than a minor police operation.

The Aragonese capital, with its forty thousand inhabitants, had no garrison, indeed Godoy had virtually depleted Aragón of regular troops. Zaragoza was not a fortress town. Its adobe walls were little more than a modest circumscription to ensure that goods entered and paid the appropriate taxes at the official gates. After a brief reconnaissance, the French commander came to the same conclusion as Palafox: the city was indefensible. Although the northern walls were protected by the Ebro, and a suburb, the Arrabal, on the river's far bank which was connected by a stone bridge to the city, provided the inhabitants with a road out to the rest of Aragón, the southern walls were highly vulnerable to attack. Lefebvre decided to storm these. Although the walls were flimsy, here and there friaries, churches, a monastery, an almshouse and a cavalry barracks protruded their solid backs through or beyond the walls. The city's castle and a few other friaries stood singly half a kilometre or so in the countryside beyond.

Before the French advance, Palafox had ordered a general enlistment throughout the region, summoning all recruits to Zaragoza. This led to popular tumults in a number of Aragonese townships where the people feared being left unprotected.[5] His call for all arms in the capital to be handed in within two days also met popular opposition, the municipal council informing him that 'the

---

* It was not by accident that two of Wellington's victorious battles in the Spanish interior took place along this diagonal at Salamanca and Vitoria.

people have been surprised and take badly the order to hand over their arms which they hold for the defence of their persons and houses'.[6] The people were well aware, as they had been during the rising, that arms were their power and sole defence.

At the same time, Palafox took a further step to legitimize his command. He called a meeting of the ancient Cortes of Aragón to ratify his position and to appoint a junta to advise him. This, on June 9, the Cortes duly did.

Persuaded that Palafox and his levies would hold off the French column at Alagón, only twenty kilometres from the city, Zaragoza's population had done little to fortify the capital before the first battle survivors began to straggle in on the night of June 14–15. Many people, and not only the wealthy, asked for passports to leave.[7] Most of the junta members newly appointed by the Aragonese Cortes absconded.[8] But the greater part of the people rallied to make good their earlier deficiency, hurriedly dragging cannon to the southern walls' three major gates, and opening musket loopholes in the walls. Meanwhile, the fifty army gunners remaining in Zaragoza were assigned to the pieces, none of heavy calibre, 'given a gratification to do their duty' and provided with a small amount of ammunition.[9] Formally leaderless now that Palafox had gone, and without any concerted plan of defence, shouting inhabitants crowded in the streets leading to the gates as the French began their attack. Some bore arms, others munitions and provisions; yet others knelt and prayed. Amidst the general confusion and excitement as the first shots were heard, the people flung themselves forward to face the enemy. They lined up two deep along the promenade outside the wall from the Carmen to the Portillo gates, and fired at the advancing enemy troop. French cannon rapidly dispersed them, and they rushed for the shelter of the gates where the Spanish army gunners were opening fire. From inside the city, more people ran forward to defend the gates. As Alcaide Ibieca, an eyewitness, recalled:

> the street to the Carmen gate was thick with people, most of them armed, and among them women, old men and boys. Now and again a group would break off to make for the Portillo or Engracia gates. Others were returning carrying the wounded on their shoulders. Women were rushing towards the cannon with drink for the gunners. Spirit reigned in every face . . .[10]

The leaderless defence soon found its own leadership. A number of men – among them two or three of the small vineyard owners who had raised the city barely three weeks earlier – effectively organized the gates' defence. Santiago Sas, a highly respected priest in the Portillo quarter, rallied his parishioners and distributed arms to defend their neighbourhood's gate, while an engineer major raised a force of men, women and priests to take up position on the rooftops and balconies of nearby houses to fire on the attackers. Another small vineyard owner, Josef Zamoray, and a cavalry major, Mariano Renovales, led the defence of the Engracia gate. 'Victory or death!' was the order of the day.

Three times the French attacked and entered the empty cavalry barracks embedded in the city wall; and three times, in hand-to-hand fighting with cold steel and small arms, the people, who were waiting, annihilated them. At the Carmen gate, the French charged to within a few metres of the Spanish cannon; several of the gunners fell by their pieces. Civilian volunteers leapt forward to replace them, reloading the guns and beginning so rapid a fire that the French infantry was forced back with heavy casualties. Still unrelenting in his determination to take the city by storm, the French commander observed the depleted defence at the Engracia gate, and ordered his Polish cavalry to charge. Pennants flying, a squadron leapt over the silenced guns and dead gunners at the gate, and swept into the city, brushing aside the few men who tried to halt them.

The cry went up, 'the Engracia gate is undefended!' The Polish cavalry turned into the widest street on their left which led to the plaza del Carmen and on to the cavalry barracks and the plaza del Portillo by the gate of the same name. But as they charged along the roughly cobbled street, from rooftops and balconies musket shot and stones rained down on them, killing a number. In the Portillo plaza, the Polish cavalry lost all sense of direction. In scenes reminiscent of the May 2 rising in Madrid's Puerta del Sol, men, women and youths rushed at them with knives, hatchets and clubs. The squadron's remnants and riderless horses galloped back the way they had come to escape the inhabitants' fury. This was the furthest the French storm reached.[11]

At the gates, artillery munitions were running short. Without being given any apparent orders, women, youth and children went round houses and artisans' workshops throughout the city demanding scraps of iron, broken glass, pieces of old clothing to put as a wad between the charge and the cannon shot, rags to bandage the wounded, candles and fuses, bread and drink for the people who were fighting . . .

> The women were exemplary: they ran between the files of soldiers and bayonets, without concern for the musket fire or the bloodshed of both sexes, bringing water and bread, cheese, almonds, wine and spirits to their brave fellow-countrymen, sacrificing thereon the little money of their day's subsistence . . . The serenity with which these heroines ran through the musket fire . . . inspired the most ardent defender, whose energy was thereby redoubled.[12]

The women's participation in the defence impressed all male eyewitnesses. They evidently had expected nothing of the sort. But women's contribution was not the exclusive privilege of the lower orders: condesa de Bureta, Palafox's cousin, fought with equal valour. She and the plebeian women might in the long term be fighting for different objectives; but in the immediate both were defending their city against French 'colonial' subjection. As another witness of the struggle put it: for the men

> the idea that they were defending their wives, their children, and their homes gave them the strength to fight; they remembered that their religion was endangered; that they were about to lose their freedom: and that on this depended the return of their sovereign, and they called down the fires of Etna to overwhelm their vile oppressors.[13]

As the sun set, and many of all classes gave up hope and were leaving the city, the French made one more determined charge. At both the Engracia and Carmen gates, they pushed the defenders back, but their advance was halted by withering fire from roofs and windows of nearby houses and narrow street openings. At this crucial moment, reinforcements arrived, one thousand Catalan volunteers and local recruits under Colonel Francisco Marcó del Pont, who entered the city on its northern side: the French had not been able to cross to the Ebro's left bank to cut off this road. The reinforcements were rapidly distributed to the endangered gates. At Santa Engracia, Major Renovales organized a counter-attack which drove out the Polish cavalry; the French infantry who had momentarily seized the Carmen gate were also forced to retreat. It was now the people's turn to attack and they pushed out beyond the gates and skirmished among the olive groves. The French commander decided to call it a day and withdrew out of Spanish artillery range to the Santa Barbara heights. In nearly nine hours of fighting he had lost seven hundred dead, thirty prisoners and six guns which could not be pulled away under the defenders' heavy fire. The defenders' losses were put at about three hundred.[14]

The people broke out in wild jubilation on the news of the French withdrawal. They had stood fast against Napoleon's army, indeed severely mauled it. The trophies of war were there for all to see, six French flags among them. Women were

> running in groups through the streets displaying the Eagles, the shakos, the backpacks, the fine shirts and epaulettes taken from the French, so that all should see that the enemy soldiers, and even their officers, had been conquered by Zaragozan arms . . .[15]

More booty was being brought in from beyond the walls as men and women set out to make a grisly profit from the enemy dead, stripping corpses of shoes, uniforms, watches and sundry valuables. And as though these were insufficient, two days later armed Spanish civilians were arrested sacking the monastical Charterhouse outside the gates.[16]

*

Although Palafox had refused to return to Zaragoza from his headquarters at Belchite, just over fifty kilometres to the south-east, he had gathered a small force of volunteers and a few regulars, and was determined to cut off the French besiegers' rear. At Épila, a part of Lefebvre's column, under a Polish colonel's command, smashed the Aragonese leader early on June 24. Palafox had now gone down to defeat twice in open battle.

In Zaragoza, meanwhile, the authorities who had played little part in the first day's combats, attempted to reinforce the city's defences and their own control over the inhabitants. In accord with Palafox's post-rising declaration that he was imposing a military command, they appointed army officers to the gates' defence, ordered Zaragozan defenders to join the military units created by Palafox after the insurrection, and to obey only their military officers. Women, children and the elderly were ordered to remain at home when the French again attacked. Exceeding their established status, women's participation in the struggle was presumably believed to be an incitement to a frenzied popular defence and lack of respect for established authority. Out of this might arise some quite unforeseen and – the authorities feared – undesired consequences.

The population took little notice of the orders. They elected their own leaders at each gate. June 16 was Corpus Cristi, one of the major liturgical celebrations of the year. But there was no procession and from eight in the morning no church opened its doors to any but women.[17] The people spent the time instead carrying out church benches, shop cupboards and shelving to build barricades in the streets; others tore down the awnings from their windows to make sacks, which were filled with earth and wool to protect the guns at the gates while some, armed with swords, patrolled the streets; yet others with spyglasses climbed towers to warn of an enemy advance . . . Those who ventured out beyond the walls cut down the olive trees to reinforce the gates' defences and clear the field for the artillery.[18] Although much of this activity was militarily useless, it showed a popular initiative which no orders from above either brought about or could countermand.

Palafox had earlier ordered his older brother, marqués de Lazán, to return to Zaragoza, giving him full authority to act in his name. As so many of the officially constituted junta members had vanished during the first day's fighting, Lazán called a meeting of the major military, civil and religious leaders, which decided to set up a military defence junta and sent an appeal to the Lérida junta for the heavy artillery and gunners which had assembled there; and on June 28, several large cannon and munitions reached Zaragoza from the Catalan city.* At more or less the same time, a few detachments of troops who had fled Barcelona and Madrid, a reduced battalion of infantry and eighty Portuguese troops who had escaped the French also arrived. Meanwhile, the intendente, Calbo de Rozas, organized supplies of food, set up an armoury and arms factory, and put friars and others to making cartridges, and farriers to turning scrap iron into musket and cannon ball. Further French surrender demands were indignantly rejected; and two men who, on reaching the city from outside, were discovered to be carrying Bonapartist propaganda were rapidly tried and hanged.

Zaragoza's defence had by now become of military–political concern for the French in Madrid. The new French ambassador, La Forest, reported on June 20 that rapid Aragonese submission was needed adversely to affect Catalan and Valencian resistance, as well as in the two Castillas where 'the Aragonese are considered Spanish heroes'.[19]

> There is a great difference between the Spanish nation today and what it was towards the middle of May. An ignorant people, who cannot abide uncertainty, have thrown themselves en masse into the opposition.[20]

* Lazán's new junta twice (June 28 and June 29) called on Palafox urgently to return. 'The circumstances are worsening . . . the people are full of mistrust . . .' the junta wrote. (AHM de Zaragoza, *Archivo Palafox*, caja 8145, 1/8².)

VALENCIA: POPULAR RESISTANCE

On June 28, two days before the Zaragoza offensive reached new heights, Marshal Moncey appeared at the gates of Valencia. Like his companion in arms before the Aragonese capital, the veteran French commander had been ordered to subdue the Valencian insurrection with a force of about eight thousand men. Believing it little more than a rapid military exercise, he chose the shortest, but by far the more difficult road from Madrid, through the mountains of Cuenca. Believing he would march on the easier route across La Mancha, the inept Spanish army commanders paid little or no heed to his actual whereabouts.

The Cuenca road to Valencia passed through two steep defiles, one across the Cabriel river, the other the Cabrillas pass where the Castilian meseta dropped down sharply to the Valencian coastal plain. When the Valencia junta learned to its surprise that Moncey was in Cuenca it sent a force of about eight thousand mainly new recruits to cut his passage across the Cabriel defile. Inexplicably, the military commander stationed most of the force at the furthest and least likely bridge and only a small force at the obvious passage. Shortly thereafter he vanished.* The French forced the bridge over the defile with relative ease: the dryness of the summer allowed their troops to find several places to ford the river and turn the levies' flanks.

Defended by armed villagers and a small, heterogeneous force of military who had retreated from the Cabriel river disaster, the second great obstacle, the Cabrillas pass, was similarly outflanked by Moncey with great loss of life to the defenders.† A hurriedly formed line of defence in the plain outside Valencia was also forced to retreat on the city. Of the eight thousand civilians gathered the day before to defend the line, only 150 remained the following morning. The rest had deserted during the night in resentment at the martial discipline and their fear of betrayal by the military leaders.‡

After these easy victories, it was unsurprising that Moncey who had already twice summoned Valencia to surrender, repeated his demand on reaching the city's gates on Tuesday, June 28. By this time the city was full of people who had fled their villages. The Valencia junta rejected the first two summons. Outraged by the military's 'treason' in not organizing the two defiles' defence, the inhabitants, encouraged and advised by artillerymen and military engineers, hurriedly began as in Zaragoza to strengthen the city's defences, dragging cannon to the main gates, digging trenches to impede the enemy advance, filling bags with earth to provide parapets for the artillery, and securing the gates with massive wood beams torn from the recently constructed bullring.

---

* The commander, Major General Pedro Adorno, was court-martialled at his own request to clear his name two years after the events and sentenced to lose his rank.
† Moncey claimed after the battle that with six thousand steady troops he could have defended the pass against Napoleon himself and the *Grande Armée*. (Oman, 1902/1995, vol. I, p. 135.)
‡ They beat to death an artilleryman whose cannon they discovered was loaded with grass. Too late it was explained to them that this was normal procedure for artillery on the move.

More than anywhere else, the smallholders from around the city had good reasons to fear the French attack. Their massacre of French residents only three weeks earlier was certain to cause massive reprisals should Moncey take the city.* But with the French forces at the delapidated city walls, a junta faction led by the captain general La Conquista vacillated in favour of surrender.

According to friar Rico – whose memoirs always stated the author's sole protagonism in important events – the people's tribune alerted some of his trusted followers to the junta's doubts and these gathered a crowd of armed people at the junta's door shouting: 'Death to all those villanous and cowardly leaders, the traitors who want to surrender the city. They must all be put to death.'[21] Hearing these threats, wrote Rico, some junta members fell to their knees before a crucifix on the wall, believing that their hour had come. Others prepared to resist the mob. Finally Rico was commissioned to calm the people, which he was able to do only on condition that the whole junta emerged and joined the defence. Having no other option but to face death at the people's hands, its members came out and made the rounds of the major gates. There they sounded out the defenders' feelings. 'War, war, we shall die rather than surrender', came the answer.[22] Moncey's last surrender summons met with a sharp riposte:

> The people of Valencia prefer to die in the city's defence rather than come to any [surrender] agreement. They have informed the junta of this and, for your information, the latter hereby apprises you of the fact.[23]

It was not the junta which had led the people, but the people who had led the junta to the city's defence. Fighting broke out immediately, the French attacking the western gates, especially the Quart with its two ancient towers. Inhabitants lined the top of the walls and kept up a heavy musket fire; but it was the artillery that decimated the advancing columns, whose flanks and rear were constantly harried by smallholders. Vicente Bertrán de Lis, one of the rising's main protagonists, was active in this skirmishing, leading a group of his 'private army'.[24] Knowing the terrain intimately, the smallholders fought the enemy hand-to-hand amongst the Turia river's reedbeds, and opened irrigation channels to flood the path of the advancing French. By evening, after seven hours of fighting, Moncey's troops had not set foot in the city.

The few regular Spanish military officers who commanded the cannon at the gates no doubt saved the situation. But the people's massive participation, and among them the educated elite – lawyers, scriveners, merchants, landowners and other 'law-abiding' inhabitants who stood unprotected along the tops of the walls by the Quart gate to fire on the French – reinforced the general determination to resist to the last breath.[25]

By five o'clock in the afternoon, grapeshot was running out at the Quart battery. Friar Rico, who was active throughout the defence, secured a large quantity of iron. But the sacks in which to load it into the cannon were lacking.

* See Chapter 5, Valencia: the June 5–6 massacres, pp. 146–9.

On summoning the neighbours to make good the need, people poured out of their houses with sheets, pillowcases, linen and woollen goods, iron kitchen utensils, crying out that if there were insufficient grapeshot they would tear down the iron balustrades and *rejas* from their windows. As in Zaragoza, women were again highly prominent in the defence. As Rico records:

> Their enthusiasm was so extreme that women of all ages and classes ran into the streets, and some took off their stockings to make sacks for the grapeshot and for the cannon wads others divested themselves of their outer clothes. And some even advanced to the batteries to cool off the cannon with vinegar and water. Their admirable and heroic ardour showed what a people is capable of when they possess a real love and enthusiasm for liberty.[26]

Only a fortnight earlier, the *Diario de Valencia* had written that 'the public considers that the fair sex can have no part in this war until her humanitarian duties are called upon'.[27] In all likelihood this was in answer to a statement from La Coruña reproduced two days earlier in the junta-originated newspaper, the *Gazeta de Valencia*, which had cast a very different light on women's role.

> Our revolution's great work is due to the dash and courage of our Matrons who were the first to throw themselves into danger and to create a public spirit [of opposition to the French]. The people rose and the women in particular rode roughshod over everything, mistreating all the troops who came out in defence of the French government.[28]

Women in Zaragoza and again in Valencia proved that the 'public's idea of the fair sex' was no more than a patriarchal myth. The *Gazeta de Valencia* eulogized their role in the defence. 'Receive, you sensitive and loving beings, your country's and our sex's sincere thanks', the paper's report concluded.[29]

As in Zaragoza, there were individuals who played a particularly valiant role in Valencia's defence. Miguel García, an inn-keeper, with a small group of companions – smallholders, by one account – made constant sorties from the city's gates to harass the enemy. García had a horse shot from under him; a garrison officer gave him his, and he continued to skirmish beyond the walls.[30]

At eight o'clock in the evening the fighting came to an end. The inhabitants spent all night reinforcing the damaged walls and gates. But the French had suffered heavy losses. Without sufficient men or heavy artillery, and with a Valencian–Murcian division now threating his rear, Moncey took the only course open to him. Early the following day he began the retreat on Madrid. This time he choose the easier of the two roads via Almansa, where another defile made his force vulnerable to attack. Despite the junta's urgent orders, the Valencia army commanders inexplicably made no serious attempt to cut off his retreat. The people could not be faulted for their distrust of senior officers.

In a postcript to the heroic defence, ten days later the *Diario de Valencia* published a curious notice: 'those false and imprudent devotees who carried off the images and other effects which had been spared the flames of the Socorro church during the French attack, have not given notice of them. As things belonging to the altar and sacristy are missing, they are kindly asked to return them.'[31] As in Zaragoza, there were local looters who stole religious treasure when the opportunity arose.

ZARAGOZA: THE HEIGHTENING SIEGE

On June 27, twelve days after the first battle, General Verdier, a French army veteran, reached the Aragonese capital with reinforcements.* As senior officer he took command of a force of nearly fourteen thousand infantry, over one thousand cavalry, and twenty cannon, mortar and howitzers. The defence now numbered some eight thousand men, who included seven hundred regulars, 170 cavalry and 250 army gunners.[32]

Only a few hours after Verdier's arrival, a tremendous explosion shook the city with a roar which could be heard forty kilometres away. Some barrels of gunpowder, which were being carted from the stores, had exploded; people ran panic-striken into the streets, barely able to breathe in a cloud of black smoke and dust. Cries of treachery were raised as men and women began to dig out survivors from the smoking rubble of houses which had collapsed. But it seemed that a spark from a negligent carter's cigar was the real culprit.[33] French patrols advanced towards the gates hoping that the defence had abandoned their posts; they were met by musket and cannon fire.

In a style and tone not uncommon to the patriot leaders, Lazán issued an exhortation to the people for tranquility, 'submission and deference to the law' and 'docility to the constituted authorities' paternal voice' to maintain the city's defence. But his unusual and revealing words that followed made apparent the authorities' dependence on the people in the city's extreme situation. 'Order, subordination, *fraternity and the intimate union of general opinion* will procure and secure incalculable advantages' (stress added).[34] The inclusion of the lower orders in 'general opinion' and the call for an 'intimate union' of all orders of society, let alone 'fraternity' between them, was quite novel. The populace had made its effect felt. But then these were desperate times.

*

Shortly after midnight of Thursday, June 30, Verdier began his first bombardment. It was to last uninterrupted for nearly twenty-seven hours. The initial panic, which – despite orders – saw inhabitants running wildly in the streets, and crowding into the Virgen del Pilar's shrine, soon gave way to a resigned calm: the French cannon was not doing great damage to the solidly built brick houses. Moreover, look-outs posted in the Torre Nueva rang the bell when they saw the French batteries firing; and civilians took cover.

There were, unsurprisingly, miracles of survival.

---

* Lefebvre's column had already been reinforced, bringing the total to six thousand men and a second battery.

Everywhere people were saying: A shell fell on my house. There were several of us there and it exploded in front of us, yet no one was hurt. An incredible thing: a miracle worked by the Virgin Mary.[35]

Others felt themselves under the protection of their patron saint, the Virgen del Pilar, who would shield God's 'elected people'.[36]

But the unremitting barrage, which intensified at dawn, did great damage to the Portillo gate, leaving the cannon there virtually unprotected, and some of the gunners wanted to spike their guns. Major Renovales ordered them back to their battery and threatened to shoot any deserter. At the Santa Engracia gate most of the gunners were killed at their posts, and their places were taken by new defenders. But the French attack on the gates was repulsed.

It is impossible to describe the haste with which people worked . . . Soldiers and civilians who had been gathered to defend the batteries ran towards them or fled. The constant ringing of the bell and the shaking of the earth heightened the horror: and it seemed as though there was nowhere to save one from death.[37]

That evening, July 1, Palafox at last returned, entering through El Arrabal on the northern side which still provided free access to the city. He brought with him thirteen hundred men and a few cavalry he had managed to raise after his defeat at Épila. He took command, establishing his headquarters in the San Francisco friary close behind the main southern defences.

At 3 a.m. on July 2 the French guns at last fell silent after one last crescendo of firing in unison. This heralded the beginning of a general French infantry assault. Six columns were moved up under cover of darkness, and before dawn launched their first attack. They were repelled. But the danger was greatest at the Portillo gate where fifty defenders had been killed or wounded. On a rumour that the French had entered the city, civilian reinforcements rushed back to the market square. The last gunners alive, who were working frantically to set their huge twenty-four pound cannon, saw the line of French infantry, with fixed bayonets, advancing at the double, and fled. At that moment, a young woman who was bringing drink to the gunners, sprang forward, seized the still smouldering linstock from the hands of a dying artilleryman, and fired the cannon, which was loaded with grapeshot: the carnage among the closely packed French infantry was devastating. Standing on the gun carriage the woman rallied the civilian defenders to the gate's defence; and they poured musket fire onto the French who wavered and then turned in retreat.

Agustina Zaragoza's bravery had saved the gate. Catalan on her mother's side, she was 'about 22 years of age, a handsome woman, of the lower class of people', as one upper-class English observer who met her in Zaragoza baldly put it.[38] Another gave a more flattering picture: 'Her countenance is mild and feminine; her smile pleasing and her face altogether the last I should have supposed to belong to a woman who had led troops through blood and slaughter and pointed the cannon at the enemy . . . .'[39] Not surprisingly, she became the symbol of Zaragoza's heroic defence, and by extension of the patriotic war.*

The battle raged for several hours; unarmed civilians, women again prominent among them, reloaded the defenders' muskets so that they could keep up a rapid fire. French guns destroyed most of the earthworks, but not a single French soldier got into the city, though many died little more than an arm's length from the Spanish guns. As a result of this latest failure, all the more surprising after his day and night bombardment, Verdier decided that only a regular siege could reduce the city; and he began the time-consuming business of digging parallel siege trenches, linked by short diagonals and zig-zags, so that his troops could advance under protection as close to the city walls as possible, and heavy siege artillery could be dragged up and set in specially dug batteries to breach the walls. But he had also to cut the city's last link with the rest of Aragón, the northern road through El Arrabal, along which supplies of food and powder still reached the city. Under cover of dark and in the space of a single night, his engineers threw a flying bridge over the river, wide enough for a cannon to pass; and fighting now extended to the city's northern side, making it nearly impossible to bring in further supplies.

Palafox and his intendente, Calbo de Rozas, put the city on a war-economy footing. All property belonging to French residents and Spaniards who had fled and did not return within a week was ordered to be confiscated. One wealthy woman was imprisoned and her property taken over.[40] Food prices were fixed at their June levels, and temporary flour mills, worked by mules, and bakehouses were set up. The inhabitants handed over their wheat and flour which was made into the inferior bread habitually given to soldiers and prisoners, and which rich and poor alike now ate out of solidarity with the defenders.[41] The well-to-do were asked to make donations and give shirts for the many shirtless defenders. The shortage of gunpowder had to be resolved by ingenuity: every mortar and pestle was requisitioned and powder was ground by hand, while groups of civilians, including women and children, carefully washed the streets to find unprocessed saltpetre and sometimes even scraped it off the walls of buildings. The charcoal required was provided by burning hemp, which grew in abundance around the city.[42] Even so, only a small proportion of the enormous quantities of gunpowder needed could be produced; and a powder factory was set up in the safety of a mountain village seventy kilometres to the southeast.[43] An edict ordered village justices to round up and return the volunteers and regulars who had deserted in the first days of the siege.[44]

Martial discipline had never been one of the civilian defenders' strong points. After over a month of confronting death by the hour, dissension arose between

* Although she was, and is, commonly known in Spain as Agustina de Aragón, her family names were Zaragoza Doménech. As a reward for her action, she was made an artillery lieutenant; she wore petticoats and a military loose coat, with one gold epaulette 'and thus arrayed has a very soldier-like appearance'. (Jacob, 1811, pp. 123–124.) Although Byron, on a brief visit the following year to Andalucía, where Agustina was then serving, did not claim to have met her, he made of her, in his *Childe Harold's Pilgrimage*, one of his romantic heroines.

military and civilians, some of the latter maintaining that courage and the will to fight justified any indiscipline, and accusing the military of cowardice. The latter responded that bravery was insufficient if unaccompanied by military skills. Both arguments neglected an important cohesive aspect of the civilian–military defence: the civilians' will and courage to fight infused the soldiers with the sense of an all-out struggle; the military gave to the civilians a disciplined backbone and the knowledge of how best to organize the defence.

Nonetheless, there was open talk of treachery to explain the defenders' little success in raising the siege, and of the Valencia junta's lack of patriotism in not sending its army on the Ebro to the city's aid.* A spy mania became widespread. 'The people began to distrust everything, making them so suspicious that they overlooked no measures to discover traitors.'[45] No one could stop a mob seizing the military governor of the Cinco Villas, who was confined to prison on suspicion of communicating with Murat, and shooting him as a traitor at one of the gates.[46] But a beggar who aimed his musket at people to secure alms was sentenced to a severe flogging.[47]

Only a volunteer captain's quick reaction in arresting a priest he overheard trying to raise men to assassinate the French being held in custody for their own safety prevented a repetition of the Valencia massacre. Arraigned before the junta, the priest pleaded for his life, alleging that an aide-de-camp had ordered the assassination. Both men were held in custody, and the guard on the French was doubled.

On the eve of the great French siege bombardment which began on the night of July 31–August 1, Palafox announced that he had just received news from the Valencia junta of a great Spanish military victory in Andalucía. He had no further details and the defenders could not know that the battle of Bailén would shortly bring them relief. Before this, nearly two weeks of bitter fighting from street to street and house to house awaited them.

The bombardment, the worst the city's inhabitants had yet had to face, continued until shortly before dawn on August 4. On the previous evening, the fifteenth-century hospital, which at that moment held over five hundred sick and wounded, as well as orphans and the insane, was repeatedly hit. The inmates panicked. Men and women volunteers – 'abandoning all attention to their own property'[48] – rushed to evacuate them; and patients of both sexes ran, hobbled or staggered into the streets in their hospital nightshirts with their bandages, crutches and splints. As more shells rained down and masonry collapsed, great numbers were killed, some literally blown apart. To add to the horror several lunatics escaped and ran shouting, singing and wildly laughing amidst the corpses. 'Hell opened its gates that day', wrote an eyewitness.[49]

Shortly after first light on Thursday, August 4, the French assault started, announced by the besiegers' sixty guns firing in unison to cover their troops as

---

* Palafox sent a commissioner to the Valencian army which meanwhile had removed itself further from Zaragoza to Tortosa on the claim that the latter town was threatened by the enemy. The commissioner reported to Palafox that he did not believe the Valencian command was prepared to come to Zaragoza's defence. (Lafoz, 1996, p. 156, fn. 397; Alcaide Ibieca, 1830–1831, vol. I, p. 307, note 28.)

they took up position. In a further six hours of bombardment, the heavy French siege guns smashed nearly three hundred metres of wall, and opened two huge breaches. Men and women defenders braved the enemy fire to carry up sacks of earth and cotton to try to fill them; to little avail because by noon the Spanish artillery was silenced, although sharpshooters were still firing from amidst the ruined walls. An hour later, Verdier gave the order to attack. French and Polish infantry rose from their siege trenches and charged. For the first time they succeeded in putting a foot inside the city walls.

But once inside they found that 'each house was a citadel from whence there came such a hail of bullets as I have never seen before', wrote the French commander in his report on the action.[50] Verdier himself was wounded in the thigh, and Lefebvre again took command. The imperial infantry's advance was slow – but it advanced. Long before this moment, by eighteenth-century siege rules, the defenders' could have surrendered with honour. But if they fought on they must expect the city to be sacked: pillage, rape, murder, arson . . . If the inhabitants did not lose their lives, they were sure to lose everything else.

As his wound was being dressed, Verdier reportedly sent Palafox a message under a flag of truce, to which he received an instant answer.

> (French) Headquarters – Santa Engracia. *Capitulation.*
> Headquarters – Zaragoza: *Cold Steel and War.**

The French commander gave the order for his troops to continue their assault. Storming houses, silencing their defenders, they advanced through a hail of musket balls, bricks, pots and pans and boiling water and oil – soon known to the French soldiers as 'garlic soup' – hurled down on them by the inhabitants. Before long, the attacking skirmishers reached the Coso, the city's main thoroughfare. There, suddenly, everything went still. The defenders' fire was silenced. Only the great bell continued to sound the alarm. Panic-stricken, the inhabitants were fleeing across the stone bridge to El Arrabal on the far side of the Ebro which the besiegers had been unable to take. They swept soldiers and civilian defenders with them in their headlong rush. Some shouted that the city had fallen, others threw down their arms, and many older inhabitants were nearly trampled to death in the crush to cross the bridge.[51]

The news had got out: Palafox for the second time had left the Aragonese capital at its darkest hour. Guarded by a cavalry detachment, he had ridden off over the bridge with his staff officers and intendente, turning over the city's command to the fusilier brigadier, Antonio Torres. 'He saw, of course, that the city was lost', wrote his elder brother, marqués de Lazán, later;[52] so much then,

---

* Vaughan, 1809, p. 22. No Spanish witness of the events, let alone Palafox, cites this exchange. But at this moment Palafox had almost certainly left Zaragoza for the second time: the exchange may therefore have been with Brigadier Torres, whom Palafox had left in command. Vaughan was not present during the siege but spent several weeks after it with Palafox, from whom presumably he learnt of it. Oman (1902/1995, vol. I, p. 165) maintains that, on the commemorative medal issued after the first siege, the words 'cold steel and war' were inscribed on the reverse.

it seemed, for 'Cold Steel and War'. But there was at least a plausible pretext for his departure. Only a few kilometres from the city's northern exit, a Catalan column of two line regiments and two to three thousand new levies had arrived with an enormous convoy of much-needed supplies; and Palafox had gone to join them.

On the northern end of the stone bridge, a young cavalry lieutenant stopped the mass exodus almost single-handed. Brandishing his sabre, he ordered a cannon dragged out and aimed at the bridge; the tidal flight hesitated as the people saw him lift the linstock to fire the gun; at that moment several Franciscan friars ran past him onto the bridge, bearing a crucifix aloft, and urging the people to return to their posts. 'Is this how you defend the Faith and God's cause?' In a few minutes, the mass panic was ended; and as the people streamed back into the city those who still remained believed that the long-awaited reinforcements had arrived.[53]

It was now the military's turn to rouse the civilians. Under a hail of fire and with only a bayonet in his hand, an engineer captain, Marcos Simonó, jumped onto an improvised cannon parapet. Seeing civilians gathered at the openings of side streets and in doorways, he shouted that they were cowards. To 'defend their wives, families and fatherland', they must come out and fight. But the civilians hesitated. Noticing several French soldiers emerging from a house, the captain cried out: 'The enemy are fleeing!' A number of civilian defenders ran to his side and put themselves at his orders . . .[54]

A small group of men, led by a friar, charged suddenly from a side street and fired their muskets at point-blank range at the head of a French column. They paid with their lives; but their suicidal charge was another signal of the defence's revival. Heavy shooting broke out on the Coso; and barricades were again raised. A Spanish cannon opened fire along the thoroughfare; and soon more were brought up to sweep the Coso with grapeshot. Many of them were adorned with a red banderole which read in large letters: Victory or Death! The French, who a moment before had appeared on the verge of dominating the city, now found the tables turned. They could not advance down the barricaded side streets; and were exposed to sniper fire from the tops of houses when they sought cover. Shortly they were driven back by a charge of Spanish regulars and civilians. Fighting turned into house-to-house combat, the French often occupying one floor, the defenders the next; staircases had to be stormed one by one, and party walls knocked through in order to advance. No quarter was given in hand-to-hand fighting; 'friend and foe all fought pell-mell and without order'. The streets were littered with the dead and dying. It was each for himself; armed only with a knife, a seventy-six-year-old carpenter attacked two French soldiers who were sacking a house after assassinating its inhabitants; he killed one and, seizing his musket, took the other prisoner. Another man crept between the dead and attached a rope to a French cannon; in the struggle the rope broke and the defenders were denied their prize. More successfully, Manuel Fandos, a surveyor of the Imperial Canal, and a few companions, undertook a lightning dash across the Coso, killing the French gunners, and dragging their cannon away to turn it on the enemy.

The French were gradually driven back, maintaining advance strongholds only in the hospital and San Francisco friary on the Coso's south side. At nightfall, these two buildings were the apex of the French-held area; the base was the three hundred metres of wall their siege guns had battered down. Joining the two, along Santa Engracia street, they held a tenuous hold. In seven hours of fighting they had suffered two thousand casualties – a high proportion for a siege army of fifteen thousand which had also to protect its lines and batteries, and attempt to close off the city on both banks. It was evident now that no rapid end to the struggle was in sight.[55]

Throughout the night besiegers and besieged worked to strengthen their defences. By morning, both sides had rough but continuous front lines, the defenders encircling the French, often with no more than a narrow street in between. Wherever there was a space, cannon had been brought up to sweep the street. To the defenders' cheers and the sound of music, the marqués de Lazán, who had left the previous day after his brother, Palafox, re-entered the city from the north with a veteran battalion from the Catalan column and a few wagons of munitions. The French had not been able to hold the northern approaches to the city; in heavy skirmishing El Arrabal's smallholders had forced the enemy off their land. The munitions arrived in the nick of time.

> On August 5th there was not a single cartridge left, or the means to make them. In such critical circumstances, it was astonishing that, though they knew it, the people were not plunged into despair.[56]

Over the city there hung a pall of smoke. In the streets, the dead lay in heaps, unburied. The August heat was intense. But nothing now deterred the defenders, encouraged by the reinforcements and munitions which they had received. While the French commander laid plans for his troops to advance house by house, since this was the 'only kind of warfare suitable for waging against these madmen', the Spanish launched counter-attacks. The intense street fighting was to last another week. As a French officer, J. Belmas, subsequently wrote:

> The besieged defended themselves with unparalled fury. We could only gain ground by setting fire everywhere, by burrowing from house to house, by piercing the walls between one and the next to establish communications and form new lines of embrasures. Often we smashed down one partition to find the enemy behind it, defending himself with the bayonet.[57]

The fighting was in fact unnecessary. Both Palafox, who returned on August 9 with four thousand regular troops and armed villagers and two hundred supply carts, and Verdier, the French commander, had received the same news. The French army in Andalucía had capitulated to the Spanish after the battle of Bailén on July 14; barely entered into his new capital, King Josef was retreating from Madrid with his army to a defensive line on the upper Ebro. A Valencian division was, at last, moving to the relief of Zaragoza.

Verdier received orders on August 6 to be ready to raise the siege; but the following day the order was countermanded. The French general staff wanted Zaragoza captured as soon as possible in order to turn it into a strongpoint in their defence of the Ebro diagonal. On the point of being dismantled, the besiegers' batteries resumed firing.[58]

Palafox had delayed his return for two days believing that the French would raise the siege. On the day he returned to the city, the news of the Bailén victory was published in a special edition of the Pocal gazette. The rejoicing was triumphal; but the defenders still had four days of street combats ahead. The French batteries continued to fire on the city. The newly arrived Catalan volunteers, in their traditional village dress of red bonnets and wide-kneed breeches, chased the enemy from the Santa Catalina and botanical gardens; divided into squads and marshalled by a conch bugle, they fought hand to hand with the long knives they preferred.

By August 12, the French had moved back all their men, with the exception of a few snipers. On the night of the 13th, the bombardment was again intense and so many fires broke out all along the Coso that they 'appeared to be but a single blaze'.[59] Shortly before dawn the following day a great explosion shook the city; as a farewell gesture, the French had exploded a mine under the Santa Engracia monastery. That morning, not a single French soldier remained in the city. On direct orders from King Josef to raise the siege and cover the left flank of his army making for the Ebro, the besiegers had started their withdrawal at midnight under cover of the bombardment. The two months' siege had cost them 3,500 casualties and an untold amount of war materiel, including their heavy batteries which they spiked and threw into the Imperial Canal. Nearly all the high-ranking French officers were wounded, killed or sick, and some regiments were commanded now by captains, as Lefebvre reported a week later.[60]

The defenders' losses in life and property were incalculable; 'the loss of women and boys was very great, and fully proportionate to that of men'.[61] 'Zaragoza will be famous for ever – but it has been destroyed for a century', wrote one of the eyewitnesses. 'They could have razed the city to the ground and finished us all off, but they would not have seen us surrender.'[62] As Sir Charles Vaughan later wrote:

> It is a very singular fact to add, that though the writer of these few pages saw in Zaragoza many a parent who had lost his children, and many a man reduced from competence to poverty, he literally did not meet with one human being who uttered the slightest complaint; every feeling seemed to be swallowed up in the memory of what they had recently done, and in a just hatred of the French.[63]

The day after the French raised the siege, August 15, was the day of the Annunciation. A thanksgiving Te Deum was celebrated in the basilica of the Virgen del Pilar, the patron saint. In a language common to many Spanish patriots at the time, one of the men who had lived through the siege wrote:

The God of the armies has elected you, valiant Zaragozanos, to lower the pride of the stupidest, most calculating, ambitious and insatiable prototype of a tyrant; the most famous troublemaker and irascible destroyer of Europe, the fevered, the frenetic Napoleon.[64]

Two days earlier, in a vein also then common, a Palafox proclamation had excoriated the French army for pillaging,* robbing churches, rape, firing crops and assassinating the innocent and defenceless. But he went on to single out the women defenders for particular praise. They had displayed a courage 'superior to all those [women] whom history has recorded', an 'extraordinary spirit' amidst danger to bring food and succour to the male defenders.[65]

As a tribute to the people's determined defence and defiance of authority, the authorities disarmed the civilian defenders at the end of the siege.[66] The former's fear of those it called 'troublemakers' was evident: armed, their continued defiance of those who were in power during the siege might lead to highly undesirable results.

Four months later Zaragoza was again under siege. In even worse conditions, the city again held out for two months until it was finally forced to capitulate.

BAILÉN: AN IMPERIAL ARMY'S CAPITULATION IN THE FIELD

On July 19 the Andalucian patriot army defeated General Dupont at Bailén. The French general, it will be recalled, had marched from Madrid on yet another pacification campaign, ostensibly to ensure the safety of the French fleet in Cádiz, but in reality to subdue the Andalucian insurrection. After taking – and sacking – Córdoba he learned that the French fleet had surrendered and that a large Andalucian army was being formed under General Castaños, who had supported the Sevillan insurrection with his troops stationed in front of Gibraltar. This news – the patriot army's number exaggerated and with the added threat of inclusion of British troops who had landed near Cádiz – the Sevillan junta ensured he received through messages sent deliberately for French outposts to intercept.[67] Dupont thereupon retired to Andújar on the Guadalquivir where he havered for a month, urgently requesting reinforcements from Madrid and preparing to defend himself, instead of going onto the offensive or retiring to the easily defended Sierra Morena defiles.†

Andújar was not a good place to hold out. The extreme summer heat and the infections which accompanied it caused twenty percent of his troops to report sick.[68]

---

* There was obviously some pillaging by the defenders also since, during the street-fighting, Lazán issued an order of the day threatening to shoot all Spanish looters. (His order in Casamayor, 1908, p. 130.)

† Napoleon's plan was for Dupont to be reinforced by a French division in Portugal and by Moncey marching down the coast from Valencia after subduing the Levant. But neither of these reached him and Dupont had to rely on Madrid despatching reinforcements from his own corps.

General Castaños used the time to train his new volunteers. While there was no lack of arms – the British forces in Gibraltar provided a considerable number – the need of uniforms and shoes was a pressing problem. Although the Sevillan army provisioner put four hundred tailors to work, they could not provide sufficient uniforms in the time necessary. The junta called on the women of Sevilla to help out. Even so, Saavedra, the junta president, and the army chiefs, decided to 'share out each uniform between two recruits, giving to one a hat, coat and corduroy trousers, and to the other the (regiment's) barracks cap, jacket and cloth trousers.'[69]

Although in their month's training, using a French revolutionary army manual,[70] the volunteers were relatively well trained, Castaños was wary of the poor results shown by volunteers in open battle, and included only ten percent of these in the force he used directly against Dupont. The remainder were posted to reserve battalions.[71]

In keeping with accepted eighteenth-century military tactics, the Spanish army commander formed a flying column under a colonel to harass the French communication and supply lines and to keep the French forces under constant observation, without however engaging in battle. This irregular corps was the first formally created by the patriot military during the war.

Dupont, meanwhile, made an uncharacteristic mistake: convinced that the Spanish would attack him in Andújar – and the appearance of a Spanish army on the other side of the river fuelled his misconception – he failed to send out a cavalry screen to inform him of the patriot army's movements. Instead, he ordered his reinforcements under General Vedel, which were holding the rear along the road, to march urgently to support him against the feared Spanish attack. In a forced march of nineteen hours along the tracks beside the Guadalquivir – instead of the royal road which would have taken less than half the time – Vedel reached Andújar. No sooner had he done so, than Dupont received news that a Spanish force – the patriot's flying column – was threatening the Sierra Morena defiles and thus the French rear and communications with Madrid. He ordered Vedel to march back immediately to defend the mountain passes. Like a good Napoleonic general, Vedel set out the following day.

Castaños had deceived Dupont: the patriot force in front of the French at Andújar was the Andalucian reserve army, aimed precisely at making the French general believe that this was to be the main point of attack. Castaños had meanwhile sent two crack divisions of veteran soldiers to ford the Guadalquivir above Andújar with the aim of taking the French from the rear. Splitting his forces was risky: had the French commander informed himself better, he could have attacked the relatively weak Andalucian reserve; instead, with the news of Spanish military activity in his rear, he decided to withdraw to the safety of the Sierra Morena which was guarded by his reinforcements. At nightfall on July 18 he began his retreat from Andújar. As Colonel Pedro Girón, of Castaños' general staff, recorded:

> It says little for the patriotism or resolve of Andújar's inhabitants that not a single person ventured to inform us of [the enemy's retreat] until 2 a.m. the following

morning; at that hour two men appeared in the commander-in-chief's bivouac, where I was also, and gave us the first news.[72]

The two elite patriot divisions had meanwhile forded the river and stationed themselves, as planned, before Bailén. Their objective was to advance on Dupont's rear; they did not know that the French general was instead advancing on them, and Dupont was unaware that a considerable Spanish force was about to advance on him. Before dawn on July 19, Spanish outposts encountered the French vanguard. The patriot forces took up defensive positions. They were commanded by two foreign-born major generals: a Swiss, Teodor Reding, and a Belgian, marqués de Coupigny. To complicate matters, both sides now also had enemy divisions in their rear: Castaños, who had crossed the river at Andújar that morning, was purportedly pursuing Dupont; and the Spanish defending Bailén were potentially threatened by Vedel's division which Dupont had ordered back to the Sierra Morena, some fifty kilometres away. But inexplicably the commanders of both these reserve forces dawdled, arriving at the battlefield too late to have any effect on the fighting.*

Dupont made the mistake of underestimating the number of Spanish troops in front of him and committing at first only the vanguard of his marching column. In consequence, his cavalry was much depleted in the first attacks. It took him time to deploy infantry from his column, which included a baggage train five kilometres long, loaded with pillaged loot from the Córdoba sacking, so Napoleon subsequently claimed, but more importantly with the sick and infirm.

From dawn until early afternoon, in the increasing summer heat, the patriot forces withstood the French attacks. In the front line of the defence was one of Reding's infantry battalions, in which Francisco Guervos, the Granada cathedral violinist and volunteer, commanded a company after being promoted to corporal and sergeant in two months. In a letter to his parents, he wrote:

> The enemy's vanguard of twelve thousand men had the fortune to take a low hill planted with olive trees around our positions. The olives saved them from even greater disaster. Our infantry was very bold: groups of thirty to forty men held off the ferocious and repeated enemy cavalry's charges . . . although with great daring numbers of their horsemen reached to within twenty paces of our batteries . . . I was lucky not to be hit by a musket ball. I had left my position to reprimand a soldier who had left the line. Immediately, the sergeant behind me was killed, crumpling to the ground. It was impressive to see the raw recruits (and even officers) politely acknowledge a grenade or cannon ball which passed over their heads.[73]

The penultimate attack was led by the French commander and all his generals at the head of his only veteran force, the Marine Guards, who were bringing up the rear. The attack was thrown back, and Dupont was wounded.

---

* As Colonel Girón observed on the Spanish side, 'the reserve, followed by the third division, moved forward much later than it could or should have done'. (Girón, 1978, p. 226.)

One final attack by Swiss mercenary troops originally in Spain's service, but whom Napoleon had pressed into the French occupation army, ended the battle. On the other side of the line were the Swiss mercenaries who had remained loyal to the patriot cause. The latter followed the Swiss custom of parading their colours and presenting arms in front of their countrymen who were about to attack them. Thereupon the Swiss in Dupont's army refused to fight and fraternized with their compatriots.[74] At that point, the patriot flying column appeared in Dupont's rear and flank, and the French commander, believing it to be Castaños' vanguard, asked for a truce and a free passage through Bailén. General Reding agreed to the former, but replied that the latter depended on his commander-in-chief, General Castaños.

Heat and thirst were the major protagonists of the battle. Even Spanish soldiers of the reserve who had not fought dropped dead from dehydration.[75] For the infantry combatants, thirst was worsened by the powder which dried their mouths when they chewed off the end of their cartridges before loading their muskets. There was no shade, and the stubble which was set alight by the fighting increased the heat. The Spanish forces, which included seventy mounted bull herders from Jerez with their long lances,* were supported by Bailén inhabitants who brought them water and encouraged their resistance. The heroine – for there had to be one who epitomized the popular struggle – was a relatively well-to-do married woman of sixty-five, María Luisa Bellido.[76] As she was carrying water to General Reding, her pitcher was shattered by a musket ball; without hesitating a moment, she brought a piece of the jar in which some water remained to quench the commander's thirst. But the French received no such popular help. When the truce was declared the French troops dispersed in search of water. Sergeant Guervos believed that, 'more than three thousand Swiss and Italians used this as a pretext to come over to our side. If the truce had lasted longer, Dupont would not have had a force to surrender . . .'

While the capitulation talks were continuing, Guervos saved a cuirassier officer's life from a Spanish soldier. 'These wretches are no better than the French when it comes to killing and thieving', he wrote to his parents. He went to the French encampment to visit the officer whose friendship he had won by his action.

> The camp was a horror; everyone dying of thirst and receiving two ounces of bread a day. We're not much better off; for three days we have eaten nothing but gazpacho for want of money to provide us our rations.[77]

As Vedel's reinforcements had not appeared on the field of battle, Dupont sued for surrender terms. The arrival at this moment, though late, of Castaños'

---

* These were volunteers, who titled themselves the Jerez Lancers. Their numbers are taken from an official army statement of strength submitted to the Sevilla junta prior to the battle (Quesada Montero, 1958, appendix 5). With the exception of their commander, who was wounded in both wrists by a musket ball, they appear to have suffered no casualties, but were mentioned in despatches for their 'very distinguished services' (Castaños to Sevilla junta, July 27, Andújar; BL, *Eg* 386/8–15).

reserve army, added to the pressure: Dupont was effectively caught between two fires. He agreed to capitulate. When Vedel at last appeared on the scene, he felt himself free of the agreement: only the Spanish threat to slaughter Dupont's troops brought him to capitulate on the same terms as his commander-in-chief.* The Spanish thus forced the surrender of more than seventeen thousand unwounded French troops; nearly two thousand more French dead and wounded were left on the battlefield. The cost to the Spanish army was just under one thousand casualties.[78] While much of the local population devoted itself to attending to the Spanish wounded, others set about looting the surrendered French troops of the plunder they had themselves looted on their unsuccessful campaign.[79]

*

By the standards of the Napoleonic wars Bailén was not a major battle. But its repercussions far exceeded its military importance. A second-rate military power, in political turmoil at the start of its anti-Napoleonic resistance, had forced the capitulation of a Napoleonic army in the field.† Even worse, King Josef, who had barely arrived in Madrid, exaggerated the importance of the defeat and the Spanish army's strength, and fled northwards with his military to take refuge on the defensive line of the Ebro. 'This foolish action, as much as Bailén itself, gave the Spanish uprising credibility and damaged Napoleon's prestige throughout Europe.'[80]

The Iberian summer of 1808 was not a good one for the Emperor. His army was about to be bundled out of Portugal by the British – a second French capitulation more important than that of Bailén, because henceforth Portugal would be British terrain; had been humiliatingly defeated in Andalucía; had failed to take the 'indefensible' Zaragoza; had been thrown back before the walls of Valencia; and had abandoned a second attempt to capture Gerona and Tarragona in Cataluña. Spanish popular resistance was proving more difficult to overcome than mere 'punitive' military expeditions could deal with.

Bailén also gave a national dimension to the Spanish struggle: apart from Andalucians, there were in the victorious army Aragonese, Castilian, and Murcian troops. Three commanders were Navarese, Extremaduran and

* The terms, anticipating those of the Cintra Convention by little more than a month, were that the French army would be returned by sea to France from Cádiz. The Bailén terms, like those of Cintra in Britain, caused considerable popular Spanish resentment, which was reflected in the Sevilla junta. In the end only the senior officers were shipped home, the rest of the French army being left to rot in prison hulks in Cádiz or to die of hunger and thirst on the barren Balearic island of Cabrera. Napoleon court-martialled Dupont who was imprisoned and stripped of his rank and honours, though on Napoleon's downfall and the restoration of the monarchy Dupont had his revenge: Louis XVIII appointed him minister of War.

† Though sometimes said to be the first, this was not the case. Napoleonic armies had capitulated at Cairo, El-Arish and Verdeiro previously. But Bailén irritated the Emperor in particular because the quite unexpected capitulation to the forces of an anti-Napoleonic insurgency damaged the Empire's triumphant image, French honour and glory. (Jesus de Haro Malpesa, 'El impacto de la batalla de Bailén en Francia. La historiografía francesa', in VV.AA., 1999, p. 161.)

Catalan. (Indeed, even José San Martín, the future liberator of Argentina and Chile, who was serving in the army as a Spanish cavalry captain, made his name by ambushing a party of French soldiers prior to the battle.) In other words, the victory belonged not solely to Andalucía, but to a much wider national (not to say international) spectrum. The Sevillan junta was well aware of this. In a manifesto issued a few days after Bailén, it reminded Andalucians that they were Spanish, and called on them to unite with their brothers on the Ebro, the Duero and the Júcar – the latter two rivers representing Castilla la Vieja, Castilla la Nueva and Valencia.[81] An anonymous poet in Sevilla wrote:

> All are going together . . . Castilians, Asturians,
> Galicians, Santanderinos and Extremadurans
> all yearn to free themselves. The triumph
> of their union achieved
> the Pyrennees
> will see them linked with Navarra
> the Basque Country and Cataluña . . .[82]

THE ILLUSIONS OF VICTORY

These early Spanish victories, however, had more baneful than beneficial results for the patriot cause. They brought the illusion – very soon to be brutally shattered – that after Bailén the Spanish army could fight and defeat the French in open battle; with two not very significant exceptions, the patriot army on its own would, in this type of combat, go down to crushing defeat time and again. The other illusion, precipitated by Zaragoza's and, to a lesser extent, Valencia's defence, was that, thanks to the inhabitants' determination, towns could withstand imperial sieges. This, at an enormous cost of lives and untold suffering, was similarly proven false. With only one important exception – Cádiz, which by its geographical situation was almost impregnable to land attack – no town would again repeat Zaragoza's first triumph; and after Gerona's seven-month long resistance in 1809, the length of time besieged towns were able to hold out diminished to little over one month and sometimes much less. This was not so much because popular resistance declined, but because the size and firepower of the army Napoleon committed to Spain increased. For sure, the dozen or so sieges tied down large numbers of imperial troops for about eighteen months. The defence of the weaker side, as the American War of Independence had shown in its first year, lay in increasing the length of the conflict and in wearing down the enemy. But the cost in prisoners, usually regular troops, of these defeated sieges, let alone civilian lives, was immense; and in the end this static defence was not going to win the war.

7

Soldiers at the Front and Rural Conflict in the Rear

THE PATRIOT ARMY'S SLOW ADVANCE

The last of King Josef's troops to abandon Madrid after Dupont's capitulation at Bailén was a squadron of cuirassiers. This 'sad relic of a proud corps' was preceded by

> A boisterous and playful crowd of children, wearing the same breast and back plates which that bloody army had abandoned in its flight, and who mimicked exactly the unruly officers' gestures, the brutal cavalrymen's yells and their barbarous prancing and cavorting . . . Acquaintances and strangers embraced in the streets . . . the hymns of victory resounded everywhere,

wrote *Semanario Patriótico*.[1]

During the two weeks between the French army's rapid retreat and the first patriot army's entrance, the Madrid burgess lived in fear of 'anarchy' without government or authorities to control the populace. In fact, nothing of the sort happened. But the Valencian–Murcian army's arrival on August 14 did little to enthuse the law-abiding. The soldiers were poorly dressed in countryman's flared knee breeches and woollen cloaks, recalled Antonio Alcalá Galiano, and their round hats were covered in bad religious miniatures.

> Dirty and dishevelled, they were fierce of aspect and violent in their ways, lacking all discipline and of repugnant appearance . . . The Madrid educated classes were filled with terror to see these threatening people abound in the streets . . .

They sang to small four-stringed guitars, and entered convents to ask the nuns for yet another religious picture to stick in their already overloaded hats, keeping their daggers always visible in contrast to the devout images on their heads. 'On the other hand, the Madrid plebs . . . looked on them as friends on whom they count in case of need,'* continued the same witness.[2]

The capital's elite looked forward therefore to the Andalucian army's arrival. This, since it had defeated the French, must be a professional army. Although some members of the Sevilla junta saw the necessity for their victorious troops to move immediately northwards in pursuit of the enemy, the victory celebrations in Sevilla and the fêting of Castaños, as the hero of Bailén, took up over a month's vital time before the army reached Madrid. Its effect on the educated classes was not a great deal better than that of the Valencian–Murcian army. Apart from the mounted Jerez bull-herders who, in their native attire, attracted particular attention, the rest of the army was of 'middling aspect – not as bad as the Valencians but not as good as the best of the French', recalled Alcalá Galiano.[3]

> When the people remembered the martial appearance of the Imperial Guard whom the defeated Dupont had taken with him, they were amazed to think that they had surrendered to these inferior looking soldiers.†

The elite's doubts as to whether these troops could again defeat a French army were shortly to be confirmed. The populace, on the other hand, was ecstatic. In front of the church where Castaños and his staff attended mass, a *manola* suddenly leapt out of the enormous crowd and embraced Colonel Whittingham with such force that both she and the British observer to the Andalucian army fell to the ground while the woman exclaimed: ¡bendito sea el inglesito de mi alma!' ('blessed be my darling little Englishman!') . . .[4]

To the people's even greater delight, the Andalucian army's 'valiant soldiers' arrived 'adorned with captured spoils': hats decorated with enemy plumage, officers' swords and even proudly mounted on the crop-tailed horses of the highly regarded French cuirassiers, reported the *Gazeta de Madrid*.

> Some were attired in complete French uniforms to show that they had looted the enemy whose life they had taken. Others bore the muskets, swords and sabres which had, on the day, been loaded and sharpened to use against them . . . The overjoyed Madrid populace mingled with the soldiers and followed them . . .[5]

The possibility that these rough and ready patriot troops might unite with the Madrid populace to cause a commotion – even to fill the capital's power vacuum – was never more than an elitist chimera, as the events of the following day proved. On August 24, with all the city's councillors dressed in the traditional black doublets and hose of Spain's golden age, a rejection of all that was French, indeed foreign, Madrid proclaimed Fernando VII king and the

---

* After incidents involving French subjects, the army's commanding general, González de Llamas, threatened to punish any soldier who insulted or demanded money from a Madrileño, whether of French origin or not. (*Gazeta de Madrid*, August 16, 1808.)
† In fact, Dupont did not have the Imperial Guard, but the Marine Guard, in his column; but it was the former's appearance which most impressed Madrileños.

authorities swore the traditional oath of fealty. It was the people who had insisted on the dress, asserted Quintana's *Semanario Patriótico*, and it was the people who gave the day its particular significance.

> They were not the purely passive spectators accustomed like mercenaries to attend the ceremonial occasions organized by the authorities or, as often as not, by a tyrant's will . . . it was the people who were this august function's glorious spirit, motif and composer. Not content with cheering their king, the populace's . . . greatest huzzas and vivas were reserved, as was only right and just, for the noble English guests, Lord Doile and Colonel Vitingham, in a display of the people's gratitude for the singular favour that their generous nation is demonstrating to Spain; and frequently cheers were heard in which 'England!' 'Spain!' and 'Fernando!' were mixed.[6]*

The following day, the city's inhabitants and troops were treated to a celebratory firework display, music in the Prado, the ascent of three hot-air balloons and two specially authorized bullfights, one in the morning and one in the afternoon, to which the soldiers who had 'so gloriously defended their country' were allowed in free and, as 'a gift to the capital's public', civilian spectators were charged only half price.[7] The Prado itself was shut to carriages so that ordinary people could 'enjoy the spectacle more comfortably'. Significant of the general feeling of new-found freedom, 8,300 tickets were sold by the two Madrid theatres for their performances on August 25.[8] There was no particular thought of the morrow; the inhabitants, assiduously assuaged by the local authorities, believed that the war had come to an end; they had declared for Fernando VII and forgotten that Napoleon did not take defeat lightly.

Meanwhile, the armies tarried in Madrid when they should have been marching north to chase the French army out of Spain. There was more than one reason for Castaños' delay. The Sevilla junta refused to authorize him to move north of Madrid or to continue to supply him.[9] The juntas' determination to keep their armies under their own control – for without an army they lacked their most important recourse to power – here demonstrated one of the true, and limited, faces of the 'national' rising. And though Sevilla subsequently denied its refusal to supply its army, there can be little doubt that it was true.† In a letter from Madrid, Castaños wrote that he was 'saddened to know that nearly three thousand of my troops cannot leave their barracks because they have

---

* 'Lord' Doile, a Spanish journalist's invention, was in fact plain Colonel Doyle posted as a British military observer to the Asturian army, although he turned this into a roving commission. 'Vitingham' was the previously named Whittingham – Spanish then having no 'W' in its alphabet.

† Foreign Secretary Canning wrote on September 5 to James Duff, British consul in Cádiz, that the Sevilla junta was 'so tenacious of their individual authority' that they had reserved exclusively for their own use British supplies which were intended for the 'service of all those Provinces that have embraced the Cause . . .' (PRO, *FO* 185/15). Notwithstanding, between June 8 and Sept 30, 1808, the Sevilla junta spent over twenty million reales on its thirty-thousand-strong army (Quesada Montero, 1958, Appendix 7: *Army Treasurer's accounts*) which, at an annualized rate, made sixty million reales. The junta's outlays, moreover, were all effected through the army Treasurer who kept exact records.

nothing to wear, and I don't count in this number those men who are in rags . . .'.[10] Both Madrid theatres gave three special performances in late August to raise money to provide troops with uniforms; they brought in 28,301 reales, a paltry sum in relation to the troops' needs.[11] The lack of uniforms and shoes would constantly beset the Spanish army whose troops often went barefoot and in rags.

Greater affairs, however, detained Castaños in Madrid. The regional juntas, led by Galicia, Valencia and Murcia, had reached agreement on the need to set up a Junta Suprema, in effect a national government, to conduct the war effort.* General Cuesta, who had so reluctantly been pressed into joining the Valladolid rising, quickly attempted to pre-empt the new ruling body. As the regional juntas' deputies were making their way to the Junta Suprema's founding meeting, he proposed to Castaños that the two generals and the duque del Infantado (who like many another authority after Bailén had abandoned the French cause and turned 'patriot') should take over supreme military command. The provincial juntas would be abolished and the authority of the captain generals and audiencias re-established. Generals with military command would pressure the Junta Suprema to appoint a regency in its place. To his credit, Castaños turned down the plot which would have been the first real *pronunciamiento* – the military's intervention in politics at a national level which so plagued the rest of the Spanish nineteenth century.[12]

Ignoring these state affairs, the Madrid proletarian youth who had burlesqued the last French cavalry to abandon Madrid took to the streets as though they were theirs. To the horror of the burgess and the authorities they cavorted naked in the Prado's public fountains, 'without heed of the presence of both sexes', and sang lewd songs which 'offended the public's sense of decorum and virtue'. The Consejo de Castilla demanded that the Madrid justices re-establish patrols of law-abiding subjects.[13]

RURAL CONFLICT IN THE REARGUARD

We must pause for a moment in the march of events to survey the rearguard, the rural world which formed the majority of the population. The still widely-held Spanish idealization that all social classes were united as one in the struggle was rapidly shown to be no more than a myth.

From the start of the war, frequent complaints from the Church and señorial lords that their vassals were not paying dues and tithes reached the regional juntas. As the lords were not receiving their dues, post-hoc logic assumed that the villagers were not paying them. In many cases this was true. But another more imperative logic was also at work: local oligarchs were retaining these impositions, especially tithes, in order to pay the war contributions demanded by the juntas, and to have sufficient food stocks in hand to meet the requisitions of the Spanish and French armies, both of which had to live off the land. In this way, these classes spared themselves the burden of being the major contributors

* See Chapter 8, pp. 201 et seq.

to the exactions levied on their villages.* But the ability to provide supplies to the armies was also a way to save ordinary villagers from military – especially French army – reprisals for failure to deliver up their meagre crops.

Bishops and cathedral chapters were particularly vocal in their protests about losing tithes. Village resistance had begun before the war, but with the conflict the refusal became more radical and widespread. The Church's right to exact such tribute was now questioned in even the smallest of places, like Herrera del Duque, far from the beaten track in Badajoz, where villagers staged a catechismal parody during their local fiesta in May, 1808. A man on a donkey, acting the part of towncrier, addressed the villagers:

> Do you believe that tithes are to maintain those who go about Toledo† in carriages with their whores and to keep priests who are no more than drones? – Yes, that is what we believe, responded the villagers in chorus.[14]

Although patriot bishops and cathedral chapters were initially often a source of considerable funds for the local juntas, popular feeling was aroused by the Church's determined refusal of any wartime sacrifice of its right to tithes. As a letter to the Junta Suprema by one who called himself Juan de Miedez put it: 'Why should the poor soldier suffer and die in the war, and the canonry with its excesses bring down the wrath of our great God on the whole Spanish Nation?'[15] Both the Suprema and the Catalan regional junta agreed with the Church and señorial lords, denying to all and sundry the right to seize dues and tithes: in their view, no change in the feudal system could be envisaged. The social status quo, it might be argued, was necessary to maintain a broad patriotic alliance against the French; but it could equally be argued that this strategy suited both juntas' conservative instincts.

Villagers on the other hand were not content solely with denying the Church its dues; land seizures, strikes for higher wages, smallholders' revolts, farmers' and juntas' counter-offensives affected various regions of the patriot zone.

Only two weeks after the Sevilla rising, day labourers in the nearby township of Carmona refused to reap the harvest on the great estates.‡ They stayed at home, alleging that their absence was due to the 'new developments'. Effectively on strike, the withdrawal of their labour increased – as they must have known it would – the shortage of field hands resulting from the recent large army enlistment. Taking advantage of the excellent grain crop standing in the fields, the day labourers were attempting to secure a raise in their pitifully low wages. On June 9 the Carmona junta reacted with draconian measures: for each day

* French army officers in search of provisions invariably seized village tithe records in order to determine the largest local landowners from whom they could exact the maximum produce.
† The village was in the diocese of Toledo.
‡ In its landholding distribution Carmona was fairly typical of latifundista western Andalucía. In mid-eighteenth century, 5.7% of owners, who included clerical institutions as well as individuals, held 76.1% of the land, and the remaining 94.3% of owners held just under 24%. (Josefina Cruz Villalón, *Propiedad y uso de la tierra en la Baja Andalucía – Carmona, siglos XVIII–XX*, Madrid 1980, pp. 90–91, Table 11–7.)

that a labourer refused to work he was to be punished by ten days in gaol and two hours in chains.[16]

Presumably this got some men back, because ten days later the junta received a farmers' memoir setting wage levels for different labouring jobs. The day before, after complaints from a number of townships about the labourers' strike, the Sevilla junta issued an edict which said it had been made aware of landworkers' 'scandalous abuse' of the shortage of hands caused by

> the indispensable necessity to defend the fatherland, religion and our beloved sovereign . . . Ignoring the level of day wages already agreed, they have tried to raise them exorbitantly, to the very notable prejudice of agriculture. The junta cannot remain indifferent to . . . or fail to restrain the avarice of these inconsiderate vassals who use to their own benefit the afflictions of their fellow workers . . .[17]

In order to contain wages 'within the limits of reason and distributive justice', the Sevilla junta ordered that all wages agreed prior to the 'present events' must be respected and local justices must enforce these, punishing if necessary those who failed to respect the agreed rates. Significantly the junta did not threaten recalcitrant labourers with the fate that Carmona had decreed; indeed it even threw them a few crumbs by recognizing that as a result of 'the actual circumstances' wages might rise somewhat: no junta at that moment could afford to create an enemy of its future rural recruits or run the risk of serious agrarian conflict.

However, even this edict did not immediately have the desired effect, because a few days later the Carmona junta admitted that 'many labourers are still in the town and will not go to the fields to work'. And those who had returned were being paid 'excessive' wages by some estate bailiffs without heed of the Sevilla proscriptions or its own. The Carmona junta issued another decree raising the punishment for each day's refusal to work to twenty days in gaol – although reference to chains was now omitted – and a fine of about five days' wages.*

The repetition of a broadly similar situation in Calatayud, Aragón, suggested that labourers' determination to raise their low wages thanks to the outbreak of war was a fairly widespread phenomenon.†[18]

---

* Thereafter, the issue vanished from the Carmona junta's record of proceedings; the majority of labourers, it must be supposed, went out to reap the harvest, lucky if they received higher day wages.

† Farmers complained to the town council at the end of July 1808, that the labourers were demanding 'excessive' wages of twenty-four reales, and even twenty-six, when the maximum for each hanegada cut had been twenty in previous years. And this was despite the fact that the corregidor had already issued orders that no wage rises be paid to day labourers. The council threatened to imprison labourers and fine farmers who did not respect the previous maximum. (AM de Calatayud, *Libros de Actas de los Acuerdos de la Villa de Calatayud*, 1808–1810, documento No. 251, July 29, 1808.) As here again no more was heard on the matter, these measures were presumably effective. However, the labourers' example spread to the town: its pastry-cooks' exorbitant price increases – 'to the public's detriment' – were roundly condemned in November 1808 by the town councillors, who decided that they would fix their prices in future.

More dramatic events broke out in Don Benito, an Extremaduran town of some ten thousand inhabitants, in November 1808. A crowd of carters, labourers and artisans gathered in the main square for the military enlistment ordered by the newly formed Junta Suprema throughout the patriot zone to raise the army's strength. Suddenly shouts were raised:

> 'Let the rich go to war, they're the ones who've got something to lose, the pasture lands! . . .' The protesters drew out knives and daggers and threatened the magistrate and town councillors who fled precipitously in fear of their lives . . .

These 'malicious mutineers' then pursued other honourable townsmen, even entering their homes to insult them, wrote an anonymous correspondent. As these men received not the slightest punishment, they felt themselves free to take over en masse the pastures and plough them. 'They have threatened the lives of any who oppose them, a threat they repeated to the new corregidor in the public square.'[19] The correspondent maintained that there was no cause in the enlistment proceedings for this tumult. But one must suspect him of being economical with the truth; wartime enlistments carried out by the local authorities frequently led to disturbances. The reason was simple: the local oligarchs' sons were all too often excused military service on some trumped-up pretext, while the poor were sent to the army.

In Don Benito, however, the landworkers' riot represented a refusal to fight in defence of the wealthy's property and privileges which were denied them; and their protest was immediately carried over into direct action to solve the agrarian problem that had bedevilled Extremadura for centuries: its vast untilled pastures which the impoverished and landless villagers, denied access to the land, rightly saw as the cause of their poverty.*

The region was one of Spain's poorest: Extremadura was the privileged winter grazing of the great flocks of transhumant sheep which were driven down from the cold northern Castilian plains where they grazed in summer. Though the corporate power of the age-old *Mesta*, the powerful group of Castilian sheep-owners, who included nobles and monasteries, had been eroded in the eighteenth century, their merinos still grazed in Extremadura and parts of Andalucía, exercising a hold over the land which prevented much of it being tilled.

The letter's anonymous author – one of the 'honourable' townsmen, without a doubt, and probably one of those who had been insulted – could not believe that the lower orders, 'usually humble towards their [social] superiors and obedient to the local magistrate', could have had the 'effrontery' to act with such wildness. There must be a 'hidden hand' behind them; and the hand he found was almost as surprising as the events themselves. A friar, Miguel Cortes de la Rocha by name – no ordinary friar, for sure, because he was a member of a

---

* One hundred and fifty years later, the problem still remained. Shortly before the outbreak of the Spanish Civil War in July 1936, thousands of landless Extremaduran villagers, under the aegis of the Socialist Landworkers' Federation, invaded the pasture lands and began to plough them.

prestigious military–religious order – had revealed himself as the instigator of the troubles after the first commotion and the authorities' flight, publicly telling the labourers in the evenings:

> 'Look, my sons, we are all equals in this world. There's no difference between you and me other than that I am ordained. Go out to plough the pastures, nobody shall punish you for it.' And so these delinquents say they have nothing to fear because (the friar) will protect them and he has many connections in Badajoz and Madrid.[20]

The anonymous correspondent then went on, perhaps libellously, to detail the friar's 'disreputable life' and wrote that it could be 'reasonably doubted whether he was religious'. A native of the township, he had said only three or four masses in his years in Don Benito, knew no Latin, was living with a young mistress, a stranger to the town, had sucked his elderly parents dry, and lived in considerable style which had led him to lose nearly all his wealth. But he was well connected by marriage with a former Madrid minister and with a present titled member of the Extremaduran junta which often used him to carry out local tasks on its behalf.

Whether friar Miguel was in fact the 'hidden hand' or whether it was not rather the 'hand of justice' that was at work must remain an open question. But if the friar in fact expressed the thoughts attributed to him then his clerical support would have been of vital importance to the labourers who invaded the pastures and began to plough them in readiness to sow their own crops.

*

The most seriously threatening rural revolt against the new authorities came in Asturias. The Fernandistas of Oviedo, the regional capital, had recruited the villagers as a hired street force to make their rising, in late September 1808, the junta's powerful opponents used the same tactic in an attempt to overthrow it.

They called on villagers to attend a popular assembly on September 25 in Oviedo. Some four hundred came, as did numerous townsfolk. After drawing up a document of popular grievances, the crowd marched to the junta's seat in the town hall, broke in to the council chamber and arrested one deputy whom they accused of treachery. They carried him off and imprisoned him in the fortress.

Although the junta had been reformed only a few weeks earlier, it basically remained an alliance of the landholding lower nobility and a handful of progressives. In order to ensure that the alliance could work to the latter's advantage, the progressives made several concessions to the majority which were prejudicial to the villagers. In a region supposedly at war, and where the hidalgos formed seventeen percent of the population, the junta abrogated a Godoy measure and reaffirmed the nobility's privileged exemption from enlistment. The whole burden of fighting in the war now fell on the commoners, the villagers in particular. But the final straw came not as the result of a junta order but of a rumour that it was about to abolish a twenty-year-old royal privilege which made it illegal to dispossess villagers of the lands they rented.

This provision had made villagers lifetime tenants of the land they held in rent. Whether or not there was some truth to the rumour mattered little. Given that the junta was dominated by the same lower nobility that had always ruled their lives, and which had just restored some of their privileges, the villagers readily believed it.

The junta meanwhile had made two powerful enemies, the audiencia and an important sector of the Church. It had curtailed some of the audiencia's rights – no doubt in revenge for its role in trying to prevent the rising; and had taken over the cathedral chapter's wealth – on the pretext that the chapter refused to pay canons and employees who were 'serving the country'.

These enemies combined forces and, cleverly, in the light of popular discontent, succeeded in introducing a 'people's representative' on the junta – which shortly afterwards abolished the post, and approved the pro-noble decrees.

Its opponents launched a counter-attack, accusing the junta of arbitrary and tyrannical conduct, misappropriation of funds and finally of proposing to abolish the villagers' right not to be dispossessed of rented land.

More than a little alarmed, the junta issued a proclamation the following day strongly denying these 'false rumours' which had caused 'popular anxiety and displeasure' against the 'legitimate authorities'.[21]

Still determined to win, the opposition planned an anti-junta coup for the following night, using the same tactics as those who had risen four months earlier. Villagers were to assemble in Oviedo and seize various strategic sites by surprise. But this time the new authorities were on the alert. Major General Francisco Ballesteros, later one of patriot Spain's more successful generals, occupied the town with his troops and artillery. Villagers who had been summoned by church bells ringing the alarm set out with their arms; but on discovering that the capital had been taken over militarily, they returned to their homes without confronting the troops.[22]

The junta arrested the people's representative and a number of audiencia employees, and set up an investigatory commission, announcing at the same time that henceforth a military force would be stationed in Oviedo to prevent any repetition of such disorder.[23]

Subsequently a different gloss was put on the events by the leading progressive Flórez Estrada and another junta deputy who, addressing themselves to the 'pacific townsfolk, landworkers and simple artisans', called on them not to be seduced in future by 'French agents' in combination with such impostors as a 'small number of this capital's inhabitants' who wanted to 'raise the entire province' against the junta. These people had sent out orders in the junta's name to the villagers 'to come armed to the capital on September 29'.[24]

As a young witness to the events, and a fervent junta supporter, later admitted, the junta had been wrong in attacking the villagers who

> had taken to arms to defend the country's Independence, but also to improve the lot of the Spanish, and to make them equal before the law. It was politically inadvisable, therefore, to create enemies of a very important class of society, and even less to create divisions and rivalry among it.[25]

EPISODES: THE VICISSITUDES
OF AN ANDALUCIAN LANDOWNER

At the beginning of the conflict, Estevan Meinadier, of French origin but a Spanish subject, was a large landowner in Puerto Real, Cádiz. Unlike most such owners, he ran the estate himself, and had turned it into a model farm. Shortly before the outbreak of war, he had brought in ten French landworkers to put into practice the latest cultivation techniques on the estate with particular attention to clearing uncultivated land to create arable. His French employees were the start of his downfall. The Cádiz junta ordered them held in a friary until they took an oath of loyalty to the new regime; when they had done so, they were returned to their work on the estate.

Shortly thereafter a lad armed with a shotgun, and a fictitious order from the junta's president, came to arrest them. Aware that it was a trick, they fobbed him off and informed the junta. The latter now ordered them to report to Puerto Real where they were put aboard a Spanish man of war anchored in the port and held for forty-six days. Meinadier provided food and drink for them and their guards to prevent the latter again mistreating the workmen as they had on the first day 'because of the general ferment that reigned in Andalucía at the time'.

It was harvest time. Meinadier was one landowner who did not benefit from the Sevilla junta's prohibition on labourers raising their wages. To get the harvest in he had to pay large increases. And once the wheat was on the threshing floor, most of it was stolen. His foremen and overseers, 'hallucinated by revolutionary fanaticism, fear or wilfulness', did not dare to oppose the thieves, who were 'encouraged by the local magistrate, and others of his faction who wanted to benefit from the fruits of his (Meinadier's) labours'.

The same fate met his olive crop. Only now the people came armed and with beasts of burden to carry the olives away, and threatened anyone who attempted to stop them. Finally, the 350 fanegas (about 550 acres) he had sown to wheat were invaded by villagers with their livestock 'to graze on as though it were waste land'.

Subsequently, Meinadier's estate was expropriated and he and his fourteen-year-old Spanish-born son were condemned to the hulks as 'suspicious and harmful' French subjects. Although his Spanish wife secured orders for his release from the Junta Suprema representative in Cádiz, the judge refused to release him, and she had to take his case to Sevilla. There, despite the judge's continued resistance, the Junta gave him an honourable discharge and fined the judge 300 ducats (3,300 reales). On his return to his estate after six months in the hulks, Meinadier found that all his valuables, farm animals and equipment had been stolen; he had lost some 750,000 reales, he calculated. To pay his debts he was forced to sell part of his land. But what finally drove him to leave the estate and Puerto Real were the threatening masses of people who gathered outside his house; on the last occasion four thousand assembled townspeople and villagers remained from two in the afternoon to eight at night.[26]

*

Meinadier was obviously hated by the locals. Why? Because of his French origins, or because he was a large landowner? There is no conclusive evidence; but it could be supposed that it was a combination of both. Here was a latifundista who, unlike the pure Spanish estate owner, was vulnerable to attack. Backed by the local magistrate, whatever his motives, the surrounding villagers could take out on him both their xenophobia and their hatred of the large estate owners who deprived them of land, reducing the majority of them to the status of landless day labourers. Perhaps even his model farm was the cause of envy and resentment. Certainly, bringing in French landworkers to instruct his locally employed labour in the latest agrarian methods would have been experienced as an insult. For a villager, maintaining the old ways was a point of pride. New-fangled 'foreign' methods, wherever they originated, were initially resisted. In any event, the field hands and others took out on him a hatred that prejudiced even their own interest, sending in their livestock to feed on his wheat fields when they could better have waited to harvest the crop and kept themselves comfortably in bread.

There was one last irony to this story. When the French occupied Andalucía at the beginning of 1810, Meinadier returned from nearby Puerto Santa María, where he had taken refuge, to Puerto Real. The port and the surrounding countryside had been sacked by the French military of all its remaining grain, straw, charcoal, firewood, olive oil, household valuables and farm equipment. On his arrival, he was acclaimed by the clergy and inhabitants who chose him as local magistrate, a post in which he was confirmed by King Josef. His French heritage now stood him and the inhabitants in good stead; and in his new post he did all in his power to alleviate the population's distress.[27]

Fatherland and Nation:
A National Patriotic Government

REVOLUTIONARY BABEL

Revolutionary circumstances usually release a babel of voices from those who were silenced under the previous regime. Patriot Spain was no exception. As the Vigo junta in Galicia put it:

> From the first moments, the inhabitants of this place began to open their mouths and to speak of the real feelings which moved their oppressed hearts, their voices expressing nothing but fervour and just hopes for their king and lord.[1]

As long as a predictable, univocal loyalty to their dispossessed king was the actual or supposed outcome of the inhabitants speaking their 'real' minds, the juntas could boast of their patriotic credentials. Neither absolutist nor progressive dared to doubt for a moment that they owed the country's anti-Napoleonic resistance and the revolution to the people's initiative. The conflation of the 'instruments' with the 'originators' of this state of affairs had been initially fostered by the Fernandistas' need of popular legitimation for seizing power locally and creating the juntas. But the lower orders' participation in the risings and their mass of volunteers for the new junta armies was taken by the absolutists as proof of the plebeians' 'uncontaminated' Spanish virtues which – in contrast to the French-influenced upper social strata – stood by their duty to religion, king and fatherland.

Most junta members, acting like the Old Regime officials many of them were, considered free speech subversive. But nothing could stop people talking. In the Madrid flea-market, for example, the rumour was rife in the autumn of 1808 that the British army in Portugal was coming to join the Spanish army. The people's comment that 'they are no better than disgraceful Frenchmen disguised as English' reflected popular distrust of Spain's traditional enemy as of all foreign troops on Spanish soil; nonetheless, the remark was considered worthy of a letter to Floridablanca, president of the recently constituted Junta Suprema, the national government, by the person who overheard it.[2] Similarly,

Galician popular suspicion of British designs on El Ferrol, the navy arsenal in Galicia, which were obviously rife, were passed on to the Junta.[3] Informing on 'traitors', rumour-mongers and French sympathizers in Madrid became rampant. There were certain women

> who not only had shown a criminal audacity in singing songs in favour of the intruder king and against our nation, but one of them is maintaining herself on the money left her by two Frenchmen with whom she lived; and another has a relationship with an unknown person, which is suspicious enough. They should be investigated immediately.[4]

In another letter to the Junta which said more about the writer's self-perception than about the perception of the traitors named, a woman wrote: 'If a woman's advice is worth anything, and begging your forgiveness for my audacity, I write to say that . . . .'[5]

The Junta soon stepped in with a warning to the Madrid police and court authorities to prevent the large numbers of people in cafes, taverns and other public places who were holding 'conversations subversive of law and order, no doubt promoted by our enemies to foment partisanship and anarchy'. They had forgotten the laws which severely prohibited such 'suspicious and prejudical' gatherings.

> To tolerate these in the present circumstances is to contribute directly to the corruption of the public spirit which is all that can save us in the terrible crisis in which we find ourselves.[6]

The Madrid justices expressed their 'unanimous surprise' at the order for, as they reported to the Junta Suprema, they had not the slightest indication of gatherings of this nature, although they would increase their vigilance henceforth.[7]

As a newly established government, the Junta Suprema, still unsure of its public legitimacy, might be excused its paranoia about public talk. But it did not understand that the new 'spirit' on which it so patently admitted that the war effort depended, equally depended on a new sense of popular intervention in public affairs. Old Regime reflexes which demanded an unquestioning obedience to authority and the trinitarian slogan of religion, king and fatherland still ruled the minds of the new authorities.

MILITANCIES: AN INFORMANT'S ARREST

Little did sixty-one-year-old Josef Guinart think he was venturing his freedom when he set off from Madrid to Aranjuez on foot with a letter for Floridablanca, the Suprema's president. A Catalan who had come to the capital in vain to find work in the mid-eighteenth century, he had joined the army and served four and a half years in the Regiment of Africa. Subsequently, he had become a wigdresser and guild member;

but more recently he had lost work due to the new male fashion of dispensing with wigs and cutting hair short. He and his wife made a modest living from their Madrid home on the main floor of No. 4, Calle Júcar, where they rented out two rooms for a total of twelve reales a day. Guinart, lodgers testified, spent most of the day in bed. But he had not forgotten that he had been brought up in the household of the engineer general who had remodelled the Barcelona fortresses of the Ciudadela and Montjuich and the Figueras fortifications. He believed that he knew their weak points and how they could be re-taken by the patriot forces. He also understood, so he thought, French military tactics, which were 'quite different to all those of the nations they had overcome'. And so on Sunday, November 13, he set out with the letter for Floridablanca, describing these matters.

He got no further than Villaverde, one of the first villages on his route, when he was detained. Had he a passport to go to Aranjuez, the local justice asked. No, he replied, but his matter was urgent. He had to deliver this letter to the Junta Suprema's president. The letter was unsealed and unstamped, noted the justice, taking him into custody. Guinart resisted arrest, which did his case little good. Obliging him to put a stamp on his missive, the justice sent it to the Madrid corregidor, informing him at the same time of Guinart's arrest. The corregidor immediately reported the detention to the Junta Suprema.

So far, there was not much to hold against Guinart. But presumably frightened by his arrest, he disowned his letter and pretended that it had been given to him by a Catalan in Madrid whose name and address were unknown to him. Even this was insufficient to cause him grave trouble. This came from another source. When Martín de Garay, the Junta's secretary general, received the information from the Madrid corregidor, he asked the royal architect in the capital to investigate Guinart. The architect talked to the Catalan's neighbours, including the actor Vicente Baca, and discovered that Guinart had had commissions and contracts from the Godoy government to transport artillery and other war materiel during the recent Franco-Spanish invasion of Portugal, while still continuing to work as a wigdresser. This was enough for Garay to order, three days later, that Guinart be taken under arrest to Aranjuez, seat at that moment of the Junta. Guinart's fate thereafter remained undocumented, but if he was still imprisoned, as was likely, he was probably released when the Junta fled shortly before Napoleon's capture of the capital a fortnight later.[8]

Guinart – perhaps no more than a self-deluded 'expert' – was illustrative of the lower orders who tried to make their voices heard to those in command of the patriot war effort. His efforts were no more successful than others before and after him.

PAMPHLETEERING: A UNITED NATIONAL STRUGGLE?

Guinart would have done better to have written a pamphlet than to try to approach the new government directly. Before – and indeed immediately after – the Junta Suprema's formation, the educated commoner elite's main form of intervention in public affairs was pamphleteering. Scores, if not hundreds, of pamphlets and tracts were written and printed at their authors' expense. This sudden explosion of opinion was a clear sign of the Old Regime's institutional collapse: its censorship had vanished in the debris, and the literate, whose voices had been stifled for so long, breathed a new air of freedom. To read all that was published 'you would have to rise at seven in the morning, when the blind pour into the streets, and not finish until eleven at night', wrote a correspondent in the *Diario de Málaga*.[9] In the majority of cases the writers used the freedom to relieve themselves of their pent-up feelings but expressed not much original thought.

Although a hard and fast line could not be drawn between them, the pamphlets fell into two broad categories: vituperative diatribes against Napoleon, the French Revolution, French influence in and domination of Spain,* sometimes in verse but more often in prose; and those primarily concerned with the type of patriot government needed to meet the country's imperative needs. Leaving the second category for later consideration, the first consisted largely of invective, insults, satire, irony, sarcasm, parody and hyperbole, in which Godoy was not spared either; but as there was a limit to the amount of virulence that most of the home-spun writers could summon up to describe Napoleon's 'despotic tyranny', they tended to repetition: the Emperor was unfavourably compared to the tyrants of antiquity (Nero, Caligula, Tamburlaine, Attila); to a tiger, a fox, a wolf. He was a cross between 'a wild beast and man', a 'tyrant sated with crimes', the 'Anti-Christ'.† He was a man of 'frenetic ambition', 'impious', 'treacherous', 'perfidious', 'barbarous'; 'Europe's greatest robber',

---

* One clerical author, addressing the wives of the well-to-do classes, fulminated against French tutors and French books for their children, French chefs in their kitchens (whose 'nouvelle cuisine' with its small servings designed to 'flatter the eyes and awaken the appetite' in place of the traditional heaped Spanish plates, had made masticating impolite), French wig and hairdressers, French couturiers, jewellers and usurers, French dances . . . all came under his critical admonitions that the Spanish should return to their old and 'authentic' customs. The author's title was significant: *Spain's Political Hygiene or Preventive Medicine against the Bad Morals by which France Infects Her* (Antonio Marqués y Espejo, Madrid, 1808).

† Napoleon's invasion of the Vatican states in February 1808, appeared to most Spaniards as the culmination of the attacks on the Church which had begun with the Revolution, and had made a deep impact, as had subsequently the Pope's support for Spanish resistance. Napoleon's recognition of French Judaism was another strong irritant. The 1808 title of a pamphlet by an Andalucian priest, *The Seven-headed, Ten-horned Beast or Napoleon, Emperor of the French. A literal exposition of Revelations, Chapter XIII* – in which the mythical beast was taken by the Church as a symbol of the Anti-Christ – was indicative of the lower clergy's feelings on these events.

the 'dragon of France', 'the Corsican upstart'; 'a small island's abortion', 'a monster spewed from Hell' . . . In short, 'assassinations, false oaths, treachery, impudent lies, corruption: all these are noble and approved means in the Napoleonic Code which illustrate his sacriligious morality'. What Spaniard could believe that the Emperor desired Spain's 'felicity', 'regeneration' and 'defence of her religion' when he had founded his claim to the Spanish throne on Fernando's forced abdication; when his troops had sacked Spanish churches, murdered priests and defiled nuns; and when, at this moment, he was preparing handcuffs and chains to take Spain's youth to fight Austria 'on the shores of the Danube'.

The enlightened's passionate hatred of Napoleon – the epithets and quotations above come from the pens of two such erudite and respected authors* – was reminiscent of lovers scorned. And though one of them, Capmany, specifically rejected the notion, many of the Spanish educated elite had in the recent past admired Napoleon as France's redeemer who had brought order out of revolutionary chaos without denying the best of the revolutionary conquests. But the Emperor's treatment of his long-suffering ally had turned admiration into abhorrence.

These authors' excessive language, however, was also intended as an instrument of patriotic propaganda to whip up and maintain anti-Napoleonic sentiment in the country. Another form of this propaganda, in question-and-answer form which made it more easily assimilable by the public at large, was the Catechism. The first of these, *El Catecismo civil*, 'a brief compendium of the Spaniards' obligations, awareness and explanation of their freedom's nature, to be useful in the present circumstances for both sexes' education', was published just days after the rising in Cartagena.†

---

* Antonio de Capmany, a notable Catalan historian, in his *Centinela contra franceses*, and Isidoro Antillón, Spain's most famous geographer in *Qué es lo que mas importa a la España?*, both of 1808.
† A version of this Catechism, under a different title, was published in a four-page supplement of the *Diario de Valencia* in early August 1808. The most important changes, which show how thinking had changed in little over two months, appear between square brackets. In the last three extracts, I have changed the original order to make a coherent reading. This Catechism was originally intended as a reply to Napoleon's *Imperial Catechism for the Use of all Churches of the French Empire*, which had been translated into Spanish in 1807 and again the following year. (Françoise Etienvre, Introduction to Antonio Capmany's *Centinela contra franceses*, p. 31, fn. 66, London, 1988.)

Q. Tell me, boy, what are you called?
A. A Spaniard, by the grace of God.
does Spaniard mean?
A. A fine, upstanding man.
Q. As such, what and how many are your
obligations?
A. Three. To be a Christian, an Apostolic
Roman Catholic, defender of the true faith,
of King and Fatherland, and to die before
being conquered
Q. Who is your king?
A. Fernando VII.
[. . .]
Q. Who is the enemy of our felicity?
A. The Emperor of the French
Q. Who is he?
A. A new and infinitely evil señor. The
covetous origin of all wrong, exterminator
of all good, the sum of all vice.
Q. How many natures has he? [Does he
belong to the race of humans?]
A. Two. One diabolical, the other
human. [It can be doubted, given his
diabolical operations].
[. . .]
Q. Who can free us from such a monster?
A. The union of Spaniards under arms.

Q. Is it a sin to kill French people?
A. No, sir, it merits praise if by this the What
homeland is freed of their insults
[. . .]
Q. What is Spain? [Who forms the fatherland?]
A. The entirety of many peoples [our peoples]
ruled by a King and governed by the same [just]
laws
Q. Are ours and all these peoples' interests the
same?
A. Yes, sir, by the natural and reciprocal
obligation of all to support and defend each
other
[. . .]
Q. What felicity should we be seeking?
A. That which the French cannot give us.
Q. And what is this?
A. The security of our rights and persons, the
free practice of our sacred religion, and the
establishment of our monarchical
government, adapted to Spain's present
customs and those of European religion.
[. . .]
Q. To whom shall we look to achieve this?
A. To Spain, which alone has this right, to
the exclusion of all foreigners.[10]

Apart from the obligatory anti-Napoleonic virulence, and the determination that the country's political salvation depended exclusively on itself, the Catechism attempted briefly to articulate two war-related problems. The need for union among the Spanish peoples whose continuing mass mobilization was necessary to man the armies needed to repel the foreign aggressor, and the question of how this could be achieved and on what basis it could be maintained. In short, the nature of the Spanish 'Nation' or 'Fatherland'. The Catechism went no further than proposing that Spain consisted of the entire conglomeration of its peoples (or communities) who had a mutual obligation to defend each other. Once they had released their venom on Napoleon, both of the earlier cited authors, the Catalan-born Antonio Capmany, the most intelligent of Spanish conservatives, and Isidoro Antillón, a determined Aragonese progressive, addressed this problem in more detail. In Antillón's words:

> We are all Spaniards . . . All members of a great family, [who] are fighting for our King Fernando, for our religion, our laws and our honour. The cause is one: one is our spirit, one is our plan, one our defence, common to all are the dangers and the victories . . . But we need a centre of this union.[11]

The notion of the 'great family' came from the Old Order monarchy. The king was the 'father' and his vassals his 'sons'. As such, all those under his rule were 'brothers' who faced common dangers together. The initial appeal to defend religion, king and country sought an overarching bond to unite Spain's peoples in terms they could easily understand and feel. Hatred of Napoleon, the perfidious aggressor, pursued the same aim. The Emperor's previous military triumphs had been achieved because he had 'fought against kings, not the people. Our situation is different . . . .' The Spanish would do well to recall what Napoleon had only the previous year told the Poles: 'A nation of eight million inhabitants, who want to be free, runs no risk of ever being subjugated.' Antillón continues:

> Spain has a population of more than twelve million souls.* Let us for this once profit from his [Napoleon's] doctrine. Let us show the world that the forces of tyranny are nothing against a million men, armed en masse to defend their liberty and honour.[12]

While the progressives shared the absolutists' view of the people's prime importance as the originator of the risings and in volunteering to fight, they saw the urgent need of going beyond religion, king and fatherland in order to maintain popular enthusiasm for the struggle. A country-wide, but provincial popular resistance had to be – but had not yet been – turned into a united, 'national' struggle which would enable Spain's peoples to release and coordinate all their human energies and material resources to free the country of the foreign invader.

In this sense, it was fortunate that Spain had been a 'state-nation', covering the same geographical territory, and occupied by mostly the same peoples, as it had been since its foundation in the fifteenth century by Fernando and Isabel (more aptly known in Spanish as 'The Catholic Kings'). Its inhabitants shared a collective identity, centred on the monarchy and Church, that had largely been forged by Spain's 150-year-long dominance in Europe. Funded by the silver and gold from the newly conquered South American empire, Spain's supremacy had involved the country in constant wars in defence of its fortuitously inherited European possessions† and of Roman Catholicism against the Reformation. While the fighting did not immediately affect the bulk of the Spanish population, the conflicts inevitably ended up doing so: the popular recognition of Spain's common enemies and of their abhorrent betrayal of the true religious faith served to foster this identity which, by the eighteenth century, was comparable – though incomparably distinct – to that of the English and French.[13] In this identity's formation, moreover, the Spanish Church's bitter struggle against the Reformation had played a singular part: as the irreducible defender of Catholicism, the Church and Inquisition raised intransigence and

---

* This was the popularly accepted figure. In fact, it was closer to eleven million.
† Brought about by the accession to the Spanish throne in 1516 of the Habsburg Carlos I, the Catholic Kings' grandson, who inaugurated his house's Spanish dynasty; shortly thereafter he was elected Holy Roman Emperor under the title of Charles V.

intolerance to the rank of sanctity. It was unsurprising therefore that these two characteristics entered into the popular collective identity.

Largely isolated by the Counter-Reformation from scientific and philosophical advance in much of western Europe, the lower orders' reliance on tradition, the way things had 'always been', became inbred: Catholic monarchy and entrenched defence of the holy faith; a (supposedly) ethnic and Catholic Spanish purity (stemming from the Jews' and Muslims' expulsion from the late fifteenth to the early seventeenth centuries), and an endemic suspicion of all that was foreign; lack of innovation and defence of the routines of daily life – these became the common people's inheritance.

The cost of Spain's golden age had its share of blame in this. The colonies' precious metals flowed in – and flowed directly out to finance the country's wars. European ascendancy and intransigent defence of Catholicism was bought at the price of a domestic socio-economic leap forward, the creation of a vital urban life and the emergence of new capitalist classes.

Spain's European dominance was finally broken by France in mid-seventeenth century. One hundred and fifty years of decadence followed: depopulation, a marked decline in agriculture, the country reduced largely to exporting wool. Not until the beginning of the eighteenth century, alongside the change from Habsburg to Bourbon absolutism, did Spain slowly begin to recover. A century later at the start of the Peninsular War the country, though for long now a second-rate European power, still retained the largest colonial empire of its time. But it was less this, less the new economic and demographic progress or even a distant collective memory of the country's glorious past* which inspired popular pride: this rested, as always, on loyalty to tradition, to the inherited Spanish identity. The extent to which, socially, this identity encompassed a feudal past was indicated by two terms still current in the first years of the nineteenth century: 'vassal', a word which had long since disappeared from the vocabulary of most European absolutist regimes,† and 'purity of blood'. The latter, a legal requirement for admission to many state posts, and to even the lowest ranks of the nobility, meant proof of several generations' 'non-contamination' by alien, non-Catholic forbears: Muslims, Jews, Gypsies or any other 'undesirable' ethnic or religious group. So deep-rooted was the consubstantial nature of Spanish ethnicity and Catholicism that an expression resumed it: 'castellano viejo',

---

* Starting with Jovellanos, some enlightened eighteenth century thought also rejected the golden age because it had seen the consolidation of absolutism. Significantly, this vision focused on an even more distant (and mythical) past prior to absolutism, in which Jovellanos, for one, believed that medieval Spain had enjoyed 'fundamental laws' which guaranteed the country's traditional liberties and had stood guarantor of a 'general will' through the power shared in the Cortes by the three estates with the king. What was needed to guarantee these liberties anew, he argued, was a return to those laws which absolutism had eviscerated.

† As a sign of the times, it has to be said that the word generally disappeared from the juntas' and Suprema's declarations, proclamations and edicts to be replaced by 'citizens' ('ciudadanos') or 'residents' ('vecinos'). In neither case, should the word be taken in its present sense but rather in its original meaning of persons of standing enjoying rights in the cities, towns or villages in which they lived. Absolutists, however, continued frequently to use the word vassal.

signifying an authentic Catholic Spaniard. (The extent to which this value was assimilated by the common people was evinced by the fact that as late as the start of the Peninsular War, artisans' guilds aped the practice of demanding blood-proof of their new members.) In so traditional a society, in the absence of a flourishing urban civil culture, the Enlightenment could hardly have been expected to penetrate deep into the social fabric: only a few years before the anti-Napoleonic war, four out of every five Spaniards still remained illiterate.

Without *their* monarch, without *their* religion, the lower orders' traditional identity at the start of the Peninsular War appeared threatened. To preserve it, they had risen and volunteered en masse to fight Napoleon; however desperate the cause, however unlikely the victory, could it have been otherwise? Which people with a sense of their old and characteristic identity would lie passively before a foreign power's military invasion? And even less so in front of an ally who had dethroned their king and threatened their religion. They would struggle to the death against an aggressive imperial army to assert the right to their traditional way of life: to protect their families, their homes, their plots of land, their scanty possessions, their cities, townships and villages: and beyond that, their time-honoured world under a Catholic monarch and Church.

Up to this time, however, their struggle had inevitably been local or at most regional. In the recent past, the word 'nation' had often been applied to their traditional identity; but it was not – and could not be – a 'nation' in the modern sense for it lacked one of the essential ingredients: popular participation in the country's governance – and the consequent sense that the people had equal rights and responsibilities for Spain's destiny.* It was this that the progressives wanted to endow the people with.

In order that the Spanish peoples felt as one nation in fighting *against* Napoleon they had also to be fighting *for* a better, participative future in that nation's creation. In little more than two months, writing on the type of patriot government needed before the Junta Suprema was formed, Antillón had gone far beyond his 'great family' notion to the start of a new nation's creation:

> To count alone on the people to contribute with their possesions, their bloodshed and all sorts of sacrifices, and not to create a just government . . . is a horrendous idea which will fill them with despair and be the cause of grave ills. Our [old] laws and Córtes recognize and admit that kings are only heads of government, and that sovereignty resides in the nation, or in its people . . . Nature did not create slaves, lords, kings and vassals: these are the work of man-made institutions and force: that is why [by nature] we are all equal . . . [The people's] extraordinary acts of bravery are

---

* In diplomatic relations between France and Spain before the outbreak of the Convention War in 1793, 'the Spanish monarchy refused to accept any mention of the Spanish "nation" in official papers. That is to say, it refused to accept French revolutionary principles because the concept of nation was incompatible with the sovereignty of the king of Spain.' (Lluis Roura i Aulinas, 1993, p. 104.)

due to the firm and well-founded belief that they are fighting for their freedom . . .
Our need for them to continue in this conviction . . . requires that we return to them
their rights of which they have been deprived . . .[14]

Among these rights was that of electing representatives in whom they had
confidence to form a government which 'restores felicity to the fatherland'. But
Antillón himself doubted the efficacy of his ideas, especially during a revolution.
'As long as the mass of the people, on whom one must count, remain in
ignorance, and for want of ideas, find themselves at home in the dark,
continuing to kiss without thought the same chains which have bound them
to their degradation and slavery', the few politically educated were preaching to
the wind. He wished that the patriotic literati wrote books of 'good and healthy
politics' in a simple and accessible style so that country people could understand
what they should expect of their present sacrifices and the dangers they ran if
they allowed themselves again to be governed by an arbitrary government.[15]

Popular sovereignty, like the modern nation, was an abstract notion to those,
like villagers, brought up to believe in monarchy and Church, a novelty which
was vigorously combatted by absolutists – and the many priests among them –
as yet another French revolutionary import. It was hardly surprising, therefore,
that the people did not get what Antillón deemed essential to their rights; and
the Junta Suprema refused him permission to reprint his pamphlet.[16]

Despite the earlier diplomatic restrictions, the word 'nation' itself was frequently used in 1808 official junta proclamations, although its meaning was
ambiguous and dependent on context. Sometimes – although increasingly rarely
– it reverted to its original meaning as the country where a person was born: 'The
nation to which we owe our birth'.[17] As an extension of this definition, it was also
used as a synonym for the entire Spanish peoples: 'All that the Nation holds
precious – its possessions, its customs, its women – are threatened.' At other times,
associated with an appropriate phrase, it referred to the Monarchy or to its
historically and juridically constituted 'state-nation'. 'The Nation's sacred rights',
for example, or 'The Nation, its laws, its Monarchs and its Religion.' These last
phrases, from a Sevilla junta proclamation of May 29, 1808, whose title, *A General
Appeal to the Nation*, without doubt referred to the Spanish peoples as a whole,
concluded with a passionate appeal to Spaniards to defend the 'fatherland'.[18]

The fatherland and patriots were no new concepts either. The second half of the
eighteenth century saw a proliferation of the educated elite's 'patriotic societies'
whose leitmotif was 'love of the fatherland'.* The War of the Convention, during
which the reactionary elements of the Church had redefined, in a counter-
revolutionary sense, the patria in opposition to the French Revolution's 'La
Patrie'; and more profoundly the anti-Napoleonic struggle, extended the meaning
of patria and patriotic in several new directions. In the first instance, love of the
fatherland descended from the educated elite's heights to the patria's plebeian
defenders; and as the conflict spread to all the regions of Spain, so the patria
extended in popular credence from local or regional allegiance to the whole of the

* See Chapter 1, p. 14, second fn.

country. Finally, the new patriots were expected to experience so burning a personal devotion to the fatherland that they would willingly sacrifice their lives in its defence. (Whether this latter asumption on the part of the patriot rulers coincided with the plebeians' real sentiments will be explored in later chapters.)

It was the patria, rather than the abstract notion of the nation, which Antoni Capmany, a curious blend of conservative and reformist, traditionalist and man of the Enlightenment, proposed as the unifying national principle of the Spanish peoples' anti-Napoleonic resistance. This was not, of course, 'La Patrie' of the French Revolution, but neither was it the diametrically opposed 'patria' of Spanish absolutist churchmen during the Convention War. His was a 'patria' full of affective appeal. Returning to the Old Regime concept of the monarchy as a family, the 'patria' became the motherland and 'the mother' its guiding symbol.* Patriots of all strata of society owed it to her to love and shed their blood in defence of the mother who had borne them.[19]

Capmany praised the villagers for not having been corrupted like the upper orders by French thought and fashions, for having remained true to

> your forefathers in character, dress and language, and the love of the land which saw your birth and which will witness your death. Now you have shown this in your bravery and disdain for your lives by throwing out the [French] robbers who threatened your possessions, honour and families.[20]

The concept of motherland could then in the first instance appeal to the villagers' basic sense of loyalty to their own community and traditions which, though far from extending to Capmany's global vision of the patria, could certainly encourage the villagers' continuing patriotism.

The idea of a motherland, never clearly defined as a concept, was a portmanteau into which progressives and absolutists alike could put some of their treasured beliefs in order to remain united in the struggle. More clearly than most, Capmany saw that the Spanish had still 'to save their skins', as he put it, warning constantly of the French military threat that awaited them in Napoleon's certain counter-offensive to reverse his early defeats. The need for unity of all strata of patriot society was essential to this endeavour. His strongly held anti-Napoleonic sentiments, so widely shared, were insufficient; but he indicated the way: conservative ideas mixed with promises of reforms held together – momentarily at least – by an emotional, and sometimes irrational, appeal to love of the patria as the mother of patriotism, the mother of all Spain's patriot peoples.

*

* This was not a new analogy, but Capmany expanded it and gave it a new context. It is curious that Romance languages feminized 'patria', whose Greek origin, 'patris', carried over into the Latin 'patria', meant fatherland.

More than erudite disquisitions on the modern nation or popular sovereignty, religion, king and country – a slogan with the advantage that one or other of its terms could be prioritized – had captured the people's heart. Indeed, Alcalá Galiano maintained that the slogan 'was everywhere repeated, written and sung'.[21]

Apart from heeding patriotic propaganda, there was one immediate and practical task, much closer to home, which concerned the villagers and rural townfolk: to defend their houses, families, crops and possessions from the ravages of the French army. This was undoubtedly a – if not *the* – major mobilizing patriotic force in the occupied or invaded regions. To see their homes and villages burnt to the ground was a sharp reminder of what the conflict was immediately about. The story of Feliciano Recoder, a Catalan administrator, may serve as a representative example.

EPISODES: FLEEING FRENCH REPRESSION

At an untimely three o'clock in the morning of Wednesday, June 8, 1808, Feliciano Recoder was woken by shouts in the streets of his home town, Molins del Rey, close to Barcelona. 'The French are coming! They're sacking the place!' Rapidly awakening his wife, children and mother-in-law, and telling them to dress, Recoder and his family fled from their house. In the dark and with their only possessions the clothes they stood up in, they climbed the mountain tracks to the hamlet of Papiol. Here they stopped, looking down on their township to observe the imperial troops' movements.

Recoder was a veteran of the War of the Convention. He had been one of the twenty thousand Catalan militia – miquelets, as they were locally known – who had responded to the mass call-up to defend Cataluña after the Spanish army had proved incapable of holding back the French revolutionaries. He had served as a lieutenant of the Mataró tercio of miquelets. In the fourteen years since then, his fortunes had risen thanks to his appointment as administrator of the toll bridge across the Llobregat river in Molins del Rey. The head of the Barcelona postal service had nominated him, and his appointment had been approved by no less than the government's chief minister, Pedro Cevallos. But he had not, so early in the present war, imagined having again to serve. Though Recoder and his fugitive family were unaware of it, the 'French' troops who were sacking their township were the mainly Italian soldiery under General Schwartz who had just been driven back from the Bruch pass. They were determined to wreak vengeance for their defeat on a undefended village within close range of French-occupied Barcelona and imperial aid if needed. After loading a train of carts with their booty, they consumed their rage in fire.

From the heights of the local castle, I saw them put Molins del Rey and other nearby places to the torch. The deplorable state I was in as I watched my house, all our valuables, clothes, household goods and possessions being burned beggars description. These had taken many hard years of work and service to earn. I was particularly sensitive to seeing all the papers relating to my work and appointment as the Administrator of the Molins del Rey bridge being laid waste by the flames.[22]

There was nothing the Recoder family could do to salvage their former home. Without food, they set off across country to escape further danger. For four days they walked northwards into the interior, crossing mountains and valleys until, 'worn out and discomposed', they reached the small village of Castellterçol, some fifty kilometres from Molins del Rey. By this stage, Recoder was

so given over to dire sentiments and in a state of such despondency as is difficult to conceive. In this crisis, this moment of such significant things, I resolved to take up arms again to defend Religion, my King and Country. I made my way to Granollers where the local junta gave me the lieutenantship of the third company of miquelets . . .

After taking part in a successful attack on the castle of Mongat, on the coast just north of Barcelona, Recoder was charged by his commanders with overseeing all the captured French supplies and conducting the garrison prisoners of war to an English frigate stationed offshore. The captain invited him to dine and showed him 'every benevolent consideration'.

His family, wandering from place to place, was without any means of subsistence, and he no longer had his monthly Administrator's salary to provide for them. Two months almost to the day after he had watched his belongings burn, he petitioned the Catalan junta for a position in the patriot postal service 'or any other compatible with his status' in order, as 'an act of mercy', to be able to support his family.

The petition, in which he related his and his family's recent experiences, ended with an invocation of the Catalan junta as 'this loving and compassionate Mother', who demonstrated her desire to do justice, and also as 'the Father of mercy' under whose 'beneficent cloak' a destitute supplicant trusted to receive a post as 'a gift from heaven'.

Did these blandishments secure Recoder his desire? The documents, as is so often the case, leave us uninformed. But Recoder's prior words, despite their invocation of the tripartite slogan, leave little doubt as to why he again came to take up arms. 'Religion' and 'King' – they are not again mentioned – fade before the patria's importance: the local homeland, moreover – the *patria chica* – and the loss of his home and possessions at the hands of marauding imperial troops.

PREPARING FOR A NEW GOVERNMENT

The great number of pamphlets and tracts opining on the appropriate government for patriot Spain had one thing in common: none doubted the need of a nationally representative body to lead the country through its greatest trial of recent times. The evidence of this need had become greater with the Bailén victory and the French retreat north: provincial juntas, devoted to their regions' defence, could not organize the supreme offensive necessary to throw the enemy back over the Pyrenees.

Already a month before Bailén the necessity had become obvious to some regional juntas. Again with surprising unanimity, three juntas – Asturias, Galicia and Murcia – proposed within ten days of each other in mid-June some form of central government or gathering of the Cortes. On July 16 – the day after Bailén, but in ignorance of the event – the Valencia junta weighed in with its proposal for a Junta Suprema. It urged speed in forming a central governing body. The war effort required it. So, too, did relations with the colonies.

> If the colonies do not depend directly on any [metropolitan] central authority, each will establish its own independent government, as has happened in Spain. Their distance, situation, wealth and the natural inclination towards independence will lead them to it if the ties which unite them to the fatherland are broken. Our enemies will then achieve, thanks to our carelessness, what they have not been able to engineer despite their most powerful efforts.[23]

Coming hard on the patriots' stunning victory, the Valencia proposal was generally accepted, especially by the powerful Sevilla junta. Very shortly thereafter, the Consejo de Castilla, in an attempt to make good its seriously impared patriotic credentials, threw a spoke in the juntas' wheel by proposing that it should take a leading role in a Junta Suprema's formation and composition. The uproar from the regional juntas, Sevilla especially, was so thunderous that the Consejo backed down.

During the three-month interregnum in major combats after the French evacuated Madrid at the beginning of August, and Napoleon unhurriedly assembled the *Grande Armée* on the French border to deal a decisive blow to the Spanish 'insurgents', the pamphleteers had a field day with their ideas and proposals on the sort of government needed. The majority seemed to have little idea of what was awaiting them. Many, those of absolutist persuasion in particular, proposed a regency. The reformists' rejection of this was straightforward:

> The stairs to the throne, which formerly no one dared tread without some more or less legitimate right of succession, are now commonly trodden by men who climb them without any such right. Their example, joined to human ambition, will excite even more the passion to dominate.[24]

On one point there was widespread agreement among the pamphleteers: whether a regency or some other form of government be created, it should be formed of a small body of men able to act decisively and rapidly. Its task would be to appoint a supreme military commander to coordinate the provincial armies in benefit of patriot military operations. Once this and other war-related matters were dealt with, the new government should settle down to resolving the country's much needed reforms. The judiciary, treasury, military, navy and diplomatic corps were still packed with Godoy's placemen who must be dismissed. Within a few months, wrote a reformist, 'the Nation will find itself renewed . . . After this peaceful and consoling revolution, the task of planning the new order of things can begin with the creation of a new constitution.'[25]

The pamphleteers, especially the newly liberated Madrid educated classes, apparently considered that there was all the time in the world to reform Spain peacefully. They were living a time of illusion, granted by Napoleon's careful preparations to crush them.

THE JUNTA SUPREMA SEIZES POWER

The Junta Suprema was finally founded with due pomp and circumstance in the palace of Aranjuez on September 25, 1808, little more than three months after the original idea had been mooted. After a solemn mass in the royal chapel, the deputies were sworn in. The provincial juntas had previously reached agreement that each should send two deputies to the founding meeting. In the preceding two days, preliminary discussions among the score of deputies who had already reached Aranjuez had led to some significant decisions, of which there remained very few documentary traces. Even deputies who arrived after the event found no account of them.[26]

The prior meeting in effect staged a political coup. Rejecting the Valencian position that the new government was to be the regional juntas' 'administrative body'; and the Sevilla junta's condition which made its deputies responsible for reporting back on all major decisions before voting, it decided that the new body was to be the nation's supreme central government. The assembled deputies were no longer to represent their individual provinces or regions, but the 'entire Nation'. To 'give itself the luster due to its functions' the Suprema collectively assumed the title of 'His Majesty';* 'sovereign authority', it claimed, had been vested in it until Fernando's return to the throne.

The upper nobility's return to power, which was observed in the provincial juntas' membership, was more than replicated in the new governing body: numerically, over half the deputies were nobles, all but a handful titled and five of them grandees. Ecclesiastical representation was the second most numerous, and included two archbishops (one of whom died before the Junta's foundation)

---

* It explained that this assumption of 'Majesty' was common to all Councils, juntas, even to the lesser among them, which represented the king. It might have added that a number of 'sovereign' provincial juntas had also adopted the same title. (AHN, *Estado*, Legajo 1C, communication from Junta Suprema to Consejo de Castilla, informing latter of decision, Aranjuez, Oct 3, 1808.)

and several canons. There was only one known commoner – Calbo de Rozas, a Madrid merchant, who had played a notable role in Zaragoza's defence and who was one of the two Aragonese deputies. Of several others their social rank has not been ascertained to this day – they may have included another commoner or two.[27] While overall, the majority of the deputies leaned towards the preservation of the absolutist status quo, there were no easily definable political lines of division amongst them.

At the professional level, the deputies covered a broader range. There were three ex-government ministers; seven military officers, again repeating the provincial pattern; an identical number of jurists; and four who had held important financial and economic posts, as intendentes, army treasurer and accountant.[28] While many of the deputies were thus not without professional expertise, they nonetheless formed a large and unwieldy body of illustrious unknowns.

There could be little doubt, however, that the Junta Suprema was a radically new form of Spanish government. It was certainly the culmination of the institutional and political rupture which the risings and the provincial juntas had precipitated, and the projection of this rupture to the highest level of state. But unsure of its 'constitutional' basis for – or unable to articulate a justification of – its seizure of power, the Junta Suprema hesitated before the instances of the Old Regime, refusing to make the institutional rupture definitive: for example, it kept the Consejo de Castilla in place and used it to make public its orders and edicts. This deeply irritated those provincial juntas which had seen in the Consejo the traitorous voice of the French during their first occupation of Madrid. But in fact, the Suprema's action was very little different from the provincial juntas' original incorporation of Old Regime figures in order to give themselves credibility with their local populations. For what was at stake here was the same search for credibility, though now at the national level.

The theoretical foundations of this new government's legitimacy were of minor importance to the public at large compared to the legitimacy it still had to win by proving its practical ability to organize the war effort. It was not theory but practice – could it defeat the invader, or at least keep him at bay? – that would legitimate popularly its seizure of power.

The Junta Suprema quickly received recognition from the state's official institutions, including (after some legalistic quibbles) the Consejo de Castilla, and from provincial and local juntas. Some of the township and village authorities were quite ecstatic. In the small coastal port of Muros, Galicia, as the local judge, Juan Antonio Navarra, reported, he ordered the tower illuminated and the church bells to ring. On the facade of the local inn where he lodged, he hung a portrait of Fernando on horseback and a Latin inscription below it: *Fernando VII, Optimo maximo/Patri Patria*.

To the bagpipes' accompaniment, the common folk's simple maidens danced, responding with affectionate huzzas to the Viva Fernando VII! Viva la Suprema Junta! which from time to time I called out from the balcony. A musket shot accompanied my cries, and rockets which I launched into the air. An English frigate

which was anchored in the port, responded with colourful fireworks until eleven
o'clock of the night . . . I had the great satisfaction to witness the ordinary people's
patriotic enthusiasm.[29]

The Suprema's establishment was celebrated even under the enemy's nose. In
Olmos de Esgueva, a village forty-five kilometres north-east of Valladolid, on
which the French were closing fast, a large ceremonial procession was held in
the streets. With a sharp sense of the military situation, the corregidor then
advised the people gathered outside that it would be 'most appropriate' to
suspend the next day's celebratory bullfight and that they should better set out
to spy on the enemy, and console and shelter the many families who had fled
from Burgos and other parts which the French had taken. 'With their customary mansuetude, the people obeyed.'[30]

One of the earliest Junta Suprema's measures was to order the Consejo de
Castilla to restore the traditional censorship on the publication of pamphlets.
The new sovereign body had no wish for public controversy which, in its view,
would only cause disunity 'among those not expert in these matters', while
permitting 'our enemy to take great partisan advantage of such'.[31] At the same
time, the Junta 'solemnly recognized' the national debt, stated that annual
taxable income would be carefully calculated, and the Old Order's tax system
simplified in as far as possible to make its burden equitable.

The first to feel the full weight of the Junta Suprema's sovereign authority
were its own constituent provincial juntas. Their titles and authority were
immediately reduced from 'Supreme' (i.e. sovereign) to 'Superior Provincial
juntas of Observation and Defence'. They were forbidden to make further
military and civilian promotions;[32] had to provide the Junta Suprema with
financial statements of their time in office, including funds still held, and
renounce the honours which they had previously used; and they were to respect
the existing laws prohibiting the de facto freedom of the press and 'in so
important a matter, not permit the least change or infraction'. The Supreme
Junta did not quite dare abolish its constituents altogether, as it might have
wished. But in diminishing their titles – and status was all-important to Old
Order minds – it subjugated them to its sovereign orders.

Although on the face of it seemingly of little importance, one of the most
drastic of the new regulations was to abolish all township and village juntas
excepting those in district administrative centres. At their best, these juntas had
allowed new men to take over municipal affairs in place of señorial placemen or
councillors with hereditary title to the post. These junta members were often the
newly wealthy – large farmers, renters, tax-farmers and the like who had their
own agenda: a hostility (in those areas still dominated by señorial dues) to a
feudal system which affected them adversely, to tithes which rich and poor alike
– though unequally in their effect – had to pay and to all constraints on a free
market in land. Although occasionally they might make common cause for their
own purposes with their locality's smallholders and tenants, they were prepared
to see the latter go to the wall. But on the juntas they represented a rupture with
the local social status quo, as was plainly indicated by the fact that they were

often at loggerheads with the still existing town councils. Moreover, they were likely to be more dynamic in aid of the war effort than the routinized councillors. To see these small-town juntas disappear was a loss of support that the provincial juntas' reformist and progressive elements could ill afford. In fact, many of the small local juntas refused to disband.* The Sevilla provincial junta supported them. 'Their members are individuals who generally are the most outstanding residents of their localities, and that not simply by status of birth and [royal] awards', it declared.[33]

To retain its singular sovereignty in the name of the king, the whole Junta had to discuss and approve suggestions from its committee members. This made decision-taking a cumbersome and slow affair. 'I lament to say that matters are going on very slowly, and the measures of the Junta are far from keeping pace with the energy and enthusiasm of the people', Charles Stuart, the British diplomatic representative, informed Canning from Aranjuez a month after the Junta's creation.[34]

As a self-declared sovereign power, the Junta had overlooked one essential: the sovereign power of money. Its founding provincial juntas had not provided it with any immediate funds to finance its own existence, let alone the war effort. The sixty-five million reales (£1,100,000) of British aid which had gone at the start of the war principally to Galicia, Asturias and Sevilla were now sorely missed by the Junta. It dispatched requests for the respective provincial juntas to remit the British monies remaining because, as it wrote, its situation was 'of the greatest need and distress imaginable'.[35]

In these early days the Junta Suprema was still unsure that its sovereignty would be respected by its provincial constituents whose role it had just downgraded. It proposed to raise a loan at four percent, which it hoped would produce sixty million reales, and which would be guaranteed by future tax receipts and silver and specie received from the colonies. One-third of this money, it supposed, would come from Madrid, and the remainder from the regional juntas.[36]

Lorenzo Calbo Rozas, the only known commoner on the Junta, was dispatched to Madrid in the early days of November to raise the capital's contribution. Five million reales of the hoped for twenty millions were urgently needed to finance the newly-denominated Army of the Centre. As a former Madrid merchant, Calbo Rozas had no difficulty in securing promises of twelve million reales from his professional colleagues. But they would provide the money only on condition that the grandees and wealthy put up their proportionate share.

> It is shameful that men with an income of three hundred thousand reales a year have the nerve to offer three hundred, when a merchant whose capital is well below this sum willingly offers twenty thousand, and a poor servant who can barely save one hundred reales a year generously gives the price of two or three shirts. The titled nobility and the wealthy should raise thirty millions in Madrid alone, and while the

* The Junta Suprema had to repeat its order on July 31, 1809.

war lasts, contribute two-thirds of their income . . . If they and other wealthy persons are short of cash, they should hand over to the mint their unused silver plate.[37]

Calbo Rozas, however, was highly enterprising. In one day, he increased the Madrid contribution from little over one and three-quarter millions to six. Again he fulminated at these 'highest persons of estate, in class, income and salaries, who proportionately offer the least', while 'those who – at the cost of the sweat of their brow – and barely have enough to live on decently freely donate the savings it has cost them many years to earn'.[38] Meanwhile, the Junta's merchant deputy did not ignore the Church's wealth. He sent a message to the Carmelite prior in Madrid to ascertain the sum of money deposited in a religious foundation in the latter's charge. 'According to my information, the foundation has eight million reales which would come in most handsomely at the moment. It could be a refundable loan.' He was cautious enough, however, to ask the Junta's opinion on the matter. Receiving no immediate reply, he added:

> The Prior, murmuring over the very mild but quite clear message I sent him, will be taking some powders at this moment. But if those musty funds vanish into thin air, it will do us no good.[39]

Calbo Rozas did not report on the outcome of this particular attempt to secure funds. But the six millions he had collected, and the Galician junta's opportune discovery of three millions more from its British aid, pulled the Junta out of its immediate financial abyss and provided the means for the main Andalucian and Extremaduran armies to advance north to meet the threatened French offensive. At the same time, Calbo Rozas also ensured the removal to safety of the gold stored in the Madrid mint; and, as a good merchant, was presently securing the most favourable price for a large consignment of salt pork for the army.[40]

Notwithstanding his success, even this entrepreneurial deputy had succeeded in securing less than one-third of the Junta's hoped for twenty millions from Madrid. Quite evidently, the Junta was not out of the financial woods. As a body, the Junta Suprema did not compare with Calbo Rozas' exemplary enterprise. Its 'mindset', to use an anachronistic expression, was that of the Old Regime: rapid decisiveness was not of the essence. More concerned with insuring themselves against the 'despotic' control by the few, its deputies preferred to delay fundamental decisions, such as appointing a commander-in-chief, which could lead to any such threat. Much concerned by the delays, Stuart again commented to Canning that he was 'disgusted' by the 'slowness of this unwieldly machine which is common to every person who has business to transact, whatever be the branch of service'.

> The people who have learned to reason, and to weigh the measures of their Government since the late Revolution, are by no means contented . . . if any reverse should take place [on the Ebro – the new front line after the French retreat from

Madrid] it requires no degree of foresight to predict that the Power of the Junta will
totter to its base.[41]

Though slightly exaggerated, this was a prescient prediction. Several deputies,
Stuart reported, had assured him that they felt very strongly the necessity of
some measure to 'calm the publick mind, [and] to re-establish the popularity of
the Junta . . .'. Accordingly, the Suprema had determined to publish a manifesto written by Quintana, 'a writer of some eminence'.[42]

The address, headed simply, 'Spaniards', dated October 26, was made public
two weeks later.[43] After rehearsing Spain's recent ills, Quintana stated that in
the Junta's formation the Spanish had won their 'greatest success, their greatest
victory'. This 'interim repository of supreme power', a new 'centre of authority'
had to confront an enemy of 'colossal strength'. He warned that the road ahead
was 'long and arduous' and that to follow it to its end would require 'prudence
and constancy . . . your enthusiasm and greatest qualities'. The Junta had
decided to raise an army of five hundred thousand men and fifty thousand
cavalry, the address continued. But its military preparations, urgent as they
were, formed only one of its aims. The other, as important as the first, was to
ensure to the people the 'great reward' for their enthusiasm and sacrifices.
Political independence was nothing without felicity and internal security . . . It
was high time that the law based on the general good came into being. . . .

> Spaniards, the fatherland must no longer sound a hollow and meaningless word to
> you . . . The Junta has already publicly recognized that a greater voice in the
> government must be accorded to the Nation, which in the king's name and cause
> has achieved everything alone and without assistance. The Junta solemnly pledges
> that you shall have this fatherland which you have so enthusiastically invoked and
> defended – nay, indeed, conquered – with such valour.

The manifesto promised that the Junta would study the necessary reforms of
the civil and penal code, projects to improve state education – 'for so long
overlooked among us' – and called on the educated elite to submit their views
on these matters to the Junta which would consider them with care. The
Spanish would know how to improve their institutions and consolidate their
liberty without disrupting the state. Quintana had judged public sentiment
acutely. The pamphleteers' insistence on the Junta as charged both with
leading the war effort and as a reforming body had seen to that. But it was the
war rather than reforms which had immediately to occupy its collective
decisions.

Although the Junta had detached deputies to the various armies, it had not
taken full control of the war effort; its generals were riven by rivalries and, most
serious of all, the logistic support to keep the troops in the field was totally
inadequate. The Junta admitted as much: 'Many soldiers are nearly naked and
exposed to illnesses which, because of the onset of winter, will cause more
casualties than the enemy'; and it called on the provincial juntas to open
subscriptions for uniforms which, including shoes and cape, cost a total of 257

reales.* An English observer reported that while the regulars and Valencian troops seemed fairly well clad, the Aragonese, Castilians and Murcians were suffering terribly from exposure. The Murcians in particular had no more than light linen shirts, pantaloons and a poncho to cover them from the rain. A terrible epidemic of dysentery was thinning the ranks.[44] Three weeks later the Junta had again to insist that the provincial juntas secure uniforms for their recruits, look to their training and organize food supplies which could be had by 'asking them of the wealthy who, being those most concerned to ensure the fatherland's freedom, should willingly provide them'.[45] The Junta's summons came at a moment when the summer's grain harvest in the Castillas and Andalucía had been the highest of the century.

Despite its best efforts, the Junta's attempts to organize the war could do little more than to take discrete measures. The task of organizing the military effort on the large scale required would have meant setting the country on an all-out war footing: requisitioning the wealthy's grain stocks – instead of 'asking' for them; forcing the rich, including the Church, to contribute to its loan; taking over tithes and ecclesiastical benefices; in short, commandeering all the wealthy's resources to fund the war and supply its armies. This would have meant the beginnings of a social revolution. Apart from the fact that its social composition countered any such radicalization, the Junta was still highly dependent on the provincial juntas' collaboration; and the demands on the wealthy might well have threatened their continuing participation in the broad patriotic alliance that ran from noble landowners to villagers and urban proletariat. Thus it remained that the poor were called to the colours to sacrifice their lives and the rich were called on to donate some part of their wealth in a cause which, as all came to recognize, served first and foremost to defend their property.

* Britain sent great quantities of uniforms which seemed often to 'vanish' before, or on, reaching the armies; not a single uniform of the eight thousand sent to Extremadura had been issued, the Junta Suprema complained to the provincial junta in April 1809. The Junta claimed that some soldiers sold theirs. (AHN, *Estado*, Legajos 67A/101, Junta Suprema to Badajoz junta, Sevilla, April 13, 1809; & 44A/151, Junta Suprema report, Sevilla, of the same date.)

Napoleon's 1808 Offensive

PATRIOT DEFEATS

Early in November, Napoleon crossed into Spain to take personal command of the *Grande Armée* of 250,000 men and most of his veteran field commanders whom he had assembled along the Ebro. The Emperor came with his strategy planned: an Austerlitz on a massive scale – to smash through the enemy's centre and to sweep up his flanks from the rear. The patriot armies were to be annihilated and all further resistance crushed – the supreme revenge for the Bailén humiliation.

Although his lightning campaign did not go exactly to plan, Napoleon's victory was total. He shattered the patriot armies or sent them reeling in retreat, great numbers of the raw troops deserting in panic. On November 24, the day after the Army of the Centre and the Aragonese armies were defeated at Tudela, and with Napoleon already at Aranda del Duero, the Junta Suprema ordered the fortification of Madrid. The capital must not again be allowed 'to submit in cowardice to the tyrant's insulting yoke'. Recalling the heroic example of the May 2 rising, it called on the population to turn the capital into the 'tomb of the enemy army', and ordered supplies and provisions to be hurried to the city.[1] Letters from King Josef's ministers appealing to Floridablanca, the Suprema's president, and other notables to avoid the country further disasters and to end their resistance were ordered by the Junta to be burned by the public hangman.[2]

On November 26, Jovellanos, now an Asturian deputy on the Suprema, on commission in Madrid to prepare the Council of the Indies for its escape, reported that the capital's inhabitants were 'living without a care in the world'. They expected the enemy to be held off in the Guadarrama mountain passes to the city's north.

But only two days after Jovellanos' visit, on November 28, the Junta issued the first of its many 'popular war' declarations, calling on all Spaniards to 'turn themselves into soldiers, to make every house an impregnable fortress'. Even numerous armies were insufficient to defeat a battle-hardened enemy.

It is necessary to resist the enemy at every step, so that each small advance costs him a victory, diminishes his forces, his soldiers' spirit and hopes. The inhabitants not only of provincial capitals but of all important townships and large villages must resist, using whatever means are at hand, even sticks and stones if there are no other arms, because everything serves when it comes to defending one's own home . . . This defensive war . . . will give the enemy an idea of what patriotism means when the people are determined to conquer or die.[3]

Yet, in truth, very little was done to prepare Madrid's defences until Napoleon, having swept aside the patriot defence at the Somosierra pass, was closing on the capital's gates. Then its inhabitants began feverishly to attempt to fortify the city, as witnessed by one high official, José García de León y Pizarro. The capital was a 'grandiose sight'.

Men and women working with their hands to lift the paving stones from the streets, to dig, fill sandbags, carry stones, to help with the defence work. In the [defence] junta, I found nothing but disorder, suspicion, and . . . dissimulated terror. So I, and many other honourable men and even women, went to work like day labourers on the defence of the Puerta de Fuencarral, and on a battery at the top of the calle de Alcalá.

Though the popular spirit was willing to emulate Zaragoza's defence, Madrid was not the Aragonese capital: in the latter it was the old part of the city, with its winding, narrow streets, that had helped to hold off the besiegers. Madrid's northeastern sector which was under threat of assault had a number of avenues leading into the city's heart. Napoleon came at the head of a far greater veteran army than the heterogeneous Zaragoza besiegers had assembled. The decisive difference resided in neither of these factors, however, but in the pusillanimity of those in authority in Madrid.

The Junta Suprema had placed the city's defence in the hands of the marqués de Castelar, captain general of Castilla la Nueva, and General Tomás Morla, a member of the Junta's military committee. But by the eve of Napoleon's attack, the popular effervescence had risen to such a pitch that the authorities, alongside Castelar and Morla, created a defence junta to organize and keep it under control. The junta included officials of Madrid institutions and four Consejo members.[5]

On December 2, Napoleon reached the capital's gates. Before launching his assault, he summoned the city to surrender, and received a defiant response: the inhabitants would die buried in the ruins of their houses rather than permit French troops to enter the city. The Emperor would have to assault the capital. But again before ordering the attack, he demanded the capital's surrender. The Emperor had no wish to reduce Madrid by force and so to create patriotic heroes of its defenders; he wanted a quiescent and undamaged capital which would peacefully swear allegiance to its Bonaparte king, his brother, and show up the patriots as a doomed, fanatic, priest-ridden horde manipulated by the English for their own anti-French ends.

As the defence junta's reply did no more than stall for time, Napoleon ordered his troops to attack. As the first shells fell on José Pizarro's home his servants fled and the house was converted into a munitions depot. Pizarro himself received an order from the man commanding the Fuencarral gate to fetch munitions for the patriots who were fighting in open country beyond the gate.

> I did as I was told. The people's docility and zeal was incredible in those glorious days: someone had only to call out and from all the balconies people threw down their iron and copper utensils to make grapeshot, woollen or cotton articles for cannon wads. The balconies were covered with mattresses ready for street attacks; the entrances to the streets themselves were blockaded with tables, rich chests of drawers, and furniture of all sorts. There was no mistrust, all the houses were left open . . . Oh my countrymen, you were always worthy of better government![6]

Instead of pressing the attack, at 11 a.m. Napoleon sent another surrender summons, offering the city a pardon, security for its peaceful inhabitants, respect for churches and clergy and 'oblivion of the past'.[7]

To the military on the defence junta it was obvious that the city could be heavily bombarded from the Retiro height which Napoleon's forces had taken; to the civilians that, if resistance continued, their homes and property would be sacked. A majority decided to send two negotiators, General Morla and Bernardo Iriarte, a member of the Council of the Indies, to treat with the Emperor. After two hours of negotiations with Marshal Berthier, Napoleon's chief of staff, the two Spaniards were taken before the Emperor who was waiting in the next tent. As Iriarte later recalled, Morla, almost prostrating himself at Napoleon's feet, appealed for mercy, humbly repeating, 'Aiyes pitié du peuple de Madrid' (Have pity on the people of Madrid).

> The Emperor turned his back on him and repeated, ten or a dozen times, 'FF' ['Fuck']
> . . . Embarrassed by this scene, I intervened and addressed the Emperor in a tone quite distinct from that of Morla's humble and lamentable voice. 'Sire, I am the brother of him who had the pleasure to sign the Peace of Bâle (which ended the War of the Convention) and to renew the links between our two nations which should never be separated one from the other. What happiness would be mine if I could obtain from a Hero such as Your Majesty the kind treatment of this people as befits your character.'[8]

Without moving, the Emperor continued the discussion with Iriarte. He threatened that if Madrid did not sign the capitulation articles by six the following morning, December 4, all those caught with arms would be executed. With these terms before it the junta spoke no more of resistance; but the news of the coming capitulation was kept secret for fear of the inhabitants' reaction. As Pizarro recorded:

> Everything was done behind the people's back, gulling them deceitfully; the people were still full of spirit and fight . . . I saw troops and their officers mysteriously

retreating from their posts, the junta inexplicably and uncertainly leaving, and finally everything breaking up . . . Determined not to remain in the conqueror's power, I decided to leave the capital and follow the fatherland's noble but desperate resistance.*

The problem was to get the people to stop firing on the enemy. This was not easy, as Domingo Traveso, a Galician in the Seminario de Nobles, reported:

In the morning of December 3, an officer of the Segovia Grenadiers appeared and ordered everyone in the Seminario to stop firing. He said this was necessary because our armies were approaching from the rear to cut off the enemy and we could be mistaken and shoot at them. But the people took no notice and did not stop firing until two o'clock in the afternoon of the same day.[10]

When it became public knowledge that the junta was about to surrender many, like Traveso – a batchelor from Cedofeita, Galicia, who had been staying with his uncle, an employee in the general accomptancy of the state – fled the capital on foot; on reaching Mondoñedo on December 26, Traveso suffered the fate of many eyewitnesses of Madrid's fall: he was detained·in the militia barracks on possible charges of aiding and abetting the enemy by spreading false rumours. He was fortunate that two young Galician bakehouse porters from Vivero arrived shortly afterwards on foot from Madrid. They not only confirmed that Madrid had fallen but added that they had fled on hearing it said – or reading it in a French edict, one of them claimed – that all youth were to be rounded up and forced to join the imperial army.[11]

On the morning of December 4, Madrid's gates were opened, and the French marched in. Remembering Murat's ferocious repression after the May 2 rising, the inhabitants had handed in their arms; they watched the troops in sullen silence. Napoleon kept the garrison to a minimum and its soldiers on a short leash. Even so there were 'excesses' and Napoleon reprimanded his army publicly: any imperial soldier caught mistreating an inhabitant, pillaging or impeding the re-establishment of order would be condemned to death by a military tribunal, he announced.[12] As a further step to avoid provocation, the Emperor only entered the city once – and then early in the morning and without fanfare – to visit the royal palace, otherwise remaining in the duque del Infantado's country house at Chamartín.

Those who had tried to leave Madrid before and during the French offensive had run the more likely risk of death at the hands of the capital's inhabitants or the villagers arriving to help in the capital's defence than from the French. José Pizarro was one of those who turned back on his attempted first flight, convinced that his life was in greater danger outside than within the capital.

Even the mass exodus on the capital's fall was not without serious risk. Marauding soldiers and parties of villagers still making for the capital to defend

* Secretary of the Council of State, and a former diplomat, Pizarro had remained at his post in Madrid during the first French occupation, but on the capital being freed after Bailén he had, like many another, declared for the patriot cause.

it were a threat to those who had a privileged look to them and were evidently fleeing. Even grandees were obliged to leave the capital on foot. And the very few privileged who fled in comfort had to contend with the people's ire. Their carriages were fired on, recalled the wife of a highly placed public servant.[13] For those on foot, the lack of food was one of the worst hazards.

Determined to put the greatest distance between himself and Madrid, Pizarro set out again on foot and reached Navalcarnero with some companions he had encountered en route. There was no food to be had. Recalling an attractive young woman whom he had known years before in an amateur theatrical production, and whose father was a shoemaker in the now almost deserted township, he made enquiries of the only young man he could find. The directions he received were correct. He rang on the doorbell. Recognizing Pizarro, an aged, poor old man opened the door and embraced him, crying: 'my dear sir, what a state you are in!' Locking the door behind him, he began to cook a chicken with rice, a dozen eggs, and put bread and wine on the table. Once Pizarro and his companions had satisfied their stomachs, the old man told them of a fellow shoemaker who lived in the Toledo hills who would help them the following day. By leaving the main road, Pizarro and his fugitive companions might escape the worst of the marauding bands; and the shoemaker sent his son to show them the right track.

> I can do no more than praise this shoemaker's truly noble conduct and generous hospitality . . . The natural moral character of this poor sort of person should put in the shade those arrogant enlightened individuals, whose knowledge is most of the time directed at no more than a contemptible, small-minded egoism.[14]

Coming from an enlightened top level civil bureaucrat – especially one as drily observant of his fellowmen as Pizarro – this was a fine testimony to the virtues of the Spanish artisan.

NAPOLEON'S 'REGENERATION' OF SPAIN

In under four weeks, Napoleon had achieved his military objectives. With the patriot armies' rout and the capital's surrender, Spanish resistance had, he believed, met its end.

Amidst scenes of mutinous soldiery fleeing for their lives, the Junta Suprema's hasty retreat, and the capital's quiescent populace, Napoleon's judgement appeared justified. In a war between states, one resounding victory, the capital's capitulation, ended the conflict. But Madrid was not Vienna or Berlin; the Spanish war was not between states – there was nothing yet that could reasonably be called a patriot 'state' – but between a national uprising and the Napoleonic order. The war had started in the regions; in part deliberately, the provincial risings had set out to fragment a Madrid-based 'despotic' state. While the capital's fall deeply affected the provincial patriot inhabitants who blamed it on the Junta Suprema's ineffectual leadership, Madrid was not the resistance's centre, and its surrender did not signify the end of the patriot cause. Resistance returned to where it had begun, in the regions.

The Emperor's view was thus ill-judged. The war was not at an end, but rather about to begin: the real, gritty, grinding and seemingly endless war. Until then Napoleon had fought and defeated, in a decisive battle or two, the potentates of Europe, not their peoples – the objects, perhaps, but not the subjects of imperial destiny. He depreciated the lower classes. Despite his military genius, which had revolutionized warfare, he could find no strategy to deal adequately with popular war. And though the imperial armies in Spain were still to win many resounding victories in the field, the end of the tunnel, the ultimate victory which concluded the war, never came. As resistance was crushed in one region, it began again in another . . .

Nevertheless, with his customary reforming zeal and confidence in his power, the Emperor decreed from his Chamartín residence a series of radical reforms to 'regenerate' Spain. At the stroke of a pen, he abolished all feudal rights, including señorial jurisdictions, did away with the Inquisition, reduced the number of religious communities by two-thirds – their properties to fund an increase of secular priests' salaries to 2,400 reales – and abrogated all internal customs barriers.[15] At the same time, he dissolved the Consejo de Castilla. Had the Chamartín decrees been put into effect, they would have changed the face of Spain overnight. But what power was to implement them? His own, the Emperor assured a gathering of city councillors come to pay him homage on December 9. 'There exists no obstacle capable of delaying for long the execution of my will . . . .' But what was 'superior' to his power, he confessed, was to create a Spanish nation under a Bonapartist king if Spaniards continued in their hatred of France which 'England's supporters' had spread throughout the country. National Spanish independence required that the king be assured of his subjects' love and loyalty.

> It would be easy for me to govern Spain and, should I be obliged to do so, I shall appoint viceroys in every province. But I do not refuse to cede my rights of conquest to the king once the capital's thirty thousand burghers . . . have proven their loyalty . . . and made known to the nation that its existence and happiness depend on a king and a liberal constitution, which favours the people and is opposed only to the grandees' egoism and proud passions.[16]

Napoleon's revolutionary inheritance emerged in strength in his decrees and these words to the councillors. There was no reason to doubt the intention of either. His decrees were among the reforms necessary to modernize Spain, as four years later the patriots' Constituent Assembly, the Cortes de Cádiz, implicitly recognized in creating a constitutional monarchy. Napoleon may also have hoped his measures would draw progressive Spaniards to the Bonapartist cause, overlooking that those who had joined the patriots rejected the concept of reform by a foreign power, even by the 'greatest of Emperors'. But they were also a marker: the reforms, which Napoleon issued in his own name without consulting his anointed king, much to the latter's chagrin, were what awaited the country if he were obliged to impose his personal rule in his brother's place. As things turned out, with Josef restored by Napoleon to the throne, the decrees were, with two exceptions – the abolition of the Inquisition and of the religious communities – never put into effect. King Josef was not strong enough, or sufficiently willing to take such drastic but necessary measures.

FLIGHT: MUTINOUS PATRIOT TROOPS

To the people at large in the patriot zone, maddened by Madrid's surrender and the armies' flight, the decrees – if they heard of them at all – were Napoleonic propaganda and they paid them no heed. The blow of defeat was all the heavier because the initial patriot triumphs had bred over-confidence and complacency. The provincial juntas' gazettes kept the news of the capital's fall from the people for as long as they could, up to a fortnight in Sevilla, and twice as long in Valencia where it was not published until January 3, 1809; but rumour always outpaced official news. The people knew well before it was announced that the capital had fallen and that its armies were in full retreat, its soldiers dispersing and mutinous. Accusations of treachery were rife. In Talavera, men of the Extremaduran army and local townsfolk assassinated the general in command of the Guadarrama passes, Benito San Juan. General Castaños, relieved of the overall command to which the Suprema had appointed him only shortly before, and ordered to re-join the Junta Suprema's military committee, was fortunate not to meet the same fate. Subjected to every kind of insult and threat in the villages as he vainly tried to catch the Junta up in its flight southwards, he found that marauding soldiery were spreading the word that 'there must be no more generals in command, and no government that gives orders . . . .'[17] Calbo Rozas, one of three deputies ordered to Talavera by the Junta to report on the Extremaduran army's desertion, wrote from Navalmoral four days after Madrid's fall:

> Such is the insubordination that officers and other individuals on the road open the Junta's dispatches. Out of curiosity, no doubt . . . It is impossible to get any news from Madrid.[18]

This merchant deputy had only a couple of weeks earlier shared with the Junta his reflections on the manner in which, despite having no armies or generals, the Aragonese, Catalans and Valencians had beaten off the French. 'They have given a cruel lesson to all those grand politicians and learned military men', he wrote. He proposed that senior officers who failed in their leadership should be court-martialled within the week and, if guilty, hanged within sight of their troops.[19] Little had he thought then that mutinous troops would shortly take justice into their own hands.

On the night of December 1–2 the Suprema had fled from Aranjuez. It put about that it was making for Puerto de Santa María close to Cádiz. It travelled down the main Extremaduran road to Badajoz when, in Trujillo, it ran out of money. The Junta invoked the patriotism of the bishop and canons of Plasencia to provide the wherewithal to continue its flight. Recognizing that the Junta's appeal had caused it the 'most painful sentiments for a service that involves our duty and honour', the bishop and canons apologized that, 'with the gravest difficulties, we have succeeded in collecting only ninety thousand reales . . .'.[20] Replenished with funds, the Junta managed to continue its flight. It had already received news of what sounded like a Sevilla junta revolt. On learning that the Suprema had fled, the Sevilla junta had called for a new junta to be formed in Córdoba of two delegates each from the Andalucian, Extremaduran and La Mancha juntas. When it became known that the Junta not only still existed, but was making for Andalucía, the Sevilla junta announced that its proposal had been intended only to create and coordinate the armed forces necessary to defend their regions should Napoleon thrust southwards after his victory in Madrid.[21] However, relations were tense enough for many Junta members and their staffs to doubt their reception in Sevilla where, in fact, it had been decided to establish the Junta; but these fears were unfounded. On reaching the Andalucian capital on December 17, the Suprema received a warm welcome.[22]

Immediately on its arrival the Junta despatched urgent instructions to Badajoz to send out special commissioners to round up the dispersed troops to defend the Almaraz bridge on the main Madrid–Badajoz road across the Tajo. If the bridge were taken, all of Extremadura would be threatened. 'Experience shows that our troops abandon even the best military positions when confronted by an enemy force not much greater in numbers.'[23]

General Galluzo, commander of the Extremaduran army, had unsuccessfully tried to blow up the bridge. When he learned that his flank had been turned by the French who, unopposed, had crossed the next bridge upriver, he inexplicably retreated some kilometres from Almaraz, leaving the bridge to be defended by only two infantry battalions of his force of five thousand men. On December 24, after only an hour's combat, the French seized the bridge. The road to the heart of Extremadura was now open.

Under constant rain throughout Christmas night, Galluzo continued his retreat southwards; on the following day the Extremadura army virtually ceased to exist. Infantry and cavalry alike 'dispersed'.* With their commander's example before them, it was hardly surprising.† The earlier scenes of routed and mutinous troops grew even worse. A farmer reflected on the desolation:

> I shall not leave the house because the great number of deserters make it dangerous to be outside. Today I did not send the mules out to plough lest they be stolen . . . Nothing is safe from the deserters, neither donkeys, livestock nor anything they can lay their hands on; they try to sell here what they have stolen elsewhere. God help us, as he may, because we have seen the evilness of those who give orders and those who obey them. (Tio Pepe, December 10, 1808)[24]

---

* A euphemism for 'fled', the dispersed were usually given ten days to rejoin the army before being considered deserters.
† Galluzo, who retreated until he had put a good one hundred kilometres between himself and the enemy, was shortly thereafter relieved of his command by the Badajoz junta, and subsequently, on the Junta Suprema's orders, court-martialled. The Badajoz junta successfully petitioned the Junta Suprema to allow General Cuesta, who had fled with the latter as a semi-prisoner after his attempted coup to prevent the Suprema's formation, to take over command of its army.

Later, the *Semanario Patriótico* gave a graphic description of the disbanded troops' exactions of their own countrymen.

> Throwing down their muskets in the fields, the dispersed left a trail of horror and abominable excesses in the villages through which they passed. They covered the shame of their precipitous flight by crying out that their officers had betrayed them, that they had fled the colours because they doubted their patriotism and loyalty . . . As they approached villages they shouted that the French were coming; frightened, the inhabitants fled their homes, and the troops then sacked them . . . there was even an individual who was seen with a church chalice which he was trying to sell. Those who passed through the village of Mengabril pillaged all the clothes and lengths of cloth, and stole the monstrance's precious jewel which was kept in the parish priest's house . . . How sad an outcome of indiscipline and the state's general disruption![25]

It seemed inexplicable that the fleeing troops should subject their own country-folk to so severe a sacking. It was as though their fellow-commoners were the enemy on whom they were entitled to take their revenge for resisting defensively in the rearguard while they had suffered the vicissitudes of battle, hardship and severe defeat at the front; as though the patriotic fervour with which they had begun the war had turned sour on them.

The junta commissioners had to redouble their earlier efforts. Antonio Fernández del Castillo, a Badajoz junta member, had been assigned to Cáceres. On December 27 and 28 only thirty-four inhabitants, including himself, remained in one of the most populous Extremaduran towns.

> I have never seen a sadder sight . . . Like a devastating and irresistible storm . . . [the town] was innundated by the pestilence [of the dispersed]. They had spread such terror among the inhabitants and those of nearby villages, that the hills and woods around were full of terrified people while their houses stood empty. The faces of the few who had not fled were marked by fear.[26]

Had regimental officers stood firm, the work of the special commissioners would have been made easier. During its brief stay in Trujillo, the Junta had issued orders that all deserters were to be arrested and, without more formalities than an 'assessor's' findings, to be sentenced to death 'without the slightest delay'.[27] But who was to arrest them? As Fernández del Castillo, reported:

> Although it is unbelievable, there are officers so cowardly that some pretend they are here on commission, while others go into hiding. On December 24, General Galluzo called for reinforcements – if no more than armed villagers; the officers listened to the appeal without the least feeling. Some vanished. Others publicly ignored the most ignominious reprimands, turned their back on the enemy and made for Badajoz. None returned to the army. I shall use the same procedures against them as against the troops.[28]

Unruly behaviour had, 'like a contagion', finally infected all classes and estates of the population, the commissioner wrote. A friar preacher of the order of the Descalzos de San Pedro de Alcántara, Gregorio de Villamiel, had been heard publicly declaiming in front of a gathering of inhabitants that the treachery of a number of generals was the principal cause of the patriots' disasters. The Extremaduran army had been well provisioned but its soldiers had died of hunger. But worst of all, the friar committed a sacrilege that offended every patriotic sentiment. He wrote to the Junta Suprema to suggest that if Spanish generals were inadequate, English generals should be appointed to lead Spanish troops.[29] No patriot could countenance the idea that foreign generals were better than their own, even when the latter proved themselves inadequate for the task. The patriot leaders continued recklessly to count on finding capable commanders, inevitably of noble origin, from the army's top echelons.

Shortly before, the Junta Suprema had itself found it necessary to draft an exhortation to the bishops of the realm to help combat the enemy's 'vile and suggestive' means of 'disorganizing our armies and filling with fear and terror our soldiers . . . who, at the beginning of our revolution, fought like heroes'. The 'brave and honourable' Spanish people had never failed to follow the clergy's leadership, it asserted.

> In no time has this been as important as now . . . With its exhortations and prayers, the priesthood must help to ensure that the government's orders are not in vain. The Junta Suprema trusts therefore that Your Holiness will contribute to this sacred aim, charging all your priests and other subjects to portray with intensity and energy from the pulpit and in private conversations our present situation, the fate that awaits us if we are defeated, the obligation that religion imposes upon us to fight for it, our king and country.[30]

Amidst its armies' disintegration and the soldiers' wild cries of 'betrayal', the Junta's need to call on religious aid was expressive of its own uncertain authority in defeat. Nonetheless, its feeling that it could not take this aid for granted was striking: was not the Church the backbone of patriotic Spain and one of the principle causes that the people were defending? Not necessarily: the Junta was well aware that some enlightened bishops in the French occupied zone had declared for the Bonapartist cause.*

The Junta had been in Sevilla barely ten days before it attempted to solve another problem which agitated it: the growing number of guerrilla groups which were forming outside its control. While the Suprema wished to encourage popular resistance, it also feared that its 'sovereign' power, from whose exercise the lower orders had been excluded, might escape into the hands of the people in arms, and that the social order would be subverted from below.

On December 28 the Junta issued its first decree creating and regulating irregular civilian combatants which envisaged them as a 'new type' of voluntary militia to 'introduce terror and consternation into the enemy's ranks'. Without

* See Chapter 13, pp. 317–19.

totally depriving them of self-initiative, the Suprema placed these newly authorized formations firmly under regular army command, giving the civilian leaders and their subordinates military rank and pay; and excluding from their members all enlisted soldiers. This was to say that deserters were not permitted to join. The new voluntary militia was an expeditious and cheap way of extending resistance at no cost to the virtually bankrupt patriot treasury; and it was given a considerable incentive by permitting these new militias 'to enrich themselves honourably from enemy booty' and 'to immortalize their names with actions worthy of eternal fame'. But the moment at which the decree was issued was so disastrous for the cause that it did not become widely known in large parts of the remaining patriot zone.

*

The Army of the Centre, commanded by Castaños until he was relieved of his command, was in little better shape than the Extremaduran army. Although only the rearguard had engaged the enemy, the long retreat after the defeat at Tudela – in which the Aragonese army took the brunt of the fighting – had taken its toll. A soldier, Alvaro de Angulo, wrote to his father from La Mancha on December 9 of the hardships the troops had suffered. Many officers and soldiers had dispersed because of their 'great hunger and tiredness'.

> After two weeks without having slept under a roof more than the half of two nights, paying a duro for a loaf of bread, losing the best part of our baggage, stealing horses one from another and – had it been possible – each others' hearts too, we have neither been told where we are going nor ordered to fight which the whole army desired . . .[31]

The army had retreated on Madrid but arrived too late to play any part in the capital's defence. Instead, its remnants had crossed the Tajo by ferry at various points upstream from Aranjuez, which had already fallen to the French, to take refuge in the mountains of Cuenca. Barely had Angulo's regiment crossed the river and reached Santa Cruz de la Zarza than it was ordered to parade without arms. As Angulo related in his letter:

> This made the troops think that they were about to be handed over to the enemy. There were shouts of 'treachery!' which were immediately followed by others crying 'the enemy is upon us!' Thereupon the soldiers fled, each as best he could, losing the remainder of the baggage and the regimental strongbox . . . I said to Perico Cuevas that I would follow him in whatever he did. That day we decided to make for Despeñaperros,* where we believe there must be people prepared to resist the enemy, whom we believe is going to march on Andalucía . . . Some officers and troops are accompanying us in the same spirit.

No sooner had the army reached the relative safety of the Tajo's left bank than a mutiny broke out. Set in motion by his troops, an artillery colonel took the lead

---

* The major pass through the Sierra Morena separating La Mancha and Andalucía.

in trying to get the army's remnants to retrace its steps to defend Madrid. But his commanders, under orders to make for Cuenca, and simultaneously incapable of dealing with the mutiny, renounced the army's command in favour of the duque del Infantado. Grudgingly, the Junta Suprema accepted this fait accompli. The new commander gave a desolate account of the troops under his command.

> I saw a ruined army, and troops who presented a most distressing appearance. Some were entirely barefoot, others almost naked, and all disfigured . . . by the most ravenous hunger . . . Many died of hunger along the roads and in the mountains. They appeared more like walking corpses than men ready to defend their fatherland.[32]

Infantado ordered that all male adults of La Mancha provide one pair of shoes each for the army, and that all arms abandoned or sold by the troops on their retreat be handed in immediately. The response was not overwhelming, for both orders were repeated six weeks later.[33]

DEFEATS IN CATALUÑA

As the remnants of the Army of the Centre were straggling into Cuenca, disaster struck the Catalan army. Its second commander in six months, General Vives, former captain general of Mallorca, had ineptly set his sights on converting into a siege the patriot land blockade of Barcelona which prevented supplies reaching the city by road from France. His army of some twenty thousand was not strong, or experienced, enough to contain the city, let alone take it. Certainly, the French commander in Barcelona, General Duhesme, was experiencing problems supplying his ten thousand men and the inhabitants; Napoleon gave the task of relieving the city to General St Cyr at the head of an army of twenty-five thousand which marched into Cataluña at the same time as the *Grande Armée* advanced on the Ebro. After a month-long siege of Rosas, whose bay provided a base from which the British navy could control French maritime supplies to Barcelona, and which finally capitulated on December 5 without Vives making more than a minimal effort to relieve the town, St Cyr pressed forward to Barcelona. The attempt to stop him at Cardedeu resulted in the rout of General Reding, hero of Bailén, and the French commander entered the city on December 17. St Cyr's victory was as much a moral as a military defeat for the Catalan army's raw recruits who had taken courage from their blockade of Barcelona. Four days later they were dealt another blow: St Cyr again heavily defeated the army which had reassembled at Molins del Rey. Having lost all of their artillery, the survivors retreated southwards to Tarragona. As the Catalan junta wrote to one of its representatives on the Junta Suprema, these two 'unfortunate defeats' had led to such general discontent – 'insubordination spread throughout a part of the army and some villages' – that it had been necessary to appoint General Reding, who had twice gone down to defeat in under a week, to the army's overall command.

One of the principal causes of our misfortunes is lack of money which makes it impossible adequately to clothe, equip and supply the army. A single province invaded by the enemy cannot maintain an army with the inadequate amount of aid that has been provided.[34]

Shortage of funds, supplies, food and clothing was endemic to all the patriot armies and remained so throughout the war. Meanwhile, only one army remained more or less in a condition to fight: the Aragonese, and that was now bottled up in Zaragoza at the beginning of the city's second seige.

THE SECOND ZARAGOZA SIEGE

Within the city walls the battle for Zaragoza was even longer and more ferocious than during the first siege. For over three weeks the fighting raged in underground tunnels, streets, houses and rooftops. One of the fiercest battles was inside the sacred walls of a church. The French had to bombard and attack a strategic house ten times before they could force the defenders out. The besiegers' artillery was relentless throughout: in one week in January alone six thousand bombs and grenades fell on the city.[35]

To save imperial troops' lives in hand-to-hand combat the French command resorted to massive underground mining to blow up the resistance. The defenders retaliated by burning houses and counter-mining. The French strategy was soon found to be counter-productive. The rubble provided them with no protection and impeded their advance. Smaller charges of gunpowder were used to shatter only a part of the outer walls, except for the large, strongly built friaries and convents where enormous mines were laid. Many defenders were buried in the ruins; and many of the besiegers were horrified at treading on limbs and corpses in their slow and painful advance. Where houses remained more or less intact, bloody fighting from one floor to another was frequent. The defenders pierced the ceilings and dropped explosives through them or down chimney flues. On several occasions, the miners of both sides encountered each other in their tunnels and desperate fights broke out with pickaxes, shovels and spades. On the tiled rooftops, the Aragonese ran with greater ease than the French; but when finally cornered more than one threw himself to his death rather than surrender.

There were other significant differences to the first siege. More than thirty thousand troops, most of them of the Aragonese army, including two Valencian divisions, who had retreated on Zaragoza after the defeat at Tudela, were assembled within the city. This force almost doubled the Aragonese capital's population, creating cramped quarters – some of the soldiers had to sleep rough under arches in the streets – which turned into a breeding ground for epidemics. In the four months between the two sieges, General Palafox had tried to turn Zaragoza into a fortified city, building a new wall, heavily armed redoubts and fortifying friaries and other buildings on the city's vulnerable southern flank and El Arrabal on the northern bank of the Ebro. The inhabitants originally showed little interest in these works:

'the smallholders and artisans believed that the best defence lay in their courage and heroism' as they had shown in the first siege.[36] But as the retreating soldiers from the Tudela defeat straggled into the city, men, women and children en masse rushed to complete the defences. Within the city entire districts between the walls and the Coso, Zaragoza's main thoroughfare, were 'labyrinths of tunnels from house to house, trenches, ditches and barricades'.[37] All houses were loopholed for muskets.

The French also had learned from the first siege. They needed from the start to invest Zaragoza from both banks of the Ebro, so as to cut off the roads which previously had allowed reinforcements and supplies to enter through El Arrabal on the river's far side. Equally important, they needed an immensely strong siege train which for three undisturbed weeks Marshal Moncey assembled in Alagón, only twenty kilometres to the north of Zaragoza. All the materiel had to come overland from Pamplona. Palafox's failure to use his numerous troops to destroy the train before it could be brought to Zaragoza was typical of the Aragonese hero's grasp of military affairs: throughout the second siege, he was never willing to risk but the smallest sortie even when the odds of turning the tables on the besiegers' limited forces were highly favourable. 'He wavered, was indecisive', Alcaide Ibieca, eyewitness and chronicler of both sieges, wrote. His lack of resolution aroused the wrath of the polymath and university professor Ignacio Jordán de Asso, who had edited the *Gazeta de Zaragoza* during the first siege. Three days before Moncey began the second siege on December 20, Asso protested to the Junta Suprema that thirty thousand troops were confined in Zaragoza while 'three to four thousand enemy soldiers' were allowed to gather supplies, artillery, munitions and pontoons to cross the Ebro.*

> The army and ranking officers all clamour to sally forth against the enemy. I must inform Your Majesty [the Suprema] most determinedly that unless corrective measures are rapidly taken, Aragón will be lost . . . I repeat that things are going very badly.[38]

The troops under Moncey's command numbered more than Asso's few thousands, but they were mainly the raw recruits who had invaded Spain earlier in the year and were not in good fighting shape, which made them vulnerable to a surprise attack; but they were shortly reinforced by Mortier's veteran army corps bringing the total which initially besieged Zaragoza to forty thousand infantry, 130 cannon of different calibres, and over one thousand engineers and sappers.[39] But hardly had the siege begun than ten thousand veterans were ordered to leave to keep open the road from Madrid.

* During the first siege, Palafox's older brother, marqués de Lazán, and his military advisers had sent an officer with the express mission of forming villagers into corps of guerrillas to prevent supplies reaching the besiegers; experts believed that only five hundred armed men who knew the countryside intimately and whose officers were prepared to take all the necessary measures would have sufficed for the task. But in this first attempt at creating an irregular rural fighting force, nothing was achieved. 'Disagreements and the incompetence of some officers in the field was, in general, the cause of failure.' (Lafoz, 1996, p. 152.) The full development of guerrilla warfare still lay ahead.

The besiegers rapidly repeated their conquest of Monte Torrero, the only height from which their batteries could bombard the city at will, and began to dig siege trenches in the bitter winter cold. Their sights were again set on the Santa Engracia gate, but this time they planned – or rather, after studying city plans, Napoleon had given the order – to attack the walls to the east of Santa Engracia – the Quemada gate and the Plaza de San Agustín – from which the besiegers would more rapidly reach the Coso which it was essential to dominate. At dawn on January 26, with Marshal Lannes now in command, fifty heavy cannon blasted three breaches between Santa Engracia and the Santa Mónica convent to the east. The following day the full-scale assault began; and though the Santa Mónica breach could not be stormed, after seven hours of fighting the other two were taken and the French were again within the city. The inhabitants once more rushed to its defence. For the next three weeks the battle raged house to house and street to street south of the Coso.

The great number of soldiers in the city had until then induced a certain popular lethargy, the inhabitants believing that the defence works and the fighting could be left to the military. Palafox's constant proclamations and edicts – sometimes threatening, at others cajoling the population – had had far less effect than the besiegers storming through the city walls. Moreover, the number of soldiers fit to fight had diminished considerably. A new protagonist had entered the scene: typhus. In the cramped conditions, with civilians huddled in shelters against the bombardment, the epidemic spread rapidly.* Within a week of the siege's start, six thousand soldiers were ill; by the time of the assault three hundred people were said to be dying each day. Food, especially meat and vegetables was in very short supply, either for the sick or healthy. Soldiers dropped dead in the streets. Corpses, the majority naked, some in sacks, were piled up at church doors and in public places, and the stench became so great that the order was given to bury them at night without coffins.[40] By close to the end of the siege the number of hospitalized soldiers had doubled.[41] The inhabitants again needed to fight for their and their families' lives.

On January 30, after so heavy a bombardment that three whole storeys of the Santa Mónica convent by the plaza de San Agustín collapsed simultaneously, burying many of the defenders, the French seized it. From there on the following day they attacked the church and friary of San Agustín just to the north. Through a hole they blew in the church wall, the besiegers charged in and took cover behind the main altar. The defenders seized chairs and benches to improvise a barricade in the nave, and occupied the side chapels, the organ loft and even the ornately carved wooden pulpit, one of the most cherished adornments of the church which was soon filled with smoke from the grenades thrown by both sides. As the stained glass windows shattered under musketfire, the organ pipes were pierced, holy statues and wooden carvings in the side chapels splintered, the French charged from behind the altar. A bloody battle was fought at the foot of the pulpit, the last defenders were shot or bayoneted to

---

* Though the sanitary junta declared that there was no epidemic, but that the sickness was caused by 'destitution, lack of cleanliness and shortage of food and beds' (Casamayor, 1908/2000, p.163), this was probably an attempt to calm the population.

death, and the attackers ran out of the church into the friary, only to find that every passageway was barricaded and had to be stormed.[42] Finally, they seized it, assuring themselves of access to two straight streets leading to the eastern half of the Coso.

That same day, Palafox issued a proclamation calling on women to fight alongside the men. (Indeed, a considerable number had already been doing so for the past three days.)

> The French soldiers will be frightened of you, ashamed of defeat at your hands . . . Your sole presence intimidates the bravest. A woman, when she wishes, makes the strongest [man] tremble . . .[43]

Numerous women responded the following day when French forces burst into the Plaza de la Magdalena on the Coso. Palafox had urgently summoned the inhabitants to the defence, and eight thousand people were waiting for them. So strong was the resistance, so withering the fire, that the French were forced to retreat.

Marshal Lannes had nine thousand troops to fight within the city; and as he periodically relieved half his force to rest for a few hours, his combat strength in the street fighting was effectively halved. This was a small number to take on an army still officially numbered at twenty thousand – almost certainly an exaggeration for many were fighting sick and could barely remain on their feet – as well as several thousand civilian defenders. But at the expense of vast quantities of gunpowder and field artillery brought through the breaches, the French advanced, more or less at the speed at which their sappers could dig; above ground, some of the more daring of these slid between the defenders' loopholes and hammered their protruding musket barrels with crowbars . . . And yet so slow was the advance that many of the French troops grew discouraged: after three weeks of street fighting they had still not taken a building on the Coso from any of their breaches.

Palafox issued one proclamation after another: his patriotic rhetoric was considerably superior to his military leadership.

As in the first siege a spy mania broke out among the defenders. Since the beginning of the second the gallows had been raised in the customary public places and not a few 'French spies'' bodies were exhibited to the public dangling from them. They were shortly joined by a storeman in whose warehouse a number of desperately needed beds were discovered by chance. He was immediately seized as a traitor and garrotted in prison that night. His corpse was hung from the gibbets carrying a notice across his chest: *Assassin of the human race for hiding twenty thousand beds.*

Finally, on February 7 the besiegers advancing from the Agustín friary reached the south side of El Coso by capturing the orphans' hospice. But this was only a slender hold. The French troops pushing slowly forwards to the Coso from Santa Engracia along the street of the same name faced a formidable obstacle: the heavily defended and fortified San Francisco friary where the besieged had workshops and a powder factory. French engineers planned to place the largest mine they had yet used under it: three thousand pounds of gunpowder. But as their sappers tunnelled they heard the unmistakable sounds of the defenders' counter-sapping which had already reached behind them. Immediately, the French ordered their mine to be placed at the end of the tunnel; and in the early afternoon of February 10 they fired it. The huge explosion blew up a large part of the friary, but as the smoke and dust settled, the church tower was seen still to be standing. A ferocious and bloody hand-to-hand battle which lasted two days began among the ruins and dismembered corpses, in the church and on its roof. French soldiers pursuing defenders across the roof tiles slipped and fell to their deaths.[44]

Palafox issued another of his long proclamations, each of which was becoming more feverish in tone. Envisaging that the defenders might abandon him and the city to its fate, in which case 'the world will abominate you', he called on them to stand firm. Any who did not would bear the 'mark of scorn on his forehead in the eyes of God and mankind'.[45]

Typhus spread to the French troops who were fully stretched in holding on to the positions they had won. They still only controlled about one-quarter of the city. On February 15, Palafox fell ill; two days later he was confined to bed. On the 18th the French, after a short siege, siezed El Arrabal on the far bank of the Ebro and dominated the stone bridge which crossed to the city. They could now bombard Zaragoza from north and south. In the afternoon of the same day, the university on the far side of the Coso was mined, stormed and occupied. Officers dragged sick soldiers from their hospital beds to make good the depleted defence; often they had sufficient strength only to fire one round before collapsing. The end was in sight.

His fever worsening, Palafox made over his command to a junta of thirty-three officers, churchmen and authorities on the 19th. They spent all night and the best part of the next day arguing about the prospects of continuing the defence. Fewer than three thousand troops were fit to fight, they were informed, and few defensible strongholds remained. Marshal Lannes concentrated their minds by unleashing the heaviest bombardment the city had yet suffered and exploding several large mines in the city; he gave the junta two hours to agree to his summons to capitulate or face a full-scale attack. The junta agreed to negotiate. Lannes granted the inhabitants a general pardon; the garrison was to march out the following day from the Portillo gate with their arms and lay them down; all civilians were to hand in their weapons and villagers were free to return to their homes.

At noon on Tuesday, February 21, the garrison marched out. Colonel Luis François Lejeune, who had participated in both sieges, observed the thirteen thousand sick men who,

> bearing the germs of the contagious disease in their blood, all hideously thin, with long, black, neglected beards and with barely enough strength to hold their weapons, slowly dragged themselves along to the beat of the drum. Their clothes were filthy and dishevelled. Everything about them gave the impression of the most atrocious hard-ships. But a sentiment of indefinable pride still flashed across their livid countenances.[46]

While the French troops looked at them and wondered aloud why they had had so much trouble overcoming this rabble, the Spaniards seemed to be counting the French ranks and 'strongly regretting that they had ever weakened before such a small number of enemies'.[47]

An even more desolate sight met the first imperial officers who ventured into the city. 'It was a horror to behold', wrote a Polish officer, Heinrich von Brandt. The infected air was suffocating, dense smoke covered the sky. Under the arches of the calle de Toledo where many inhabitants who had lost their homes took refuge,

> there lay children, old people, the dying and the dead, household furniture of every description, and starving domestic animals all in an indescribable confusion. In the middle of the street there was a heap of corpses, many in a state of complete nudity; here and there were braziers where a few poor wretches were cooking their food . . . The children above all, thin and with eyes bright with fever, were painful to see.[48]

Shortly before his own death at the battle of Essling a few months later, Marshal Lannes reflected on the siege, wondering if in truth it had been necessary to put an end to such heroism. 'To conquer a throne [in Spain] a nation has first to be destroyed', he commented, not without a sense of historical irony.[49]

*

On Napoleon's express orders that he be considered a rebel, Palafox, who had received the last rites, was transported to the Vincennes fortress in France where, imprisoned, he spent the rest of the war.

At the end of the siege, six thousand corpses were said to be lying in the streets awaiting burial. A modern study of parish records shows that just under 3,600 parishioners perished, just over eight percent of the inhabitants. Many more – especially villagers whose deaths were probably not recorded – almost certainly increased the numbers. But the recorded parishioners' deaths, and the lowest number of births so far in the new century, effectively wiped out the previous five years of the population's growth. More surprisingly, within the next five years under French control, the inhabitants recuperated all the siege's losses. Marriages after the end of the siege rose in the rest of 1809 to an all-time high for the new century, nearly doubling their 1800–1817 average, and deaths in 1810 fell to a new century low; births in the latter year were ten percent above average. Despite its two sieges, Zaragoza was one of the few places where at the end of the war the population had grown by nearly two percent since the conflict's start, and eighteen percent above its 1800 figure.[50] Though the majority undoubtedly continued to hate their French occupiers, the relative peace the inhabitants enjoyed was, as the growth figures showed, an unexpected boon.

EPISODES: BRITISH RETREAT[51]

While Zaragoza's inhabitants were engaged in their bitter struggle to stave off the enemy, ill-starred events were taking place far to the west where a British army, under the most renowned British field commander at the time, General Sir John Moore, was fleeing for its life in front of Napoleon and one of his best-known marshals, Soult.

A few days after Moore had taken command of the British forces in Portugal, he had ordered them to advance into Spain. On November 13, he reached Salamanca. Three days earlier Napoleon's offensive had shattered the centre of the patriot armies and the imperial army had taken Burgos. The British troops' arrival impressed Joaquin Zaonero, a Salamanca diarist who, nearly a year earlier, had witnessed Junot's army's march through the town on Portugal: the British infantry, he wrote, seemed 'insuperable'.

> This is the best army that can be found, as much in its men, as in their discipline, submission, uniforms and arms; they receive a good daily ration of food and pay. Their punishments, though, are cruel. For the least offence they receive one hundred or one thousand lashes from which many die. And their religion is no more than a chicken's cackle. They hold their masses of a Sunday . . . without more ado than a chaplain in an ankle-length cassock and a drum on the floor . . .[52]

Moore had a high regard for the Spanish people. As he had demonstrated during an earlier command in Sicily, he was hostile to absolutism and to governments that brought no benefit to the people. But in Salamanca he was surprised to find a lack of enthusiasm for the anti-Napoleonic war which he had been led to believe fired the hearts of all true Spaniards.

Nor was he alone. A local wrote to Floridablanca, the Suprema's president, on December 6, 1808, to complain that 'everything here has gone cold'.

> All the young men are in their houses and the horses with their owners. If some were in the army they have been sent home. The people are frightened, and say to each other, 'what is going on? . . . Treachery! Treachery! . . .' Seeing our leaders' inactivity and weakness, our allies, the English, are most dispirited. I've heard them say that the people are well-disposed, the Spanish soldier is strong and spirited, but the leaders are impaired, and the generals a bunch of ignoramuses.[53]

Moore had to wait three weeks in Salamanca before his artillery, which he had sent on a circuitous route from Portugal because of the poor state of the roads, caught up with him. Meanwhile reinforcements sent from Britain under General Baird had disembarked at La Coruña. Despite the Galician junta's initial reluctance to allow foreign troops in their land, the locals turned a pretty penny from them. They sold horses to the British at 'excessive prices', the junta reported, while

in the city's squares, cafes and public stalls, the troops are being charged scandalous sums for products and food. It is necessary to correct this procedure in respect of allies who have so generously come to sacrifice their lives in order to consolidate our independence . . .[54]

The Galician junta ordered its Coruña counterpart to take the necessary measures to prevent this scandal continuing and to punish those who contravened them.

*

On December 10, five days after his artillery had reached him, and in the knowledge that Madrid had capitulated, Moore marched from Salamanca to strike a blow at Napoleon's lines of communication to the north of the capital. 'We had no business being here as things are, but, being here, it would never do to abandon the Spaniards without a struggle', he had written on November 26.[55]* Meanwhile, the Emperor's armies were poised to continue their advance southwestwards from Madrid into Portugal, seizing en route Extremadura and possibly Sevilla, before converging on Lisbon. The immediate course of the war would thereby swing dramatically in Napoleon's favour. But on Monday, December 19, the day before the Zaragoza siege began, the Emperor finally received various reliable but much delayed reports on the British movements. Immediately ordering Ney to march north against Moore on the following dawn and diverting his army from the assault on Extremadura and Portugal, he assembled every available soldier into an eighty-thousand strong force to crush the British who totalled less than half that number.

On learning the news of Napoleon's pursuit – thanks to General Romana's intelligence – Moore decided to 'make a run for it' as he had always supposed he would be obliged to do. The order for a general retreat on the evening of December 23 disconcerted the Spanish officers attached to Moore's army. The engineer commandant of El Ferrol, whom the Galician junta had ordered to assist General Baird, wrote that

* In fact, Moore was disobeying his government's orders to establish a 'bridgehead' in Asturias, a strategically important province, as Napoleon also insisted, since it provided ready access to Galicia to the west, Castilla la Vieja to the south, and the Cantabrian coast centred on Santander to the east; and could easily be supplied by sea from England. If things went desperately wrong, the British navy could evacuate England's only army in the field without great difficulty. Moore made a serious mistake in not following this plan; but he set little store by the War Office's strategic thinking, and decided to pursue his predecessor's plans to strengthen the Spanish armies which were about to face Napoleon's attack from the line of the Ebro. His full forces arrived too late to do so.

it was not very decorous for the undefeated British Army, which had solely been in the rearguard without engaging the enemy, to retreat and leave a defeated Spanish army [the Galician] in the vanguard. The British were turning their back on the field of honour . . .[56]

The order to retreat was also highly unpopular among the British troops. Many of them were veterans of the previous year's British victories over Junot's forces in Portugal. The idea of running away, without firing a shot, from the enemy whom they had defeated a year earlier, wrote a Highland Light Infantryman,

was too galling to their feelings . . . rage flashed out on the most trifling occasion of disagreement. The poor Spaniards had little to expect from such men as these, who blamed them for their inactivity. 'Why is not every Spaniard under arms and fighting? The cause is not ours: are we to be the only sufferers?' Such was the common language, and from these feelings pillage and outrage naturally arose.[57]

Looting of villagers' houses for food, and any object that would fuel the troops' bivouac fires, began almost immediately on the retreat, a precursor of the much worse that was to come. Doors were torn down, the villagers' sparse furniture burned. Drunkenness, which had been a problem on the advance, increased in retreat. In Benavente, the troops brought up barrels of wine discovered in vaults beneath the main square and shot holes in them, drinking from the wine running down the gutters. Moore issued a strongly worded order in which he blamed officers for not controlling their men. Protected by a rearguard of cavalry and light infantry which held off the enemy, the heavy infantry and artillery continued the retreat, in constant rain along roads that turned into a quagmire of thick mud, but without being troubled by the French.

In Astorga, a walled town in which later Spanish forces held off French besiegers for a month, the British troops and the Spanish liaison officers hoped Moore would make a stand. If not in the town itself, then on the 1,200-metre high Manzanal pass beyond it on the main road to La Coruña. But, unable to find a defensive position that could not be flanked, and running short of provisions, Moore pushed the retreat over the pass.

Although Soult's vanguard cavalry and the British rearguard cavalry were involved in constant skirmishing, the French had not caught up with the main British army. In Astorga, Napoleon realized that Moore could only be retreating on Galicia, not Portugal, and on the pretext that urgent business summoned him to Paris, he dropped out of the pursuit, leaving Soult and Ney to finish off the work. From Valladolid on January 17 he departed from Spain in great haste, never again to return.

Having arrived direct from England without campaigning experience,

Baird's division, with the exception of the Guards, fell to pieces in the village of Bembibre, about forty kilometres west of Astorga.

> Bembibre exhibited all the appearance of a place lately stormed and pillaged. Every door and window was broken, every lock and fastening forced. Rivers of wine ran through the houses and into the streets, where lay fantastic groups of soldiers . . . women, children, runaway Spaniards, and muleteers, all apparently inanimate . . . while the wine, oozing from their lips and nostrils, seemed the effect of gunshot wounds.[58]

The British rearguard tried to get the drunken soldiers to their feet and on the march westwards. But the two-day advance that Moore had stolen on the French was lost. The French cavalry were now upon the British. In Bembibre, they rode through the lines of the drunken soldiers 'slashing among them as a boy does among thistles'.[59] More than three hundred British were taken prisoner, most of whom bore sabre wounds.

The scenes of drunkenness, pillaging, looting and general disorder were repeated at Villafranca. They were far worse than anything seen among the Spanish armies' 'dispersos'; Spanish troops were frequently reported to be dying of hunger – something never reported about the British who died rather of drunkenness. What Moore saw in Villafranca incited him to another strong proclamation. He again told his officers to 'put an end to this disorder'. While some plundered, others straggled and many fell down dead drunk; the rearguard, in which Hanoverian dragoons, though often hard pressed, played a singularly important role, held off the enemy. The remainder of the army did no fighting; it had to march – and march fast – through sleet and snow. But it was retreating not on mountain tracks but along a main road. It was on the second of the road's two major passes, the Pedrafita, that the most dramatic accounts appeared in many soldiers' memoirs of the retreat. Most of them concerned the scores of women camp followers and their children who had accompanied the army from Portugal. Ensign Blakeney saw a group of soldiers lying in the snow by the roadside. He approached to get them to their feet to continue the retreat.

> In my coming up a sad sight presented itself. Through exhaustion, depravity or a mixture of both, three men, a woman, and a child all lay dead, forming a kind of circle, their heads inwards. In the centre was still the remains of a pool of rum, made by the breaking of a cask of that spirit. The unfortunate people must have sucked more of the liquor than their constitutions could support.[60]

One of Moore's staff officers picked up a baby still suckling at her dead mother's breast under an overturned bullock cart, wrapped it in his cloak and rode off with it. Other officers stopped and lifted up two-day-old twins struggling in the snow beneath a second cart on its side: the woman who had been riding in it, and the mules pulling it, were dead.

By now great numbers of Moore's army, including some officers were marching barefoot – or unable to keep up because of their bleeding feet. Shoes disintegrated in the churned up mud. Dysentery was rife, exhaustion common. Officers fell asleep as they marched. With only one day's bread ration remaining, and Soult on his heels, Moore ordered a twenty-four-hour forced march of seventy kilometres to Betanzos, close to La Coruña, where he expected to find British transports waiting to embark the army. With the exception of the Guards and the two reserve brigades, which had alternated as the rearguard and frequently faced the enemy, the remaining regiments which reached Betanzos were 'disorderly, the officers negligent; the whole army . . . disorganized in the most disgraceful manner', wrote a senior British officer.[61] Behind the regiments came the thousands of sick, shoeless, exhausted, the plunderers, marauders and malingerers. And what had the looters stolen? Money, but also

> brass candlesticks bent double, bundles of common knives, copper sauce-pans hammered into masses, every sort of domestic utensil which could be forced into their packs were found upon them without any regard to value or weight . . . On this day upwards of fifteen hundred robust marauders . . . passed through the rearguard of the reserve.[62]

From the motley array of loot, it was obvious that the villagers had suffered the greatest plundering. Most of the latter fled their homes as the British retreated, leaving houses unattended which, on the flimsy pretext that the villagers were withholding due aid, the soldiery considered ripe for plunder. Defending the villagers against accusations of 'their inhospitable reception of us, and the concealment of provisions', a British officer put it:

> Do those who are most loud in their complaints honestly think that an army of 30,000 Spaniards would be better received in England than we were in Spain? I doubt it much. The people, dispirited and alarmed, began to look to self-preservation as the primary or sole object of their care.[63]

The Junta Suprema was outraged by Moore's retreat.

> It is with the greatest bitterness that the Junta has witnessed the British Army's conduct . . . it could have retreated with Romana's army to the mountains of Galicia and there stood firm.[64]

But as much as the British retreat, the Suprema feared that La Coruña's fall would give Napoleon ready access by fast-sailing ships to the Spanish South American colonies to alarm and undermine their confidence with false news about the patriot cause.[65]

The British army, at last in reasonably good order after Moore had again issued a strong warning to officers and troops, reached La Coruña to a warm welcome. Men and women set out, as in the defence of Madrid, to try to strengthen the city walls against the French attack which they realized was imminent. But the transport ships Moore had ordered from Vigo had not arrived. The British were going to have to make a last stand. Moore drew up the army on a ridge about three kilometres outside La Coruña near the village of Elviña, while Soult occupied a ridge in front. The following day, the transports put into La Coruña. Early in the afternoon of January 16, when evacuation of the sick, baggage, cannon and cavalry was planned to begin – previously over two thousand horses and draught cattle, in so sorry a state that they were not worth shipping, were stabbed and shot to death or finally driven over a cliff[66] – the French attacked. There was heavy fighting for Elviña which was taken and re-taken; as he was directing a counter-attack Moore was struck by a cannon-ball that severed his left arm and shoulder – a fatal wound from which he died a few hours later. He was buried that night in La Coruña. After three hours of fighting, the battle ended with both armies occupying more or less the same positions as they had before it.

Under cover of dark, and the ruse of bivouac fires kept blazing through the night by a few men, the British retreated from the battleground and began to embark on the transports. Shortly thereafter La Coruña surrendered to the French; it had no forces with which to defend the city.

How many men did Moore lose on his expeditionary campaign? Figures ranging from just over three thousand to just under six thousand have been advanced, roughly between ten and twenty percent of his force. Of these under one thousand were lost in the only major battle Moore fought at La Coruña.[67] The retreat had been a high price to pay to save the only British army that then could be fielded against Napoleon on the continent.

However, the sacrifice had its positive aspect. It kept Napoleon from advancing south to capture Sevilla and Lisbon; gave the Junta Suprema a breathing space to reorganize its defeated armies, and tied up two French army corps – Soult's and Ney's – in the northwestern extremity of Spain. After submitting initially to the capture of their country, Galician villagers rose en masse and led the French to withdraw, never to return: the only instance during the war when a popular rising precipitated the enemy's withdrawal from an entire region.

The Contagion of Defeat: Popular Revolts and Local Resistance

The patriot armies' defeats and the fall of Madrid infected the rearguard's lower classes with a desire for revenge which they wreaked principally in assassinations and tumults against their own juntas, two of which they overthrew. Though confined to only a few places, the assassinations nonetheless took a toll of at least fifteen lives – the majority of them suspected French sympathizers – in those regions which felt most immediately threatened by the enemy's advance: Lérida in western Cataluña, Extremadura and La Mancha.[1] These killings usually contained an element of defiance of local juntas or the authorities. On December 16, in Badajoz, for example, the entire junta turned out to try to prevent the slaying of two French prisoners of war who had just been brought under escort to the city gates:

> No sooner did we arrive on the scene than the shouting and clamour redoubled, and the mob roundly insulted us, calling us no better than sycophants [of the French]. In the midst of this confusion, and defying all respect for authority, the two prisoners were beaten to death.[2]

Three more people – two Spaniards and a Portuguese, an alleged French spy – were later dragged from imprisonment and assassinated. At the same time, probably aided by the mob, eleven common prisoners escaped from gaol. The Junta Suprema expressed its revulsion at these assassinations, and ordered the guilty to be expeditiously punished. The Catalan junta had not waited on the Suprema's orders: in Lérida, seven of the chief culprits were punished within forty-eight hours, and four more detained within the next four days.[3] But in Badajoz, the investigation was hindered by the refusal of 'honourable' witnesses of the events – which took place in broad daylight – 'to testify against the principal authors of this horrifying catastrophe, whether out of compassion or fear'.[4] Unruly behaviour had, 'like a contagion', infected all classes and estates, as the Badajoz special commissioner in Cáceres had earlier remarked in another context.

MURCIA: THE PEOPLE OVERTHROW THE JUNTA

When it came down to serious popular opposition, most juntas were – at least momentarily – powerless. Murcia, a small provincial capital, was a good example. Beginning on December 26, artisans, shopkeepers and liberal professionals were prominent among a crowd which forced the junta president – the city's corregidor and intendente – and the junta's military councillor, a lieutenant general, to surrender their commands; abolished the honourable volunteers militia, raised and commanded by a local noble; and attacked the bishop. Having to all intents seized power, they characteristically handed it over to another local noble, the marqués de Villafranca y los Vélez and, by marriage, duque de Medina Sidonia.

Popular fears that Murcia was to be left undefended before an enemy which, after taking Madrid and Toledo, was thought to be advancing across La Mancha on the regional capital, lay at the tumult's root. The removal of field artillery from the city, the requisitioning of privately held arms and – in the midst of the tumult – infantry deserters, wrongly identified as artillerymen, being conducted, roped together and under armed escort, from the capital gave substance to the lower classes' fears. The junta, moreover, had made itself unpopular by imposing a war tax of one and a quarter reales daily on each head of family in the city and villages, and had applied much 'pressure and humiliating distraints' to ensure the tax's collection.[5] But the people's fears and distrust of the junta were manipulated in typical Old Regime fashion if not by Villafranca, then almost certainly by the Junta Suprema's deputy and local representative, marqués de Villar.[6]

On the day after Christmas, two popular and peaceful demonstrations demanded that Villafranca take over the junta's political and military command. In the evening, a mass of people marched up to his house in the pouring rain, bringing with them the postal courier who had just arrived. They insisted that any suspicious letters be opened and read aloud.[7] At that moment a thin man, with sunken cheeks in a brownish-skinned face, wearing a cape and top hat,* came through the crowd and said that the courier had brought documents for the intendente, Clemente Campos. 'To his house!' the people began to shout. A regimental adjutant, Gerónimo Valle, was ordered by his colonel, who was present, to accompany the crowd to ensure that no harm befell the intendente's guard drawn from the regiment. When the adjutant reached the intendente's house, people were shouting: 'attack the guard!', 'force them inside!' Valle pushed his way to the front. 'Gentlemen, contain yourselves. What is it you want?' 'The ceremonial mace', came the shout. A corporal touched Valle's shoulder: 'here it is' and handed him the intendente's symbol of office.

Almost immediately thereafter, according to Valle, who was latter arraigned for his part in the events, the intendente appeared before the crowd.

---

* The top hat was a relatively new emblem of the better-off commoner, or those who had pretensions of appearing so.

> I have no desire to command. I am a true Spaniard and a respectable man. I have no need of more guards than the people of Murcia. Take my mace. I beg of you only one consideration: please leave us in peace because my wife has just given birth . . .[8]

Subsequently the intendente saw matters less equanimously. His staff of office had been forcibly seized as the result of an 'iniquitous plot' to deprive him of the junta's presidency, to which Villar, the Suprema's representative, had given his approval the following day. 'The consequences of this bad example are evident from its similarity to a democracy', he wrote to the Suprema, going on to finger the ten men who, he claimed, were the real troublemakers: an apothecary, two carpenters, a tavern-keeper, a surgeon, a noted doctor, a weaver, a master woodcarver, a scrivener's assistant, and one other man whose trade or profession he did not state.[9]

The crowd, whose leaders were armed with staves, blunderbusses, shotguns, swords and carbines, next made for the military councillor's house and shouted that he surrender his mace. Lieutenant General Julián Retamosa appeared with his staff of office which, with the crowd's approval, Valle took. No sooner had the general retired inside his house, than a voice shouted: 'and the general's sash!' The crowd took up the cry. The general sent a servant down with it and handed it over to Valle who wrapped it around the two maces.

When Valle handed them over to the Suprema's deputy, the latter passed them on to Villafranca: 'As the people have elected your excellency as their political and military leader, as these insignia demonstrate, I, in the name of Fernando VII, bestow them on you.' A one-eyed man in the crowd called out: 'And if you don't govern well we shall take them from you.'[10]

Although up to this point there could be little doubt that the crowd – and possibly Valle – were working in concert with Villar, the comment indicated that the people had their wits about them. The events of the following day reinforced this idea.

At 10 o'clock the next morning, more grave incidents occurred outside the episcopal palace.* As the bishop's employees were preparing to distribute tithe grain and alms to the poor, a small, red-faced man in a green cape strode up. A mason, commonly known as the 'Governor', he shouted to the men to stop giving out wheat and insulted them roundly. To the two or three poor who had already received their portion, he ordered them to return it to the stack, and the granary's doors to be shut.

> This is what the people want. All the grain must be sent to the army, he cried. Then, turning on the episcopal porter, he said: why are you not wearing a cockade? You're man enough for that, do the same as the rest of your class . . . Then the apothecary who was standing close by told the porter to get back to his room lest worse happen . . .[11]

Under arrest, the mason in question, by the name of Marin, testified to the investigating magistrate that he had just come out of the episcopal palace lavatory as the alms distribution was beginning.

* Murcia was in the diocese of Cartagena, and though the bishop resided in the regional capital, he was known as the bishop of Cartagena.

It seemed right that the wheat which was about to be handed out should go to the army, because here everyone can work and improve their lot. The accused did not intend to insult anyone; had he thought he might do so, he would have preferred to bury himself underground, being, as he was, no more than a very poor man who could eat only when he worked . . .[12]

Marín's action attracted a large crowd to the bishop's residence. And what comments had he heard them make?, the investigating magistrate asked the forty-six-year-old apothecary, Manuel Gómez, identified by the intendente as one of the city's 'most wicked' subjects and who was detained in gaol on suspicion of participating in the events. The people were saying that the bishop 'should be confined to a friary and receive only twenty reales a day, and all the rest of his income should be devoted to the war effort'.[13]

Villafranca condemned the insults against the prelate's decorum and respect, and ordered the arrest of those responsible. While the bishop gave way to the popular demand no longer to distribute alms to the poor and send the proceeds to the army, he also gave vent to his ire. He informed the Junta Suprema that he had suffered

the most sacrilegious and degrading insults that could be made to a vagrant or criminal. The people wanted to confine me to a friary and seize my mitre . . . [while] others have distorted my actions to give them a criminal appearance, to make them appear as though I do not use my tithes to support the public cause.[14]

But the bishop was careful not to say as much to the Murcian public. Two days after the worst of the tumult, he issued a printed statement in which he listed all the money the bishopric had contributed to the war effort and on alms since the beginning of the war. Privately, he begged Villafranca to have the case against his denigrators dismissed or, if that were impossible, that none of the accused be punished. Christian charity was informed by the experience that it was impolitic to antagonize the Murcian lower orders.[15]

The revolt, however, was not yet over. Wednesday, December 28, its third day, began with the people's altercation with a former junta member who had torn down an anti-junta pasquinade at Cuatro Esquinas, the city's centre, and ended with the closing down of the honourable volunteer militia. The latter was highly unpopular. Its colonel, conde de Campo Hermoso, was known for his incompetence and arbitrary conduct, which affected all the city's inhabitants, and particularly the subordinate classes.

But there was another reason, not confined to Murcia, for the regiments' unpopularity. It was supposed to be made up of those who, for whatever reasons, were not eligible for military service. But in fact it was the refuge of many young men, especially from the privileged classes, to escape enrolment in the army.

There is no reason why youth who are fully capable of serving in the army or those who have got married to avoid military service, or hidalgos looking for ways out of joining the army by interpreting His Majesty's orders in their own interests, should be allowed to enlist in the honourable militia in order to escape their responsibilities.[16]

This complaint by the newly enlisted Murcia plebeians showed that they were not prepared to be oppressed by the better-off who were dishonourably escaping the call to the colours by joining the honourable volunteers regiment. To make matters worse the latter's duty officer – a 'chubby young blond fellow' – had the previous night arrested a wigdresser when he went to ask for the volunteers' drums.[17]

Two carpenters and a baker made for the guardhouse. Juan Meléndez, a master carpenter in the silk-spinning factory, one of the intendente's 'wicked men', demanded to see the officer in charge. The latter, a lawyer, admitted the carpenter to his presence. He did not know Meléndez who at first had his cloak wrapped round his face.* But later the duty officer saw that he was tall, brownish-skinned with a mark on his lip. The newcomer told him to come out onto the staircase.

> There he opened his cloak. He had bulges in it which appeared to be firearms. On his left side there protruded a dagger or knife hilt. Taking off his hat, he said: 'The people order you to close down the guardhouse and to come with me to the marqués de Villafranca's . . .'[18]

Recognizing that the man before him was one of the leaders of the previous day's tumult, and that he came determined to achieve his ends, the duty officer consented: the few volunteer soldiers under his command had no ammunition, and there was still much popular disorder.

In the presence of the Suprema's deputy, the master carpenter handed over the volunteer guardroom's keys to Villafranca. 'The people considered it right to shut the guardhouse. This gentleman was the officer on duty . . . .' 'Meléndez, you have done a very bad thing', Villafranca replied. 'If the people wanted this, they should have asked me first since they have placed the government in my hands', the lawyer–officer recalled him as saying.

'Well, the thing is done now', responded Meléndez, 'and there is no remedying it', letting Villafranca understand that he had no regrets.[19] Without more ado, the honourable volunteer regiment was disbanded.[20]

The two carpenters and the baker were arrested, with many others, at the beginning of April 1809, nearly three months after the events. Of the first dozen or so men who were gaoled by the investigating magistrate for their alleged participation in the tumult's various events over half were master craftsmen – those usually called upon by the pre-war authorities to put down the revolts of their journeymen and apprentices, none of whom figured among the recorded number of Murcian accused. The working elite's dissatisfaction with their social superiors in the old junta's organization of the local war effort – and it was not much better under the new – had reached critical proportions. As an anonymous correspondent wrote to the Suprema:

---

* This was the habitual way the lower orders prevented others from identifying them.

If the provincial juntas had been created correctly, and the artisan and farmer had had a vote on them like all the others who should not have it, things would have been different . . . In Murcia only the unhappy artisans are enlisted, for the rest nobody has to serve . . .[21]

For long thereafter, Murcian politics remained polarized between 'old' and 'new' juntas. Obliged to send two ranking officials to restore a minimal unity, the Suprema became the target of popular anger by also reinstating the 'old guard' alongside the new. As one friar, Alejandro Valentín Castillo Zapata, recorded:

The people are very disdainful. They say: on our own authority we overthrew the former junta and we had just and powerful reasons for doing so . . . What reasonable motive has the Suprema to derogate what only a short time earlier it approved . . . [and to press for the arrest of those] who took part in the events – persons who deserve to be applauded rather than punished?[22]

But this, the friar continued, was an 'everyday occurrence in Spain at the present time . . .'. Murcia was experiencing what had happened in Valencia, Granada and other 'notorious places': their juntas, assuming a 'feigned patriotic air and a burning zeal' to the prejudice of the public cause, had punished many hundreds of 'good, true and innocent patriots' to prevent an outcry against their corrupt obstination and conduct. Unless the Suprema took the most serious measures to remedy these ills, the lower orders would, without any doubt, take over the whole government. 'They will cure these problems easily . . . .' Preaching to the wind: the Suprema was the supreme example of what the writer complained of.

CÁDIZ: THE JUNTA DEPOSED

There were few critical junta members, especially progressives, who did not suffer imprisonment at the hands of their fellows. The above writer's reference to Valencia concerned the anti-progressive junta coup staged by the region's former captain general, La Conquista, on December 29, 1808, when he arrested Vicente Bertrán de Lis and father Rico, leaders of the original anti-Napoleonic rising, along with most of the Bertrán group, on trumped-up charges of 'disturbing public order and clashing with the authorities' during the latter rising. The accused were shipped off to Mallorca, though eventually most were found innocent.[23]

During the Cádiz riots in late February, 1809, the plebeians, to the insistent cries of 'we want no more juntas like this', deposed the Cádiz junta, demanding its members hand over their badge of office; forced the criminal judge out of office; and assassinated the commandant of the excise forces. At the same time they released Tap y Nuñez, one of the leaders of the rising in Sevilla, from the infamous Santa Catalina castle in which he had been incarcerated by the newly formed Sevilla junta shortly after the rising.*

* See Chapter 4, p. 96.

Ostensibly a popular revolt against the announced arrival of a patriot 'Foreign Legion', made up principally of deserters from the imperial army, it was almost certainly manipulated initially by some members of the honourable volunteers regiment, who feared that they would be forced, by the Foreign Legion's replacement, to leave Cádiz to join the regular army.* But the rioters, who were armed by sympathetic soldiers and sailors, went far beyond this limited aim: they started by demanding the keys to all the official correspondence of the Catalan Suprema deputy and representative in Cádiz, the highly unpopular marqués de Villel, in order to examine his communications with the Suprema; demanded that the Foreign Legion be banned from the city, a measure immediately agreed to by the authorities, and that the city's artillery defences be improved; they ended by confining Villel under guard in the Capuchin friary with the intent no doubt of forcing him from the city. True to his 'populist' principles, Tap y Nuñez twice harangued the rioters in the friary which had become their headquarters, presumably congratulating them on their overthrow of the junta and inciting them to take over the city's government themselves.

The paradoxical aspect was that, on Villel's initiative, the Suprema had seriously concerned itself about Tap y Nuñez's release from prison since the Sevilla junta refused to give any valid reason for his incarceration. But on learning of his participation in the revolt, the Suprema ordered his continued imprisonment and new charges to be brought against him. The riot was brought to an end by religion and armed force: clergy and military deployed in the streets to pacify or deter the rioters. Though a month later, an army captain reported from Cádiz that the city's 'lowest classes' still remained ready to 'disturb public tranquility'.[24]

From the available evidence it is impossible to deduce exactly the extent to which the rioters' hostility arose from resentment at having placed in power a new set of rulers who were little or no better than those of the Old Regime (being usually of much the same social strata), or whether their protest was principally aimed at their new rulers' ineffectiveness at organizing the war effort to protect them from the enemy. Most probably both these reasons were inextricably intertwined.

DISTURBANCES IN THE COUNTRYSIDE: LA MANCHA

If the Junta Suprema was to be believed, La Mancha's villages were rife with 'assassinations, disobedience of magistrates and serious disturbances against the authorities'. It appointed a Granada High Court judge to travel through the region to investigate the situation because of the 'critical and extraordinary circumstances'.[25]

Just over a fortnight before the judge, Francisco León Bendicho, set out on his commission, Toledo had been taken by the French without resistance; this opened the way to the enemy light cavalry which set out on exploratory patrols

---

* The regiment as a whole, however, participated in putting down the revolt.

southwards towards La Mancha. But the mass of the French army had been diverted to Castilla la Vieja and León in pursuit of the British forces under General Moore and was not about to attack. Nonetheless, fear of the enemy's advance reigned in villages and townships deep into La Mancha.

The judge began with an escort of four hundred light cavalry. Given the chronic shortage of patriot troopers, this was a huge force. Almost immediately his escort was ordered north to reinforce the patriot vanguard. After 'very disagreeable' talks with the cavalry's major, Bendicho persuaded him of the importance of keeping his escort to ensure 'public order' in the rear. The real reason emerged a few days later when a new general ordered the escort to the west, and the judge accompanied it 'because my person was not safe without it, due to the influence which the previous scenes of ferocity still retained in the people's minds'.[26]

While fearing for his personal safety, Bendicho was, for a high court judge, curiously reticent about providing concrete evidence of this 'ferocity', or of the 'considerable number of assassins and the evil-intentioned' he had arrested who were 'fomenting this province's insurrections'. He reported only one arrest of a man who had seriously wounded a magistrate in the countryside near Almagro.[27] But when it came to a confrontation with the provincial junta of Ciudad Real over the extent of his remit, he acted with insufferable arrogance – filling endless pages to the junta and Suprema on a trivial matter of precedence and status.[28] Obviously imbued with a sense of his self-importance as a judge and a Suprema commissioner, his positive patriotic influence on villagers and town inhabitants, in which the Suprema had trusted, could only have been of small value.

He nearly met his downfall at the hands of the patriot tribunal of public security in Sevilla. His failure to explain the 'grave excesses' of the deposed French-born corregidor in Almagro were sufficient for the tribunal to consider the judge's conduct highly suspicious and to demand his recall for investigation. The Suprema softened the punishment to a reprimand, and Bendicho continued in his post – almost certainly as much hated as the French – until he fled before the enemy in April 1809. The actions of one Old Regime judge were of no special social significance other than as an indication of the human material on which the Junta Suprema counted to assure itself of popular support. Blind obedience to patriot authority – like obedience to the eighteenth-century absolutist reformers – was, in this view, the villagers' essential duty. Popular mobilization had therefore to take place outside of the authorities' ambit. The contrasting events in two townships, which Bendicho reported but did not investigate, were significant of the social divisions taking place in La Mancha. In the face of the French threat, a local lawyer in Villanueva de los Infantes revolted against the provincial junta and the Suprema because neither could do much to defend his locality; in Carrión de Calatrava, a noble of a famous house staged a coup to reinstate señorial domination.

Villanueva was an important agricultural township, the head of the Montiel administrative district, lying about thirty kilometres due east of Valdepeñas in the southern half of La Mancha. Nearly sixty percent of its population was engaged in the dry-land grain farming typical of the area. Artisans formed one in twelve of the working inhabitants. Although the population of 5,700 had declined since the end of the seventeenth century, Villanueva remained one of the more densely populated municipalities of La Mancha, including a high proportion of day labourers; and for that reason no doubt, like other places in the region, the township had earned a reputation for rebelliousness.[29]

The increasing numbers of smallholders and tenants who had lost their lands to large farmers and had been reduced to day labouring had heightened social tension in La Mancha for a number of years before the war. Labourers, who still remained proportionately far below the numbers in Andalucía and Extremadura, resorted to acts of violence against the large farmers' lands, ripping up their crops and putting axes to their olive trees.[30]

The call to patriotism was insufficient to reduce the social tension: all those without property to defend knew only too well – indeed it had been stated by none other than the Junta Suprema – that the landowners and wealthy had the most to lose from a French victory. Nevertheless, by resisting the French, the proletarians stood to lose a great deal more: theirs and their families' lives, their women's honour and the desecration of their cherished religion – a threat more than enough, in the absence of an army to defend them, to put doubts in the mind of all but the bravest. Even the Suprema recognized the problem of convincing villagers to engage in their self-defence.

It was in this situation that the Villanueva lawyer and member of the local junta, Antonio Josef Cabañero, declared the township's independence from the provincial junta and the Suprema. He issued a call to all the neighbouring villages to send delegates to a meeting to agree on a common defence policy. His refusal to accept the provincial junta which, like the majority of its kind, had not thought to include members from its principal townships, led him to reject its emissary sent to resolve the local dispute unless two of Villanueva's junta members were given seats on the provincial junta. But his defiance was reported to have gone much further: he had 'captivated the people's simple minds and especially that of the junta's president', had taken over all public funds and used 'armed force to seize all the king's possessions', that's to say, all those to which the Suprema had entitled itself.[31] A strong personality in a situation like this could become an indisputable leader. But what was equally evident was that, in the absence of a strong patriot national government, local autonomy again inevitably came to the fore. And this autonomy, just as inevitably, denied the inhabitants' duty blindly to obey the patriot authorities. The strength of wartime resistance depended as much on this local disobedience – or rather, local initiative – than in obedience to the central authorities. In the last instance, the latter could do very little to protect individual villages or their surrounding rural areas.

When, in the summer of 1809, the French occupied villages in Villanueva's neighbourhood and the patriots fled to the hills, the township's junta president and magistrate, who was earlier said to have been in Cabañero's thrawl, swore allegiance to King Josef. This the local junta members in hiding, including Cabañero, would have forgiven him, believing he had acted out of 'fear or stupidity'; but what they could not forgive was that he had travelled to Madrid, taking with him a commoner under a noble pseudonym, to swear personal fealty to Josef on behalf of Villanueva's nobility and commoners.[32] Duplicity, it appeared, was but another form of personal defence.

*

The Carrión coup, in the heartland of the Calatrava military–religious order's domains, momentarily deposed a local magistrate appointed by the provincial junta in place of the previous señorial administration. Members of the order had come under attack at the beginning of the war from one of the first patriot guerrilla leaders for having failed in 1808 to help villagers fight Dupont's army as it crossed La Mancha to Andalucía.

Carrión de Calatrava, not far distant from Ciudad Real, was a village of some two thousand inhabitants, one in five of whom was a day labourer. It was one of the many, centred on Almagro, over which the military–religious order had held sway since the seven-century-long reconquest of Spain from Islam's domination. In Carrión, early on the morning of Friday, March 18, 1809, a noble, Antonio Portocarrero, accompanied by his brother, a friar of the order, and several other persons, affixed a public edict proclaiming that he was asuming the judgeship in order to control 'the revolutionaries and discontented' who had 'disturbed public tranquility' since the new magistrate's appointment. Henceforth, his edict proclaimed, gatherings of three or more people were prohibited under pain of a fine and imprisonment, and 'revolutionaries and tumultuous people' would be punished under the full rigour of the law. Portocarrero's acolytes assaulted the existing magistrate who quickly resorted to a cavalry colonel for help; after ascertaining from the local priest who was the village's rightful magistrate, the colonel arrested Portocarrero. He was found to have a pistol on him, and his dagger was discovered thrown into a corner of his place of confinement.[33]

The coup's importance was more symbolic than real. But it demonstrated the determination of an important sector of the landed classes not to lose their señorial domination over 'revolutionary' day labourers and the like.

*

As a result of these multiple disturbances in the patriot zone, the Junta Suprema issued, on February 3, 1809, new orders on the suppression of riots. No society or government could exist unless its members were to 'submit to the law and respectfully obey the authorities whose duty it is to enforce it'. Henceforth, riot leaders and those who offended magistrates would be shot out of hand; and their followers sentenced to two hundred lashes and ten years in a penal colony. The lightest sentence was forcible enlistment in the army to fight in the positions most exposed to danger. It became an offence to pass on 'seditious' comments about magistrates or the authorities, to detain or open the mails, to call anyone a 'traitor' in public. The armed forces were to assemble immediately on the scene of a riot; parents and guild masters were responsible for keeping their children or journeymen and apprentices out of the streets; and guild officials were to put themselves at the authority's orders to restore public order. With the exception of enlistment riots, which continued unabated, the number of other riots certainly declined – though whether this was due to the new ordinance or to the increasing demands of the war was open to question.

FROM RIOTS TO LOCAL RESISTANCE

Barely ten days after its riot ordinance, the Suprema issued its second call for total 'popular' war on the enemy. The entire population was summoned to become soldiers, fighting with stones, bricks and boiling water if no other means were at hand. The new order implicitly revealed the problems of convincing villagers to engage in their self-defence. Noting with 'great sorrow' that provincial juntas had failed to observe, or even communicate, its earlier call to the villagers, and that none had fully carried it out, the Suprema, in its new appeal to the provincial juntas, commented:

> The result has been disastrous. The enemy has invaded many provinces without the slightest risk to himself . . . It is essential that villagers stop deluding themselves: sterile willpower is insufficient to gain their freedom. What is needed is to fight – and to fight valiantly . . . The villagers must be convinced of the fact that only their resistance can save the Country . . .[34]

Even allowing for the hyperbole common to Suprema proclamations, the Junta's doubt about villagers' determination to resist was patent. Yet how should they be convinced that they must defend themselves and their villages in order to prevent sackings and robberies by the enemy? If they fought and lost, they were certain to be the objects of reprisals. Why should the landless day labourers and rural artisans expose themselves to the threat of dying to defend the property of the privileged? Needing to maintain the patriotic alliance of the wealthy and the impoverished classes, the Suprema – made up as it was of the privileged orders – did not address this problem, other than to offer an annual reward of 320 reales (approximately half of a labourer's yearly wage) to those who, in their village's defence, killed or took prisoner an imperial soldier. Welcome as such a sum might be – though there was no record that it was ever paid – the Suprema's constant and consistent refusal to permit any change to the established socio-economic order militated against the proletarians' general determination to defend the patriotic cause.

In terms of village defence, nevertheless, there was one factor which negated this argument: the organic solidarity of village life when confronted by external threat. Even the most impoverished villager felt that his or her home place – usually their village of birth – was as much theirs as that of the wealthiest farmer or landowner. Attachment to locality was perhaps even stronger among the poor who barely ever ventured beyond its purlieus. Without expressing it as such, this was what the Suprema was in fact counting on in its appeal to local defence, at the same time as it defined the external threat in the shape of the 'barbarous imperial soldiery's looting and rapine' – a theme unremittingly harped on in all the patriots' declamations (though it could equally have been used about the British on their retreat to La Coruña or about the conduct of the Extremaduran army's 'dispersos').

Like its first call in late November 1808, for all-out civilian resistance at the French threat to Madrid, its second, in February 1809, come when the Suprema was in panic at the possibility of a French invasion of Andalucía. After Moore's army had evacuated La Coruña in January, Galicia had unresistingly fallen to the imperial forces. The French armies were now free again to pursue Napoleon's original plan to advance southwards on Extremadura and Andalucía, and into Portugal, while the Suprema was still desperately trying to form new armies to resist them. In fact, Napoleon, with characteristic strategic sense, ordered Soult to use his new Galician base to invade Portugal and wrest it from British control. However, the Junta's call for 'popular' war corresponded once again to a moment when it feared that its own existence was threatened; and contained more of a desperate demagogic appeal than the determination to support and carry out such a war, the popular consequences of which would be unpredictable.

The Suprema's dictum to villages and townships on their self-defence ran to forty-nine articles on the practical details of the means of resistance, some of which were taken from Zaragoza's and others from Cataluña's example. The most striking perhaps was that they enjoined local magistrates to prepare the necessary defence measures though these were to be assisted by 'persons of accredited knowledge' in such matters who were to be appointed by the provincial captain generals. In other words, popular defence was to be kept well under control of the existing authorities: it was not to be a popular uprising against the French. This overlooked one important aspect of local life: on the threat of a French attack many local authorities were the first to flee. In one aspect, however, the Catalan example was cited with admiration: villages should form sometents, on the Catalan model, for their self-defence. This sort of homeguard should be paid out of village funds, and if these were insufficient, local landowners should advance the necessary money which would be repaid out of the first tax monies received by the municipality. In this scheme of things, the propertied would lose none of their income, while the day labourers and rural artisans risked their lives to defend their villages.

EPISODES: VILLAGE DEFENCE

Under certain limited conditions, townships could and did defend themselves in the early days of the war. Villacañas, a place of 4,500 inhabitants, in southeastern Toledo close to La Mancha, held off French light cavalry for five days at the end of 1808. Lying between the main roads to Andalucía and Valencia, Villacañas was one of fourteen villages belonging to an ecclesiastical señorío, the priory of San Juan. An agrarian township, where nearly one thousand men worked on the land, two-thirds of them day labourers, Villacañas was of no particular strategic importance to the French who already had their cavalry in

Madridejos to the south. The inhabitants of the latter and other places along the Andalucian road had fled on the imperial troops' approach. Not having seen a French soldier, those in Villacañas stayed put, 'in great tranquility or rather criminal inactivity', as a subsequent account of the events termed it.[35]

The inactivity ended on the evening of December 20, 1808. Guided by a local man, sixty French cavalry silently entered the township and formed up in the main square. Their captain demanded that the magistrate provide them with two men to lead them to Alcazar de San Juan, the district's chief town, thirty kilometres or so to the south, for which they were leaving immediately. Distrusting their intentions, the inhabitants suddenly fell on them with any and every weapon that came to hand, killing two troopers and their horses and putting the rest to flight. The people, who suffered no losses, pursued them into the countryside, but in the snow and darkness lost sight of them. This access of popular fury was typically attributed, in the subsequent report (by a participant in the events), to the inhabitants' renowned patriotism, their hatred of and anger at these 'bandits whose only precepts are sackings, violations, desecration and devastation'. If this were the case, why had the inhabitants quietly basked in their 'criminal inactivity' only the day before?

The writer gave a small, but better clue to another important aspect of this sudden attack. Among the inhabitants were a number of men who had served in the army, to whose orders the inhabitants – especially the 'rustics' as the correspondent put it – willingly deferred. Had these been retired army officers, it would have been customary to specify their rank. But there was no mention of rank, not even of the military man who was popularly elected as 'General' to lead the defence. It was conceivable therefore that some of these men were dispersed soldiers of the Army of the Centre, and by now virtual deserters – whom the writer did not want to refer to directly in order to save them from reprisals. These soldiers' well-documented desire to avenge their humiliating retreat after the battle of Tudela may well have precipitated the attack.

Whatever the case, Villacañas was now committed to defend itself against the inevitable French reprisal. That night the inhabitants seized the arms stored in the town hall, and posted sentries to alert them to a surprise French attack. As was their habit in these situations, some of the local authorities decamped, leaving the township to its fate. Nonetheless, a few 'more or less distinguished persons', among whom were the report's author, and a number of priests and friars remained to participate in the defence.

The following day, December 21, two hundred enemy cavalry appeared shortly before noon to take the township. The enemy opened fire with such ferocity that 'it sounded like cannon shots'. The fire was returned from behind the walls which enclosed underground rooms on Villacaña's outskirts and hastily dug trenches. The battle lasted over three hours; the defenders nearly ran out of cartridges, but the 'God of battles' came to their aid by the discovery of some musket balls, powder and cartridges held by the inhabitants. Unable to advance, the French finally sounded the retreat. This victory over 'the victors of Austerlitz, Jena and Marengo' enthused the population. Their patriotism

> made them determined to resist whatever number of French attacked the township. They were perfectly united in their aim – the only essential in such circumstances. In order to triumph, the whole peninsula should have pursued this aim from the start, and should at the present still pursue it . . . The people said, We shall triumph or die before surrendering . . .

On the following two days, French cavalry detachments approached the township to observe if it was still defended. Seeing that the defences had been improved – new trenches had been dug, more embrasures opened in the walls, every sort of cart and carriage used to form ramparts in the streets should the French succeed in penetrating the outer defences – the French cavalry withdrew without offering to fight.

Even so, the French cavalry general ordered the township to surrender and swear allegiance to Josef Bonaparte. 'Some people argued that, in order to avoid worse consequences Villacañas should submit; but others, more sensible, rejected their arguments.' By this time the inhabitants had armed themselves with every conceivable weapon: muskets, shotguns, blunderbusses and pistols; swords, halberds, lances, pikes, sharpened iron staves and billhooks attached to long wooden poles . . . 'a selection of quite extraordinary weapons'. The military men divided them into groups to defend the township. On Christmas day, the French cavalry again appeared in force. By now totally confident, the defenders shouted at them to attack; when the French held back, the infuriated inhabitants suddenly rose from their defensive positions and attacked them, putting the enemy to flight and pursuing him into the countryside. 'Since then we have seen no more of him.'

*

Villacañas became an heroic patriotic episode, cited as an example of local defence in the Suprema's call for all-out popular war. Without denying the bravery and determination of the township's inhabitants, it must be said that French light cavalry was not the adequate military force to subdue a township's resistance. It was not intended as such, as its lack of cannon demonstrated. It was the Napoleonic army's exploratory 'screen', ranging far ahead of the infantry to gather information of the enemy's positions and the possibilities of exacting food supplies. At a moment of the Spanish armies's dispersion, it was a force sufficient to occupy undefended townships; but not to overcome those which stubbornly resisted.

To cite Villacañas as exemplary in terms of local resistance was consequently somewhat of a Suprema deceit. Should the French infantry, supported by cannon, attack a township or village, the consequences were almost certainly to be much graver for its inhabitants. But as long as the patriots defended the interests of noble landowners and large farmers, their concept of popular resistance could go no further than to envisage that the plebeian inhabitants of villages and townships should – as in Villacañas – patriotically sacrifice their lives in an all-out resistance to the French. Real popular war would have made very different demands on the dominant social structure: greater representation in provincial juntas, or even in the Suprema; the end of noble domination of the army's officer corps, the abolition of señoríos and their feudal domination; the conviction that defence of the fatherland was the defence of a more just and equitable future instead of the defence of an existing hierarchical society . . . If the patriots, exemplified in the Suprema, did not envisage this sort of popular war, it must be said that the villagers did not generally demand it either. Under the Church's influence, when they were willing to fight it was to defend the past, not the future.

LOCAL DEFENCE AND THE AUTHORITIES

The Suprema's injunction that local magistrates take charge of their place's defence – part of the Old Regime's hierarchical order – was shown up in the village of Torrejoncillo, in northern Extremadura, which a troop of forty-two French cavalry reached on December 31, 1808. Instead of calling on the three thousand inhabitants to defend their village, the two local magistrates ordered them to open their doors to the French and not to demonstrate the least sign of resistance, threatening any who disobeyed with sentence of death. They themselves went out with a white handkerchief attached to a stave to meet the French troop.

Scandalized by this 'reprehensible and intolerable' surrender of the village to 'the atrocities this canaille habitually commit', and aware that the French troop was too small to subjugate the place, two villagers began to shout: 'Go for them!' Thereupon the people attacked the cavalry with knives, stones and any sharp instrument that came to hand, driving them out of the village and pursuing them for some distance while the magistrates still tried to calm them. Once matters were again safely under their control, the magistrates ordered the arrest and imprisonment of the two men who had raised the cry to attack the French; and sent word to the latter that they were holding prisoner those who had been responsible for the assault. 'That was the punishment that these innocent men, who were only trying to defend their country, religion and August Sovereign received'; and they were still under close guard in gaol when the witness to these events, one Clemente Terrón, left the village four days later. However, the magistrates would shortly change place with the two patriots: on receiving Terrón's report, the Suprema sent immediate orders to General

Cuesta, commander of the Extremaduran army, to have them arrested and ensure they were tried.[36]

*

By the winter of 1808–1809, not a single patriot army still stood unbeaten and intact. The advice proffered at the start of the war by the Sevilla junta on the only strategy to combat Napoleon – to avoid pitched battles and to wear the enemy down by every other means – had not been heeded by the Suprema or its army commanders.

Increasingly, however, the people were taking the struggle into their own hands. Bands of rural guerrillas were forming in different parts of the country to wage their own irregular war on the enemy. As a symbol of this new type of struggle, an unidentified Spaniard sacrificed his life in a suicidal explosion in the port of Santander where he blew up a number of gunpowder barrels and 130 boxes of ammunition to prevent them from falling into French hands. Spanish and British sailors then landed from a cruiser and sacked all the port's warehouses, leaving nothing of worth, the Bonapartist authorities reported.[37] The rapidity of the Anglo-Spanish incursion after the explosion suggested that the suicide bomber's action had been planned in agreement with the cruiser.*

---

* It must be said that no other such case was documented, to my knowledge, during the war.

1809

THE RAVAGES OF WAR

In many regions 1809 was, until the famine of 1811–1812, the harshest year of the war. Almost without exception, civilian deaths rose and births declined, dramatically reversing the population growth of the two previous postwar years. In what could, at that moment, be called the frontline regions, deaths between 1808 and 1809 increased by over two and a half times in Cataluña, more than doubled in Castilla la Nueva, rose by over one-half in Extremadura and more than one-quarter in Castilla la Vieja. Annual population losses ranged from seven percent in Cataluña – a tremendous drop in one year – three and a half percent in Extremadura and two percent in Castilla la Nueva. With the exception of the latter region where the loss came almost exclusively from a sharp increase in deaths, the combination of lower births and higher mortality largely explained the decline.* In Cataluña, births in 1809 fell to their lowest point of the war – indeed, of the whole period from 1800–1817. In terms of annual population loss, 1809 was not only the worst year of the war in Cataluña, but the worst in the eighteen-year period from the beginning of the century.

Everywhere, the deaths were generally caused less by enemy fire than by the ravages of war. Despite the Suprema's call for all-out local defence, the constant French incursions of villages and townships to requisition food struck panic into most inhabitants and sent them fleeing for safety to remote hills, barren lands, outlying refuges. Here they had to live rough, exposed to the elements, with insufficient food or polluted water. The toll on young and old was enormous. In the cold winter months of 1809, fifty-five percent more people died in Castilla la Nueva than on average.† High death rates continued through the summer: disease struck down both the aged and the under-sevens. More young children died than in any other year of the war.[1]

* The extent of depopulation is almost certainly somewhat inflated because the regional population figures do not record those who fled their homes to places of greater safety or those who were absent because of imprisonment or for whatever other cause (Author db/ *Demography*: Regional population, 1800–1817).
† As explained earlier, the average is of the entire 1800–1817 period.

It was in Cataluña, however, that the death toll reached shocking heights. More under-sevens died proportionately than at any other time between 1800 and 1817. Adults suffered even worse. Judged by villages in the Tarragona area, deaths began to rise in November 1808, and thereafter climbed relentlessly month after month until May 1809, when they reached over five and a half times their average for that month. Even though the rate began to decline slowly thereafter, it was not until November that something approaching normality returned. In the year from November 1808 to October 1809, three times as many villagers in the area died as on average.

In Extremadura, bordering on Portugal, the first full year of the war exacerbated a population crisis which since the turn of the century had plagued the region, one of Spain's poorest. In 1809 deaths rose to their second highest point of the war and births fell.

Advancing, retreating or merely stationary, and without firing a shot, the armies brought death and disease to civilians. The township of Chinchilla, southeast of Albacete, explained to the Suprema that

> since the Army of the Centre has been here, this town and its neighbouring villages have been devastated. Food and supplies have been paid only by receipts and bits of paper. The costs have risen by having to care for six hundred ill soldiers. Due to this, sickness has spread so rapidly among the small number of the town's inhabitants that within less than a week two hundred people have been laid low, and the contagions continue to spread.[2]

Contagious diseases and lack of hospitals decimated civilians, and reduced the fighting strength of the armies. In April 1809, five thousand soldiers were in Catalan hospitals with 'putrid fevers' resulting from lack of proper clothing and the miserable conditions of the previous winter's campaign. The army's commander-in-chief ordered a ration of brandy for his troops to increase their nutrition 'in order to prevent in part the spread of disease'.[3]

Naturally, nothing was more feared. In March 1809, the Sevilla junta commissioned a doctor to report on how contagious diseases in La Mancha could be prevented from spreading to the Andalucian capital.[4]

By October 1808, Napoleon had pushed nearly three hundred thousand troops into Spain in an attempt to put down the insurrection. (The number rose by another fifty thousand to its maximum in the summer of 1810.)[5] Depending on circumstances, the Spanish army had around one hundred thousand men. Without counting the British army's sporadic incursions, some four hundred thousand 'useless hands' had to live off a countryside which, before the war – when most of the available labour was working the land – struggled to support its own population. It was fortunate for Napoleon – and the patriots – that the conflict began in a bountiful agrarian year: the highest grain crops of the new century. A famine year in 1808, or even a year of below average crops, and it is doubtful that the war could have continued for long, unless Napoleon renounced his dictum that imperial troops had to live off the land, as he was forced to do in Cataluña, a region traditionally deficient in grain.

Although in principle the Spanish military paid for its supplies, the patriot treasury was usually in such dire straits that the payments, as in Chinchilla, were not in cash but receipts. (Some of the wealthier made a good living from this: they discounted heavily the villagers' paper and collected the full amount – or as near as they could get for it – from the treasury when the Mexican silver ships arrived.) Short of hands, the villagers had to support, virtually free of charge, two, and sometimes three, destructive armies as well as Spanish guerrilla forces and try to keep themselves alive. In consequence, a vital – indeed *the* vital – issue of the war turned on the control of limited food resources.

In 1809, the villagers' inevitable inexperience in this matter no doubt increased their number of deaths; lack of food exposed them to dying cruelly of disease. Some, of course, died at the hands of imperial troops in their raids to exact supplies but they were the minority. The sort of thing that happened in these French forays – the following example is from the village of Pueblanueva, southeast of Talavera de la Reina – was described by a member of the Toledo junta in hiding, Martín de la Cerda. On November 24, 1809, French infantry, accompanied by cavalry, entered the place and seized eight to nine thousand head of all type of livestock, as well as over seven hundred fanegas of barley.* They also looted some houses. Three days later, as he was writing his account, they were seizing a further ninety-two fanegas of barley and looting three more houses.

> There is not a saint they have not burned, a woman they have not abused and they have killed some men who refused to give them what they wanted . . . This has to be seen to be believed.[6]

Despite these barbarities, the loss to the villagers of their whole herd of livestock and no doubt a large part of their barley reserves was an even greater blow. In just a few days the village economy was shattered. How the villagers were to live thereafter could be barely imagined. But they and township inhabitants learned to become more resourceful. They hid their crops and livestock from any and every army that crossed their lands. Toledan villagers sowed their grain by night to prevent soldiers of one side or another seizing their seed corn.[7]

Though in 1809 several regions suffered heavy population losses they were exceeded in the two Castillas, southwestern Andalucía and Extremadura by those of the pre-war famine and malaria epidemic. From mid-1803 to mid-1804, Extremadura lost five percent of its population, each of the two Castillas just over four percent and southwestern Andalucía, struck also by yellow fever, slightly more than three percent. The first full year of war in these regions was less deadly than a peacetime famine accompanied by disease.†

During the war (as in the pre-war) there were wide regional differences. For example, Valencia, in the patriot rearguard, lived (in comparative population terms) as if the war barely existed in 1809. Though a small rise in mortality –

* A fanega equals approximately 1.5 bushels.
† The famine occurred during the peace following the treaty of Amiens, 1802, a peace which in Spain's case lasted until 1805.

among young children especially in early spring and mid-summer – brought a population decrease, the mere 0.2% was the lowest of all the regions. Marriages were buoyant, reaching their highest point since the turn of the century. Month after month throughout the year, with the single exception of November, when the patriot army went down to its heaviest defeat of the war at Ocaña, they exceeded their average. Conceptions followed the same pattern, though at a lesser rate.

Felicitous Levante! Valencia still had three years before its population experienced the full rigours of war and enemy occupation with demographic results as disastrous as elsewhere.

POPULAR ATTITUDES TO THE WAR

Death was usually involuntary; marriage and conception – intimate individual choices however limited by contemporary constraints – frequently spoke more tellingly about popular expectations and fears than the lettered elites' scanty references.

This was demonstrated in several regions from the onset of war. Marriages, the area of greatest personal choice, dropped in Cataluña throughout 1808 but the decline was particularly notable in February, when Barcelona was first occupied, in May during the abdication crisis – two of the usually highest marriage months of the year – and in July and August after the risings and the effective declaration of war. From the moment the French army marched on Madrid in March 1808, marriages dropped in the two Castillas. Extremadura's situation was yet more extreme. From May, the month of the anti-French rising in Madrid and the Bourbon abdications, weddings plummeted below average for twenty-nine straight months with only one exception. Almost without respite Extremadura remained a frontline region.

This downturn in marriages, which continued generally throughout 1809, seemed to require no explanation: the youth had gone to war, leaving their fiancées behind. However, in many regions patriotic conscription lagged. Young men, who should have been in the army, were still at home and took advantage of this to get married and thereby claim – sometimes only temporarily – exemption from the call-up.

The extraordinary number of deaths in 1809 should, paradoxically, have served to increase the matrimonial rate as it expanded the 'market' for second marriages, very common at the time, of widows and widowers.* Over and above the Old Order's structural demographic ebbs and flows the decline

---

* Following the example of the absolutist enlightened reformers, the Suprema implicitly assumed an unwillingness to limit demographic growth: population increase meant more power to the state, more potential tax-payers to the treasury. Married men were only called up if there were insufficient batchelors and widowers without children to fill the assigned quota which was fixed at four regional recruits per one hundred souls; married men with one or more children were virtually exempt. For those who had no desire to serve, marriage and parenthood were thus an incentive to escape the rigours of military service.

indicated that the people in 1809 did not look on their future with much hope, certainly not enough to consider their conditions propitious for marriage. Even in the heady days of the previous year, when a patriot victory seemed assured, villagers were evidently doubtful; and 1809 increased their fears. Although a patriot victory had receded to an uncertain horizon, they could not be certain what a rapid Bonapartist triumph would bring in its train. Accustomed to the Old Regime's political certainties, and the continuities of their daily lives, villagers and townsfolk lived in doubt and fear of what lay ahead.

A rise in conceptions* in the spring of 1809, after nine months of decline in the two Castillas, was seemingly at odds with a popular sense of anxiety about the future. The drop had begun just after the risings in the summer of 1808. While fertility was subject to many more physical constraints than marriage, the simultaneity of the decline – and of the subsequent recuperation – in two such large regions was notable. (In Castilla la Vieja, the decrease was particularly marked in the autumn of 1808 during Napoleon's invasion.) Moreover, like marriages, the trend was exaggerated in Extremadura, where conceptions declined below average for twenty-six straight months from May 1808. Most remarkable was the case of Plasencia, a town of some five thousand inhabitants in northern Extremadura, not far from the main Madrid to Lisbon road, where not a single marriage or conception was recorded in the autumn of 1808, a phenomenon that had not occurred even during the worst of the pre-war famine years. The panic at the Emperor's offensive appeared evident.† Arguably, the two Castillas' simultaneous reversal of the conception decline – spring was traditionally the highest fertility period of the year – expressed in both occupied and patriot zones the other face of anxiety: popular hope in a quick resolution of the conflict and an end to a threatening uncertainty, albeit under a new king. A similar recuperation in springtime fertility in patriot-controlled Andalucía – for the first time in the new century and at precisely the moment when the region felt under constant threat of French invasion – suggested that this was so. Disillusionment with the Suprema had reached such a pitch that the majority of couples in the patriot rearguard, which still included southern Castilla la Nueva, could well believe that their and their family's fate would be better if the war, irrespective of victor, were brought to an end.

With all the more reason, the inhabitants of occupied Castilla la Vieja hoped for the conflict's conclusion to rid themselves of the constant anxiety caused by the intrusive imperial military presence. But in both Castillas it may be equally true that the recovery in conceptions was a further sign of the ravages of war. Couples began to 'make good' the drop in the birth rate due to the earlier decline in fertility.

Though a popular desire for the war's end was disappointed, the above average recuperation fed through into a demographic recovery in both Castillas in 1810–1811.

* Baptisms backdated nine months.
† Possibly, some women may have given birth in villages to which they had fled after the town was occupied by the French nine months after Napoleon's invasion of 1808 (See José Antonio Sánchez de la Calle, *Plasencia. Historia y población en le época contemporánea (1800–1990)*, Caceres, 1994).

THE PATRIOT ARMY:
DEFEATS, AND MORE DEFEATS ON THE BATTLEFIELD

The year ended as it had started with the main patriot army routed and in flight. With the exception of a couple of small victories – Alcañiz, in Aragón, and the re-occupation of Salamanca for a fortnight; and, fought together with the British, the stalemated battle of Talavera – the year brought nothing but defeats, the final and most disastrous of which took place at Ocaña in Castilla la Nueva, opening the road to the conquest of Andalucía at the beginning of 1810. Most of the battlefield defeats could be attributed to two factors: the field commanders' incompetence and their lack of coordination; and the fear inspired in largely untrained troops by this ineptitude which allowed French cavalry to descend on their rear. The Junta Suprema's policy of 'permanent war on all fronts at all times', adopted after the battle of Talavera, failed. Despite serious recruitment delays, the Junta managed to assemble masses of raw recruits to form the appearance of large armies which, under their Old Regime commanders, were thrown willy-nilly into open-field combat against seasoned imperial troops. The cavalry was the patriot armies' weakest point. The lack of sufficient horses, given the mid-eighteenth-century turn to mules as the country's major traction,* aggravated the situation. But even reasonably mounted, the patriot cavalry was often the first to turn tail. The infantry – stolid, but militarily untrained, village recruits – could stubbornly withstand frontal attack, but when the patriot cavalry fled they had not learned to manoeuvre to reduce the enemy threat from the flank or rear.

The battle of Medellín on March 28, 1809, was a prime example. Marshal Victor, under orders to advance on Extremadura and Andalucía, and to help Soult who had marched from Galicia into Portugal to confront the British army now under General Wellesley, was met on March 28 outside Medellín by General Cuesta, commander of the Extremaduran army. On the Suprema's orders, he had just been reinforced by the duque de Alburquerque with twelve thousand men. Together the two forces numbered twenty-two thousand against Victor's eighteen. Successful at first in forcing the French back, the two Spanish columns sought to re-engage the enemy, advancing at a different pace, and leaving gaps in their line. The French cavalry saw their opportunity and charged; the Spanish cavalry turned tail, and the French outflanked the patriot force. When the enemy troopers appeared in their rear, the Spanish infantry panicked and fled the field. The massacre of the routed lasted all day, turning the battle into a slaughter. The Spanish lost ten thousand men, three-quarters of them dead and wounded; some battalions were annihilated down to the last man. It was Spain's historically worst military defeat so far on its own territory.[8]

Not surprisingly, the rank-and-file had little confidence in their generals, and

---

* It is worth recalling that even the nobility's carriages were mule-drawn; in place of oxen, the mule, rather than the horse, had become the main animal power in the last half of the previous country, as a result of which horsebreeding had declined. An impressive quantity of mules were imported through Cataluña from France each year to maintain the necessary numbers which Spain itself could not provide.

the latter little confidence in their largely untrained men. Just as bad, many regimental officers seemed to have little stomach for fighting in these circumstances. In January 1809, the Suprema ordered the many officers who had come to Sevilla on the pretext of illness to return forthwith to their regiments, and forbade any officer to be absent from his post. The wounded and sick amongst them were to be attended to in army hospitals. (These officers' lives had evidently been eased by the custom of drawing campaign rations while in the rearguard, a practice which the Junta had also to forbid.[9]) Finally, the Suprema threatened to execute any officer who deserted.[10]

Alerted six weeks later by the tribunal of public safety to the continuing presence of many officers in Sevilla, which the population took badly, the Junta again issued immediate orders for them to return to their regiments.[11] The problem was not new, and nor did it seem to have been cured under the Suprema's rule.

> Desiring to put an end to the scandalous abuse of officers leaving their posts on all occasions, and especially on a day of action, in which [the Junta Suprema] sees an intolerable lack of discipline, of insubordination and above all one of the principal causes that our military actions do not correspond to the bravery and constancy of our troops who, with so many less obligations and advantages, are giving proof of their love and fidelity to our King and Country . . . (preamble to Suprema order, November 17, 1808)[12]

As the date of this order makes clear, the problem had existed from the time of Napoleon's offensive, if not before. Exactly a year later, in November 1809, it still evidently continued. The Army of the Centre's generals who, at Ocaña, had just suffered an even worse defeat than that of Medillín, reported to the Suprema that 'some regiments had had very few officers to lead them' on the decisive day.[13] The high command was obviously looking for every possible pretext to explain the rout; but this one had a familiar ring. The Junta once more ordered all officers to their posts.

Alongside these defaulters, there were many officers who fought bravely at the head of their men; though how many took the time to supervise their training was another question. The Suprema's order in April 1809, that all troops, whether armed or not, must train seven hours a day should have been superfluous.[14] The Junta also fulminated against infantry officers who had evaded the summons to hand over horses suitable for the cavalry and ordered them to ride only mounts that were 'two fingers' under the requisitionable height. Similarly, the Suprema was 'outraged' that officers had arrogated to themselves more batmen than were officially permitted and had provided them also for their wives and families who remained in the rearguard. These batmen had to be returned to their regiments forthwith or be treated as deserters.[15]

In the spring of 1809, the Junta floated the idea that selected officers should be sent to Prussia – whose army since Frederick the Great's time had been the Spanish military model – to perfect themselves in the art of war; but the minister of war turned down the suggestion 'because of the present circumstances', presumably referring to the recent Medellín disaster and the threat of a French invasion of Andalucía.[16]

The harshest criticism of the officer corps and the army in general came from Jovellanos, the Junta member for Asturias. In a memorandum to his fellow deputies a few days after Medellín, he wrote among other things that the officer corps should be purged, and NCOs and others who had distinguished themselves on the field of battle promoted to officers.

> It is not good enough to take the broom only to the heads [of the armies], it is necessary to take it right down to the lowest officer ranks . . . There has been great abuse in the use of our armies. We look only to numbers, when it is not the numbers of men, but their skill and bravery that win victories. We clamour for more muskets to arm men, and we do not attempt to train them in their use. There are thousands of enlisted men everywhere, and yet there is not a single depot to train them.[17]

His call for a 'training army' went unheeded at the time. The moment was too fraught to withdraw veterans from active duty to train recruits. As Jovellanos himself continued: 'the [Medellín] disaster of March 28 has put the fatherland in danger. That misfortune was the result of a lack of unity . . . The Junta must recognize that it is impossible for us to find two generals who can effectively cooperate together.' But now that the Suprema had appointed Cuesta supreme commander, it must trust him, give him ample powers. 'In the situation in which we find ourselves, it is everything or nothing.'*

The Suprema's policy of calling on raw recruits to reinforce armies allowed Cuesta to replace his force's ten thousand Medellín losses in a couple of months. At various times, the Junta clearly expressed the belief that only 'great masses of troops, aided by villagers' could defeat the French. 'We must oppose tactical superiority by numbers, [military] skill by enthusiasm, and then the fatherland will not be exposed to its present crisis', the Suprema officially informed its deputy and commissioner in Cataluña in the late winter of 1809.[18] This was a revolutionary military strategy without revolutionary politics: popular 'enthusiasm' was predicated solely on anti-French sentiment, not on the lower orders' defence of revolutionary conquests. Approving the Extremaduran call for a mass general rising to help stave off the French military threat four days before Medellín, the Suprema cited favourably and at length Galicia and Cataluña as prime examples of this strategy, which had killed more French than any other, and called for their example to be followed *as long as the rising is orderly . . . and does not propose to go beyond its implied objectives* (stress added).[19] In other words, as long as it contained no threat to the status quo. Within these limits, the Suprema envisaged that a mass rising would

> produce heavy damage [to the enemy] because he cannot push forward small forces and will encounter frequent and fearful obstacles to devastating the countryside,

---

* Immediately after Medellín, the Junta Suprema promoted Cuesta, who was wounded in the battle, to captain general of the army and effective supreme commander.

collecting supplies and exacting forced contributions from the villagers . . . The French are used to fighting against disciplined troops and to engaging in battle with armies. Above all they fear the villagers, who attack and then scatter before them without presenting a force on whom to employ their terrible tactics.[20]

Cuesta rejected this policy, pointing to the military difficulties of the people's mass arming. Indeed, he had a shock in store for the Suprema. Only a month after Medellín, this new supreme commander proposed abolishing the existing Extramaduran junta and establishing a new one for the defence of Badajoz 'in which neither the people nor the the old junta members have any influence'. Surprisingly, the Suprema's military junta agreed. Informed of the matter, the Suprema immediately reacted with shocked indignation, countermanding both its own military junta and Cuesta. Though it had seriously curtailed the provincial juntas' powers, the Suprema was always aware that its original authority emanated from them: and it was not prepared to see any of them sacrificed to the whims of a general who, despite Jovellanos' plea to place their full confidence in him as the new commander-in-chief, many Suprema deputies continued to fear as a potential dictator.[21]

MILITANCIES: A SECRET MISSION TO MADRID

When Salustiano Andrés de Embite, an infantry captain of the Tiradores de Murcia, set off on the Suprema's orders from Sevilla for French-occupied Madrid on January 29, 1809, he knew he was on a perilous mission which, as a military officer in villager's disguise, might end before a firing squad shot as a spy. The Suprema's instructions were wide-ranging: from ascertaining French military forces and fortifications in the capital to making contact with high officials of the Old Regime to persuade them to leave Madrid for Sevilla. But the crucial issue was to discover the Bonapartist government's policy towards the colonies.[22] Embite had had no hesitation in accepting the mission. He was brave, as he had shown in the defence of Madrid, where he succeeded in breaking through Napoleon's troops and rallying his men to fight again at Aranjuez.[23] Captains were two a penny and any who wanted quick promotion had to prove themselves ingenious, efficient and daring.

With a trustworthy companion, Vicente del Campo, whom the Suprema had allowed him to choose, the captain's troubles began at Manzanares, about half way through the Mancha.* There he was warned that the French were thick on the ground not far to the north, the road was untravelled in consequence, and he was advised to take a safer but more circuitous route. He ignored the advice because it would take too long but, as a precaution, donned his villager's guise, and hid on his person all the documents and gold he carried. The people's terror at

---

* Villacañas, whose inhabitants had fought off the French cavalry, lay about sixty kilometres to the north of Manzanares. (See Chapter 10: pp. 245 et seq.)

the enemy's advance was so great, he later reported, that nobody would help them venture north, until the captain learned that a calèche had just arrived from Madrid. Imagining that the driver must have a French pass, the captain approached him and found that he was willing to sell his authorization for the return trip to Madrid (the Suprema had provided Embite with funds and documents to procure money from local justices). Though the pass was for the driver alone, Embite and his companion pressed on the following morning: the captain gambled, correctly, that a single pass would be sufficient.

French patrols soon stopped them. Embite showed the pass and said he had gone to leave his wife in Mora, and had forgotten to report to the local French commandant. The officer in charge was understanding but told them to remain until further orders. Embite and his companion looked for ways to escape; but at that moment the outpost received orders to retire northwards and they were free to continue their journey. Luck accompanied the daring, and the two men finally reached Madrid. But not before seeing some horrifying sights on the road entering Aranjuez:

> Three poor men had been hanged and were dangling from trees . . . At the beginning of the long bridge [across the Tajo] four more had not only been hanged but had been nailed through the breast to the tree trunks . . . In neighbouring villages, as we heard, fathers and husbands had seen their daughters and wives raped and even sons their old mothers . . . Everything that had been beautiful in the Aranjuez palace and gardens had been burned or destroyed by the French army . . .[24]

In Madrid more trouble awaited them. Embite returned to former lodgings to find them already taken. His companion was received by an ironmonger to whom he had been recommended until at six in the evening of the first day he was told he had to leave. Fear was greater than patriotic hospitality, and del Campo was obliged to spend the night in an inn, a dangerous move because all new arrivals had to be registered with the police. The next day he fled Madrid in the company of some muleteers, not to return.

Greater luck as usual attended Embite. A 'generous and patriotic merchant' took him in, provided for all his needs and refused to leave his side during the week he spent on his mission. On the vital issue of discovering the Bonapartist government's policy towards the colonies another stroke of luck put in his hands – he did not report how – a 'position' paper by Miguel Azanza, the new king's Treasury minister and a former viceroy of New Spain (Mexico). Arguing that Spain without the Indies would forever be 'an impoverished country without authority or defence' in the world, the new regime must do nothing to antagonize the inhabitants which could only encourage their aspirations for independence such as already existed in Puerto Rico, Cuba, Vera Cruz (Mexico) and other places of the northern colonies.

As soon as they know by whatever means about the latest events in Spain the inhabitants will become as impassioned as the Andalucians and other regions' people who have been attempting to defend themselves and will join in their common cause . . .

Azanza's paper was designed to stave off any attempt to make the colonies swear fidelity to the new monarch, as the inhabitants of the Bonapartist zone had been obliged to do. He reported that the king's three councils, in joint session, had unanimously rejected a prior attempt to do so as 'inopportune'. He recognized furthermore that the colonies had from the start thrown in their lot with the Sevilla junta which had told them not to obey any royal council's orders. If now they learned that the Emperor in person had conquered Madrid and placed his brother back on the throne,

it is impossible that the Council of the Indies could persuade the colonies' inhabitants that it has freely decided in the national interest [to impose the oath of fidelity]. The Junta [Suprema] or the other juntas which still exist are certainly in frequent correspondence with the colonies and will have told them that the juntas are invincible and whatever else they feel is needed to maintain their and the colonies' union . . .

Whatever the outcome of the present struggle, Spain must preserve the Indies . . . When the Spanish provinces [in revolt] admit defeat or change opinion and come to agreement [with us] . . . When the colonies' inhabitants do not receive conflicting reports from Spain, but hear a single authoritative voice speaking . . . then it is almost certain that Spain's and the colonies' unity will remain assured through ties of family, custom and interests; and those in the Indies who promise themselves a better future under a different form of government will be overcome. Meanwhile, the divisions in Spain must not be permitted to pass to the colonies and foster plans for independence.[25]

Though it illustrated a Bonapartist political view of what was necessary to preserve the colonies, Azanza's report was already outdated by the time Embite got hold of it.* On learning of the beginning of the war and the creation of regional juntas in the metropolis, many of the South American colonies had formed their own juntas which sooner or later would lead to independence movements. Embite's report to the Suprema's general secretary answered one other important question: the state of mind of Madrid's population.

Here it is necessary to divide the inhabitants into the same classes the social order uses to consider mankind. All those who previously made up what was

---

* Josef was formally king of Spain and the Indies. On February 18, 1809, ten days after the paper was written, the government issued a decree obliging all of the 'kingdom's officials and military to swear loyalty to the king or else they would be considered to have resigned their posts'. There was no specific mention of the Indies, whereas an earlier decree of October 1, 1808, stated that 'the peoples of Spain and the Indies will swear loyalty to the king'. (Artola, 1989 (1), p. 97 fn. 16 and p. 98, fn. 18.)

called the plebs – tradesmen, retailers and employees, even those of the courts of justice – are spirited and abhor the French domination more than ever. The large merchant houses and their employees support the new regime out of fear. Amongst the inhabitants at large, there are many declared supporters of our enemies, I was assured.

After a week in the capital, Embite was informed by a sympathizer that his presence there was known to the police, and another friendly informant told him that a man in muleteer's disguise had been taken prisoner. Believing that this might be his companion del Campo, he decided to leave. Again his merchant host came to his aid, securing a pass from the Spanish police – an easier matter than from the French military – to leave the capital with his servant. Taking on his host's guise, Embite left Madrid the following day to return to Sevilla which he reached without great trouble.[26]

Once he had presented his report, he petitioned the Suprema in Old Regime style to grant him a recompense for his efforts: to be appointed one of its aides-de-camp and promotion to lieutenant colonel. In May Embite received his reward of the promotion and reinbursement of the money he had spent from his own pocket, some five thousand reales.

PATRIOTISM AND THE LABOURING POOR

At the very beginning of the conflict, when Marshal Moncey attempted unsuccessfully to force Valencia to surrender, the carpenters who had recently raised a new bullring in the city refused to pull it down to provide the wooden beams necessary to reinforce the antiquated gates and walls. In the end the inhabitants pulled it down. At first sight, the carpenters seemed opposed to defending their city at the expense of destroying their own work, even if this gave the enemy an advantage. But was it so?

Other fortification works suggested another, more complex response. In the small village of Villarta de los Montes, in the Toledo hills, the imperial forces suddenly moved to attack. On the first day, the villagers came out to dig a trench to defend the bridge across the Guadiana river; on the second day, to a patriot officer's despair, only a few labourers appeared.

They said they had seen where the trench was to be dug, adding insolently that they were not going to dig it. I called the local justice who said that the villagers demanded a day's wage for the work, and he did not have the authority or money to pay them. If they refused to dig it there was nothing he could do. This magistrate was a weak and indecisive man . . . I berated him for not obeying the royal order on [local] defence, but it was all useless and so I left . . .[27]

It was the same story on a larger scale during fortification works in provincial capitals like Badajoz, Sevilla and Cádiz. In the first of these, under real threat of French attack after the Medellín defeat in the spring of 1809, the workers did not turn out in full to strengthen the walls. Despite demanding lists of labourers' and tradesmen's names from every neighbourhood, two days later this had still not had the desired effect, for the military governor had to order all male inhabitants to the defence works under threat of a fine.[28]

In Andalucía, despite similar fears of a French invasion, work on fortifying Sevilla was slowed perceptibly 'for want of hands', the brigadier in charge of the works reported. The situation became so extreme that the cathedral chapter and Franciscan friars themselves offered to work to 'set an example and stimulate others'. The workers' refusal to turn out – or if obliged to turn out, their refusal to work – was described in one of the police reports the Junta Suprema ordered the Sevilla criminal justices to submit daily:

> There is considerable discontent among the people owing to their being obliged to work on the fortifications because, as the workers say, they are not being paid for their labour. One of the magistrates has reported that on his rounds many of the workers were sitting on the ground until someone of authority approached who could reprehend them, whereupon they pretended to work, only to sit down again once the person had passed. 'Quiet, lads, quiet', they said.[29]

Although the sit-down strike did not reappear in further police reports,* the Sevilla fortifications, which were to prove of little effect finally, were not completed until the following August, six months later. In Cádiz progress was even slower; here it was not artisans but day labourers, mostly Galicians, who did not turn out because, in the words of Francisco Hurtado, an engineers commandant, 'they can earn more as porters at the Customs, Corn Exchange, fish market and the like than they can on a day labourer's wage – which has already risen to eight reales. Their avarice is such that they will not work on the fortifications.'[30]

On the neighbouring Isla de León, the governor warned that there was no money to pay the day labourers for such works. 'The consequences of this must be taken into account, for the labourers have no other means of subsistence than that which they earn by their daily work.'[31]

In January 1810, just before the Suprema's demise, it sent conde de Ayamans, its Mallorcan deputy, to speed up and complete the Cádiz fortification work that had been going on for over a year. He ordered all the surrounding townships and villages to send labourers 'with their clouts' to work on the fortifications 'at the same daily wage as they receive from individual employees'. Within four days he had 440 men working on the caño del Trocadero's defences.[32]†

*

* At least not in the remaining records from which many of these daily reports are missing.

† Valencia adopted a similarly realistic approach. The trenches (around the walls) had been completed. 'They were started thanks to voluntary subscriptions and townspeople working unpaid; later all the inhabitants had to contribute financially, and when this proved insufficient, the treasury gave certain sums.' (AHN, *Estado*, Legajo 36P/338, Valencia, intendente Aspiroz's report to Junta Suprema, Sevilla, April 17, 1809.)

Not so long before, the labouring classes who were now disinclined to build defences had enthusiastically participated in, or welcomed, the popular uprising against the Napoleonic invasion and the Godoyistas in power and volunteered en masse for the army to fight for their king, religion and fatherland. Little less than nine months later they refused, even in so fundamental a matter as their home towns' defence, to sacrifice a day's wage to the struggle. An attitude of defiance towards their patriot 'betters' was apparent in their dissent. They threatened the latter with allowing the French to seize the towns and appropriate their property. This was perhaps no more than a form of pressure to receive the wage they believed their due. They – the labouring hands – had no property to lose. Significantly none of the places had yet suffered the dramatic effects of French occupation.

It was obvious that a long string of patriot military defeats had undermined popular enthusiasm and morale. The lower classes' sacrifice of life and well-being in an ineffectually led army of which they formed the majority – and were the major sufferers – was known to all. Those with conscripted sons or relatives had seen how the local privileged used their power to keep their sons from the military's grasp. The Junta Suprema's misconduct of the war had led to widespread disillusion with this new form of government. Save in the most extreme of circumstances – the last Gerona siege for example – proletarian patriotism could not feed on labourers' empty stomachs; but there was a further, and more complex dimension to their understanding of patriotism.

At this historical moment, patriotism could – if only still just – be distinguished from nationalism. The Enlightenment's reformulation of antiquity's love of one's country and the willingness to sacrifice one's life for it demanded liberty, equality before the law and justice. Absolute monarchy, which considered the country its feudal domain and its peoples as vassals, distinguishing legally between privileged noble, the ecclesiastical orders and commoners, could not create a patria. Without liberty, equality and justice there could be a *country* but no *fatherland*.[33]

The 1808 risings were generally assumed by their Fernandista organizers to be the work of a 'patriot' populace. The major problem less than a year later was to maintain this sense of patriotism. To suppose that altar and monarchy dominated their sole sense of 'patriotism' was to imagine that the lower orders were unable to form their own ideas of what patriotism should mean.

A popular protest in the township of Vivero on the north Galician coast shed some light on these matters. At the beginning of the war, the corregidor's measures to form defence squadrons manned by retired soldiers and township inhabitants and his order that all privately held muskets be handed in for their use brought a formal complaint signed by fifteen members of the community. They protested that 'men of influence and power' were exonerated from serving when it was they who should be the township's most determined defenders, and if they were not willing or able to undertake this themselves, they had the financial means to provide it.[34]

As it was, the burden of defence fell on the 'weak shoulders of men who live only by their work and industry', they wrote. Elsewhere, local defence in the name of 'religion, fatherland and *liberty*' (stress added) had been organized to alleviate the burden on those who 'groan under the oppression of labour in order to stay alive. For that reason no one should be exempt from what, in justice, is an obligation on all.'

The situation, continued the protesters, had been worsened by forming all those with military experience into a separate township guard, leaving the squadrons without anyone capable of training them. It was they, the untrained, who would be exposed to death and desolation in the dangerous outposts. In other words, the untrained labouring classes were to defend the rich on the basis of the latter's 'patriotic' demand to defend a fatherland from which, de facto, they were excluded. They rejected their social superiors' patriotism outright. Instead, they put forward their own patriotic demand: equality of sacrifice in the war effort.

This was an equality which their presence as 'street troops' during the Fernandista-led or inspired risings of 1808 had left their social superiors on the newly formed regional and local juntas with no option but to heed: the juntas' initial call to arms had unanimously summoned all men – *without distinction of class or status* – between the ages of sixteen and forty-five to report for military service. The labouring poor expected no less than that the powerful and the rich would contribute equally to the war effort. And they had been deceived. They had not seen the privileged commit their means, their wealth, their sons to fighting the common enemy. Nor had the Suprema offered them any tangible advantages for defending the patriot cause. To the contrary, the new government defended all the Old Regime's rights and privileges: señorial and Church prerogatives over the land, social privilege, subordination of the labouring classes. The Cortes, were it finally summoned, might bring reforms; but most reforms, as workers knew from the past, could prejudice as much as help them. Meanwhile, they understood full well that the patriot elite – which was not about to go short of a meal for itself and its families – was primarily defending its own interests at their expense; and at the same time demanding of them a sacrifice for the patriotic cause which they had already paid a hundred fold on the battlefield. Why then should they forgo a day's wage that kept them and their families alive? Or demonstrate a patriotic zeal which their betters denied to themselves? The Vivero protesters' last claim, in a pure Old Regime style, demonstrated that it was equality of sacrifice – not social equality – that the lower orders demanded. They complained that the defence squadrons

> arbitrarily mixed individuals of whatever trade or position, the unvirtuous and the indecent with the more decent who have responsibilities which distinguish them in the social order, a distinction created by nature, the soul, craft or skill . . . The respectable, honourable man . . . will then not find himself put on the same level as a lowly tradesman, a dolt or a despicable inferior.*

* They could point to La Coruña, for example, where the newly formed urban militia included one company exclusively of nobles, with noble commanders, and another was reserved solely for merchants. These two companies were to receive no pay, whereas the remainder, made up largely of 'poor artisans', were to get the same pay and rations as soldiers. (Martínez Salazar, 1953, p. 97.)

The protest's dominant tone was unmistakably that of the master craftsman, concerned about his social status and honour, though it cannot be supposed that all fifteen signatories came from this social stratum. Their statement can be read in two, not necessarily antagonistic, ways. In the first, as the craftsmen's continuing defence of their status against the enlightened reformers' attack on their corporative guilds' control of production and their fear that a Bonapartist regime would carry this to its extreme – the Revolution had abolished the guilds in France. In this respect, it was significant that in many parts of the country artisans and journeymen had formed an important proportion of the first volunteers to fight Napoleon.

A second reading demonstrated that their claim to a new social status reflected on their right to a particular vision of patriotism. Their substitution of 'liberty' for 'king' in the hallowed patriot tripartite slogan was the most significant of these. The fatherland without liberty did not exist. While social distinctions might be 'natural', they were also created by the 'soul, craft or skill'. As spiritual liberty, the soul could be patriotic, even if actual liberty was unknown; by 'craft or skill' they were as distinguished in the social order as those who occupied this position by 'nature' and thus they had a right to tell their apparent social superiors their patriotic duty. To reinforce their argument, they claimed that in 'another country' – presumably France – they would enjoy 'noble status', a hyperbole in Spanish society where the distinction between the noble-born and the ignoble labouring poor remained marked not only before the law but in society as a whole, especially in Galicia where the lower nobility, the hidalgo, formed the dominant class.

Isolated by land, Vivero was a port where many foreign ships put in; and so it was often better connected to the exterior world than, for example, the closed rural world of the Galician interior. Despite their Old Regime defence of social inequality this contact with the outer world appeared to have allowed the protesters to imbibe something of the French Enlightenment and the first phases of the French Revolution. Moreover, Vivero was one of the largest areas of royal – rather than minor noble or ecclesiastical – lordships in Galicia, which gave it and its hinterland a certain independence; and also added a further significance to the substitution of liberty for king.

However exceptional, the Vivero protest illuminated an Old Regime cast of mind overlaid by – or rather already imbued with – a number of progressive ideas. It would be foolhardy to suppose that this was equally true of the labouring poor everywhere. But what was certainly true was that the Vivero men's dominant demand for equality of sacrifice was widely shared. This was the real meaning of the labourers' refusal to work unpaid on their towns' and cities' defences. The popular complaints about the injustices of military conscription reinforced this view.

In the first months of the war, patriot Spain could call on three-quarters of a million single men of conscription age, well over half of whom were sixteen to twenty-five-year olds, the age group which had shown the greatest willingness to volunteer at the start of the conflict, and eighty-seven percent of whom were under forty.* This demographical base should have been more than sufficient to raise an army of half a million *unmarried* men alone. In part this was borne out by the massive enlistment, much of it voluntary, immediately after the uprisings, which provided more than sufficient troops to make good the depleted army regiments and even to form new ones. The introduction of conscription was thereby delayed until November 1808, during Napoleon's invasion. In its need for fresh recruits, the newly created Junta Suprema followed the Old Regime's conscription procedures. With their superficial appearance of equality – the drawing of lots of those deemed eligible to serve – the system was inherently plagued with manipulative possibilities. To obtain the number of men needed the new central government fixed quotas for each province, without certain knowledge of their total population or of how many had enlisted from each at the start of the war; and a proportion of the quotas was in turn allocated to each village and township by the provincial centres. Lacking any administrative structure to manage conscription, the central government and provincial juntas were forced to rely, as had the Old Regime, on local magistrates to decide who should be included in the drawing of lots. This inevitably led to favouritism, manipulation and corruption at local level to exempt the sons of relatives, friends and of local oligarchs. Even though the Suprema insistently reiterated that there were to be no exemptions except for the physically incapacitated the abuses continued. This inequality of sacrifice resulted in widespread popular disturbances, protests and disaffection.

Conscription became so plagued with protests that the Junta Suprema ordered in May 1809 that each province create a grievance junta to investigate the complaints; as late as December 1, 1809, in the Sevilla military district, the list of all those whose cases were outstanding and their villages of provenance covered two dense pages of handwritten text.[35]

One of these, from Puebla de Guzmán, south-western Andalucía, was fairly typical. The conscripted protested that the local magistrates had exempted thirty-four men who should be serving. A priest, Lorenzo Gómez Romero, who came from the region, explained that in this village

> the magistrates' or the caciques' . . . intrigues to free their sons (probably without the slightest grounds) and those of their allies and supporters, have created a high state of ferment in this village . . . H.M. [the Junta Suprema] should realize that these villages' original sin can be reduced to three points: Who should give the orders; who should steal the most; and who should pay the least.[36]

The Rev. Gómez, who had offered his services to the Suprema as a roving commissioner to the region's villages to speed up enlistment, round up deserters and search for horses needed by – and under expropriation for – the patriot cavalry, reported that up to ten thousand reales were being paid in Sevilla by

---

* These figures, are based on the Godoy census of 1797, from which I have deducted Castilla la Vieja, the Basque country, Navarra and Madrid capital (unfortunately equivalent Barcelona figures were lacking) as being under Napoleonic domination.

local oligarchs to free a son. Faking infirmities and rapid marriages were other means:

> Juan de Bargas, a magistrate, has two sons. He freed one by claiming that his teeth were not good enough to bite the end from a musket cartridge; and the other he married off a month ago, although the couple is not yet living together. The villagers are mutinous about such goings on . . . I told Bargas and another magistrate (who had paid a bribe to free his son) that they were no better than villains, and the villagers' disgust was just and well-founded.[37]

Though nowhere was the refusal to serve in the army as passionate and determined as in Cataluña, conscripts there echoed their fellows' words throughout the patriot zone in a petition to the Catalan junta: 'Convinced though [we] are of the necessity and obligation to serve the king and to reinforce the principality's army', a group of conscripts from Riudoms wrote that thirty-three local youth who should have been called up had been exempted. 'Many if not all of these have not the slightest legal right to exemption. Justice demands that the necessary measures be taken to examine their reasons and to declare these insufficient . . .'[38]

Conscription was unpopular everywhere. Nonetheless, the majority of the labouring classes outside of Cataluña were prepared to accept it as an ineluctable wartime necessity, as long as it was carried out justly and demonstrated social equality. Still, a large minority of deserters rejected it – large enough certainly for the Junta Suprema to state, with unconscious irony, that they made it appear as though people were being forced into the patriot army against their will.[39] This was almost certainly close to the truth. Conscription was a coercion which in normal circumstances manual workers would have done their utmost to avoid:* none better than a Catalan military doctor, Josef Antonio Viàdér, who lived through the Gerona siege, to describe a wartime soldier's living conditions:

> passing from extreme heat under the sun to rain, snow, wind and damp . . . day and night in wet uniforms, sleeping on the open ground, or on soggy straw; going months without enjoying a bed or having a change of clothes; drinking bad water and worse wine, eating poor bread made from inferior flour poorly kneaded and baked; making do on rotten meat, and fish and fruit of low quality; ordered to march and engage in violent exercises . . . and living in constant fear of his life:[40]

---

* The pre-war soldier was popularly thought to be the 'scum of the earth', his life harsh in the extreme, subject to very severe discipline, poorly paid (when paid at all), and always hungry on meagre rations. He deserted, robbed, drank, gambled, whored and committed crimes, the Inspector of Infantry admitted, 'with the premeditated idea of improving his lot in penal servitude'. (Lt. General, Franciso Javier de Negrete, 'Estado en que se hallaba la Ynfantería Española en fines del año 1801 y principios del de 1802 . . . por el Ynspector de dicha arma . . .', cited in Andújar Castillo, *Los militares en la España del siglo XVIII: Un estudio social*, Granada, 1991, p. 94.)

It was little wonder therefore, that many patriot conscripts, faced not only with such conditions but also with the prospect of being thrown untrained into battle and the likelihood of violent death, were highly reluctant to serve, and that Spain's largest conscript army up to that time suffered high rates of desertion. While desertion was common to all European armies, revolutionary or absolutist, what was new to Spain was the volume of the phenomenon. Though fewer in number than conscripts, regular army officers also deserted. After having several times had to order officers back to their regiments the Suprema finally instructed that officer-deserters be shot. (Those who turned themselves in were reduced to the ranks.) With such examples before them, it was scarcely surprising that ordinary soldiers abandoned the colours. The Junta's attempts to prevent it – threatening first to shoot all deserters, then offering rewards for their capture and finally punishing rank-and-file deserters with an additional eight years service – were of no real avail.[41]

Of those waiting to be conscripted, some mutilated their trigger finger; others fled. Almost despairingly, the Ecija junta in Andalucía reported in mid-1809 that a 'considerable number of lads fit to serve have fled into the countryside, taking refuge on estates or other lands whose owners have no means to prevent them'.

> Many have also fled to the islands in the [Guadalquivir] river where, because of hunger, need and not being able to go to the villages, they have committed excesses. Only a strong armed force would be capable of dealing with those who have formed bands, to end these ills and to bring the men in.[42]*

Many others in Andalucía and Extremadura took refuge in military hospitals, presumably with the connivance of the attendants;[43] in Galicia hundreds if not thousands sought safety in neighbouring Portugal;[44] in Cataluña they escaped to northern Valencia[45] or, if they had the means, to the Indies.[46]

Deserters, wrote an anonymous correspondent from the village of Mollina, Andalucía, 'are carrying on disgracefully with the women here because the parish priest has married a deserter twice . . . They are getting married in this place not to have to go to the war.'[47] All over the country, many hastily married in the hope that for the next nine months there would be sufficient single men to fill the quota by which time they, as the husbands of pregnant wives or as fathers, would almost certainly be exempt.

The most exhaustive list of means to avoid conscription and the requisitioning of horses came to the Suprema from a correspondent in Benameji, Córdoba. He recorded that those who had sixty fanegas of land or their renters were being exempted. This in itself was causing numerous crafty instances of false land deeds being drawn up. Not only had marriages increased enormously – in neighbouring villages there were as many as nineteen in one day – but the blame

---

* Lacking military force, the junta proposed a legally accepted mode of achieving its ends. The fathers and mothers of all those who had refused to report were to be arrested until their sons turned themselves in. Meanwhile, a party of trustworthy locals would try to round up the deserters in the countryside, being paid by the head for each one taken.

lay with parish priests whose interest in marriage fees was a major stimulus. Moreover, these priests, knowing full well that there was no contact with the papacy, were engaging in another 'crafty practice', charging one hundred reales or more for the preliminary procedures to secure marriage dispensations. This was creating a great number of scandals and sinful conduct because unmarried couples, who had no hope of receiving a dispensation, were living together, often with children. The number of friars had suddenly increased, a dozen having become novices from the township in the last three months alone. Local surgeons were telling potential recruits what illnesses to simulate and even giving them caustics to create sores and ulcers. Horses were being hobbled to make them lame or having patches put on them to burn their skin to prevent them being taken for the cavalry.[48]

The problem in Cataluña, was especially acute. When military conscription was finally introduced at the beginning of 1810, just under ten percent of the enlisted in Vich, for example, deserted; and the following year the percentage doubled.[49] But heavy desertion had begun earlier among the volunteer militia who were inducted into the Spanish army's line regiments: up to thirty percent in one case, and almost all within the first few weeks. Throughout the war, it was estimated, five hundred Catalans deserted on average every month from the regular army, most of them new conscripts.[50] On this basis, over the four remaining years of war after conscription was introduced, the total of twenty-four thousand deserters would have been almost as high as the number of army troops serving in Cataluña at any one time.

Desertion from the army did not necessarily mean abandoning the struggle; the men might join a guerrilla group where the possibility of booty and plunder, licitly or illicitly got, made good the lack of army pay and offered relief from military discipline. Others turned to outright banditry; the deserter become guerrilla turned bandit was a not infrequent phenomenon during the war.[51]

The losses of the Spanish army in Cataluña through desertion, it might be imagined, would have been off-set by the constancy of the volunteer miquelets, the militia which the Catalans raised in place of the Spanish-led army; but it was not so. As elsewhere, volunteers felt free voluntarily to return home. The cleric Francesc Rovira, one of the most prestigious Catalan guerrilla chiefs, wrote of his surprise at the 'continuous and scandalous' desertion in all his divisions, adding that within a short while 'I expect to be left without any men other than those of my own corps. And even there, the example is bound to have a deleterious effect.'[52]

The volunteers deserted, Rovira wrote, because they complained that frequently they went without pay and often lacked food. 'If that were true, my lads would have deserted a long time ago', he scornfully added. Nonetheless, Tomás Veri, Suprema deputy for Mallorca and its sometime representative in Cataluña, informed the Junta that fewer miquelets would abandon the colours if there were sufficient money to pay them.[53] He was proven right by Joaquín Sagrera, a Terrassa cloth manufacturer, who in a very short time raised a force of deserters and dispersed by offering to pay them a peseta a day out of his own pocket and to provide them with a ration of bread to defend the town.[54]* Veri's

---

* The Catalan peseta was worth four reales.

report was an admission of the impossibility of maintaining a large volunteer force on a regular footing without funds.

But there was no stopping desertion. By the spring of 1810 the rate had increased to such an extent that it was reported to be one of the major problems of Cataluña's defence.[55] Dr Bosch i Cardellach, of the village of Bràfim, noted in his diary on May 18:

> Our troops' desertion is scandalous. I have counted three thousand men who have passed through Bràfim in the past three days going back to their homes.[56]

The Suprema's insistent orders to local magistrates to round up deserters and return them to their regiments usually fell on deaf ears. Everywhere desertion was heaviest at harvest time.

Colonel Carlos Carbantes, an officer who had spent four pre-war years hunting down smugglers and delinquents in Andalucía, explained that labour shortage on the land was the principal reason that deserters were not turned in. The latter's parents and friends

> depend on or respect their patrons, the local authorities, who need these deserters to work their land because there is a lack of young hands. They protect them, therefore, and their parents give them shelter. These magistrates have no other aim than to look after their own interests.[57]

It would be erroneous not to suppose that the labouring classes were fighting for altar and throne: in sermons and confessionals parish priests instructed them in defence of their 'fathers' religion'; in their hearts they believed that their new king would alleviate their intolerable poverty. In practice, they defended their homes, families and lives from the enemy's depredations. The deserters who, despite the seemingly contrary evidence certainly shared these beliefs, were a minority. Willingly or unwillingly, the majority accepted their fate as enlisted troops against an 'impious' and destructive enemy.

But the self-serving village wealthy's conduct in seeking to free their sons from conscription and to use deserters for their own ends bore no relation to the working poor's idea of equality of sacrifice as the basis of the patriotic war effort. Their large-scale desertion could not for sure be explained solely by their social superiors' egotistical example. But whether they served or deserted, these labouring hands could not but be aware that the well-to-do classes were unprepared to sacrifice their wealth or their sons to the war effort, at the same time as they called on the poor to sacrifice their livelihoods and lives for the patriotic cause.

PLOUGHSHARES INTO SWORDS: AN ARMOURERS' STRIKE

Resistance to the patriot government and elite continued with go-slows and obstructions at the very heart of the war effort: arms manufacture. The shortage of muskets had preoccupied the Junta Suprema from its first days. It lacked sufficient to arm the thousands of volunteers who flooded to the colours in the initial enthusiastic response to the risings.[58] England provided 160,000 muskets by November 1808, with the promise of more to follow.[59] But the new recruits, ill-trained or untrained in their use, quickly damaged them, and the dispersing troops habitually flung them away. With its smooth bore barrel, the musket was a relatively simple firearm. Its effective range was about one hundred metres. It was designed not so much to be aimed at an individual target as to be fired by troops in volleys. Its elementary character, however, had compensations: the cartridges, consisting of a cylindrical paper twist containing powder and ball, were easy to make by hand; the soldier bit off the cartridge twist, poured the powder, ball and the paper as a sealing wad into the muzzle and rammed it all home; a flint's spark set off the priming charge in the pan. A trained Spanish infantryman could fire four rounds every three minutes,[60] his mouth and lips becoming parched and blackened in the process by the powder.

A musket's manufacture, however, was a slow process, involving five master armourers, each a specialist in a different part (barrel, lock, stock and butt, brass furnishings and bayonet). The most complex part, the barrel, required rolling and forging a trapezoidal sheet of special iron and of specific thickness, which then had to be drilled out to the correct size for the ball, and its asperities removed by hand filing. A skilled armourer might make three to four barrels a day. Traditionally, each master and his journeymen worked from the master's home, periodically handing in their finished components to the 'factory' and collecting new raw materials, the cost of which were deducted from the contracted piece rate for each part. The factory tested all the pieces and any that were unserviceable were broken by the examiner, the master having to make good the deficiency.[61]

The Basques, with their large concentration of iron ore mines, and to a lesser extent the Catalans, were the specialists in the trade. During the Convention War, when the French revolutionary army occupied the Basque factory, a considerable number of Basque armourers were moved on government orders out of harm's way to the Asturian capital, Oviedo, where a new factory was established. But in 1808, both Basque and Asturian factories had for different reasons stopped production. The former region was again occupied by the French (whose muskets used a smaller size ball), the latter for lack of Basque iron. The Suprema did not want to depend on Britain (perhaps doubting the new ally's continuing commitment)* or on any other foreign source for its supplies. It decided therefore to order provincial juntas in its Andalucian and Levante rearguard, which had no tradition of firearm production, to create arms factories.

Half a dozen juntas responded immediately. Almost all were in the same position as Granada, where the five so-called local armourers 'could barely

---

* England itself ran short of muskets, and the government was obliged to ask the East India Company to make over their large supply of a shorter-barrelled, cheaper arm, made to a less demanding standard than the British army's. The Company agreed. Most of the muskets sent to Spain were therefore of this latter type.

make an individual part or two – and even then badly – but none knew how to construct a whole musket'.[62] Only the drive and initiative of some junta members, especially in Granada and Valencia, and their search for a few qualified armourers wherever they could find them, managed to push their projects forward with some success. Not surprisingly, their understanding of a factory was of a place in which the whole manufacturing process was undertaken by wage labour. A considerable amount of time was inevitably taken up therefore in building or conditioning the workshops, and even more in making the necessary special tools – drills, files and vises which were unobtainable locally. In its first nine months, the Granada factory almost exclusively made tools, but it had not had to buy any abroad, it proudly added.[63] This was all very well; but it barely responded to the urgencies of the moment: very few new muskets were in fact produced in the year before the Andalucian factories fell to the enemy in early 1810, though great numbers of damaged firearms were reconditioned.*

Following the Granada's junta's earlier example in its own province, the Suprema in August ordered all armourers, blacksmiths, locksmiths, cutlers and iron workers in general in Sevilla, Jaén and Córdoba provinces to report to the Sevilla or Granada arms factories with their tools.[64] This caused an outcry from farmers and rural local authorities, who claimed that they were needed to make and repair agricultural tools, and from the craftsmen who complained that their livelihoods and families were being ruined.

Despite this labour conscription, there were no documented labour problems in Granada or most of the other new factories. This was reserved for Sevilla. Indeed, as the Granada junta pointed out at the end of 1809, in the six months since its factory had been completed, a labour force skilled in a trade never before locally undertaken had been created. Youth who had entered as apprentices had become proficient journeymen in crafts that normally required four to six years' apprenticeship. The pressure of war showed that the Old Regime's artisanal routines could be surpassed. It also demonstrated among Basque armourers brought to Sevilla how entrenched these routines could remain.

In Sevilla, an artillery colonel of thirty years service, Francisco Dátoli, who had helped establish the Oviedo factory, was in June put in charge of musket production. The Suprema, which provided the funds, had initially entrusted the setting up of a factory to two Sevillan brothers, the Gutierrez, one of them an armourer of apparently little technical knowledge. On his first inspection of their plant, Dátoli found that only six muskets, four of them without bayonets, had been made. In his report to the Suprema he avoided sharp criticism because, as he circumspectly put it,

---

* Valencia, another relatively successful factory, with the same number of workers as Granada, had by October 1809, produced 250 new muskets, and reconditioned over twelve thousand, having had to spend less time than Granada in setting up its factory in the newly built municipal slaughter house. (AHN, *Estado*, Legajo 36P/343, Valencia junta report to Junta Suprema, October 19, 1809.)

in the present critical circumstances, anyone who does not fall in with the people's or an individual's ideas is – as easily as unfairly – distrusted, since all believe that only they know what is best.[65]

This particular view of the difficulties – perhaps even the personal dangers – of the moment did not prevent him from setting out to bring Basque armourers from Oviedo and the Basque country to Sevilla to set up an efficient arms factory. He already had twenty-six Basque masters and fifty journeymen, but he needed many more to establish a factory which, as he hoped, would employ three thousand workers. Opportunely, three infantry captains, two of them veterans of the second Zaragoza siege, and two Basque civilians separately volunteered to smuggle armourers and iron out of the French-occupied Basque country.

Captain Manuel Eguaguirre y Redín was the most experienced in this matter, having twice undertaken such a mission, the last time bringing out half the number of masters Dátilo already had at his service. Eguaguirre, who had no doubt that the unemployed Basque armourers would follow him because they had families to support, planned to hide them in woods close to the coast until they could be taken off by ship to Asturias from one or other small port.[66] By early August Dátilo had seventy-six Basque armourers on hand.

With his experience of transferring Basque armourers to Oviedo and setting up the new factory, Dátilo did not expect the problems he had to confront with the first of the armourers to arrive. Almost immediately they complained that they were unable to work because they could not set up forges in the places where they were lodged. Many were accustomed to start working at night, and they wanted to be out of the city's centre. Dátilo sought a large house to accommodate them and the hundred or so family members who had accompanied them. Within a short time, the armourers demanded that the rooms be partitioned so that each family could have its individual living space because of the incidence of fevers and the danger of these spreading to their families by having to live at miserably close quarters. Meanwhile, they and their journeymen were receiving a day wage although in their first two months they did not produce a single new musket, with the exception of three hundred assembled from English barrels and locks.

Understanding that the only way to get them to produce the quantity and quality of muskets required was to respect their traditional work practices, Dátilo pressed ahead drawing up a piece rate contract. But when he presented it to the masters, giving them three days to sign, all five armourers' guilds refused to put their names to it. Among their objections, they stated, quite reasonably, that they needed first to know what they would be charged for the raw materials required to carry out their work, claiming that prices, wages – even washing a white shirt – cost double what they were accustomed to paying in the north. Moreover, they were unused to the Andalucian summer heat which would cause them illness and reduce their productivity. Finally, they asked for a Basque-speaking priest to attend to their spiritual needs; and a mass to be said on holy days.

A near month-long struggle between Dátilo and the armourers ensued. The Suprema took a direct hand in the matter, threatening the armourers that if they did not sign within three days they would be deprived of their craftsmen's rights 'within His Majesty's dominions' and returned to their home regions at their own expense.

Unawed and unabashed, the master armourers reiterated to the Suprema many of their earlier objections and rejected the accusation that, because of the privileges they had enjoyed in Asturias, their refusal to sign was a result of 'our not wanting to concede anything in circumstances where all vassals have had to suffer'.[67] They ended by writing that they were willing to sacrifice their lives if the Suprema demanded it of them but rejected all allegations that they were disloyal to the royal service.

Incensed no doubt by these last lines – for no one was asking the armourers to sacrifice their lives, and their loyalty to the royal service could certainly be questioned – Dátilo replied to the craftsmen the following day: 'Let me tell you, exaggerated expressions of patriotism and the greatest will to serve the cause are very common, especially when the facts demonstrate the exact opposite . . .'. Though under extreme government pressure, the Basque masters continued to hold out. They now said they wanted to live in their own houses with rooms to establish their shops. Dátilo agreed to find them housing once they had signed. Finally, the masters, among whom the barrel makers were the most militant, appointed a Basque judge of the Sevilla audiencia to represent them. To assist him in his task, Dátilo drew up an extensive account of the prices, costs and profits of each trade in Oviedo and those proposed in Sevilla.

The judge, Domingo Letona, was helped by the Suprema which agreed to accept his claims on the armourers' behalf, and to pay them for the days that the stand-off had lasted. At the same time it stated categorically that Dátilo's original price of 201 reales for a completed musket and bayonet must stand. As the Suprema had restricted its own freedom by announcing acceptance of the judge's findings, it – and Dátilo, too – had to accept a four-real increase in the barrel makers' piece rate which brought a musket's price to 205 reales, eighty-five percent higher than the Oviedo price.

The armourers' contract was finally signed on August 7. The masters' agreed piece rates – from which they had to pay higher journeymen's wages and material costs – rose on average by two-thirds. The master barrel makers more than doubled their Oviedo piece rate. Dátilo calculated that the master who produced a monthly maximum of 120 barrels would make a net profit of 1,500 reales a month in Sevilla as compared to just under one thousand in Oviedo. This was no small increase: it equalled the pay of a serving colonel without command of a regiment; three-quarters of an army auditor's, and half of a newly appointed provincial intendente's salaries.[68] And compared to the thirty reales a day a master armourer received in Cádiz it was riches.

In the five months that remained before Sevilla was taken by the French, the Basque armourers could have produced at the most forty percent of their annual Oviedo output: 520 muskets.

Understandable as it was, the Suprema's decision to be independent of foreign musket supplies cost it dear. It underestimated the difficulties of setting up arms factories de novo in regions without any tradition of arms manufacture, and the cost that such autarchic production entailed. Granada alone spent 600,000 reales to set up its arms factory, in tool-making, wages and the beginning of musket production. In the year to the end of 1809 it had produced a total of 370 new muskets and five hundred barrels in varying stages of completion. (The Oviedo factory turned out thirteen hundred new muskets per annum which could have been raised to fifteen hundred.) Taking Granada's cost attributable to musket production alone, each firearm came out at a cost of over 900 reales, more than four times Dátilo's contracted Sevilla price.[69] For the money spent on the Granada factory alone, which was only a fraction of the Suprema's subsidies, the latter could have bought nearly six thousand East India Company's muskets.*

Despite various setbacks, the factories were a serious attempt by local juntas to respond to the Suprema's order to innovate a previously unknown manu-facturing process to resolve a crucial military problem. The juntas accepted the premise of independence from foreign supplies – even to the point of delaying their own musket production by spending invaluable time in making their own specialized tools. The Suprema's war 'commandism' was extended most sig-nificantly to the 'conscription' of all iron workers in Andalucía: there could be little doubt that, in some extreme circumstances, it was prepared to consider a sector of the civilian populace's mobilization as part of a total war.

But its relatively lenient conduct of the Basque armourers in Sevilla demon-strated that the Suprema was not prepared for an outright confrontation with a determined and dissenting labouring group. This was evidently also true of another trade working on war materiel: the gun-carriage makers in the Sevilla arsenal. The latter's weekly production reports referred frequently to

these workers' continuing absence which seriously threatens production . . . in terms of not completing on time royal orders for gun carriages and other military materiel which, but for their absence, could be produced.[70]

As Dátilo pertinently observed, the Suprema's armament policies were plagued with inconsistencies, like many of its other wartime actions. But then, the Suprema would always temporize to retain an apparent patriotic unity, and especially to avoid disruptive conflicts in the rearguard, which would threaten to split an absolutist–reformist coalition whose only raison d'être was the anti-Napoleonic struggle. And, as under the Old Regime, there was nothing it feared more than a popular revolt.

The labouring poor or, in the case of the Basque armourers, the labour elite, had no such scruples. They were not prepared to sacrifice their immediate livelihoods in the name of a unity which they knew best served the wealthy's immediate and long-term interests. They had a daily living to earn at whatever the cost to the war effort.

*

* Their cost to the British government was approximately £1–14s (102 reales). See H.L. Blackmore, *British Military Firearms 1650–1860*, London, 1961, p. 138. I wish to thank Michael Baldwin, Head of the Dept. of Weapons, Equipment and Vehicles, at the National Army Museum, for providing me with details of the cited book.

One other productive undertaking demanded by the Suprema of craftsmen was the making of saddles and tackle for the increased number of cavalry it proposed to raise. Unlike musket production, saddle making was by no means an unknown skill in Andalucía and Levante, and presented few problems other than those of price. In January 1809, the Suprema nonetheless took the precaution to order all craftsmen in Sevilla and Córdoba provinces to report to Sevilla city 'without excuse, pretext or delay' to work on saddle making.[71]

The saddlers were a different kettle of fish to the Basque armourers. For a start, they were established in their own 'country' and had none of the new-comers' doubts about unknown conditions, costs and the weather. They grasped the chance to compete to increase their normal limited production for the wealthy and to take advantage of being fully employed.

Whether the Suprema's conscription and centralization was cost-effective was another matter. The price of a saddle and tackle in Sevilla was reported to be of the order of five hundred reales, whereas Jerez masters quoted 420. In Cádiz and neighbouring townships, craftsmen were prepared to work for four hundred, and finally for as little as 360 which 'leaves the craftsman with only a short surplus but no gain'. Domingo González was a leading Cádiz master saddler capable of making fifteen complete sets in ten days, and was producing them at the basic price to support the war effort.

> All your majesty's [i.e. Suprema's] vassals have the indispensable obligation to contribute, according to their capabilities, classes and states, to the fatherland's service. It would seem, Sir, that I have fulfilled this obligation . . .[72]

González, who wrote that as a result of his war work his shop had 'lost its good standing', petitioned the Suprema to reward him with the title of royal master saddle and tackle maker, chief special saddle maker to the cavalry of Cádiz and its district, and to award him the wage or pension which 'shall please your Majesty'.

The Suprema's response was not recorded. But the petition was in no way out of the ordinary. Great numbers of the educated elite who believed they had sacrificed their personal well-being to the patriot cause petitioned the Suprema for recompense in the form of vacant official posts, stipends, honorific titles or other public marks of recognition. In this instance a craftsman followed their example; even so, he did not forget the monetary sacrifice which his patriotism had cost him.

A BONAPARTIST PEACE INITIATIVE

It was not only Spanish generals who disrespected official orders; Napoleon's marshals, though better field commanders, were equally disobedient when it suited them. After his Medellín victory, Marshal Victor, believing that the patriots' crushing defeat could be exploited as political leverage on the Junta Suprema, halted the conquest of Extremadura and Andalucía which he had been ordered to carry out by King Josef and only briefly moved to help Soult in

Portugal. He thought instead to strengthen a prevailing spirit among some Spanish Bonaparte ministers* to bring the patriots to surrender. Without unanimous expectation of success, the Bonapartist government in Madrid agreed and despatched Joaquín María Sotelo, a former patriot, as its emissary.

From Mérida, Sotelo sent a low-key letter to the Junta, stating that 'various honourable Spaniards, who cannot look with indifference on the absolute dissolution of our beloved country', had persuaded King Josef to undertake this initiative in order to spare the country the evils of French military occupation. He placed much emphasis on 'the horrible effects' of military conquest on the occupied provinces, and the desire to save Andalucía from the same fate. He offered nothing concrete, however, other than the request that the Suprema appoint one or two deputies to begin talks.[73]

The Suprema responded in fulminating style. Recalling its 'sacred oath to the nation', it said that if Sotelo were invested with powers sufficient to treat of 'the restitution of our beloved king and of the French troops' immediate evacuation from all Spanish soil', he should make them public in a form recognizable by all nations. Then, 'with our allies' agreement', the Suprema would listen to him. Negotiations on any other basis, which would not save the state, could only be degrading to the Junta which had solemnly promised to 'be buried in the ruins of the monarchy rather than listen to any proposition that lessened the Spanish people's honour and independence'.[74]

And there, despite a few more exchanges, the matter rested. In his last communications, Sotelo commented that if the 'evils' he was trying to resolve could only be treated on the Suprema's conditions, this was tantamount to refusing even to listen to proposals for their resolution. 'If the Junta does not consent to the proposed conference, I shall have the eternal pleasure of having endeavoured to secure the good of our beloved country, although with the bitterness of not having succeeded . . .'[75]

MILITANCIES: JOAQUÍN MARÍA SOTELO

Like many of his high administrative contemporaries, Sotelo had so far had an agonizing war. The 42-year-old solicitor general of the pre-war Bourbon Council of War had escaped from French-occupied Madrid shortly after the national patriot rising the previous year, leaving behind his pregnant wife and children.

From the beginning of the French intervention in Spain, he had given vent to doubts about Napoleon's ulterior motives and had taken certain military precautions to foil his plans, his wife later wrote. Indeed, his experience in Portugal during the Spanish–French invasion of 1807 had led to disgust with the French occupation; but he had returned from Portugal to French-occupied Madrid, where he had been appointed to

---

* Cabarrús, the Finance Minister, had, for example, recently sent duque de Alburquerque a letter calling on him to think of his country's good and justifying his own Bonapartist collaboration; and other ministers had written letters to various patriot juntas in the same sense. (Artola, 1989 (1), p. 132 et seq.)

the Bonapartist supreme tribunal's section of the Grace and Justice ministry. Though he never took up the post, his appointment was published by the Bonapartist-controlled Madrid press. He had opposed Murat, evaded swearing loyalty to the new regime and had managed – feigning illness – to avoid being sent to Bayonne as a deputy to Napoleon's constitutional congress, his wife added. Shortly after the May 2, 1808, rising in Madrid, he had offered his resignation from his post, which the war minister, O'Farril, refused to accept.[76] Finally, he had fled the capital.

From Talavera, the first unoccupied town he reached on his escape, he wrote to the captain general of Extremadura in 'proof of his fidelity and patriotism', to say that he had left his employment, family, and all his belongings to serve his king and country, and desired to return to his native Sevilla. This was an intellectual rather than a natal loyalty. Born in 1766 in Almeria, of a Madrileño father and an Andalucian mother, he was of the 'third' and youngest generation of pre-war enlightened reformers. From the age of thirteen, he had enjoyed a brilliant career at the University of Granada, receiving outstanding degrees in jurisprudence and canonical law, and was appointed professor in both subjects. But from 1786, he had become attracted to Sevilla – his mother came from the nearby township of Utrera – because of its literary and intellectual vibrancy. He moved there and was well-known and personally respected among his peers as one of the small, but influential pre-war group of enlightened literati, most of whom were in 1808 using their pens to support the patriot junta.

As a result of his letter to the captain general, the Extremaduran junta gave him a passport to return to Sevilla. But popular rumours in the Andalucian capital about his loyalty to the patriot cause – so great at the time were the suspicions of Madrid officialdom's collaboration with the French, especially when their appointments to posts under the new regime had been published in the Bonapartist press – led Sotelo to petition the Extremaduran junta to clear him officially of charges of 'anti-patriotism'; this indeed it did, as subsequently did its Sevillan counterpart.[77]

The patriots' victory at Bailén and the French evacuation of Madrid in early August 1808, occurred while Sotelo was still clearing his name. General Castaños ordered him to the capital, stating that he was needed 'for matters of importance to the country and the prompt restitution of our beloved king, Fernando VII, to the throne'. On his return to Madrid he was again cleared of 'anti-patriotic' charges by the war council itself.

However, no sooner was the Junta Suprema formed than the patriot Gazeta de Madrid alleged that he had refused allegiance to the new government; to refute the allegation he petitioned the Suprema, describing himself as 'a faithful citizen whose acts have given many proofs of his patriotism'.[78] The Suprema cleared him and ordered that its finding be published in the Gazeta; but in the general confusion of the patriot armies' defeats and Napoleon's imminent capture of Madrid, it never appeared in the paper's pages. Barely a week after writing his petition to the Suprema, he was again fleeing Madrid to escape the Emperor. This time he bundled his wife, María de las Mercedes Porres, his three children, father-in-law and other relatives with no more belongings than the clothes they were wearing into his carriage, a dangerous form of escape at that moment.* Sotelo left on foot. By chance he was overtaken by his friend, Juan Antonio Almagro, a lawyer, who was travelling in a coach. Shortly, his wife's carriage caught up with them. Her father, the marqués de Castilleja, proposed that, before leaving, Sotelo and Almagro should pay their respects to the Suprema in Aranjuez. They agreed and quickly found an empty calèche whose driver agreed to take them there.

> On coming within sight of Valdemoro, Lieutenant Colonel Joaquín Ovalle, at the head of a few [Spanish] soldiers, obliged all those on the road to return to Madrid . . . This misfortune could not be made good on the 2nd and 3rd of December, because – as is well-known – the people forbade anyone to leave, and those who attempted to do so were treated as traitors. They even fired on carriages carrying wives and children to safety.[79]

After lying low in the capital for five days, Sotelo once more escaped on foot, accompanied by several companions, including Almagro. Before reaching Alcorcón, they and the large crowds in flight from the capital were warned by retreating Spanish troopers that the French were ahead and killing all those they seized. Everyone left the main road and scrambled in a wearying escape over ploughed fields to bypass the township; once on the other side, Sotelo and his companions believed it safe to rejoin the main road. They were mistaken. A party of French cavalry caught them and threatened them 'with the ultimate horror of an untimely death' if they did not return to Madrid. En route back to the capital, and again in Madrid, French soldiers robbed Sotelo of twenty-three ounces of gold, his gold watch and the jewellery he carried on him. The bloodstained streets were still full of dead bodies from the capital's aborted defence. His wife, who had taken refuge with her father in Cádiz,

> spent many miserable days in the cruel uncertainty of his fate. Since her husband was in such an awkward situation in relation to the perfidious French, her misery received no comfort from the news that he was back amongst them . . . He was a person who – even physically – was the least able to withstand the rigours of flight.[80]

In fact, as she subsequently discovered, Sotelo had gone into hiding in the capital. He refused absolutely, wrote his wife, to seek the new

---

* See Chapter 9, pp. 213–14 on the dangers faced by those who left the capital by carriage shortly before and during Napoleon's attack on Madrid.

regime's protection, even at a time when, as seen from Madrid, the war appeared virtually over:

> French divisions were pouring out in December, 1808, towards Extremadura, Andalucía, Valencia; the patriot armies were thought to have scattered; the villages were believed to be in a state of anarchy, and the Suprema hunted down. The English army's (i.e. Moore's) arrival in Castilla saved Spain, forcing Bonaparte to withdraw the forces that otherwise would have entered towns and cities before the news of their approach even reached them.[81]

Convinced by past experience of her husband's patriotism, his wife had no hesitation in petitioning the Junta Suprema, in January 1809, for financial help. Sotelo, she explained, had for the past year received no salary for his official post – a common enough occurrence at the time. The Suprema acceded to her request, given 'the particular services' her husband had done for the cause, and ordered her to be paid one month of Sotelo's salary due. Thus neither his wife, nor the Suprema, had any doubts about his 'patriotism' at the beginning of 1809. In clandestinity in occupied Madrid, meanwhile, Sotelo still maintained hopes of escape with his friend Almagro, though such an attempt without a Suprema passport would have been highly perilous: a villager had only to remember the *Gazeta's* original accusation that he had refused loyalty to the Suprema and which the paper had not had the time to correct before Madrid's capitulation. Many were assassinated for less. Believing it dangerous for Sotelo to flee in these conditions, Almagro escaped alone in February with the promise that, once in the patriot zone, he would organize Sotelo's escape. He was as good as his word, approaching Garay, the Suprema's general secretary, and other deputies to secure a passport for Sotelo which he planned to leave for him in the first unoccupied village outside Madrid. He also contacted a trustworthy postal courier to assist in his plan.

Unwittingly, however, Almagro was Sotelo's downfall. The former sent his friend a letter from Andalucía telling him of his attempts to rescue him. The courier, who brought other letters also, was denounced by 'a bad Spaniard' and a list of all those to whom he had delivered correspondence was discovered on him. In the middle of Wednesday night, March 29, all those listed were arrested and imprisoned, though Sotelo was only found after another friend was deceived into revealing where he was living. Like all the other prisoners, Sotelo was kept incommunicado for three days. On the following Saturday, April 1, a police commissioner took him after ten o'clock at night to General Morla's* dwelling where he was to be held under house arrest; a day or

---

* Morla had been charged by the Suprema with Madrid's defence against Napoleon; he was one of those who signed the capital's capitulation, and thereafter remained in Madrid in the Bonapartist service.

two later, a French and a Spanish officer with an escort arrived with a carriage, and between them Sotelo was taken off to Mérida in Extremadura to open peace feelers with his companions-in-arms.

This sequence of strange events had its antecedents. After a council of ministers' meeting on April 2, at which King Josef had heard several of his ministers express the opinion that the moment was opportune to sound out the patriot terrain and take the initiative in peace feelers, the king charged the war minister and General Morla with selecting suitable persons for the task. On April 3, the minister presented Sotelo's name, which met with no objection. As the French ambassador, La Forest, put it, 'he has committed so many misdemeanours which require pardon that for these alone he will find all the avenues to the enemy open'.[82] In this convoluted comment, the ambassador confirmed Sotelo's adhesion to the patriotic cause.

Up to this time he had neither sworn loyalty to the Bonapartist regime – an absolute requirement of any official who hoped to retain his post – nor participated in any of the public acts which were obligatory on them. Why then had he undertaken to carry out this Bonapartist mission? Had he in the couple of days between imprisonment and setting off, been 'turned'? It was very unlikely. Sotelo was highly principled. If he had ever managed to escape from the capital, he no doubt would have served the patriot cause, while probably dissenting from the Suprema's politics. But caught in Madrid, his enlightened rationality informed him – as it did most Spanish Bonapartists – that the French army's conquest and occupation was disastrous for Spain. As a high official of the Council of War, Sotelo was particularly sensitive to the ravages of the conflict. General Morla, an intelligent, if not perhaps overly courageous, former patriot, would certainly have reinforced Sotelo's opinion. Anything was better than allowing the French army – and the continued resistance which threatened civil war – to destroy the country when what was urgently needed was Spain's reform. Patriots and Spanish Bonapartists were equally agreed on this necessity – though not on the means of achieving it. Many Bonapartists, furthermore, were fully aware that the French army's occupation, attacks on civilians and exactions were disastrous for their cause, fuelling further patriot resistance; but at the same time they were forced to recognize that without the French army their regime would be overthrown by the patriots within days or weeks. This was their Via Crucis, which they could never escape throughout the war. Having infringed every Bonapartist edict and law, Sotelo was in no position to refuse the assigned mission, unless he were prepared to pay for it with his life. As his wife, who ardently defended her husband through thick and thin, commented in a fine comparison:

Like so many others, he yielded before an irrestible force as did our adored King Fernando when he renounced the throne and recommended that his vassals obey the oppressor. It was no crime of Sotelo's not to sacrifice his life, for this could not save the country, and neither the law nor any prior example demanded it.[83]

Peace, on the other hand, was a worthy cause which could save his country. Four years before, shortly after becoming the Sevillan Academy of Literature's director, he had begun his political career with an expression of his desire for peace: 'A felicitous and fortunate peace, capable of restoring fertility to our countryside, industry to our cities, commercial activity and happiness to our nation.'[84] A year later, Spain was again at war – and had been at war, albeit on different sides – ever since.

Sotelo's failed peace negotiations raised a calumnious, vituperous outrage against him in the patriot zone. In a Manichean atmosphere where only 'good' or 'bad' Spaniards, 'patriots' or 'traitors' existed, and a 'turncoat' was condemned to hell's fire, libelled and slandered on all sides, it would have been impossible for him to have attempted to return. Meanwhile, his situation in Madrid remained uncertain, if not dangerous; but he could do no more than remain there. A year later, having earned sufficient credibility with the new regime, he was appointed one of a number of Bonapartist royal commissioners, in his case of Jerez, after Andalucía was conquered. Meanwhile, his wife and children were but a crow's flight away in patriot Cádiz. His friend Almagro, who had gone to such ends to escape and organize Sotelo's flight from Madrid, also served the Bonapartist cause in Andalucía.[85]

A CONVINCED BONAPARTIST: ANTONIO RIVAS

Sotelo's was an extreme but not exceptional case. In many instances, families were divided by geography and ideology as they were over a century later in the Civil War of 1936–1939. Among the more notable of them, conde de Montijo's younger brother, conde de Teba, who had been instrumental in the Sevilla and Cádiz patriot risings, went over to the Bonapartist cause in Sevilla; the disputatious, progressive Sevillan member of the Suprema, Tilly, had members of his family living under – and acknowledging – King Josef in Madrid; some of the better known Sevillan literati, Sotelo's friends, sided with the Bonapartist camp after Sevilla's surrender in 1810. Even more striking was the fact that the southwestern Andalucian landed classes kept – deliberately or coincidentally – a foot in either camp: after the region's fall, some of their members fled to patriot Cádiz while others remained behind to claim their family's estates to prevent them from being taken over by the Bonapartist regime.

A less notable, but more riveting case, was that of Antonio Rivas, Bourbon corregidor of Trujillo, Extremadura, in 1808, whose wife stubbornly refused to follow him into the Bonapartist camp. From the patriot point of view, Rivas was suspect from the beginning. He rescued a considerable number of French subjects, civilian and military, from patriot persecution. Surviving the 'stormy slings and arrows of fortune' until December of 1808, the approach of Napoleon's army led the local junta to denounce him as 'suspicious of infidelity to king and fatherland'. The patriot military commander, General Galluzo, before his own ignominious retreat in front of the imperial forces at the Almaraz bridge over the Tajo, had him arrested. Accompanied still by his wife, and under escort, he was taken in the direction of Sevilla, although subsequently he was returned to Badajoz when it became clear that the French were not to advance that far south. The Extremaduran tribunal of public safety began proceedings against him. These had not advanced very far when Marshal Victor invaded Extremadura in the spring of 1809 before the battle of Medellín. Once Victor reached close to Mérida – from where Sotelo had conducted his abortive peace negotiations – Rivas managed, with his prosecutor's complicity, to get permission to travel there for a few days to help his wife, a member of whose family was seriously ill. In Mérida he defected to the French army; and Victor appointed him the town's corregidor.

His wife, Joaquina Orozco, however, resisted his 'bad conduct' in going over to the Bonapartists, and defended herself against his and various French military officers' 'aggressions', the latter attempting to force her to accompany her husband in his decision. With 'great constancy she freed herself, steadfastly rejecting the enemy's offers of great opulence or their threats', she later wrote. Effectively she repaid her husband's desertion by deserting him, and demanded of the Junta Suprema that it make over to her half of Rivas's possessions which had been embargoed on his arrest.

In both Sotelo's and Rivas' case, their wives showed greater loyalty to the patriot cause than did their husbands. Rivas faithfully served the Bonapartists, becoming again corregidor of French-occupied Trujillo where he organized a petition to the Junta Suprema calling for an end to the war. But he gave up the offer of a criminal judgeship in Valladolid to return to his wife and family after Sevilla, where the latter were living, was captured by the French early in 1810. His wife, he said, had 'demanded his protection', and he had complied. An accredited Bonapartist husband, in a French-occupied zone, had become an undeniable asset; even more so after his wife's earlier patriotic stance. In 1812 Rivas' submission to become a supernumary judge, albeit unsalaried, in Madrid was rejected by the minister of Grace and Justice on the grounds that it was neither 'just nor respectable' that anyone serve unpaid or that posts be created before their necessity was proven. However, he was assured that his case would be kept in mind.[86]

12

Popular Territorial Liberation Struggles: Galicia and Cataluña

GALICIA AND FRENCH RETREAT

The repeated defeats of patriot armies in open battle led to irregular civilian warfare of two distinct types. The most common were the initially small guerrilla bands which, though they usually had certain territorial allegiances, ranged far and wide: mobility was essential to their capacity to strike at the enemy by surprise and evade capture.* Of a different order, although using the same type of irregular warfare, were the partisan groups who defended their territorial interests against the French. Galicia and Cataluña were prime examples of this. The Galician–Asturian army, then under General Blake, and operating alone on the Vizcayan–Santander border, had been heavily defeated in Napoleon's November 1808 offensive. Blake's battle losses of three thousand were nothing compared to those suffered in a harrowing retreat – far more arduous than Moore's – over tracks in the Cantabrian mountains. By the time he reached the relative safety of León, two-thirds of his remaining army had simply 'dispersed', as Spanish dispatches habitually put it. Blake was replaced by General Romana who took over the seven thousand troops remaining.†

After the British army's evacuation early in 1809, La Coruña capitulated to Moore's pursuer, Marshal Soult, without resistance. Thereafter all the major cities and towns fell like a pack of cards: within a fortnight the French were masters of Galicia. Instead of taking refuge in the mountains to organize resistance, the Galician junta disintegrated and vanished. Scarcely able to believe the news of the region's lack of resistance, the Junta Suprema excoriated

---

* See Chapters 14 and 17 for a detailed study of the guerrillas.
† Romana had taken his time about returning to Spain, having spent two months in England after his rescue from Denmark in mid-August. He arrived in La Coruña on October 19, 1808, accompanying the new British envoy to the Suprema, John Hookham Frere. (AHN, *Estado*, Legajo 72A/74, Galician junta to Junta Suprema, La Coruña, Oct 19, 1808.) Romana later confided to General Moore that 'had he known how things were, he neither would have accepted the command of the Galician army nor have returned to Spain'. (PRO, *WO* 1/236, pp. 253–254, Moore to Castlereagh, Dec 31, 1808, cited in Esdaile, 1988.)

the Galicians, calling them 'wretches who lacked the strength to fight or the courage to die . . . La Coruña's surrender at so little cost will for all eternity recall to the world your nullity and infamy.'[1] Appointing a special mission to enquire into the causes of this collapse, the Suprema could little imagine that within a few months it would be hailing the Galician people as heroes, an example for all patriots to emulate, although continuing to consider as traitors the former local juntas of large towns and cities.

Napoleon's plans for Galicia's domination, a hasty outcome of Moore's pursuit, were deficient in an area where he was usually strong: geography, the lay of the land. (He was certainly not alone: one of the Suprema's early orders had been to make an accurate map of Spain.[2]) He was misinformed about the state of the roads and the speed at which his troops could move between major towns. To prevent further English landings, control of the Atlantic coast and its ports was his major concern. Much of the Galician hinterland, especially in the south, was left unoccupied. Moreover, once he had secured the region's submission, Soult was under orders to invade Portugal from Galicia and Ney was left in command of an occupation force which was not large enough to control the whole countryside.[3]

Napoleon also allowed preconceptions to misinform him about the villagers' religious loyalties. As usual, he believed that the upper clergy – in this case the bishops – controlled the 'ignorant and fanatically religious' villagers, and his commanders were given orders to cultivate and win over the prelates. But it was not they who exercised influence, but rather the parish priests and the permanent ecclesiastical institutions: monasteries, friaries and cathedral chapters which incarnated Galician tradition.[4]

Equally – if not more – important for local Galician resistance was the fact that, though the countryside was still profoundly señorial,* villagers, who made up eighty percent of the population, had enjoyed for nearly half a century virtual hereditary land leases. This meant that they and their heirs had the legally sanctioned use of their plots, even if they were not legally their owner and had to pay rents and dues to their lords. As long as they complied with their feudal obligations, the land to all intents and purposes was 'theirs'.[5] It was they, not their lords, who had introduced the two new crops – maize and potatoes – which had dramatically alleviated the food shortages of the past. In this sense, legal ownership of the land was not the villagers' sole criterion: legal ownership of the land's *use* was what mattered. A villager 'lived better or worse depending on the extent of the land he could work; a renter with five hectares did not envy the smallholder with half a hectare, even though it were his own'.[6]

There was, for sure, a long anti-señorial tradition and constant legal battles between villagers collectively and their lords over feudal dues, from which the former tried to free themselves or at the worst convert them into real rents

---

* In the second half of the eighteenth century, approximately fifty percent of Galicians lived under secular señorial control, thirty-seven percent in episcopal and monasterial señoríos, and ten percent in royal lordship. The military orders held another two percent. (Saavedra, 1994, p. 54, table 2.)

related directly to the land; and many villagers involved in legal disputes used the war situation to refuse to pay these dues to their ecclesiastical lords.[7]

Throughout Spain, territorial resistance was almost always stronger where villagers enjoyed the virtual right of property over the use of the land than where they did not. This was not suprising: these villagers feared that 'their property' was at stake. One other condition of Galician local resistance was the custom of beating the parish bounds. Most parishes had a considerable extent of commons – generally hilly forest land – which were an essential and invaluable part of the villagers' difficult livelihoods. Unclearly delineated, these were often invaded at nightime by neighbouring parishioners. Gangs of youths from fifteen-years-old and upwards – and most parishes had one – set out to guard their commons and fight the invaders with whatever primitive means they had to hand. The gangs, to which only batchelors were admitted, had their youth leaders, their own meeting places, customs and rites. There was thus a gang tradition of defending their parishes against all intruders.[8]

As long as there was no direct threat to their parishes and lands, Galician youth evaded joining the army with as much determination as their counterparts in other regions. But they were more fortunate than most: they had a neighbouring country, Portugal, where there was no language barrier, to which to flee. Traditionally one of the major Galician migrant destinations – the population density and natural growth in relation to agricultural resources made migration obligatory for many young Galicians – Portugal gave shelter to an estimated eighty thousand of the region's 'surplus' inhabitants.

Many hundreds, if not thousands, of young villagers fled their homes and conscription to join their compatriots in Portugal. Aware of the potential recruits and deserters in the neighbouring country, the Galician junta first called for volunteers among its native population in Lisbon. A meagre ninety to one hundred men came forward, of whom a quarter deserted before they set off. The junta admitted to the Suprema that it had taken the measure because of the need to man the army; as soon as Romana's tattered force had reached Galicia, all the soldiers from the region had 'set off for home', he reported.[9]

After the poor showing in Lisbon, the junta asked the Spanish consul in Oporto in the autumn of 1809 to detain and hand over 'a goodly number of Galicians apt for military service', only to find that their commissioner's attempts were sabotaged by the Oporto authorities and Portuguese and British merchants who kept, he claimed, 2,500 Galician servants hidden in their houses. Of the thousand or so men who were finally returned to Galicia most were illiterate villagers; great numbers deserted on the march back.[10]

La Coruña city councillors urged parish priests to arouse the patriotism and honour of the deserters among their flocks to return to the colours before a military commission came for them. To ensure itself of sufficient conscripts, the junta dropped the army's required five-foot minimum height by two inches.[11] Before their priests' efforts could have much effect, the smallholders observed one of the more striking cases of 'patriotism and honour' which went awry. The Literary Battalion (as it was always popularly called, though its official title was the Royal Volunteer Battalion of Santiago Light Infantry) of one thousand student volunteers, mostly of the lower nobility, raised at the start of the war by Santiago University, stirred patriot hearts in and beyond Galicia: here was privileged youth setting an example. The students made sure, however – as indeed they did elsewhere – to secure serious advantages from their future heroism; each year served in the battalion would count as a completed academic year.

By the time they and the Galician army reached León, the first province to the east of Galicia, in the early autumn of 1808 and before engaging in a single combat, they were much 'less ferocious and enthusiastic than when they set out', observed the Rev. Juan Antonio Posse, a Galician parish priest in a village near León.

> Many no longer wanted to continue. Their commander (an army colonel, who had been promoted on the spot in Santiago to brigadier) found himself in the dire necessity to send many of them home. The majority left with their uniforms almost in tatters; others became beggars. Many of the latter came to me, pretending to be ordinary people. I gave them what I could.[12]

General Blake, the Galician army commander at the time, sent home a further 350 in September 1808, after the defeat at the battle of Río Seco, 'because of their lack of spirit and willingness to sacrifice their lives for the cause'.[13] The battalion was reformed with a mixture of the remaining students and soldiers, and thereafter performed creditably.

THE STRUGGLE'S START

With its news limited to the surrender of the major Galician cities, the Suprema had good cause for its condemnation of the region's lack of resistance, but it did not recognize the beginnings of a sporadic rural anti-French struggle from the moment the imperial forces invaded the country. This started solely in places exposed – sometimes brutally – to the presence of French troops:* it was by the Pedrafita pass on the main road to La Coruña – the scene of so many dramatic accounts of Moore's retreat – that the first recorded resistance took place shortly after the British had struggled – and straggled – up it in sleet and snow. Formed by three local notables, a partisan group killed over forty imperial soldiers in various actions at the end of January 1809, freeing in their course a number of British prisoners, and finally ambushing the brother of the French military commandant of Lugo. In reprisal, imperial troops burned several neighbouring villages, which stiffened local resistance; but also resulted in the permanent stationing of three hundred French soldiers on the pass.

Above all, this patriot defence of the Pedrafita was aimed at cutting French communications with Madrid in which it proved quite successful. As Antonio Eiras, one of the original organizers put it:

---

* The same, of course, was true in other regions. The defence of Villacañas in south-eastern Toledo was a case in point. (See Chapter 10, pp. 245 et seq.)

The [enemy's] loss of mail was a bad blow for them . . . The villagers in their redoubts on the pass, reinforced by others from the burned down villages, made fun of the enemy troops. Many times they forced them to flee in retreat. At least one hundred of our men were killed, but this was not considerable in relation to the numbers the enemy lost.[14]

On the southern road to Orense and Vigo, along which a smaller part of Moore's forces had marched, Romana's raggle-taggle army had followed, seeking refuge close to the Portuguese border. The French army pursued, and mauled it twice, but did not finish it off. En route, the imperial troops made their usual demands for supplies and committed abuses. Around Valdeorras the villagers' fury rose to such a pitch that it was not difficult for local priests and hidalgos to form them into a partisan group. Many villagers had escaped to the snowbound mountains to be freed of French oppression. As Eiras reported:

All of us complained of their pillaging, sacrileges and violence . . . They treated iniquitously those who had remained in the village. After making them do the most degrading tasks, they forced them to carry haversacks on the march with them for days on end. Burning for revenge, our anger was raised still more when two hundred dragoons put to the sword all the villagers of Salas, without sparing the priest, the elderly or the young . . .[15]

A district junta was created under the Casoyo parish priest's supreme leadership, helped by his brother, Juan Bernardo Quiroga, and the district's military commandant. The partisans were divided into five groups, each with a captain at its head. Their greatest triumph came on January 31, when they attacked ninety-six French troopers, killing or capturing all of them. Displaying great heroism, women fought the cavalry alongside the men.

Two small northern coastal townships and their surrounding countryside were the next to offer open resistance: Ribadeo, on the Asturian border, and Vivero, an isolated medieval port at the end of a long bay well to the west. French troops deployed from Mondoñedo, the nearest town, reached Ribadeo on January 25, 1809, and demanded, as was their habit, rations of bread and wine; some 'honourable and distinguished patriots' incited its inhabitants to resist their demands and to unite in their locality's defence. Within twenty-four hours villagers from outlying parishes armed with shotguns, pikes, sickles, and other edged weapons had gathered in strategic places on the troops' return route and set about the small French column which, it was reported, lost sixty of its 150 men in continuing skirmishes.[16]

The consequences of the neighbouring parishes' participation in Vivero's defence were sharper. A column of seventy French cavalry entered the township on January 28 to a chilly reception. The commander's orders were to ensure that the local civilian, military and ecclesiastical authorities swore allegiance to King Josef; his proclamation to that effect aroused the inhabitants' anger. Nonetheless, despite prior defence preparations, Vivero's 2,700 inhabitants and local authorities made no move to defend themselves for a week. However, after midnight of the morning on which the authorities had been summoned to swear allegiance, five thousand villagers from neighbouring parishes and hamlets gathered on the heights outside Vivero and began a lively fire. The French cavalry force was already in a state of fear: 'they read in the inhabitants' faces their inner anger at their presence, and posted sentries at night . . .'.[17] Heavy rain interrupted the villagers' attack for four hours. At 5 a.m. they advanced on the walled township. At the same time, its inhabitants began to fight the French. Within an hour, the enemy had suffered eight dead, forty-eight prisoners, including their commander and his officers, and a number wounded. Only eighteen of the original seventy-four troopers managed to escape, the majority of them being cut down in the countryside beyond Vivero.

Once they felt themselves the masters of the township, the villagers went on the rampage. They demanded that all existing authorities be dismissed and threatened to kill the corregidor, firing at his house. They wanted no corregidor, they clamoured, unless they appointed him themselves to 'do and undo' as they themselves desired. Nor any more scriveners.* Shouting that the local junta members were French sympathizers, they assaulted the houses of two of them, both naval officials. They knew full well that the local junta had been set up, as in many other places in Galicia, by the dominant elite – in this case the municipal council – essentially to control any 'popular excesses', but without the most minimal popular pressure or participation.[18] Thus even the Dominican friary did not escape their fury; they dragged out five casks of wine to drink, using the brothers' glasses and serviettes, before going on to loot the home of a rich merchant, the French and Danish vice-consul, which they stripped of every movable object. Several locally respected men, who tried to calm the mob, were manhandled, and one was wounded. Even the hastily assembled junta's offer of food and drink for all the villagers was insufficient to calm them.[19]

Many of these same villagers had, a decade earlier, burned down the recently created Sargadelos iron-ore foundry; at the instigators' trial it was alleged that the incendiarists had cried 'Long live freedom, long live France, death to the factory and its owner!' though the accused claimed that the cries were 'Long live the king and death to Ibáñez!' (the foundry's merchant owner).† Finally, in view of the prospect of the French army's certain vengeance on the township, the villagers were pacified and prepared to defend themselves and Vivero. The vengeance was not long in coming, and this time in strength. Some two thousand imperial troops pushed through the civilian-manned defences on

* Scriveners were Galician villagers' particular object of hatred, since they often used their official positions and knowledge to feather their own nests at the villagers' expense.
† Antonio Raimundo Ibáñez, an Asturian-born merchant, was assassinated at the beginning of the war in Ribadeo on the rumour that he had manufactured handcuffs in his re-built foundry. Its burning down was, in fact, inspired and organized by the local hidalgo elite and certain priests who assured villagers' discontent at the demands and conditions made on them by Ibáñez, with royal approval, to cart firewood and provide other services for the foundry. The local elite was concerned that the peasantry would abandon the land – and thus reduce their own income and wealth – to work for the foundry. (On this affair see González-Pola de la Granja, 1994.)

the outskirts and seized Vivero on February 18, putting it to the sack for over three days. Two hundred people were slaughtered, but the majority of the population managed to flee to the hills.

In Vivero and Ribadeo, it was villagers from parishes in the surrounding countryside who provided the townships' main fighting force, though in neither case had the French troops carried out the customary seizure of their crops. The villagers around Betanzos – Moore's last halting place before La Coruña – were far less favourably placed since the French army was thick on the ground and forced them to feed it, adding insult to injury by frequently seizing the best oxen or cows which had drawn their cartloads of supplies. Aggrieved, these villagers one night took their revenge in an action that remained part of the region's collective memory: at an agreed hour they rose in the last week of February and massacred all the French officers and men in their parishes, burying them in the pine woods with their accoutrements and effects, and immediately dispatching their horses to Romana's army in Ribadavia in the south. According to tradition, 199 French were killed, one wounded corporal escaping to report the massacre.[20]

Local resistance in the south was precipitated by Soult's march from the Atlantic coast to the city of Orense where he crossed the Miño river to invade Portugal. Once the example of local resistance was set, it developed rapidly into a widespread uprising, taking advantage of the absence of Soult's troops, and gathered great numbers of rural recruits with the aim of expelling the enemy from their territory.

The mass of combatants were villagers; but they were raised and led by their social superiors, in many cases parish priests or local magistrates, and subsequently by a number of officers sent for the purpose by the Junta Suprema or detached from Romana's Galician army. After the initial moments of resistance, they were generally organized by parishes, in companies and battalions with sergeants and corporals, and commanders whom they elected. As could be expected the latter were 'individuals who, by their gifts, authority and bravery', the villagers recognized as worthy of respect. The best shots among the youth were selected for the few firearms available.[21]

THE COUNTRYSIDE ATTACKS THE CITIES

News of such events was spread far and wide to rouse villagers to the struggle. Parish priests played an important part: the pulpit became 'a political tribunal, confessionals served to transmit slogans, orders and news of the war. Altar cloths hid firearms. Altar boys made scapulars for those about to die and cartridges for those about to kill.' Flysheets, the periodical press, songs served the same end:

> The worst of all, lads,
> Is that hangman France works,
> To prevent us being Christians
> And to turn us all into Turks.

So my priest says
Let our clenched fists make a rod
For the Fatherland and King.
And prepare ourselves willingly
To die for God.[22]

This composition, with its many more stanzas, was sung all over unoccupied Galicia, especially in the taverns where the villagers gathered to talk and exchange news. The young and the not so young began to join their local partisan groups. A participant in the struggle described the workshops set up in the friary of Santo Domingo to equip these new village recruits. 'A group of shoemakers and tailors, under the direction of the prior and two members of the local junta, were working to clothe and shoe them. Carpenters were busy in a workshop making musket stocks and artillery gun carriages. Everything was so well ordered that it looked like one of the king's arsenals.'[23]

The uprising spread rapidly. The French use of cavalry detachments to control villagers – Ney had begun his renowned military career as an enlisted ranker hussar – did not prove effective in tight situations where they could not easily manoeuvre, as in township streets or in the narrow valleys and mountainous Galician terrain. In more favourable cavalry circumstances, the partisans fled before them, reformed and attacked them from the rear. But the stretched occupation forces' need to cover a large region with the maximum speed gave Ney little other choice.

The partisan bands, like those at the Piedrafita pass, had to all intents and purposes cut communications between the French garrisons, isolating them. The lack of news of how their fellows did in other towns served to lower the troops' morale,[24] as did the partisans' harassment of their patrols and the small but steady additions to their death toll. Moreover, they had everything to fear from the village irregulars who did not respect the conventions of war. They were, however, spared one additional fear: Romana, incredibly, did not bring his army – which by this time, thanks to new volunteers, numbered nine thousand men – to the partisans' aid, even when they were beseiging a major town like Vigo. He earned the Galicians' scorn for constantly evading combat and the sobriquet of marqués de la *Romería* (a procession to a shrine) for his marches and countermarches to keep at a safe distance from the French. In the early stages of the rising before his excessive caution became clear, a number of partisan chieftains consulted him and asked for help; and in the absence of any supreme Galician power, he took over this role, confirming local leaders' appointments, supporting the fusion of different groups, ordering punishment of those who refused to serve. Though not participating directly, he became the partisans' organizational centre of reference. His best service to the cause was to detach Captain Bernardo González, a native of Orense, from his army to lead the partisans of Ribadavia and O Carballiño. Under the nom de guerre of Cachamuiña, he became one of the rising's most important leaders, and one of the first to decide to attack the French-garrisoned cities. This bold move, with a force only of poorly armed villagers, was made possible by the small garrisons

Soult had left behind when he invaded Portugal; nonetheless, for untrained irregulars simultaneously to besiege three of the main towns in the southwest immediately on their formation was a novelty repeated nowhere else.

Pontevedra was the first to fall after a two-week siege. Cachamuiña had organized partisan leaders in a number of neighbouring insurrectionary villages to join forces to take the town. No sooner had Pontevedra been taken than the victorious forces left it to join the siege of Vigo, a larger and more important city port to the south; and – temporarily, as it turned out – the French reoccupied Pontevedra.

Meanwhile, another leader also to become famous, the parish priest of Vilar y Couto, Mauricio Troncoso y Sotomayor, had rebelled against Soult's requisitions of foodstuffs, wine, meat and mules for his army on its march to invade Portugal. He told his parishioners not to provide the supplies and invited them and neighbouring hamlets and villages to join him in armed struggle against the French. Two small French detachments which came to collect the provisions in Vilar y Couto were beaten off; the battle with a third, larger contingent lasted three days.

Little more than an isolated hamlet of scattered houses around a parish church just north of the river Miño, Vilar y Couto became the nucleus of an army which grew to over 7,000 strong. By the end of February, Romana had appointed Troncoso 'general' of his newly raised army. Shortly thereafter he laid siege to Tuy, downriver on the Miño, where the French garrison numbered four thousand.

At the same time, the parish priest of Valladares, Juan Rosendo Arias Enríquez, and two Franciscan friars, along with several local hidalgos, raised the countryside south of Vigo. They issued a proclamation, also signed by Troncoso, ordering all men able to bear arms to report within twenty-four hours or face a firing squad. Their siege of Vigo began on March 8, the same day as Pontevedra's investment, but it was a week before all the region's partisan bands had gathered to join it. Vigo and Tuy were the only two French-garrisoned places in the south. Though much larger than the latter, Vigo was more lightly held by a scant fifteen hundred imperial troops. After the partisans, under two of their Franciscan friar leaders, brothers Villagelíu and Giráldez, had thrown back a French attempt from Pontevedra to raise the siege and attacked the city itself which they could not take, the situation turned more unfavourable to the French: two British frigates arrived off Vigo to help the besiegers whom they supplied with a certain amount of munitions. Surrender talks began, but the French commandant, fearing that some of the village partisans would run amok, refused to surrender to civilians. Cachamuiña, Lieutenant Pablo Morillo (raised from the ranks on the Bailén battlefield for his bravery, and one of the officers dispatched by the Junta Suprema to assist the Galician patriots) and a retired captain, Francisco Colombo, who had raised the village of Cotobade, arrived from Pontevedra to take over the negotiations, and to advise the besiegers. But as the negotiations dragged on, some partisan leaders believed that the garrison was playing for time. On the night of March 27, with Cachamuiña and the two Franciscan friars at their head, the partisans again attacked the city. Within an hour, the French surrendered. The next day, more than eight hundred imperial troops, led by their commandant, Chalot, formally surrendered to Captain Coutts Crawford of the frigate Venus who took them prisoner.[25]

After their victory, the partisans hastened to the siege of Tuy where for nearly a month the Couto parish priest, Troncoso, had led his army. The immediate effect of this strengthened force was that Troncoso was relieved of his command and replaced by Lieutenant Colonel Manuel García del Barrio, the senior officer sent by the Suprema to Galicia. This was taken very badly by the other partisan leaders, especially when del Barrio decided to lift the siege in the face of a combined attack by Soult in Portugal and Ney from the north. With only two thousand men with firearms, the rest having only lances, axes and clubs, del Barrio's decision made military sense. But the local partisans refused to join him in his retreat. They elected friar Giráldez as their commander, who asked Cachamuiña, now the new military governor of Vigo, for munitions to continue the siege. Happily for the partisans, Soult's column commander realized that there was little possibility of holding the town for long, and the marshal needed its four thousand men. He evacuated the garrison and its artillery across the river Miño. On April 17 there was not a French soldier left; southern Galicia was free of imperial domination.

The advantages enjoyed by the partisans in the unoccupied enemy south were revealed in the north where the occupation force was a great deal more numerous. When the small port of Corcubión just to the east of Cape Finisterre raised an army of villagers under its parish priest to resist further enemy exactions, a French infantry column from Santiago evaded the defenders and burned the village to the ground, slaughtering a great number of its inhabitants. The British frigate *Endymion*, which the Corcubión junta had called upon for assistance, could do little to help.[26]

THE MIÑO DIVISION

In the south, the third and last stage was potentially the most difficult: to confront the French in open battle. Here at last, though not on his direct orders, a portion of Romana's army participated.* A detachment of two thousand men, whom he had left under General Martín de la Carrera in Puebla de Sanabria, on the extreme south-eastern limits of Galicia, joined the partisans, bringing with them nine cannon and a few troopers. A group of guerrillas under José María Vázquez, of Salamanca, who was known for daring attacks in Castilla la Vieja, also joined the Galicians.[27] By this time, the partisans alone numbered fourteen thousand, of which those formed by the parish priest, Troncoso, comprised the largest nucleus; and together with the newly arrived troops, the whole force turned itself into the *División del Miño*, commanded by Carrera. Its immediate objective was to take Santiago de Compostela, a symbolic town for all Galicians, indeed for most Spaniards, as the (supposed) burial place of St James, the Apostle, one of the two patron saints of Spain.

* Romana himself was at this moment in Asturias, where he abolished the junta before being surprised by Ney who chased him out of the principality.

With Morillo as its chief of staff, the new division, taking with it ten thousand men, advanced north along the coast road towards Santiago. The city was defended by General Macune of Ney's army with nearly three thousand troops, fourteen cannon and three hundred cavalry. He chose to engage the insurgent force on open terrain, supposing no doubt that there his disciplined and trained troops would have the better of the village partisans. On May 23, at the campo de la Estrella, he joined battle with the division which outnumbered him by over three to one. For once, weight of numbers told; he was defeated. Carrera's report on the battle read:

> Santiago is ours . . . After an hour of firing we tired of this suffering, and I ordered Morillo to charge the enemy on the right flank while I led the other columns on his front . . . Morillo succeeded in entering the city and cut down the enemy in the streets, pursuing them for more than a league. We have suffered few losses.[28]

The French were reported to have had six hundred dead and wounded, including among the latter Macune himself. However satisfying this conquest, it was premature to offer great thanks. The division could take a city but were unable to hold it. Ney reconquered it barely a fortnight later in his last desperate attempt to put down the insurrection.

Meanwhile Soult, who had suffered defeat by Wellesley at Oporto and made a harrowing escape – even worse than Moore's – over the Portuguese mountains, reached Lugo, the easternmost provincial capital of central Galicia. At a stormy meeting, Ney argued that their task was to suppress the Galician rising; at this moment, he held no more than La Coruña, El Ferrol, Mondoñedo and Lugo. Soult responded that the main objective was to force the British out of Portugal. Each was doing no more than express Napoleon's original orders. Finally, they agreed that while Ney would push the insurgent army back to Tuy, and send a column to Orense, Soult would pursue Romana and force him to fight or retreat, and would also make contact with French forces in Zamora and Astorga.[29]

FRENCH WITHDRAWAL

Ney returned to Santiago which he took without a battle, the partisans having retreated south of Pontevedra to strong defensive positions at the Sampaio and Caldelas bridges across the Oitabén river on the main road to Tuy. The former bridge had been cut on Morillo's orders and the latter was heavily blockaded. On June 7–8 all Ney's attempts to force a passage for his twelve hundred cavalry across the swollen river's fords were beaten back by the Miño Division's ten thousand partisans and soldiers who held the far bank in well-prepared positions. A gunboat from an English frigate also participated in the defence. As great numbers of the insurgents were still without firearms, they used, it was said, every artifice of war: cannon hollowed out of oak trunks, bound with iron rings; improvised bows and arrows made from umbrella spokes; clay pots painted bronze to appear like cannon mouths . . .[30]

Soon realizing the high cost to his eight-thousand-strong corps if he continued to press the issue, Ney called off the attack and returned with his troops to Santiago and La Coruña.

Though little more than a minor victory – Vigo's earlier siege and capture by village partisans without military help was more significant of the uprising's strength – the Sampaio battle had consequences far beyond its military importance. While Ney waited in La Coruña for Soult to join him, the latter, on hearing the news of the battle, decided to abandon Galicia and march to neighbouring León. Ney was left in an untenable position, with little other choice than to evacuate the region also. By July 3, he had removed his force from Galicia; behind lay the popular insurrection which two of Napoleon's most famous marshals had been unable to repress. Galicia was free of the French army which, throughout the rest of the war, would never again set foot there. After achieving this reversal of Napoleonic fortunes, the majority of Galician villagers returned home to tend their land and look after their livestock. The parish priest Troncoso, lately 'general' of the Miño forces besieging Tuy, also returned to his village to continue to care for his spiritual flock. The popular rising brought no social change in its train. The dominant rural classes – hidalgos and clergy – retained their hegemony over the villagers. In part this was due to the fact some of these classes had participated in the struggle to expel the French, fighting as they were to preserve their privileges. Troncoso, however, was highly critical of them. He had expected, he wrote in a summary of his activities to the Suprema's defence minister, Pedro Cornel, that the 'arduous enterprise' of ousting the French would have been supported by local magistrates at the head of their villagers, and dispersed army officers who would have led the 'rough plebeians' who made up the Miño army.

> The wealthy and enlightened should have contributed to maintaining order, always so difficult in such cases, and with their wealth could have helped to feed the many poor who made up the army's largest number . . . But with great sorrow the writer must say, that with a few exceptions, it was not so. The wealthy's promises . . . were never kept . . . What damage they did to the cause! Keeping themselves and their wealth to themselves, they left the poor to fight alone.[31]

The villagers were well aware of their role. As one of them from Lugo later stressed, it was they who had 'kicked the French out of Galicia and back into Castilla'.[32] They had no doubt of their united strength; but that strength had had to be mobilized by their social superiors before it became effective.

CATALAN POPULAR RESISTANCE

> O Peuples d'Espagne! Que vous seriez laches, si vous ne preferiez la mort au joug d'aussi cruels devastateurs. [Oh Spanish people, how cowardly you would be if you did not prefer death to such a cruel and devastating yoke.] – (Inscription found on the

interior wall of a house occupied by a senior French officer in Vich when General
Blake took over the same quarters in August, 1809.[33]

The territorial liberation struggle in Galicia lasted six months; in Cataluña it
continued for six years. Popular resistance to the French occupation in 1809 had
aspects quite uncommon to the Galician struggle, the greatest of which was in
the relationship of forces. Once Soult had left Galicia on his invasion of
Portugal, the French were left with one soldier for every seventy Galicians;
after St Cyr's army entered Cataluña to reinforce the small French force there in
the autumn of 1808, the imperial army had one soldier for every twenty-three
inhabitants. Despite this enormous difference, large areas of Cataluña remained
at the beginning of 1809, like southern Galicia, unoccupied, including all the
major towns with the exception of Barcelona.

Moreover, the Catalan people's struggle faced dangers unknown to the
Galician resistance. Zaragoza's fall in February 1809 left the French army free
to move from neighbouring Aragón into western and southern Cataluña to
carry out Napoleon's aim of subjugating the main towns which his armies in
Cataluña had been unable to achieve. This danger was perceived from before
Zaragoza's fall; and the Suprema ordered General Reding to lead his army of
Cataluña to the Aragón capital's relief.[34] But Reding did not carry out the
order, and under Catalan pressure to secure a victory over St Cyr, he instead
went down to defeat. The year 1809 began then as the old year had ended, with
the army's third rout in pitched battle in as many months. At Valls on February
25, Reding, the hero of Bailén, lost not only the day but his life,* the remnants
of his army retreating in disarray on Tarragona.†

As elsewhere, the defeat at Valls finally proved that the army in Cataluña
could not take on the French in open battle and led to a re-thinking of military
strategy. Henceforth the army's tactics would have to approximate those of
irregular war, in which a considerable number of Catalan villagers were already
engaged; irregular war was more appropriate to the village-raised militia
(miquelets) and sometents who knew their countryside intimately and who
could be stiffened by small numbers of regular troops. But the new strategy
contained a major contradiction: irregular war was to be centred on or around
the main unoccupied towns which were to be turned into defensive fortresses.
To exchange mobility and the enemy's constant harassment by a static defence,

---

* He died in Tarragona two months later of wounds received in hand-to-hand combat
during the battle.
† It was left to his successor, General Blake, whom the Suprema appointed to the overall
command of the Catalonian, Aragonese and Valencian armies, to carry the offensive into
Aragón and hold back General Suchet's advance into Cataluña. After his only victory of
the war at Alcañiz on May 23, 1809, which forced Napoleon's general back to Zaragoza,
Blake was ignominiously twice defeated by Suchet near the Aragonese capital (María and
Belchite, June 15 and 18) when he attempted a flanking movement to cut off the French
commander's communications with France. Though these defeats resulted in the usual
dispersal of the patriot army, Blake's intervention in Aragón delayed Suchet's invasion of
Cataluña by nearly a year, the time it took the French commander to undertake Aragón's
'pacification' – a 'pacification' which, moreover, was never complete.

inevitably led to a siege mentality on the unhappy Zaragoza model. The French, well armed for sieges, were sooner or later certain to take the town and a large number of military prisoners which depleted the army of much needed veterans. As could be expected, therefore, this resulted in a succession of Catalan siege defeats in the coming years, without for all that eliminating the popular anti-French struggle in the countryside.*

THE SIEGE OF GERONA – MAY TO AUGUST

On May 5, 1809, French troops laid siege to Gerona which had already repulsed two imperial attacks the previous year. For seven months, the town held out in the longest siege of the war – with the exception of the later French blockade of Cádiz. Gerona was the major key to the control of the main road between France and Barcelona and to keeping the Catalan capital and its imperial occupiers supplied with French provisions.† Unlike Zaragoza, Gerona was a fortified town – for centuries the principal Catalan strategic defence on the road from the French frontier. It lay at the foothill of rocky heights whose outcrops above the town held a series of defensive fortresses and redoubts. The heights dropped sharply to a plain watered by the river Ter which, washing Gerona's north-western walls, provided a further natural defence. Though its defences had been neglected in the late eighteenth century in favour of the Figueras fortress further to the north – which the Napoleonic forces had taken by guile in early 1808 – its outer fortifications on the north-eastern heights remained impressive. The principal of these, the Montjuich fortress, was guarded by three advance redoubts; across a ravine on the heights lay three more forts. But the town itself was protected by no more than its medieval walls, thick but not built to hold heavy cannon, and containing few redoubts of consequence.

General Verdier, who had led the first attempt to beseige Zaragoza, was in command of the attacking force. The experience had taught him to be exceedingly wary of Spaniards fighting behind town walls. Instead therefore of attacking Gerona from the Ter plain which was the most obvious point of assault but would have involved fighting his way up narrow streets and crossing a stream which ran through the town under fire from the fortresses on the heights, he chose instead to subdue the latter first. Because of its stubborn defence – an ill-judged attempt to storm the Montjuich fortress through a breach in the walls cost Verdier over one thousand casualties – it was not until the beginning of August that his cannon finally pounded the fortress into

* One interesting – and strategically correct solution – was provided in March 1810, when Marshal Augereau besieged Tarragona; Enrique O'Donnell, then commander-in-chief of all Catalan forces, adopted a guerrilla strategy, sending a column from the city to occupy the enemy's rearguard, and cutting the French communication lines. After a fortnight, Augereau raised the siege on the pretext of shortage of food and returned to Barcelona.
† Despite Napoleon's dictum that his troops must live off the land, in northern Cataluña and Barcelona his forces had soon discovered that they could not do so since the land did not provide them with the necessary food and fodder.

submission, its garrison retreating to the town. Meanwhile, other imperial troops had established siege batteries around the plain to bombard Gerona itself.

> My dear friend . . . From our garden for the last four days we have been able to watch the enemy perfectly as they approach to establish their batteries. Tonight we believe they will regale us with bombs and grenades . . . and not content themselves with but a few . . . They are setting about a siege which by definition must be cruel . . . If need be we women will defend the walls . . . Goodbye, friend of my heart, recommend us to God in your prayers; perhaps this will be the last letter of mine you will read . . .[35]

The writer was the young, unmarried daughter of the Pastor family, one of Gerona's illustrious houses, of whose first name no more was known than that it began with a 'J' with which she signed her letters. A fortnight later she wrote to her friend of her hope that 'God will not permit Gerona to become a second Zaragoza . . . Courage, come what may, nobody dies until their time comes.' To emulate, indeed to surpass the length of the Zaragoza sieges, was precisely what the town's military and political governor planned and often referred to. General Mariano Alvarez de Castro, a 'severe, taciturn man of a puritan cast of mind',[36] confronted the siege with a fanaticism that could be ascribed in part to his Convention War experience and his recent disgust at Barcelona's servile surrender – especially of the capital's Montjuich fortress which he had commanded in early 1808 – and in part to his determination, at the age of sixty, finally to inscribe his name on the tablets of history by refusing to capitulate. He was prepared to see Gerona's defenders put to the sword, the town sacked and burned, its inhabitants killed, pillaged and raped rather than destroy his remaining chance of military fame. One of his senior officers, Brigadier Blas de Fornás, subsequently characterized him as an 'officer without true military talent',

> but with an extreme confidence in Providence – almost, one might say, a believer in miracles . . . but I must confess that his heroism always seemed to me that of a Christian martyr rather than of a professional soldier.[37]

The town he was so determined to defend, though a provincial capital, had a population of some eight thousand inhabitants in 1808,[38] and was smaller than many in Barcelona's industrial orbit. It lived off the land – most of those who laboured on the señorial estates were sharecroppers – and was known for the quality of its mutton and lamb. Day labourers formed the largest part of its active population, followed by textile workers; more than half of the artisans were guildsmen. While this gave the guilds a certain social importance, their existence did not indicate a thriving economy: Gerona's economic prostration had been worsened by the Convention War.[39]* The town was notable for one other social aspect: its great number of clergy – one of every twelve

* With the exception of five master printers, not a single other master employed a journeyman. The major guilds were shoemakers and cobblers, carpenters, tailors and masons. (Simón Tarrès, 1985, p. 151.)

inhabitants in 1797 which was more than four times the Spanish average; the cathedral chapter became one of the principal bases of resistance during the siege.[40] It was, in short, a small rural town, civilly dominated by a self-perpetuating elite and religiously by a large clergy, which had missed out on Barcelona's industrial revolution, and with a long history of suffering sieges. Despite his military staff's reservations, General Alvarez was certainly professional enough to organize the volunteer civilian defence on military lines from the start. Eight companies of one hundred men, each under a captain, whom he collectively named *La Cruzada* (The Crusade): one was made up of students, another of friars, and another of secular clergy. Garrison officers trained them to load and fire a musket; nothing more was expected of them, and they generally defended the less vulnerable town walls and bulwarks. Carpenters, masons and labourers were also organized into three companies whose tasks were to strengthen and repair the outer walls, and in the first part of the siege especially, when the besiegers' artillery fired mainly incendiaries, to put out fires. Other civilian volunteers took over guard duties and the like to relieve the garrison of minor tasks.

One other novelty, taken on the initiative of two garrison officers' wives and quickly accepted by Alvarez, was the organization of women volunteers into a company to fetch the defenders food, water, brandy and munitions and to assist and accompany the walking wounded to hospital to relieve soldiers of these duties. The Santa Bárbara Company, as it was officially called, consisted of 120 'young, robust and male-spirited women, without distinction of classes', as Alvarez's founding order put it, divided into four squadrons each under a woman commandant. His consideration of women's abilities did not run to the belief that they could be left to organize themselves or to comply with their military duties. He entrusted the company's organization and its orders of the day to two male commissioners. In carrying out their duties under fire – and not infrequently bearing the wounded on stretchers on their shoulders – five of the company's women were killed and eleven wounded during the siege.[41]

Having organized the women volunteers, Alvarez had a large part of the civilian population under his control; like most of the educated elite, whether military or civilian, he disliked and feared nothing more than the lower classes 'getting out of hand'.

> My friend: After three days of incessant bombardment . . . the houses are almost all destroyed; but in spite of everything you would be overcome to see the common folk, and especially the women, walking along the streets or at their doors, dodging the cannon-balls and laughing at them . . . It seems that [the Spanish army] has abandoned this unhappy city, but our spirits are not lowered. If we receive no help, we may go down to defeat; but we shall not live to see it . . . We prefer to die or to be killed first . . . if you learn that your friend has died, console yourself that this was probably her true destiny, that she preferred it to living in perpetual slavery[42]*

---

* Her letter was dated June 6. Most of those who lived through the siege put the date of the first heavy bombardment a week later, June 13 or 14. Did the author perhaps confuse the date?

As in Zaragoza's second siege, the initial Gerona garrison of just over 5,700 men
– more than half of them regulars, the remainder miquelets – largely outnumbered the male working population. In popular terms therefore the defence
bore little resemblance to the first Zaragoza siege of the previous year, where the
people fought under their own leaders from the start in a determined whirlwind
to repulse the French at the city's very gates and in its streets.

Both Gerona's besieged and besiegers firmly believed that the Montjuich
fortress was the strategic key to Gerona's fate. Alvarez ordered it to be defended
at all costs; and even when his engineers commandant inspected the battered
defences and advised him that the only course was to abandon the fortress, he
again repeated his order. For five more days the defenders held out until they
saw a vastly superior imperial force preparing to attack. The Montjuich
commander gave the order to evacuate and retire into the town. Shortly
afterwards a series of tremendous explosions tore the remains of the fortress
apart as the defenders' slow-burning fuses set off the powder kegs they had
planted in the walls. Montjuich's seven-week defence had cost the garrison over
five hundred dead and more than four hundred wounded.

In fact, the loss of the fortress signalled only the end of the siege's first stage;
the second would continue for a further four months.

SPANISH AND CATALAN RESENTMENTS

The Gerona siege occupied the French army in Catalonia to the virtual
exclusion of all else. To Barcelona's south there was little fighting. But the
Spanish-led army did nothing to relieve the town. Almost inevitably in the
circumstances, popular Catalan sentiment rose, expressed mainly through
hostility to the Spanish military on its soil, its officers and men considered
truculent and cowardly braggarts. This enmity was recognized by General
Coupigny, the acting military commander, in March 1809. 'There reigned a
total and disagreeable anarchy and a deep-rooted opposition to the Castilian
troops', he wrote.[43] While the Catalans' initial reaction was to vote with their
feet – deserting from the army or finding pretexts for not serving – the Castilian
military's hostility to the Catalans was openly manifested from the start.
Sergeant Francisco Guervos, a Bailén veteran who numbered among Reding's
Granada division ordered to Cataluña in one of the Suprema's first military
measures, was an articulate example of this. Barely arrived in Cataluña, the
former Granada cathedral violinist wrote to his parents that every day he hated
the Catalans more and more.

> They have no other God but money, and to get it they would sell their fatherland,
> their parents, their saints and everything else . . . I can assure you that were it not for
> the nation's honour and interest to wage the war to the end, there would be no one
> outlandish enough to take up arms to defend these despicable people. They abhor the
> very name of soldier . . . instead they have gangs of thieves who, calling themselves
> sometents, devastate villages almost like the French and pillage with greater ability
> than they. At general headquarters I have seen various bands of them in rags and

tatters, covered in filth. (Their rags to allow them to flee all the faster, their filth so as not to spend the slightest money) . . .[44]

Guervos was in fact a privileged urban Andalucian, who had been promoted from sergeant to lieutenant in command of an infantry company, and was able to afford in Cataluña to keep a horse, a groom and a barber–tailor.* His relative prosperity came by issuing letters of credit on his Andalucian family to Catalan civilians and clergymen. He was thinking, he wrote his parents, of taking on a third servant, a wigdresser.[45]

Guervos, then, was hardly likely to sympathize with poor villagers in tatters fighting to defend their lives, homes and families, or taking revenge on rich villagers who had exploited them as hired labour. However, after the experience of defeat – taken prisoner at the battle of Valls, Guervos managed to escape and rejoin the army – his letters became, if not more sympathetic to the Catalans, at least deeply aware of the hardships the villagers were suffering.

The army which Guervos so staunchly defended did not come cheap. The additional taxes imposed to try to fund it – on top of French exactions – tarred the Catalan junta in the people's eyes with the same brush as the army itself. As General Blake informed the Suprema on August 8,

> No resources remain in the villages . . . Nothing but near desperation and the people's unhappy clamours . . . The troops have nothing to subsist on, and are hated for being a burden on the inhabitants . . . Even the most fertile imagination is unable to suggest ways of exacting what is needed.[46]

A few days earlier, Guervos wrote to his parents:

> If you could see the greater number of this principality's villages and townships you would be overcome with horror at the devastation they have suffered at the enemy's hands. Everything is in ruins and amongst the rubble you can find the images of saints and dead children lying together. There is nothing but desolation everywhere.[47]

THE PEOPLE'S SUFFERINGS

The villagers' hardship could be judged by their population losses. In the hardest hit, these rose well above the already enormous Catalan seven percent decline in natural growth from 1808 to 1809. In the village of Bràfim, on the much-marched route between Barcelona and Valls, one in six of the population died in the winter months of 1809, the local doctor reported in his diary.[48] Parish records suggest that the death rate for the whole year was even higher: 18.5 percent of the population. Births also declined, though not so drastically. As a result, natural growth in 1809 dropped by a catastrophic 16.7 percent over the previous year when Bràfim had reached its maximum population figure in the new century.

The immediate cause of the massive number of deaths, an epidemic of

---

* Regrettably, Guervos gives no indication of the source of his family wealth.

'catarrhal and gastric fevers' in Dr Bosch i Cardellach's words, could not be disassociated from the wretchedness of war: the village had already suffered the first of its eight French sackings, and the inhabitants had fled to the mountains for the third time in as many winter months. Over the six years of conflict, the villagers abandoned their homes no less than seventeen times – the last of which was on the Spanish army's advance to 'liberate' them. Three years after the war's end, Bràfim had still not reached its 1800 population figure.

Other villages suffered as much or more. The war was bleeding most villagers dry. They appeared to be the protagonists of the struggle, but in reality they were its victims. The same could be – and was, justly – said of villages in many other parts of Spain; but in Cataluña there was barely any respite. Everywhere villagers were forced repeatedly to flee their homes, to suffer French sackings, punitive exactions and fines. Nonetheless, they continued to resist: their determination to defend their homes, families and forefathers' religion was encapsulated in a small incident at the beginning of April 1809, close to Granollers, in the Vallés. Here, as imperial troops advanced, local villagers posted themselves on the heights. The French general sent an aide-de-camp with a message: his troops only fought other troops, not civilians; in consequence the latter should leave their weapons and go home, and no harm would come to them. If not, he would attack . . . The villagers replied that they only took orders from the Spanish commander-in-chief, whom they would inform. Until his answer arrived, they would remain on the heights but were prepared not to attack the French as long as the latter ceased hostilities in the surrounding villages. If this 'just proposal' were rejected

> the villagers will use every means at their disposal to rid themselves of the invader . . . They will never surrender to a power which has demonstrated no other right than that of force. General St Cyr and his worthy companions can cover themselves with the sad glory of reducing this country to a pile of rubble; like cannibals, they can enjoy the pleasure of treading on the corpses of those they have killed; but neither they, nor their Master, will ever be able to say that the Vallés villagers surrendered to the yoke which the whole Nation justly rejects. This is their answer, given by those who occupy the said heights.[49]

Although the style and language used in Spanish was hardly that of the plain villager who, like as not, was barely literate and spoke only Catalan, the defiance and determination to defend themselves was patent. But with good sense they were also prepared to secure a truce in hostilities, however short, against troops who, on previous incursions into their villages, had assassinated their inhabitants in cold blood and burned down their houses, violated their women and desecrated their 'forefathers' religion', plundered and pillaged, as their statement also asserted.

SOCIAL CONFLICT

The better-off villagers of the same Vallés region had not only to confront the French troops but their own forces. Though the Spanish army was odious to

Catalan villagers, many of their own volunteer miquelets and sometents were soon equally hated for their pillaging and aggression towards their own countrymen. In August 1809, the local justices of the Vallés district jointly 'and with much grief' complained to the Catalan junta about the miquelets' conduct.

> The outrages, thefts, and humiliations they commit and inflict are as numerous as the farmers' houses they pass, without the owners being able to oppose their execrable conduct . . . the miquelets point their muskets and threaten to kill them if they try to prevent the pillaging.[50]

One farmer who had the temerity to seize a miquelet who was robbing him, took the militiaman to his commander, expecting to see him punished. Instead, the commander arrested the farmer and let the miquelet go free.[51]

Similar reports about the miquelets' misconduct were received from a number of places. A trial of four militiamen in Granollers in August 1809, on charges of attempting to steal various flocks of sheep, implicitly showed that, unlike the Galician uprising, a secondary conflict using the same irregular tactics was being waged in Cataluña under the cover of war. The well-off knew that they could count on the Catalan junta's rigorous defence of property rights, tithes and feudal dues – in short of the Old Regime's status quo. But great numbers of the miquelets were impoverished village landworkers who had, in the past, been exploited by wealthy farmers and monasterial *señorios*. The war had put the dominant boot on the labourer's foot. Armed but not subject to military discipline, these rural militiamen took the law into their own hands and to their own advantage, for want of money if nothing else, since most of them received little or no pay for defending their homeland. The first witness at the miquelets' trial, a butcher in Mollet, close to Granollers, testified that two months earlier they had attempted to force him to give them his flock but had been prevented from their 'criminal designs' by the local purveyor and a cashier. They had, said the butcher, already tried to steal other flocks.

The militiamen then went to a nearby pasture and tried to rob a shepherd of his flock. The latter informed the tribunal that he had mendaciously told them that the sheep belonged to the municipality and that if they stole them he would have to pay to make good the loss. This was sufficient to deter the miquelets. They had then proceeded to a another pasture, declared a third witness, where they had told those minding the flocks that since the sheep would shortly be taken by their owners to the relief of French-occupied Barcelona – a documented practice (see below) – the militiamen would do so themselves. An argument arose. The miquelets pointed their muskets at the shepherds; the owner–witness's brother offered them money – a peseta to begin with, a duro subsequently – to take themselves off, but the militiamen refused. The owner's brother sent a message to the local justice. He appeared on the scene with a number of locals, and the miquelets fired at them, not hitting any however. Overwhelmed by the number of villagers who had gathered, the militiamen made off.[52]

It was notable that the thieves' principal violence was reserved for the large sheep owners and their alleged sale of their flocks to the enemy-occupied capital. By comparison, the deceitful poor shepherd had been let off lightly. The wealthy farmers were accused of anti-patriotic profiteering at the people's expense: they were thought, no doubt correctly, to be turning a handsome profit from an illicit trade. The thieves could do the same or, in a patriotic sense, prohibit it by keeping the flocks to feed their own men. Either way the well-to-do would lose out. Little better than brigands, these miquelets nonetheless demonstrated a certain social consciousness.*

In fact, the village militiamen were fighting two wars. In the first, like all Spanish villagers, they took to arms to defend their homes, their families, their lives against the French invader who was trying to dominate their homeland. Beyond their historical memories of hostility to France, they believed in Fernando VII's cause – that in the new and young king the much-needed reforms which would alleviate their lives would finally be enacted. They defended their 'forefather's religion' and their local traditions. These were sufficient causes for believing in the struggle's righteousness. But at the same time they were fighting to redress the social inequalities they had suffered – as hired labour, sharecroppers or tenants of the privileged in the past.

*

Cataluña had a long history of armed groups roving the countryside: gangs of bandits and smugglers, miquelets and sometents, and it was to be expected that with the practice of irregular warfare banditry and smuggling would resurface during the Napoleonic war. However, the supply of provisions to the enemy in Barcelona was a particularly flagrant affair with some sometents around the capital acting to protect and profit from it. The Mataró junta informed the Catalan junta that

> In the village of Tiana, there is a farmer called Felio Rovira who raised a number of [sometent] companies which originally were useful to the struggle. Today they have become the primary smugglers of foodstuffs into Barcelona, signing passes bare-facedly in return for the money they demand. They have gone so far as to threaten the life of the village mayor, who is one of the most honourable of men . . . Another similar group has now appeared there . . . and the competition between them has reached the point that they have shot at each other in order to keep this lucrative business . . .[53]

When they were well-led by Catalan commanders who had earned their respect – through their skill, fighting success and social status – the 'volunteer' miquelet companies fought alongside the army as well as any troops; and as irregulars were formidable enemies. Often aided by village sometents rallied for the occasion, the militia contantly fought or harassed French foraging forces and columns

---

* Unfortunately, the available documents do not record their own defence or the tribunal's findings.

attempting to control the countryside as had the Galician villagers. St Cyr, the new French commander-in-chief, testified to the constant drain on his forces by their attacks. By the middle of February 1809, little more than three months after his army of twenty-five thousand had crossed into Cataluña to reinforce the French occupation forces, which were then barely holding on to Barcelona and Figueras, he calculated that his troops had 'used up two million cartridges in petty skirmishes and suffered a very appreciable loss in operations that were practically worthless'.[54]

Worthless they no doubt were to the task of subduing Cataluña; but in terms of the patriots' war aims, of controlling the countryside and depriving the enemy of vital food supplies, while at the same time causing a steady drain in imperial casualties, they were far from worthless. In May 1809 alone, irregular forces pushed back or scared off six enemy sorties from Barcelona into the neighbouring countryside. On May 6, an enemy force of one hundred Italian infantry and a few cuirassiers were known to the miquelets – communications between patriots within and without the walls of the Catalan capital successfully evaded the occupying army's vigilance – to be setting out to escort a wagon despatched by General Duhesme, Barcelona's French commander. Forty miquelets and the same number of Spanish regular cavalry were detailed to lie in ambush in woods outside Hospitalet. They allowed the imperial escort to pass – its numbers for a single wagon testifying to the French command's insecurity – and then attacked it from the rear, taking thirty-four prisoners, the wagon, arms and horses and pursuing the remainder until confronted by superior enemy forces.[55] This was but one of the small, 'worthless' incidents which made up the war on the ground.

*

Popular resistance was never as total, homogenous and univocal as the phrase implied. The miquelets and the sometents, who were not strictly subject to army discipline, shared many military disadvantages which a writer to the Catalan junta observed had started because

> this war began back to front, due to Barcelona's occupation by the enemy. Miraculously a handful of people without order or discipline stopped the enemy at the Bruch pass, and thus the idea progressively took hold that, in disbanding the regular army, [the war could be fought] without generals, cavalry or infantry. The crime of desertion was considered a virtue and remains so to this day. The first bodies of miquelets did not fight with the coordination and method of those in 1794 [during the Convention War] when there was a line army which brought order and discipline. (Antonio Borràs, January 29, 1809)[56]

So little had Catalans accepted conscription into the Spanish army, that 'some people try to form sometent companies to avoid the call-up', wrote a Mataró junta member. 'And they attempt to oblige villagers to maintain them. Many justices complain that neither they nor their orders are respected since the conscripted refuse to join the army and flee their homes. The justices ask this junta for help to make them see reason, but we have no force or any help to give them.'[57]

As a village-raised force the sometent also inevitably became an expression of local 'politics': public favours – privileging the privileged by giving them command – and private grudges against individuals could be worked out through them. As an example of the latter, Martiniano Clara, a fifty-five-year-old illiterate village baker in Besalu, whose miquelet son had earlier been killed in action, found that his other son and bakery lads were called up as sometents, leaving him without any help. He was unable to bake the bread needed by the village's inhabitants, or the rations of passing military forces. 'Perhaps moved by some unfounded resentment', the local junta had then included his name in the drawing of lots and he had also been selected to serve as a sometent. He appealed against this 'injustice' to the Gerona junta, which ordered that he not be obliged to serve.[58]

*

In the 'intestinal' war, as one contemporary writer termed it, that was being waged at the same time as the war against Napoleon, it was significant that complaints about land-related problems – villagers' non-payment of rents and dues – formed only about one sixth of the total protests received by the Catalan junta between November 1808 and June 1809.[59] Rather than attacking the señorial and land-owning system outright, it seemed that miquelets and some-tents tried to enrich themselves directly at the expense of the village rich: it was an individualist rather than a social revolution. At the local level, however, juntas' retentions of tithes to pay for their self-defence were far more frequent. Tithes, as Dr Bosch of Bràfim commented, were the first resource on which village juntas laid their hands. This illustrated that the better-off were as hostile to the Church's exactions as were the poor smallholders: feudal dues – despite the señores' eighteenth-century attempt to increase the latter – were considered by villagers as part of their contractual land rents. Tithes, on the other hand, were seen as an unjustifiable imposition by a Church which enriched itself at their expense.

The popular agitation against the more prosperous villagers also reflected the latter's lack of zeal in assuming their local responsibilities in the face of war. The Catalan junta was inundated with reports from municipalities informing it that newly appointed or elected councillors refused to take up their posts. Comprehensible at the personal level – it was they who had to treat with invasive imperial forces and attempt (often at the risk of their lives) to prevent a sacking or worse – their collective refusal did not testify to great patriotic selflessness. As the people's principal representative on the Olot township council complained to the Catalan junta:

> The large landholders and those who do not work for a living take advantage of all possible excuses to refuse to serve the public . . . [and] offer frivolous pretexts not to occupy public posts.[60]

Of the sixty-two municipal complaints received by the Catalan junta in the spring of 1809, forty percent concerned at least one councillor who had refused to take up his post or who petitioned to be excused from filling it.[61]* The Catalan junta was having none of this, and ordered them to take up their positions under threat of a fine.

The intestinal war was fought not only between poor and rich villagers, but between the new organisms of local power – the juntas – and those of the ancien regime – the town halls. The former considered themselves emanations of popular power appointed to lead the war effort; the latter, rejecting the assumption that the juntas had taken over all their powers, fought to retake their previous legal rights. In general, the Catalan junta sided with local juntas.

*

Great numbers of the better-off fled Cataluña for Mallorca, which remained unthreatened by the French, and points further off. This was particularly true of the Barcelona burgess who escaped from the capital, having in general first paid a hefty fine to the French command for the privilege of joining 'the insurgents'. The capital's landed denizens were put on the line: the Catalan junta threatened to expropriate their estates if they did not leave the city to live on them. (Ten nobles reported their return to the Catalan junta between November 1808 and June 1809, although it must be assumed that others did not inform the junta.) The occupying French military's policy of ridding the capital of possible oppositionists and of expelling the indigent to save food, increased the exodus; the capital lost about two-thirds of its pre-war population of one hundred thousand.[62] In its place, Mallorca became patriot Cataluña's main trading port. Compared to the turn of the new century, the number of ships calling at Palma annually more than doubled during the war.[63]

*

Despite five attempts in seven months† by the capital's internal resistance to liberate Barcelona, their planned night-time risings were never able to coordinate effectively with the exterior Catalan forces which were to advance to support them. The resistance's ineptness – 'as soon as any plans were agreed upon they immediately became public knowledge [in the capital] down to their last details' – did not do much to encourage an armed intervention which most Spanish military commanders, with the exception of the Catalan partisan leaders Milans del Bosch and Juan Claros, believed 'one of the most risky enterprises' they could face.[64] Nonetheless, the Barcelona acting captain general's and the majority of the audiencia's refusal in April 1809 to swear allegiance to Josef as the new king of Spain kept high the resistance's hopes; and plans were laid for another urban rising on the night of May 11. But when the moment came, the military forces from outside the city did not appear. The French rapidly found traces of the abortive attempt and arrested eighteen alleged plotters, among them seven clerics. A military court sentenced five of the

* It should be observed that municipal complaints declined sharply the further away they were from the junta's seat at the time. Thus the percentage cited here effectively concerned villages and townships close to Tarragona or in a line from there to Lérida.
† November 8 and December 10, 1808; March 7, May 11 and June 6, 1809.

accused – a doctor, a priest, a currency broker, a treasury bond official and a sergeant – to death: the French took their revenge principally on the educated elite whom they suspected of organizing the revolt. As the condemned were mounting the scaffold, the cathedral bell unexpectedly rang out the tocsin. Four artisans, a carpenter, a locksmith, a mason and an esparto plaiter, had gained access to the belfry and, with farriers' hammers, struck the bell in a call to the population to defend itself. French troops immediately surrounded the cathedral: the carpenter managed to escape, but the three others were trapped and forced to hide under the organ's bellows. Tricked after seventy-two hours into revealing their presence, they were soon thereafter climbing the scaffold themselves.[65]

On the last attempted rising on the night of June 6, the regular troops finally moved; a Catalan vision of the Spanish army was expressed in what followed:

> As the division approached up the rise from St Feliu, some of the troops fired, and the word spread immediately that the French were coming. Despite it being a false alarm, or better put, an intrigue, a part of the cavalry vanguard turned and fled, trampling down the infantry behind. Some of the troops began to fire at one another, some threw down their arms and ran, the drummers forsook their drums, there were injured and in a disorderly stampede all finally took to their heels, forgetting their most sacred duty.

As a result Juan Claros's and Jayme Jatjó's (irregular) divisions had to abandon their positions, and 'the sometents, seeing themselves deceived yet again, cursed the troops and their commanders . . . quite justly, because one of their groups, led by the Englishman, John Evans, had reached the powder stores on Montjuich, from where they had fired on the fort; the soldiers' preciptious flight exposed them to being cut off'.[66]

THE SIEGE OF GERONA: SEPTEMBER TO DECEMBER

Well aware that the major danger to resistance lay as much in the inhabitants' health as in the besiegers' attacks, medical precautions were taken from the beginning to prevent the outbreak of epidemics of the sort which had led to Zaragoza's final defeat. The dead were to be buried in the newly consecrated cemetery outside the town, not in churches and friaries as had been the custom; streets, hospitals and barracks should be kept clean, stagnant water beyond the western walls must be cleared. The inhabitants should live as 'moderate and frugal a life' as possible.[67] Until August, the measures were successful. Dr Josef Viadér, chief hospital doctor, reported that no serious epidemic existed up to that month. Of every one hundred hospital patients, only five died.[68]

The increasing hardship of the besieged was conveyed in the doctor's reports. In September the number of hospital deaths rose to one in fourteen; dysentry, scurvy and 'putrid fever', or typhus, began to affect the inhabitants. In October, as famine threatened, the figure increased to one in eight; in November and the first ten days of December, when Gerona finally capitulated, it reached just over one in four.[69]

Despite Alvarez's many appeals for help, the Spanish army made no serious attempt to force the French to raise the siege. During the first two months, Blake was engaged on his disastrous Aragón campaign, where he had taken a large portion of the army of Cataluña to join Aragonese and Valencian forces. The majority of these had scattered and dispersed after the Belchite defeat. Obviously chastened by his recent rout, on his return to Cataluña he was in no mind to risk yet another defeat against an enemy twice his number, although the Suprema, in response to pleas and reproaches from the Catalan junta, expressly ordered him 'at the expense of any sacrifice and by all possible and imaginable means – even raising a levée en masse – to speed to the town's help'. Announcing that it had no intention of abandoning Gerona to its fate, the Suprema added that it was including an extra two million reales and all the treasury's gold to the six millions it had embarked for Cataluña. But when the ship arrived it brought only five millions in all. Had the extra two million reales arrived, Tomás Veri, the Suprema's commissioner in Cataluña wrote, 'they would perhaps have been sufficient to sustain a mass sometent to reinforce the army for the time required' to relieve Gerona . . .

> To make no attempt to help the town is tantamount to opening the gates of Cataluña to the enemy, to lose all hope of recuperating Barcelona, and to destroy the Catalans' spirit which is kept alive by their belief in an effort to raise the siege. And who will be capable of reviving them again after a year of such calamities?[70]

Nevertheless, the military made several attempts to get reinforcements and supplies through to the town. The greatest success, on September 1, was Blake's. His plan for four different forces to collaborate to put a train of fifteen hundred supply mules and large reinforcements into Gerona succeeded beyond measure and out-manoeuvred St Cyr. Colonel Enrique O'Donnell staged a ferocious feint against the defensive imperial lines which St Cyr, assuming that he faced the Spanish army's full-scale assault, pulled his forces back to confront, leaving a gap in the line. In torrential rain four thousand patriot troops, who had escorted the train from Olot, slipped through the gap, fought their way with the convoy through the siege lines and into the town, their passage much helped by Rovira's and Claros's miquelet guerrillas and eight hundred of the Gerona garrison who sallied forth.

The townspeople's overwhelming joy at this sudden supply of food rapidly turned to disappointment. The nearly three thousand new reinforcements left by the commanding officer from among the troops who had entered with the convoy consumed much of the food themselves. The siege mentality was like a dam which, owing to the earth carried in from its contributing rivers, silted up and reduced its capacity. Nonetheless, the inhabitants were heartened by the show of aid and by the besiegers' subsequent eleven days of inactivity, which they used to repair the town's defences. Encouraged by the enemy's lack of action, neighbouring villagers again risked their luck to bring in scanty supplies over mountain tracks which for those who could afford them provided some additional relief.[71] As it turned out the September 1 breakthrough was the last important external aid Gerona received. Two other convoys the same month were beaten back before reaching the town. Between June and September most food prices, with the exception of wheat and barley, had at least trebled, a contemporary diarist noted, and some, like the cost of a fowl, had risen over twenty times. Alvarez's order that prices, other than those of food brought in by villagers, were not to be increased had little effect. Supply and demand at a time of scarcity were stronger than patriotic appeals.[72]

Alvarez's lack of military talent at the head of the defence, in his staff subordinate's words, was made good by his fanaticism. The French revolutionary wars had to a large extent revolutionized counter-revolutionary warfare by introducing the people as a determining force; the former idea of a passive population under siege had gone.*

> No one had previously considered what the defenders can do when they unite valour and ingenuity; how much they can slow down the besiegers' work by continuous sorties, or how many ways there are of defending a breach. The previous error was to suppose that everything depended on the artillery.[73]

His very fanaticism led Alvarez to use these new tactics – and often to very good effect. Unlike Palafox in Zaragoza, he organized frequent sorties to delay the siege works. To an officer who was to command one of these and who asked on what point to retreat were he forced to do so, Alvarez tartly replied: 'To the cemetery.'[74] He was able, moreover, to imbue the inhabitants, many always ready to believe in miracles, with his military version of 'martyrdom' in an unyielding defence.

By mid-September, the besiegers had opened three wide breaches in the town's north-eastern walls. The prior month's bombardments had been so fierce that it was said that only one house in the town still stood intact. In the afternoon of September 19, after a further morning's heavy artillery fire, the imperial troops launched their much-awaited assault. Behind the breaches, the defenders had prepared a second line of defence, cutting wide pits, constructing barricades and opening loopholes in houses. In bitter fighting, some of it hand to hand, the garrison's regular troops and miquelets threw back the attackers who suffered over six hundred killed and wounded to the defenders' 250 casualties.† As an eyewitness, Narcis de Camp y de Font, wrote to the Catalan junta:

> Though everything stood to be lost in the two hours of fighting, the town remained calm. People stood at their doors to give the wounded a sip of the little good wine they still retained, the best cordial there is. The Santa Bárbara women's company's went to

---

* Spanish history could be called on for two such refusals to surrender to besiegers: Numancia and Sagunto. In both, the inhabitants after long sieges set fire to their places and perished in the flames rather than surrender to the Romans in the former, and to Hannibal in the latter.
† The only senior officer to be killed was Rudolf Marshall, an Irishman, who had left home and family to fight in the war; he had particularly chosen to go to Gerona where he was made a lieutenant colonel of the Ultonia (Ulster) regiment, and was put in command of defending one of the most important breaches. His last words were reported to be that he died happy to have defended 'the cause of so brave a nation'. (*Diario de Gerona*, September 23, 1808.)

the breaches to fetch the troops munitions, water and whatever wine could be had, and to bring back the wounded. Men of the *Cruzadas* were on the walls . . . The whole town was at work . . . And the prize for all of this is not to know whether the town will be rescued before it dies of hunger, for famine is nearly upon it . . .[75]

The victory was hailed as Gerona's 'great day'. The imperial forces would not again try to storm the place. Instead they attempted to starve it into submission. This change of strategy, combined with Blake's two further fruitless attempts to relieve pressure on Gerona – in the last, on November 1, he was defeated with the loss of two thousand men and thereafter retreated from the scene – made the end almost inevitable; but still the starving town held out for a further six weeks.

Every day from late September, a number of the garrison's and population's horses were slaughtered – Alvarez was the first to offer his – to provide meat for the troops, the population and the sick. The bishop ordered a soup kitchen to be opened at his expense to feed the poor.[76] Hungry army infantrymen began frequently to enter inhabitants' houses demanding, as 'charity', bread and wheat.[77] By the beginning of October, the spectre of famine became a reality. The mills were not producing sufficient flour to provide bread; Alvarez inspected them. As he came away, an inhabitant called out: 'Sir, do not be distressed, we will eat dry grains of wheat if necessary.'[78]

The French command was now taking measures in the heights above the town to prevent villagers getting through with food: cords with bells and guard dogs to alert sentries to anyone passing over the mountain tracks. Marshal Augereau, who had finally taken command from St Cyr in the first days of October, reinforced this new tactic with constant bombardments and feint attacks to wear down the population's morale. To save food, the Gerona junta ordered beggars and all those without means, women and children under sixteen, people over sixty, the walking sick and those who had taken refuge in the town, to leave when the opportunity arose.[79]*

In spite of widespread hunger, it was not the inhabitants but the garrison officers who first broke ranks. They complained bitterly that they were receiving neither food nor pay. To pacify them, Alvarez called a meeting of the town's notables and guilds on October 4 to raise sixteen thousand reales to provide them with food and pay. Though this sum was not forthcoming, those in attendance committed the nobility, clergy and guilds to contribute ten reales a day.[80] At the beginning of November, the junta had to ask that this payment be repeated. To survive the populace was by now eating almost anything – or nothing because of the exorbitant prices. As J. A. Nieto Samaniego, a doctor in charge of military hospitals, recorded:

---

* Two hundred families accompanied Lieutenant Colonel O'Donnell, who had reached Gerona with the remnants of the last abortive supply train at the end of September, and broke out a fortnight later. Despite his initial success, his column was attacked by imperial forces and many of the fleeing civilians were captured (Pla Cargol, 1962, p. 169).

Cats and mice were considered exquisite dishes and sold for a good price . . . A fowl fetched an ounce of gold, a pair of half rotten thrushes twenty reales, a jar of bad brandy seventy reales, and a jug of wine forty to fifty; as to greens, a handful of celery leaves, wild chicory or poppies, the only vegetables we could obtain . . . sold for similarly exaggerated prices. And there was no question of bargaining: the first buyer snatched them from the seller's hands.[81]

A refugee from occupied Barcelona who had reached Lérida offered to manufacture dried broth cubes for the beleagured hospital inmates. Each cube would make four cups of wholesome meat or chicken broth, he wrote, and because of their small size and weight they could be easily taken into the town in sufficient quantities to make broth for 2,500 men a day. But his offer to the Catalan junta, to which he sent four experimental cubes and informed it of the manufacturing process came, like other aid, too late.[82] Heavy rains and cold weather in October worsened the inhabitants' plight, scurvy, dysentry and fever weakened their half-starved bodies. The homeless poor, and those whose houses had been shelled, slept out; every night some of them died. Others dropped dead in the streets. For days their bodies lay unburied, adding to the pestilence. The sick were confined in over-crowded hospitals; the rain leaked through their tiled roofs. No medicine remained to treat the patients. Dr Viadér recalled their plight:

> Most of them lay on the bare floor for want of straw, benches or beds; a minority had palliasses which had rotted. All were without nightshirts, sheets, bolsters or blankets . . . [The hospitals] were a cruel source of contagious disease. Such great numbers died that it can be affirmed that of every hundred seventy-five were the victims of these conditions.[83]

A quarter of the garrison troops fell ill; and as the still-active soldiers could no longer be relieved, they too became more readily exposed to sickness.[84] By the end the original garrison had lost two-thirds of its men.[85]* 'In general, every face bears the pallor of approaching death', Dr Nieto Samaniego reported to Alvarez on November 29.

> [The inhabitants'] voices are listless, their steps slow, their breathing frequent, their pulse weak; they suffer from an excessive despondency, not only physical but of natural pride and amour propre. They have little inclination for social intercourse; and the little they have serves only to relieve grief, to brood on their hunger, to think of their harsh fate . . . [and] the cruel abandonment to which we have been reduced, leaving us to die in hardship, barrenness, famine and sickness or by the terrible besieger's sword.[86]

---

* The imperial army was also suffering heavily through sickness. By October 1, Verdier's army was down to four thousand active troops but by combining these and St Cyr's forces Augereau had some twelve thousand soldiers against a steadily dwindling garrison. (Oman, vol. III, pp. 49–50 and 55.)

There were hardly any pregnant women to be seen. Menstruation, the same doctor reported, was frequent and excessive. 'Many women have seen their new-born die of hunger, clinging to their milkless breasts.' The streets were torn and deeply holed by cannon fire, and the holes were full of excrement washed by the rain from the cesspits of roofless houses. The remains of human diarrhoea were everywhere; and adding to the pestilence were the human and animal corpses buried in the ruins.[87]

By now the defenders' guiding spirit, Alvarez, was himself suffering from fever and was delirious much of the time. Yet he rejected out of hand all offers of terms – as he had done throughout the siege. The town, its garrison and inhabitants could perish of hunger or at the enemy's sword: he would not surrender.

Despite their great suffering, it was once again not the inhabitants who lost heart, but rather the officers, eight of whom, including three lieutenant colonels, deserted to the enemy on November 19. They informed Marshal Augereau of the town's state and that Alvarez was insane and dying. Heartened by the news and determined to hasten the end of the siege, Augereau offered to treat, but Alvarez again rejected surrender. The French commander began to batter a new breach in the walls, and took the redoubts above the town, seriously threatening the garrison's last forts on the heights and Gerona's inner defences.

But the immediately decisive factor was Alvarez. On December 8 his health worsened notably and he suffered a fit of delirium. Drs Viadér and Nieto Samaniego confirmed the seriousness of his condition, and the next day he was given the last rites. The junta appointed his second-in-command, Julián de Bolíbar, in his place. At a meeting of military commanders and junta members early on December 10, amidst a bombardment which had begun at dawn from all the enemy batteries and with constant requests arriving for reinforcements at the breaches as the imperial troops attacked, and members' discouraging accounts of the state of the defences, the lack of wheat stocks, the unlikelihood of receiving any external aid, the majority voted to seek negotiations to ensure that the population and garrison were not put to the sword after a successful new assault. Colonel Fornás, who had led the Montjuich defence and commanded many of the garrison's sorties, was called on to negotiate.

Meanwhile, the bishop called a meeting of clerical dignitaries, professional men and guild representatives to inform them of the state of affairs. The guild members, who had been one of the mainstays of resistance, expressed great opposition to negotiations. Guildsmen had been responsible originally for raising Gerona; their 730-odd members had defended the town – masons, carpenters and allied trades in the three special companies which repaired breaches;[88] their officials had ensured that members reported for duty in their Cruzada companies; and the guilds had contributed money to the defence and to the officers' food and pay. But they had not been consulted on the army envoy's dispatch to seek terms; with the exception of Alvarez, the officer corps had revealed itself as the defence's weak link.

Extended to a wider meeting, the military junta informed the assembly that, even with civilian help, the garrison was too weak to hold off an enemy attack on the breaches, and that negotiations had begun to avoid the population's slaughter. But if the inhabitants were determined to continue resistance, the garrison was prepared to die alongside them. While these discussions were still in progress, the French general appointed by Augereau to draw up the capitulation terms arrived. He was amazed to find himself the object of questions from junta members in the midst of an increasingly chaotic meeting which had not reached agreement on whether to surrender. Minds were finally focused by Colonel Fornás recalling that, under his agreement with Augereau, he was due in a short time to return to the marshal with the town's answer. Finally, agreement was reached; Fornás returned, terms were reached: the town would capitulate on the following morning, December 11.[89]

At midnight, four hundred soldiers and civilians, including women, tried to escape from the town. As they waded the Ter, French guards gave the alarm, shooting broke out, many were killed, a few managed to escape, and the majority fled in panic back to the town.

At the appointed hour the next morning, just under 3,400 officers and men marched out and laid down their arms. Behind them 1,090 officers and troops, including Alvarez,* remained in hospital.[90] The original and reinforced garrison's 9,400 troops had suffered nearly five thousand casualties, of whom approximately one thousand had died.[91] Such was the state of the soldiers who surrendered that 'the besiegers felt ashamed to have been held at bay so long by dying men', an imperial eyewitness observed.[92] Despite the capitulation treaty, 119 clerics were subsequently deported.

It was the civilian population, however, which had suffered most. One in five died – nearly sixty percent more than the garrison's deaths. This high civilian mortality rate was caused less by enemy action than by hunger, sickness and the infrahuman conditions in which people had been forced to exist.[93]

*

As predicted, Gerona's surrender deeply affected the Catalan population who blamed the Spanish army for not having raised the siege. It was easy to make Blake the scapegoat and he certainly deserved a fair share of the blame.† However, it was also the case that the Suprema's war minister had ordered him not to risk his small force in certain defeat; and the Junta, after ordering him to 'speed to Gerona's defence', had later written that it had intended him to do only what, in his military judgement, was 'possible'.[94] In any case, he had given the Catalan junta long warning of his refusal to take on the besiegers with his outnumbered army;‡ had the junta acted decisively, it could have used south-

---

* Alvarez was first taken to prison in France and then inexplicably returned to solitary confinement in a dungeon in Figueras castle where he died almost immediately. It was widely believed at the time that he had been executed. (Toreno, 1838/1916, p. 223.)

† Two days before Gerona's fall, he resigned his command on grounds of illness, but in fact because of his differences with the Catalan junta.

‡ Colonel Veri had done his utmost to secure reinforcements for Blake from Valencia, but the regional junta refused, saying it had no troops to spare. (AHN, *Estado*, Legajo 38E/388[6], Tarragona, Sept 16, 1809.)

western Cataluña's seven-month freedom from enemy attack to raise levies to reinforce him. But it was easier for the junta to write letters of protest than to take resolute action. Finally, it realized that its own prestige was at stake and summoned a congress on November 20 in Manresa, which decided to raise a mass sometent levy and a ten million real loan to support it. By the time even a small force could be assembled, it was too late: Gerona had fallen. The failure to go to the besieged town's aid led to a series of incendiary anonymous letters and pasquinades protesting about 'the betrayal of Cataluña', the Spanish army's passivity, the junta's resort to conscription, and urging the need for Catalans alone to take up their own defence. Some of these were signed by 'The Tiger of the Catalans', and repeated themselves, in Catalan or Spanish, in almost identical terms.

> Take to arms, Catalan people and our sound will frighten the Spanish military and humble French pride. I shall be your leader – The Tiger of the Catalans.[95]

The tiger was little more so than on paper, but after Gerona and the failure to recapture Barcelona, there was little doubt that distrust of, and desertion from, the Spanish army notably increased. Gerona's capitulation was just the first of the four Catalan sieges which all went down to defeat.

13

The Church at War

ABSENCE OF A UNIFIED FRONT

We are not now engaged in an ordinary war . . . No, this is a voluntary war of religion, in which all who are capable of taking arms must willingly enrol, and offer themselves in sacrifice to God if that is the Almighty's wish. It is a war in which the rich must offer all their wealth and jewels without a thought, as the Church is about to offer all its silver . . . Moreover, to ensure us of all Heaven's fervour, we must preach the complete reform of [the people's] customs: if we do not do so, how shall we distinguish ourselves from our dissolute and disbelieving enemies? . . . This is a time of penitence . . . (A Prelate's Proclamation to his Parish Priests, 1808)[1]

This was the language that could be expected of an absolutist bishop. There was nothing new in it; it had been used by predicant monks and friars during the previous war against the French Revolution, which they had similarly declared a religious war. What was singular about the proclamation was that it did not represent a nationwide clerical response to the anti-Napoleonic struggle as might be supposed.

From the start of the conflict, the Church failed to adopt a national collective stance – a general ecclesiastical call, for example, to rally clergy and people in a crusade against the 'infidel' invaders. The Church's 'silence, inactivity and insensibility' to the popular will to defend religion had 'made the people lose heart, and not without reason . . .' wrote an unnamed correspondent to the Suprema.

Scandalized by the enemy's insults and profanations of their temples, altars and ministers the people in their zeal would have faced any danger or sacrifice to avenge them. Had the ministers of the Church raised their standard and exhorted the faithful in their defence this would have happened . . . The motif of religion profaned was more than sufficient for all Spaniards to adopt the motto, Victory or Death.[2]

Who better than the head of the Church to rally popular resistance? But the primate of Spain, Cardinal Luís Borbón, a close relative of the deposed royal family, was at that moment a member of a pro-French junta of public tranquility in Toledo. An enlightened – though personally weak – cleric, there he would have stayed had it not been for the patriot Bailén victory; like many another highly placed personage, he then changed his mind about Bonapartist prospects in Spain and turned coat to become a patriot supporter. Even so, it was only two months later, in September 1808, that he issued his first pastoral to his diocese calling on his parishioners to take to arms like 'the Israelites and Spanish provinces' in defence of religion, king and fatherland.

Cardinal Borbón's attitude graphically illustrated the ecclesiastical split. Although the Church was a truly national institution, a state within the absolutist state, the question of whether it could have been the vector of organized national resistance seemed dubious in the light of its lack of political and ideological homogeneity and of a coherent territorial organization.*

When Toledo was captured by the French in December 1808, shortly after Madrid fell to Napoleon, Borbón fled south with the Suprema in front of the imperial troops, leaving full powers to the cathedral chapter which in turn delegated them to the auxiliary bishop and two canons. Covering an enormous area in the heart of Spain, the Toledo primate archdiocese was the country's largest, and its wealthiest. Most of its northern part was in French-occupied territory, but the southern still lay in patriot hands and its various vicariates were unable to communicate with Toledo.

This ambiguous situation lasted until April 1809, when the Bonapartist regime in Madrid decided to exert greater control and ordered the chapter to elect one of its nominees to hold delegated powers. The chapter at length complied, the cardinal retaliated by appointing two trusted canons to the same post and a number of 'flying vicar generals' to the patriot front lines to maintain contact with Toledo. From this new and even greater diocesan confusion, a pragmatic compromise was struck. Depending on the circumstances, the cathedral chapter consulted either the Bonapartist or Borbón-appointed governors, and thus lived relatively untroubled for a further year. In this condition, compounded by the cardinal's indecisive character, it could hardly be expected that Toledo would afford clerical direction to the patriot struggle.[3]†

At the start of the war, the Church included its share of both vehement Old Regime clerics and politically circumspect reformists who had counted on the prewar state to implement Church reforms; but alongside a minority of 'afrancesados' – the most notable of whom was the inquisitor general and archbishop of Zaragoza, Ramón de Arce – the Church had its share of episcopal contemporizers with the Bonapartist regime in the occupied zones who remained to care for their flock or who adopted one of the only other positions open to them: Render unto Caesar the things which are Caesar's . . .

* See Prologue, pp. xiii–xviii, on the state of the prewar Church.
† In 1810, the Bonapartist regime, aware that the chapter remained in contact with Cardinal Borbón, declared his archbishopric vacant and prohibited communication with him under the strictest punishment; the majority of the chapter thereafter obeyed King Josef's orders, creating further diocesan problems. Borbón tolerated the situation in order to avoid increasing the upheaval, demanding however that his appointees continue communicating with him, which they did.

The bishop of Valladolid, one of the very early Bonapartist supporters (though at the same time highly doubtful that the patriotic rising left him much scope for pressing King Josef's case), issued a pastoral to his diocese in July 1808:

> Jesus Christ did not ordain himself as a judge in secular matters . . . To serve God and not to obey the king, to love your neighbour and to offend against a single man, are contradictory acts, products of a bad conscience. Those who serve God and love their neighbour will be faithful and obedient to their sovereign.[4]

The criticism of the Church's 'inactivity' appeared then to stem from the failure of a general ecclesiastical call for a religious war or from the demands of a 'theological interpretation' of the ongoing events. Very shortly after the national risings, of which he would probably have been unaware at the time, Pope Pius VII called on the Spanish clergy to 'rouse themselves' and look at the evil the 'impious' Napoleon had caused France. In a pastoral on June 7, 1808, which contained many allusions to the books of the Maccabees* and the Apocalypse (which became the touchstone of later patriot sermons and religious writings – afrancesado bishops tended rather to the New Testament) he warned all Spaniards of the dangers to religion they faced from Napoleon, 'that sinful man and son of damnation'. He told Spaniards that the war was just and that they should fight for 'king, country and the law' and to 'avenge the injustices done to Spain and its princes . . .'[5]

In the whirlwind of the risings – in which individual clerics played a not inconsiderable part in awakening and maintaining a spirit of popular resistance – until the victory at Bailén, many indecisive bishops followed Borbón's suit and did not commit themselves to the patriot cause. In this they were little different to many high government functionaries and members of the nobility. However, the dozen or so prelates who were presidents or members, alongside an even greater number of canons, of the provincial juntas assured a part of the Church with patriotic credentials.

Nonetheless, in 1808 a considerable number of clerics showed publicly that they were reluctant to deny their evangelical duties and preach a religious war in outright support of the patriot cause. In Sevilla a few days after Bailén, a Carmelite friar, for example, preached a sermon, under the ambiguous title, 'Should we hope or fear?' in which, though admitting that this was a scandalous theme for a religious minister to pose, he tried to persuade other clerics not to resist the French. 'Have they not seen that the cancer of defending the throne, state and fatherland is certain to bring the Church's ruin?' he asked. He ended his sermon, however, giving thanks that 'due to our faith' the patriots had won victories 'without the means to do so', showing that he had little trust in their ability to withstand the French. On the same day in Sevilla, a canon and member of the Granada junta gave a sermon in which, after rehearsing Spain's

---

* Judas Maccabeus led a religious revolt in Judea against the Syrian Seleucid king in 165 BC. The four books – the first two of which form part of the Apocrypha – contain many references to the defence of religion and the right of avenging injustice.

history since the seventh century, he praised 'the Maccabean spirit' of the troops who were heroically defending the country. In the absence of a national Church response to the war, everything depended at first on individual clerical initiatives. Significantly, however, there were few recorded appeals for a religious war.[6]

The change came with the crisis at the end of 1808 when Napoleon crushed the Spanish armies, took Madrid and seemed set to capture most of the country. The Suprema considered the Church's efforts insufficient and called on it for an organized endeavour to enthuse the people's will to resist. The first such appeal to prelates and the heads of religious orders came as the Junta fled south before Napoleon's offensive. The clergy, it said, 'have the greatest interest in and are the first who are obliged to defend religion . . . The Suprema expects you to employ all your zeal, suasion and patriotism to revive the people's spirit . . . .'[7] Subsequently the Junta called on missionaries to go out to preach in favour of the patriot cause, 'as our kings have bidden in equally calamitous times'.[8]

Rather than these Suprema appeals it was no doubt the fact that the majority of the lower clergy, secular and religious, feared Napoleon's imminent domination; this determined them to declare a Holy War, a 'Crusade' against a godless invader, 'the most heretical of all heretics'. A torrent of vituperation and abuse poured out on the enemy in sermons and writings, much of it sustained by a theological interpretation of Spain's history in which the divine will was the prime mover of events. In this ideology, which drew a veil over the many material interests that the divinity was unlikely to attend to, 'Spain is suffering the lash of punishment because it provoked the terrible hand of God against itself.' And thus: 'The Most High, who is the God of fury and vengeance, is reaching out anew to Spaniards to convert them.'[9]

Coming from what was generally assumed to be the most Roman Catholic of countries, this was bewildering. But it also was not new. Since the turn of the century all the disasters, epidemics and famines had proven God's wrath with the Spaniards for having turned from his path. The war was the latest – and greatest – of these punishments, inflicted by the very country whose example had been responsible for corrupting an age-long Spanish religious tradition: France, 'from [which] all evil, all pestilence, all ruin has come to us. . . .'[10] None other than the last Suprema president, Archbishop Laodicéa, addressing patriot Spaniards on his assumption of office, resumed the values of theological history with copious references to Israel's fate when its people strayed from the face of God, and to Spain's past victories as his standard bearer. The people must 'sanctify this war to oblige God to favour our cause'.

> The [holy] faith shows us that war is one of divine justice's greatest scourges wherein is seen the hand of God and his fury to make this nation amend its impious ways, to be appeased only by prayer and penitence . . . Let us weep at the insensitivity which, in midst of outrages to our holy religion, of our villages' desolation, of our provinces' oppression and of the ruin which threatens the kingdom, does not recognize the need to set our customs aright, of which God, through the fruit of our new and extraordinary tribulations, is attempting to make us aware . . .[11]

This was relatively restrained in comparison to some exhortations, the arch-bishop having proved himself a fairly moderate Suprema member; and it was published at an extreme moment of crisis in the war, with the enemy preparing to invade Andalucía. Nonetheless, it illustrated the theological stance that Napoleon was little more than God's scourge to return Spaniards to their old ways, for Catholic devotion was inherent in the nation's customs and was not a matter of choice: religious toleration – which many feared the Bonapartist regime would introduce in the occupied region – was anathema. God, not soldiers, won battles, though the archbishop did not totally ignore human agency, exhorting the nation's clergy to aid military enlistment and the for-mation of clerical guerrilla bands.

The token of this theological position was almost always women's 'immodest' dress.

> Like the proud women of Israel, some Spanish women, in their confident arrogance, expose themselves in their dress far in excess of Christian modesty and decorum. Provoking the wrath of Heaven with the whims of your lust, you bring on yourselves dishonour, orphanhood, mourning and the final extermination.[12]

Shortly before, the bishop of Santander had tried to have the Suprema legally outlaw feminine 'immodesty'. But he met his match in the former vicar general of Toledo, who had become the Suprema's secretary-general. In his report on the bishop's proposal to 'bury legally and forever in Spain women's nakedness', Pedro Rivero advised the Suprema that 'every law which is at odds with a kingdom's public and general opinion is not obeyed or is evaded in such a manner as to make a fool of the law', and 'in turn reflects on the government's power'.[13] The Suprema agreed with its secretary general who, as an enlightened cleric, granted society's agency a power which the theological interpretation of events tried to deny it.

Many of the lower clergy were less concerned in their sermons with theo-logical arguments about God's wrath on the Spanish than to incite them to fight.

> In our present straits, it is imperative that we unite all our strength. We must hasten to take up arms; all deserters and those who shelter them or prevent military enlistment are unfaithful to the fatherland and religion . . . Friars and clerics will join the struggle . . .[14]

From early 1809, in the occupied regions of Castilla la Vieja, Navarra and Aragón, about half the bishops fled their dioceses for the safety of the patriot zone. Many of them went disguised as ordinary priests, some on foot. The eighty-three year old bishop of Segovia, for example, hid in a friary in the Guadarrama mountains for five months until he was warned that a detachment of French troops from Madrid was on its way to arrest him. Fleeing at night, he rode over the sierras, down into the Tajo river valley and up into the Toledan hills until he reached the patriot outpost of Horcajo de los Montes where he rested from 'the ailments and disorders of this long and tiring journey on horseback which . . . it seemed impossible for me to have endured. But I am comforted that I did so rather than tarnish my old age . . . by setting Spanish youth an example of weakness . . . .'[15]

The Suprema was 'horrified' by the Bonapartist bishops' 'scandalous' conduct. Who could have believed that among those few individuals, 'whose perversity, ambition or weakness' had led them to 'embrace the party of Europe's oppressor', there should be numbered prelates of the Church?

> Even more so does it seem impossible when the tyrant's and his satellites' outrages to our August Religion, to the faithful's Venerable Father, to our most holy and sacred institutions, are taken into account. No, it is not credible that the Lord's anointed . . . should use their high and sacred ministry publicly to maintain that perfidy is justice, godlessness piety, inhumanity clemency, violence a legitimate right, pillage generosity, devastation happiness.[16]

The Suprema ordered that all the Bonapartist clerics' property, temporalities and rights were to be seized immediately and that they were to be tried for high treason if caught. As the Bonapartist regime also expropriated prelates who did not return to their dioceses in the occupied zone, the Church's institutional heads were generally in little position to lead the struggle.

By default, this was left to rural parish priests who shared their village parishioners' fate at the hands of the French forces. They were the only clerics who usually stayed at their posts at times of imperial incursions. This clergy was materially affected by the enemy troops' exactions since, against the Bonapartist government's express orders, the portion of tithes on which they lived were usually seized by the military along with the villagers' crops; and with the increased resistance to paying tithes – and local authorities' retention of those that were paid to meet exactions from both French and Spanish armies – the parish priest was hard put to stay alive.* In this he was no different to the majority of his parishioners.

As long as the patriot resistance was principally rural-based, depending on villagers for recruits and crops, village priests were in fact as important to the cause as Church prelates, indeed perhaps more so for their direct influence on the local population. (The Bonapartist regime also recognized this and tried, unsuccessfully, to win them to its cause.) What was at stake was to ensure the Church's survival which required in turn the fatherland's survival. To an unlettered public, the parish priest was the divine and terrestrial conduit summoning villagers to continued resistance for God-given aims and the sheer need of physical survival. Sermons were their major form of rallying the people. In the villages where imperial troops seized crops and livestock, damaged churches and committed other crimes, they provided parish priests with ready-made patriot propaganda. But even in those that had not yet experienced

---

* In 1800, Toledo diocesan tithes amounted theoretically to 7,500,000 reales a year; in 1812 the amount had dropped to 217,000 reales – although this sum came only from the areas under relatively solid Bonapartist control. (Higueruela del Pino, 1982, p. 46.)

the enemy, the news of their *razzias* elsewhere was sufficient; from a small, isolated Sevillan village, the local priest wrote in June 1809:

> Though my parish is poor and has few parishioners, the [Suprema's] orders for special and solemn celebrations on H.M. Fernando's saint's day were observed with a solemn mass and Te Deum . . .; and the following day another service in honour of our brothers killed in the present war. All this in order to ask mercy of God, to honour and glorify him for the outrages which the vile French heretics perpetrate.[17]

The Suprema was well aware of parish priests' importance in maintaining the people's spirit of resistance. In gratefully rejecting one such's offer to serve in the army, the Junta told him that 'in your substantial duties as a parish priest you can do more good for the fatherland by inspiring your parishioners to fight and resist tyrants than you can by enlisting in the army'.[18]

*

It was, without a doubt, the Bonapartist regime's dissolution of the religious orders which provided the patriot lower clergy with a common bone to chew. Foreshadowed by Napoleon's Chamartín decrees of December 1808, King Josef's minister of ecclesiastical affairs, the Spanish conde de Montarco, spent considerable time with his advisers carefully planning the matter in order to lessen opposition to the dissolution, though the need to reduce Spain's sixty thousand friars – the Bonapartist figure, which was fifty percent higher than the usually accepted number[19] – had been widely recognized by enlightened secular *and* religious clergy, as well as by the government, from long before the war. (The patriots would subsequently also propose a reform restricting friars' numbers.)* An early Bonapartist measure was to promise all those friars and monks who left their cloisters voluntarily a pension of 2,200 reales. Only about seven hundred accepted the offer;[20] many more fled in the face of imperial army incursions and did not return because their religious houses had been burned or destroyed by the occupying troops.

The 'near-run' battle of Talavera in July 1809,† and the awareness that the majority of the Spanish regular clergy was implacably hostile to the new Madrid regime, brought a readiness to seize the moment for reform. 'Neither the consideration we have shown until now . . . nor the sincere promises we have made to grant [friars and monks] our protection and favour, have sufficed', the preamble to the dissolution decree declared.[21]

---

* Though the reform was never approved by the Cortes of Cádiz, it would have prohibited all communities in uninhabited places, or more than one community of a given order in a town, forbidden the restoration of monasteries or convents with less than twelve professed members, regulated the size of convents (350 nuns) and monasteries (60), disallowed the creation of new communities or established religious houses to acquire new property. (Rodríguez, 1996, pp. 130 and 136; Callahan, 1984, p. 101; Lovett, 1965, vol. II, p. 480.)
† See Chapter 15, p. 348.

The ex-friars, who were supposed to return to their places of birth, were not permitted to hear confession, preach or to form associations in order to prevent the more influential among them from conspiring against the regime, even if only in the confessional or in sermons. Those who 'by their suitable and healthy political principles' showed their willingness to accept Bonapartist rule – and swore fidelity to the new king – were however allowed to become members of the secular clergy which did not endear them to many parish priests. The majority, on the other hand, who considered the regime's conditions humiliating, tried to keep alive as organists, elementary schoolmasters, farm bailiffs and the like while the more unruly and dissatisfied often joined patriot guerrilla bands.[22] Ex-regulars' hostility to the reform was increased because the Bonapartist state, nearly as short of funds as the patriots', was unable to fulfill its promise to provide them with a living, giving them credit notes on practically valueless disentailed ecclesiastical property.[23]

In the particular wartime conditions, the reform turned against the Bonapartist regime. Although earlier the regulars had been belligerent in their opposition to Josef's government, they had then to some extent been controllable in their monasteries and houses; dispersed, control became virtually impossible.

THE CHURCH AND THE SUPREMA

By 1809 the Church in the patriot zone assumed a hand in public affairs which, at least since the war of the Convention, it had not exercised. In large part this was a result of the authorities' need to endow the patriot struggle with a common ideological bond for its disparate supporters. Nowhere was this more true than of towns under siege, of moments of extreme military crisis or temporary triumph. In Sevilla, for example, the Suprema and provincial juntas ordered eight special religious ceremonies to be celebrated in nine months of 1809, seven of them between March and July alone; three of the latter included public veneration of Saint Fernando's incorrupt body which was uncovered in the cathedral especially for the occasion;* and a further three were public rogatives, each lasting nine days, 'to implore the God of the Armies to ensure the success of our arms'. Churchmen played their part with fervour in all of these, gathering under their banner in processions through the streets and religious services a new collective public of military, clerics and lay persons, of which they became, as it were, the ceremonial masters.[24]

The Suprema's request that missionaries go out to preach in favour of the cause quite probably stemmed from a friar's letter informing the Suprema that in Carmona, a township close to Sevilla, influential locals were spreading defeatist talk. Brother Josef Meléndez-Valdés proposed the great benefits to be derived from 'preachers and religious ministers preaching the truth of the

---

* For the first of these on March 22, 1809, the royal chaplain informed the Suprema that the cathedral did not have the money to assume the costs, which the Junta was thus obliged to bear. (AHN, *Estado*, Legajo, 27F/290[1-3].)

matter (since the cause is so just) and inspiriting the people among whom they enjoy so much influence'.[25]

The Suprema's request brought a reply from the prior of a religious order in another nearby township. The secular and regular clergy had denied their profession of faith, he wrote.

> I attribute precisely all the evils which have affected, and still affect us, to the sins of us who are ministers of the faith . . . We have still not returned to our duty as clergy, it being necessary to carry forward our reform in order that such missions &c may bear their full fruit.[26]

When the final crisis loomed and Andalucía was about to be invaded, the Suprema again appealed to bishops to send priests, prebendaries and other church dignitaries to the army 'with the purpose of exhorting the troops and officers to fulfil their respective obligations and to improve their habits'. The fatherland's defenders must learn military discipline 'and become accustomed to the duties which religion imposes on them'.[27]

From the start of the war, some provincial juntas had been ready to intervene directly in ecclesiastical affairs. The Granada junta, for example, declared that Spanish bishops could make full use of their facultative powers to confront the critical situation created by the impossibility of communicating with the Pope, then Napoleon's prisoner in France, or the Roman curia. Cardinal Borbón protested at this lay 'intervention' in ecclesiastical matters: the juntas' sovereignty, in his view, was limited and temporary and did not extend to 'regalist' sway over the Church. Undaunted, the junta even intercepted some of the cardinal's mail.

The Suprema's major grievance with the Church came, however, over the most material of matters: gold, jewels and silver plate – ecclesiastical treasure. Despite its great institutional wealth, the Church, which thanks to some of its prelates had contributed handsomely after the uprising, now barely gave anything to the cause it was supposed to call its own. The prelates of Valencia and Cuenca, the former with prewar revenues of close on two million reales a year and the latter with but one quarter of this amount, were exceptions. But the archbishop of Granada categorically refused to contribute more than the four hundred thousand reales he had already given when the Suprema called on him to provide for the maintenance of troops from his diocese serving in Cataluña 'in order to help them secure Barcelona's surrender'. He said that his alms kept alive 'the poor of all classes, many of them honourable families, in a country whose poverty makes it the Galicia of Andalucía'.[28] Charity at home was evidently more important than a distant war.

One reason, no doubt, for the decline in the prelates' war contributions was that patriot bishops who had fled their dioceses no longer controlled their revenues or had seen them expropriated by the Bonapartist regime; another that clerical revenues had in many cases dropped very considerably because of the widespread resistance to paying tithes or their expropriation by local authorities to pay for exactions levied on villages by the French military. In order to identify the local landed wealthy, the French made a practice on entering an unknown village of immediately seizing the tithe books. To defend themselves and their villages, the wealthy could offer payment collected from the community's tithes instead of seeing their own resources plundered.

But the major reason for the church's refusal to contribute its great wealth in treasure – silver plate in particular – lay elsewhere. Its patriotism did not run to trust in the Suprema: neither its organization of the war nor its promises of refunding the silver after the war were credible. Moreover, if the conflict went the wrong way, it was certain that the Bonapartist regime would not pay back the valuables the clergy had contributed to the struggle against it. Church treasure was better kept by those whose duty it was to look after it.

Thus the popular sacrifices called for in the name of religion were not reciprocated by the Church in the one area where its contribution would have weighed heavily in the patriots' favour. Enormous amounts of treasure remained locked away or hidden not only in the great churches and monasteries, but scattered over parishes throughout the land. The Suprema's efforts to unlock this fortune to pay for the war were of no avail.

In its first appeal, on April 4, 1809, the Junta called on the Church to hand in all treasure not strictly required for religious services 'for the just and religious objective of avoiding or diminishing the risk of its being stolen by the French troops in their sacrilegious atrocities'. The treasure would be considered part of the national debt and repaid as soon as the 'present critical circumstances come to an end'.[29] Clerics were not deceived: the call was in fact a way of obliging the Church to pay a large part of the war effort. While some prelates sent their cathedral treasure for safe keeping to provinces less exposed to immediate attack, they notably did not hand it over to the Junta. Cuenca, which had suffered a French sacking at the beginning of the war, was an exception; so, too, was Salamanca province which despatched over two thousand kilos of church silver to Sevilla.*[30]

In general, however, so little notice was taken of the Suprema's appeal, that it was obliged to repeat its demand, expressing its 'grief' at the Church's refusal to heed its previous order. The outcome was no more favourable, for in December

---

* Even during the siege of Gerona, the cathedral chapter was initially more than reluctant to hand in silver not required for religious services to coin money to pay the troops. Apart from sacred vessels, the chapter alleged, there was 'little cathedral silver and what there is is of little weight'. Under pressure from the local junta it surrendered two of the major altar's candle sticks and two of ten ceremonial staves. Finally, in the increasingly critical situation, the chapter caved in and turned over two thousand and seventy ounces of silver. (*Libro de resoluciones capitulares de 1807 a 1812*, entry for June 26, 1809, in Marqués Planagumá, 1959, Gerona, p. 341.) Cathedral chapters were generally more tight-fisted than bishops. For example, the bishop of Sigüenza, who had fled to the patriot zone, offered to fund more than four thousand men from the nearly six hundred villages and townships of his diocese, each place selecting one man out of ten to become a guerrilla. He would be their commander-in-chief. There is no evidence, however, that anything came of this. The bishop of Cuenca also offered financial aid to the resistance. (AHN, *Estado*, Legajo 16/2¹/29 & ibidem 21,25 & 27; letters of June 1809 to Antonio Colmenares, special Suprema commissioner for Soria, Guadalajara, Molina and Aragón.)

1809 the Junta again issued an order for treasure to be handed in as part of new war measures.[31]

In Cataluña, similar demands by the provincial junta also had little effect. But the abbot of the famous monastery of Montserrat informed the Suprema that he had 'certainly contributed more [funds] than anyone' to the Catalan military effort, handing over monastery treasure, while maintaining in silence the amount, 'in order to avoid invidious comparisons, excuses and other taxpayers' speculations'. During the rising, the monastery had aided the 'thirty or more' villages over which it exercised señorial lordship, and continued to support their forces in proportion to the rents it received from each.

> Counting this and ordinary and extraordinary war contributions, and the amounts which the licentious liberty, the arbitrariness of renters and their dependents retained and still retain, the Monastery has left not one-third of the rents which it received in ordinary times, and which were never as high as vulgar foolishness, exaggerated devotion or personal distemper claimed.[32]

Shortly after his report, the abbot engaged in a serious struggle with the provincial junta in defence of the monastery's ecclesiastical and señorial rights. The neighbouring township of Monistrol, confronted without prior notice of their arrival, had had to victual three thousand soldiers and sometents on their way to the relief of Gerona; to do so the town hall had laid hands on wine and other foodstuffs due in tithes or rent to the monks, and had allowed doors of the monastery's archives in the township to be torn down. Other places had also seized agricultural produce due to the monastery. Monistrol scathingly rejected the monastery's protest and appealed to the provincial junta which supported it publicly.

These illegalities, thundered the abbot, had 'very grave and detrimental consequences' for ecclesiastical property and señorial rights:

> especially now when the common people flatter themselves on their desired freedom from paying tithes and from the clergy's just ascendancy . . . Heaven, it is to be feared, will not bless the civil authorities' efforts in the just common cause if they do not . . . literally comply with indispensable canonical law . . .[33]

The abbot's claim of his outstanding contribution to the Catalan war effort may have been true; but his invocation of divine threat, his evident concern to conceal the monastery's real wealth from its señorial subjects' suspicious eyes, and his outraged attempt to bring the 'licentious' villagers to heel, illustrated the lengths to which the higher clergy defended itself during the war, especially in Cataluña where a 'war' against feudal rights was being simultaneously waged within the wider Napoleonic struggle.

The bulk of Church treasure remained where it was – in town and village churches, jealously guarded by local clerics. Once, but then only briefly, the Suprema took direct action, sending a judge and a canon to La Mancha to secure Church silver which on their last incursion the imperial forces had itemized but left in place. In their brief excursion to fifteen townships, the Suprema commissioners netted over one thousand pounds of silver in weight – an average of sixty-six pounds per township – which they carted back for the Suprema's use.[34] Had such expedient action been used throughout the patriot zone, the treasury's difficulties would have been lessened. But intent on keeping the patriotic alliance together, the Suprema could not – or would not – take drastic measures against ecclesiastical or private property.

EPISODES: RESISTANCE: A CATALAN PARISH PRIEST

Sixty-six-year-old Pere Solanllonch had served uninterruptedly as Pierola's priest since the age of thirty. The village of about five hundred inhabitants lay just south of the Bruch pass where the imperial column had met its first Catalan defeat at the hands of armed civilians and military. It was sufficiently off the beaten track, however, for many neighbouring village families to seek refuge there. Nonetheless, on one of the occasions when the Napoleonic troops occupied Igualada, the nearest township, they spread through the neighbouring countryside 'robbing and sacking without pity'. The priest wrote notes of the events in different parish records, depending on the clerical function he had just performed: baptismal, confirmation and burial records, church accounts and tithe books all served at one time or another.

On July 31 imperial soldiers descended for the first time on the village.

> They came with such fury and cunning that as I fled from my house, a French cavalryman on a white horse and another on foot with drawn sabre saw me. 'There's the priest . . . Kill him! Kill him!' I heard the foot soldier shout. By the skin of my teeth I managed to escape.[35]

His church and rectory sacked, for forty nights of the village's three months' trials and tribulations, Solanllonch noted, he slept in a hut on the edge of his lands to escape danger. But he never abandoned his parish or parishioners throughout the whole time, escaping yet once more with his life.

> Vigilance day and night had to be extreme in order to escape such an enemy's cruelty. We posted a few lads up in the sierra de las Rauredas . . . to raise a white sheet as a flag, and when the French tried to come down, they fired three musket shots . . . That was the signal for all to flee their homes. Almost every day the enemy made as though to descend on us. What frights, what escapes, what losses! This torment and affliction continued from the day of St James [July 25] to October 10, 1811, on which day the French retired to Barcelona with their spoils . . . Many, many neighbourhood people remained without a change of shirt, without bread to eat or wine to drink. [The soldiers] flung the hogsheads down and smashed them: not even a robber, no, no one would do that. Oh what a bad time of it we had!

Summoned by the French commandant in Igualada to report to receive orders, he paid no heed: 'Let him go to hell,' I said to myself, 'that little ferret can wait for me. What does he think, that at sixty-six years of age I need orders.'

In all, the imperial soldiers made three razzias on the village, each time sacking the Church and rectory 'leaving me as fleeced as a new-shorn sheep'. The soldiery had taken all his food stores. His brother advised him not to go to the rectory after the third raid; but the priest insisted. Tears came to his eyes when he saw the destruction wreaked. 'But courage!' he said to himself, 'he who really trusts in God is never completely downcast.'

EPISODES: THE EX-FRIAR AND NAPOLEONIC SECRET AGENT

Less edifying was a former friar's garrotted corpse on public display in Sevilla's plaza de San Francisco on the early morning of April 15, 1809. Round his neck a sign informed the curious that he had been executed for forging papers in Fernando VII's name. Luis Gutiérrez's eventful, thirty-nine-year-old life had come to an end at the executioner's hands. Twenty years earlier he had fled his order and the Inquisition for revolutionary France, settling just across the Spanish border in Bayonne, a convenient town for a born intriguer to exercise his literary talents against his country's civil and religious authorities. His first coup was to write a vicious attack on the Spanish political system and the Inquisition, and then to engineer the Spanish government's purchase of the manuscript in order to avoid its publication in France and its certain clandestine distribution subsequently in Spain. Later he founded and became the chief editor of the *Gaceta de Bayona* which was a stalwart Spanish organ of French propaganda, especially during the Bayonne constitutional assembly of 1808, which brought Gutiérrez his golden opportunity: at the French government's behest, he forged letters from the imprisoned Fernando and his brother Carlos addressed to the Mexican viceroy, informing him that it was the king's wish that a regency in his name be created in the colony which would be saved for his throne should Napoleon succeed in imposing his brother's rule on Spain. To prosper, this plot needed British acquiesence and assistance. By August 1808, Gutiérrez, under the pseudonym of the baron de Agra, was in London, with a small retinue in attendance, claiming to have foiled French vigilance and escaped in a British man-of-war. He had several meetings with George Canning, foreign secretary, who agreed to forward the documents to the viceroy and support the plan; surprisingly for such an acute mind, Canning appeared to have fallen totally for the plot which had been very carefully designed to attract British interest. Fearing revolutionary anarchy above all, and desiring a small, effective government, Canning had pushed for a regency in Spain; British support for a similar governing body in Mexico would hinder Napoleon's claims to Spain's South American empire and would, it could be supposed, bring British trade similar rewards to those granted in Brazil by a grateful Portuguese royal family which had been taken to safety there in a British warship. However, at the time it was hatched, the plot had quite other objectives for Napoleon: if successful, it would undermine the metropolitan juntas' self-assumed authority to act in Fernando's name and deal organized Spanish resistance a serious blow. A regency in Mexico could claim to be the only body authorized by the king, making the formation of a patriotic central government highly problematic. At this time, Napoleon was also planning to 'emancipate' Spain's empire to keep it as free as possible of British influence. A regency, therefore, was the future government already in place.

However great – or feigned – his trust in 'Agra', Canning could not be seen to act in Mexico without the newly created Suprema's knowledge and insisted that Agra return to Spain to inform the Junta of Fernando's written wish. If he went, it would be to his doom, the ex-friar knew. He boarded a British ship bound for La Coruña at Portsmouth and disembarked at Plymouth; but two of his retinue remained on board and were arrested when they reached Spain without passports. It was not long before the patriot authorities had discovered who they were dealing with.

Gutiérrez–Agra got wind of the arrests before Canning and escaped from Britain on board a ship bound for Lisbon. But his pursuers were by now more alert than he. Placed under patriot surveillance from the moment he reached Portugal, he and his 'secretary' were issued, as a blind, with Suprema passports to Sevilla; the intention was to see whether he would lead his observers to other French agents. Instead, the two men went north in a vain attempt to take refuge in Soult's army which had invaded Portugal from Galicia. They were arrested before they could reach the imperial invaders, incarcerated in a Lisbon prison and from there taken by coach to Sevilla where they were handed over to the tribunal of public safety, the Suprema's special court to investigate and try suspected French sympathizers. Except for his break with the Church, Gutiérrez did not deny his past, alleging in self-defence that all his actions had been undertaken to avenge himself on the French. It did him no good: he was a man condemned to death from the moment of his arrest in Portugal. Four days after his execution, his secretary met the same fate.

While alive a bit player in the great events of his time, Gutiérrez's posthumous fate was considerably grander. Before the war, he had published anonymously in France a violently anti-clerical novel, which circulated secretly and to such great success in Spain that it ran to three editions in as many years. But after his death, and still anonymously, a further twenty Spanish editions, translations into French, German and Portuguese, stage adaptations and romantic ballads were published up to the 1850s. Gutiérrez became a nineteenth-century best-selling author. His novel, which concerned an innocent young girl's misadventures at the hands of a lecherous archbishop of Sevilla and of Inquisitorial fanaticism, was a deep-felt plea for religious tolerance.*

DIVINE WONDERS

Prodigious phenomena contributed to keeping alive a spirit of Providence's intervention on the patriot side. A Valencian farmer's eighteen-year-old son, who, alongside his work in the fields, had demonstrated a vocation for the priesthood and had taken his first vows in the Franciscan order, was conscripted at the beginning of the war and killed in battle almost immediately during the French advance on Valencia. Salvador Torrent's corpse lay high up on the wooded heights of the Cabrillas pass, some locals reported to his smallholding parents in Chirivella, a village close to the provincial capital. Nearly four months after the battle, they set out to find his remains, passing in horror the skeletons of other corpses consumed by beasts and birds of prey and the summer's heat. To their astonishment, they found their son's body lying incorrupt on the ground in the form of a cross, its head on its right shoulder, its arms outstretched, one foot over the other, naked but for the cord of the Franciscan order. They carried him down on their shoulders and brought him home where for three days his corpse was displayed to a numerous public of all stations of life before being buried in his order's habit.

> The young man's well-known morality and the prodigy of his corpse . . . offer to the Patria's glorious defenders an example worthy of imitation and a laurel leaf to the Religion [which] makes a man forget dangers and be prepared to risk his life for his Country . . .[36]

*

Despite prelates' exhortations of penitence, the population at large – if a number of parish priests can be believed – were not in a particularly penitent mood. Many churchmen did not believe that the lower orders or even the middling classes were responding to the theological proposition that Napoleon was God's scourge to return Spaniards to the Catholic devotion inherent to the nation's customs. Clerical complaints about the lack of respect for religion, immorality, and the breakdown of Catholic custom began early in the war, and increased as the 'ungodly' French dominated ever larger areas of Spain. In 1809 one priest wrote to the Junta Suprema:

> Couples living publicly in sin without the rites of marriage have become common in a great number of villages, and they include individuals of good standing of all classes

---

* The novel is titled *Cornelia Bororquia o la víctima de la Inquisición*; two new editions have been published in Spain since 1987. (See Gérard Dufour, 'Andanzas y muerte de Luis Gutiérrez', *Historia 16*, no. 228, pp. 33–39; English translations of the forged Fernando VII documents and Canning–Agra correspondence in PRO *FO* 185/15 *General* 1808, and the denouement in PRO *FO* 72/64/288–289; on Gutiérrez's capture, transferral to and trial by the Tribunal of Public Safety in Sevilla, AHN, *Estado*, Legajo 29G/204³⁻¹⁰.)

and states. Blaspheming and other vices are increasing scandalously. Women have forgotten their modesty, and their extravagant, indecorous dress has been the downfall of many. These women should be severely punished . . .*[37]

Another cleric observed in the same year that

We cannot win the war unless God delivers up the enemy into our hands. How can a soldier who is in mortal sin have the courage to fight when he knows that a bullet may send him straight to hell? . . . And if they win a victory many generals barely attribute it to God, or to the Virgin's intercession, or to the rest of the saints, but to natural forces like their soldiers' bravery, enthusiasm and daring, treating them as though they were invincible which only God can be.[38]

In the French-dominated zones, parish priests complained in the later years of the war that the villagers who had made their peace with the occupiers had adopted their habits. Some French soldiers entered a church with modesty and devotion,

but the majority blasphemed against God and the Virgin, against all the saints without the least shame; the vileness with which they speak of divine providence; the temerity with which they laugh about immortality and hell, the irony with which they condemn the gospels, their satires against Christian virtue and morality . . . and in short the total breakdown of our customs.[39]

The youth in particular, especially in the towns, were reported as being the most affected by the change, 'senselessly imitating the lascivious distractions previously unknown among us, and the sensuality of our barbarous oppressors'.[40]

One parish priest, of the village of Lozoya, in the sierra de Guadarrama, north of Madrid, blamed not only the French but the example set by the guerrillas who found refuge there. The latter's behaviour was 'free and unbridled', the former's 'irreligious and tyrannical'; and soon the effects of both were felt. The local youth began to steal cattle and other livestock, and to live hidden in bands, robbing unwary travellers. The parish priest decided there was no option but to flee his parish: he had already been threatened with a dagger during confession.

The village was living in a state of promiscuity. Nobody obeyed the religious precepts. Children's education was totally ignored. Many parents could not be obliged to send their children to school or to catechism classes. Couples came to me to get married

* Many marriages were endogamous, and when relatives were involved, required papal dispensation. But, having been sequestered by Napoleon, the Pope was no longer able to provide this. The Bonaparte regime in Spain solved the problem by giving bishops the right to issue dispensations, but the monarchist Church hierarchy on the patriot side refused such a solution, leaving fiancés with only two options: to delay their marriage until the Pope was restored to the Holy See or to live together in the hope of marrying one day.

without ever having been to confession; worse yet, many on their death beds were without knowledge of the sacraments that would save their souls. It was impossible to make or oblige many parents to fulfil their religious duties. Their lives reached a state of demoralization in which custom and tradition were quite ignored.[41]

RELIGIOUS OBSERVANCE

These complaints all stemmed from the clergy, the majority of whom were parish priests of the villages and townships where they were serving. Though there was no reason to suspect that they did not tell the truth as they saw it, their focus on events was obviously unilateral. Measured by whether one of the Church's proscriptions – the Lent commandment of sexual abstinence – was observed to a greater or lesser degree during the war provided more objective evidence that their complaints were in general unfounded, at least among couples if not village youth.*

Pre-war, despite the proscription, during the forty-six days of Lent from Ash Wednesday to Easter Saturday inclusive, sexual abstinence was not particularly marked. Depending on region, Lent conceptions constituted on average between ten and fourteen percent of annual conceptions, Extremadura representing the highest and Castilla la Nueva the lowest. Measured by this yardstick, the wartime averages in a total of seven regions showed very small changes despite the increased emphasis from 1809 of the Church's summons to the population to mend their religious ways in order to win the war. As could be expected, the averages also sometimes reflected the regions' population growth or loss as was the case in the disastrous year of 1809 when Lent conceptions dropped in line with the latter in all seven regions.†

Lent wartime averages did, however, show certain tendencies compared to pre-war. In six of the regions they ran counter to or exceeded population growth, rising in Castilla la Nueva, Extremadura, the Basque country and Valencia and declining in south-western Andalucía and Castilla la Vieja. In other words by this measure wartime religious observance was higher in the two latter regions than in the other four. Understandably: Castilla la Vieja was historically the heartland of Catholic Spain, and southwestern Andalucía had been the centre of patriot resistance for over a year (1809–1810).

In the remaining regions the war's dislocations and the breakdown of absolutism's civil and clerical controls over the people evidently fostered a

---

* The two usual ways of assessing religiosity, the number of Easter communicants, and diocesan visitors' reports on parish priests, were inapplicable during the war since lists of the first were not often kept and visitors no longer made their pre-war tours of inspection on the bishops' behalf. In the sense used here conceptions were baptized and recorded births backdated nine months. As this ignored abortions, stillbirths and the newborn who died in the usual forty-eight hours before baptism, the figures understate reality.
† Bearing in mind that slow social changes are best measured by the century rather that by comparatively short periods like the war, the minute percentage movements of religiosity during the conflict may in fact be no more than chance statistical results, a possibility confirmed by computer tests to determine their level of randomness. See Appendix 3, Popular Social Change and Table 3.5.

slight decrease in religiosity. But the overall averages obscured certain moments of relative declines which, in the historical context, were noteworthy. Between 1810 and 1812, in both Castillas and Andalucía Lent conceptions rose to wartime highs. In these three years, the French extended their occupation; by early 1812, they dominated – though they could never entirely control – the largest extent of Spain they were to hold. The popular perception that, despite the ongoing guerrilla struggle, they were there to stay with the consequent loss of the Church's previous power, could well have accounted for the downturn. Change was inevitable and the Church could not prevent it.

Reinforcing this perception, another important event took place during these years. A reforming Spanish regime began to emerge in Cádiz where the patriots under French siege held a Constituent Assembly which culminated in the proclamation of a new constitution late in Lent, 1812.* But the event had long been foreseen. Opposed to absolutism, the constitution appeared to many, especially the absolutist clergy, as a check on the Church's former power.

In 1812 and 1813, in one of Spain's most devout regions, the Basque country, Lent conceptions soared while population growth dropped.† Until then, as in the pre-war, Basques had observed the proscription with a certain rigour. What had changed? In the first instance the war itself. From early 1812, precisely at the height of their apparent control, the French occupation was shown to be vulnerable: known to all, Napoleon was withdrawing troops for his Russian campaign; guerrilla activity rose to its maximum in neighbouring Navarra and the Basque country itself, and a fortnight before Lent Wellington captured the border fortress town of Ciudad Rodrigo, the first step of his latest campaign in the Spanish interior. Perceptibly the war was taking a new turn. It was now possible even to imagine victory in which, under a new constitution, the Old Order and its dominant Church would have no place . . . By the following year the war was plainly about to end in an allied victory: barely a fortnight into Lent, Josef Bonaparte evacuated Madrid never to return. A triumphant peace would ensure that the patriot constitution was put into effect, undermining the clerical ultras and their Castilian centralism which the Basques deplored.

In this view, popular wartime religiosity depended rather largely on the fortunes of the war at different moments and visions of what the future might hold. On external events, in other words, rather than on internalized religious sentiment, in keeping with a past where, in much of Spain, a ceremonial Church pervaded the exterior world without undue concern for the inner spiritual being.

*

* See Chapters 16 and 18.
† The two-year average rose by 1.8% above the wartime average. The Basque Church was in several important ways different to that of Castilla. It was neither a big landowner nor a señorial presence and was much closer to the small farmers, from among whom most of its clergy stemmed. It also placed more emphasis on religious devoutness than on the baroque rituals of much of the rest of Spain.

The postwar Inquisition's tribunals added another dimension to the question of wartime religiosity since they explored religious 'subversion' during the conflict. One accusation in particular predominated both before, during and after the war. Called 'propositions' it covered a multitude of sins: heretical, erroneous or scandalous utterances, for instance, that transgressed religious dogma by, to cite one example, declaring that ordinary fornication was not a sin. In 1815, ten Inquisition tribunals throughout the country received denunciations of persons accused of propositions. These had more than doubled over the pre-war number.* This could well have been because 'verbal heresy' was the easiest accusation to make and the hardest to disprove. But their regional distribution gave the lie to the Spanish clerical assertion that the French occupation had been solely responsible for the growth of secularization.

Most strikingly it was precisely in those regions which the French had not occupied – Galicia and Murcia – or occupied only for a relatively short time like Andalucía that headed the list of the highest number of propositions. In Sevilla, for example, they rose six-fold. But those regions which had been occupied the longest or for nearly the whole war varied little from their pre-war levels. The exception was Cataluña where the number rose by nearly two-thirds: the severity of the social conflict which was fought there under cover of the anti-Napoleonic struggle was no doubt responsible; and the postwar desire for revenge on the part of the well-to-do and ultra clergy was sufficient cause for the increase of accusations.

The disparities between unoccupied and occupied zones could be interpreted in a number of ways: on the one hand, those who had suffered the French occupation for a long period would be little inclined to denounce the religious 'crimes' of persons who had been known patriots, while notorious collaborators with the Bonapartist regime had either fled or been killed. Intimately aware of the difficulties of the times, the majority who had not actively participated on one side or the other provided little scope for potential accusers who would fear that the tables could be easily turned on them. In the unoccupied or briefly occupied zones, there were fewer restraints. The great number of accusations compared to pre-war – though the war and postwar years extended over a greater time span – could be explained by the fact that people had no excuse for their sacrilegious verbal behaviour.† Added to which was an unknown factor: many of the denunciations, it could be imagined, corresponded to personal wartime vendettas which were pursued in the repressive post-war climate.

* The fact that they were recorded by the tribunals did not mean that the accused had been found guilty (a few, indeed, had been absolved) or that their cases, which went back to the war, had been completed.
† See also Appendix 3, Table 3.3.

Origins of the Guerrilla

One of the first recorded guerrilla leaders was a self-confessed illiterate, Diego López Membrilla, whom his companions elected to their command after the people had risen in several townships of La Mancha and fought against Dupont's rearguard in 1808 on its march to Andalucía. In a proclamation, he said that the ordinary people 'maintained a good number of wealthy men' with their dues and rents on the lands belonging to the locally dominant Calatrava military–religious order.

> But on this occasion little good did it do you to protect your cause. These (rich) men did nothing to help you, did not place themselves on your side and raise an army of your courageous brothers . . . [In future] they shall contribute with their wealth to protect you so that you may conclude the great enterprise that you have undertaken. (Itinerant headquarters on the Guadiana [river], June 27, 1808, by order of señor Diego Lopez Membrilla, who does not know how to write.)[1]

Romantic myth had it that the guerrilla (or 'small war') – like the anti-Napoleonic rising – was the major popular response to Napoleon's invasion of Spain. And in Membrilla's case with the added spice of social criticism. There can be no doubt that the lower orders played a significant part in the rising and guerrilla; but in neither case were they the exclusive protagonists. The educated elite played an important role in both. One of the earliest partisan leaders, for example, was a Basque-born friar who formed his party in Castilla la Vieja very shortly after the outbreak of the war. Juan Mendieta (who fought under the *nom de guerre* of 'El Capuchino', in honour of his religious order) staged a particularly spectacular coup in capturing General Franceschi, Napoleon's brilliant light cavalry commander, in June 1809. Franceschi was travelling by coach with dispatches from Marshal Soult to King Josef in Madrid. As he passed through Zamora, where Mendieta's friary was situated, the friar's band held up the coach and, after a struggle, seized the general. A couple of months later the friar took prisoner at no great distance from Valladolid a French detachment commanded by an aide-de-camp of General Kellerman, military governor of the Castilian capital. Irregular warfare had an age-long history; the guerrilla was of a more recent vintage, with its own particular historical causes.[2] From the mid-eighteenth century, the regular and increasingly professionalized armies on which absolutism based its power paid much greater attention than in the past to the principle of mobility. Small military groups reconnoitred and probed the enemy's lines, seizing prisoners to gain information on their opponents' strength, movements, food supplies and battle plans. When fighting in their homelands, local villagers acted as guides and informants. This type of war, named by the French 'la petite guerre', or 'small war', was adopted as a standard military strategy of the Old Regime's armies and became 'as common as pitched battles or sieges'.[3] Translated into Spanish, a great number of treatises on the subject, especially French, used in their titles or translations the literal Spanish equivalent of 'small war' – 'guerrilla'. This military connotation was the Spanish word's principal meaning at the outbreak of the Napoleonic war.

Only one further step was necessary: the expansion of the 'little (military) war' to a civilian strategy of armed resistance which recalled the age-long tradition of irregular warfare. Although it was often believed that, because of its Spanish name, the guerrilla as a civilian phenomenon was a Spanish innovation arising out of the Napoleonic conflict, there were recent forerunners in French anti-revolutionary movements: the Vendée and Chouannerie of 1793–1801; the Calabrian insurrection of 1799, and indeed the Spanish war against the French Convention (1793–1795). During the latter conflict, it was villagers in south-western France who took to irregular combat when their homes and lands were threatened by Spanish regular troops. In French revolutionary times, when their own armies failed them, or they had none, a population determined to resist had little other option than to fight with the only means to hand: a 'small war'. What distinguished the Spanish guerrilla in the Peninsular War was thus not its originality but its *extent*. It was the first time that the guerrilla became a nationwide form of resistance and a sanctified right of self-defence.

PRECONDITIONS OF SPAIN'S GUERRILLA WARFARE

Sanctified or not, self-defence had for long been a self-assumed right under the Old Regime. In the difficult times of the late eighteenth century, villagers had to defend themselves, their homes, crops and livestock from a proliferation of bandits, smugglers, highwaymen, robbers and thieves. Many locals were skilled in the use of firearms as a result. In coastal and border areas, armed smugglers, often in large bands, were prepared to fight it out with excise men. Volunteer civilian forces raised by the government tried to put them down. The result of this strife was that a great number of township and village inhabitants had experience of fighting in small, self-organized bands; or in officially approved militia-style 'regiments', and this practice they could put to good use in the anti-Napoleonic struggle.

Self-defence was one precondition for armed popular resistance. Two others were the military's state at the outset of war and the question of land 'ownership'.

The Spanish Military

The army's humiliation during the War of the Convention in which, after initial success, it was defeated by the French revolutionaries, brought on an identity crisis among officers who, on the one hand, admired the French army with which some had trained and alongside which others had fought as allies, while, on the other hand, they intensely hated the revolutionary ideals that informed the French army. Their accepted view of the world had been overturned: yesterday's allies, the French, were today's enemy, and the former enemy (Britain) now an ally.[4] The same happened in 1808. In their disoriented state it was hardly surprising that in general the Spanish officer corps went through the Napoleonic war 'without being able to understand or support either the new strategy of mass warfare or the tactics of guerrilla war. They had been trained for very different suppositions than those it was their lot to live through.'[5]

The patriots' unexpected victory in open battle over General Dupont at Bailén, in the summer of 1808, almost entirely achieved by pre-war Spanish regulars and mercenaries, seemed to make thoughts of irregular warfare unnecessary. In the autumn and winter of 1808, the situation was reversed: the series of crushing patriot defeats in pitched battles during Napoleon's campaign again made urgent the question of how to fight the war. The troops' lack of trust in their commanders, which was reciprocated by their officers, did not encourage the 'dispersed' to return to their regiments. The guerrilla offered a solution, not as a new military strategy but as an alternative to being thrown into pitched battle and almost certain defeat, and to the general hardships of military life.

Land Ownership

In certain regions of Spain, the villagers enjoyed property rights or the virtual right of property over the use of the land. The long sweep of smallholders and 'use-owners' from Galicia along the Cantabrian coast, dipping into parts of Castilla la Vieja, and continuing to the Basque country, then ran inland to northern Navarra and, passing through Aragón, reached its culmination in Cataluña.*

It was in these regions that the greatest guerrilla resistance arose. They were also rugged frontier areas – by sea or land – with villagers used to defending themselves – either as law-abiding subjects or outlaw-smugglers and bandits – with, above all, 'their' land and crops to defend. The socio-geographical difference of border and hinterlands explained in large part why irregular warfare came to be concentrated mainly on Spain's periphery while the major

* At the turn of the century, of the 75% of the active population engaged in land work, nearly half were renters and one-fifth smallholders and 'use-owners', although many of them were little more than subsistence farmers. In Galicia, Vizcaya, Navarra, Aragón and Cataluña about half of the land-working population owned or held the 'use-ownership' of their plots. Outside these regions the proportion dropped to between 10 and 25%. (Census of 1797.)

regular army battles were fought on the plains of central Spain.* It also explained why the majority of the great guerrilla forces all originated north of a line drawn along the Duero river.

In Galicia and Cataluña,† the overwhelming majority – over ninety percent in Galicia – of those engaged in irregular warfare came from their respective regions and did not basically move out of their territories; and once the Galicians had accomplished their aim of forcing the French to withdraw, most of them returned home to their former occupations. This illustrated the difference between popular territorial liberation struggles in these two regions and the guerrilla: irregular warfare was not therefore the guerrilla's exclusively differentiating definition.

HIGHWAYMEN OR PATRIOT GUERRILLAS?

Starting early in 1808, villagers ambushed imperial couriers and aides-de-camp on their solitary missions across the country, seized their horses and saddle-bags, took their lives or made them prisoner, and turned in their booty to a patriot authority in the hope of a handsome reward: an ounce of gold, for example, which a Castilian shepherd received from the Ciudad Rodrigo junta for killing a courier and bringing in his horse and correspondence. The line between highwayman-bandit and patriot guerrilla fighter was pretty thin at the start; and for some it remained so until the end.

The first recorded interception of Bonapartist mail took place in February, 1808,‡ two months before Juan Martín, a smallholder from Fuentecén, a small village on the Duero in Burgos province, and a former corporal in the Convention War, began his sorties, accompanied by two companions, to capture French couriers on the Burgos–Madrid road, a practice which led to him eventually becoming the guerrilla leader best known to patriots and Bonapartists alike, and in command of several thousand men. El Empecinado, as he was always known,§ soon gathered a group of a dozen men, which included his three brothers. On horseback – he captured a great number of horses in an operation in Segovia province to provide for his group – he and his men roamed over Castilla la Vieja, cooperating with the armies when they could: he was at the early battles – and bloody defeats – in his region and in Salamanca when Sir John Moore was waiting there in the autumn, unsure whether to advance or retreat.¶ In the meanwhile he

---

* The Andalucian guerrilla, after the region's occupation in 1810, began in the same sort of geo-social conditions as in the north: mountainous border terrains in Ronda and Málaga, known for their smuggling activities, and the Alpujarras in Granada, though later it extended widely through the region. La Mancha produced many groups, but they never matched the eventual size of some of those in the north.

† In its region's defence, Cataluña developed several important guerrilla bands; but they operated within the overall concept of territorial defence.

‡ See mail interceptions, Chapter 17, pp. 408–10.

§ Martín was born in Castrillo de Duero through which flowed a stream blackened by the local mud or 'pecino' as it was called. All the township's inhabitants therefore shared this nickname in the neighbourhood, which has come in Spanish to mean 'determined', 'stubborn'.

¶ He handed over to Moore French correspondence he had captured and received eighteen thousand reales in return, which he used to buy more horses for his party.

attacked the French garrison of Roa, a township in his home territory – together with another guerrilla leader destined to become famous: the priest Jerónimo Merino – but they were put to flight. Shortly thereafter he captured a treasure trove of French booty. More men joined his party: by December his band numbered thirty. He returned to his home territory and ambushed forty dragoons on a food-gathering expedition: they were all killed. A small company of gendarmerie was his next target: he took them prisoners and sent them to Valencia. He had learned a lesson from the fate of his first French prisoners. He had sent them under the guard of half his party to ensure their safe arrival at the nearest small town; there they were murdered by the inhabitants, the guard presumably doing little to protect them.[6] Vengeance was the original password of popular resistance. The rules of war were for those whose job it was to make conventional war.

About one in six of all the parties recorded during the war were founded in 1808 in various parts of the country. All of them began as small local groups of only a few individuals gathered around a leader to whom, like a clan chieftain, they owed loyalty and respect. The party's fate and ultimate growth – or disintegration and disappearance – depended almost entirely on the chief's success in the field, the capture of booty, arms and – especially – horses.

LEGITIMATION

While they wished to encourage popular resistance, the authorities also feared it, lest the people in arms subvert the social order from below. In consequence, one of the Suprema's first decrees on reaching Sevilla after its flight before Napoleon's 1808 offensive attempted to regulate the guerrilla groups which had begun to form.* But in the chaotic condition of the moment the decree remained unknown in the greater part of the patriot zone.

In the following months, the number of civilian combatants – and the danger of their being shot out of hand by the imperial forces as armed bandits – had so obviously increased that the notion of 'legalizing' the guerrillas as recognized, albeit non-uniformed, militiamen found favour in the Suprema. Under a new decree they were to become 'land privateers' on the same legal lines as those which applied to maritime privateers.† The decree of April 17, 1809, was justified because

> using the lowest and vilest forms of guile . . . Napoleon took over our principal fortresses and imprisoned our king. Is it not evident that civilians must unite to combat these hosts? . . . Force must be repelled by force, and the arms used must be the same . . .[7]

This decree 'militarized' the guerrillas only as a pretext to protect them. It did not suggest new measures for putting them more firmly under military or civilian

* See Chapter 9, p. 220.
† These required a royal or governmental charter; without one they would be considered pirates and be automatically condemned to death.

political control. The Suprema sent a paper to French army commanders to inform them of the 'just and powerful causes' for engaging in 'land-privateering'. It was hard to imagine that a nation which only twenty years earlier had

> proclaimed with the greatest energy the Rights of Man and defended with no less enthusiasm the independence of nations, should have degenerated in so short a time to the extreme of attacking and attempting to destroy those principles which are the basis of civil society and have been recognized and canonized by all cultivated nations and by the philosophers of all centuries. (Junta Suprema, Sevilla, May 1809)

The regency, which in 1810 succeeded the Junta Suprema as patriot Spain's government, adopted a series of regulations in 1812 to bring under even more direct military supervision the growing guerrilla strength, having already incorporated most of the 'great' parties – in numbers and leadership – into the regular army.[8]

If there was any tradition of Spanish civilians taking up arms and fighting their own war in self-defence it could perhaps be said to have come from the Catalan sometent, the volunteer village 'home guard' who were called out to defend their locality and had inevitably to resort to irregular warfare. But it is unlikely that their example was well known to the people outside of Cataluña. For example, the originator of the Suprema's policy of legalizing partisans as officially authorized combatants under the invention of 'privateering by land', Vicente Alcalá Galiano, the royal treasurer, did not appeal to some historic Spanish (or Catalan) tradition; he wrote that the idea had come to him from the Cossacks on the Vistula and Napoleon's maritime privateering to enforce the Continental blockade.[9] Nor did Alcalá Galiano, or his predecessor who drafted the Junta's first regulations on the guerrillas in late December, 1808, use the word *guerrilla* or *guerrillero*. Formations of civilian combatants were called parties or teams ('partidas' or 'cuadrillas') in the first document and exclusively 'cuadrillas' in the second.*

Although guerrilla warfare had certain Spanish preconditions, it was another myth, put about by mainly foreign nineteenth-century writers, that its way of fighting suited an anarchic, individualist Spanish temperament. Rather, the guerrilla corresponded to a number of pressing objective situations: the regular patriot armies' continuing and crushing defeats in open battle, the state of the military, and the will of many conscripts and regulars who had served in the army to continue the struggle in better conditions. This explained why it became a widespread popular response in the Napoleonic war.

GUERRILLA STRATEGY AND TACTICS

In contrast to popular territorial liberation, the guerrillas were distinguished by their constant and continual attacks on the enemy wherever he was to be found,

---

* 'Cuadrilla' was widely used for groups of smugglers or labouring teams in general. It was not until later in the war that the word 'guerrilla' became current.

unbounded by strict territorial considerations. While their origins, recruitment bases and general perspectives were almost always territorially conditioned, their objectives were not – in the immediate at least – to recuperate home territory but to use it to prevent the enemy seizing or moving through it unopposed and without cost. It required an uncentred spatial control, in which the guerrilla passed through and over the land without occupying any part of it. Although such mobility was exceptional, in the two years (1810–1811) of its existence, Miguel Díaz's party, 'Fernando VII's Flying Column', as it called itself, fought actions across the whole of Spain south of Madrid, from close to the Portuguese frontier in the west, to the Valencian–Aragonese borders near the Mediterranean in the east. Made up of about 140 mounted and foot men at its maximum, this was just one of a number of ordinary parties. Starting its actions in the south of La Mancha, it ranged over approximately five hundred kilometres from west to east and three hundred north to south: an area of fifteen hundred square kilometres.[10]

Knowledge of the terrain rather than possession of it was at the heart of success. Spain's rugged and often barren topography took on a new life and significance in this type of war; Colonel Schépeler, the Prussian military attaché in London who fought with the allies, considered it ideal for civilian guerrillas:

> The mountains are harsh and barren, but scaleable for the agile Spanish who find refuge in them. There are immense plains in the interior, scored by valleys, but not so deeply that they cut off one part of the country from another, or offer a regular army points of advantage against the guerrilla. And although the mountains and plains are traversed by innumerable streams . . . they can be crossed at will, as can the large rivers in many places especially in summer. This terrain is truly well disposed for a guerrilla in all senses.*

The guerrilla's self-appointed task was a permanent and incessant 'little war' of erosion, of wearing the enemy down, of keeping his troops constantly alert and in fear of surprise attack. It was continuous warfare over time and space. It went on unremittingly day in and day out, year in and year out: there were no 'campaign seasons' as in the regular armies, with interludes between, no distinction between day and night. Space was a place of forced marches over little known or secret paths. 'I get no rest at all', noted Julián Sánchez uncomplainingly after forty-eight hours of constant movement and actions.[11] The guerrilla fought not for the great victory that would deny the enemy 'their land' but for the small and harassing 'victory' that could be won from the weakest links in enemy columns, their vanguards and rearguards, to capture food supplies, livestock, arms and munitions, horses, carts, looted wealth, high-ranking officer prisoners. The guerrilleros tended to attack only when they outnumbered their immediate foe and stood a good chance of victory: apart

---

* Schépeler contrasted this with 'a terrain too divided into parts' which was unsuitable for a long-lasting guerrilla since the enemy could occupy a few vantage points to hinder and impede it; such a terrain was more suited 'to war carried on by regular army parties'. (Schépeler, 1829, Vol. 1, p. 75, fn. 2.)

from mobility and surprise, they held the initiative on when and where to attack. Almost always short of ammunition, the Navarrese guerrillas, for example, went into combat with only one cartridge. Apart from the lack of ammunition, the time taken to reload a musket would lose the guerrilla the advantage of surprise. This was the reason for the Navarrese Espoz y Mina's tactic of the single volley at the start of the ambush, and thereafter hand-to-hand fighting with edged steel: bayonets, daggers, lances, sharp, steel-pointed iron bars, an occasional captured sword . . . a countryman's style of fighting which cost the enemy, unused to close combat, more casualties than the attackers . . . 'We have to win and win quickly, with few losses', Espoz y Mina explained.[12]

Unlike the territorial liberation struggle, the guerrilla knew better than to try to defend static positions. When the enemy occupied and garrisoned townships and villages, this dispersal of forces achieved one of the guerrillas' aims: the French command was left with fewer men to throw against the main armies or with which to pursue the guerrillas. When the enemy marched on without leaving a garrison, he gained no additional foothold in the countryside. When, caught between these two profitless options, he burned down the villages, more recruits joined the guerrillas. Whatever the enemy did could be turned to the guerrillas' advantage.

The guerrilleros armed and mounted themselves in the first place mainly at the enemy's cost. *Mobility, rapidity, surprise* was their strength in attack, retreat and dispersal. A lion's heart, a fly's stomach, and a hare's feet – this was their self-image. Their speed of flight in different directions was as important as their surprise in attack. For this very reason, considerable numbers of guerrilleros – at least half if not more of the small parties, as the Junta Suprema recommended – were mounted; and the infantry was enjoined to spring onto the horses' haunches in case of need. But horses were hard to come by; and many had only rough-and-ready saddles and wooden stirrups and nags at the best.* El Empecinado made a point of ensuring that his cavalrymen carried a spare set of horseshoes with them.[13] The general practice was that a guerrillero who captured a mount from the enemy or secured one by licit or illicit means kept it and joined the party's 'cavalry'. Although overall the proportion of guerrilla horsemen to foot did not exceed one in six, by 1811 the more than nine thousand mounted guerrillas became the equivalent of Napoleon's light cavalry which the patriot army grievously lacked: apart from their unceasing attritional attacks, the guerrilla was the army's 'eyes', its screen stretched out far into the enemy's rear to gather information on his movements; this, indeed was one of their major functions which even critics of their military usefulness, like Wellington and most of the patriot higher command, came to appreciate.

The guerrillas also needed their own 'eyes'. Some – like Javier Mina in Navarra, the priest Jerónimo Merino fighting around Burgos and Francisco Abad Moreno, 'El Chaleco', in La Mancha – received considerable help from

* Wellington asked the Junta Suprema in September 1809 to buy three hundred mares for the British Army, but turned down all but seventy of the first 196 requisitioned as not being up to the army's standard. Communication from Spanish War Minister, Cornel, December 21, 1809 (AHN, *Estado*, Legajo 39D/179).

spy networks run by patriots in their zones of operation who provided them with information on enemy strength and movements and sometimes 'directed' their operations. The effective guerrilla and its leader's prestige depended on trustworthy intelligence for its success; reliance on hit-and-miss tactics or chance rarely succeeded.

*

In regions like the Basque country which had in recent decades been hard hit by economic setbacks, the 'social' war seemed sometimes to take precedence over the struggle against the French. Here a relatively stable agrarian economy had entered a structural crisis of land shortage and rapid population growth and the rural unemployed had become vagrants, vagabonds and even bandits. Occupied from the initial moments of Spain's invasion, the Basques, like the Navarrese, had not initially risen: with the high number of imperial forces on the ground there was little hope of success; and the Basque elite, concerned mainly with the preservation of their self-governing rights which Napoleon's Bayonne constitution had agreed provisionally to respect, and the dire state of their region, hoped that a temperate response to the French occupation would be more profitable to their interests than a declaration of war. It was thus not until after Bailén that a successful rising finally took place in Bilbao in August 1808. And one of the major reasons that it took place at all was, as elsewhere, the high level of French impositions and exactions.

Small guerrilla bands began to form from late 1808 and early 1809. The latter year and the following two were economically even harsher than the preceding period. Grain prices rose and output fell. Criminality increased, and the incipient guerrillas and bandits grew in numbers. To out-of-work and vagrant youth the former offered, if not a land of milk and honey, then one of food, drink and a weekly wage of twenty reales, as some adolescents testified to the Bonapartist extraordinary criminal tribunal in Bilbao. By the autumn of 1809, guerrilla incursions into villages – especially those of difficult access to the French – were becoming frequent. Six guerrilleros took over the village of Munguía on Epiphany, 1810, cutting off its entrances and mingling with the many inhabitants celebrating the feast day, saying they had come to kill the local magistrate who, along with the rest of the village authorities, rapidly went into hiding. A village landowner and former cavalry officer who witnessed the street scene said that 'never had he seen a more disorderly and unruly group of men, whose drunkeness, their running hither and thither, their shooting of arms and shouted threats not surprisingly frightened many people'.

As a rule, at this stage, between fifteen and thirty armed men, some mounted, others on foot, would seal off the village entrances and take over the main square. They had come, they quickly made it known, to 'deal with' a number of local notables of dubious patriotism. The notables in question hid, fled or tried to temporize; it made little difference because their belongings, money, clothes, arms, private papers and archives, even their beds on occasion, were seized. They could be happy to escape with their lives. Meanwhile, the guerrilleros recruited among the indigent young and could usually count on enlisting a good score of them.

Alongside these chaotic, lawless small groups – 'bold, daring and perverse men, who will do whatever comes into their heads' said a landowner who had been threatened with death by a group – there emerged a number of guerrilla leaders who commanded respect by their discipline, conscious commitment to the anti-Napoleonic struggle, tactical skill and personal bravery. They had no hesitation in shooting spies and traitors, in punishing rogue guerrillas, in pursuing 'an eye for an eye and a tooth for a tooth' reprisals. But they took good care of the relationship with the villagers and issued receipts for the food and services received – though whether the villagers were ever able to cash them in is highly doubtful.[14] A guerrilla tactic to deceive the enemy was to order village authorities to prepare rations for several thousand men on the following day. Learning of this from their spies, an outnumbered French column would make off; the guerrilla then struck in an altogether different direction.

THE GUERRILLAS' SOCIAL PROFILE*

At their most basic level, the guerrilleros could be separated into three general categories depending on the manner in which they were created. Those who took up arms without any authorization from either civilian or military authorities could be called *partisans*; those who asked for and received official authorization to create new groups under one of the two Junta Suprema's decrees, especially the second, could be termed *privateers*; and within them was a sub-category of *outlaws*, mainly pardoned smugglers, whom the Junta Suprema also called on to participate in the guerrilla. Finally *religious crusaders* was the name given to officially authorized groups led or formed in their majority by clerics. Guerrilla, when it entered the Spanish language in its new use, became the generic name for all of these.

Partisans formed eighty percent of the recorded guerrillas.† On this evidence, the authorities' policy of encouraging and sanctioning the creation of new groups in order to retain control of the guerrilla movement was not strikingly successful. But once the decrees were widely known, increasing numbers of would-be guerrilla leaders asked permission to form their groups. At the very minimum one in five guerrilleros came from the privileged classes: the clergy, military, professionals (lawyers and doctors mainly) and civilian authorities – administratives and civil servants. Students were also well represented. Clerics made up forty percent of these classes, but only eight percent of the guerrilleros total. The elite's presence was more marked among the leadership than in the rank and file.

Overall, the labouring poor outnumbered the educated classes. Smallholders and land-use owners formed nearly half of the latter's members. But the most striking aspect of the labouring classes was the absence of the rural proletariat – the agrarian day labourers – who at the turn of the century made up just under one half of Spain's land-working population. This can be ascribed to two

* For detailed figures see Appendix 4, *The Guerrilla*, table 4.4.
† In the author's database of 751 guerrilleros.

factors: their proportion of total land workers was lower in the north – Galicia, Asturias and the Basque country had under twenty-five percent, and Castilla la Vieja between twenty-five and fifty percent – than in Andalucía where they reached eighty percent.[15] The fact that they had nothing to lose and were the last to fear a Bonapartist takeover in terms of ownership – they would have to labour to earn their daily wage whichever regime was in power – was the second factor. As Gaspar Melchor Jovellanos, a Junta Suprema member, speaking about the Andalucian rural proletariat, put it: 'these provinces in which the people are mainly composed of day labourers, are miserable and indifferent and *without any patriotic spirit . . .*' (stress added).[16]

Among the partisans – those who became guerrilleros without either civilian or military authority – labouring men outnumbered proportionately the privileged classes, demonstrating the fact that the former had been first into the field and had asked permission of no one to wage their own 'little war'. At their head, as always, were smallholders and land-use owners; and these, as a percentage of their recorded participants, provided as many chiefs as did clerics who headed the elite's number of leaders.*

Though overall the lower orders provided fewer chiefs than their social superiors, it was from among the former that many of the great guerrilla leaders emerged: their parties came to number several thousand each, and their chieftains, whose military exploits in confounding the imperial forces became legendary, demonstrated an instinctive sense of irregular war and how to lead their men. They showed an agility of tactical thinking and flexibility of action that should have put the Spanish noble military hierarchy to shame; and most of them were promoted by the patriot government to the military rank of brigadier at least.†

Among the privileged classes' leaders in all three types of guerrilla it was those with experience of commanding pre-war who generally commanded in wartime: clergy, military and civilian authorities/functionaries.

With their ideological hostility to imperial 'hereticism', reinforced by the Bonapartist abolition of monasteries and friaries, the lower clergy's leadership role was hardly surprising: probably close on two-thirds of clerical guerrillas were former monks and friars. The military, however, was a different matter.

The soldiers on active service in 1808, whose ranks were recorded, were overwhelmingly officers. Captains were the most numerous amongst them – nearly one-third of the total. (A captaincy was a watershed to which many might ascend and few transcend.) However, another twenty-five percent were regimental commanding officers or above: lieutenant colonels, colonels and a brigadier. The majority of these had taken part in the Zaragoza sieges and had been promoted by José Palafox, the Aragón commander, who had dispatched them to raise local contingents to come to the aid of the Aragonese capital. Others had escaped from the French after the second siege and the city's surrender in early 1809. Their experience of an open city's outright resistance

---

* For an explanation of proportional social representation, see Appendix 4.
† The high clerical percentage, it must be recalled, was in no small part due to the formation of the 'religious crusades', guerrillas led by or made up of clerics

had taught them that where urban inhabitants, led by their own local leaders, determinedly fought, using whatever means came to hand, they had stiffened the military's resolve which, in turn, provided a steadying and rallying force for the population. The combination of civilian spirit and military discipline could serve equally in the rural guerrilla.

The military presence in the parties was reinforced by deserters or 'dispersed' troops. With every battle defeat, soldiers (and officers) fled in all directions to escape the enemy and (theoretically) to live to fight another day. Many of these who were willing to continue the struggle joined a guerrilla instead to escape the army, its officers whom they did not trust – the great majority Old Regime nobles – and the constant battlefield defeats, harsh military discipline, hierarchical command and lack of supplies, food especially. In a well-organized guerrilla they could expect a regular day's pay, usually higher than in the army, a share of captured booty, sufficient food, and an absence of strict military discipline.*

Yet another sort of deserter was to be found in the guerrilla ranks – deserters from the imperial armies in Spain. These were almost invariably non-French troops. German, Italian, Dutch, Polish, even Russian conscripts deserted in considerable numbers, many of them joining the large guerrilla parties. Some British deserters or stragglers were also to be found among them. Of those whose reasons for joining the guerrilla were recorded,† one in four claimed that he had been a 'disperso'. (If other known dispersos, whose motives for joining the guerrilla went unrecorded, were added to the above, deserters would have formed between thirty and fifty percent of the total.) Nonetheless, regular military men followed by smallholders, land-use owners and artisans formed the majority.

The only other motive for joining the guerrilla which came close to that of desertion was the experience of collective violence at the hands of the imperial forces, often with personal consequences: the death of close relatives, the abuse of female kin, forced labour in carrying or carting for the occupying army, the forcible seizure of food supplies and an infinity of individual indignities. Many of the outstanding parties' leaders, however, shared an experience which conditioned their choice of taking up arms: the Convention War. Three of the large party leaders – El Empecinado, Julián Sánchez, Miguel Sarasa – and Gerónimo Saornil, the leader of a medium-sized party in Castilla la Vieja – were veterans of the war; and Espoz y Mina had felt its harsh effects when the French revolutionaries invaded his native Navarra.

Guerrillas' Age

Although the average age‡ was 25.9 years – the youngest guerrillero registered was ten and the oldest sixty – it was, as in the massive army volunteer enlistment at

* Of friar Mendieta's nineteen guerrilleros captured by the French ten were 'dispersos': four small farmers or land use-holders; a friar, a cobbler, a barber and three of unknown trades.
† The sample was a regrettably small: twelve percent of a total of 751 recorded guerrillas.
‡ Based on the ten percent of those whose age was recorded.

the beginning of the war, the sixteen to twenty-five-year-olds who predominated, forming almost two-thirds of the total. (The sixteen to twenty-year-olds alone formed forty-seven percent). The overall average was raised by the much higher age (near thirty on average) of the educated classes.

Generally speaking then the labouring poor's guerrilleros were considerably younger than their privileged counterparts, which reinforced the latter's leadership role. Given that life expectancy at birth for all Spanish males was no more than 27.3 years,[17] and that half of the national population was aged twenty-five or under (but only twenty-eight percent lived to reach more than forty, and just over fifteen percent to reach more than fifty), it was little wonder to find youth at the forefront of the labouring classes' guerrilla contingent.

15

From the Battle of Talavera
to the Suprema's Demise

In July 1809, General Wellesley's British army of Portugal, in conjunction with General Cuesta's army of Extremadura, began an offensive along the Tajo river towards Madrid. On the 27th and 28th the allies won what both patriots and the British government considered the 'victory' of Talavera. It was the largest and bitterest battle the British army had fought in sixteen years of war.[1] A *Te Deum* was sung in celebration in Sevilla cathedral, and Wellesley was elevated to the peerage as Lord Wellington, viscount of Talavera, by a grateful Tory cabinet. The victory was not, however, as clear-cut as the Anglo-Spanish forces might have achieved. In a fierce and bloody battle, Marshal Victor made three determined attacks on the allied lines and was beaten back, only narrowly more than once, with the loss of some seven thousand men. But the imperial troops inflicted heavy casualties also: Wellesley lost 5,400 – one in four of his combatants on the field. At the end of the day, the allied forces made no attempt to pursue the enemy which had retreated only a short distance.

Instead, after a few days, it was the allies who retreated, under threat from Soult advancing on their rear, leaving free the neuralgic centre of Spain to the enemy who was at liberty to begin his attacks southwards again. The situation was worsened at Almonacid on August 11 by the defeat of the patriot army of La Mancha, which was supposed to have supported the allied offensive but arrived too late. Within a few weeks, according to a patriot agent, French officers were openly laughing in Talavera about the battle just outside the town's walls. They had successfully attacked a force double their strength, they claimed. Although at one level this was sheer bravado, at another it represented a strategic truth: the imperial forces remained in command of the Tajo river, Madrid's natural defence against attack from the west or south. But the patriot agent in Talavera wrote:

> . . . such is the faith and enthusiasm of all us unhappy and ignorant people that together, as though with one voice, we say: *Our forces will come like lions one day and all will be avenged.* A few, who claim to be more sensible, exclaim: What is the purpose of their coming just to retreat?[2]

The battle's outstanding effect on the allies was to worsen their relationship, which began with Wellesley's distrust of Cuesta;* a distrust which deterioriated into mutual recriminations, charges and counter-charges; and ended with Wellesley – now Wellington – retreating at the end of the year from the Spanish–Portuguese border back into Portugal, not to reappear at the head of an army in the Spanish interior for two and a half years.

Before his retreat, the Extremaduran junta attempted to prevent him from withdrawing his forces totally from their region.[3] The Suprema reacted violently to the junta's 'insubordination' in treating with foreigners – violating the Junta's diplomatic privilege; its anger was increased by the fact there had been discussions in its military junta about giving Wellington command of the Extremaduran army. The Suprema deputy, Antonio Valdés, had approved the idea 'as long as Wellington is prepared to remain on the offensive'. But another deputy, Rodrigo Riquelme, of Granada, forcibly rejected the proposal.

> It is not part of the British system to make active war against the French . . . It should not be forgotten that after Talavera the English general [Wellington] withdrew his forces from those of Cuesta . . . The British government has realized that the Spanish Nation's struggle against the Tyrant [Napoleon] is altogether unequal, that all the sacrifices it makes are useless, and might as well be thrown into the sea . . .[4]

No more was heard thereafter about the proposal.

*

Much of the earlier recrimination revolved around Spanish food supplies for Wellington's army. When in January 1809, shortly after its arrival in Sevilla, the Suprema appointed Clemente María Rodríguez director general of the kingdom's royal provisions, whose task was to supply the armies, he found the office like a 'skeleton in its death throes', without funds, staff, and any knowledge of the armies' or their commissariats' whereabouts.

> The only ready money I found in the till was sixty-one thousand nine hundred reales. There was no accounts staff, no one to take charge of distributing supplies . . . How great was my surprise and bitterness, my worry and fear! . . . Instead of the twelve million reales a month that in peacetime H.M. government assigned to this office, I received [from the Suprema] only two million six hundred and forty-six thousand from March 1 to June 30 . . .[5]

Before the battle at Talavera was even joined, Wellesley believed that the Spanish were wilfully withholding food supplies. 'It is ridiculous to pretend that the country cannot supply our wants', he wrote. His own lack of prior

---

* Before the battle, it appeared, he would have been prepared to see the Spanish commander defeated without coming to his aid, although Cuesta did not repay him in kind: during the fighting, in which his troops were little engaged, the Spanish commander detached two divisions and a battery of heavy artillery at a crucial moment to give the British considerable support (Muir, 1996, p. 98).

intelligence about the villagers' situation in northern Extremadura, which had suffered the ravages of two French armies, not to speak of the patriot army and General Moore's artillery column, was patent. Not to have taken this into account was a serious mistake for any general who planned to campaign in the poorest region of Spain. A British informant – perhaps an agent – who travelled through the area shortly after the battle, reported to his minister of war that

> from Mérida to Trujillo there was no cattle . . . [the villagers] had not enough oxen or any animals to thresh out their crop . . . [I saw in Trujillo] the unpaid bills of some miserable wretches who were starving though in possession of regular receipts to a great amount for provisions furnished to Gen. Hope [commander of Moore's artillery in 1808] . . .[6]

However, there was no doubt in the mind of a patriot lawyer, Laureano Escamilla, from the small village of Erguijuela in Extremadura, who witnessed the scenes in the rearguard before and after the battle, that there had been criminal incompetence in supplying the patriot armies. Lack of food, in particular, had been the cause of 'thousands of soldiers deserting, falling ill or dying', he wrote to the Suprema. The officers and authorities responsible should be severely punished.

> Soldiers and villagers see these guilty men, endure them and can do nothing about them. They do not know how to complain or dare not do so, and their only sad consolation is to say that everything is lost because of the bad Spanish government.[7]

The most excoriating military criticism came from the Suprema-appointed junta of La Carolina, responsible for the defence of Despeñaperros, the major pass in the Sierra Morena from La Mancha to Andalucía, and of the army operating before it. After the latter's rout at Almonacid, junta members saw patriot soldiers fleeing all over the countryside like 'flocks of discomfited pigeons . . . who reached the sierra devastated and broken in spirit . . . There has been no other military nation up to now which has conducted war in the manner we have been doing.'

> Our generals are absolutely ignorant of how to unite their forces, totally lacking intelligence and the art of coordinating a plan of campaign . . . This junta is convinced of the necessity of restraining and reducing to moderate limits the whims of military despotism. Events have shown that we have no generals in whom such unlimited power can be safely confided.[8]

There was certain irony in this. The report was signed by, among others, the junta's president, Juan Carlos Aréizaga, who was shortly to lead – through his incompetence – the patriot army to its gravest defeat.

MILITANCIES: LORENZO CALBO DE ROZAS –
A MERCHANT PATRIOT

The Suprema took very seriously the accusations that it had failed the allied armies in the matter of food supplies. Within two days of the Talavera battle, it ordered its 'troubleshooter', to use a contemporary phrase, Lorenzo Calbo Rozas, to Extremadura to investigate. The former Madrid merchant, who had been Zaragoza's intendente during the city's first siege, and was subsequently appointed a deputy for Aragón to the Suprema, was one of the few Junta members who was prepared to take an active role in attempting to resolve concrete problems. Like many another Madrid merchant, Calbo was a Basque by origin who, in 1798 at the age of twenty-five, migrated to the capital at the start of what was to become a highly successful and prosperous business career. By the beginning of the war, a decade after reaching Madrid, his fortune was estimated at four and a half million reales, including six houses in Madrid, which easily put him among the richest twenty-five percent of the capital's merchants.[9]* His business interests extended from Málaga, Cádiz, La Mancha and Alicante to Lisbon.[10]†

As an active progressive, Calbo was exceptional among merchants. At the very beginning of the Suprema's existence, it was he who had raised in Madrid part of the loan which the Junta desperately required to continue the war effort; and during Zaragoza's second siege, he forcibly advised the Suprema that if it did not send reinforcements to relieve the city, he would resign his Suprema post and return to Aragón to fight with musket in hand.[11] In the spring of 1809, the Junta asked him to report on the manufacture and distribution of army uniforms, including those sent from England, because many troops wore still unclothed – the Suprema believed that many recruits sold their uniforms.[12] He submitted proposals to the Suprema for the reform of the patriot administration, which he called 'dim and abusive', and most of its employees 'negligent or inept'.[13] It was not surprising therefore, that the attempt to resolve the armies' supplies should fall on him. An ardent supporter of summoning the Cortes as rapidly as possible and of immediate press freedom, he had used his privileged position as a Junta deputy to bypass the Suprema's attempted control of the press and publish an attack on army officers' neglect of their troops' training and other military wrong-doings. The Suprema retaliated and ordered the paper closed.[14] The article earned Calbo considerable unpopularity with the military, and his absolutist Suprema colleagues were, no doubt, only too pleased to commission him to take on the prickly task of dealing with the allied armies' food supplies.

* On merchants in general, see Prologue, pp. xxiv–xxvi.
† The Bonapartist regime expropriated three million reales of his Madrid wealth for his adhesion to the patriot cause.

Calbo's mission began in much the manner in which it was to continue: his carriage broke down less than three leagues out of Sevilla, from where he had set off at two in the morning, and the postilion's saddle collapsed soon afterwards. 'I fear that this trip will take longer than I had intended', he wrote to the Junta's general secretary.[15] After a month's stay he returned mortified and frustrated. The new army commander, General Eguía – Cuesta had resigned for health reasons shortly after Talavera – refused, as did his interim intendente, to provide him with such elementary information as the number of daily rations needed by his army. He believed they themselves did not know. 'Here everyone does whatever they desire' – it is a 'theatre of disorder and confusion'. No one obeyed orders. He had given the strictest instructions that villagers were to be properly paid for carting supplies to the army, and were not to be distrained or subjected to other extortions which made them reluctant to undertake the work. In spite of his 'solemn promise', he had received nothing but complaints from villagers that the old practices continued.

Meanwhile, the Extremaduran junta in Badajoz excused its failure to supply the armies by claiming that, 'like the most ordinary of people', it did not know their whereabouts or their fate.[16] The previously cited British informant found a month later that Badajoz had plentiful stocks: the junta's president, a priest, informed him that – apart from the stores accumulated in the spring when, after the Medellín defeat, the French had threatened the border fortress town – Sevilla had recently sent further supplies. None of these, except biscuit, had been forwarded to the armies. 'Badajoz is determined to become a second Zaragoza', he wrote, putting his finger accurately on one of the main supply problems.[17]

Weary of his fruitless struggle, Calbo turned his energy to trying to improve the lot of hundreds of military sick and wounded who had been sent to a hospital in an abandoned Franciscan friary in Medellín. Though Calbo had given two weeks' warning to the military hospital service, neither the Inspector nor the employees had done anything to prepare the place or to care for the patients, who were without palliasses or sheets. Calbo procured these and then had to attend personally to feeding the inmates. He busied himself 'in this disagreeable but gratifying task, for anyone who appreciates the character of the Spanish soldier knows that he suffers more than sufficient causes of discontent to disgust him and lead him to desert'.[18]

*

Patriot military hospitals were one of the early disgraces of the war which the ordinary soldier experienced directly. During his brief tenure as the Central Army commander of the troops in La Mancha, General Cartaojal gave the thirty thousand sick and wounded under his command only six hours in which to be evacuated southwards from field hospitals which were in a general state of disorder. As a result of the urgency, five thousand soldiers had died, wrote Fr. Alonso de la Puebla in a scathing report after being ordered as a member of La Carolina junta to investigate military hospitals.[19] All such matters immediately becoming a question of competence and power, the army's intendente, making the most of his twenty-two years of service, criticized the report and the priest's proposed reforms. Confronted by its own war minister's opposition, the Suprema, with its customary back-pedalling before established precedent, rescinded its recent order passing control of military hospitals to the junta and reverted to the intendentes' command decreed nearly three quarters of a century before.

But the problem, as usual, lay elsewhere: doctors and hospital workers were owed 630,000 reales in back wages; and the latter were living in such a state of poverty that they lacked even a change of clothes. Some went out at night and, pretending to be beggars, tried to receive sufficient alms to buy a pound of bread; others went in gangs to steal the broad beans farmers had just planted to sate their hunger, wrote the Comptroller of Hospitals.[20] If this was the state of hospital employees, the situation of the sick and wounded was not hard to imagine.

> I can see no reason why the hospitals should be looked upon with such indifference, or why these wretched soldiers' infinite clamour against those who are the cause of their great need should fall upon deaf ears . . . Are these miserable men of a different hierarchy when their illnesses and wounds have been incurred in Our Defence? Why do they find themselves victims of the disputes and mad ambitions which should be far from our thoughts today?[21]

Lorenzo Pérez, a priest who had been appointed Administrator of military hospitals in Úbeda, Jaén, protested to the Suprema's secretary general that funds were needed to help 'these poor men who are worthy of every consideration'. He reported that, without advance notice, as many as two thousand sick soldiers had reached his town on a single day from other nearby military hospitals, and they were still arriving as he wrote. The local junta had done all it could in the early days to help fund the hospital; but the army's intendente had subsequently insisted on taking over the task despite his lack of funds. Lorenzo Pérez had provided what money he could from his own small benefice and, when this was insufficient, had pawned some of his family's jewellery to succour the 'destitute humanity' in his hospital.

Overwhelmed by these and other reports on the hospitals' state, the Suprema ordered its finance minister to make funds available to remedy the situation. Whether or not these were actually paid – indeed, whether there were any funds available to do so – is not recorded.

Public concern about military hospitals was evident; battles took place in distant places but the wounded and maimed were there in the rearguard for all to see. Many soldiers complained that they were released from hospitals before being full cured. When intendente José Canga Argüelles, a member of the Valencia junta, decided that a 150-bed convalescent home was needed for these men, and took over a country house and gardens outside the city walls for the purpose, his appeal for its funding met a massive public response from the Valencia population. Eighty thousand reales were raised; significantly more poor people contributed than the wealthy, although the latter's contributions – especially the bishop's fifteen thousand reales – provided the bulk of the funds.[22]

PUBLIC OPINION

Calbo's concern with press freedom and forming public opinion, shared by all progressives, meant public involvement in the affairs of state. Under the Old Order the general public had been passive spectators of the kingdom's political affairs, their views and participation in the country's governance neither asked for nor desired. In propitiatory recognition of the 'people's' role in the rising, the Suprema had, from its inception, appealed to all 'citizens' (i.e. respectable members of society) to make their views known. This had opened a small space for their involvement in governmental affairs which was simultaneously constricted by the Suprema's refusal to decree the freedom of the press.

That a public opinion was, nonetheless, beginning to take shape – but not necessarily the one Calbo would have desired – cannot be doubted. As a comment by an Andalucian Capuchin friar, brother Pablo de Vélez-Málaga, suggested, this involved all sectors of society:

> In Jaén and neighbouring villages, people of all classes and condition, from the bishop's secretary to the commonage, talk of the events of the day with the freedom of members of the House of Commons, and this not only in private but openly in public places . . .[23]

Perhaps this was due to the Jaén junta's laxity or its opposition to the Junta Suprema, shared with its superior, the Sevilla junta. But as brother Pablo, the son of a very poor family, learned to his cost, this freedom did not extend to his native Andalucian village. The local junta of Vélez-Málaga detained him for speaking his mind publicly on political events, especially for singing the praises of the forthcoming Cortes, searched and placed his parents' house under armed guard, and submitted the friar to a six-day 'trial', having sworn to secrecy all junta members and others attending it as though the case concerned lese-majesty. The main witnesses for the prosecution were fellow friars to whom brother Pablo had talked. The local junta was convinced of the latter's guilt; but the Suprema's special commissioner in Málaga, Antonio Cortavarria, sensibly called it a case of 'little seriousness since only some imprudent expressions, without further importance, are at stake'. Nonetheless, brother Pablo was confined to a special cell for friars in need of punishment in the Málaga Capuchin friary.[24] The restrictions on public opinion which questioned a univocal patriotism remained very sharp.

The progressives wished for a public opinion carefully moulded by literate patriots along progressive lines, not anarchic and critical discussions among the plebs which were likely to be destructive and demoralizing to the patriot war effort. One of those who made a serious attempt to educate his fellow country-men was Rev. José Blanco, the political editor of the *Semanario Patriótico* founded by Quintana in 1808. (As a leading member of the Suprema's staff, the latter gave up the editorship during its publication in Sevilla in 1809.) In a series of articles entitled *Política*, Blanco set out to recuperate words like 'liberty' and 'equality' tainted in the elite's notions by their association with the French Revolution.

> Men of bad faith, who try to keep the public in a state of passive despondency, and those who shudder fearfully at the thought of innovation, put it about that liberty means disorder, and equality anarchy . . . There is no madness greater than to confuse freedom and lawlessness. Never do men enjoy less liberty than when there is no order . . . Political liberty consists of a nation being subject only to those laws which it has willingly recognized . . . There is no monarch, however unlimited his power, who can oppose a people's unanimous opinion.[25]

'Equality', Blanco continued, was in material and social terms impossible, even undesirable, for the poor's ambition to equal the rich in wealth and power had historically caused rivers of blood. 'While the people can barely achieve a miserable subsistence', condemned to 'work and poverty', they believed that happiness belonged to the privileged. 'It is necessary that the poor understand that society does not condemn them to this horrendous inequality; and that the superiority in wealth, honours and might which indispensably must exist in society, is not directed at nullifying and rendering unhappy the inferior classes.' For if material equality was impossible, equality before the law was not only possible but necessary; and it was this that would change the workers' and indigents' condition. Under legal equality, they could, if they would, make their way in society by their own capabilities and ingenuity on equal terms with the wealthy.

> The state in which . . . one class overflows with wealth and others are without the means to earn a livelihood is close to total ruin. This horrible inequality which brings low its victims, turns the most prosperous regions into uninhabited deserts which only wild animals will devour.[26]

In the meantime, the labouring poor should 'remain in the place that Providence has assigned to you: and when the time comes for your voice to be heard, do not clamour to strip others of their positions'. Poor comfort in reality, but a fair index of what awaited the lower orders from the progressive elite.

In the autumn of 1809, as political strife over setting up a regency in the Suprema became acute, two other newspapers began publication in Sevilla in support of the reformist cause. *El Espectador sevillano*, edited by the poet Alberto Lista, was not long in producing a definition of public opinion:

> It seems to us then that public opinion, defined with the greatest possible exactness, *is the general voice of a whole people convinced of a truth which they have examined through discussion.* It must be *general* in order to produce its great effect: since truth known only to the wise and unknown to the nation serves no purpose.[27]

This 'general voice' could not make itself heard without freedom of the press and an assembly in which 'an examination through discussion' could take place openly. Meanwhile, public opinion lacked a public avenue to those in power.

The Suprema recognized this. It proposed to set up an office, ostensibly to inspect mail intercepted from alleged or actual Bonapartist supporters, but also secretly to read all private mail to check on the 'people's public spirit'.

> The pen expresses the soul's feelings which are communicated to relatives and friends with the good faith these relationships inspire . . . [Letters] which give news of the people's state, of individuals among them, or of any other part of the realm, of the enemy's behaviour towards the people and their's towards him, in short everything which gives an idea of their morale, and the real physical and material state of the realm's countryside and homes . . . should be classified and graded according to category.[28]

Though the proposal was marked 'approved', there was no documentary evidence that it was ever acted upon. In fact, it became a case of the hunter hunted. The Sevilla junta was discovered opening and reading the Suprema's mail, especially from Cádiz, and note being taken of the information it contained, as a junta member informed the Suprema. The latter immediately ordered Sevilla not to open any mail other than that addressed directly to it.[29]

In the circumstances, the letter to the Suprema came therefore to be one of the major access routes for the expression of individual comment and criticism. The Junta received (and filed) over four hundred of these, many of them in the early months of its existence.* Three-quarters were anonymous. To the present-day mind this refusal to put one's name to a letter has a contemptible, even sinister ring. But to individuals unused to the freedom of expressing to authority critical opinions of its conduct and fearful of retaliation – the case of friar Pablo de Vélez-Málaga showed that this was no idle threat – it was a protective recourse. Another reason for anonymity was expressed by a writer who, criticizing the Suprema for not informing the nation of serious reverses, wrote simply that he (or though unlikely, perhaps she) was 'a person of no consequence'. It was precisely because most of the writers could have said the same that the letters are significant; and because, as another correspondent put it, 'it is still impossible to write the truth'.

---

* The following observations are based on a classification of one hundred letters, those which most incisively expressed their comment and criticism. There are many other letters scattered throughout the Suprema's files, but this block, contained in AHN, *Estado*, Legajos 52A to 52H, contains the major themes.

As could be expected, the greatest number concerned the Suprema's conduct of the war, and especially its dilatory activity. Criticisms of the military, the socially privileged and provincial juntas followed.*

> The Nation fears and weeps because it does not see the government making the extraordinary efforts demanded by the extraordinary circumstances and great risks to the fatherland . . . How much more was done when the Provinces acted separately. With what slowness [the government] acts when everything should be activity and burning fire . . . Why not arm the nation en masse?

The situation was better, remarked another correspondent, before there was a Suprema.

> The labouring poor have courage and energy, and cannot look on with indifference at what is happening . . . Unless more active measures are taken, the nation will be obliged to shake off this oppressive yoke, as it did in May [the Madrid uprising of 1808].

The Suprema's war leadership and its confidence in the old class of generals came in for frequent criticism:

> Get rid of these old, lazy, ignorant, timid and indolent generals: let those of courage, virtue and real merit command the armies instead of these grandees of pure and illustrious birth. I ask only one thing: that an ordinary sergeant in gaiters be put in command of twenty thousand infantry, two thousand horse and one thousand artillerymen and be given the absolute right to pursue the enemy, on condition that no military commander is of higher rank than a sergeant . . .

The view that sergeants would make better commanders than noble generals was frequently expressed, reiterating the enlighteneds' pre-war anti-noble stance. The government's expenditure on wages and salaries also came under attack. The four to five million reales that were spent on these could maintain four to six thousand soldiers a day, complained one correspondent. Even Godoy had not robbed the state of this amount. 'If we are all asleep, let us go to bed and leave the French to come and dominate us.'

Public awareness that the rich were not contributing their just share to the war effort was evident in a number of protests the Suprema received on the score:

> Shamefully, it is the better-off classes that have shown the least patriotism . . . The truth is that we owe everything to the classes which have nothing to lose . . . From the others we can expect nothing, generally speaking. Have we not seen the paltry, mean contributions they have made . . . Nothing about taking over private and Church

---

* The many protests about the form of military conscription and the few about and from the Church appear in chapters 10 and 13 respectively.

silver plate? It seems, I repeat, that we are not at war, that we want to leave all the wealth to the French . . .

The war profiteers were the target of special criticism. They were accused of being the cause of the soldiers' hunger and lack of uniforms:

> The military purveyors think only of becoming rich at the expense of the poor soldier who sacrifices his life for the fatherland . . . These purveyors should be sentenced to death after scrupulous investigation into how they have come by their wealth when before supplying the army they were poor, almost of a venal class . . . [The soldiers' lack of food and clothing] makes the youth resist joining the army, and explains the violence with which they have to be taken from their villages . . . for there are some who say, even if they drag me I shall not go . . .

Finally, a single voice was raised in favour of irregular warfare in place of pitched battles.

> The only thing that is of use to us is to make the enemy waste the time which he wants to gain. This can be achieved by occupying strong points where tactical manoeuvres, of which the enemy knows a great deal and we do not, are useless or inapplicable. By continuous alerts which tire the [enemy] soldier . . . and offensives, depriving him of provisions by all imaginable means, which leave him in hunger . . .

THE SUPREMA'S DEMISE

Shortly after Talavera the Suprema conceived a new plan for a massive autumn attack on Madrid. It defended the idea of permanent war on all fronts at every moment, and, despite the difficulties, it had by the early autumn of 1809 succeeded in increasing the number of its regular forces.

In the west a forty-thousand strong patriot army would keep Ney occupied around Salamanca; another, under the duque de Alburquerque, now in command of the Extremaduran army, would threaten Soult in the Tajo valley, while the decisive thrust, unthreatened by flank attacks, would be launched by a reinforced Army of the Centre across La Mancha direct on Madrid. A mass rising of villagers in unoccupied Cuenca province was to support the main offensive. On paper it read splendidly; in practice it ended, for the same reasons as always, in the gravest of disasters.

Lack of coordination doomed the first part of the plan. In the west, the army, although it defeated an imperial force southwest of Salamanca on October 18 and for a fortnight occupied the city which the French had evacuated, had revealed its presence three weeks before the Army of the Centre moved into La Mancha; on November 28, it went down to defeat at Alba de Tormes. The Extremaduran army, depleted to reinforce the Army of the Centre, advanced on Talavera but was easily held off. When at last, on November 8, the fifty-thousand-strong Army of the Centre, the greatest yet assembled by the patriots, began to advance across the plains of La Mancha, its flanks were not as secure as the plan had assumed.

Speed and surprise were now of the essence. The army, into which much British aid had been poured in cloth and muskets, was commanded by General Juan Carlos Aréizaga, who had given a good account of himself in one of the only two patriot victories of the year: in defeating an imperial attack on Alcañiz, Aragón, earlier in 1809. As a result, he had been appointed president of La Carolina junta, in which post he was one of the signatories of a blistering report on Spanish generals. (See above, p. 350.) But there was another imperious reason for speed: La Mancha had been so ravaged by French and Spanish armies that the villages' food stocks were exhausted. The French had but recently carted off all the grain and other foodstuffs they could lay their hands on. Two members of La Carolina junta, with personal knowledge of the region, were detailed to accompany the army in the hope of being able to provision it; but they reported that the situation was so desperate that they could find no supplies.[30]

By November 13 the Army of the Centre had reached La Guardia, some fifty kilometres south of Aranjuez on the Tajo river. There it inexplicably halted for three days before continuing on to Ocaña, only twenty kilometres to the north. From La Guardia, Aréizaga urgently addressed the Granada junta, maintaining that his forces were in a 'deplorable state for lack of shoes and almost devoid of uniforms', and appealed to it to supply him with shoes.[31]

Shoes – the bane of all infantrymen's lives! The British foot soldier carried two pairs with him: even so, he needed the constant attention of cobblers amongst his companions to keep him from going barefoot. The Spanish conscript, if he was lucky, had only one pair. To make good the deficiency, the Suprema had ordered esparto sandals – which also became popular with British troops – and a rudimentary type of laced leather overshoe used by hunters in the cold and wet Castilian winters – to be manufactured to replace the insufficient infantryman's shoe. English aid in this respect was not of much use. 'The heel of the Spaniard generally projects much, and the foot is longer than that of the English peasant', observed a British note at the end of a request for renewed supplies.[32]

It was remarkable, nonetheless, that a commander-in-chief of a major offensive should only take notice of his troops' barefoot and near-naked state when he was approaching the enemy's positions.

The Suprema's special commissioner to the army, Juan de Dios Ravé, a military officer and a Suprema deputy for Córdoba, confirmed that many of the men were shoeless. But as he had refused to accept this as an excuse from the Castilian and Extremaduran armies for their tardiness in protecting his army's flanks, he could not claim exemption to his own rule: 'Let them march like many of our troops, barefoot', he exclaimed.[33]

It was probably the fear that the enemy on his flanks, especially Soult in the Tajo valley, had not been closely enough engaged by the Extremaduran army to keep him from attacking the Army of the Centre which brought Aréizaga to delay his march on Madrid. His advance guard had crossed the river Tajo, and six thousand Cuenca villagers and townsmen, armed with primitive weapons, who had responded to the mass mobilization ordered by the Suprema, reached Tarancón, fifty kilometres to the east of Ocaña. Their task was less to fight than to present a diversionary threat to split the enemy forces. They had barely arrived when Aréizaga ordered them home, informing their leader, the Cuenca junta president, that they were not needed. However, the volunteers provided the army with a large quantity of shoes, esparto sandals and leather overshoes.[34]

Then came three days of torrential rain which held up the bulk of the army again. These delays gave Soult time to gather his forces. Abandoning the advance on Madrid, Aréizaga recrossed the Tajo, while Soult, with thirty-four thousand men, advanced. On November 18, the most important cavalry engagement of the whole war took place with a total of seven thousand cavalrymen, the Spanish being pushed back to Ocaña which the infantry had now reached. Here, on flat terrain, his flank unprotected by any natural advantage, incomprehensibly and without military necessity, Aréizaga decided to give battle the following day. Poorly led, without clear orders and a decisive overall command, the Spanish army was at a disadvantage from the start. Soult immediately exploited the undefended flank and his cavalry turned it. The Spanish soldiers panicked at finding themselves attacked from the rear. The army was totally destroyed, losing ten thousand dead and wounded and twenty thousand prisoners, including three generals. The commander-in-chief came down from the belfry where he had been watching the battle; he was smoking a cigar and held a field glass in one hand. He mounted his horse and calmly rode off south without leaving any orders . . .[35]

Once again, the Suprema's trust in a regular army commander led to a sacrificial slaughter and loss of its raw recruits. The Junta could not put together another such army immediately; Andalucía now lay open to the French.

Although it took the imperial army time to organize Andalucía's invasion, on January 13, 1810, as the French began their attack the Suprema announced that it was moving to the Isla de León, Cádiz's immediate hinterland, allegedly to prepare for the Cortes' opening on March 1: the inhabitants of Sevilla were not deceived, seeing it as a flight from the advancing enemy. Ten days later almost all the Suprema's members left Sevilla for the Isla. Those who went overland were threatened and insulted, and sometimes fortunate to escape with their lives: villagers believed the common rumour that the government was abandoning them. They had not forgotten the Portuguese royal flight to Brazil aboard an English man-of-war little more than a year earlier. Those Suprema delegates who travelled down the river Guadalquivir were more fortunate, reaching their destination without trouble.

Despite the more than a year that the patriots had been given to complete the defences of the Despeñaperros pass in the Sierra Morena on the main road from La Mancha to Andalucía they had not been finished. The French were clear of the pass after a couple of hours of fighting. Sevilla fell much as it had risen in June 1808, with a popular insurrection, the seizure of arms and the invasion of the chamber in the Alcázar where the Suprema had sat. The crowd agitatedly demanded that a regency be immediately set up.* Francisco Saavedra, former

---

* The mob had previously released the conde de Montijo and Francisco Palafox, two of the main plotters against the Suprema in favour of a regency, from the prisons to which the Junta had condemned them, and called on them to be members of the regency.

Suprema treasury minister who had remained in Sevilla as a member of the local junta, was among those who tried to calm the people.

> Their clamour was finally reduced to forming a military commission for Andalucía's defence and for General Blake to take command of the Army of the Centre . . . Despite the fury which is always characteristic of these tremendous popular upheavals, they can be calmed down and the people's confidence restored to the point of even handing over with the greatest docility the arms they had seized to veteran soldiers who were unarmed . . .[36]

The following morning a mob again assembled at the Alcázar, once more demanding a regency. They were led, Saavedra informed the Suprema's president, by an Aragonese priest.

> We told the people that for the moment such a demand was out of order. The people allowed themselves to be persuaded, and even turned their anger on the inflamed instigator of their demand . . . But what most infuriated the people was the news that in Cádiz ships were waiting to embark the Suprema delegates, taking with them great quantities of money, silver and jewels.[37]

To satisfy the people, the Sevilla junta dispatched one of its members to Cádiz forthwith to order the governor not to permit any such manoeuvre. On the Suprema's departure, the regional Sevilla junta proclaimed itself Supreme – its final revenge for the months of dissension that had occupied the two since the Suprema had taken up residence in the Andalucian capital. It promised to organize the patriot defence. But as the enemy approached it too fled. A few French cannon shots sufficed. On Thursday, February 1, 1810, Sevilla surrendered without a fight.

*

As in the first imperial invasion of Andalucía, the second also mistook the relative importance of Sevilla and Cádiz as their major objective. In the early days of the war, the French had marched from Madrid on Cádiz with the aim of relieving their fleet bottled up there for three years since Trafalgar. The end result was their defeat at Bailén. In 1810, as Andalucía lay defenceless at their feet, the choice again lay before them and at the last moment they selected Sevilla. The patriot capital was a more tempting prey than the great city port on its rocky Atlantic isthmus. By this decision they brought upon themselves an unsuccessful siege which lasted nearly two and a half years. Although initially garrisoned by only eight thousand men, Cádiz was virtually impregnable by land: a river and marshes protected its approaches and it could not be starved into submission since supplies could be brought in by sea. Furthermore, the small garrison was more than doubled in size from the very beginning by the duke of Alburquerque's initiative in force-marching his twelve thousand troops from Extramadura into Cádiz the day before the French appeared.

The Suprema deputies gathered on the Isla de León – some, including the president, Archbishop Laodicéa, had to be summoned to go there[38] – had many months earlier collectively elected the Isla as their place of exile should Sevilla be threatened. It was a semi-island joined to the Cádiz isthmus, protected by the swamps on the far side of the river Petri from where any land attack would have to come. In the circumstances, it was as safe a place as could be.

Here on January 27, 1810, the progressive merchant Calbo de Rozas, who had for so long stubbornly defended the Junta against the absolutists' demand for a regency and had called for the immediate summoning of the Cortes, himself called for a regency to be formed. The Sevilla riots, he admitted, had plainly shown that the Suprema had lost the people's confidence. Calbo set about formulating the internal regulations by which a five-man regency, under General Castaños, would be governed.[39] On January 31 the regency took office and the Suprema ceased to exist.*

Few regretted its disappearance. And yet for the sixteen months of its existence, it had, despite its many drawbacks and failures, kept the military struggle alive against very great odds. It had managed to recreate large armies after massive defeats, and though these were never likely to deal the French a decisive blow, their threat could not be ignored by the imperial forces. Its major defect in this field had been to leave its armies in the hands of the old noble officer corps. The Junta had also encouraged civilian guerrilla war, even if its aim had essentially consisted in trying to control what was already becoming a large-scale phenomenon by 1809. In general, however, it must be said that its concept of 'revolutionary' war was highly unrevolutionary, and it did little or nothing to mobilize the lower orders whom it feared as much as – if not more than – the French.

None of the regents, with the exception of Francisco Saavedra, who was old and ill, was a leading politician. Without an elected Cortes to legislate, the regency seemed unlikely to be any more adept at running the war than the Suprema and, new to power and fearing progressive reforms, it was even less likely than the latter to summon the Cortes.

The former Junta delegates became the targets of a vicious campaign of denigration; many suffered the mortification of having their baggage searched for stolen funds before they embarked on a frigate for Galicia. But the worst treatment was meted out to the more progressive among them, including accusations of corruption and embezzlement of funds. Calbo's Talavera mission turned out more personally disastrous than he could have imagined. He was arrested by the new government and confined under close detention on board a frigate in Cádiz and then in the San Sebastián castle in the same port. His wife and secretary, among others, were also imprisoned. Within a month of proposing its creation, he found himself a prisoner of his creature. His high-placed absolutist enemies took their revenge on a progressive, using trumped-up

---

* Apart from General Castaños, the other members were the Bishop of Orense; Francisco de Saavedra; Antonio Escaño, Minister of the Navy in the Suprema; and Miguel de Lardizábal y Uribe, a native of Mexico. Calbo had stipulated that one of the five members should come from the South American colonies.

allegations that on his Extremaduran mission, and earlier as intendente in Zaragoza, he had embezzled public funds for his own speculative trading operations. Held incommunicado for nine months without charges, he was released in October 1810; but this was only the beginning of a three-year-long battle to restore his reputation. 'A man's life is nothing if he cannot live with honour', he wrote.[40] (He had the good fortune to survive: conde Tilly, a Sevillan-appointed Suprema delegate who was also incarcerated, died in prison.)

As to the Cortes, which was due to convene on March 1, it did not finally assemble until September 24, 1810, and then only because serious pressures were brought to bear on the regency. The greatest of these came not from Spain itself but from the South American colonies where the Suprema's demise was taken to mean the end of Spanish resistance. To defend themselves from Napoleonic domination, the creoles of Buenos Aires, Caracas and elsewhere, created supreme juntas on the Spanish model, which remained loyal to Fernando VII but not to any current Spanish government.[41] Their incipient revolt turned, in September 1810, into a full-scale rising against the Spanish in Mexico, led by the priest Miguel Hidalgo y Costilla, who nonetheless initially recognized Fernando VII as king. As a number of more far-sighted patriots and Spanish Bonapartists had feared since the start of the war, the conflict's consequences had undermined Spain's jewel in the crown, the greatest territorial empire of the time.

16

1810–1811

Compared to the extreme and generalized civilian suffering of 1809, the following two years were less rigorous. With the exception of Galicia, Cádiz and the Levante, and parts of the northern Cantabrian coast and Extremadura, the French in principle controlled Spain, though in reality they dominated only those areas they physically occupied. Most of the heavy fighting was now confined to the Spanish periphery: the southern Catalan Mediterranean coast, where Marshal Suchet made slow but inexorable progress in reducing the last urban foci of resistance: Tortosa and Tarragona, and prepared to besiege Valencia; and on the Spanish–Portuguese border. The most significant military action took place not in Spain at all but in Portugal. Napoleon's victory over Austria at Wagram, in July 1809, left the Peninsula as his only field of military operations. The Emperor used the opportunity to reinforce his armies in Spain to their highest strength of the whole conflict and to attempt to chase the British out of Portugal. By the beginning of 1810, the imperial forces in Spain numbered 360,000 men (with an effective strength of 287,650), formed into eight army corps commanded by some of Napoleon's most experienced commanders.[1]

In 1810, the population began to make good the losses of the previous year. A sharp drop in the death rate, a moderate rise in the birth rate, and a great upswing in marriages were the most striking elements of the recovery. In Castilla la Nueva, for example, deaths fell by half between 1809 and 1811; births rose by twelve percent and marriages in 1810 increased by over fifty percent compared to the year before to reach their highest annual number of the whole war. Castilla la Vieja's progress was smaller but it had suffered less; even recently conquered Andalucía showed broadly similar tendencies though the birth rate remained very low.

The most exceptional change, however, was in Cataluña, where deaths dropped by sixty percent in 1810 compared to the previous year, births rose by one quarter, and marriages by more than one half. At the opposite end of Spain, Extremadura received a little relief: although deaths continued to outnumber births as they did for every year of the war except the first, mortality dropped by over one-fifth in 1811 compared to 1809, births rose more than ten percent and marriages a considerable thirty-eight percent.

These positive population figures showed two things: a natural tendency to make good the disasters of 1809 and the population's general belief that the 'normality' of the French occupation had become a fact of life. This 'normality' remained 'abnormal' in that arbitrary French exactions, requisitions and war taxes remained severe. But pitched battles and French victories had receded from the immediate experience of the greater part of the country. Except for Navarra, bordering on France and flanking the main imperial communications route, where the guerrilla movement was taking a threating aspect for the Bonapartists, French military governors in Castilla la Vieja were content to hold the large cities on the route: their inactivity against rural resistance was criticized by Josef's Spanish officialdom, but as long as the countryside did not rise to threaten their hold on the cities, in Castilla la Vieja at least, they made only the occasional *razzia* into the countryside without great conviction of definitively putting down the rural resistance.

*

These were the years when the imperial forces expected to win, and in all reason should have won the war in the Peninsula. However, in battle terms, their impressive number of troops was deceptive: not even a quarter of their effective strength could ever be asssembled by the French command for a single battle: sixty thousand men was the maximum and that was for the decisive battle of Vitoria in 1813. The rest were tied down in occupying the country, protecting lines of communications and escort duties. An entire army corps was needed to keep the high road between the French frontier and Madrid open from guerrillas. The journey from the Spanish capital to the French frontier that had taken three days before the war, now took eleven, and for large military convoys, with an escort of three to four thousand men, cavalry and artillery, Madrid to Paris could take as many as thirty-seven days. In Andalucía, Soult needed seventy thousand men to maintain his hold over a region where a guerrilla movement had begun almost immediately after its fall. The number of parties formed became the largest of any of the regions.

Though many Spaniards in the occupied zones had no doubt come to the conclusion that the French were there to stay and that further resistance only imperilled their lives or worsened their living conditions, a large minority of the population continued to fight. In the absence of sizeable patriot armies – after Ocaña, the patriots could never again raise forces totalling one hundred thousand – and with an ineffectual government confined to Cádiz, it was during these two years that the guerrilla became not only a significant fighting force, ensuring that enemy troops who otherwise would have formed larger armies to throw at the Anglo-Portuguese forces had to be retained in the rearguard, putting the smaller allied armies on a closer numerical parity with the French;[2] but equally, the guerrillas' small though resonant victories served to raise the population's morale and will to resist.

Nonetheless, relief that the war was more or less at an end seemed the dominant note. Andalucía in general had put up no real resistance; it was a moment when much of Spain's labouring classes gave signs of retreating into apathetic acquiesence of a fait accompli: the Bonapartists observed this in the spring of 1810.

> For a short time, villagers recognized their real interests, threw off these enemies of the people [the guerrillas] or tried to persuade them to return to their homes to take advantage of the king's pardon for their past mistakes and to enjoy all the advantages which his government offers.[3]

In the time it took the smallholder Espoz y Mina to consolidate his hold on the Navarrese resistance in 1810 and prove that a great guerrilla was in the making, guerrilleros went home, villagers were demoralized and the temperature of resistance fell notably. After Andalucía's fall, a large part of the population seemed for a moment stunned into resignation; the armies' virtual demise as a fighting force and the imperial troops' impact on the rural world were the decisive factors in maintaining the guerrilla alive. Until then, it could be said that the guerrilla had been an auxiliary to the army; even its greatest coup could not match a battle won. But the patriots had now lost almost every battle but the first and by the beginning of 1810, the army was a discredited and spent force. All that remained were the guerrillas. They had rejected the army's regular warfare for a style of their own, and this had brought them military honours and officer's rank. To renounce the struggle would have been to dishonour both the cause and their particular place in it.

Without them, they knew, the rearguard's resistance would crumble. The guerrilla was the crystallization of the villagers' will to resist. It was the only form of combat available to the weak against the strong. The guerrilleros were the villagers' kith-and-kin. They were used to fighting in straitened circumstances. When the guerrilla failed, the rearguard's spirit and determination dropped. Keeping resistance alive was one of the guerrilla's main aims.

> Despite the philosophers and politicians, who weigh up the balance of forces, the advantages and disadvantages of their field positions, the armies' greater or lesser skills – even whether their cause is good or bad – the guerrillero will win because the philosophers do not take into account . . . the presence or lack of fighting spirit which is needed for victory . . . (*Semanario Politico, Historico y Literario de la Coruña*)[4]

The Bonapartists were shocked and angered at 'our misfortune' in witnessing the guerrilla's strengthening re-emergence. They recognized it as a rural reaction; support stemmed from the villagers. But they pinpointed it concretely on the guerrilla's thefts of the well-to-do's property, and sale of the stolen goods to the lower orders locally or in neighbouring villages.

> These evil men, aided by some of the inhabitants, enter the villages and sack the houses of the rich whom they call traitors, taking their owners with them to assassinate later or often in the village itself. They then carry off in triumph everything of worth, in money, livestock and other effects, certain that they can sell them at low prices in neighbouring villages if not in the village where they have committed these

horrors . . . There would be fewer men of this ilk if they were sure they could not find buyers, and there would be no buyers if the local magistrates arrested them and handed them over to the courts . . .[5]

This slim pretext for the guerrilla's increasing numbers appeared at first sight like a displacement theory which refused to recognize the truth that the imperial occupiers' exactions were the cause of the Bonapartist 'misfortune'; and it might have applied equally to French and British soldiers who made a fair picking from this sort of trade.* But perhaps it was precisely in implying the considerable difference between the soldiery's and guerrilla's aims that the Bonapartist government theory signalled a fact worth taking into account. Since the guerrilla's objective was to eliminate village authorities' collaboration with the occupying force, their seizure of the well-to-do's property was a punishment or a warning to them of the vengeance they could expect if they sided with the enemy; and the sale of their property an acknowledgement of the impoverished social order under which most of the lower classes of villagers lived. In a rudimentary manner, then, the guerrilla found itself waging a 'social' war with the objective of ensuring the majority of villagers' support for the patriot cause by redistributing wealth from rich to poor and – by the use of terror – restraining the rural wealthy from collaborationism. The 'sale' of the wealthy's goods was a piece of social revenge that was a means to maintaining alive a popular spirit of resistance.†

Though the guerrilla, which had to fund itself, no doubt made its turn on these deals, it was not from these small village takings that much money was made. It was rather from the sale of large-scale expropriated crops, the collection of fruits and tithes on wine, rents and feudal dues from Bonapartist landowning supporters that even some of the reputable leaders, including El Empecinado, amassed small fortunes during the war as was to be expected by the criteria of the times.[6] But there was undoubtedly another reason, which the Bonapartists seemed unable to fathom, for the guerrilla's attack on the village wealthy. Local oligarchs were buying up at low prices expropriated lands, including those of the former religious houses – the National Property, as it was called by the Bonapartist regime which put them on the market in an attempt to reduce the national debt – and village commons and grazing which councils were being forced to sell to pay the exorbitant French demands for money and

* For example, in the village of Azucayca, close to Toledo, French soldiers stole some mules, and the following day produced them in the village plaza to sell. 'Their owner complained bitterly. As a result villagers seized the mules, and punched the soldiers in the face. The military governor of the place ordered the soldiers arrested and offered to have them punished, which calmed down what otherwise would have been the start of a revolt.' (AHN, *Estado*, Legajo 40/255, report from Josef González de la Torre, the Suprema's lookout on the Toledo front heights, to Junta Suprema, Aug 5, 1809.)

† 'This is a war of poor against rich', recognized General Cafarelli, who spent a fruitless time hunting down the guerrilla leader Espoz y Mina in Navarra, in a letter to Marshal Berthier, in which he referred to the guerrilla's plundering of the wealthy. On the ground Cafarelli saw the situation far more clearly than the Spanish Bonapartist ministers immured in Madrid. (Cafarelli's statement is from *Dictionnaire Napoleon*, ed. by J. Tulard, Paris, 1997, in the entry under 'guerrilla', written by J.R. Aymes, pp. 849–852 and cited by Moliner i Prada, 2004, p. 95.)

food. The better-off class of villager or wealthy townsman was profiting from enemy measures at the expense of the poor villager, the smallholder, the long-term tenant who could not afford to buy the land on offer and was losing his traditional rights to the village's communal lands.

MASSÉNA'S DEFEAT BEFORE WELLINGTON'S PORTUGUESE DEFENCES

After Andalucía's conquest, Napoleon turned his attention to the British in Portugal. As long as Wellington remained there he was a threat to the Emperor's Spanish flank. In April 1810, Napoleon created an army of Portugal, under Marshal Masséna, to carry out his plan of expelling the British, and sent nearly 140,000 more men to Spain – though only twenty thousand of these were new troops; the remainder were replacements to bring the three army corps under Masséna up to strength.[7] He thought at first to lead this army himself, but his divorce from Josephine in December 1809, and his marriage to the Arch-duchess Marie Louise of Austria, focused his mind on dynastical matters rather than on military leadership.[8]

One of Napoleon's oldest and most able commanders, the one-eyed André Masséna was in no hurry to conquer Portugal – Napoleon had ordered him not to take Lisbon too swiftly 'as I could not feed the city [before the harvest] with its immense population accustomed to live on food brought from the sea';[9] and Masséna had first to cover his Spanish flank, in particular Asturias: Oviedo, the capital, was taken and retaken four times and though imperial forces occupied most of the principality they were never fully able to consolidate their hold. At the same time the French had to besiege and reduce Astorga in León which, due to its stout resistance, caused them heavy losses; and then the fortress towns of Ciudad Rodrigo in Spain and Almeida in Portugal. Despite the urgent pleas of Ciudad Rodrigo's governor, Andreas Herrasti, Wellington, whose vanguard was close by, refused to commit any troops to help raise the siege which lasted two months. After the British commander's refusal to come to the Suprema's aid during the disastrous Ocaña offensive, or to the defence of Andalucía, the Spanish were incensed and in consequence refused to provide Wellington with information on French movements.[10] As Wellington retreated deeper into Portugal, there were many Spaniards who recalled Moore's 'inglorious' retreat in 1808 when he, too, had refused to engage the enemy. Ciudad Rodrigo finally capitulated on July 9, the Spaniards losing 460 killed, nearly one thousand wounded and four thousand prisoners.*

---

* Wellington, it must be said, was not prepared to risk Britain's only field army on an enterprise which he was not certain of winning, since even a costly victory might give the British government the excuse to withdraw the army, which he was convinced would be a military error. The peninsular bridgehead, he believed, was dividing the Emperor's military strength which might otherwise be directed at more direct conquests abroad. And he had prepared defensive plans to beat off Masséna's threat which he had foreseen for over a year. Napoleon was unaware of the extent of these – a major intelligence failure – and under-estimated the number of Wellington's troops, which by June 1810 numbered thirty-three thousand British and German rank-and-file and ten thousand more by November.

Masséna, whom Napoleon had also placed in command of all northern Spain in order to use its military resources for the offensive, had an effective fighting strength of sixty-five thousand before the invasion proper began. But he could not use the thirty thousand imperial troops stationed in the north of Spain – indeed had to reinforce them – for fear of guerrillas in conjunction with the remaining small Spanish regular forces disrupting his communications with France.[11]

After reducing Almeida, Masséna waited a month for reinforcements and supplies. The former did not arrive. Although the Emperor had ordered his generals to afford him all the help he required, General Reille, the military governor of Navarra, diverted some of the reinforcements which crossed into Spain in August to his own flying columns which were fighting the three thousand guerrillas raised and led by Espoz y Mina in the region. The reinforcements helped Reille to harry the guerrillas for over two months in a series of forced marches and counter-marches over mountainous terrain, until, with only half of his men left, Espoz y Mina was obliged temporarily to leave Navarra, cross the Ebro and take refuge in Castilla la Vieja.[12] Mina had nonetheless delayed Masséna's reinforcements which, when Reille finally despatched them, arrived too late to be of any effective use.

Wellington made one stand against Masséna on September 27 at Buçao; more decisive than his victory, however, was the scorched-earth policy, a traditional Portuguese practice before an invading army, which Wellington enforced. Unable to hold Coimbra, he obliged its forty thousand inhabitants to withdraw in front of the British troops, carrying with them everything that could serve the enemy.

> Old people, lame and sick people, women just risen from childbed, children, and whole families with all their belongings packed either on bullock carts, mules, horses or donkeys, were to be seen mixed up with all kind of beasts, among which pigs, owing to unruliness and horrible cries, were the most conspicuous. Now and again, the cry would arise that the French were coming, and then the young girls would implore all those who were riding to help them upon the saddle with them. Ladies, who, according to the custom of the country, had never perhaps left their homes except to go to Mass, could be seen walking along, three in a row, wearing silk shoes and their heads and shoulders covered only with thin scarves.[13]

Masséna's army, now down to fifty-seven thousand men,[14] depended on supplies irregularly brought from the rear on roads which were in a terrible state, suffering severe deprivation as a result.

In mid-October Masséna found himself facing an impenetrable challenge. The Anglo-Portuguese army and eight thousand Spanish troops whom General Romana had marched from Extremadura, were ensconced behind two parallel fortified lines of earthworks, blockhouses and hundreds of cannon some twenty miles in front of Lisbon and guarding all access to the Portuguese capital. Wellington had been constructing these fortifications, the Torres Vedras lines, for over a year: the first line was held by the Portuguese militia while the Anglo-Portuguese field army was held back to counter-attack if the French managed to break through at any point in order to decimate the enemy weakened by the assault.[15]

Although the scorched-earth policy was not carried out close to Lisbon with the thoroughness Wellington had hoped for, and Masséna's army was able to hold out for a month in front of the lines and three further months in Santarem on the Tajo where food was more plentiful, only Masséna's steely determination kept the French army in Portugal. Despite Napoleon's order to all his field commanders to help him none did except Soult in Andalucía who finally moved in February, scraping together as many men as he could without threat to the loss of his Andalucian fiefdom, and besieged Badajoz which after five weeks tamely surrendered to him on March 10, although the border fortress town had men and supplies sufficient to hold out another month. Five days earlier, Masséna's army, having received no further reinforcements, began its withdrawal, committing harrowing atrocities in the Portuguese villages en route. The invasion cost the French some twenty-five thousand men, about sixty percent of whom fell victims to starvation, disease and the Portuguese irregulars.[16] Although Masséna had failed in his major objective, the French had in the course of mid-1810 to the spring of 1811 succeeded in taking three of the major Spanish–Portuguese fortified border towns: Ciudad Rodrigo, Almeida and Badajoz. Until Wellington had subdued these, he could not move into Spain. General Beresford's failure to recapture Badajoz in May 1811 effectively confined British forces to Portugal for the rest of the year and they failed to present any threat to the French armies in Spain.

JOSEF IN ANDALUCÍA

After Andalucía's fall, King Josef made a triumphal entry into his newly conquered territory. Constantly derided by his 'subjects' with derogatory sobriquets – Pepe Botella was the most usual* – he was, surprisingly, received with popularity by the Andalucian local elites who had been aggrieved and frustrated by the Junta Suprema's incompetence in leading the war effort and the run of military defeats. The war had at last receded, the Andalucians had not yet suffered the full rigours of French military occupation, and they believed for a time that peace at any price was an improvement on the immediate past. Josef, a legal man by training and a wealthy merchant by profession, was Fernando VII's antithesis: a moderate liberal who wished to reform his new kingdom and improve its people's lot. Cultured, amiable and generous to a fault – Napoleon envied his older brother's cultivation and success with women – Josef's well-intentioned desires were undermined by one serious defect, as Napoleon also saw. A civilized monarch – too civilized, too gentle a man, perhaps – he lacked the mettle, the strength of character to impose himself as king in the difficult conditions of the Spanish struggle. 'He is fond of pleasure but does not value military glory enough', was a Napoleonic general's succinct summation of his character.[17]

---

* Pepe is the common version of Josef (or José), and Botella ('bottle') because he was said to drink heavily.

But now, with his – and not his brother's – conquest of the largest and most populous patriot region, Josef allowed himself to believe that he had achieved military glory, had imposed his regal will. He deluded himself. Important as the region's addition to his rule might be, his conquest, brought about and maintained by French bayonets, precipitated a popular resistance – the formation of the highest number of guerrilla parties recorded in any region, while his failure to take Cádiz allowed the patriots a stronghold from which to begin their own constitutional reforms. Very shortly, moreover, Napoleon showed him who was the real ruler of Spain.

In the immediate, Josef, who was not without vanity, bathed in his clamorous Andalucian reception, the popular recognition of his sovereignty which was so strenuously denied him elsewhere. The reception Josef received in Córdoba, he assured General Suchet, surpassed in allegiance anything he had ever received in his former kingdom of Naples.[18]

EPISODES: A COUNTRY MARRIAGE

On his procession, Josef had passed through the rural township of Bujalance where the authorities had turned out in full to welcome him. Among them was Pedro de Torres y Coca, an hidalgo who, in representation of the nobility, had received from Josef's hand a ring which, as he subsequently wrote, was the 'gem he would always most highly treasure'.

Learning earlier that Josef was in Granada, he set out to lay himself, in the idiom of the day, at his sovereign's feet and kiss hands. But his good intentions were frustrated only two leagues from his destination when he was held up by sixteen 'bandits' who several times during the night threatened to execute him and his retainers. They accused him of having hidden in the farmhouse where they had discovered him a great quantity of money to hand over to Josef. Finally, they robbed him of five thousand reales in money and clothes and all of his gold. In these straitened circumstances, he had felt it impossible to present himself to the king and had returned home with the hope of being able to pay homage when Josef reached Jaén or Andújar which were closer to Bujalance.

These events he related in a petition to Josef which indeed had another, quite different purpose: to beg the king to order that a wrong done him by the regal commissioner* in Córdoba be righted. The latter had embargoed all his wealth, household goods and olive crop at the demand of doña Joaquina Dozta, whom his brother, don Diego Francisco, had married at the age of forty twenty years earlier. Joaquina was half her husband's age, of 'unknown antecedents and very poor', he added. His brother's entailed estates brought in over thirty thousand reales a year.

---

* This was a new civilian post created by Josef to head each province's administration.

Despite the difference in age, my brother who is a meek man, allowed Joaquina to flatter him into making over his estates' management to her which she carried out for seventeen years. She did not respond with the gratitude and love which such a privilege merited but avariciously amassed wealth for her widowhood because they had no children. Not content to leave him without the money for those occasions that society offered his peers, she treated him like her ward and even denied him her table and bed.

Two years earlier, Diego Francisco clearly saw that he was losing his income and peace of mind, revoked her powers and made them over to his brother. A lawsuit followed immediately to legalize the change to which the justices agreed. In accord with his social status, Diego Francisco also claimed his living costs from his wife.

Realizing that she had to pay not only his past costs but the expenses of the lawsuit, and that she would no longer control her husband's income, Joaquina took action. It was at the start of the war, and the Córdoba junta had just been formed. 'Thanks to the work of some of its delegates', Torres y Coca alleged in his petition to Josef, 'she succeeded in procuring an absolute decree to have her former rights restored, and that her husband should be interned in the monastery of El Fardón, situated in a deserted, uninhabited place. She had no consideration for the fact that this would have killed my brother because of his great age and poor health.'

Diego Francisco learned of her manoeuvre, fled Bujalance and after a few days appealed to his brother for help. The latter agreed and hid him in a number of different country farmhouses and hamlets, paying for his food and his repeated and costly illnesses. Diego Francisco offered to reimburse his brother for the considerable costs involved as soon as he had again taken possession of his estates. Joaquina meanwhile continued in her former position, until in 1810, learning that French troops were approaching Bujalance, she fled, leaving behind the money she had amassed. On the day of Josef's visit to Bujalance, Diego Francisco appeared in the township to ask the corregidor whom the king had appointed to return his estates to him. This the official did without more ado, and Diego Francisco took charge of the olive crop which was then being picked, and sold the oil to repay his brother for the two years he had maintained him.

But Joaquina was not prepared to sacrifice her well-being. She went to Córdoba and convinced Josef's regal commissioner to repossess her of what she had lost, including the olive oil her husband had sold. As Diego Francisco was not well enough to travel, his brother went to Córdoba in his place to inform the commissioner of events and to present a petition that he revoke his order. He received a dusty answer, telling him to return home to await a decision which, when it came, was shattering: a complete embargo of all his property. He was, he informed the king, penniless and unable to pay the labourers who had gathered his own olive crop, to whom he owed six thousand reales, or the millers who were pressing oil from it. If anyone should have had their possessions embargoed, it was his brother who had reclaimed his estates and sold the oil, he wrote.

Finally, Pedro de Torres y Coca begged the king to issue a royal decree to the Bujalance corregidor that not only should the embargo be lifted but that his brother's right to administer his own estates be recognized 'at least until such time that a court can consider the case and reach a decision'.

> In this manner the supplicant will receive . . . the justice which His Majesty is well known to accord his loyal vassals, among the first of whom is the present petitioner. He prays to God incessantly that Your Majesty's precious and important life which is so necessary to this monarchy may last a great many years.[19]

The outcome of this case is not on record. But it was not uncommon for a wife to administer her husband's property when he was considered incapable or too idle to do so.

NAPOLEON'S COUP: DIVIDING SPAIN

As Josef continued his triumphal tour, a bombshell struck: Napoleon decreed on February 8, 1810, that all the regions north of the Ebro – Cataluña, Aragón, Navarra and the Basque country – were henceforth to be ruled directly by his own generals. Shortly, he added Burgos and the Valladolid-Palencia-Toro district, and Andalucía, where he gave Marshal Soult supreme civil and military command. Josef was to be left with nothing but Castilla la Nueva, Extremadura, and a small portion of Castilla la Vieja and, as his only forces, the Bonapartist Army of the Centre and the few Spanish regiments he had created, mainly of prisoners of war who were voluntarily prepared to enrol, often with the idea of deserting to the patriots whenever the chance occurred. Nothing probably did the Bonapartist cause in Spain more political harm than Napoleon's decree which he justified by the high cost of maintaining the French army there, and the Spanish administration's failure to gather sufficient revenues to pay for it. While this was probably true, it fooled no Bonapartist or anti-Bonapartist Spaniard. The Emperor had divided Spain along the Ebro and his next move would be to annex the northern part to France. This had been one of his first plans for Spain which he explicitly rejected in the Bayonne constitution where the country's territorial integrity was guaranteed, an integrity which Josef always stressed in his vain attempts to win his subjects' hearts and minds.*

---

* 'The unity of our Holy Religion, the Independence of the Monarchy, the integrity of its territory and the freedom of its citizens are the conditions of the oath I took upon receiving my Crown. It will not be debased on my head', he had announced on his second entry into Madrid, in January 1809 (AHN, *Estado*, Legajo 3004).

Josef sent various emissaries to Paris to try to persuade his brother to reverse his decision and accept the terms of the Bayonne constitution, threatening to abdicate otherwise. But there was no changing the Emperor's mind. The Spaniards had not accepted the constitution, he retorted, and Josef had kept the throne only thanks to the French armies' presence. He did not therefore feel any obligation to respect the constitution.

In November 1810, during Masséna's Portuguese campaign, Napoleon was even more brutally frank.

> The King of Spain would be very little if he were not the Emperor's brother and the general of his armies. He would be so little that a mere town of four thousand souls would be stronger than all the supporters he may have in Spain. Even his guard is French. Not a single Spanish officer of repute has shed his blood for the King.[20]

Napoleon's reference to the number of Josef's supporters was obviously understated for ironic effect. What was certainly true was that the country had not rallied to the Bonapartist cause. The regime was faced with an irresolvable contradiction. Because of popular resistance, only the French army on the ground kept it in being; but by its actions that very same army undermined any possibility of the new government winning positive public acceptance or legitimation. Spain was occupied by a foreign military power which was visibly more concerned with imposing its will and sacking the country's resources than with improving its lot.

AFRANCESADOS

Those who supported the Bonapartist regime were well aware of the contradiction. If they supported the new regime it was generally for one of three reasons: opportunism; careerism or the need to earn a living, irrespective of who was in power; and genuine political belief in the reformist policies Josef tried to implement.

There were considerable numbers of the first two categories who, once their region was conquered, changed coat and went to work for the new regime. Judge Francisco de León Bendicho, of the Granada high court, for example, had served the Suprema as its commissioner to La Mancha and subsequently on the important La Carolina junta which oversaw the patriot Army of the Centre's activities. Although as commissioner, he did not prove to be particularly decisive or valiant, refusing to continue investigating the villages' 'dangerous turmoil' without a cavalry escort, he later redeemed himself by collecting a considerable quantity of parish church plate and jewellery from La Mancha for the patriot cause; and was one of two La Carolina junta members sent to the Mancha to find food for the army on its abortive Madrid offensive which ended in the rout of Ocaña.

After the Suprema's flight, he returned to the Granada High Court where, in June 1810, under French occupation, he was the criminal courts' chief justice. Two months later he had risen to become the court's dean. Something then went wrong. Possibly because of his past connections with the Suprema, General Sebastiani, Granada's imperial commander, arrested him in his home and ordered him to be sent to Madrid to be placed at the government's disposition. From this moment at the beginning of September 1810, until fifteen months later, evidence of his fate vanished. Then, equally suddenly, he reappeared in December 1811 as president of the Málaga extraordinary criminal tribunal, the Bonapartist court which tried guerrillas, bandits and the like. The court's life was languid: no one was sentenced, let alone executed during his tenure of office which ended exactly a year later in 1812 with his appointment to the equivalent Madrid tribunal. As part of new justice reforms, these courts were very shortly abolished, and Bendicho was last heard of, in April 1813, as a judge on the Bonapartist provisional Madrid court.[21] He was a judge who evidently believed that, with the same impartiality, he could try 'dissidents' of one side or the other.

The ideologically committed afrancesados were a different case. Most were usually enlightened men of the old generation – this was particularly true of those in government – who had believed in reforming Spain from above: 'everything for the people without the people', had been enlightened despotism's policy. Reform without disorder, in other words. They considered themselves as 'patriotic' as the patriots, if not more so, inveighing against a fratricidal war which they envisaged as destroying the country and preventing the reforms which the great majority of Spaniards knew were needed. The nation's geographical indivisibility was as important to them as to the patriots. Though they recognized the inevitability in the circumstances of the French army's presence they in fact disliked it, seeing it clearly for what it was; but they could also not forget that for over a century France and Spain had been allies, and that Britain, with her threatening designs on the South American colonies, had been the natural enemy. Only Napoleon was strong enough to keep the British at bay.

Some ideological afrancesados – there were not many of them in all – had like a number of patriots begun the war on the other side. The rising, the mob in the streets, the fear of revolution had brought the former into the Bonapartist camp; while the patriots' victory at Bailén in the summer of 1808 had kindled the hope among others that resistance was not only possible but could triumph. Until the war hardened the lines, the divisions were often very thin. It was more the means of how to achieve them than the reformist ends which separated them.

MILITANCIES: FRANCISCO AMORÓS
AND THE FRENCH ARMY

The friction between Spanish Bonapartist government officials and the French military was exemplified by Francisco Amorós, an ideologically convinced afrancesado (and ex-Godoy supporter), and General Thiébault, the French military governor of Castilla la Vieja. Amorós, who was the king's regal commissioner in Burgos, unceasingly complained to Josef's government about Thiébault's military inactivity against the guerrillas and his active attempts to take over the region's civil administration. On one occasion in the summer of 1809, a convoy of 110 carts of munitions heading from Burgos for Valladolid, with a small escort, was successfully intercepted by several guerrilla parties which had united for the attack. 'One thousand wretched men, poorly armed and led made a fool of five thousand excellent soldiers whom this general [Thiébault] has at his command, without knowing how to use them', Amorós informed the king, adding that the general had not had the courtesy to receive him as the monarch's representative.[22]

By September 1809, the situation between the two had become even more critical. A petty incident gave a good idea of the tension. The Burgos police chief appointed by Amorós arrested a local tailor for 'comments subversive to honourable opinion'. Thiébault immediately ordered his release. The police chief handed in his resignation which Amorós refused, and the former re-arrested the tailor. Thiébault again sent an aide-de-camp to release him; but the tailor now refused to leave prison because he feared the consequences and 'respected, as he should, his natural [i.e. Spanish] judges'. Whereupon Amorós ordered his release because of his 'honourable conduct' and the police chief again resigned and was replaced by another Amorós appointee.[23]

Thiébault retaliated in a decree placing all police matters and Spanish troops serving the king under French military command. He informed Amorós that General Kellerman, governor of all northern Spain, had ordered that no general measures be taken without his permission. Amorós riposted by sending Thiébault the king's orders on his appointment as regal commissioner.

Amorós saw only too clearly that the new regime needed the imperial army to consolidate its rule, but at the same time that the army was in large part responsible for the regime's failure to ensure the people's loyalty. Although armed force was necessary, the French army could not achieve the latter aim. More was needed.

> The great gap between the triumphant French conquerors and the Spaniard impoverished by the war and resentful of its ravages, but indomitable because of his concerns and tenacious temperament, must be reconciled by persons loyal to and fervent in the royal service if the king is to become the sovereign of all Spaniards.[24]

However, six weeks later, with Thiébault's decree round his neck, and further experience of the French army's actions, Amarós was doubtful that even the previously well-disposed would support the Bonapartist regime.

> Some French military commanders are now so hated for their behaviour that the Spanish refuse even to accept any benefits they offer. Military governors refuse to allow . . . the Spanish authorities to carry out Your Majesty's and ministers' civil and political orders . . . as the [Bayonne] constitution guaranteed. The people's displeasure and irritation will become general as a result.[25]

The French military's determination to control the civil administration, he continued, had in Burgos led them to line their pockets with a 'considerable portion of the royal revenues', a foolhardy practice which could only end in trouble. It was not only embezzlement but French military exactions which concerned Amorós. A delegation from the township of Belorado had recently made the fifty-kilometre journey to Burgos to complain to him personally about the exactions Thiébault had imposed. They had travelled this distance, he reported to the king, because they feared to put their complaint in writing. Thiébault had threatened to burn Belorado to the ground if they remonstrated about what he had extorted from the inhabitants.[26]

When two Burgos hospital employees deserted their posts, Thiébault ordered all the hospitalized sick to be sent to prison. Even worse, it had come to Amorós' attention that in the Basque town of Mondragón the local French commandant ran his own court of justice.

> In his horrible tribunal a man's life depends solely on whether or not he has one hundred reales to pay for his freedom . . . This officer has an obsession to be known as they military commandant who has condemned the greatest number of people to death . . .[27]

Finally, Amorós, who had already asked to be relieved of his post which he had occupied for little more than two months, wrote to various government ministers saying he was leaving Burgos for Madrid to report personally on the state of affairs with the French military in Castilla la Vieja.[28]

BONAPARTIST REFORMS

One of Josef's demands of all those employed by his regime was that they swear allegiance to the throne. This might seem a fairly normal procedure, but in the circumstances it was bitterly resented by most Spanish officialdom and kept not a few from serving him.* The patriots had made it abundantly clear that all those who swore allegiance would be considered traitors. Indeed, a change had come about in the language they used to describe those who served the Bonaparte government. At the start of the war, these were 'bad' Spaniards; by 1810, they had lost their right to be called 'Spaniards' at all. By this change, the patriots demonstrated that, in their minds, the very essence of 'Spanishness' was anti-Bonapartist.†

* The San Sebastián corregidor wisely left it to the individual's free choice whether to swear or not (AGS, *Papeles del Gobierno intruso, Gracia y Justicia*, Legajo 1130, n.n.) but he seems to have been alone in doing so.
† The word 'afrancesado' had been used before the war, usually pejoratively, to label those who followed French fashions and customs. The first use of it to indicate a follower of the Bonapartist cause that I have found dates from May 1809, in a letter from Cartagena which denounced a number of local people to the Suprema for being 'afrancesados'.

A Galician supporter of the new regime, who titled himself a Spanish patriot, expressed many afrancesado concerns in a public appeal to his fellow Spaniards to end the useless bloodshed which was 'devastating the country' and encouraging the 'horrors of anarchy' to defend the indefensible:

> The preservation of the privileged classes, whose unjust authority runs counter to the country's well-being . . . and some clerics, who without conscience or virtue are vassals' lords and look only to their own interests . . . these are the two classes which today make their unhappy compatriots believe they have taken to arms in defence of religion and the former king, when in reality they are sending them to their deaths to continue their abuses down to the very last victim.*[29]

Napoleon's 1808 Chamartín reforms – the Inquisition's abolition first and foremost – met with the Galician author's full approval. The Inquisition had 'excessively brutalized the nation . . . and contributed not a little to Spain's progressive ruin' in the past. 'Who cannot bless the Emperor for eliminating it?' Similarly, the abrogation of feudal rights was a great step forward because the lords exercised a power in their domains greater even than a sultan's and certainly more extensive than the king's. For Spaniard to fight Spaniard was one of the 'worst outrages' imaginable, in his view. 'Let us leave this to those alone who have interests to defend . . . while the rest of us return to our ordinary tasks . . . to live in peace, if ever we can achieve it one day.'

Many on both sides had once admired Napoleon as much for his administrative talents, the domestic peace and reforms he had brought to France, as for his military genius; and during the war these committed Bonapartists wanted his legal code introduced in Spain. But even they recognized that it could not be imported wholesale; a royal decree establishing a committee to prepare legislative proposals necessary for its introduction was created in 1809, but the junta charged with the task of adapting it to Spanish conditions was still at work a year later.[30] Almost certainly, like Spanish objections to the Bayonne constitution which had resulted in Napoleon's accepting changes, vested interests were at work; most afrancesados believed that Spain must reform itself in its own manner, in which they differed little from the patriots. The end result was that, with or without reforms, the code was never introduced by Josef, though certain changes contained in the Napoleonic Bayonne constitution – the start of an independent judicial system, for example – were instigated. Other reforms, like the division of the country into prefectures, each with its prefect, were taken over from France.†

---

* The anonymous author was writing in the midst of the 1809 Galician uprising which led to the French withdrawal from the region.

† The existing town halls were to be replaced by municipalities elected by local men of property, industry or commerce chosen by lot. But there was one other important innovation: the corregidor, who was not elected but appointed by the government, was no longer to play any judicial role, or the justices have any part in local administration. (AGS, *Papeles del Gobierno intruso, Gracia y Justicia*, Legajo 1109, n.n., decree recalling to justices and corregidores the separation of their functions, Madrid, November 5, 1810. On the question of the separation of the judicial and administrative powers in general under the regime, see Muñoz de Bustillo Romero, 1991, pp. 73–80.)

In some cases, like the abolition of the religious (and military) orders, and of all noble titles with the exception of those recognized by Josef,* the new regime went further than Napoleon had himself proposed for Spain in his Chamartín decrees. Señorial rights, as the Emperor had decreed, were also eliminated† and so, too, were special jurisdictions except for commercial transactions and 'for the time being' the military. All the old state Councils were decreed out of existence, the Consejo de Castilla being replaced by a twenty-five member Council of State. Hanging was abolished; in future only the garrotte would be used, and the regime looked into ways of making this more humane (though the Madrid corregidor refused to pay for the work).[31]

The government concerned itself with primary education, 'the teaching of the Christian doctrine and the three "Rs"', and in the larger towns created secondary schools in buildings which had been taken over from those who had fled or in expropriated friaries or convents. In Madrid it set up a girls' school also. The reform of prisons was another objective actively pursued, at least in Madrid and Sevilla, where overcrowding and unsanitary conditions were rife. Old prisons, both for men and women, were shut down and expropriated friars' houses often used to replace them. It was not the government's policy to 'keep offenders for a long time in prison', the Justice Minister, Manuel Romero, informed the king, recommending a royal pardon for a women prisoner.[32]

Urbanism was of particular interest to Josef and in this he was followed by many of Napoleon's generals who were in command of cities. The king, for example, knocked down a warren of streets in front of the Royal Palace in Madrid to make today's Plaza de Oriente and, to clear access to the Plaza Mayor, built two new squares for vendors' stalls.

But in one important aspect the regime, which believed in 'an owner's sacred rights', prejudiced Madrileños' daily living conditions by freeing rents in expropriated property bought from the state, and in allowing landlords to evict tenants in arrears with their rents. This brought a flood of protests, including those from women schoolteachers. Rosa Sánchez who taught poor children in the Buen Suceso and Baroneja quarters of the city, appealed to a judge to seek a compromise with her landlord who was threatening to throw her out of her room, 'given the importance to the public of the work I do'.[33]

Recognizing that the government lacked the money to pay teachers in charity schools and other educational establishments, and that their evictions did 'grave harm to the public good', the interior minister proposed that evictions should be judicially prevented, but the justice minister disagreed. Although the law gave tenants forty days' grace before eviction, unscrupulous landlords often did not respect this, and evicted them on a few days' notice. The protests continued but there was no evidence that the government took action.[34]

* In Sevilla in 1810, he recognized a slew of marqueses who had sworn allegiance to the throne, many of them concerned no doubt to retain their titles. (AGS, *Papeles del Gobierno intruso, Gracia y Justicia*, Legajo 1104.)
† Although not all French military governors obeyed this reform, in particular Suchet. (See Chapter 17.)

Raising agrarian production was a constant concern. In 1809, Josef had distributed unused land of the Aranjuez royal estates in plots to local villagers. At the end of the following year, the superintendent of the royal household in Madrid, the comte de Miot de Melito, reported that the plots had 'reached the extreme of producing nothing'.[35] The villagers, the French intendente of Aranjuez informed him, 'continue to destroy not only the woods, but the palace itself, the guards' and all the other houses scattered over the vast domain', despite his threats to oblige their municipalities to pay for the damage done. Meanwhile, the French garrison commanders

> want only to be provided for their table with everything they desire and when they do not get it, they try to extort it. The local justice is not strong enough to stand up to all the kicks and blows he has received [from them] and there is no one who wishes to take his place. (Le marquis de Varese, Aranjuez intendente)[36]

But there was another reason for this state of affairs: the guerrillas. They 'taxed' any smallholder who worked a plot. Ninety of Tomasito's party arrived one spring day in 1811 in Añover del Tajo, accompanying a patriot war commissioner, and relentlessly demanded thirty-five reales per fanega of un-irrigated land from each villager who worked the king's estates. These belonged to H.M. Fernando VII, whose rights were being abused and the true government of Spain and the Indies had authorized a commission, which extended to another four villages, to demand these monies from those who were unlawfully working H.M.'s lands, the war commissioner's proclamation stated. Those who could not pay were obliged to hand over their draught horses, and some were arrested until they paid up. The guerrilleros stayed until nearly nightfall because they could not secure money from a number who had given their horses. Before they left, they returned the horses to their owners, saying that they would return in a few days to collect the payment 'without failure', and the kingdom's Cortes gathered in Cádiz would determine what should be done with the crops when they were gathered. In all, they collected 5,500 reales from Añover, according to a receipt they left, before crossing to the southern bank of the Tajo.[37]

But it was in Andalucía that the major agrarian effort was made. Mariano Urquijo, Josef's first minister, complained in July 1810 that

> we are at present so confined to Madrid alone . . . that materially we cannot exist, and shall have to go to Andalucía for food . . . because the insurgents and their English friends barely allow us here to procure supplies to maintain the army . . . La Mancha is a theatre of bandits and the poor. Our provinces are full of thieves and people on the move . . . We shall, I repeat, have to obtain food from Córdoba and Sevilla.[38]

Urquijo's complaints must be taken with a grain of salt because he was pointing out the adverse effects of Napoleon's division of Spain to his fellow minister, Miguel Azanza, who was in Paris trying to persuade Napoleon to revoke his decision. Moreover, it was a letter intercepted by the guerrilla and may have been tampered with before being published in the official patriot *Gaceta de la Regencia*. Nonetheless, the importance in the government's mind of Andalucía as a source of food was almost certainly not exaggerated. The grain harvest of 1810 was nowhere nearly as abundant as the record 1808 crop.

The regime's regal commissioner for Andalucía, conde de Montarco, was particularly preoccupied by the state of agriculture which was not as flourishing as Urquijo might have thought. A great deal of land was untilled, there was a shortage of day labourers, estates went unrented, and French army exactions as usual took an undue proportion of the crops. Montarco's first measure at the end of 1810 allowed anyone to till unused land, provided they first asked the local corregidor; except for the land's owner or tenants, no one was to be given preference.

The initiative received little or no response – in Ronda, for example, no one applied for land. This may have been due to fear of guerrilla reprisals – the Ronda serranía was one of the first of the Andalucian guerrilla areas – or to villagers' passive resistance to any innovative measure, especially one initiated by the Bonapartist regime when the war's outcome or even end remained uncertain, or to a combination of these. Montarco decided that more drastic measures were needed and ordered in July 1811 that all fixed land rents should be reduced by one quarter for that and the coming year, with the exception of those which had been voluntarily reduced by more than that amount. Landowners' perquisites of chickens, pigs, straw and the like were reduced by one-third. Moreover, twenty-five percent of village or common lands could be tilled.

This plan for increasing production also came to naught because municipalities were obliged to buy seed corn sufficient for the increased tillage. Most of them were by now so poor that they had no money to spare on agriculture. In November 1811, Montarco made one last attempt. Farmers were to be handsomely rewarded for switching to the cultivation of new crops which yielded more than one harvest a year like potatoes and certain cereals easier to grow than wheat. As eight months later the French military withdrew from Andalucía, the outcome of this initiative remained unknown. There can be little doubt however that if Montarco's reforms had taken root, Andalucian agriculture, and with it some of the traditional social structures of the agrarian world, would have radically changed.[39]

*

Josef, once more on the point of abdicating in March 1811 – 'my presence here is today completely useless', he wrote to the Emperor[40] – decided at the end of the month to go to France on receiving the news of the birth of Napoleon's son and heir; the Emperor had asked him to be the child's godfather. Relations between the two brothers had by now become so strained that Napoleon barely communicated directly with Josef, leaving this to his chief of staff, Marshal Berthier. In late April Josef set off. Many afrancesados believed he would never return. He was already in France when he received the Emperor's order that he was not to leave Spain; he ignored it and continued to Paris. There in a long and stormy meeting on Spanish affairs, Josef succeeded in winning some concessions.

Napoleon granted him five hundred thousand francs until July 1, and a further one million francs per month for the rest of the year. Half of this was to fund the Army of the Centre which henceforth was guaranteed to be under Josef's direct command, and more importantly, one-quarter of all the tax funds collected by the imperial armies in the regions which, under Napoleon's division of Spain, depended on Paris, was to be handed over to Madrid. Justice and the administration of these regions was in future to be carried out in the king's name; and all French army commanders were now to report to Josef on their military and political initiatives. In other words, the king regained some degree of authority over the land he was supposed to reign.[41]

Though there could no doubt about the regime's willingness to bring in reforms, there was always something improvised about those which were enacted. Like the division of Spain into prefectures, which was intended to show Napoleon that Madrid still controlled the *whole* country's future, they tended often to be reactions to immediate situations, not part of a general and considered plan. In the circumstances, probably little more could be expected: dependent on French bayonets to remain in being, subject to Napoleon's diktats, to imperial marshals' political caprices, to shortage of funds and the ebb and flow of the war itself, it was hardly surprising that the regime had an air of provisionality about it.

PATRIOT REFORMS:
THE CONSTITUENT CORTES OF CÁDIZ

On Monday, September 24, 1810, the unicameral Cortes assembled – or rather those deputies who had managed to reach the Isla de León, usually by sea – in the church of San Pedro and took the oath to 'carry out faithfully and legally the task which the Nation has entrusted to you, preserving the laws of Spain, yet modifying if necessary those that must be changed for the good of the Nation'.[42]

The claim to sovereignty had been at the heart of the provincial juntas and the Junta Suprema. But none had claimed, as the Cortes immediately declared in its first decree, that it represented popular national sovereignty. As the nation's sole elected legislature it separated the executive and the legislative – the judiciary would follow shortly – and was the first real rupture with the Old Order, in which the monarch had incorporated all three functions in his divinely appointed being. The nation's will, expressed in the legislature, was thus set above the monarchy which became the executive to whom the former could delegate such powers as it saw fit. At the same time, in its first measure, it recognized Fernando VII as Spain's sole and legitimate king, while turning the regency into the executive branch of the government and titling itself 'His Majesty'. The Old Regime's adherents, like the Bishop of Orense, one of the regents, were not surprisingly incensed at this usurpation of monarchical rights which heralded the creation of a parliamentary monarchy. He denounced the Cortes' declaration of sovereignty, accusing it of turning the king into 'the nation's vassal' and asserting that its assumption of an omnipotent power would 'consummate the Nation's ruin and even offend Religion'.[43] The deputies responded by confining the bishop to a monastery for six months; but the introduction of religion as a political issue from the Cortes' inception did not bode well for the future.

Of the just over one hundred deputies who had assembled, nearly one half were substitutes for those who had not yet been able to reach Cádiz or whose election had been delayed because they were in the French zone. They had been elected by their fellow countrymen who had sought refuge in Cádiz.* Twenty-six of these substitutes represented the South American colonies and two the Philippines. As little by little the elected deputies arrived their numbers rose to 233. Of these approximately one-third were clergymen (although only five among them were bishops), a handful of titled nobility, another handful of merchants and property owners, and a majority of mainly professionals – lawyers, professors, government officials, physicians and literati. One social stratum was entirely absent: the lower orders.

The commoners and clerics who made up the greatest number of deputies were in general moderate reformers who knew what measures they wished to see enacted although they had no overall parliamentary plan for achieving them. It was only as a small group among them proposed one reform after another, which was usually approved by the majority, that it became clear that a new political order was taking shape which was very different from that of the Old Order's absolutism. In this view, freedom – political and civil – was the only basis which would bring a lasting and just felicity to the nation and ensure that despotism could not again rule the country. The vassal of the past must become the citizen of the future. Equality – not Jacobin social equality – but equality before the law and equality of opportunity went hand in hand with liberty. Equality before the law meant sweeping away the maze of legal privileges enjoyed by the two upper estates, the nobility and Church, as well as that of distinct institutions, and opening up to all Spaniards the freedom to rise in society as the reward of their own abilities, merits and virtues. In a word, the reformers were proposing a *meritocracy*. The citizen would be free when he – for women did not form part of the political theory – enjoyed the same legal rights as every other citizen, without the exclusions which the privileged had imposed on him in the past.

The outstanding reformers came soon to be known as 'liberals', the first time the word had been applied to a political grouping, and after a time their opponents were named 'serviles', that was to say servile to absolutism. There was one other important aspect to this nascent liberalism which remained an essential tenet of its ideology thereafter: the rejection of state intervention –

---

* Except for those from unoccupied regions, the majority of mainland deputies were originally substitutes; in large part this was due to the fact that it was only in June that finally the regency, under pressure of the Cádiz and other provincial juntas, and the serious news of the South American colonies' increasing dissidence, summoned the Cortes to meet two months later, giving little time for elections to be held in those regions where the former Suprema's instructions to elect deputies could not be put into effect. Little by little, elections were held even in most French-controlled regions, demonstrating the imperial occupation's porousness over large parts of the country.

inherited then as a reaction to the enlightened reformers' attempts to involve the state in resolving all the problems which held back Spain's economic growth. Individual interest, not government laws and regulations, were the stimulus for progress, the liberals maintained: and individual interest could only be assured by the hallowed right of property and by the free market in every aspect of economic life. All 'monopolistic' interests, such as the guilds, which set prices and determined the labour market in their trades, were to be abolished.

Within three weeks of the Cortes' assembling, it began discussion on a proposal to free the press. The issue had been aired by Calbo Rozas in the Suprema without success; but the Cortes was a different matter. Three deputies made particularly powerful speeches in favour: Agustín Argüelles, a thirty-four-year-old Asturian hidalgo lawyer; José Mexía, born in Quito and professor of medicine at Lima University; and Diego Muñoz Torrero, an Extremaduran cleric and former rector of Salamanca University, who summed up the argument in favour with the words: 'the right to examine a government's actions is an imprescriptible right that no nation can renounce without renouncing its nationhood'. The Cortes approved press freedom, but it was a conditioned approval which applied only to the expression of *political* ideas. All religious writings had still to receive the consent of prior censorship, although this was removed from the Inquisition to the bishops. Moreover, a supreme censorship junta was created – along with provincial juntas of the same nature – to guard against abuses of press freedom, political or otherwise, and see to it that the accused were prosecuted by the courts.[44]

Freedom of the political press turned out to be a double-edged weapon for the liberals. Amidst a plethora of newspapers which sprang up in Cádiz, the liberals' opponents ensured that their own press took every opportunity to attack the progressives, to proselytize and make adverse propaganda, while the liberals paid the price of their most radical wing running afoul of the censorship junta which sent a couple of them to gaol for several weeks. Moreover, the liberals, with their visceral fear that the common people should inflect or infect their political agenda, made no attempt to find new graphic forms to attract their support, relying on the Old Order's classic art styles in their papers or pamphlets. Where a Goya was needed to bring alive the disasters of Absolutism, the old genre of classical print, even if intended as criticism, subtly reinforced a continuity rather a rupture with the past.[45]

The question of the colonies had arisen on the day after the Cortes assembled. The American deputies had put forward the need of accompanying the Cortes' decree establishing its national sovereignty with a statement that the colonies' inhabitants held equal rights to those of the metropolis and conceding an amnesty to those who had taken part in the recent events. In a secret session, the Cortes agreed.[46] But it came too late and was not enough.

A previous problem re-emerged only a fortnight after the freedom of the press was approved. The Cortes appealed for volunteers to build fortifications and for the recruitment of ten thousand men for the army. The results were nugatory. The liberals had no more learned the lessons of the past two years than the Suprema members had in their time. Meanwhile the Cortes set up a Constitutional Commission of nine lawyers and six clergy, of whom ten in all were Spanish and five Spanish-Americans, presided over by the liberal cleric Muñoz Torrero. Liberals and their opponents* were about equally represented; the ultra absolutists had only two members.

When, in December 1810, well-founded rumour had it that Napoleon intended to give a Bonaparte princess in marriage to Fernando (in fact, the latter had beseeched the Emperor to do so and had been turned down), the Cortes acted in united determination to prevent it by passing a motion that a Spanish monarch could not marry without the knowledge and approval of the Spanish nation.

Although a number of liberals had put forward motions at the beginning of 1811 to abolish feudal land rights, it was nearly a year since its inception before the Cortes began to debate the question which directly concerned the majority of the population.† At stake were the two forms of señorial domination of the rural world. The first, and by far the most extensive, was a lordship's jurisdictional rights which did not necessarily bear any relationship to actual ownership of the land but granted the right to appoint local justices and municipal councillors who could be expected to do their lord's bidding in any dispute with his vassals. Such disputes inevitably arose over the lord's other feudal rights to dues and tributes from those working the land, rights which also included the monopoly of mills, smithies, baking ovens, brothels,‡ grazing, of hunting and shooting . . .§ The lord might be an individual or an institution, a bishopric or monastery, for example. Most of the rights, which belonged originally to the monarchy, had been sold to them in the past by near-bankrupt kings to raise funds.

The second type of señorial holding was that of the land itself which a grateful monarch had originally bestowed on a noble vassal who had distinguished himself in the monarchy's service, usually in a military capacity. The land ceded the crown's rights over uncultivated land which belonged to neither a municipality nor an individual. At the beginning of the nineteenth century, these señorios were not usually directly worked by the owner, heir of a long distant forebear, but parcelled out into holdings or even smallholdings and

---

* The anti-liberals, it should be noted, were not hostile to all reform and at this time there was a large floating vote which did not divide along pre-defined 'party' lines.

† In the meanwhile it enacted some significant minor reforms: judicial torture was abolished; instead of remaining the exclusive preserve of the nobility, military colleges – and thus the right to become an officer – were opened to commoners; the provincial juntas were each reduced to a body of nine *elected* members, apart from the intendente, and presided over by the local captain general; Cortes deputies were forbidden to hold other official positions, and with a few exceptions a maximum wage of forty thousand reales a year was decreed for state officials.

‡ On the duque de Osuna's Andalucian domain, the township and village brothels were among the most profitable concerns and, to increase their revenues, the dukes attempted to wrest them from the municipalities and incorporate them into their señorial prerogatives, fixing the prices and wages of the employees. The brothels were clearly differentiated by their colour and other external signs from the ordinary village house. (See Atienza Hernández, 1987, p. 126.)

§ For a more detailed account of the señorial system, see Prologue, pp. xviii–xix.

rented out. Where the owner was also the jurisdictional lord he or she would collect dues and tributes, which had over time often become confused with rents. To complicate matters still further, señorial domination could vary in detail in different parts of the country without losing its basic purpose of extracting the landworking population's surplus. 'Nothing contributes more greatly to the unhappiness of villagers than to be subject to jurisdictions and particular señoríos', said a Valencian deputy, Antonio Lloret, who came from a señorial township.[47]

The simplest political solution to these forms of rural domination was to abolish all types of señoríos and reincorporate them as crown property, repaying the owners who could show that their original title was legally foolproof. This, indeed, was what the deputy for Soria, García Herreros, proposed in a motion at the beginning of a long and intense debate which led to the noble deputies collectively asking for the only time in the Cortes' history that the terms of a motion be clarified. This they soon were by another proposal by García Herreros which demanded that only señorial jurisdictional rights be revoked and that land recognized legally to belong to the señor become his or her private property. This took into account the fact that the señor's forbears had often over the centuries expanded their señoríos by abuse of their power and the forceful recognition of rights over land that had neither been ceded by the crown nor bought from individuals. Their legal ownership of señorial rights would have to be proven.

Pre-war, as land values rose, villagers engaged in lengthy legal disputes, lasting anything up to half a century, to reclaim these rights, which involved the nobility in considerable costs and conflicts with townships and villages in their señoríos. The more acute among the nobility had come to realize that they would be better off as private landowners rather than as the señorial incumbents of disputed land. Rising rents would offset any loss of dues and tribute. It was this awareness that led them not to fear the liberals depriving them of feudal lordships as long as the former confirmed them as property owners; and this was one of the reasons that had made their wartime 'popular front' alliance with the liberal reformers possible.

Heirs of the eighteenth-century enlightened reformers, the liberals had no time for the 'idle' nobility as it had been called by their intellectual forebears. But on the señorial issue the liberals were not prepared for a showdown with the nobility. It could be argued that the necessities of the war forbade any such rupture among the patriots. But in fact the liberals, in agreeing to abolish only jurisdictional señoríos, were trapped in their own ideology: their determination that there be one – and only one – law before which all Spaniards must be equal meant that special jurisdictions, such as those of the jurisdictional lordships, had to be abolished. And their insistence on the sanctity of private property meant that they could not deprive any individual of his or her right to enjoy and use it for the felicity of the nation as a whole. The proposal that all señoríos be taken over by the crown quickly dropped from the debate. Ideology dominated – as it was later to dominate the Cortes' debates on the Constitution and the rupture between a reforming and a defensively reactionary Spain. And it was permitted to dominate during the señorial debate by the absence of a large-scale villagers' movement, like that of the French Revolution, demanding the distribution of the nobility's domains which would have pressured the liberals into more radical action. As it was, the decree of August 6, 1811, abolishing señorial jurisdiction did nothing to reform the landowning structure of Spain since the señores continued to hold their large domains, converted now into private property. Moreover, the decree contained two fatal ambiguities. Whether those señoríos which were both territorial and jurisdictional were abolished because of their latter status; and whether it was the señor or his vassals who had to produce the evidence of rightful ownership to disputed land.

*

With a history of anti-feudal struggle stretching back to the sixteenth century, the Valencian countryside was the focal point of renewed conflict between señorial domination and the villagers from the very beginning of the war. Many villagers stopped paying dues and tributes, alleging in part that their contributions of food supplies and money to the 'national' cause made further impositions impossible to meet. A Suprema decree in 1809 expropriating the rents of all those suspected of siding with the Bonapartist regime, whose whereabouts were unknown or who received rents in other parts of patriot Spain became a useful instrument in their hands, since many of the titled nobility had señoríos in provinces outside Valencia* or lived elsewhere; interpreting the decree with considerable latitude, local corregidores instructed the villagers not to pay them rent.[48]

While landownership was an important element of the anti-feudal struggle, the latter was marked by another factor: it was the large farmers who led the conflict and were the most vocal in their protests at señorial domination. They resented having to pay dues and tributes to the lord, who profited at their expense and labour; members of the local oligarchies, they wanted to be free agrarian entrepreneurs, unsubjected to their lord's restrictive rights and justice.

The Cortes' August decree added fuel to the flames. It did not satisfy the villagers who wanted land, and it dissatisfied all those who had made their living from the señorial system. Moreover, it was rare in Valencia for there to be a clear distinction between jurisdictional and territorial señoríos. Unlike in Castilla, where the señores' income came almost exclusively from rents, in Valencia by the end of the eighteenth century, dues and tributes accounted for half of their income. In consequence, the decree's ambiguity as to whether this meant the abolition of both or only of the jurisdictional aspect, allowed villagers to accept the former interpretation. Though the question of whether it was the señores or their vassals who had to present the documentary proof of their alleged rights was a complicating issue, for most villagers all señoríos had been abolished.† As a lawyer representing the Valencian señorial landlords wrote:

* Or more correctly, the kingdom of Valencia which included Alicante and Castellón.
† In effect, the historical peculiarities of the señoríos' formation was likely to make them liable to incorporation in the crown.

Since the August decree was published in Valencia, my plaintiffs' villagers rejected
with vulgar or insulting gestures not only the jurisdiction but also the prerogatives and
prohibitions which the decree left to private owners. They used violence to usurp the
provisions which it granted to owners and which did not fall under jurisdictional
abolition: our share of the crops, the payments due . . . from [land] contracts freely
made . . . Many also had the temerity to take over our buildings and property . . . In
Alberique they went so far as to take over the owner's and justice's houses . . . and put
to public auction the boat, inn, shops, baking ovens and mills, and also the owner's
own rooms, and to smash the coat of arms in the portico and replace it with the title of
plaza de la Constitución . . .[49]

Elsewhere, townships, especially in the Alicante señorío of the conde de
Altamira (who, under his other title of marqués de Astorga, had for a time
been the Suprema's president) set up 'popular juntas' to run local affairs in place
of the count's administration. There was no shortage of anti-feudal incidents
throughout the patriot zone; what was lacking was their fusion into a mass
movement to ensure that the Cortes abolished the señorial system in its totality.
Given that a large number of small and medium-sized farmers were armed and
fighting in the guerrilla, their absence from the political scene was the more
striking.*

The Cortes, meanwhile, found itself confronted with another question of
land ownership. What to do with land which was not owned individually but
collectively, such as village commons? But also entailed estates and eccle-
siastically owned land. The Cortes only found time to debate the first. The
ideological liberal argument was that the commons should be sold to the
highest bidder without any type of restriction.† Those deputies who put this
view admitted that only the wealthy would benefit, but they believed that in
the long run this would be to society's advantage. However, they ran into
criticism from their own fellow liberals. Returning to the enlightened reformers' argument that a state's wealth and strength depended on the size of
its population, García Herreros stressed that a population increase was
meaningless if the additional people were poor and wretched. They must
be part of families with their roots in the land if the state's wealth were to
increase. Thus a motion was tabled in 1811 that one-third of the commons
should be sold in small plots, and all that were not sold should be distributed
among the landless and small tenantry. The more radical liberals raised the
limit to one half of the commons.

* This question is discussed further in the following chapter.
† The Catalan deputy Aner had proposed in 1811 that landowners have absolute
freedom to do what they wished with their properties; they could be enclosed, planted
to whatever crop the landowner wanted or left as pasture, rented out at a freely
agreed sum, and its produce sold at whatever price the market would bear. With the
abolition of internal customs and suppression of locally fixed prices and embargoes
of recently harvested grain for local supply and storage, the freedom of the agrarian
market had become absolute. This decree suffered the same fate as the distribution of
the commons, but it was certainly the most drastic socio-economic proposal put
forward by the liberals.

The state will gain a great amount if the number of owners is multiplied, if ownership is extended to those who presently do not own land, and if not a single plot is without its distinct owner.[50]

The motives underlying this motion were not only to increase private property and agricultural production (and thus the state's revenues) but to reward those villagers who had fought in the war. But the decree, published at the beginning of 1813, came too late to have any effect: Fernando's return from his French exile the following year and the restoration of absolutism put an end to it.

17

The Invisible Army:
Guerrilla Successes and Failures

Like a net through which no French soldier who for a moment left his column or garrison could escape, an invisible army spread out over almost all of Spain. (Miot de Mélito, superintendent of Josef's royal household)[1]

One of the most spectacular guerrilla coups of the war was the result of endurance and speed of march. The French infantry had been trained under Napoleon to march fast; but as General Reille reported on taking up his command of Navarra in July 1810, the guerrillas marched twice as fast.[2] Francisco Espoz y Mina, who had taken command of the party formed by Javier Mina, his student relative, after the latter was captured by the French in the spring of 1810, had in one year created a force of four thousand guerrilleros, despite a long period of harassment and pursuit by French forces which had not only driven him from Navarra but dealt him a severe defeat as he and his men attempted to return from Castilla in the autumn of 1810. Dispirited, the guerrilleros had filtered back into their home region. Shortly afterwards a successful ambush in the Carascal pass, a favourite guerrilla position, of a French munitions train guarded by thirty gendarmes provided the guerrilleros with the arms and munitions they desperately needed; and the withdrawal of some of the extra French troops – intended to reinforce Masséna in Portugal and which Reille had drafted into the region as a counter-insurgency force – provided them with time to regroup, refit and rest.

To reimpose discipline was another matter.

Espoz y Mina ordered that all his men be shorn of their long hair, like army conscripts; long hair, braided or held behind the ears was a mark of independence allowed in the army only to officers. Despite his subalterns' fear that the men would mutiny at the humiliation of having their hair cut, he turned the

* I should like to express my indebtedness to the work of two US scholars, Rod Alexander and John Lawrence Tone, for their detailed studies respectively of the Aragonese struggle and Suchet's pacification campaign; and Mina's guerrilla in Navarra, for many of the ideas expressed in this and subsequent chapters, even if not explicitly acknowledged.

event into a masterly display of egalitarian authority: when all his men were shorn, he sat down in front of them and had his own hair cut.[3]

The guerrillas, like the armies, contained their fair share of rogues, villains, troublemakers and the lawless, as Espoz y Mina confessed.

> You have no idea of the sort of people I have. I am in the sad situation of having to count my continued existence by the minute. I have to use several cartridges of a sudden to make myself feared, and when I am alone I see before my eyes a raised hand and dagger about to pierce my heart.[4]

Coming from one of the guerrilla leaders who was said to be more feared in his native Navarra than the French themselves, this was strong language. As a Spanish colonel whom Mina rescued by a surprise attack from a prisoner of war column on its march to France described him:

> Mina is a man of average, slightly blond looks, well-built, about five foot one inch in height, and of few but direct words. He is between twenty-eight and thirty years old, if not more. He does not like women, and would not allow one to be a member of his division. He sleeps only two hours a night, and always with his pistols readied in his belt. He remains shut in his room on the few nights that he goes to a village. He attracts much attention but is very reserved.[5]

After being shorn, Mina's men were issued with new uniforms: brown jackets and trousers, tall black hats and hemp espadrilles which was to be the standard uniform of the Navarrese Division, as Mina called his force. In uniforming his men, he was no different to the majority of guerrilla leaders, since one of the first things they tried to do was to replace with standard uniforms their men's captured pieces of imperial military outfits and shakos – a cylindrical or conical hat with a peak and a plume – which they wore on top of villagers' clothes. The reason was simple: the leaders wanted to be recognized, both by the patriot authorities and the enemy, as official military detachments. As such, they asked the patriot authorities to grant them and their subordinates military rank, and to receive money and aid. From the enemy, they wanted their men who were taken prisoner to be granted the same rights as any regular soldier and not considered, as they only too often were, brigands and gallows-carrion.

The major guerrilla leaders were not men who rejected authority or discipline per se, indeed they often tried to impose better discipline on their forces in the search for greater combat effectiveness, using dispersed soldiers to train their men and officers to lead them when their numbers rose beyond a single leader's control. They gave their guerrillas military-sounding titles – the Castilian Scouts, the Sharpshooters of Cantabria, the Hussars of Iberia – and as far as they could organized their parties along military lines into companies, battalions, regiments, divisions. But one factor would always prevent them from becoming totally militarized: the guerrilleros' loyalty to a charismatic leader. When wounded, as Espoz y Mina was, his men felt leaderless and relapsed into a generalized inactivity.

Their leaders' military inclinations were not reciprocated by the Spanish regular army officers in general. They claimed that the guerrilla was detrimental to the regular army because it recruited the young, protected deserters, encouraged indiscipline and demoralized the enemy-occupied rearguard by its exactions and incursions into villages. Some of these arguments were no more than received ideas. Guerrillas operating around Valladolid gathered up dispersed soldiers and deserters who had not returned to their regiments and as a punishment

> branded their foreheads with the letter 'D' and told them that if in three days they had not reported to the nearest army or party they would be shot and they and their parents and closest siblings would be declared traitors, lose all their property and be branded with the letter T.[6]

The guerrillas' military critics overlooked the fact that the enormous desertion from and dispersal of the regular patriotic armies had begun in late 1808 when the guerrilla had barely started to form and was the outcome of a refusal, on the one hand, to serve in an army in which the privileged orders (including officers) frequently managed, in one form of another, to evade having to face the enemy; and where, once in the army, the ordinary recruit had no other resource than to flee in defeat. It similarly ignored the social problems caused by conscription. It was an open question whether the dispersed soldiers would necessarily, or without considerable restraint, have rejoined the army under commanders they did not trust and who did not trust them. The constant complaints to the authorities about 'dispersed bandits' was an indication that they would – as many indeed did anyway – have become outlaws instead. Or landworkers whom local oligarchs were prepared to protect to secure the labour they needed.

Many guerrilla leaders initially adopted an authoritarian attitude towards villagers, which was not especially surprising in a society where the enlightened, the state and the Church had, pre-war, all ordered the lower orders to obey their instructions on almost every aspect of their public and private lives. But when carried too far this guerrilla 'commandism' was an unaccepted but actual admission of failure. Unable to win the population's support by victories over the French, their forced exactions from villagers, whom they refused to defend from imperial extortion, isolated and marginalized them, as it did the villagers, from the struggle. These parties tended not to last long; their chieftains were betrayed, or captured and sometimes shot by those guerrilla leaders who, sharing the villagers' social origins, fully understood their motives for taking to arms. It was this type of leader who prevented the rearguard from accepting the occupation as an uncontestable inevitability. Two elements were necessary to achieve this. The constant threat to collaborators' lives, or even to those who sought refuge in 'neutrality'. The imperial forces were too thin on the ground to protect all those who were – or would have been – prepared to collaborate; the guerrillas were only sufficiently strong enough to pick off some of them but the example was sufficient. Who could know where they would strike next? The second condition required victories, however small, over the occupation forces, especially on their foraging expeditions. News of these travelled fast. Without these triumphs the villagers resented the guerrillas' impositions, knowing full well that they had still to confront the enemy's exactions.

*

After another winter of renewed French counter-insurgency, when Mina was obliged to disperse his four battalions of one thousand men each to the safety of the mountainous northwest of Navarra and the eastern Pyrenees, with the occasional exception to strike a blow, it was not until May 1811 that the French counter-insurgency again slackened off, and Mina could assemble his four battalions once more. The moment coincided with his receiving the news from his fifth Alavese battalion commander* that a French convoy of over one hundred carriages of French sick and wounded, more than one thousand Spanish and British prisoners of war, and Marshal Masséna's booty from his abortive Portuguese offensive was leaving Vitoria on May 25 for France. The marshal himself was part of the convoy. The escort alone numbered 1,650 troops.

Mina did not hesitate. There was little enough time. He knew the column would have to traverse the Arlabán pass on the borders of Álava and Gui-púzcoa. In an eighty-five-kilometre forced march over rough terrain in two days and a night, he led his four thousand men to Arlabán. Once the column was well into the pass, Mina employed his usual tactics: an initial volley of one musket round per man and then a bayonet charge.

Two hundred and forty of the escort were killed and 160 taken prisoner. The rest fled back along the road they had come. Almost all the one thousand prisoners were released,† and seventy carts captured, the effects and money they contained worth four million reales. Quantities of gunpowder and munitions of which the guerrillas were always short were also seized. Masséna, who had tarried in Vitoria, was warned by the fleeing escort of the attack. The guer-rilleros retired 'laden with gold and portmanteaux full of rich apparel', Mina wrote.[7]‡ It was the biggest guerrilla victory to date.

GUERRILLA NUMBERS

At one or another time during the war over 330 parties were formed. Their number and the rudimentary state of membership figures made problematic the

* This battalion in the southernmost Basque province of Álava was formally part of Mina's Navarrese division but rarely fought alongside the other four.
† The fifty-eight British prisoners, instead of seizing the opportunity to escape, retrieved French muskets and fired on the guerrillas, the imperial general Cafarelli reported. (Tone, 1994, p. 120, fn. 39.)
‡ The first report received and passed on by the British Assistant Commissary in La Coruña, George White, spoke of the guerrillas as having 'instantly put to death six Spanish women' travelling with the convoy. All Spanish men fighting with the French were automatically killed by the Navarrese division when captured. (PRO, *FO*/72/116/ 36v–37. White to William Hamilton, Foreign Office undersecretary, La Coruña, June 29, 1811.)

calculation of their exact numbers at their height in 1811–1812. In this period, however, one fact stood out: the vast majority of guerrilleros were now enrolled in one or other of sixteen 'great' parties with a combined strength in 1811 of approximately 47,000 infantry and cavalry.* Averaging just under three thousand guerrilleros each these large parties formed over eighty-five percent of the total. The overall number of *active* small and medium parties had declined: eleven medium-sized groups (of between 250 and 999 members) accounted for a further 5,400, and twenty-nine small bands (of up to 249 members) amounted to nearly 2,400. The total number of guerrilleros in the field in 1811 would thus have been about 55,500.†

This was a high figure. At a time when the four remaining Spanish armies, excluding Cataluña for which no data existed, reached just over seventy thousand men present under arms in the summer of 1811,[8] the guerrilleros represented a nearly matching strength. As the majority of the large parties were in the north, five of these, numbering over thirty-three thousand foot and cavalry, were officially enrolled by the patriot government as the Seventh Army operating from the borders of Galicia eastwards to the French frontier.‡

Among the guerrilleros nine women were recorded, including Francisca de la Puerta, who fought with two well-known male-led groups in La Mancha and Extremadura and petitioned the authorities in 1810 for permission to form her own party which was not granted, though the Extremadura junta awarded her a medal of honour. Catalina Martín, the niece of Toribio Bustamente, a well-known guerrilla leader with whom she fought was promoted to a cavalry second lieutenant by the Junta Suprema after distinguishing herself in several actions. Francisca de Ipiñazar and Dominica Ruíz accompanied their guerrilla husbands; the latter, the wife of another known leader, Alonso Ignacio Cuevillas, was said to have killed three imperial soldiers with her own hands in Santo Domingo de la Calzada.[9]

Other women, without being in the guerrilla, played equally important roles in the resistance. Rosa Aguado, General Kellerman's Spanish mistress while he was governor of Valladolid, was a patriot spy. On being arrested later, she stated clearly that her imprisonment was due to the 'singular services she had done for the good and true Spaniards, who loved the fatherland, against the French intruder government'.[10] Three Valladolid sisters, known collectively as

---

* The fact that the large parties' size (in rough terms) was recorded with greater frequency and accuracy than those of the smaller parties permitted this approximation of the total number of guerrilleros. Detailed tables will be found in Appendix 4.

† José Gómez de Arteche, in his massive military history of the war (*Guerra de la Independencia. Historia militar de España de 1808 a 1811*, vol. 2, p. 125), estimated a total of fifty thousand, including Cataluña and Galicia which do not figure in the above calculations. Moreover, another fifty-six parties were recorded as having been active in 1811, but not one of these had members' figures for any single year of the war. In all likelihood, they were small parties since it was these whose figures usually went unrecorded. Were this so, applying to them the small parties' average number of 84.9 members in 1811 would have added another 4,754 guerrilleros, bringing the total to 60,285.

‡ It consisted of the Porlier, Longa, Espoz y Mina, Merino and Renovales divisions with Jáuregui's Guipúzcoan brigade part of the latter. The cavalry made up about eight percent of the 7th army. (Barthèlemy, 1995, vol. 1, pp. 259–261.)

the Ubonas (from their family name of Ubón), looked after and helped poor Spanish military prisoners, and probably also acted as spies for the guerrilla. After the war, one of the sisters, María, was given a life pension by the government for her services.[11] In fact, many other women in Madrid and elsewhere helped Spanish military prisoners to escape or sheltered them when they had done so.

THE PARTIES' REGIONAL DISTRIBUTION

About one in six guerrilleros fought in regions outside of their own. And one in five of these fought in more than two other regions: the Cantabrians and the Navarrese were the most active on this front, mainly in Aragón, Asturias, the two Castillas (especially la Vieja), the Basque Country, and Extremadura. The Cantabrians, under Brigadier Porlier, the rank to which the Suprema had promoted him and the best-known of the military guerrilla leaders, defended three fronts: the Basque to his east, the Asturian to his west, and the Castilian to his south. In Navarra, the main danger came from Aragón, which Espoz y Mina was determined to control.

These regional 'transfers' were not part of some larger tactical plan, but responded to the conflict's exigencies or those of the individuals concerned. They reinforced the truth, stressed earlier, that it was not 'home territory' that the guerrillas were defending in the first instance, not even their own plots of land, but the right of passage over the face of their own country.

People who had moved little beyond the perimeters of their home villages, found themselves suddenly thrown into unknown territories which formed part of a country threatened by the same hostile forces as those which they faced at home. They found themselves coexisting with others confronted by the familiar needs of earning a living from an ungrateful soil, saw crops unknown to them – potatoes and maize for the southerners in the north, rice and citrus for the northerners in the south; heard unknown languages and dialects, and customary names for weights and measures different to those they were used to; but everywhere they confronted the same enemy, the heretic invader who requisitioned villagers' livestock and crops, pillaged their villages, sacked their houses and desecrated their churches. The more they moved the more they found everything was the same.

This new mobility, which was not exclusively a guerrilla affair – army service also provided it – reinforced an awareness that for all its diversity Spain was one country, one nation, and that only the union of its diverse parts could achieve its present objectives.

CRITICAL MASS

In 1811, El Empecinado, a small farmer who became the best known of the guerrilla leaders, wrote that the day of the small party was more or less over. They could no longer do as much damage as they had at the beginning of the struggle. The early guerrilla movement of surprise attack and rapid dispersion in search of a small victory had led to its own counter-insurgency tactics, and produced fewer benefits as a result. His comment was borne out by the facts: the concentration of guerrilla parties continued strongly between 1811 and 1812. The total number of medium and small parties, as well as those of unknown category, declined by over half while the large parties held their own, though also not without some loss of members. Overall, the number of guerrilleros dropped by nearly six percent in 1812. The French withdrawal from Andalucía in that year was certainly in part responsible for the decline both in numbers and small parties.

The sheer weight of men which the large parties had come to command was leading them to the formation of a critical mass which inevitably changed their aims and perspectives. They were beginning to seek a centred spatial control, to hold down territory, to become more like a popular territorial liberation movement. Critical mass, however, was not a question of sheer numbers alone. Of equal, if not greater importance, was fighting experience. After years of hand-to-hand combat, the guerrillas were battle-hardened veterans who were no longer frightened of the French troops, having killed, captured or put them to flight on so many occasions. As an experienced French counter-insurgency general who led the 'Infernals' (so named by the French for their notorious anti-guerrilla tactics) wrote after suffering a heavy defeat at Espoz y Mina's hands:

> I confess to your excellency in all honesty that the brigands of this kingdom [Navarra] merit the name of veteran soldiers. They can compete with the best of our armies, for the continuous battles and victories have made them lose their fear of us. (General Soulier to Marshal Suchet, February, 1812)[12]

The decline of eighty thousand imperial troops in Spain during Napoleon's Russian campaign* reduced French military pressure on the guerrillas and opened a space for a new sense of territorial conquest. This was best expressed by Espoz y Mina's blockade of Pamplona, the Navarrese capital. Decreed in December 1811, the blockade was put into serious effect in the early months of 1812. Its aim was to cut off the capital and its French garrison from the rest of the region. Marker stones, guarded twenty-four hours a day, were set up on all the major roads into the city at a distance of about one and a half kilometres from the walls: no one was to be permitted to carry money, food or merchandise beyond these markers towards the capital. Its inhabitants were allowed to leave the city to live in the guerrilla zone but not to return: those who remained in Pamplona were declared enemies for as long as the war lasted. 'The volunteer detachments guarding the line will shoot anyone they see approaching, without orders or communication; and whether wounded or not the offender will be hanged immediately from a tree', said Article 10 of Mina's blockade decree.[13]

* In May 1812, the French had 230,000 troops in Spain. Six months earlier the figure had been 310,000. Napoleon in fact only withdrew the twenty-seven thousand men of the Young Guard and Polish regiments for his Russian campaign; the remaining deficit of fifty thousand soldiers not replaced, was due to battle and disease. (Glover, 1974, p. 190 and footnote.)

This in a year when food was already growing short meant considerable hardship for the Pamplona population, and hardship also for the small farmers who marketed their produce in the capital, but it was a clever territorial move. It visibly demonstrated to the population that total belligerency was demanded of them by a guerrilla that was in civilian as well as military command.

Earlier, in another brilliant stroke, Mina had taken over Navarrese custom posts and chanelled their tolls – three million reales a year, he estimated, including a monthly 'contribution' of one hundred ounces of gold from the French customs post at Irún to allow French goods to cross the border – into the guerrilla movement to pay his men's wages, buy arms and munitions, uniforms and other equipment. Although he was quite capable of levying forced contributions from townships which had proven themselves unwholeheartedly behind the cause, and of obliging the villagers to provide his men with food, he used the customs money to avoid having to impose monetary taxes on the mass of the rural population. In order to rally the Aragonese to his guerrilla, Mina pledged that he would put an end to the excessive French taxation, requisitions and pillage.[14]

At the beginning of February 1812, the British navy provided Mina with two twelve-pound cannon and two four-pounders in a drop-off in the Bay of Biscay. For a week, the guerrilla humped, hauled and heaved the precious artillery pieces over mountain paths and tracks in enemy occupied territory with the division spread out covering the flanks to a considerable depth to prevent a surprise French attack. When they reached their objective – Tafalla, one of the Navarrese towns most heavily fortified by the French – the twelve-pounders were not long in opening a breach in the castle walls which, after an abortive guerrilla assault, was still sufficiently threatening to induce the imperial garrison to surrender the following day.[15]

General Reille, who had chased Mina very hard and pursued a repressive policy in Navarra in the same year, saw the writing on the wall. The mobile column which Napoleon had ordered as the chief counter-insurgency weapon, was losing its fighting efficiency, he observed. Until then, numerically inferior imperial columns had been able to engage and put to flight guerrilla bands. But the latter's combat experience was beginning to tell and they were defeating increasingly large French columns, many of which were manned by raw conscripts or troops unfamiliar with the terrain. Until more troops were available, Reille noted, the imperial inferiority could only be made good by cavalry and artillery units – which were impossible to deploy in rugged terrain.[16]

THE BATTLE FOR FOOD

The battle for provisions was vital to the guerrilla war – indeed to the conflict itself. Napoleon's policy of 'war feeding war' – in other words that his troops be fed and paid by local requisition – was viable for an army on the march but became a very different matter when, in a poor agrarian country, it turned into an army of occupation. Nothing was more likely to keep a rural guerrilla alive and fighting than French exactions of food and money in an impoverished countryside.* Moreover, if the guerrilla could prevent the French requisitioning supplies, they did the enemy as much harm as by forcing a column to flee or killing a score of imperial soldiers. To deny the enemy their daily subsistence brought the guerrilla – who also had to live off the land – the popular support it needed, added new recruits to their cause, and left the enemy hungry, unpaid and demoralized.

As their power increased, so by 1811–1812 the guerrilla increased the French army's illness rate by their stubborn defence in the war of provisions, preventing the enemy from providing full rations to his troops. This they achieved more often by seizing imperial supply columns – flocks of sheep, beef on the hoof, convoys of wheat carts – than by preventing the French soldiers' requisitions; as a result the French military's sickness rate of twenty percent in Spain was higher than on campaigns in central Europe. In January 1813, Suchet had to reduce the bread ration from twenty-four to sixteen ounces because the guerrillas had collected most of the available surplus from the harvest and hindered the transportation of what little grain the French had managed to accumulate; and in the early summer of the same year one-quarter of his infantry reported sick.[17] The guerrilla sapped the enemy's morale – imperial troops had little faith that they would conquer the 'invisible' army in this constant, never-ending struggle which forced them into long, tiring and fruitless marches over rugged country only to find that the enemy had vanished into thin air; or even worse, if they encountered the guerrilla face-to-face they feared a terrifying fate. Untrained for this sort of work, conscripts had little stomach for it: the guerrilla's existence encouraged the rate of desertion in the Napoleonic ranks. Even in major cities, regular French troops felt under constant threat. 'Little by little we are going to be destroyed . . . We shall all die here', wrote an infantry sergeant major to his father in France shortly after Sevilla's occupation.

> We shall never destroy these bandits . . . Without hesitation and in broad daylight, an inhabitant will kill a French soldier he finds on his own in the street . . . The other day a drunken soldier who was stabbed to death had more than thirty dagger wounds from head to stomach . . . Like others, he died in the *cruellest* of torments. The armed villagers commit the most brutal barbarities. They cut their victims' ears off and stick their genitals in their mouths . . .[18]

---

* A decade later, when French troops again occupied Spain to restore Fernando VII to the throne after three years of liberal rule under the 1812 constitution, Louis XVIII's regime admitted that Napoleon had exacted from the conquered countries 'twice as much as was needed to supply his soldiers.' Well aware of the outcome, the restored French monarchy decided that its troops in Spain must buy their food in local markets and avoid at all cost requisitions, violence and pillaging 'as this will be a way of winning over the population' and of avoiding a popular rising. The monarchy's view was proven correct: where only twelve years earlier, a guerrilla had fought the French occupation tooth and nail, this time there was no popular insurgency, though other factors were also responsible. (See R. Sánchez Mantero, *Los Cien mil hijos de San Luis y las relaciones franco-españolas*, Sevilla, 1981, pp. 39–45, cited by de la Torre, 1991, p. 93).

Shortly before, a lieutenant colonel of the Imperial Guard, who had been promoted to colonel to command a line regiment, had suffered this fate in a village not two leagues from Sevilla before he could take up his new posting. After six in the evening no troops in the Andalucian capital dared to venture out of barracks.* The French occupation army was in a wretched state, the sergeant major confessed to his father. The soldiers had been three days without bread. No uniforms, no shoes, no shirts were reaching them from France . . . 'I have seen many soldiers die of vermin, I saw one with a hole in his armpit eaten by lice which had laid their eggs in it, others die of chagrin and misery.' It was quite probable that sickness – human louse-borne typhus in particular – decimated the imperial ranks more heavily than the guerrilla. Suchet's third army corps alone, which was one of the best equipped and supplied, lost an estimated thirty-six thousand men – or one sixth of its strength yearly – to illness between 1810 and 1814.[19] At an annualized rate, this was the equivalent of nearly twenty casualties a day.

In the ongoing battle for provisions, the French exacted more than 150 million reales in food, fodder and monetary taxes from the Navarrese population alone. The bulk of this fell on the villagers. This amount represented two years of the region's average pre-war annual agarian, commercial and industrial production; spread out over five enemy occupation years, the sum was the equivalent of forty percent yearly of the region's principal income. Just under half the total sum was requisitioned from villagers solely between February 1808 and July 1811, in rations of bread, wine and meat for the imperial troops and barley and straw for their horses.[20]

It was the area of small farmers' predominance in La Montaña – the rugged northern part of Navarra – which most resented enemy exactions and sought to resist them; and it was this region, giving on to the foothills of the Pyrenees in the east, that formed one of the major guerrilla recruiting bases and refuges throughout the war. With its gorges, hidden valleys and series of mountain ranges of up to two thousand metres high, it was ideal guerrilla country; French superiority in arms and military organization was largely neutralized by the terrain. La Montaña was over-populated at the time for the subsistence farming on which it depended because the usual outlets of migration or emigration had been cut off by the war, and there was no shortage of potential guerrilla recruits who shared a common cultural heritage: like Espoz y Mina, they spoke Basque. With the exception of Pamplona, the region's capital, there were no major towns: the people lived in small villages or hamlets scattered over the countryside, which made the

---

* Nine months later, an incipient urban resistance movement was discovered in Sevilla by the French who tried at a special military court nineteen people from a wide range of trades and professions: four artisans, six workers, a merchandise packer, two muleteers, a farmer, two shop lads, a scrivener, and two women, one the wife of an accused artisan. The charges against them were of spying for the patriots and inciting imperial troops to desert. The scrivener and a gold-thread weaver were sentenced to death; six, including both women, were ordered to be put under police surveillance; four workers at the artillery arsenal were to be tried again by a special French court martial, and the remainder were acquitted. (Gómez Imaz, 1910, appendix, pp. 366–368.)

imperial army's task of tax-collecting and requisitioning all the harder and more hazardous.*

The only opposition in Navarra to imperial domination lay in Espoz y Mina's guerrilla which grew exponentially year by year, until it became by far and away the largest in Spain. Though the Navarrese Division had also to be fed by the villagers, their requisitions were much more modest than those of their enemy – thirty percent of the total compared to the imperial forces' seventy percent; and only seven percent overall of the guerrillas' were exacted by armed force. At the same time, the guerrilla paid (in fact, issued receipts) for nearly three times as much food received as they seized by force.[21]

All French-occupied regions suffered heavy monetary imposts and seizures of foodstuffs to pay for the imperial war and to keep their troops victualled. Between 1810 and 1814, Suchet extracted from Aragón forty-one million francs – just under 150 million reales – the same amount as in Navarra, though the Aragonese population was approximately three times the size of the former.[22] Santander, on the Cantabrian coast, was another province harshly pillaged by the French where feeding, supplying and paying for their occupation took up seventy-five percent of the province's costs.[23] It was one of the main battle-grounds of Juan Díaz Porlier, a young naval officer who had fought at Trafalgar and subsequently transferred to the army. By 1811 he had a force of several thousand men. The Bonapartist provincial police chief had no doubts about it:

> The situation is looking worse and worse throughout the province . . . the miserable inhabitants have nothing to eat because of the guerrilla's requisitions of foodstuffs and enlistment of recruits.[24]

On top of the French exactions, which were the main cause of the misery, and the guerrilla supplying itself, foodstuffs that could be of use to the enemy were expropriated. In Castilla la Vieja, the different bands carted off the grain as soon as it had been threshed. Writing to the Bonapartist police minister, Pablo Arribas, his Valladolid informant reported:

> The conde de Torreblanca's bailiff has had his whole grain crop in Cubillos seized, leaving him in its place a Junta [Suprema] decree which ordered the parties to requisition all those whom they believed to be Bonapartist supporters or who lived in the French-occupied zone. (Josef Timoteo del Monasterio, Valladolid, September 20, 1811)

Though even the early small parties had been able seize a certain amount of food requisitioned by the imperial troops, or to ambush enemy detachments on their exaction raids, villagers could not be adequately protected until the guerrilla became a large and veteran force that dominated the countryside and fought the French in open battle.

---

* By contrast, southern Navarra was made up of plains watered by the Ebro with large farms, agro-towns and a high percentage of day labourers.

POPULAR SUPPORT

Mina's three guerrilleros, who escorted the French prisoners to be exchanged, arrived in Pamplona with their arms and revolutionary insignia, and after being presented to the [French] Governor were allowed to walk through the capital's streets, squares and public gates . . . A numerous crowd gathered and followed the three bandits, crying Viva Mina! Viva Mina! . . .[25]

To say that the guerrilleros swam like fish in a sea of villagers would be exaggerated. To the guerrilla, the villager 'owed' the fighting man his foodstuff for risking his life daily to protect the run-of-the-mill non-combatant villagers, whose principal resolve in the harsh war conditions was to retain as great a portion as possible of their agricultural reserves. If the guerrilla protected the villagers from enemy plunder, well and good, the former's demands could be seen as an insurance policy, and what the guerrillas took, the French were denied. But so, too, were the villagers. And if the guerrilla could not or would not protect them, leaving the villagers still to face enemy impositions, then they were no more than another armed pestilence to feed.

The large partisan bands appreciated only too well the need for villagers' support – they had many men and horses to feed, required good local intelligence and guides in unknown territory, refuges and deposits for arms and stores, and a rural population that did not betray their presence to the enemy. They understood very clearly that rogue guerrillas who were no better than bandits did them a great deal of harm by undermining village support and, when they did not shoot them out of hand, they arrested them, going so far on occasion as to hand them over to enemy justice.

Gerónimo Saornil, whose party came to number nine hundred by 1812, fought in Castilla la Vieja, mainly in the area around Valladolid. A youthful veteran of the Convention War, he had been released by the rising from a Valladolid gaol at the beginning of the war, where he was being held on charges of robbery or smuggling, and took to the hills where he formed a group of partisans. In the spring of 1812, he caught nine men in the act of robbing some passers-by in Medina del Campo and arrested them; he believed they were the same group which a few days earlier had robbed and killed four people. He penned a letter to the local Bonapartist corregidor, explaining that he held these men prisoner.

But I have no safe prison for them, nor does my style of life permit me to take them with me to put them on trial. This is why I have decided to hand them over to Your Honour so that they may be formally tried and receive the punishment befitting their crimes in accordance with the law. I trust therefore that you will tell me where you would wish me to turn them in . . . (A flying camp, May 1, 1812, Geronimo Saornil)[26]

This was a service, his letter added, which was as important to the patriots as to the Emperor's troops; convinced of this, he had detached a number of parties to hunt down and arrest thieves and murderers to 're-establish in this manner

public order and tranquility'. He would continue to hand over to the Bonapartist authorities all those who committed such grave crimes, he concluded.

Nonetheless, there were very many villagers' complaints about guerrilla exactions and brutality. For example, the party of Julián Sánchez ('El Charo') from
Salamanca, whose aid Wellington appreciated sufficiently to incorporate him
into his army, was accused of arbitrarily demanding rations and other exorbitant
supplies, and when the local magistrates did not provide them of tying them to a
tree in the square or on stands resembling scaffolds in the village outskirts and
giving them a severe beating until they accepted their demands, thus 'satisfying
their evil aim of doing harm for its own sake'.[27] The terrorizing of local authorities
which was part of the guerrilla strategy could also affect the ordinary villager
whose food supplies the magistrates, in order to save their own lives, would
commandeer to satisfy the guerrilleros' demands. Nonetheless, popular sympathy with the guerrilla was expressed in the traditional *coplas* (four-line songs)
which were invented – often by women – to be sung to well-known tunes.

> Mina is my life,
> Longa is my love,
> Don Gaspar de Jáuregui
> Fills my heart

or

> Since the priest Merino
> a general was made
> Spain's urgent interests
> Are no longer delayed*[28]

A smallholder (Mina), a master artisan (Longa) and a poor Basque shepherd
(Jáuregui – who significantly was given the title of don, perhaps only to fill the
stanza adequately) were the guerrilla leaders the common people celebrated.
There were no similar songs saluting Spanish noble generals.

The guerrilla leader, El Empecinado, was very rapidly turned into a national
hero, epitomizing the anti-Bonapartist struggle. A number of plays about his
exploits were written and performed in Cádiz theatres from 1810 on. The
guerrilla struggle was felt by common patriot folk – or at least those who did not
live under its exactions and terror – to express the essence of popular resistance
to the Bonapartist regime.

MILITANCIES: THE FORGING OF A GUERRILLERO[29]

Matías Calvo was an Aragonese doctor's son from Lecineña, a large
village about thirty kilometres northeast of Zaragoza in the Monegros

---

* This is a very free translation: the Spanish reads: Desde que el cura Merino/se ha
metido a general/los asuntos de España/van marchando menos mal.

steppe lands. In 1801, aged nine, Matías was sent to grammar school in Zaragoza. 'God endowed me with an average talent but made of me a bad but quite intrepid student who, in my time off, got up to pranks and fights . . . [but] never of a nasty kind . . . .'

At the university, he read philosophy, as had Javier Mina, the founder of the Navarrese guerrilla, who was three years older than he and whom Matías probably knew. But Javier seemed to have been no direct influence on Calvo; it was his relative Espoz y Mina, who succeeded Javier on his capture in 1810, who made an impact. After the 1808 rising and general enlistment Calvo, as a university student, was immediately made a sergeant in Fernando VII's Royal Infantry Regiment. 'At that time one can say that there were few men in Spain capable of commanding a company let alone a battalion, but when we saw the enemy we thought we would eat him alive simply because he was the enemy. What ignorance!'

Matías took part in both the defences of Zaragoza, in the first fighting at the Carmen gate which was one of the most vulnerable openings in the city walls. But halfway through the second siege he, along with several others, deserted, jumping from the city wall at night and making off across the countryside towards his home village. 'No words can describe the state of the city by then . . . everything was in ruins . . . .' His return home was worse than the besieged city he had fled. French forces were attacking and sacking the village where three thousand patriot civilian reinforcements had assembled to relieve Zaragoza. Thirty-seven inhabitants, men, women and children lay dead in the streets and houses, and the sanctuary of Our Lady of Magallón was ablaze.

Escaping with young villagers up the high wooded hill to the sanctuary, Calvo saw below him, stretching out over two kilometres or more, the French forces sweeping forward, leaving swathes of dead Aragonese volunteers behind them. A few artillery pieces were still defending the sanctuary. In his hurry across the square in front of it he did not notice that one of the 'artillerymen' was a woman, Lorenza Marcén, helped by her fifteen-year-old son, Nicolás Seral. Both were killed in the final French attack.

Matías' parents lived by the sanctuary but they had fled. After sleeping in the sierra, eleven of the bolder youth made a cautious reconnaissance of the village: the French had evacuated the place.

> Oh, heavens above! Words fail me. We looked at one another as we passed the first houses . . . there was a corpse lying in the street, two more further on. A man who had been ill in bed at home lay dead . . . There was not a house in the village with an unbroken chair, a table, not even the smallest thing; everything was smashed, all the doors and windows as well. It was horrible to walk down the streets.

That night the youth made a fire in the public square with the firewood prepared by the French troops to warm themselves. Matías lay down on a stone bench between the arcades. When he awoke he found himself alone in the midst of a dark, cold, silent square. He recalled that his erstwhile companions had spoken of a house where they could spend the night and he set off to find it. But they were not there.

> I did not know where to go. I seemed to remember that the last place we had spoken of was by El Coso. I went down the calle Mayor to the corner of the Coso and the calle Baja, but I did not see or hear anyone. It was enough to frighten even the most courageous . . . Passing a door all you heard was a dog howling . . . Through another door I had already seen a man with his throat slit, and others shot to death . . . When I reached the calle Gimeno, my courage failed me entirely. A man who until that moment had known neither fear nor danger, my eyes were suddenly blind with terror. I believe that if I had not had the luck to see a light emerge into the street . . . I would not have come out of the village alive. I was convinced that something even more frightening had happened and that my companions had fled.

His young companions welcomed him back and shared out the little food they had found: two doves and a chicken inside a large feather-lined wicker basket which must have belonged to the general commanding the French troops. 'The experience made me realize that I was beginning to live, that it was impossible to continue to exist as I had until then . . .'

In a literary memoir this new state of consciousness would almost surely have heralded a change in personal attitude and activity. A sixteen-year-old who had been gaoled (for his anti-Godoy student actions), experienced most of the Zaragoza sieges, an attack and the sacking of his home village, a night of panic, and two winter months in the Sierra de Alcubierre where his family and the other villagers took refuge thereafter, would be prepared to throw in his lot with the guerrillas. But this was not Matías' case. After Zaragoza's fall on March 29, 1809, and the patriot military defeats three months later in their attempt to encircle Zaragoza, there were virtually no guerrillas to join. General Suchet succeeded in slowly but surely eliminating the small bands like that of Anselmo Alegre, an ex-smuggler whose ten-year sentence to the galleys had been pardoned by the patriots for fighting as a guerrilla leader in the sierra de Alcubierre.

Matías neither went to war immediately nor followed his father's medical profession.* For the next two years he lived with his parents in Leciñena, helping his father attend to the local sick and those of the neighbouring village of Perdiguera, all of whom were living rough. Matías' village was permanently occupied by imperial forces, and their French commandant became a firm friend of his father, don Cosme, who had cured him of a painful illness.

---

* This, which Matias did not explain, may well have been because of the excessive number of doctors and the very poor training they received, with the exception of Salamanca and Valencia universities: university medical faculties were frequently shut down for those reasons.

From the time of the cure the commandant came to our house every day after our meal, because his only pleasure was to talk to my father . . . They conversed in Latin. I must say that my father was famous for his command of the ancient language. Whenever new imperial troops arrived, the commandant immediately posted guards outside our house to ensure that no one entered or bothered us in any way.

Once General Suchet was fully occupied with besieging the towns of southern Cataluña the columns of his troops diminished,

and the Spaniards began to raise guerrillas in all parts, waking at last from the lethargy in which they had been enveloped . . . Aragón's liberation came from the west, from Mina's side, from the borders of Navarra. Mina exercised control over the Aragonese parties and appointed José Tris, *Malcarado*, as their chief.

Matías' father's death at the age of forty-eight in 1811 left the family with three sons, of whom Matías was the oldest, three daughters and a mother. 'All señores without careers and little money.' In his new circumstances, Matías chose the profession of arms.

Almost immediately one of Mina's officers asked me to accompany him, in fact, offering me a horse and arms . . . That very afternoon I was part of his group of twenty horse and fifty soldiers in the sierra of Llanaja whose task was solely to recruit people and send them to Navarra for training . . . Our orders were that if we saw a French force we thought we could defeat we should attack it and until 1812 all of us came out of these encounters unharmed, by which time we could do to the French what they until then were used to doing to us. Then, sometimes, we would go into the villages at night – until then we always slept in the woods – but wheat was so dear in 1812 that . . . a kilo of bread cost sixty centimos whereas a guerrilla's daily pay – and this was good pay – was ten centimos a day.

Probably because most of his guerrilla companions were illiterate, Matías from his earliest time in the party had been made the receiver and distributor of the company's rations. 'As a result I never went short of wheaten bread . . .' This showed little solidarity with the rest of his troop whom he always contemptuously called 'those people', though he was referring to the Navarrese whom he considered as far greater fighters than his fellow Aragonese, and to Mina's custom of mixing veteran and recent recruits in the division's forces.

At the beginning of June 1812, Mina sent the Aragón cavalry a commandant accompanied by twelve men and a sergeant whose task was to take over the small cavalry force and form a regiment to be called the Aragonese Hussars. Until two months before, most of the Aragonese cavalrymen continued on provincial recruiting missions, remaining in Aragón, under the command of José Tris, an Aragonese guerrilla leader of somewhat dubious reputation. Indeed, Matías did not record the incident by which Tris went down in guerrilla history. In April 1812, Espoz y Mina had passed into Aragón after a second handsome victory at Arlabán,* in the Basque country, when he was nearly captured during the night in lodgings in the village of Robres. There was no doubt that he had been betrayed, and there were a number of different stories as to how he escaped. One of these had him surprised alone in his rooms by a French cavalry detachment. While the French tried to break down the front door, Mina rushed out with a stave in his hands, and as he battered the nearest foes into submission shouted: 'Lancers to the rear! Cavalry sergeant, take the first squadron to the left!'[30] Thinking that it was they, not Mina who had been trapped, the French withdrew just long enough to allow the guerrilla leader to escape on horseback.†[31]

Mina wreaked a terrible vengeance for his near escape. Believing that Tris and six town officials had betrayed him, he had them shot. Nothing in his actions or in the French correspondence suggested that the Aragonese guerrilla leader had betrayed Mina, or that he was a traitor. A scapegoat, however, he certainly was. But Mina had not finished. With his usual speed and decisivenesss, he ordered all the magistrates of the villages who should have warned him of the French attack to be hanged forthwith. On being informed that the Lecineña parish priest had told a patriot cavalry officer, whose handsome uniform he had mistaken as French, that, according to the local justice, there were a great number of Navarrese dispersos in the region, Mina also ordered the priest and justice shot. Such was Espoz y Mina's authority, nonetheless, that not only did his own men accept this rough and ready justice, but the members of Tris's band made no objection to being taken over by Mina and stayed under his command even after their former leader was shot.

*

One guerrilla battle Matías never forgot, for it was his first as a sergeant, was an affair that was typical enough of the sort of 'battle' that the guerrillas were frequently engaged in and which would in normal circumstances have barely made a footnote in a history of the war. But Matías related it as though it were a major victory. One June day of 1812, he was ordered by his new commander to go to Huesca (the capital of the Aragonese province of the same name which was in French hands) with four mounted men to see if they could provoke the French garrison – said erroneously to be made up of not more than thirty cavalry – into battle. His commandant believed that twenty of Mina's cavalry – Matías' company strength – would be sufficient to deal with

---

* See p. 393 for his first Arlabán victory.
† The most likely story is that an aide, who was captured, gave Mina time to get to his horse. The incident cost the guerrilla eighty captured, sixty dead and the loss of 150 horses.

them because the Navarrese Division by now felt it could handle greater numbers with ease.

Quite probably Matías was chosen for the mission because he knew Huesca well, the town being only a few hours on foot from his native village, or because he and the men were not yet fitted out in the glamorous Navarrese cavalry uniforms which the latter could now afford, while the Aragonese-based men were still dressed little differently to the villagers. With his four soldiers, Sgt Matías made his way in the dawn through Huesca's streets, his and his men's arms hidden under their capes, while he thought of some student prank from his tavern days in Zaragoza to set matters alight.

'We reached the market at last and there we shot dead a *gabacho* [the common Spanish name for a Frenchman][32] who was just leaving a meat stall. The rest of the French troops in the market ran for their fort.' Quite cold-bloodedly, the guerrilleros celebrated the death with some glasses of spirits in the market liquor shop. Then they left at a canter.

At about the time that Matías had set out on his mission, the guerrilla leader Joaquín de Pablo, 'Chapalangara', set out for Huesca with two companies of his Aragonese infantry guerrilla and forty horse. The infantry took up an ambush position around the Huesca gates. From beyond the city walls Matías and his guerrilleros allowed themselves to be seen, and soon a French gendarme cavalry squadron sallied forth. Specially trained to maintain (French) civilian order and put down bandits in rural zones, the gendarmes could see that they were outnumbered by the two hundred infantry. 'When we reached our rendez-vous with our chief he asked me: "How many are there?" and I replied, "quite a few", without giving him any more details. I would have been taken as a coward to have said more; in that division you had to be cautious.' As he was admiring the 'gendarmes' high-spirited looks', Matías saw that there were not thirty but nearly eighty horsemen. Chapalangara's infantry advanced on the enemy, while the guerrilla cavalry was ordered to take up position behind the French to cut off their retreat into the town. On seeing the number of infantry ahead of them the enemy wheeled about to retire on Huesca, only to encounter the guerrilla horse. The infantry continued forward . . .

> The minutes seemed like eternity until we got the order to charge. We had advanced some five hundred paces to find gaps in the stone boundary walls of the fields through which to set upon the enemy . . .

The French cavalry fired two rounds at the Spanish as they charged – the first with their carbines, the second with pistols. 'The first round broke our commandant's leg and the second killed a brave cavalryman of our army whom I did not know until he was dying, but his comrades told me was a courageous man.' The rest of the fighting was hand to hand with sabres and infantry bayonets. Matías' sabre had over one hundred parrying chips slashed into it, and his commanders came to look at it . . . 'I knew thereafter that my companions had no equals in all the armies.' The French cavalry finally broke through the Spanish lines and retired into Huesca with thirty casualties against twenty for the guerrillas. The latter's wounded could take comfort from the fact that Espoz y Mina took great care of them, for he believed that a well-trained soldier was his most valuable asset.

*

Four years earlier, Palafox had ordered frightened and improvised Aragonese troops to defend Zaragoza. The tables had turned now, Matías reflected. Then, Palafox had been unnerved by the constant defeats and it was the Spanish who took refuge in the cities; now it was the Spanish who were ready and prepared to take on the enemy in open battle. Severe discipline, austerity, courage and the sharp intelligence of those in command had made of the Navarrese Division a formidable and frightening force, even for the most experienced imperial troops.

> Officers used to say to me that I was cut out for a military career. But they were mistaken. I was not really courageous, and I did not distinguish myself in any of the many other actions in which I took part. But nor, I must say, did I ever leave my post or fail the mission assigned to me. I was never rash, but nor was I a coward . . . where others expected me to be they found me. That was my whole campaign, I had a great passion to pursue a military career, but in a few moments all my plans were brought to nought.

Matías remained a guerrilla sergeant for the rest of the war.

MAIL INTERCEPTIONS

One of their major tasks – indeed, as has been pointed out, the origins of the guerrilla movement itself – was the interception of enemy mail. Preserved in the Madrid National Historical Archive among the Junta Suprema's documents is a collection of 1,626 intercepted letters.* Only twenty-eight date from 1808; but in 1809 the figure rose tenfold and in 1810 trebled that of the previous year. The highest number, it must be said, were private Spanish letters, followed by Bonapartist government mail. Amongst the intercepted French correspondence from within Spain were a number of letters from French generals and regional commanders to their counterparts or hierarchical superiors reporting on and complaining about the state of their region usually because of the increase in guerrilla activities. There were even a few personal letters to her husband in Madrid from the king's wife who remained in France. But there were no concrete French military orders.†

* In fact, scattered throughout the eighty-six legajos of the Junta Suprema's records in the same archive are a number more but I have not included these in this analysis of intercepted mail.
† Possibly such intercepts were filed by the government's military juntas separately from civilian intercepts or by the respective patriot armies to which they were passed on; if that were so, they do not exist in the General Madrid Military Archive either.

There could be no doubt that such orders were intercepted, since an increase in the French use of a cipher for many military communications was notable by the beginning of 1812. A collection of fifty-two such dispatches – not all in cipher (which a British intelligence captain cracked) – was received and compiled by Wellington's command between March 1812 and March 1813.[33] Since one of the guerrilla's main objectives was to inform on the enemy's war plans and movements, the absence of a section devoted exclusively to intercepted military orders is striking.

But one letter in particular was remarkable, less for what it said than the circumstances of its interception.

EPISODES: A DEATHLY INTERCEPT

One of the first guerrilleros in the north, Juan Fernando Echevarría, a young man of good family, was also one of the first to be captured by French troops in March 1809. A Basque, he had begun his guerrilla with a score of men in the uplands of the neighbouring province, Santander, where he called his party La Compañía del Norte (the Northern Company). The conditions of his capture with two of his men were never made specifically clear. The three were taken to the prison at Mercadillo until they could be sent to Bilbao. Between fifteen and twenty of his men tried to rescue them from the gaol, but the provincial vice-commissioner of police, the abbot of Siones, and villagers and prison guards fought them off for three-quarters of an hour. The following day under the command of a French sergeant who, recognizing the quality of his person, let Echevarría ride his horse on his word of honour not to escape, the captives set off, the two other guerrilleros on foot. Their route took them through the township of Balmaseda. After attending mass in the parish church, Echevarría asked his guard to be allowed a few minutes with a family friend who lived there. The meeting was very brief, just long enough for Echevarría to beg the friend, Joaquín María de los Azuelas, to write to Juan Fernando's brother to ask the latter to try to secure him a royal pardon; Azuelas sat down to do so immediately.

> They say that this king is so compassionate that, on prostrating oneself at his feet, his charitable heart may respond to an appeal for clemency. My friend . . . you should not neglect this task . . . because it is a matter of your brother and you should put forward his extreme youth . . . And speak to Abril, who is a general, and to Amorós* to see if they are able to secure your brother's pardon . . . Here my friend we have suffered considerably and I in particular because my house was one of the seventy-five whose sad lot it was to be burned to the ground in this poor and now very unhappy village . . . Much patience is needed . . .[34]

* General Abril was the French commandant of Bilbao at the time; Francisco Amorós was a Bonapartist councillor of state, and at the time royal commissioner of the Basque Country and Burgos.

This letter never reached its destination. It was intercepted by guerril-leros – quite possibly by Echevarría's own men – and eventually was forwarded to Sevilla where it ended in the Junta Suprema's files. In May 1809, little more than a month after his capture, Echevarría was sentenced to be hanged: the Bilbao extraordinary criminal tribunal was set up especially to try him and his associates, the first of these courts which were to become a standard instrument of Bonapartist anti-guerrilla 'legal' repression. Whether any representation was made on his behalf to Josef remained unknown.

*

The quantity of the guerrilla mail interceptions in 1810 – 963 – did not increase their quality: forty percent of the intercepts were private letters mailed from within Spain and to a small degree from France. However, the Bonapartist regime suffered heavily, particularly in official corre-spondence with Andalucía. Ministers accompanying Josef on his official tour of the newly won region complained constantly that correspon-dence from the capital was not being received. On July 27, 1810, for example, the entire Andalucian mail from Madrid was seized by a guerrilla party at Villarrubia de los Ojos. But it was by no means a problem confined to Andalucía: 'Despite the proximity of this town [Guadalajara] to the capital and court [Madrid], it is as though we were a hundred or more leagues away in relation to the mail . . .'[35] wrote the Guadalajara prefect in 1811; while the king's regal commissioner to Andalucía, on his return to Sevilla on September 21 in the same year, after visiting the whole region with Marshal Soult, reported that he had received no correspondence from Madrid since June 26 and no orders since August 5. 'I very much fear that the mail will be lost because of its constant interception especially around Granada and Málaga.'[36] Part of the problem, the Bonapartist government maintained and probably not without reason, was that the majority of postal couriers in Spain were Spanish and out of fear handed over their dispatch bags to the first person to stop them.[37] They had plenty of incentive to do so, since their lives were usually at stake. Bonapartist officials, when they could, used the French military's postal system which was protected by the army – in November 1809, the entire Third Regiment of the Vistula was detached to safeguard correspondence.[38]

Mail interception was not all-weather work, however; in autumn and winter throughout the war intercepts dropped to only a small percent of their spring/summer highpoint. Thus guerrilla effectiveness depended to a considerable degree on the year's seasonal weather.

REPRISALS

The question of reprisals arose from the start of the war, demonstrating the conflict's popular ideological nature.[39] While with some exceptions the regular troops kept more or less to the levels accepted by eighteenth century rules of war, reprisals on occasion rose to barbarous heights among the opponents in the guerrilla struggle. As irregulars and 'brigands', the guerrillas received no quarter from French troops who saw in each villager their potential assassin; and village combatants gave none where they could expect none and saw in every imperial soldier a pillager and sacrilegious invader. Some guerrilla leaders moreover justified the tactic of an eye for an eye, a tooth for a tooth, as the only means to force the French to recognize the guerrillero as a bona fide combatant. Only a dehumanized foe could be stabbed in the back or strung from a tree; only a dehumanized authority could order the guerrilla to attack enemy hospitals among its normal targets.*

El Empecinado, a former corporal in the Convention War, was the supreme guerrilla observer of the rules of war in relation to his prisoners, and General Hugo, Victor Hugo's father, who spent a fruitless time pursuing him, respected him for it and treated his guerrilla prisoners in the same manner.†

In Navarra – and to a lesser degree the Basque country – the spiral of violence was more acute than in most of the rest of Spain. A succession of French generals, frustrated by their lack of success in putting an end to popular Navarrese resistance on the borders of France, turned to terror. Guerrilla corpses were left to hang for days in trees alongside major roads to intimidate the population; but soon their bodies vanished overnight and there were French soldiers' corpses hanging in their place. 'Vous pendez les nôtres. Nous pendons les vôtres', said a placard pinned to their chests. In revenge, the French commander of Navarra, General d'Agoult, ordered fifteen of the fifty-seven monks held in Pamplona to be executed and their bodies to be strung up publicly for twenty-four hours.[40]

Although a successor, General Reille, won two significant victories over Espoz y Mina's guerrillas in the autumn of 1810, he racked up the violence by several notches; lists of those absent from their homes without good reason were the most useful police source of information. Over 3,300 people from the capital and surrounding villages were imprisoned in Pamplona: some villages had up to thirty percent of their inhabitants incarcerated.[41]

The guerrilla's repression of local civil authorities to keep them in line was one counterpart to the occupiers' repression. Ears and noses cut off, foreheads branded, tarring and feathering were frequent forms of physical punishment. Spanish 'traitors' serving under French colours were regularly executed. But French prisoners had been respected. However, on December 14, 1811, Espoz y Mina issued an order that all French officers and soldiers captured, with or without arms, in battle or not, would be hanged and left along the main roads.

---

* The regency government's *Rules for Guerrilla Parties* of July 11, 1812, stated specifically that the guerrillas' tasks 'are constantly to cut the enemy's communications, intercept his despatches and convoys, and attack his hospitals and warehouses'. The decree is cited in Horta Rodríguez, 1984, p. 186.
† General Hugo was a veteran of the Vendée and Calabrian anti-insurgency campaigns which both ended favourably for the French regime. But he was unable to overcome El Empecinado.

This was in response to an increased wave of repression decreed by Reille in which 150 guerrillas and 60 non-combatants were recorded as having been executed between July and October 1811. Moreover, Reille had nearly six hundred guerrillas' relatives arrested, and the gaols were so crowded that he deported three hundred civilians to France on a single day in October – bandits who were fit only to 'finish their days in some distant dungeon'. His successor, General Abbé, who relieved Reille in November, had a further sixty-seven guerrillas and their relatives executed in the first nine days of December.[42]

On January 11, 1812, Espoz y Mina put his threat into execution. He had just decisively defeated Abbé and his two-thousand-strong column outside Sangüesa, inflicting six hundred casualties. That day he took no prisoners. And thereafter, when the French executed a guerrilla officer, four French officers held in Mina's prisoner-of-war camp were shot; for every rank-and-file guerrilla, twenty imperial soldiers were executed. As the French by now were losing more men to the guerrillas than vice-versa, Abbé stopped treating Mina's men as bandits; and Mina returned to his former system of giving quarter to captured enemy troops. The barbarous cycle was finally laid to rest for the last years of the war.

ARMS

Always short of arms, munitions and money, the Spanish government bottled up in Cádiz could do little to aid the large and distant northern guerrillas. The first regency, which took over from the Junta Suprema, asked Britain to supply arms and money direct to the 'Corps of Troops and of Peasants' in these regions because the distance from Cádiz made it impossible.[43] A large part of this aid was channelled from La Coruña eastwards along the coast, either by land or sea. The assistant British Commissary, George White, to whom the guerrilla chiefs, Porlier, Longa and Espoz y Mina all addressed requests for arms, ammunition and shoes, stated unanimously that they could employ 'to the greatest advantage any number of Arms that may be sent them'.

White gathered together a shipment of materiel to be sent by sea, which included ten thousand pairs of shoes, two thousand muskets, pistols and swords, and wrote to his London superior:

> I am convinced that their distribution will have the effect of greatly encouraging those meritorious Parties who meet with so little consideration from their own Government that their only expectations of assistance and encouragement are directed to England.[44]

Another less obvious source of munitions for Mina, as well as for El Empecinado and Brigadier José Durán, leader of a large party in southern Aragón, were sent by mule trains from Valencia, where the British agent, Pedro Tupper, was in charge of the operation.

It affords me great satisfaction to receive the thanks of all the Authorities of the interior acknowledging . . . that the brilliant advantages obtained [by these guerrillas] over the Enemy since November [1811] could never have been achieved without my exertions . . .

he wrote to Henry Wellesley, British minister to the regency, ten months later.[45] Tupper also appointed his old associate and one of the three brother conspirators of Valencia's uprising in 1808, Manuel Bertrán de Lis, to venture deep into the interior and bring back information, including the state of the guerrillas, from the enemy rearguard. These services, Bertrán later wrote, 'involved danger to his life every day he was engaged on them'.*

Along the Cantabrian coast and the Bay of Biscay, the transport of guerrilla and regular Spanish and British forces by a small Anglo-Spanish naval squadron stationed at La Coruña and El Ferrol, in unoccupied Galicia, kept the French coastal defences under threat from the summer of 1809 till the end of the war. In July 1810, and again in August, British frigates appeared off the coast, and landed strong guerrilla raiding parties;[46] the failure of two well-known partisan chiefs to join Porlier brought the first raid to an end after four days, but it gave the afrancesado intendente, Joaquin Aldamar, a serious fright.

I, and those like me who desire nothing but peace, came to fear that this province was absolutely lost. The plan was without doubt to raise and arm the people . . . I congratulate myself . . . to see frustrated the plans of the enemies of peace . . . and to be freed from the sadness of witnessing the punishment which, had the marquesillo [Porlier] remained in the province, would have been meted out to so many poor victims of the [guerrillas'] resentments and passions . . .[47]

So pervasive was the guerrilla presence in the province that the intendente could find no trustworthy person to carry his letter, even when 'rolled in a paper small enough to be hidden from the searches and examinations that all have to undergo from the cuadrillas as they close around the province from all sides'. Finally, he found a French military detachment marching to Burgos to take it on the first stage of its travel to the justice minister and the king in Madrid.

TAKING THE WAR HOME TO THE ENEMY

Although both Mina and the Catalan irregulars raided Pyrenean France from time to time, they did not think seriously about cutting at the enemy's

---

* In impoverished political exile in London in 1826 Bertrán, a Cortes deputy during the 1820–1823 liberal revolution, appealed to Canning, Foreign Secretary, and subsequently to Wellington for financial assistance, enclosing Tupper's sworn testimony to his having carried out the missions entrusted to him and observing that his intelligence work on behalf of the British had been carried out without remuneration. His appeal was consistently turned down. (PRO, FO 72/324/121 and 153–154 for his memorial to Canning and Tupper's supporting statement; also his drafts in Spanish of his appeal to Wellington, from which the quote is taken, among his private correspondence which I thank the marquesa de Marañón for allowing me to consult.)

underbelly in a joint invasion, something Napoleon came to fear unduly.* It was a strategic guerrilla error which demonstrated two aspects of the war.

A defect which the large guerrillas shared with the army was their difficulty of combining for joint operations. While the smaller parties often collaborated to increase their strength for a particular coup, the larger they grew the more they tended to be sufficient unto themselves, even when formed into a single army. Poor communications between them contributed to, and resulted from, this situation. In August 1811, three large guerrilla parties and the same number of irregular military forces, two of them Catalan, numbering in all twenty thousand men, stood in or on the borders of Aragón; this was five times the strength of the imperial counter-insurgency columns in the region which could easily have been swept out by the combined force. Or more daringly, this large irregular cohort, which did not take action in Aragón, could have crossed into France and campaigned in the lower Pyrenees, the sort of terrain they were accustomed to, and possibly have relieved pressure on Valencia which was about to be invested by Marshal Suchet. But which commander would lead such a combined force? Espoz y Mina, who by this time controlled most of Aragón north of the Ebro, and his counterpart, Durán, on the river's southern banks were neither likely to concede such a prominent role. Moreover, the former was determined to keep Catalans out of his new Aragonese dominion.

The second shortcoming was common to the Spanish struggle in general. The major objective, as was pointed out earlier, was not Napoleon's overthrow, but to rid the country of its Bonapartist regime and the French army which kept it in existence. Not to have taken advantage of Napoleon's invasion of Russia in 1812 to threaten France's southwestern borderlands was an admission of this aim; it was also an indication that the Navarrese guerrilla's 'critical mass' was more concerned with its region's (and Aragón's) territorial liberation from the French occupation forces than in a wider strategy of attacking the enemy's bases across the frontier.

Admittedly, Mina's division – even united with Catalan irregular forces – could not hope to hold a part of Pyrenean France for any length of time; but the anti-Napoleonic propaganda effect of a serious offensive across the Pyrenees would have served notice on French public opinion that the Emperor was engaged on two fronts simultaneously and that his home rearguard was threatened. The fact that Wellington, who was concerned solely with defeating Napoleon, was no more aware than the guerrilla of the advantage of advancing into France after his 1812 victory at the battle of Salamanca, certainly made it invidious to criticize the latter with their smaller forces and different concerns. Nonetheless, Wellington's failure did not excuse a strategic guerrilla omission.[48]

* In March 1811, Mina escaped French encirclement in northeastern Navarra by taking refuge in France where, in the region of Alduides, he found a sympathetic reception. (See Tone, 1994, pp. 126–127, fn. 62.) On other occasions he briefly crossed the Pyrenees into France, forcing Napoleon to mobilize the national guard to prevent further incursions: some of the border townships had supplied Mina with supplies and guides to the French side, demonstrating a sympathy with his cause which was a highly sensitive matter to the Emperor.

EPISODES: FORCED RECRUITMENT

Forced recruitment to the guerrilla was by no means unknown and, after being captured by the French, many guerrilleros used this as their excuse for having joined a band. A striking case of resistance – indeed not only to joining a guerrilla but to fighting for king, religion and country in any form – was provided by a man who later became notorious as El Empecinado's jailer before the famous guerrilla leader was hanged by Fernando VII's restored absolutism.

Gregorio González was a twenty-year-old at the outbreak of the war, and the only son of a well-to-do family in the village of Roa, in the province of Burgos. His father had died and the womenfolk depended on him to look after the large family estate. He and his mother were determined to keep him from any form of armed service and they succeeded, paying bribes if need be to ensure that Gregorio was not conscripted into the patriot army. By 1811 the situation had become so difficult, however, that his mother advised him to get married to avoid having to serve, and he faithfully obeyed. However, shortly afterwards a new threat appeared in the shape of El Empecinado's brother and co-founder of his guerrilla, Damaso Martín. By sheer threat of force, Damaso enlisted Gregorio in the guerrilla and took him off. His mother was having none of this.

> Her displeasure at my enforced absence, her fear of the danger I was being exposed to and her trepidation that I would leave my already pregnant wife a widow were so great that she packed her bags and, obliging my father-in-law to accompany her, set off after me. She caught up with the guerrilla in the village of Riaza [not far distant], where she arrived at a most opportune moment, and her pleas and efforts on my behalf were so successful that she succeeded in having me granted a total dispensation from armed service.[49]

What this may have cost the family coffers Gregorio González left carefully obscure.

GUERRILLA-INFLICTED CASUALTIES

The guerrillas have caused more losses to the French armies than all the regular troops during the war in Spain. It has been proved that they murdered one hundred of our men per day. Thus, during the period of five years, they have killed more than 180,000 Frenchmen, without losing . . . more than 25,000. (General August Julien Bigarré, aide-de-camp to King Josef)[50]

Though the question of guerrilla-originated casualties is virtually uncharted terrain, and no official statistics on French losses in the war have been compiled making it impossible to reach a global estimate, Bigarré's statement was certainly exaggerated in terms of the numbers of dead alone. (Had he written 'losses' to include wounded, captured and missing he might have been closer to the mark.) In Navarra, it has been estimated, 16,745 enemy soldiers were killed or captured by Espoz y Mina's divisions between 1810 and the end of the war, 9.2 men per day. Including wounded, the figure rose to a conjectural fifty thousand enemy losses, about 27.5 men a day, a high figure.

By way of comparison, throughout the whole war in neighbouring Aragón the French suffered just over 7.5 guerrilla-inflicted casualties per day; and from the fall of Zaragoza in March 1809 to September 1811, when General Suchet, the French commander in Aragón, managed if not to destroy the guerrillas totally, at least to bottle them up, the French losses averaged no more than 4.5 men per day.[51]*

There were, however, considerable variations in this rate at other times of the war. Thus during Suchet's four-month campaign to take Valencia (September 1811 to January 1812), when he left Aragón weakly garrisoned, a resurgent guerrilla put out of action a daily average of twenty enemy. In the whole Ebro valley, the average reached thirty-five per day. This rate – of over one thousand men a month – almost equalled Suchet's losses of the previous two and a half years.[52]

Napoleon's determined attempt, on the eve of his Russian campaign of 1812, to put an end to the guerrilla threat in his rear and their periodic raids across the Pyrenees into France, also ended with high daily losses. The specially created Army of the Ebro† lost 2,500 men, an average of twenty-two a day, over the sixteen weeks that its campaign lasted.

To try to set such losses in perspective, a comparison with the casualties suffered by the French in two regular army battles – one, for example, from the early stage of the war, Talavera (1809), and the other from almost the ultimate, Vitoria (1813) – is instructive. In both cases, the French confronted allied armies of which the British under Wellington constituted the major fighting force. The average French losses in the two battles was 14.4 percent of their total forces involved, with a death, prisoner and missing rate of 4.3 percent, and a wounded rate of 10.1 percent.‡

However, the comparative interest lies in annualizing the Talavera and Vitoria losses, including wounded. Over one year, these ran in crude terms to twenty and just under twenty-two soldiers per day respectively. But the two battles taken together lasted only three days. If the time span is factored in, the French losses in one year for the total of both engagements ran at a daily equivalent of 125.5 men; and thus over four years, the timespan of Mina's Navarrese Division, at 31.4 a day.

---

* Suchet's subordinates may well have attributed guerrilla-inflicted deaths and captured to desertion which would explain the very low number.
† See pp. 426–7 for this special army.
‡ The losses at Talavera were: killed 761; prisoners/missing, 206, wounded 6,301; total 7,268; at Vitoria: killed 756; prisoners/missing 2,829; wounded 4,414; total 7,999. (The figures are from Oman 1903/1995, Appendices, Vols II and VI). For different reasons the Talavera prisoners were understated and the Vitoria prisoners overstated. Taking the two battles together, it has been assumed here that the differences cancelled each other out.

During limited periods, guerrillas in the Ebro Valley, as has been seen, inflicted a broadly similar rate. But the Navarrese claim to have caused roughly comparable average losses day after day for four years, especially in 1810 and the first half of 1811, when for nine out of fifteen months French military pressure was so great that Espoz y Mina was obliged to disperse his guerrilla, was of a different order. By including the wounded, especially of the walking wounded who succeeded in escaping with the help of their companions and lived to fight another day the estimates were open to exaggeration. But the majority of casualties consisted of wounded – seventy percent of the losses at Talavera and Vitoria combined – and guerrilla estimates which included them must be viewed with initial caution.

The Navarrese figure of 9.2 enemy killed and captured per day is therefore a more reliable figure from which to start. At the two battles jointly these losses accounted, in crude annual numbers, for 12.5 men per day; and in weighted terms (over four years) for 9.4. On this calculation, the Navarrese guerrilla caused similar enemy losses in killed and captured as those which resulted from the pitched battles.

Neither Navarra nor Aragón were typical of the guerrilla movement, the one highly mobilized and the largest of all, numbering by 1811–1812 ten thousand men, the other virtually quiescent for the previous two and a half years; their figures consequently represented two extremes. But despite such regional ups-and-downs it could be supposed that the remaining guerrilla movement, with four and a half times Navarra's numbers, was capable of causing sustained daily losses of killed and captured at least double that of the Navarrese: in other words eighteen per day. Throughout five years of war then, and including Espoz y Mina's four-year-long struggle, the guerrillas would have accounted for forty-six thousand French losses without counting the wounded.

If the guerrilla proportion of enemy dead and captured to wounded were generally similar to that of the two battles (1:2.3), a further 106,000 losses would have been inflicted, bringing the total to 152,000 over the five years, or eighty enemy soldiers per day. In that case, the guerrillas would have caused just one half of the hypothetical French losses during the war;* and the Navarrese claim of fifty thousand total killed, captured and wounded would have accounted for one-third of these.

Although the overall figures including wounded, are not far short of those advanced by General Bigarré for guerrilla-inflicted deaths alone, they remain, it must be stressed, highly speculative. As for the general's guerrilla 'losses' of twenty-five thousand – by which it must be assumed from the context that he was referring to deaths – if the same proportion of killed and captured to wounded were applied as in the two battles the guerrillas would have sustained a

---

* The author's inclination is to accept Muir's estimate of three hundred thousand French losses, although other conjectures run from two hundred and forty to six hundred thousand. The only figure that is definitely established is that of the 71,000 foreign imperial troops involved in Spain who suffered 46,200 losses – sixty-five percent of their total. (Emsley, 1993, p. 146 and Muir, 1996, notes 9 and 11, p. 421.)

further 57,500 losses, a total of slightly over eighty thousand in five years or an average of forty-five per day. A rate in other words of just over half that wreaked on the enemy . . . But the proportion's plausibility does not signify that it is more than conjecture.

GUERRILLA WAR AND REVOLUTION

Though by no means exclusively plebeian, as has been seen, the guerrilla formed the only *popular* Spanish armed force during the war. Its major leaders (for contemporaries and historians alike) were of plebeian origin: landworkers and small farmers like Juan Martín, 'El Empecinado' in Castilla la Nueva; Espoz y Mina in Navarra and Julián Sánchez, 'El Charro', from Salamanca; the 18-year-old shepherd Gaspar de Jáuregui, 'El Pastor', in the Basque country and the rural parish priest Jerónimo Merino in Castilla la Vieja, alongside the Burgos master ironworker, Francisco Longa, in Cantabria. (Four army officers, Juan Díaz Porlier, in Asturias and Cantabria, Mariano Renovales in the Basque country, José Joaquín Durán, in Castilla la Vieja, Navarra and Aragón and Ramón Gayán also in Aragón, were the outstanding exceptions.) By the end of 1811 Mina, apart from a few towns still physically held by the French, virtually ruled his native Navarra, while other leaders – El Empecinado was a case in point – dominated the main military resistance in Guadalajara and neighbouring territories up to the gates of Madrid.

This guerrilla military ascendancy raised an important but seldom addressed question. Why did this plebeian armed force not act on the political situation of the moment? Could, for example, the patriot Cádiz Cortes' decision of August 6, 1811, to abolish only the jurisdictional aspects of the señorial system on the land, satisfy these village guerrilleros? In effect, the Cortes had proposed no profound social change in the señorial agrarian world other than to deprive the señores of the right to appoint magistrates and municipal councillors and to collect certain dues and tributes which pertained to their lordships' rights. For the rest, the same señores would now own the land over which they had exercised feudal privileges if their legal rights to ownership could be sustained.

The Cortes debates had given a fair indication of the lack of any substantial reforms to be made to the basic structure of land ownership, and it was clear that the villager did not stand to gain much – indeed, as will be seen, stood rather to lose a great deal – from other legislation which was to 'liberalize' the rural world by opening it to market forces. The August 6, 1811 legislation might alone have been thought sufficient to generate protest among the village guerrilleros and ensure that they used their military strength to attempt to amend, reform or radically change it and to put in its place a land reform act.

But the guerrilleros made no move to cash in their armed force for political power; indeed, there was little evidence from the 1810 elections to the Cortes in the occupied zones – when the guerrilla strength was, of course, considerably less than two years later – that they made much effort to ensure that some of their own number were elected.* For all their leadership and organizational skills, most of them would have agreed, sincerely or ironically, with El Empecinado: 'I am an ignorant fellow; I am sorry that God did not give me more talent, or fortune more learning, but I am not to blame.'[53] In other words, national heroes they might be, but the ability to represent the nation in debating its future was not part of their self-conceived mental attributes. Apart from self-depreciatory jibes, there were objective conditions which explained, though not necessarily in order of priority, the guerrilla absence from the political scene.

News from the constitutent Cortes might take a month or more to reach Navarra which was about as far from Cádiz as it was possible to get by land in Spain. For many months at the start of his guerrilla leadership, Mina had had virtually no contact with Cádiz at all, and though the government came to admire and reward his military exploits, it never seemed to overcome a certain suspicion, fuelled by the Navarrese refugee elite, of the 'governmental' measures he took to achieve his ends: his take-over of Navarrese customs posts, which yielded his guerrilla several million reales a year, was a case in point.

But as Mina acerbically pointed out,

> no titled noble, no owner of an entailed estate or man of property, no renowned name came forward to raise the banner of resistance . . . around which all the youth who desired could rally . . . So what could be expected of men like us who for the greater part knew only how to handle a spade, a mattock and pruning shears, and whose only commercial experience was of selling the harvests our small plots produced?[54]

For a long time Mina's main contact with patriot Spain was through Valencia, arguably the most manifestly anti-señorial region of Spain. But Navarra was not señorial Valencia: except in the southern plains, some seventy percent of Navarrese villagers owned the land they worked, and 'use-owners' made up most of the rest, even the relatively small proportion of señoríos being rented out on inheritable leases.[55] In Valencia, on the other hand, the señores derived at least half their income from dues and tributes.

This difference which, with the exception of Galicia, was true of most of the north and northeast, explained why the large guerrillas did not become directly involved in the agrarian questions being debated in Cádiz. Another factor also held them back. The guerrillas appeared as the patriot army disappeared as a fighting force. But this did not mean that institutionally the Spanish army had disappeared for good as the large guerrillas' insistence on attempting to militarize their parties demonstrated. Thus, while their leaders and subalterns were being incorporated into the officers' ranks, it was difficult, if not impossible, for them openly to sustain political positions which their military

---

* An exception was the Rev. Casimiro Javier de Miguel, parish priest of the Navarrese village of Ujüé, who was the secret power behind the region's incipient guerrilla movement and organized a widespread anti-French espionage and supply system without himself becoming a guerrillero. (Tone, 1994, pp. 63–64.) Though whether he was elected to escape from Navarra, where his activities had become well-known to the French, or as a guerrilla representative is a moot point.

superiors did not support, let alone to intervene militarily in the Cádiz proceedings.

Finally, of course, the threat of disunion, the difficulties guerrilla leaders experienced (like the military) in cooperating effectively, the possibility of open civil war and the threat of complete surrender to the French would all have weighed heavily on any thought of using guerrilla military power to shape the country's future. This was not to say that at the local regional level there were not accusations of guerrilla leaders wishing to take or exercise power. Apart from Mina, El Empecinado for example was virtually accused by the Guadalajara junta in 1811 of wanting to make himself the region's supreme commander and of disobeying its authority. But these were fairly exceptional situations.

POLITICS

As the above implied, regrettably little was known about the political attitudes of even the better known leaders *during* the war itself. The most that was likely to emerge was whether they proclaimed the new 1812 'liberal' constitution to their men and had them swear allegiance to it – not an insignificant political fact, for sure, but one that had an obligatory element to it which detracted somewhat from the authenticity of the political sentiments expressed by the act.

It was *after* the war that the leaders expressed their politics by declaring themselves liberals, monarchists or absolutists, or in other cases trying to weave an uncommitted path between the political options which, with Fernando VII's abrogation of the 1812 Constitution and the return to absolutism, were now at the forefront of the political divide which the war had opened in Spanish society.

More than twice as many ex-guerrilleros fought as royalists against the liberals' restoration of the 1812 constitution during the revolution of 1820–1823 as fought in support of it.* The fact that two well-known guerrilla leaders – El Empecinado and Espoz y Mina – came out for the liberals and a third, Porlier, had a year after the end of the war risen in their cause, may have obscured the historical vision that liberals were a minority in the guerrilla movement at large. Although generalization on an exiguous sample is hazardous, it could be argued that, as the crystallization of popular resistance, the guerrilla represented widespread popular sentiment in which defence of the monarchy without constitutional restrictions instead of the political innovation of national sovereignty, seen as a foreign import, was the keystone. This political option, which included defence of religion, did not, however, exclude the serious reforms expected of Fernando's restored reign. Undeniably, the rural population, from which a majority of guerrilleros stemmed, wanted an improvement of its lot; but the liberals offered them so little – abolition of jurisdictional lordships without total relief from feudal dues and tithes; a free

* The assertion is admittedly based on a very slender sample: sixteen ex-guerrilleros (2%) of the total of 751 recorded in the author's database, eleven of whom fought as royalists and five as liberals.

agrarian market in which the señores became outright landowners and villagers stood little chance of acquiring land – that their political reforms held hardly any popular rural appeal.*

*

Had the Spanish 'revolution', so consistently invoked by most sectors of the fragile patriotic alliance of Old Regime supporters and reformists – had this revolution extended to the labouring poor, the military effectiveness of the Spanish anti-Napoleonic war effort would have been deeply reinforced. But the revolution was not a social revolution. Its luck was that the poor were prepared to fight for reasons of their own: to defend their families and lives, their plots and homelands, their customs and traditions, their forefathers' religion, their monarchy. Their determination was best expressed in the struggles for popular territorial liberation and guerrilla warfare. To this extent, the patriots were fortunate in having their support. But in the long run, as Mina himself said, the war was finally won 'in the snows of Russia'.

COUNTER-INSURGENCY

The insurgency's success was everywhere in direct relation to the counter-insurgency's insufficiencies. Many of these arose from Napoleon's failure to confront the basic problems of guerrilla warfare. It was not a new military problem; the Vendée and Calabrian insurrections had been forerunners from which lessons could and had been learned. One of Napoleon's generals, Suchet, was capable of keeping the guerrillas in Aragón quiet for nearly two years; another, Reille, though less successful in Navarra, kept Mina on the run for nine months and defeated him heavily on two occasions. Why then was French counter-insurgency in general apparently so ineffective?

The first question was whether it was as ineffective as it appeared. Of the guerrillas, whose wartime death was recorded,† one-quarter were killed in action or upon being taken prisoner. This did not say much for the counter-insurgency's combat effectiveness. But when account was taken of the fact that two-thirds of the guerrillas known to have died were tried and sentenced to death, it would seem that at another level the anti-guerrilla struggle was rather more successful than was usually believed: the level of French intelligence networks must have been high; informants among the population more plentiful, and anti-guerrilla sentiment and collaboration with counter-insurgency measures greater than was generally imagined.

* The relationship between the guerrillas' political stance and popular sentiment was to some extent corroborated a decade later in the first Carlist civil war (1833–1839) which pitted a moderate liberal monarchy against a sui generis Catholic absolutism. The number of ex-guerrilleros who then backed the former compared to those who had fought against the liberal revolution a decade earlier was almost exactly reversed. Like most of the nation (outside the Basque country and Navarra which were the foci of Carlist support), former guerrilleros had evidently come to accept a moderate liberal reformism in the face of an absolutist option.
† See Appendix 4.

But the nub of the problem lay in Napoleon's politico-military strategy towards Spain. He envisaged it as a wealthy colony to be exploited for his larger ambitions and overlooked the country's actual conditions. He never provided a viable counter-insurgency policy. This error resulted in helping to keep the guerrilla alive. In the first place, his refusal to appoint a commander-in-chief to plan and coordinate on a national scale the counter-insurgency (and the anti-British struggle) was a prime mistake. He believed that he could control the war from Paris through a series of provincial commanders, many of them principally concerned with their own parcel of territorial power and frequently in dispute with one another. The result was the extreme difficulty of mounting a *unified, consistent* and *simultaneous* counter-insurgency campaign over several provinces or entire regions, a difficulty increased by the Emperor's observance of artificial provincial boundaries as the limits of territorial military commands. In consequence, the guerrillas could usually find secure refuges along provincial or regional borders where none of the provinces' French commanders, knowing that the effort was useless since the guerrillas would simply move into the neighbouring province, was prepared seriously to campaign. The mistake was compounded by dividing power within the political regime Napoleon had created to replace the old Bourbon monarchy by his segregation of the Spanish provinces north of the Ebro from his brother's kingdom to that of his own in Paris. Not only did this arouse popular resistance in the affected regions at the possibility of their being formally incorporated into France, but added yet more generals in politico-military command of provinces.

Yet another of Napoleon's errors was to believe that if Spanish resistance to Bonapartist domination of Spain had been irreducible since 1808, only military force could subdue it. And while in general the assumption of Spanish resistance was correct, Napoleon made no attempt to formulate alternative policies which would give the population good reasons not to support the guerrilla. Military pacification and taxation, repression and requisition, were the only nostrums on offer.

The counter-insurgency had to fight without better weapons or communications than the enemy. Artillery and cavalry were of little use, in fact were often counter-productive in the rough terrain where most of the operations took place. Therefore the French had either to deploy highly superior numbers or highly-trained troops if they were to defeat the guerrillas. Every time they detached large numbers to the counter-insurgency campaign they obliged the insurgents to disperse; but even with an occupying force of three hundred thousand men divided into distinct provincial commands, it was not often that they were able to assemble sufficient troops for a sufficiently long campaign – a campaign which had indeed to be virtually constant – to maintain their enemy's dispersal. And as they moved troops from one region to another the guerrilla filled the vacuum they had left.

Napoleon believed that a single campaign would eliminate the guerrillas. He was projecting state war against popular war. Powerful but brief sweeps never suppressed the insurgents for long: they disappeared in small, dispersed companies. He was convinced, on the basis of the Vendée, that mobile columns were the military answer, and in this instance his generals followed his orders. Napoleon was hostile to static garrison troops, and was constantly ordering regiments to be moved from one command to another just when the troops had become familiar with the terrain in which they had to fight. The result was to slow down the counter-insurgency: commanders delayed in dispatching their best troops to another, usually rival, general, and often did not fill their ordered quota of men, leaving the other command even more under strength than before the change was ordered.

Though Napoleon took the 'brigand' threat seriously enough, especially when they raided French territory, he never came to believe in the guerrillas' fighting capabilities, and his counter-insurgency was manned mainly by inexperienced conscripts who were the most likely to be terrorized by the guerrilla tactics of surprise attack, ambushes and hand-to-hand fighting. Moreover, the conscripts heard enough stories of the guerrillas' brutality to live in mortal fear of their enemy, and were easily demoralized by the constant losses – small detachments of their regimental companies, including individual companion conscripts – who were suddenly missing after a minor military operation to collect taxes or requisitions of food. The counter-insurgency required troops already hardened to living in a hostile environment and trained to accept that their own lives were under constant threat from even the most innocent-looking villager.

EPISODES: REVENGE

Francesc Torné i Montserrat, a twelve-year-old Catalan veil-weaver, was returning one day to his home in Reus from a visit to a nearby mill where he had gone to see if his father's flour was ready whon hc was stopped by a French patrol. They asked him where he was coming from, but as he did not speak French he neither understood the question nor was able to answer. Believing that he was a 'mountain brigand', they immediately ordered him to kneel on the ground and readied their arms to shoot him. Luckily for the lad, the French sergeant in command, seeing that he was only young, put an end to the matter and told Francesc to get up. 'Allons', he said, gesturing to him to get on his way home.

A few nights later he had his revenge for the great fear he had experienced. The two imperial soldiers billeted in his house were in a drunken stupour in bed, dead to the world. Francesc and some companions grabbed first one and then the other, carried them outside and threw them down the well. Then they filled a great sack with earth and rocks and threw it in after them. Shortly, some of the soldiers' companions arrived, asking for them. Francesc said they had recently left, but he did not know where. The following evening the companions returned saying the two soldiers had not been seen all day, gathered up their arms and equipment and left.

This, and the following incident, were stories told many years later to his son, who wrote them down.[56] Like most family stories they were almost certainly much embroidered in the telling, or even outright fabulations. But they revealed, if not 'the truth' in this particular case, a more general truth by no means confined to Cataluña: an enemy aggressor created a popular resistance in its homelands ready to resort to individual acts of great violence against a hated invader. Francesc was again returning home at nightfall from the countryside with some landworking friends when they heard a noise behind them. They turned and saw five French soldiers carrying vegetables and fruit they had stolen. Allowing them to catch up by the aptly named Devil's Reservoir, Francesc gave a signal, his friends dropped their own baskets, and attacked the soldiers with their mattocks, wounding three, two of whom fell to the ground. The other, with his face badly injured, fled with the two unhurt soldiers towards Reus. Francesc and his friends threw the remaining two into the reservoir and then fled themselves, entering the town from another direction as though nothing had happened. A French patrol was ordered out to catch them; but all it found was two corpses floating on the water . . .

*

To return to the broader theme of counter-insurgency, Suchet, arguably Napoleon's most successful commander in Spain, observed that this sort of war required battle-trained soldiers used to fighting in small units, lightly equipped and rapid, acting by surprise and led by experienced officers who were both audacious and prudent: 'These are men who are almost always out on missions; and they have to be able to bear the most painful marches and the harshest conditions . . .'[57]

In Suchet's view, the mobile columns replicated the guerrillas' own tactic of sweeping over the countryside when what was needed, he believed, was to *occupy* it; and he garrisoned as many strongpoints in his territory as his military strength, which was rarely overwhelming, allowed, and kept the same troops in the same towns for as long as possible. This had a dual objective: his soldiers not only knew their combat terrain but could fraternize with the local population, helping to reduce conflictive situations and extend the flow of intelligence on guerrilla movements. This tactic was not totally successful either, but on several occasions his garrisons held out long enough to pin down guerrilla forces or expose them to counter-attack from relief columns.

He realized early on that to win the guerrilla war he had to win over the population. Aware that looting, thieving and violence were inevitably brutal forms of alienating villagers, he kept his troops on a very short leash to prevent them pillaging. Above all, he knew that he could not pacify Aragón, create a civil administration, pay and feed his troops while great numbers of dispersed soldiers from his two victories over the patriot armies near

Zaragoza in 1809 swarmed in the countryside. He made the guerrillas his main target of attack.

Soldiers, he knew, spent their pay almost as soon as they received it. As a result, he effectively paid them every five days: the rapid turnover of money helped to keep the Aragonese economy afloat, while simultaneously discouraging the troops – many of whom in other armies were not paid for months – from acts of violence against the population. The main question then was money. But he was also prepared to take drastic retributive measures: to burn to the ground or deport the entire population of a village if it did not contribute its taxes or bring in the harvest or where his soldiers were shot. Suchet also believed that he had to attract the Aragonese with positive policies, and he did so by leaving much of the local administration, especially tax collection, to the old authorities and rewarded them with a greater share of responsibility in disposing of the region's resources.

> I was convinced that as I could not cover the whole country with my troops, it was in the army's interest to concern the people in preserving the national product by giving them one quarter of the region's income . . . the people had no interest whatsoever in allowing themselves to be stripped of it by the brigands . . .[58]

He raised six companies of fusileros – the pre-war volunteer anti-brigand militia – paid for by an extra tax, praising the Aragonese as courageous fighters and, in one of his most popular measures, ordered that the army's stores be opened to those communities whose crops had been ruined.

> The people know at last the protective power that is being offered to them, they rise against the 'brigands' . . . the farmers have sown their fields everywhere, the land is being cultivated, even industry is showing some progress.[59]

Suchet relied also on the mobile column, often made up of squadrons of gendarmerie, trained to patrol and control the French countryside, as the major link between his strongholds, which were often no more than fortified convents or friaries. But he attempted to improve their performance on the ground which had often to replicate the guerrillas'.

From Paris, Napoleon could not himself handle the small detail of an anti-insurgency war when matters of greater moment occupied most of his thinking. This was evident from the degree of insubordination which he tolerated – unknowingly in many cases – from his generals in Spain. Quite possibly, had he taken personal command of the counter-insurgency campaign, ensuring sufficient troops and making provincial generals cooperate at regional levels he might have succeeded in putting paid to the majority of the northern guerrillas. But this required a strategic decision which for reasons of international affairs (his marriage to Marie Thérèse of Austria, his plans for invading Russia) he was unable or unwilling to take. Compared to these, Spain was a secondary affair.

Many of the Emperor's commanders were more concerned with holding to ransom rather than executing any patriot they believed could raise the money to pay. To make ready cash was more important to them than shooting patriots which brought them no returns other than to create more martyrs and to reinforce the enemy cause. Napoleon was also faced with a military problem that put the counter-insurgency's priority in question. Who was the main enemy? There could be no doubt that the Anglo-Portuguese army was the greatest of the three threats which confronted his domination of Spain: however much of a nuisance, the guerrillas could not and would not win the war on their own. The renewed Spanish army and the guerrillas together were a force to be taken into account, but one that was hardly likely to threaten the withdrawal of the imperial forces from the country. The Anglo-Portuguese army, on the other hand, was capable of winning battles which could threaten imperial dominance. And if the latter were joined by the Spanish army and guerrillas the threat would be seriously increased. Despite the failure of Masséna's campaign, in 1810–1811, to throw the British into the sea, the Anglo-Portuguese army was blocked in Portugal until early 1812 by the French capture of the major fortress towns along the Spanish border; as a result the French were left a choice of isolating and defeating one or other of the Spanish forces as the first step in defence of the country. By 1812, some of Napoleon's generals were advocating that the guerrilla was the major enemy to be destroyed.[60]

Indeed Napoleon agreed with them. He had no wish to see the guerrillas cross the Pyrenees while he was campaigning in Russia. The Army of the Ebro, which he created with the express purpose of 'pursuing the guerrillas to extinction', was particularly aimed at eliminating the border raids from Cataluña which he had just annexed. This new army of thirty-six thousand men he placed under the command of General Reille, a veteran counter-insurgent general. The armies of the North, Cataluña and Valencia were ordered to help – another sixty-four thousand troops on paper. One hundred thousand soldiers in all, the largest single army the French had tried to put together in Spain. Apart from these men, Napoleon planned that an additional division of conscripts and national guardsmen protect the French frontier from the irregulars' raids. The most significant change in Napoleon's thinking was that the new army should not be restricted by provincial boundaries and was to cover natural geographical areas of operation.

As usual Napoleon expected Reille to break the guerrillas' back in one swift campaign, following his own plan which tried always to crush the enemy with a single blow, and ordered Reille to coordinate closely with General Decaen in Cataluña. But instead of helping Reille, Suchet, the Aragón army commander who had just scored an outstanding victory in taking Valencia, and Decaen began to dismember the Ebro army. Suchet, who had won his marshal's baton after his victorious siege of Tarragona, ordered Reille to send two regiments to replace the Polish regiments which he had had to send on the Russian campaign; while Decaen took two other regiments from lower Cataluña. Before he even started, Reille lost one quarter of his army which was reduced to twenty-two thousand men.

Napoleon always underestimated the guerrilla's staying power. 1812 was a famine year and Reille's troops could not secure sufficient supplies in any one zone for more than a few days; where they could not eat they could not fight, and Reille's sweeps grew ever more limited; his incessant movements to feed even his reduced army made it impossible to crush the guerrillas along the Ebro. Suchet again intervened, ordering Reille to protect only his own territorial base, Aragón. By the beginning of May, Reille had only fourteen thousand men left. On May 6, 1812, the army was wound up after four months of operations, having lost two thousand five hundred men.

REPRESSION: THE EXTRAORDINARY CRIMINAL TRIBUNALS

Article II

Assassins, thieves, the armed rebellious, the seditious, rumour-mongers, spies, recruiters for the insurgents [patriots] and those who are in communication with them, or those who are found with daggers and sharp-edged weapons upon them, if convicted will be hanged irremissibly within twenty-four hours and without the right of appeal. (Bonapartist decree creating a new court, the Extraordinary Criminal Tribunal, Madrid, February 16, 1809).[61]

The courts which the Bonapartist regime considered essential to control the incipient guerrilla movement at the beginning of 1809 tried over two thousand accused during their three years of existence (one year less in Andalucía which was taken in 1810). Of these close on four hundred received the death sentence. The unremitting nature of the repression was demonstrated by the fact that, with the exception of 1809 when the extraordinary tribunals were created piecemeal in different provincial capitals and sixty-one prisoners were sentenced to death, in 1810 and 1811 the figures were over one hundred annually. A diarist in Valladolid carefully, if laconically in the style of the times, recorded the executions for the latter year.

Jan 1, 1811. 'El Galleguillo' was brought in a prisoner this morning. At four in the afternoon, more or less, he was shot . . .

Jan 9. Five men, one of them a surgeon's son, were publicly garrotted in the Campo Grande . . .

May 23. A soldier, said to be an escaped English prisoner and a spy, was executed by a firing squad in the Campo Grande . . .

July 30. Three men, one of them the son of a local inhabitant, commonly known as Fantasías, were garrotted in the main square. Another was a lathe worker . . .

August 2. A priest, chaplain to Saornil's party, and taken prisoner, was garrotted in the main square . . .

Sept 22. A German, said to have deserted and joined a guerrilla, was executed by a firing squad . . .

Dec 8. Early in the morning 'Chagarito' and two accomplices who had been captured by the French the previous night were brought in. Chagarito revealed the names of this city's inhabitants and those of other places who, through force or out of fear, had supplied or helped him. The other two were honourable and gave no names. Chagarito thought his revelations would save his life. The extraordinary tribunal was fair and acquitted all those he had informed against. Chagarito and the other two were sentenced to death and garrotted in the main square on Dec 24. Chagarito's corpse was quartered and the pieces stuck up on the country paths into the city.[62]

These were but some of the thirty public executions in the Castilian capital in a single year – though only half of them were known guerrilleros; and the eleven who were executed by firing squad had certainly been sentenced by French drumhead courts martial, since the extraordinary tribunal condemned its victims to the garrotte. In Jerez de la Frontera, where before 1810, eight years could pass without an execution and the average was one a year, the extraordinary tribunal condemned forty-four men to death in thirty months.[63] Overall, Madrid was the bloodiest. It sentenced to capital punishment one hundred accused for various activities, including resistance, in its four years of existence; 1809 was the harshest year. The Valladolid tribunal came next in severity with seventy-one, more than half of them in 1810.

The extraordinary tribunals had two quite distinct origins, one Basque, one French. In 1799, the Basque elite had become so concerned by the increase in rural criminality in its country that it had approved a special law to judge and execute bandits and thieves which gave the prosecution thirty days to prove guilt and thereafter no appeal, complaint or other recourse was admitted before the death sentence was applied to all those above the age of sixteen. Soon after the beginning of the war this special law was resuscitated to try the first Basque guerrilla captured.*[64] The exceptional increase in highwaymen, brigands and the like which the war spawned was also used to justify bringing back the 1799 law.

The second source stemmed from French Republican and Royalist plots against Napoleon in 1803. The future Emperor had thereupon set up special summary criminal tribunals in France to try traitors and assassins, armed robbers, arsonists, vagabonds and re-offenders. These tribunals' sentences were carried out immediately and without the possibility of appeal.

The majority of those judged and sentenced to death by the extraordinary criminal tribunals in Spain were not, however, guerrilleros. The Bonapartist regime – like the French army – did not distinquish between 'bandits' and 'guerrillas'. For both they were one and the same. In consequence, it was often highly difficult to differentiate – in the brief descriptions of their crimes afforded by the summary of their cases – whether indeed these were highwaymen or guerrillas. They were tried for armed hold-ups: but whether their ultimate purpose was to steal their victims' money or to use it to further the patriot

* See pp. 409–10.

struggle was usually left in doubt (indeed, there were parties for whom the difference was of little import). Considering therefore only those who were officially identified as such, approximately twenty-five percent of those condemned to death were indisputably guerrilleros.*

Only in 1812, when the French were in obvious danger and had abandoned Andalucía did total death sentences drop back to fifty-nine, close to their starting point. Over and above the tribunals, the French military held their own courts martial which sent to their deaths an unspecified number of real or suspected guerrilleros. Usually, Bonapartist and French military respected their rough codes of justice; but occasionally the latter resorted to the barbarities of which they accused the 'brigands': the minor Aragonese guerrilla chieftain, 'Pesoduro' was tortured, and his hands – cut off while he was still alive – were publicly nailed up; on the scaffold the rope broke several times before he was finally hanged.[65]

The courts' magistrates, prosecutors and staff were exclusively Spanish – drawn from the legal profession and frequently from criminal courts, including, in Andalucía especially, those tribunals which the patriots had set up to try people accused of supporting or materially aiding the Bonapartist regime.† The latter were established in most patriot-held provincial capitals, and although they did not publish figures of their executions and sentences it was certain that they did not condemn to death anything like the number sentenced by the Bonapartist extraordinary tribunals.

The guerrillas took their revenge on the tribunals' justices by seizing them – often as they made their way to take up their posts. Thus the presidents and judges of both the Ciudad Real and Málaga tribunals were captured before they could reach their destination to set up their court. Three hundred guerrilleros, most of them on horseback, attacked Valdepeñas in La Mancha in May 1810, and took the Ciudad Real justices prisoner, sending them under guard, the Bonapartist local authorities supposed, to Valencia. Two years later El Empecinado captured the prosecutor and a judge of the Cuenca tribunal.

Guerrillas also seized a Madrid tribunal judge who was taken to Cádiz where he was publicly hanged by the patriot government; and the secretary of the Bilbao court was sequestered. A good measure of the tribunals' unpopularity was the difficulty some had in finding executioners

---

* As the records did not always prove that the sentence was carried out, I have included all those who were condemned to death unless they were officially pardoned. As the records for the forty-four executed in Jerez de la Frontera are missing from the archives from which the other figures were taken, they have been excluded from this computation for lack of evidence concerning their status as guerrillas or outlaws. However, local municipal records showed them to have been executed. (AM de Jerez de la Frontera, *Grupo Justicia*, 'Ajusticiados desde 1686 a 1850', Memorandas núm 6, doc. 10.)

† Very shortly after the Junta Suprema's formation in September 1808, it created what was initially known as the Tribunal de Vigilancia which was reformed under the name of the Tribunal de Seguridad Pública in Sevilla on the Suprema's arrival there.

to carry out the death sentences. Ciudad Real and Guadalajara complained that they could find none and Jaén informed the justice ministry that the local executioner would accept no less than three thousand three hundred reales a year with certain perquisites which he claimed went with the job.

WOMEN SENTENCED

Two hundred and sixty-eight women appeared before the tribunals to be tried for various offences, nearly sixty percent of them before the Madrid court. (Bilbao, with less than twenty percent, trailed well behind in second place.) Just under one in three were found not guilty which was perhaps not exceptional since many were brought before the court on mere 'suspicion' of being involved in some illegal activity. However, the charges against one in five of the accused were quite plainly connected to the guerrilla and patriot cause in one way or another. Manuela Salazar received eight months in prison in Madrid for marrying a man who was popularly accused of being an ex-guerrillero, and Manuela Uriarte, also of Madrid, was tried on charges of 'slovenly behaviour and of having been in the insurgent [patriot] army'. She was acquitted on all charges. Another seven women were given various sentences of from one to two years for involvement in the killing of a French dragoon. Carrying mail to the guerrilla, providing intelligence, storing arms and ammunition in their houses, implication in the theft of a French officer's horse or the sale of two stolen mares figured alongside the more banal charges of receiving stolen goods and the like. Helping Spanish prisoners of war to escape from the columns being conducted to France and aiding and abetting deserters from the imperial armies were also quite frequent charges. At least one woman, Francisca Artiago, was sentenced to death in 1810 by the Valladolid tribunal for having stolen, in the company of others, five thousand reales' worth of goods from a French mess.*

One of the more outstanding cases was brought by the Bilbao tribunal against a group of five women and three men, all from Elorrio, in Vizcaya, who carried out armed robberies in houses around the township and were in contact with the guerrilla in the hills of Urquiola. The youngest of the women was fourteen-year-old María Josefa de Iturbe who, dressed as a man, was known to have just returned from the hills where she had accompanied the guerrilla on their missions immediately before the robberies took place. She was the only one of the women against whom certain proof existed that she had taken part in the crimes. Moreover, the group was alleged to be known to have stolen six or seven cart-loads of cloth bales the previous January and to have kept them in their houses where they sheltered the guerrillas, gave them help and

---

* As the only documentary proof of her sentence is her Madrid sister's petition to spare her life, her fate is unknown but it is unlikely that she would have been executed.

accepted jewels in payment. Judging by their family names, the group included two brothers and their sisters. Two of the women, against whom no concrete proof was offered, were sentenced to ten years in gaol, two others to eight and María Josefa de Iturbe to six. Two of the men were given ten years each in prison and the third was judged to have spent sufficient time in gaol prior to the hearing to have served his sentence.

18

1812–1814

THE FAMINE YEAR: 1812

The scourge of dearth returned to decimate the population in 1812. The 1811 grain crop was poor and bad weather in the Castillas delayed reaping and threshing the little grain that stood in the fields. In war-stricken Cataluña, the death rate began to increase from the middle of 1811. The French, having taken Tarragona in June after a two-month siege which ended in a ferociously bloody sacking, now occupied all the major Catalan ports, preventing the import of grain to a region normally deficient in wheat.

In Madrid the old monarchy had always been frightened of bread riots. From the second half of the eighteenth century, they had created storage facilities of one million fanegas (just over 1.5 million bushels) of wheat in Madrid to ensure that the capital's inhabitants should have sufficient bread at a more or less constant price. But in the spring of 1811, prices began to rise as wheat supplies from the two Castillas, which until then had been adequate, fell off. The increase was worsened by bakers short-weighting loaves. Popular opinion had it, a police report said, that the wheat shortage was caused by the government which had ordered all available supplies to be sent to the French army in Burgos, or more significantly, that the guerrilla had captured the grain on its way to the capital.[1] The latter rumour was true; guerrilla bands which now showed themselves openly within a short distance of the capital had seized several thousand fanegas of wheat being transported from La Mancha: the battle for food supplies was being remorselessly waged.

Price increases began to affect other essentials, like olive oil, vegetables and pulses. As the population's discontent grew, another more subversive rumour was heard: the increases were to pay for celebrating the king's saint's day on March 19.[2] Aware of the danger, the interior minister informed the Madrid corregidor that the king would not permit celebrations that raised the price of any essential foodstuffs and ordered that those spreading the rumour be punished. At the same time the government secured assurances from the bakers to maintain the standard price; but the assurances lasted only a few days and the cost of a 2lb loaf rose by over one quarter of a real, or some sixteen percent.*

While at the turn of the century, a Madrid labourer spent nearly three- quarters of a day's wage to secure two days' food, of which bread was the main ingredient,† at the beginning of 1811, if a police commissioner's report was to be believed, the labouring classes had the wherewithal to buy food. 'The populace is calm because they have money, and if they do not have more it is because people of distinction are lacking it.' In other words, employment was not as plentiful as it might have been but for the war; but it was sufficient for the labouring classes not to suffer unduly.[3] Though the report may have been nothing more than the commissioner's attempt to ingratiate himself with the regime, there had been no deep popular discontent with the new monarchy. The cheap bread – cheaper in Madrid than in the neighbouring provincial capitals – and bullfights by which Josef Bonaparte had attempted not unsuccessfully to woo Madrid's inhabitants were, as the spring price rises showed, coming to an end.

Before they did, however, the lower classes continued to enjoy themselves. Theatre takings remained high; in the Maravillas quarter, site of the artillery depot where so much blood had been shed in the uprising on May 2, 1808, the only public dance hall, La Estrella, was always full of soldiers 'and the freest women of the surrounding neighbourhoods'. Public propriety was somewhat wanting, however, the police commissioner reported.

> Modesty and decorum which should be maintained at all public functions are not sufficiently in evidence, and this cannot be remedied because some of those present have drunk a surfeit of wine which results in an excess of kissing and hugging . . . I have warned the female proprietor . . .[4]

Gambling was the other major popular distraction. The government tried to outlaw card games, especially 'cané' which was a particular favourite among the Madrid labouring poor. When an out-of-work master carpenter, Juan de Bastiyeta, with five children to provide for was granted permission by the Madrid corregidor to organize a simple game of fortune with sweetmeats as prizes, the latter was immediately reprimanded by the police minister for acting beyond his limits and against royal regulations. Despite their rigorous hostility to the lower classes' uncontrollable gambling, the Bonapartist authorities nonetheless received a healthy income from the Madrid gaming-house licences they approved. An 'inveterate vice', as the Ocaña police commissioner called it, gaming was widespread and one of the 'greatest evils' of La Mancha; and in Sevilla, where the regal commissioner, conde de Montarco, tried to put an end to it, his efforts led nowhere because, as he informed the government, the

---

* In today's terms, a Castilian pound equalled 460 grams. Thus a 2lb loaf weighed a little short of a kilo.
† During normal times a labourer would consume more than 1lb (Castilian) of bread a day. Judging by Madrid hospital returns during the 1812 crisis, 1lb of bread and the same amount of meat was considered necessary per inmate daily. (Espadas Burgos, 1968, pp. 619–621.)

French occupation forces derived too much money from it to allow its prohibition.[5]

To appease the Madrid lower classes for their increasing hunger, carnival celebrations, which the Bourbon monarchy had banned for over forty years, were permitted by the king in February 1812, and were held in traditional style with three days of masked balls.

> Yesterday the people had great entertainment in putting on masks and strolling along the Prado in groups in ingeniously splendid dress, despite the short notice they were given that the celebration was to take place. Last night, a large crowd attended the theatre of the Caños del Peral for the public ball, and the people amused themselves in an orderly fashion . . . For a moment everyone forgot about the high cost of bread and the other burdens that are tormenting them.[6]

Indeed, judging by the amounts taken by the Caños theatre on Feb 10th and 11th – nearly thirty-four thousand reales – there was still money available for pleasure.[7] But by the end of April so few people were going to the theatre that the other main Madrid stage, the Coliseo del Principe, took in on April 29 only 381 reales. Possibly the program was not sufficiently attractive; but it was more likely that hunger and shortage of money – those who still had cash were having to pay four or five times the pre-famine prices simply to stay alive – had reduced one of the Madrileños' major attractions.[8]

Already in January, to the local authorities' amazement, a young beggar woman found dying in the street could not be admitted to the women's hospital because there was no room left for even a single patient.[9] In March two corpses were discovered in a room in the Santiago neighbourhood; a man who had died of dysentery and a woman, who looked after him, who had got drunk and died.[10]

Meanwhile the king had donated half of his civil list to acquire wheat at any price, and ordered the government to bring in grain from its own warehouses. Madrid's large stores had been progressively depleted by the treasury even before Napoleon's invasion. Special taxes on the country-wide network of grain storehouses – which had originated in the middle-ages and had been much expanded in the eighteenth century – in order to raise money to back the depreciating value of government bonds (the *vales reales*) had left many of them, including Madrid's, without the funds to purchase grain. From the beginning of the war, what remained of the stocks had been mainly used to feed troops. In the countryside, government exactions exacerbated the shortage.* In consequence, when the dearth began there were virtually no wheat reserves in the capital on which to call.

Lacking a national market and an adequate road system to move wheat cheaply from areas of surplus to those with grave shortages, pre-war wheat prices had always fluctuated wildly depending on supply. In a bad harvest year

* In June 1811, the Bonapartist government imposed a 'tax' of nearly one million fanegas (1.5 million bushels) of wheat on those areas of the two Castillas it controlled 'to provide for the necessities of the state and the cost of the war'. (AGS, *Papeles del Gobierno intruso, Gracia y Justicia*, Legajo 1128, n.n. Decree of June 23, 1811.)

they could be four hundred percent higher in the Castilian interior than in good years, although on the coast, where wheat could be imported, the rise might be only fifty percent.[11] A sharp increase in the price was therefore to be expected in Madrid where in mid-May 1811 a fanega of wheat was fetching between sixty-six and eighty-eight reales; a year later it was being sold at between 400 and 490.[12]

At the beginning of March 1812, the Bonapartist secret police reported that

> almost every day [we] find poor people dying in the streets. Sickness is increasing daily. Three swollen corpses have been taken from the San Lorenzo prison . . . There are great numbers of prostitutes plying their trade on the banks of the river [Manzanares].[13]

Until April the inhabitants' resignation and patience was remarkable. Bread, which only the wealthiest could afford, was openly carried and sold without protest among a starving people.[14] The previous month the government had been forced to recognize that the measures taken so far, which included funding a special commission to provide soup and healthy, plentiful food for the most needy at accessible prices, were inadequate and it doubled its monthly subsidy to one hundred thousand reales. Private donations were called for and received: but over and above the eleven thousand poor who were helped, three thousand of the subscribers also received the advantages of subsidized foodstuffs. Indeed, by this time even some government judges, whose salaries were always in arrears, were reduced to begging.[15]

On April 7 and 8, the poor finally lost patience. Several bakeries were asaulted and the government had to call on armed force to subdue the assailants, some forty of whom were detained, before peace was restored.[16] The government, whose free market economy principles forbade it to control prices, began to clamp down on the bakers with inspections to ensure that they were not hoarding wheat to raise bread prices. However, more energetic measures were needed. At the beginning of the month, the secret police – all of eight individuals* – informed the government that

> sickness continues to devastate the population; the hospitals are overflowing with patients, and the populace is exasperated by hunger and misery. Despite this, the people's spirit is running high and very seditious conversations are heard, both among the lower orders and decent persons who talk of nothing but enemy victories and their certainty that soon all the countries dominated by the French will be liberated . . . There was very little wheat in the grain market yesterday . . .[17]

---

* They were helped by the police patrols of each neighbourhood, which also reported each day on their operations, although the information they provided was of dubious quality. 'Of the seven agents of my patrol, only one can write tolerably, the rest can only sign their names', wrote a neighbourhood police commissioner, Anselmo Revega, in December 1809, to the police minister. 'And Your Excellency knows how many reports there are to be written.' (AGS, *Papeles del Gobierno intruso, Gracia y Justicia*, Legajo 1146, n.n., Madrid, Dec 11, 1809.)

Some way had to be found to prevent the capital starving to death and to return its inhabitants to their previous acceptance of the regime. The interior minister, rejecting the idea of mixing wheat with rice, maize, potato or carobs – potatoes were already too dear and carobs in large quantities caused 'acute colic' – decided that only an inferior quality of bread, which included a large amount of bran, could be baked. Although there was a degree of social equality of sacrifice to the measure, since this was the sort of bread used to feed ordinary campaigning soldiers and gaol prisoners, the people remained dissatisfied. Believing openly that bakers were making undue profits from the new measure, they demanded that the government fix the price of a standard 2lb loaf.[18]

Even the new sort of bread did not end starvation. May 1812 was almost certainly the most deadly month. Among the few sources of relief were the long queues at the remaining convent doors for a cupful of watery soup which at least warmed empty stomachs. Enterprising sorbet wafer-makers turned their talent to setting up street stands where they cooked 'sandwiches' from grass pea flour and onions which cost a quarter of a real. Although recognizing that these stands were tolerated for the 'good of the poor', the secret police wanted them banned because neighbours were suffering from the smoke of the burned oil and fat and the stands could be the source of fire. 'Public order and salubrity demands that these so-called sandwich stands be prohibited.'[19]

Though the secret police report did not recall it, a most surprising scene had taken place at one of these stands a few weeks earlier when the people lost patience with their long suffering. A priest bearing the viaticum was on his way to give the last rights to a dying person. In normal times people uncovered their heads in respect, or knelt in the street at the sight of the eucharist. But now indignation and exasperation had reached such a point that, as the priest passed a stand on the corner of the Calle de la Fe, the owners began to throw spoonfuls of dough at passers-by.[20] Public order required no repetition of such disgraceful scenes.

But the stands were allowed to remain. In the secret police view they were the cause of 'thousands of disturbances because the Madrid youth, desperate with hunger, robbed them and prevented people passing by in the streets'.[21] Nonetheless, one of Goya's horrifying prints of the capital's starving inhabitants in his *Disasters of War*, in which a woman half-raising herself from the street to receive something to eat from a group which appears more impoverished than she, is captioned: 'Thanks to the grass pea flour'.* The secret police could no doubt still eat, but the stands provided the poor with a little basic sustenance.

Meanwhile, the famine's 'terrible ravages' continued unabated; the secret police reported that 1,996 adults had died in May.[22]† 'Hunger is the principal enemy of this country', the king wrote. If all available troops were not called

* On Goya's *Disasters of War* see Chapter 19.
† The figure's preciseness was explicable by an earlier police order which, from at least June 1810, required all Madrid parish priests to report the number of baptisms, marriages and deaths on a daily basis. (AGS, *Papeles del Gobierno intruso, Gracia y Justicia*, Legajo 1145, n.n., Madrid document of June 1810, which refers to this order.)

upon to protect the coming harvest, 'the danger exists that the fields will be devastated and the harvest burned which will make inevitable the evacuation of Spain'.[23] His fear had been precipitated by reports that Wellington was pursuing in Extremadura the burnt-earth policy he had used in Portugal during his defence against Masséna two years earlier.*

The schoolboy Ramón Mesonero Romanos would never forget the desolate scenes of people dying openly in the streets in full daylight, wives and children crying beside their husbands' and brothers' corpses lying on the pavement from where they were collected twice a day by parish carts.

> Even the air smelled of the noxious gases of the dead and seemed to extend a funereal shroud over the population. One simple memory will suffice: in the three hundred paces between my home and my primary school, I counted one day as many as seven corpses and expiring bodies, and I ran home crying to throw myself into my anguished mother's arms. For several months thereafter she did not allow me to return to school.[24]

Mesonero Romanos also recalled that French troops stationed in the capital were generous to the numerous starving beggars in the streets; Goya in his *Disasters of War* insinuated the same. But under the bitter title 'They are of another breed' the artist depicted better-off Madrileños callously ignoring the starving, skeletal poor. Goya's captions – nearly one in five of his stark black-and-white Disasters' engravings are of the famine which, living in Madrid, he witnessed – tell the story: 'There was nothing to be done and he died'; 'Vain laments'; 'The worst is to beg'; 'To the cemetery'; 'It is no use crying out'; 'The beds of death'; 'Corpses piled up'.

The prospects in June of a promising new harvest relieved the capital's situation to a considerable degree as more wheat and flour began to reach Madrid. Most of the supplies could only have come from the previous year's harvest, demonstrating a constant aspect of famine years: the hoarding and hiding of grain to benefit from high prices which in turn worsened the dearth and the lower classes' suffering.

The number of deaths in the ten months between September 1811 and July 1812 was put at twenty thousand.[25] In the light of the secret police number for May 1812, this was exaggerated: it assumed, on the basis of one of the worst months, a similar mortality rate for every month that the famine lasted. But only a parish by parish count, which remains to be carried out, could arrive at a figure closer to the truth. Nonetheless there could be no doubt that in these ten months the Madrid poor suffered their worst period of the war.

*

But it was not only the capital which suffered. Compared to the previous year, deaths soared by as much as eighty-five percent in southwestern

---

* Wellington could pursue such a policy and offer Extramadurans food in place of their burned crops in no little part thanks to the supplies of US wheat and flour he was receiving, despite the American embargo on trade with Britain during the Anglo-American war of 1812.

Andalucía*, the hardest hit; by nearly sixty percent in Cataluña where, on top of the 1809 decline, population growth fell to its lowest level of the war – indeed, the lowest of the entire period from 1800 to 1817; by fifty percent in Castilla la Nueva and just under the same amount in Extremadura, and by one-third in Castilla la Vieja; only the northwestern regions were spared the famine's worst rigours.†

The havoc of war heightened the effects of the poor 1811 harvest. Had the country not had to support the French army – or rather, had the latter not requisitioned all the grain its commanders could lay their hands on – 1812 would have been a year of scarcity and hunger, but not of famine. As it was, the general death rate hid important local differences: villagers and townsfolk in Tarragona province, for example, suffered only about one-third of the overall Catalan increase. Three places only a few kilometres apart in La Sagra, the grain-growing Toledan plain southwest of Madrid, bore out these disparities at the micro level: in the village of Lominchar mortality rose in the year by fifty percent, just a little over the provincial average; in Esquivas the increase was 170 percent and in Cedillo over three hundred percent. (These two latter figures suggested that epidemics must have killed many inhabitants who were weakened by starvation.)

In some areas, the under-sevens suffered disproportionately. In the city of Sevilla, as in Barcelona province, their deaths rose to the highest levels of the war, in the latter case more than doubling the 1800–1817 average. Debilitated by lack of food, the young were even greater prey than normal to the dysentries and other illnesses which the summer almost inevitably brought. The simultaneity of the highest mortality in southwestern Andalucía from April to June and in Cataluña from May to July – just before the new harvest when the previous year's meagre wheat stocks had been consumed and at the beginning of the summer heat – testified to the plight of the young. But here again their dire straits were not uniform: in Castilla la Nueva generally it was the adults who died – child mortality actually declined by nearly ten percent over the previous year. Parents sacrificed themselves to keep their offspring alive. The three Sagra villages showed once more the differences that existed in one small locality. In Lominchar, the under-seven's death rate fell by one-third compared to 1811; in Esquivas on the other hand it rose by nearly 150 percent and in Cedillo by sixty percent.

Despite the uneven distribution of the spectacular mortality, the famine, which saw villagers along the Ebro in Aragón reduced to eating bread of acorns and millet mixed,[26] was responsible for fewer deaths and missing than those which resulted from the French occupation in the first full year of the war. In 1809, all regional mortality, with the exception of unoccupied Andalucía and Valencia, was higher than in 1812.

---

* Cádiz capital was excluded from this figure because, although under French siege until mid-1812, it could import wheat. These and all following figures are from the author's db, *Demography*: Regional population growth, 1800–1817.
† Navarra and La Rioja suffered mortality increases of twelve percent, Galicia half that amount and the Basque country nine percent.

SEVILLA

Confidential patriot agents in western Andalucía reported to the regency in August, 1811, that the harvest had been very unproductive and that 'great distress is apprehended'. By the early autumn the agent in Puerto de Santa María, a cleric, wrote that the first signs of famine were showing in the townships of Ronda, Morón de la Frontera and Utrera and neighbouring villages. 'I give one month and a half for the great Famine to appear which is to be the deliverer of Andalucía – a plague most fortunate, if it delivers Andalucía from one of the most insupportable scourges ever suffered by heaven's vengeance.'[27]

The agents' reports were passed on by the regency to Henry Wellesley, British minister plenipotentiary to the Cádiz government and Wellington's younger brother, who forwarded them in translation to another older brother, the Marquess of Wellesley, who was the British minister for foreign affairs at the time. 'The people here are very much out of spirits. They expect to perish this winter for want of bread, for it is already dear.' A normal 2lb loaf was fetching seven reales, the Sevilla patriot agent reported in October 1811. Three months later, it reached ten reales. Wheat was to be allowed to enter the city from any quarter available 'to avoid fatal consequences'. After visiting the Cartuja to inspect the stocks available, Marshal Soult, Napoleon's supreme commander of Andalucía, ordered that only one sort of inferior bread should be baked.[28]

Sevilla enjoyed one advantage that Madrid lacked. It was a port connected to the Atlantic and to Córdoba in the interior by the river Guadalquivir; though upriver from Sevilla the river was not navigable to ocean-going ships, it could be used by boats except in years of drought.

The great famine duly appeared as predicted, but it could not be said that it delivered Andalucía to anything but fearful mortality and distress. The French army, as usual, looked after itself by requisitioning grain, and importing flour from the Barbary coast in US ships to the great scandal of Wellesley and the regency which promised to 'put an end to a traffic so advantageous to the enemy'.[29] Even so, many of their troops also went hungry. The guerrilla battle for food was waged with the same intensity as elsewhere. The partisan leader Saldivar intercepted a convoy of one thousand fanegas of wheat, forty thousand reales and the jewellery of a French colonel's wife in December. Shortly before it was claimed he had nearly captured Soult himself on his evening ride from Sevilla to Buenavista; the marshal was saved by a shepherd's warning. 'The shepherd has had more curses heaped on his head than he has hairs upon it . . .'[30]

To alleviate the city's wheat shortage, the *Gaceta de Sevilla* reported that fifteen boats had brought wheat – the equivalent of one hundred cartloads – down the river from Córdoba, despite the difficulties of navigating the Guadalquivir. The form of transport saved twenty reales a fanega, the paper claimed.[31] As wheat in Córdoba was also in short supply and was selling at 220 to 250 reales the fanega in January 1812, according to the patriot's Sevilla agent, the policy served little more than robbing Peter to pay Paul. Moreover, the paper warned speculators who hid wheat stocks in the hope of selling them more dearly that French army stores were more than sufficient to feed Sevilla until the coming harvest. Possibly this was no more than propaganda to reassure the inhabitants that everything was being done to keep them from starvation.

But such was the lower classes' state – 'a multitude of miserable people whose faces more than their clamours proclaim their horrifying poverty' – that Marshal Soult ordered cheap soup kitchens to be opened in January 1812. All civilian and military authorities who received a fixed government salary were ordered to subscribe to a charity committee with a minimum of one day's pay per month. With more foresight than in Madrid, Soult ordered that all civilians with less than five hundred reales a month could not subscribe.[32]

Earlier, a party of French dragoons who had just arrived in Sevilla from Almendralejo, Extremadura, said that the township was 'in the greatest misery. They themselves had given the inhabitants half a ration to prevent them perishing from hunger', the Sevilla patriot agent reported.[33]

Children were the major victims in Sevilla. Their death rate rose by over eighty percent of the 1800–1817 average while adults' increased by just over one-third of the average. The under-sevens' mortality began to increase from the beginning of 1811 before the famine began, due to what the *Gaceta of Sevilla* called 'a convulsive cough'.[34] The great difference between the adult and child death rate during the famine indicated that it was illness – whether this same one or another – which, added to the debilitating effects of the lack of food, caused the enormous number of children's deaths in 1811 and 1812.

MILITARY SUCCESSES AND DEFEATS: THE FALL OF VALENCIA

The imperial seizure of Tarragona in June 1811 had brought despair and despondency in Cádiz; the South American deputies to the Constituent Cortes were saying all was lost and were 'planning independence', the French were receiving money from the Tarragona locals, and grandees with estates in Valencia – now threatened with invasion – were talking badly about the government, Wellesley reported to London. 'The word treachery was in the mouth of every Catalan', Colonel E.B.J. Green, the British military agent in Cataluña had informed him. Some three thousand Catalan recruits had instantly deserted from the Spanish army.[35] A council of war summoned by the commander-in-chief had decided that the Spanish army should abandon Cataluña.

Despite the pessimism, the British envoy reported at the same time that 'the large majority of the merchants and of the lower classes of the People [in Cádiz] are determined enemies to the French'. In January 1812, worse came. Suchet, who had won his marshal's baton at Tarragona, captured Valencia. Napoleon had insisted to Suchet on his particular interest in the city and its region in order principally to use its resources, little impaired by the war, to fund his Russian campaign.[36] In the rearguard for the first three years of the war, Valencia had been a hotbed of intrigue. General Romana's younger brother, José Caro, an ambitious frigate captain, plotted, in temporary alliance with the Bertrán de Lis brothers who wanted to create a more popular junta, to depose the absolutist captain general of the region; Caro aspired to take the latter's post. The Suprema agreed to Caro's appointment as military second-in-command, but when it ordered him in 1809 to join General Blake's army in Aragón, he and the Bertrán brothers contrived a night of popular disturbances to prevent Caro from leaving, and Blake having been defeated twice by Suchet, the Suprema gave in to the threat: anything was better than the populace in the streets unless they were defending their cities from the French. The intrigues were sharpened by Romana, a member of the Valencian aristocracy, who also wanted to become the region's captain general. Moreover, the possibility that Suchet would advance on Valencia from Aragón added an element of fear to Caro's urban support and to the genuine popularity he had won among smallholders around the city for lifting certain imposts on their produce; any attempt to make him move from Valencia was seen by the lower orders as a betrayal. But it was he who was shortly to betray their trust. In March, 1810, Suchet, under orders from King Josef, made a half-hearted attempt on Valencia. Shortly before, the captain general of Cataluña, Enrique O'Donnell, had called on Caro to move to the defence of Tortosa which he feared Suchet was about to besiege. Finally Caro was obliged to lead a ten-thousand-strong force from the Levante capital to ward off Suchet. He advanced at a snail's pace northwards up the coast to occupy a strong position* from which he could threaten Suchet in either direction. But one hundred hussars of the French vanguard put the Valencians to flight and Caro, aware that his aura of power, already undermined, had vanished in defeat, mysteriously vanished himself, disguised as a friar, to resurface in Mallorca.[37] The roving British military adviser, Major General Doyle (to give him the rank to which he had been promoted in the Spanish army) had been critical of the Valencian army for over two years. It was under the command of 'bad' officers of all ranks, he reported in the autumn of 1810, and the Valencian division's conduct during the Tarragona siege had been 'most disgraceful'.[38] In Cádiz, Henry Wellesley had been pressing the regency to allow British officers to train Spanish recruits, as they had successfully done in Portugal, but had come to the conclusion that

> so difficult would it be to overcome the prejudices and the pride of the officers at the head of the Spanish Armies as well as many of the leading persons in Spain, that I am firmly of the opinion, they would prefer subjection to the French, to receiving assistance in this shape, however advantageous, from Great Britain.[39]

However, Wellesley was proven wrong and the regency set up a new depot in Cádiz under Doyle, where British officers and NCOs trained Spanish recruits. While this was a useful step, there was nothing to be done about the generals

---

* That, at least, was Suchet's view expressed in his *Mémoires*, cited by Ardit, 2003, p. 5.

who led these men; and it was under the command of Blake,* the Spanish general who had fought and lost more pitched battles than any other patriot general, that the Valencian army of some thirty thousand confronted Suchet's second – and this time serious – attempt to take the city with about the same number of men in the autumn of 1811. Blake attacked him north of Valencia on October 25 but was heavily beaten and driven back to the regional capital. Suchet then had to wait two months for reinforcements from Cataluña, and Blake remained inactive, other than to order El Empecinado, the guerrilla leader, and Villacampos, a military officer commanding a flying column on the Aragón–Valencia border, to join him in the city. Some of El Empecinado's men did so; but their leader was far too experienced a guerrilla leader to allow himself to be shut up in a city about to be besieged. Blake's order showed how little he understood of the popular struggle: instead of deploying the guerrillas to attack the besiegers in the rear, he displayed a traditional defensive siege mentality.

During the two months of military inactivity, Blake played his cards (if he had any) close to his chest. But it soon became evident to the inhabitants that he trusted only the military and did not count on the people in his plans. The enthusiastic popular participation which had been so important in the city's first defence in 1808† was not to be repeated.

Suchet began the offensive on the night of December 25, 1811. On the day after, the city was encircled by eight French divisions. Three days later, Blake tried to break out to save his army, but the attempt failed. The rumour that he had fled led to the creation of a patriotic junta whose members were mainly clerics and artisans who voiced the people's discontent to Blake's face. By New Year's Day, the situation inside Valencia was extraordinarily tense. Food was short and prices rose sharply. On January 3, soldiers mutinied and sacked many of the friaries which had been turned into barracks and a number of private houses, while others sold their muskets and cartridge pouches to get money for food.‡ Three days later, Suchet summoned the city to surrender. When the

---

* Colonel Green, English military adviser to the Catalan army, expressed confidentially to his friend Colonel Bunbury what was probably a common English perception of the Spanish army leaders: 'One of the most dangerous Parties in Spain, certainly the greatest enemies to the British are, and have been from the Commencement of this War, the Irish [Spanish of Irish descent] officers, which have been found established here . . . it's a delicate thing to state, but I have no hesitation in saying that all the Irish who have been found in this Province [Cataluña] have been either declared Enemies or suspicious, as results have proved.' (PRO, *WO269*/259–263, Feb 22, 1812). The comment totally overlooked the military role played by Enrique O'Donnell in the siege of Gerona and subsequently as captain general of Cataluña.

† See Chapter 6.

‡ Only two days before the siege began, Pedro Tupper, the Anglo-Spanish junta member, had landed, within the enemy's sight, one thousand barrels of flour, seventeen hundred quintals of fish, as well as shoes, stockings and powder which Wellesley had sent him from Cádiz. 'The troops inside of Valencia have therefore with this supply, provisions for about a month, but I fear the inhabitants will be much distressed in the course of ten or twelve days . . .' Tupper reported. Evidently the troops did not receive the provisions. (PRO, *FO*/72/129, Wellesley correspondence, pp. 60 et seq., Tupper to Wellesley, Denia, Dec 31, 1811.)

summons was rejected, the French commander began a violent artillery barrage, which increased in intensity on the following two days; many public buildings were damaged. Blake had not ordered any precautions against a bombardment. On January 8 the city capitulated. Sixteen thousand Spanish military, including Blake, were taken prisoner.[40]

Pursued by French cavalry which cut off his return route to the city, the enigmatic British 'consul', Pedro Tupper, had escaped by the skin of his teeth during a tour of the western lines manned entirely by guerrillas on the first day of the siege. He rode across country to Cullera and then to Denia, which was subsequently captured without resistance. Fulminating against his fellow junta members who had vanished, most of them to their homes, Tupper made his way to Alicante, one of the few provincial capitals which the French never took, where he tried to set up a new junta to encourage resistance. Once occupied – Gandía was the most southern Levant coastal city occupied by Suchet's army – guerrilla parties emerged almost immediately in the Valencian region.

Despite the Bonapartist abolition of the señorial system, or the Cortes' measures against señorial jurisdictions, Suchet adopted the strategy that had served him well in Aragón: he left the Valencian feudal system intact to provide the funds he needed. In order to maintain their rights, the Valencian señores paid handsomely on their vassals' backs: two hundred million reales which Suchet demanded from the region as an 'extraordinary war contribution', and which by the beginning of 1813, had been paid, half a million reales from the capital and an obligatory loan of a further two millions. He gathered sufficient funds to send money to the Madrid government, to re-equip not only his own army but that of the centre and south, to send aid to the French army in Cataluña, and find two millions to help Josef during his time in Valencia (see below).[41]

The population as usual paid a high price for the French occupation. The province's deaths in 1812 more than doubled compared to the previous year – the famine no doubt contributed to this figure – and population growth dropped by over three percent. In 1813 mortality rose a further eighty percent over 1811, and natural growth declined by another 1.4 per cent. These were the heaviest consecutive Valencian losses of the period from 1800 to 1817.*

EPISODES: SUCHET'S CLERICAL REPRESSION

A week after capturing Valencia Suchet ordered all the city's friars to be deported to France. He blamed them for having incited Valencia's resistance, and thus having prolonged the siege.

At three in the afternoon of January 15 all the regular orders were required to present themselves at San Francisco, where [we] remained until five o'clock. Then under an escort of grenadiers [we] were taken to the friary of Santo

---

* The figures exclude Alicante and Castellon provinces and come from author, db/ *Demography*: Regional population growth, 1800–1817.

Domingo where, in a conglomeration at the gates, [we] spent the night while the French made out lists and checked them.[42]

In the dry, objective language of the times, Brother Pelegrin Benavent, a Franciscan friar who was among the many hundred deported, related that at six in the morning of the following day, guarded by a grenadier company and a group of fusileros, they were marched out of the city while the old and infirm were segregated; the remainder started on their long trudge to captivity in France.

Brother Benavent was one of the friars who had tried to prevent the Valencian populace's massacre of the French in the Ciudadela in 1808. For his efforts, he had been forcibly ejected from the fortress by the smallholder supporters of Canon Calvo, the ultramontane cleric, whose hostility to the ruling junta led him to encourage – or at least religiously endorse – the mass assasination.*

At three o'clock on the afternoon of the 16th, the prisoners reached Sagunto, north of Valencia, to be enclosed in a ruined church full of manure where they were given some raw meat and soldiers' bread but no means of cooking. They slept as they could among the ruins; in the morning they were ordered to fall in:

> They checked each one of our names against their lists of the four hundred and seventy-one of us. Then they called out Brothers Pedro Pascual Rubert, the head of the Capuchins, Gabriel Pichó, master of noviciates, and the Dominicans Faustino Igual and Vicente Bonet. These they executed by the river bank, while they read out to us the marshal's [Suchet's] orders on prelates.†

The column then took to the road again. Some of the friars were barefooted. When they reached the village of Nules in the afternoon they were confined in a friary's church which the French military had turned into a barn. The local town hall provided them with great pots of excellent haricot beans, and pitchers of water and they were able to eat and drink properly for the first time on the march. The next day as they passed through the village of Villareal on their way to Castellón they were much moved by the fact that the villagers had all locked their doors, but from their balconies and windows they dropped loaves of bread, raisins, figs, oranges, sausages and even money. 'Some of the friars collected as much as eleven pesetas and others filled their cloaks with food.' That evening at sunset in Castellón two Dominicans, who were accused of trying to escape, were taken out and shot.

* See Chapter 5.
† Probably because of the trauma of the shootings, Benavent repressed another friar executed: José de Xérica, who was in fact the head of the Capuchins; Bonet was the provincial head of the order of Nuestra Señora de la Merced (Our Lady of Mercy).

After roll-call the following morning, with drums beating at the head of the column, grenadiers marching next and another squad following up at the rear, the fusileros in two files along either side of them, the friars set off again.

> We and the carts carrying the old and infirm were in the middle . . . But the French commandant's pity on us had gone so far as to increase the number of carts, so that one hundred and forty of the weakest could ride . . .

At their various halts, the local town halls, priests and women provided them with food, wine and water to wash. 'The women especially went to great pains, making hot chocolate to comfort us . . . The commandant and his officers equally displayed great humanity by allowing us all the consolation and comfort that we were offered.' In Ulldecona, just within Cataluña, the women brought bread, wine and pots of cooked rice, 'although the majority of the inhabitants did not have bread for their supper; but they gave us so much that we had more than enough for our needs: in truth, the people's charity was exceedingly great.'

In Tortosa, where their stay was prolonged by snow in the interior, the food shortages were so acute that after a few days their rations were cut back; but 'against all obstacles' the French column commander managed to get them restored.

> Our pious commandant not only allowed some of us from all the orders to go into the city to seek the charity that the humane inhabitants were prodigal in offering, but permitted groups of four friars at a time, accompanied by a guard, to go out for walks and to buy everything we needed.

Friar Benavent sallied out into the somewhat 'lugubrious' town a number of times: in best enlightened form, he set about measuring the width of the Ebro – its flow, which he also wanted to calculate, was impossible because the current was too great – the length of the bridge spanning it and the number of ships in the port.

Five friars were freed in Tortosa; two others died a natural death and one was killed when he fell from a roof where he had climbed in order to rid himself of the fleas and lice 'as indeed we all did'. But the French commandant and the regiment guarding them was relieved. On February 17, the column set out again with the addition of sixty prisoners of war, including some officers; the marches were longer now, up to seven hours or more a day, until they reached Zaragoza five days later. There they were allowed a day's rest before setting out for France.

However, before they had marched two days, an Aragonese guerrilla party was sighted. The new commandant gave the order immediately to lighten the carts and all the prisoners on foot and their escort began with the utmost speed to retrace their steps to Zaragoza. By the time they reached the Aragonese capital, Benavent had fallen ill with fever and was taken to the military hospital 'where the worst misery was the flea-ridden beds'. On March 14, the French military governor informed him that Suchet had granted his freedom. But he still had to convalesce in a private house before he could set out on his return to Valencia. Meanwhile, he again began describing and measuring the outstanding Zaragozan monuments and recording the city's major aspects.

Once recovered, Benavent, in the company of three other friars from Jaca, in Aragón, started out from Zaragoza on foot. As they passed through a number of villages not far distant from the city, their eyes fell on cemetery walls where the back bones, ribs and shinbones of those executed by the French were still plainly visible. Finally, some days later, brother Benavent reached Valencia.

NAPOLEON'S SECOND BOMBSHELL

Although unaware of the victory, on the day Valencia fell Napoleon decided on Cataluña's de facto annexation to the French empire.* It was a decision long foreseen and feared: by Catalans who would now be subject to imperial conscription, and by Josef's Spain which saw his kingdom further dismembered. However, since the early days of the war, the Bonapartist regime had had virtually no contact with Cataluña which, in its northeastern corner of Spain bordering on France fell more easily into the Paris than Madrid orbit. The Emperor's motives for this move, which he had been planning for two years, were mixed. On the eve of his Russian campaign, he wanted to protect his southern flank from invasion by an Anglo-Catalan force by extending France's frontier to the Ebro. And, as in Valencia, he needed all the resources he could wring out of Cataluña by placing it firmly under centralized French control. Indeed, the latter process had been continuing apace for some time with high French treasury officials imposing the Napoleonic tax system, and finally the appointment of a senior French official as secretary general of the Bonapartist Catalan government. Administratively then Cataluña had been run by French officialdom for some two years before the annexation decree which took the process a step further. The region was to be divided into a northern and southern area at about the level of Barcelona, and subdivided into four departments, as head of which Napoleon appointed two French intendants of state and four French prefects. Sub-prefects and director generals of the various services were also French. What the change in effect meant was that Napoleon replaced by a civil regime the previous military government responsible to him since his first bombshell of Feburary 1810 segregating the provinces north of the Ebro.[43]

The virtual annexation did little to win over the Catalans to the Napoleonic cause. In an official report, the prefect of one of the new departments, that of the

* His decree reorganizing Cataluña's territorial division was published on January 26, 1812. It studiously avoided the word 'annexation' or 'union' but the Emperor's intention was clear enough.

Ebro estuary (Bouches de l'Ebre), explained that the Catalans' hatred of the French lay 'in very old disputes' which went as far back as the seventeenth century. These historical facts were still clearly remembered by the Catalan people, he wrote. Moreover, French emigré priests had informed Catalans of the 'barbarities' committed by the French Revolution which had increased Catalan hatred of France. The prefect added that the Catalans detested the Castilians almost as much as the French, because of the War of the Spanish Succession at the begining of the eighteenth century (as a result of which Cataluña had lost its self-governing rights), 'their national jealousy, their spirit of liberty and independence, and their natural distance from the [Madrid] court and its intrigues'.[44] The new French administration ran into many local difficulties in controlling the population: the mayors of five villages near Gerona were arrested for collaborating with the patriotic Catalan junta; and where, as in Besalu, junta-appointed mayors had been dismissed, the French administration could find no one prepared to replace them. Even the fishermen of Barcelona were refusing to collaborate.[45]

The Cortes of Cádiz had refused to see the Spanish army withdraw from Cataluña, and had appointed General Lacy to its command. To reinforce the army, the latter had incorporated all irregular units into regular service.[46] The British frigate captain, Edward Codrington, on the Catalan station, had no hesitation in writing him a letter reproaching him for his decision.

> The sentiments of the people upon the coast now appear to me to have undergone a decided change and that confidence which lately prevailed has given place to a very alarming dejection in consequence of a few thousand French occupying their Towns with impunity and their being, as they alleged, deprived of the means of defending themselves by the determination your Excellency has lately adopted of abolishing altogether those Companies of Partidarios [irregulars] who have harassed them so considerably in all their movements.[47]

Lacy replied that because one part of the coast was occupied it did not follow that the country in general would submit to its oppressors; and sent Codrington gazettes to prove his point. The frigate captain answered, thanking him for the newspapers and said they confirmed his view that

> whenever the Catalans are well commanded they will always act with their characteristic Bravery, whether as Regular Soldiers, Somatenes, Partidarios or simple Peasantry. But instead of concluding that because they have fought so well it is wise to make them Soldiers by Force, I cannot help thinking that attention to their wishes, and a kind consideration ever for their prejudices, is due to them, for their perserverance, and the sacrifices they have so long continued to make . . . Considering the eventual happiness of the people as the only legitimate cause of all warfare, it appears to be more than ever necessary to consult their feelings by whom that Army is to be kept efficient, and when personal Service is almost the only remaining sacrifice which they have to offer to their Country. . . . Nor can I forget that your Excellency then agreed with me on the necessity of attending to the sentiments of the people and

attributing the failure of your predecessors to a want of that particular consideration . . .[48]

BRITISH VICTORIES AND RETREATS

Despite Suchet's victories, the war was not to be won on the Mediterranean coast but in the heartland of Spain. The day Valencia fell, Wellington began his break-out from Portugal where he had been confined since 1810 by French occupation of the major Spanish border fortresses during Masséna's offensive. On the night of January 19, 1812, he took Ciudad Rodrigo, the northernmost fortress town, after a ten-day investment at a cost of five hundred casualties; the Anglo-Portuguese troops lost all discipline, looting and pillaging the town remorselessly until the following day. The French commanders of the central and northern armies, Marmont and Dorsenne respectively, were unaware of the town's siege until January 15, and a rapid allied advance after its capture might have caught them unprepared. Napoleon had depleted the imperial army in Spain for his Russian campaign, but more importantly had not replaced casualties or the sick: in consequence, the French army's effective strength had fallen from just under 300,000 in July 1811, to 230,000 in May 1812.[49] Since the army was trying to hold down the country, its effective fighting strength was further reduced.

Always cautious Wellington next turned his attention to the southernmost fortress town of Badajoz, which the Anglo-Portuguese army had failed to capture the previous summer, though in fact its strategic position was unlikely to play a part in an offensive in central Spain. Its capture on April 6 was rather a diversion – unless Wellington planned to attack Soult in Andalucia.[50] The British losses were tremendous; the assault's carnage was followed by a British carnage of the population, a sacking that went far beyond the rules of war. It made no difference to the drunken soldiery that they were murdering, pillaging and raping their Spanish allies; even worse was that Wellington took no serious measures to prevent what, in effect, was the most horrifying night of the British Peninsular War.[51]

In June, from his northern Portuguese base, Wellington at last launched his offensive on central Spain, occupying Salamanca, where his fifty-thousand-strong army was held up for ten days – as long as the siege of Ciudad Rodrigo – by the determined resistance of three convents which the French had fortified. Once the convents were reduced, Wellington moved on the river Duero where he was outmanoeuvred by Marmont, who forced the Anglo-Portuguese army back. For several days, the two armies marched side by side less than half a mile apart. A month after leaving Salamanca, Wellington was back on the hills around the village of Arapiles south of Salamanca which he had previously occupied, and was prepared to retreat on Portugal.*

* Wellington had been kept well-informed of Josef's correspondence with Marmont and other generals by guerrilla intercepts.

Over-confident that the Anglo-Portuguese would continue to withdraw, Marmont attempted to outflank Wellington's positions and over-extended his lines. Wellington took full advantage of this error. The battle, on July 21, resulted in a triumph for Anglo-Portuguese arms and heavy losses for the French. It was a decisive victory for it opened the road to Madrid. Josef fled to the safety of Suchet in Valencia. On August 12 – preceded by the guerrilla forces of El Empecinado, Chaleco (Francisco Abad) and El Médico (Juan Palarea) who were received by cheering crowds and all the city's church bells ringing (El Empecinado was the real hero of the day for his victories in the capital's environs) – Wellington entered the Spanish capital to the huzzas of the population which only a few months earlier had been dying of starvation and was still short of food.[52]

For the second time of his reign, Josef, his court and a mass of followers fled the capital as a result of a battle. Their three-week peregrination, many of the king's followers on foot, turned into a nightmare of heat, thirst and dust as they crossed the drylands of La Mancha.

In a highly sensible manner, the local Madrid authorities dealt with the sudden change of power by negotiating a pact that there should be no reprisals and a simple handover to a new set of aldermen.[53]

*

The run of Anglo-Portuguese victories, culminating in the occupation of Madrid, temporary though it turned out to be, brought new spirit to the Spanish popular resistance. The more perspicacious guerrilla leaders understood well that Napoleon's invasion of Russia could only favour them by reducing the number of imperial troops who could be brought to bear. From the beginning of the year, bands of guerrillas ventured ever closer to Madrid, harassing the capital's outskirts and making it unsafe for the French to venture much beyond the city's walls. 'Much annoyed', the French increased their guard and night patrols, reported the Madrid patriot confidential agent to Cádiz.[54] The fully uniformed guerrillas advanced to the Puerta de Toledo and to the far side of the river Manzanares where they were plainly visible to the inhabitants; a French colonel who was riding along the river was attacked and barely escaped with his life. The Bonapartist authorities and secret police reported the guerrillas' attacks on a number of nearby villages.

The famine also had its effect on villagers' hopes of joining a party where they knew they would be fed. As the capital's secret police reported on April 3, 1812:

Yesterday, the party of [Luis] Gutiérrez passed through Villaconejos on its way to Colmenar de la Oreja; it was accompanied by a great number of unarmed people who had left their homes to seek food, and they begged to be allowed to join this bandit's party.[55]

WELLINGTON AND JOSEF

While Wellington in Madrid debated his next move – for, important as the capital's occupation undoubtedly was, he still had French armies to the north and south of him – Josef in Valencia had no doubt that either Suchet's or Soult's armies must reinforce central Spain if he were to defend his kingdom. His choice fell on Soult's army of over seventy thousand troops, and the French marshal was ordered to evacuate Andalucía. Reluctantly, Soult agreed, and in August the great pull-out began, accompanied by a huge baggage train of looted treasure. The siege of Cádiz which had lasted thirty months was lifted; at the beginnning of October Soult joined Josef and Suchet in Valencia.

Wellington decided to advance north, leaving a sizeable force in Madrid to protect his rear from Suchet and Soult. He intended to crush the French army which he had so decisively defeated at Salamanca. But instead of offering battle the French withdrew north of Burgos, leaving Wellington to face the city's ancient fortifications, strengthened to a degree by the French, and an imperial garrison of two thousand. Though lacking a proper siege train, he decided to invest Burgos instead of finding his way round it and driving against the main enemy army. His siege wasted a month and failed. Meanwhile, the French had been reinforced by contingents from the Army of the North, which was mainly occupied holding the guerrillas at bay, and Josef and Soult were advancing on Madrid: separately, Wellington and his rearguard in the capital were each outnumbered. In late October, both began their retreat on Salamanca where they joined forces. There, however, the French outflanked Wellington, forcing him to abandon Salamanca and continue his retreat to the Portuguese border with an army now as ill-disciplined, demoralized and disorderly as Moore's on his retreat in 1808. After nine months of campaigning in Spain, the allied offensive ended back where it had started, having gained only two strategic advantages: the Anglo-Portuguese army was no longer locked into Portugal by the French hold on the Spanish fortified border towns; and Andalucía had been freed of occupation. But in a year when Napoleon was bogged down in Russia, and could not reinforce his armies in Spain, Wellington's opportunity of dismembering the French armies and advancing to the Ebro, if no further, was foiled by a city of old walls and a couple of thousand troops within.

THE 1812 CONSTITUTION: THE GREAT LEAP FORWARD

In heavy rain and under an intense bombardment by the French besiegers' cannon,* on Thursday, March 19, 1812, the fourth anniversary of Fernando VII's elevation to the throne, the Cortes proclaimed the constitution after seven months of debate. It consisted of 384 articles in ten chapters, and stated that

---

* Thanks to the Suprema, which had overlooked moving the Sevilla arsenal to Cádiz, the French were able to cast special howitzers whose range allowed them to bombard the north and centre of Cádiz though their shot often failed to explode. Fearing bombardment of La Isla de León, the Cortes voted to move out of range to the church of San Felipe Neri, Cádiz in early 1811. The bombardment continued throughout that year, often at night to terrorize the population. In 1812 the poor inhabitants most exposed to the fire were moved to a tented encampment out of range. 'In all my life I have never known more continuous public gaiety than in Cádiz during the spring and summer of 1812.' (Alcalá Galiano, 1886/1956, p. 402.)

sovereignty resided essentially in the nation which was defined as 'the union of all Spaniards in both hemispheres'. Laws were to be the same for all regions of Spain and the colonies. But the constitution went further in its claim to national sovereignty – which had been accepted at the Cortes' initial gathering – by declaring that the nation was not and could not be the 'personal patrimony of any individual or family' and that the Cortes alone had the 'exclusive right' to establish its fundamental laws.

This was disputed by the three monarchist arguments which had been earlier used against the juntas' and Suprema's assumption of national sovereignty. First, that such sovereignty could only be exercised while the nation was bereft of a monarch; secondly, that having sworn allegiance to Fernando VII, as the Cortes had done, sovereignty could not *essentially* reside in the nation; and finally, that once having bestowed their sovereignty on a monarchy, the people could not dispossess it to recover their original sovereignty.

The liberals answered that the constitution provided for a 'moderate monarchy'. What in fact it provided was a rupture with the Old Order. The separation of legislative, executive and judicial powers was enshrined as a fundamental principle, and in consequence the monarchy's former rights were reduced to the executive. A popularly elected unicameral national assembly, which was to meet for three months annually in Madrid, was to become the legislature. Although the king could veto Cortes laws for two years running, his veto was automatically over-ridden if the assembly upheld the law at a third successive session. He could appoint ministers, but these were responsible to the Cortes for the constitutionality of their acts. Many other restrictions surrounded the king. He could not hinder the Cortes' assembling, leave the country, marry, abdicate or enter into an alliance or commercial treaty without the Cortes' consent.

Deputies to the national assembly were to be elected by equal electoral districts of seventy thousand resident male voters. Only servants, those without known means of support, bankrupts and criminals were excluded. Deputies had to be at least twenty-five years old, and to enjoy an adequate income from their own property; members of the regular religious orders were disbarred from standing. In effect, the constitution instituted a mediated universal male suffrage.*

At the same time, municipal councillors were to be elected, and all hereditary council membership abolished. Taxes were to be paid by all Spaniards in proportion to their assets and irrespective of status; and finally, primary schools were to be created in all townships to teach children the three 'Rs' and the catechism.[56]

While the constitution gave equal rights to Spaniards and colonials, who now formed 'a single monarchy, one and the same nation, one sole family', it did not grant the full political rights of 'Spanish citizenry' to people who did not originate within the territorial limits of this 'single nation', that was to say slaves

* 'Mediated' because voting was indirect; parishioners voted for electors to their administrative district who in turn elected the deputy. Women did not get the vote until 1933 under the Second Republic.

or even freed men of African origin. Despite Agustín de Argüelles' passionate arguments in favour of abolishing the 'infamous traffic' of slavery, the Cortes rejected the proposal as it later again did an abolitionist motion put by Isidoro Antillón. It accepted rather the liberal Peruvian deputy Mexia's argument that immediately to free 'an immense multitude of slaves, apart from ruining their owners, could result in disagreeable consequences for the State'.[57] Liberal liberty thus went so far and no further.*

*

Although the constitution proclaimed Roman Catholicism to be the nation's exclusive religion which would be protected by 'wise and just laws' and the practice of any other religion prohibited – the liberals expressed no desire for religious freedom – it was the question of religion, and the Inquisition in particular, which dominated the remainder of the Cortes' life. And not only of the Cortes, but of much of the country at large.

'What news of Cádiz?' became a common salutation among many villagers and townsfolk. As the Cortes debates turned to religion, and parish priests' sermons to politics, so popular argument grew in intensity. Worst of all, as the vicar of Ciudad Real observed, was the temerity and lack of responsibility with which people expressed their views despite their lack of information . . .

> Although we do not know definitely what is going on in Cádiz, neither do those at the helm of government have any idea of what is happening in the provinces. One needs a great amount of kindness and prudence to live now in these villages, where public writers' and journalists' views on everything are confused with those of the government . . . [The people] do not think, they only know how to obey because that is the only education they have received . . . To give them freedom is to lead them to anarchy . . . The tribunes of Cádiz are so divorced from reality that they will end up as victims of their own ideas . . . When the people begin to hear and see what they have not seen or understood, the results will not be good.[58]

The vicar had a point: the liberals never envisaged seeking the nation's subsequent approval of their constitution. They acted as absolutely as an absolute monarch, imposing their constitution and conflating self-claimed national sovereignty with the national will. As great a leap forward in its creation of a constitutional monarchy as it undoubtedly was, the constitution was a partisan construct which did not seriously attempt to create a framework in which non-liberals could create political channels to the state.

This became clear when the absolutist Bishop of Orense announced that he would swear loyalty to the constitution only on condition that his right was respected to demand revisions at a later date of a number of aspects he found objectionable. The Cortes responded in fulminating style, declaring him unworthy of the name of Spaniard, and ordered his immediate expulsion from Spain. The assembly then approved a motion that it would mete out the same

---

* Slavery was not abolished in its last stronghold, Cuba, until 1885.

punishment to anyone who refused to swear unreserved loyalty to the constitution. From his Portuguese exile, the bishop retorted that to impose the constitution on the people without their sanction was to make slaves of free men. For the constitution to be valid, he subsequently argued, it must be ratified by newly elected deputies and approved by the king – or 'is he no longer king?'[59]

The debate over the Inquisition was the most acrimonious of all. The Holy Office had been inactive during the war for lack of an inquisitor general (only the Pope, with whom it was impossible to communicate, could approve the appointment; the previous inquisitor, Ramón José de Arce, Archbishop of Zaragoza, was an ardent afrancesado).

While the liberal deputies in general were not anti-clerical, the Inquisition was the bane of their lives since the Holy Office – or fear of it – had for so long controlled their freedom to read and write. Freedom of the press – more papers were published in Cádiz in the years of the Cortes than in the whole of Spain's eighteenth century[60] – resulted in a polemical style of journalism, broadly divided into pro- and anti-liberal, which reflected the growing antagonism between the two factions in the Cortes and the fundamental division that had surfaced in Spain during the French Revolution and festered just below the surface for a generation before.

As the anti-liberal press and its frequent clerical contributors honed their attacks on liberal policies in the Cortes, many of the more progressive liberal newspapers responded in kind with a violent polemic on the Old Order's supporters and the Church. Their attacks went beyond anti-clericalism to the heart of religious belief. When Manuel Alzáibar, a close friend of Mexía, published an article that lambasted the notion of the soul's immortality and followed it up with an even more impious attack, many liberal deputies were so horrified that they wanted the matter referred to the Inquisition, despite the fact that in matters of religion the Cortes had agreed that clerical censorship was to be exercised by bishops.

Another pretext for the ultra monarchists to pursue the Inquisition's continued existence was the scandal caused by the publication of Bartolomé Gallardo's *Critical and Satirical Dictionary* in reply to an earlier dictionary written by two ultra anti-liberal deputies.* Gallardo, a progressive liberal, was the Cortes' librarian. A self-confessed secularist from an early age, he had a sharp mind and as sharply stylish a pen, and he satirized his opponents to great effect. The work was considered scurrilous, subversive, anti-clerical, and insulting to certain members of the ecclesiastical hierarchy. Even a leading liberal deputy like the conde de Toreno thought it 'inopportune,' 'indiscreet' and 'scandalous'.[61] Gallardo was sent to gaol by the Cádiz provincial censorship junta within a week of its publication on April 15 and remained there for three months, suffering the same fate as most of those whose ideas were considered too extreme for orthodox patriotism. A year later the ten copies of his work which had been seized were burned. To take on the Church from an advanced liberal stance was bound to be a perilous affair.

* Its title was *A Reasoned Dictionary and Handbook for the Information of Certain Writers who by Mistake were Born in Spain.*

MILITANCIES THE MAKING OF A
LIBERAL PROGRESSIVE: BARTOLOMÉ J. GALLARDO[62]

Born in 1776 to a none-too-wealthy Badajoz farmer and his wife, and educated at home by priests, Gallardo was a prodigious student who was admitted to Salamanca University at the age of 15. Without consulting him, his parents wanted the young Bartolomé to study for the priesthood so as to take up a chaplaincy that was in their gift; once aware of their designs, Gallardo steadfastly refused to comply, causing a serious rift with his parents, but demonstrating a determined independence which was a trait of his life. When both his parents died, leaving him penniless, he was fortunate to be taken under the wing of a university librarian and fellow Extramaduran, who secured his admission to a university college and no doubt encouraged his protegé's enthusiasm for books. Quite soon, in his study of philosophy and literature, Gallardo became fascinated by anatomy and began to study medicine, which was less remarkable than it might seem. The Salamanca medical faculty was the most open of all to new forms of teaching and innovation of research; moreover, Gallardo spent many hours a day in his college library reading on everything that took his attention, and a work on anatomy was among these; but it was past Spanish literature that most attracted him and from which he distilled a pure Castilian style and idiom for his own writing. At the same time he read widely among the French *philosophes'* works including, clandestinely, those banned by the Inquisition, among them Voltaire and Rousseau. In his last year of seven as a student, he demonstrated his acid pen and mastery of Castilian by publishing a satire on the local Salamanca newspaper which brought him to the attention of the enlightened bishop of the city, Antonio Tavira, who, after going to some lengths to arrange a meeting, was sufficiently impressed to become Gallardo's friend and protector.* The twenty-two-year-old student responded with an epigram, as he called it, in French, dedicated to the bishop:

> Je ne suis nullement devot,
> Monseigneur, ne vous en deplaise;
> Etre profane, c'est mon lot:
> Ainsi, quand votre main je baise,
> Je n'y vois la main du Pasteur,
> J'y vois la main du bienfaiteur†

Gallardo's claim not to be devout, which he would repeat for the rest of his life, was no doubt true. He had rejected the priesthood at a time

---

* After graduating, Gallardo was given a post in the Salamanca municipal administration without having solicited it; the bishop was probably responsible.
† A slightly free translation might read: Devout I am absolutely not,/Monseigneur, and may it not displease you a jot;/To be secular is in life my lot:/Thus when I kiss your hand,/It is not the pastoral hand I see,/But the benefactor's I take to me.

when many of similar social origins made a career of the Church. As a man of the Enlightment, he was hostile to the Church's secular power, its counter-enlightenment friars and priests, its baroque rituals and the superstitions and miracles in which the devout believed. The Inquisition was a particular *bête noire* for its censorship of books, and he courageously stood up to it. Moreover, his anatomical studies were making a 'sensorialist' and materialist of him. He considered himself a 'Voltairean', and also no doubt had a clever young student's desire to shock, a side of him that at a later age he never totally lost. But, taking account of the precision of his language, lack of devoutness did not mean that he was an atheist. Even when presented with the intellectual opportunity – in philosophica–medical terms – to deny the existence, or at least the importance, of the soul, he refused as a young man to take the leap. Although there were a small number of other enlightened Spaniards – some of them in high governmental positions – who would have subscribed privately to Gallardo's lack of devoutness, they were more cautious than he in expressing it; in general the Spanish Enlightenment did not question the Catholic, Roman and Apostolic faith in which they had been brought up, though they questioned the practices of the Spanish Church which embodied it.*

Although, finally, Gallardo did not graduate as a medical doctor, his first two youthful translations were of French medical works. The first, on hygiene, or medical prophylaxis, a matter then much in vogue among the European enlightened as an important part of state policy on health, was written in 1785 by a Lyons surgeon, M. Pressavin. The latter, as Gallardo presumably knew, had played a not insignificant role as a deputy to the National Convention and as a member of the Jacobin clubs until 1793. Gallardo had himself chosen to translate the book;† and in his translator's preface he paraded his medical erudition by pointing to the book's limitations in the light of subsequent discoveries, but more importantly insisted on his efforts 'once and again to illuminate the almost ignored elegance of Spanish'. Three years later, in the prologue to his second translation of a work by Jean-Louis Alibert, a leading figure of the French 'philosophical' school of medicine and an outstanding clinician, which concerned the relationship of medicine to the 'physical' and 'intellectual and moral' sciences, he returned to his claims for Castilian. 'It is well known', he wrote, that 'our language has

---

* Always an extremist in his polemics and politics, and during the war frequently accused of impiety by his absolutist and clerical enemies, no court before which he appeared condemned him explicitly on this account. Even in his satirical *Dictionary*, he showed himself critical in part of the reform movement in the Spanish church, but he did not 'write it off' as he was accustomed to do with his many enemies. He also had a curious habit in his younger days of residing in friaries at critical moments of his life – perhaps because he felt safer with a religious 'alibi'.

† Its title in part had a peculiarly modern ring: *The Art of Preserving Health and Prolonging Life, a Treatise on Hygiene*; the translation was a success and was reprinted twice.

great advantages over French, singularly in its grandeur and extravagant wealth of expression.' At the same time, his new prologue permitted Gallardo to express himself more clearly on scientific and philosophical matters:

> The overall conclusion of [Alibert's] Discourse is that all generally well-organized men contain within them the *physical potential* to rise to the *greatest heights of thought*; and that the *difference of talent* which we note among them depends on the different *circumstances* in which they find themselves, and the *different education* they have received. The importance of *education* is therefore once more exemplified.

Subsequently, in two entries on the 'Senses' and on 'Sensations', written for a Spanish medical dictionary, Gallardo commited himself almost totally to the most advanced French theory of the day in which vague metaphysical explanations – even the soul – had disappeared in the need to explain the instinctive and intellectual sensorial processes. Surprisingly, however, Gallardo re-introduced the soul as a substantive element. Possibly, the young writer, who did not sign his contributions, was covering his tracks to ensure that he was not hauled up before the Inquisition.

Soon after the publication of Gallardo's second translation, his Salamanca publisher ran afoul of the Inquisition when he proposed to publish a new edition of his deceased brother-in-law's poetry, which the Holy Office had banned 'for its excessive licence in the order of ideas'. The publisher resorted to his translator and friend, Gallardo. The young man had no hesitation in writing a *Memorial in Defence of the Posthumous Poetry of D. José Iglesias de la Casa*, having it printed and signing it with his name, and dispatching it to the Inquisition in Valladolid and the other tribunals of the Holy Office. In it Gallardo argued that 'as moralists, spiritual doctors are permitted in the same manner as corporal doctors to call things by their proper names'. That said, and citing an Iglesias poem as an example, he added that there was nothing gross, lascivious or obscene in his love poetry. Nonetheless, the Inquisition confirmed its ban, as well as ordering all copies of the *Memorial* seized. It was a courageous act on Gallardo's part to confront the Holy Office on behalf of a friend, and it cost him much enmity among his Salamanca adversaries who called him 'an excommunicated heretic' and a Voltairean in an attempt to make his life difficult with the local clergy. He responded in what was to become his classic counter-attack: a ferocious and biting satire of his enemies.

In 1801, he had a stroke of luck and was appointed interpreter to a French division returning home from supporting the Spanish Army in Godoy's short war, on Napoleon's demand, against Portugal. As a result, he spent two months in Bayonne, where a French abbé befriended him and extended his knowledge of the *philosophes'* works.

Like the poet José Quintana, though by a different route, Gallardo assimilated the ideas of liberty and hispanicism which made it impossible for him and others of his enlightened generation to accept that Spain's freedom should be the work of any other than Spaniards themselves. And this was one of the reasons that they had no hesitation in rising against Napoleon.

It was, without doubt, his *Dictionary* which first brought Gallardo notoriety. In it he substituted his own definitions for his opponents' entries in their dictionary. Under 'P', where the anti-liberals, among other things, had defined the 'People', as a 'collection of figures or puppets to be used by their puppet-masters, *according to the philosofes*', he re-wrote the entry. After rehearsing the ancient view that some men were born with blue blood and others with red, he continued that the study of man's nature had proven that villeins and gentlemen were all made of the same matter: the definition of the people, 'at its highest and most sublime', was synonomous with the nation, and was also used to mean 'the people's sovereignty'.

> In a more humble sense (though never contemptuously because there are no lower people in Spain), is meant the ordinary citizens who, without enjoying particular distinctions, incomes or posts, live by their trades; and although they do not exercise official positions, they have the option to do so and access to the highest posts and decorations with which the fatherland rewards merit and virtue . . . These were the people who, on May 2, unarmed, cursed and abandoned by the weak government of Madrid, threw themselves on the perfidious Murat's hosts, raising the first cry for Spanish independence . . . The voice of liberty triumphed and triumphs. The proverb which says that *the people's voice is the voice of heaven* has become sacred. Eternal glory to the people of Madrid, and to all the peoples of Spain![63]

Despite his progressive thinking, Gallardo adopted the orthodox liberal view of the people and the constitutional creation of a meritocracy. There was no question of the Rights of Man. The people collectively were praised for their anti-Napoleonic resistance; thereafter, they were a mass of individuals who by their own merits and virtue could – like Gallardo himself – ascend to the political elite. The only equality offered them, and this was no small matter, was equality before the law; the only liberty offered them was that of the free market.

*

THE INQUISITION ABOLISHED

The Cortes referred the matter of the Inquisition's reinstatement to its constitutional committee which, in 1812, reported that the Holy Office's secret procedures were incompatible with the constitution and it should be abolished.

Bourbon absolutism had used its state power to control the Church, indeed had expropriated part of its wealth, and to no little degree had emasculated the Inquisition.[64] The anti-liberals saw that, like absolutism, the liberals were reinforcing the power of the state and feared for the Church, which they identified with the institutions of the Old Order that they were determined to defend. They might not want a return to state absolutism, which had attempted to oversee and reform the Church; but even less did they want a liberal state which was certain, in their view, to do even worse. As a result they fought to preserve the clergy's corporate identity and its privileges against both. They identified Catholicism exclusively with the counter-revolution, anti-liberalism and the legitimate dynasty.[65]

The ecclesiastical wrath of all but liberal clerical deputies and a small number of bishops, who had argued for the Inquisition's abolition, was immense. Writing under the pseudonym of 'El Filósofo Rancio' ('The age-old philosopher'), the Dominican preacher, Francisco de Alvarado, added fuel to the fire with his critical letters to an absolutist deputy which attacked the heretical French *philosophes* and the Enlightenment and stated, among many other anti-liberal indictments, that Spain would not be content until the Inquisition cleansed the country of '*philosophes* in the same manner as it had cleansed it of Jews'.[66]

But it was not only clerics who attacked the Inquisition's abolition. As a manufacturer, Antonio García Colado, wrote to a newspaper from Siguenza:

> If this country has ten million inhabitants, nine of them at the least want the Inquisition to continue in existence. I can assure you that despite the great devastation which, in a city like this we have suffered at the hands of the French, and there is not one of us who has not been left five times or more with nothing else than the shirt he stands up in, there is not one inhabitant who does not feel the same suffering at the abolition of the Holy Office.[67]

Despite these attacks and a much reduced majority of only thirty, when most moderate bills could count on double that number, the Cortes approved the Inquisition's abolition in February 1813,*[68] four years after Napoleon had extinguished it in the Bonapartist zone. Another decree expropriated its property. An order to read a Cortes proclamation explaining the Inquisition's abolition to the nation on three consecutive Sundays in all churches met with outright opposition, even the threat of excommunication, from many bishops. And when the Papal Nuncio protested to the regency, he was expelled from Spain.[69]

EPISODES: THE POSSESSED[70]

On Corpus Christi, one of the Church's great holy days, the religious procession in the village of Tosos was unexpectedly disturbed by eight

* The ultra-conservatives comprised only some twenty of the fifty conservative deputies, the more moderate of whom voted on some reforms with the liberals, for the political lines were not clearly drawn. (Lovett, 1966, p. 469.)

local women who demonstrated all the signs of being possessed by the devil. They made 'extreme and wild gestures' and 'frenzied movements' . . . A week later more than thirty village women were manifesting similar symptoms and accusing one woman, Joaquina Martínez, of being the witch who was responsible for their state. Very quickly, most of the villagers and the so-called doctors among them firmly believed that Martínez was a witch; and one 'possessed' male made two attempts on her life. The unrestricted violence of the possessed women soon drove Martínez, her husband and a mutual friend, out of the village.

It was mid-1812. Tosos was little more than a hamlet of three hundred souls close to Goya's birthplace of Fuendetodos south of Zaragoza. It lived mainly from its vineyards which produced grapes for the neighbouring and well-known local wine-producing centre of Cariñena.

As a result of this mass possession, the parish priest, Mateo de León, was overwhelmed by demands for exorcism which he and his friar assistant began to carry out. Before the outbreak had become widespread and Martínez had been generally identified as being the cause of the problem, she had already offered to exorcize a number of the possessed who had gone to her house. There she had applied to them the usual 'divine' impedimenta of reliquaries and religious medallions; but she had also used more mundane practices like touching and caressing their private parts. The priest who was subsequently commissioned by the Zaragoza archbishopric to investigate the case wrote of 'the ease with which Martínez had taken these women to her house, and even lain in the same bed with them'.[71]

Orgasms were a traditional part of popular exorcisms carried out on village women at the time by expert female exorcists at a famous sanctuary at Zorita, in Castellón: 'these exorcists knew the purely physiological effect that orgasms produced, and they took advantage of the subsequent soothing lassitude to calm the possessed'.[72] Sexual desire had formed a large part of two of the most famous exorcism cases in the seventeenth century: the nuns' possession in the Madrid convent of San Plácido in 1628 which brother Francisco had tried to exorcize with kisses and caresses, and the possessions which had taken place in the Aragonese valley villages of Tena between 1637 and 1642. According to the inquisitor who had investigated the latter, they were caused 'by an illness resulting from refusing to satisfy the sexual desires of one Pedro Arruebo'.[73]

As the number of exorcisms demanded of him by the Tosos possessed increased, the parish priest felt it incumbent on him to inform his religious superiors in the Zaragoza archdiocese of the events. The answer was not long in coming and was somewhat surprising to the uninitiated. The exorcisms were to stop forthwith and the possessed – 'troublemakers', the auxiliary bishop called them – were to be punished. Their fathers and husbands were to keep them busy working, and not allow them a moment of leisure; they were to be bathed in cold water . . .

'If they don't mend their ways at home, they must be shut into their room or punished in some other manner. If in church or in the streets, the justices must gaol them . . .' Their signs of being possessed 'are highly equivocal and could well be due to natural causes' or hysteria, an illness whose distinct symptoms were at the time beginning to be identified.

Here, then, were the alleged witchcraft's victims being disavowed, threatened with punishment by the highest clerical authority, and the 'witch' exonerated. When the priest read out the bishop's letter to those involved, they and their parents and relatives rioted and the priest fled the village for three months to save his life.

The villagers paid no heed to the clerical authorities. Martínez and her husband appealed to the bishop for protection and he in turn ordered the civil authorities to arrest the 'possessed' which they steadfastly refused to do. They explained that to put 'the popular will' and the 'common good' above all other considerations, meant supporting the possessed in the name of the people against the 'witch', Martínez. The villagers' welfare was more important than one person's fate. 'If Joaquina continues with her outrages she will be killed by these mad or possessed women, and the village inhabitants can never be held responsible for failing to prevent what could not be prevented', the parish priest, the local junta of 'probity' – an assembly of the village aldermen – and the justices of the peace wrote jointly to the bishop.[74]

There was an evident clash here between the enlightened eighteenth-century prelates and the popular religious beliefs of the majority of villagers. Whereas two centuries earlier the Church had been at the forefront of witch-hunting, the Enlightenment of the last quarter of the eighteenth century had come to consider witchcraft as a superstition, an absurd idea explicable only by the lower orders' lack of culture and inadequate religious formation.*[75] Indeed, after reading the evidence, the archbishopric's legal assessor judged that, far from considering Martínez a witch, she was a good, God-fearing woman who took communion regularly, and against whom nothing could be held despite the ignorant villagers' suspicions.

One woman in particular was Martínez' main accuser: Antonia Ramo. The two women had been close friends; both were in the business of selling foodstuffs to the villagers. Ramo was a woman well-considered in the village. Many witnesses confirmed that she always attended all religious devotional acts, was well-educated and polite, and that her conduct was morally and politically irreproachable. She, too, was a God-fearing woman who went to communion regularly. Some witnesses, however, recalled earlier symptoms that she was 'not quite right in the head'. Why should these two women have

* The start of a change had already been notable at the beginning of the seventeenth century when scepticism about witchcraft was beginning to be expressed by inquisitorial and bishops' justices, although belief in it persisted strongly among the lower clergy.

quarrelled to the extent that Ramo would fall into a possessed fit every time she saw Joaquina?

The 'witch' was said to have a 'warlike', 'proud' and 'masculine' temperament. She came from a neighbouring village which, in Spanish terms, always implied rivalry, and had arrived in Tosos poor and burdened with children. For a time the village authorities had given her the task of looking after its horses. In the village she was nicknamed 'The Charge-Beater' which had overtones of the heroine of Zaragoza's first siege, Agustina Zaragoza, who, when an artilleryman had fallen at the breach, took his place and fired the cannon to beat back the enemy as they charged through the gap in the walls. Nicknames were an important part of villagers' perceptions of others.

Paradoxically, the archbishopric recommended both women for their religiosity while condemning Ramo's persistent and unflagging charge that Joaquina was a witch, an accusation that nothing would make her retract. Joaquina, on the other hand, always maintained that the 'possessions' were fraudulent and caused 'by the defence of highly concrete interests', though she did not specify what these were.

No coherent explanation of these events was put forward by the initial ecclesiastical investigation which provided only random clues – and probably with good reason. Zaragoza was under French control and there was a close understanding between the ecclesiastical and military authorities.* A part of the problem between the two women seemed to revolve around the war and there was little reward to be gained for the clerical hierarchy by digging too deeply into the causes of events that had occurred in a hamlet of no particular consequence.

The original investigating commissioner, Rev. Manuel Pasqual Bernard, the Cariñena parish priest who was appointed by the Zaragoza ecclesiastical authorities, pointed out two war-related incidents without, however, expounding on them. 'It has come to my attention that in those years of revolution some violent deaths took place here', he wrote in order to explain that the threats to kill Joaquina must be taken seriously, 'as this is a village where such scandalous conduct can occur'.[76] Evidently then at the start of the war some villagers had been suspected of lack of loyalty to the patriot cause or personal vengeance had been vented on the assassinated. This had not been forgotten. But the tables had turned in the past two years when the French indisputably controlled Aragón; Marshal Suchet had even extinguished the guerrilla threat. In 1812, at the time of these events, however, the Aragonese guerrillas were re-emerging with gathering strength. Arguably, this renewed resistance and the fear of French military reprisals

---

* The archbishop, Ramón de Arce, as was noted earlier, was an afrancesado who was obliged in 1816 to seek exile in France; at the same time, as the last pre-war appointed inquisitor general, he was a staunch defender of the Holy Office, illustrating the contradictory tendencies that could exist in one and the same person.

was splitting the inhabitants into two opposed camps, each represented in their different ways by Joaquina and Antonia.*

Soon the commissioner discovered from the local parish priest's evidence that on one occasion a French military patrol had arrested him and Antonia Ramo and taken them to a nearby village.[77] But the commissioner neither asked, nor did the priest offer, any reason for the arrest which occured on an unspecified date after Joaquina had been driven from the village. What might have explained such an action? It was unlikely that the junior commander of what would have been a small imperial force sent to the village would act on his own initiative unless it were a question of taking the authorities hostage for non-payment of taxes, tributes or requisitions. While the priest was obviously a local authority, the same could not be said of Ramo. Moreover, the priest did not suggest that the arrests lasted long. Did the Zaragoza ecclesiastical authorities propose to the French military the expediency of removing these two troublemakers from the hamlet – or at least of frightening them by the possibility of expulsion from Tosos? A mystery certainly hung over both these events.

It was only after the war that a priest who was investigating the matter – which continued unabated, war or no war, under the Cortes de Cádiz's liberalism or Fernando's absolutism – came closest to providing an intelligible reason:

> During the French domination, dissensions between the said villagers arose, one of the best-known being between A. Ramo and Joaquina Martínez.† Because of the one's envy of the other's shop, Ramo began to put it about that Martínez was selling a bedevilled cheese and that all who partook of it would be possessed. At the time it happened, either because of the fear of French outrages or for other reasons that belong to the medical realm, many women and some men suffered disorders which were notable for [the afflicteds'] extraordinary movements, so that Martínez was pursued to death.[78]

Fear of French outrages, which were current in the first years of the war, were by 1812 not as likely to occur in Aragón unless villagers supported the patriot movement. The postwar investigating priest's association of village dissension under French occupation with that of Ramo and Martínez appeared to point to their interconnection (unless his report were no more than one of those common Spanish early nineteenth-century stylistic elisions of disparate events). Though it was

---

* As María Tausiet puts it in her book: 'The concept of the village as an entity of defined personality, the importance [the local authorities] gave to the expression of the "popular will" and consequently to the defence of the "common welfare" above all other considerations revealed the extent to which the possessed were identified with the new revolutionary cause or, at least, a real and uncontrollable situation.'
† The names are given inaccurately as 'N. Ramos' and 'N. Martínez'.

imaginable that in little more than a hamlet the two women's rivalry arose from the one's envy of the other's success with her bedevilled cheese, different loyalties in the war were more profound; and Tosos was obviously split in its political allegiances between French and patriot supporters. These divisions crystallized around the two women's dissension in which the villagers' 'general will' stood by the possessed.

While the participants' motives, and the village's inner workings in which these motives were played out, remained obscure, it was clear that in one small village the daily stress, fears and divisions caused by the war resulted in an outbreak of mass psychosis which conceivably was a defence mechanism, a projection of the 'enemy devil' onto the 'other', the 'outsider witch' who must be driven from the community or face the threat of losing her life when all would again be well.

Military Victory and Political Defeat

THE DECISIVE BATTLE: VITORIA

In May 1813, Wellington, whom the Cortes had appointed Supreme Commander of the Spanish armies, again moved into Spain. This time it was he who constantly turned the French army's flank from north of the Duero, forcing the enemy to retreat. On Napoleon's orders, Josef, who had returned to Madrid after Wellington evacuated the city the previous autumn, had moved his capital from Madrid to Valladolid, but he made no attempt to defend it or Burgos, whose fortress the French blew up in their retreat. Though nominally in command of nearly one hundred thousand men in central Spain, Josef (again on Napoleon's orders) had lost a part of his forces to the Army of the North which was tied down fighting Navarra's and the Basque country's guerrilla insurrection; and Josef desperately needed it before facing Wellington's seventy-five thousand allied troops in open battle.[1]*

In the hope that the northern army would rapidly join him, Josef halted at Vitoria. His army of just under sixty thousand took up a not particularly strong position. Wellington attacked on June 21, 1813, and the French army was totally routed. Josef fled to the safety of France, never to return. He was accompanied by many thousand supporters and persons who feared patriot reprisals for having collaborated with his regime. Around the battlefield, the enormous baggage trains carrying French plunder lay shattered, and as allied troops looted the looters, the ground was rapidly adrift in paper: French military and civil documents of all types trodden into the earth or blown by the wind.

Among the booty taken by the British were more than two hundred pictures the French had seized from Spanish palaces, convents and churches: paintings by Velázquez, Titian, Correggio, Murillo and many other sixteenth- and seventeenth-century artists. The president of the Royal Academy in London

---

* After the Russian disaster, Napoleon had withdrawn Marshal Soult and twenty thousand veteran soldiers to fight in Germany.

was amazed at their sight: it was worth having fought a battle for them, he said. Although according to the rules of war the plunder belonged to the victors, Wellington insisted that this artistic treasure be returned to his ally Spain; Fernando VII turned down the offer and made him a present of what was a veritable museum.[2]

The battle's outcome might have been different had the French armies united, had Suchet been ordered to follow Soult in evacuating Valencia and Aragón (as he was shortly forced to do anyway), and the Army of the North (which after Vitoria escaped into France) had reinforced Josef to face the greater of the two enemies.

The road to France now lay open to Wellington. A quick advance could have taken him to Bayonne, the main supply depôt for the French armies in Spain. Instead, he laid siege to San Sebastián and Pamplona: their garrisons of three and four thousand respectively presented no threat to his army, while the cities' investment cost several months – and heavy casualties in the case of San Sebastián, which was taken after stubborn French defence on September 8, thoroughly sacked without thought that the victims were Spanish allies, and finally set fire to.

Napoleon, who on August 27–28, had defeated the Russian and Prussian armies at Dresden, meanwhile sent Marshal Soult to command the remnants of the French army on the Spanish frontier. Taking advantage of Wellington's preoccupation with the two sieges, he surprised the supreme commander by attacking him, not as he expected across the Bidasoa river which formed the Franco-Spanish frontier, but through the Pyrenean passes. Soult had an effective army of eighty-five thousand men in whom he had inspired new confidence. For nine days of very hard fighting, known as the battle of the Pyrenees, Soult's offensive was only finally stopped in two bloody battles (Sorauren, July 28 and 30) within sight of Pamplona's walls. The battles cost Soult thirteen thousand men and Wellington just over half that number. Spanish guerrillas incorporated into the army, and battle-hardened regulars fought with great bravery to hold Soult off. Though his troops were dispirited by their defeats, Soult made one last attempt by attacking San Sebastián on the day the allies stormed the city: he was thoroughly defeated at the battle of San Marcial, losing four thousand men. The majority of the allies' 2,500 casualties were Spanish.

Even so, Wellington did not take advantage of his victory, allowing Soult a month to regroup his army and throw up defence works along the Bidasoa. The five weeks it had taken to achieve the great Vitoria victory had turned into five months (July to November) of fighting in and around the Spanish frontier. Although there was no question, as after past victories, of retreating to Portugal, like most of Wellington's peninsular campaigns this one also ended in a strong anti-climax.[3]*

* Wellington finally crossed the Bidasoa at the beginning of October 1813, and surprised Soult, turning his right flank, and putting his army to flight. Had Wellington continued his advance that day, he could have taken St Jean de Luz ten kilometres to Soult's rear and turned the line of the Nivelle, the next river. Instead he gave Soult */cont'd over*

END OF THE WAR: FERNANDO VII'S RETURN
AND THE RESTORATION OF ABSOLUTISM

While the allies continued to fight in the northwest, important political events were taking place in the rest of the country. In September, the constituent Cortes adjourned and elections to an ordinary Cortes were held in a greater number of unoccupied provinces than had been possible in 1810. In many provinces the vote was clearly manipulated by local oligarchs. At the same time the liberals of the Constituent assembly boycotted their opponents' attempts to move the new Cortes to Madrid, fearing that they lacked a popular base in the capital. When the Cortes finally gathered in the capital in January, 1814, the liberal majority had been sizeably reduced but the liberals had no intention of relinquishing power. (None of the deputies who had sat in the Constituent Cortes was permitted to stand for election.)

A profound unpredictability hung over the new assembly. A month earlier, Napoleon had freed Fernando to return to Spain. Popular premonition, fear – or desire, whipped up by absolutist clerics – of a confrontation between parliament and king and of absolutism's restoration had a startling effect. Religious observance suddenly increased: in five regions, all experiencing population growth, Lent conceptions dropped sharply in terms of the usual small changes, indicating that the Church's proscription of carnal relations during Lent were now again being more widely observed.* The change was borne out by historical evidence. In Valladolid, Castilla la Vieja's capital, a special religious fervour reigned in May, 1814, and a far greater number of inhabitants than usual attended cathedral services and other religious events.[4]

---

cont'd/   another month's breathing space to reorganize his army while he waited for Pamplona to fall. Crossing the Nivelle cost the allies more than three thousand casualties. Once again, Wellington did not resolutely pursue Soult, but again waited a month before attempting to cross the next river, the Nive. This led to hard fighting, with Soult attacking first one half of Wellington's army which had crossed the river, and then the other half. Though the allies finally threw back the French, it was at the cost of five thousand casualties. Wellington then went into winter quarters. Three battles in two months had barely advanced the allied army more than thirty kilometres into France. He did not resume operations until February 1814, investing Bayonne, Soult withdrawing to give battle at Orthez. Wellington stormed his strong positions at the cost of another two thousand casualties. Soult fell back on Toulouse. On April 10, 1814, Wellington attacked the city's outer defences, suffering 4,500 casualties. Not wanting to be besieged, Soult slipped away during the night, and Wellington entered Toulouse to great royalist welcome. On April 12 news arrived of Napoleon's abdication and the end of the war. Wellington's slow advance cost the allies nearly fifteen thousand casualties, large numbers of them Spanish. (Muir, 1996, pp. 299–305.)

* Fernando's release was common knowledge well before Lent. On Lent conceptions as a measure of religiosity, see chapter 13, and Appendix 3. It should be added that this access of religiosity did not last long. In the two postwar years, accompanying population growth in all regions, Lent conceptions began marginally to return to above their pre-war levels in Andalucía, Castilla la Nueva, Cataluña and Extremadura. Only in the Basque country and Valencia were they significantly higher. The sole exception was Castilla la Vieja which remained slightly lower, its religiosity finally untainted.

The people's presentiment was correct. As a condition of Fernando's release, Napoleon demanded that he sign an alliance against the British. The treaty also stipulated that as a counterpart for the withdrawal of French troops from Spain, Britain must follow suit; and that afrancesados would regain their positions and be restored to their previous social status. Fernando, who had done little else in his enforced exile at Valençay but attempt to ingratiate himself with Napoleon (while his uncle knitted and tore out pictures which he considered obscene or irreligious from the books in Talleyrand's extensive library), sent an emissary to Madrid to sound out the regency, over which his cousin, Cardinal Luís María Borbón, primate of Spain, now presided. The regency's response was clear: the Cortes of Cádiz had, in January 1811, decreed that it would not recognize any treaty signed on foreign soil by the captive king. The emissary was sent back with a letter and a copy of the decree. Napoleon's manoeuvre was only too patent. After his defeat at Leipzig in October 1813, he was willing to withdraw his army from Spain in order to prepare for a last stand in France and to rid himself of the British threat on his southwestern border. At the same time he was trying to split the British–Spanish alliance.

On February 2, 1814, the Cortes, in which on the question of the king's return the liberals still commanded a large majority, approved a decree which stated that Fernando would not be considered free until he had sworn an oath to the constitution which would be handed to him on reaching the frontier. Moreover, no foreigner at all, neither an armed force nor any afrancesado, even a servant, would be allowed into Spain. The decree further ordered Fernando to follow a strict itinerary from the border to Madrid, whither he would be accompanied by the regency's president.

On March 22, Fernando crossed the frontier into Cataluña, a part of which was still occupied by Suchet, and two days later reached the Spanish army in the principality. But he did not follow the Cortes' itinerary to follow the coast road south to Valencia and then to Madrid. His enthusiastic reception everywhere led him to assert his independence and visit Zaragoza where he remained for five days. His two communications to the Cortes were of a studied ambiguity. Finally, on April 16, Fernando entered Valencia to extraordinary scenes of popular rejoicing: unhitching the horses from his carriage, the people pulled the monarch's coach through the streets.

Earlier the same day on the road into Valencia, the regency's president, Cardinal Borbón, had driven to Puçol, a nearby township, to present his cousin Fernando with a copy of the constitution. Their carriages met and both men alighted. Each waited for the other to advance. Finally, the cardinal moved, and Fernando held out his hand to receive the kiss of obeisance. The cardinal hesitated. Angrily, Fernando said, 'kiss!' and the cardinal obeyed. It was a symbolic victory for Fernando which would shortly turn into reality.

From well before Fernando's arrival in Valencia, his uncle Antonio who had gone directly to the city from Cataluña, had been plotting on his behalf. A number of ultra monarchist deputies were involved also. But the real conspiratorial power was General Francisco Javier Elío, the monarchist captain general of the region, a post he had exercised from Alicante before Suchet withdrew from Valencia. He had travelled to Aragón to meet Fernando where he had incited the latter to recover 'absolute power'. On the day after Fernando's arrival in Valencia, as he made his way to a Te Deum in the cathedral along the streets lined with troops, General Elío stopped in front of the crown's regimental flag and held it aloft.

> Your majesty, I beg you to stop to show you a sight worthy of yourself. These stains which you see on the flag are those of the severely wounded officer who saved it from the enemy at the battle of Castalla. This crown covered in blood is that which the loyal army has shed in order for you to recuperate the crown; the blood remaining of all Spanish soldiers will be spilt to secure you on your throne in the fullness of your natural rights.[5]

Elío's pronouncement could hardly have been clearer. It was followed by what came to be known as the *Manifiesto de los Persas*, a letter to Fernando from a score of ultra deputies which called on him not to swear the constitutional oath. 'Absolute monarchy . . . is a work of reason and intelligence', the manifesto declared. 'It is subordinate to divine law, to justice and to the fundamental law of the state. It was established by right of conquest or by the voluntary submission of the first men who elected their kings.'[6]

On May 2, the Valencia populace, incited no doubt by the ultras, smashed the tablet naming one of the main squares the plaza de la Constitución, substituting for it the Real plaza de Fernando VII, while conversely in Madrid the atmosphere was joyous during ceremonies for the completion of the new hall where the Cortes was to assemble. The inhabitants of all classes had worked or paid to complete the hall on time to celebrate the popular May 2 anti-French rising of 1808. On the facade of the former monastery, between statues representing Religion, Fatherland and Liberty, was a marble tablet inscribed with the words from the constitution: 'The power to enact the laws resides in the Cortes together with the King.'[7]

Two days later, Fernando staged his coup. His decree, though not published until May 11 in Madrid, abolished the 1812 constitution and all the Cortes' decrees, and he reassumed absolute power. Anyone who advocated obedience to the constitution or the Cortes' decrees would be guilty of lese-majesty and punishable by death.

Fernando was making a serious mistake, Henry Wellesley, British ambassador to the regency, believed. Shortly after Fernando crossed into Spain, Wellesley sent 'A Most Secret and Confidential' despatch to Lord Castlereagh, the British Foreign secretary.

> In the actual state of Parties at Madrid the only safe line for the king to take is to accept the Constitution and to declare his determination to govern according to its regulations . . . By adopting this line of conduct he will insure the good will and support of the Nation and may, by degrees, be enabled to effect such changes in the Constitution as are necessary.[8]

A week later, he added significantly in a further despatch to Castlereagh: 'the king has nothing to offer the Nation in place of the Constitution'. Coming from Wellesley, whose meddling in patriot political affairs had been a thorn in the side of the Cádiz Cortes, this was unexpected support for the constitution, for which he had shown no particular enthusiasm, expressing the view that it was not 'consonant with the general feeling of the Nation'. Instead he had devoted his attention in Cádiz to protecting British interests as he saw them. These included opening Spain's South American colonies to British trade, intriguing to replace the regency by one more sympathetic to Britain, having Wellington appointed as supreme commander of Spanish forces, and protesting at the dispatch of ten thousand Spanish soldiers to put down the colonial insurrections. And if his demands were not met, he had threatened the regency and Cortes with withdrawing the British garrison from Cádiz and suspending British loans. But his meddling – with the exception of the patriot diversion of troops from the main ground of the anti-Napoleonic conflict to the colonies – had met with the British government's disapproval and the warning that it did not want to become involved in Spain's internal affairs.[9] In self-defence, Wellesley affirmed categorically that had it been known at the beginning of the war

that the Spanish Nation could be brought to the brink of ruin, not by the military successes of its Enemy, but by the continued misconduct of its Government . . . (and if for that reason) the authority of the Government has not hitherto been respected in the country, it is solely to be ascribed to the neglect of all the measures necessary to assist the exertions of the People, and to the want of public confidence in the regular Army and its officers . . .[10]

A perspicacious comment; as indeed were his views on Fernando's return and the political options before him. 'The King will be in difficulties if he rejects the Constitution', he reported to Castlereagh in another 'Most Secret and Confidential' despatch from Valencia on April 19. But Fernando, he added, was prepared to use force to achieve his ends.

On May 5 Fernando left Valencia for Madrid, where he had appointed the ultra General Eguía captain general to publish his decree and to take the measures he had ordered. General Elío, at the head of an army division, which included the British colonel at the head of the Spanish troops he had trained, escorted the king, his uncle and brother who had been held by Napoleon at Valençay. Everywhere en route Fernando was met by cheering crowds who usually proceeded to smash the tablets in their main squares celebrating the constitution.

On May 11 the Madrid captain general informed the Cortes president that the king had dissolved the assembly. As the president was one of the signatories to the *Manifiesto de los Persas* he readily acquiesced. That night the persecution began with the arrest of all the leading liberals whom Eguía, supported by troops, could lay hands on. The arrests continued the following day in Madrid and the provinces. That day a few hundred of the mob, probably organized by the conde de Montijo, whom Fernando had dispatched to the capital earlier to stir up anti-liberal sentiment, tore down the stone naming Madrid's plaza Mayor the plaza de la Constitución, and dragged it to the Cortes shouting 'Viva Fernando VII!', 'Long Live Religion!', 'Down with the Cortes!' 'Viva la Inquisición!' They then wrecked the Cortes chamber and obliterated the word constitution from the facade.[11]

When Fernando entered the capital through triumphal arches, with troops lining the streets, he received for the second time an enthusiastic reception. After six years of war and suffering, their 'beloved' king was back on his throne. The fundamental liberal attempt to restructure the country had collapsed. The war which, with the exception of Suchet's continuing occupation of Cataluña,[12] was finally over in Spain, had in the end, it could be thought, changed nothing.

And yet, in truth, the end of the Napoleonic war marked the beginning of the real intestinal conflict. The country's educated classes were now divided into two warring camps. The reformers on the one hand, the ultra conservatives, backed by the Church, on the other. Three nineteenth-century civil wars and the greatest of all in the twentieth, followed by forty years of Franco's dictatorship – more than a century and a half in all – would be needed before this division could be sufficiently healed in a modern constitution which permitted the free interplay of parliamentary politics under a constitutional monarchy.

Fernando's new reign, accompanied by six years of ferocious reactionary repression, was the beginning of this open conflict. The Inquisition was restored, freedom of the press abolished, the pre-war councils of state re-established and municipal government again left in the hands of the old oligarchies. The regular clergy recovered its monasteries, friaries and property. Though the landed señores did not recover their jurisdictional rights – the only advance which the absolutist restoration took over from the Cádiz Cortes – they could continue to exact dues and tributes as in the past. Wellington, not exactly a liberal himself, visited Madrid after the final victory over Napoleon to try to persuade Fernando to moderate his repression against the liberals. He was unsuccessful. What could be expected, he commented later, of a king who every day partook of his afternoon tea in the company of nuns?

MILITANCIES: GOYA AND THE *DISASTERS OF WAR*

Goya's eighty-two engravings of the *Disasters of War* – not the artist's original title* – have been and frequently continue to be taken as literal documentary evidence of the conflict's brutality, especially of French repression. This was mistaken: it turned Goya into a 'naturalist' before his time;[13] he was rather a 'visionary of the real'.[14] As in his two emblematic paintings of the May 2 Madrid rising and its repression on May 3, he did not document events as much as imagine them and their horror. Goya was sixty-two at the outbreak of the war, deaf and for

---

* This was: 'Fatal consequences of the bloody war in Spain with Bonaparte and other striking caprichos'.

nearly a third of a century had been official court painter to Carlos IV. Of humble origins – his father was a Zaragozan master gilder who died in poverty, and his mother was from an impoverished minor Aragonese noble family – until the age of forty Goya lacked any wide culture. Aged twenty-eight, he was called to Madrid to paint cartoons for the royal tapestry factory; his later friendship with Jovellanos and other enlightened reformists like Bernardo Iriarte, both of whom he painted and each of whom took separate sides in the war, eased his entry into the world of the Enlightenment. Like them, he was of a generation whose poets and playwrights attacked the social abuses of the absolutist regime, and like them, in his desire for reform, had initially supported Fernando VII. He was more daring then most of his contemporaries, however, criticizing directly in his series of pre-war engravings, 'Los caprichos', the Church's malign influence in fostering the people's ignorance and credulity, among many other social ills. While he vigorously depicted the lower classes' festivities and labours, a part of him distrusted their susceptibility to superstition, religious customs and attachment to traditional ways of thought and habits.

Throughout the war he remained in Bonapartist Madrid, with the exception of a brief excursion to Zaragoza, at General Palafox's request in the autumn of 1808, to depict the inhabitants' heroic defence of the Aragonese capital at the end of the first siege; this project he never carried out, other than to include in the *Disasters of War* an impressive etching in stark black-and-white of the siege's heroine, Agustina Zaragoza, standing on dead artillerymen to fire their silenced cannon at an invisible enemy. 'What courage!' he titled the engraving.

On his return to Madrid, which meanwhile surrendered to Napoleon, he swore 'love and allegiance' to King Josef, along with thirty thousand other heads of family. He had little choice if he wanted to continue in the capital where lay his main possibilities to earn a wartime living by his art. Considerable numbers of his enlightened pre-war friends served the new regime, and like them Goya was by no means unaware of the advantages that Bonapartist rule could bring to Spain. Napoleon's Chamartín reforms which abolished feudal rights, did away with the Inquisition, and reduced the number of religious communities by two-thirds confirmed this. But by 1810, when he began work on the *Disasters of War*, the imperial army's sacking, pillaging and outright oppression of the country had alerted many Bonapartist politicians to the fatal dangers this military policy contained for the new regime. Without the army it could not consolidate its sway; with *this* army, its legitimacy was constantly undermined.

Throughout, Goya remained deeply ambivalent about the war, its aims and means. His critical vision of reality was expressed in the palette and brush, in his engraving tools and copper plate. (Because of the war he was so short of the latter that he cut up two beautiful landscape engravings to use the reverse sides for four of his *Disasters*.)

On the one hand he heard numerous stories about the French army's brutality – he must have had large gatherings of friends in his house which, according to the inventory drawn up on his wife's death in 1812, contained over fifty chairs; he had learned to lip-read and the subject of conversation was bound to be about the war, making it easier for him to understand. On the other, the patriots' defence of religion and reliance on the Church did not enamour him to their cause. Moreover, what all the enlightened of his generation most feared had come to pass: once their fury was unleashed the lower orders proved as capable of abominable atrocities as their oppressors. The cruelty of the supposedly 'civilized' French enraged him. The savagery of the villagers and guerrillas confirmed his worst dread. In the sense in which it would be understood today, he found it impossible 'to take sides'.

This was made easier by his isolation in Madrid. Had he lived in the patriot zone things might have been different. But in the capital he depended for news on his afrancesado friends and acquaintances. News and rumour went hand in hand as they did in the patriot zone – exaggerated in both, depending on circumstance. Despite his marginal comment 'This I have seen' on a number of the *Disasters*' plates, many modern historians suspect that he indulged in a certain poetic licence. But whether he actually witnessed some of the events he depicted – and it is indisputable that he lived through the horrifying street scenes during the 1812 Madrid famine – is in fact irrelevant. His artistic imagination, the expression of his intimate feelings, was what counted. This allowed him to add at the end of the series on massacres and mutilation a number of satirical prints – 'the striking caprichos' on his old anathema, the Church – which come as a surprise to the horror-hardened twenty-first century viewer. Goya certainly intended them as a criticism of the Church's return to power – and its popular acceptance – and of the restoration of absolutism.

To Goya and his contemporaries 'caprichos' meant the free expression of the artist's imagination and interior sensibility – usually expressed in small prints, drawings or paintings – in contrast to the commissioned paintings and portraits which provided their living. In this sense – and this strict sense alone – the *Disasters* were of the 'capricho' genre. The artist's harsh black-and-white depictions of death, brutality, rape and starvation which appeared a realistic rendering of the horrors of the war often expressed rather his own anguished and contradictory feelings about the conflict's 'fatal consequences'. This did not make them less impressive; but it did not make them a documentary record of Spain's Napoleonic war. (While not denying the conflict's barbarities, it must be recalled that these were not the exclusive preserve of French troops and Spanish guerrillas. British soldiers on Moore's retreat, at Ciudad Rodrigo, Badajoz and San Sebastián were also equally barbarous, though they did not figure in the *Disasters*.)

'This is what you were born for' Goya wrote in the *Disasters* (12)*
under a pile of partially stripped corpses, possibly French soldiers by
their remaining long trousers, shoes and a fallen flat hat which some
imperial infantry wore. Above the dead an unarmed villager staggers
forward, blood spewing from his open mouth, arms outstretched in a
typical Goya gesture and about to fall on – and join – the corpses. There
is no question mark to his caption, as some commentators have
supposed; it is a bald statement of fact.

'Charity' says another below naked corpses being thrown into an
open ditch or grave (27); 'Rightly or Wrongly' – suggesting the artist's
ambivalence – depicts two villagers, armed only with a pike and a
dagger attacking imperial soldiers about to fire their muskets at them
at point blank range. One of the villagers is already bleeding at the
mouth (2). The following plate has a villager with an axe about to split
open a French soldier's head. A later engraving shows a villager about
to rape anally with a pike a naked dead or wounded imperial soldier
and a woman lifting a club to beat the body, while spectators
impassively look on. Significantly, it is entitled simply 'The Populace'
(28).

Women figure in the dualistic role of vengeful furies and victims: first
one is seen stabbing an imperial cavalryman she has unhorsed: 'The
women inspire courage' (4). But immediately the following caption
expressed Goya's intimate sense of the people's threat: 'And they
are like wild beasts' appears under a woman holding a baby against her
back and spearing a French soldier with a pike while behind her other
women, one preparing to hurl a rock, attack a small party of troops (5).
Another engraving (9) shows women in both roles: an aged mother is
about to stab an imperial soldier in the back as he attempts to violate her
daughter: 'They do not want to' reads the caption: – 'Nor they' – 'And nor
do these' – as women become solely the victims of outrage and rape
(10, 11). The imperial troops' 'Bitter presence' (13) represents yet
another woman being dragged to her fate. 'There is no longer time'
has French soldiers, swords drawn, seizing the women of men they
have killed (19). The preceding scene (18) is one of the series' most
poignant. A village couple, handkerchiefs to their faces, stand on a slight
rise overlooking a group of naked corpses – their fellow villagers
perhaps. Again the central body is depicted with outstretched arms.
'Bury them and keep quiet' reads the title . . . This 'quietism' does not
last long. Despite Goya's dislike of the clergy, a scene of a friar being
stabbed in the chest, bears the caption: 'This is bad' (46). The artist's
imagination encompassed the event but not its justification.

Goya did not engrave the *Disasters* in the order which he finally chose
for the series. In the course of the decade he worked on them his style

---

* The numbers in parentheses refer to the engraving's number in Goya's order of the
series for publication.

became more powerfully precise and dramatic. Significantly, French atrocities were the new style's theme: hanging and quartering, severing corpses in half, impaling, mutilating and executing figures bound to a tree (31–39). Usually an imperial officer or soldier is watching, a satisfied look on his face. One execution scene (35) over the title 'One cannot tell why' is striking. In fact, the reason hung round the majority of the eight men's garrotted necks: not in the illegible placards each of them bore denouncing their crimes but in the weapons they used to carry them out: daggers, knives, swords, pistols . . . Goya's imagination did not illustrate the fact that these were certainly victims of the Bonapartist extraordinary criminal tribunals which garrotted its victims while the French military generally shot them. In the artist's mind, as French military fortunes in Spain grew more desperate, their barbarity increased.

In 1809, Goya received a commission from the capital's authorities to paint an allegory of the city of Madrid, which included a medallion of King Josef. Goya completed this early the following year. Two and a half years later when Wellington entered Madrid after his victory at Salamanca and Josef fled to Valencia, the king was painted out and replaced by the word 'Constitution' to celebrate the 1812 liberal constitution which had been proclaimed in Cádiz. But Wellington's victory was short-lived and Josef reoccupied the capital. His portrait was again painted in, once more to vanish the following year after he definitively evacuated Madrid, and 'Constitution' reappeared. Its life was little longer than the first; in 1814 Fernando VII's portrait was painted in the medallion. Rather than an allegory, the painting became one more of the war's many ironies.*

Although never officially a court painter to Josef, Goya was decorated by the king with his highest honour in 1811. He also painted a number of afrancesados, among them Antonio Llorente, one of Josef's Spanish councillors, a canon and former secretary of the Inquisition in Madrid, whom the king commissioned to write a history of the Holy Office from tribunal documents taken over after its abolition by Napoleon. This, and the portrait of a handsome young French general Nicolas Guye (who fought under General Hugo in unsuccessfully hunting down El Empecinado, the outstanding guerrilla leader) are among Goya's most vibrant. His several portraits of Wellington are less so.

Encouraged no doubt by the new patriot constitution and the likelihood of French military defeat, Goya hoped to publish his 'Fatal Consequences of the bloody War . . .' as he had wished for his 'Caprichos' twelve years earlier: the latter's sale had been stopped and the plates handed over to the king to prevent his persecution at the

---

* Finally, after an unsuccessful attempt to recover Goya's original portrait of Josef, the words 'Dos de Mayo' were painted in the medallion; and thus it remains to this day.

Inquisition's hands.[15] He needed to make good his delapidated finances due to the war. But on absolutism's reimpostion – the most 'fatal' of all the war's consequences – he feared for his freedom. Having pulled one set of numbered proofs, which he gave to his friend Ceán Bermúdez, and which bear their titles in pencil, most probably by Goya himself, he set the *Disasters* and their accompanying 'striking caprichos' aside and turned to a safer subject: a series on the art of bullfighting. At the same time he proposed to the patriot regency 'to perpetuate the most notable and heroic actions and scenes of our glorious insurrection against the tyrant of Europe'. The regency gave him a monthly allowance of fifteen hundred reales and his expenses to carry out the project 'in consideration of the great importance of so worthy an enterprise'.[16] Six years after the events, which he had not directly witnessed, he produced the two magisterial and best-known paintings of the war, *El Dos de Mayo* and *El Tres de Mayo*, two paintings on the capital's May 2 rising and the French executions which followed it.* His artistic genius was such that, unlike any other Spanish painter of the time, he captured the indelible essence of both events, as well as much of the detail: for example, in *The Second of May*, the number of women around the combatants in the Puerta del Sol, one of whom appears to be helping to unseat a mameluke.† Amidst the blood and gore of the execution scene of the third of May, two aspects of the central figure can be observed: his wild face and characteristically outflung arms in the presence of death and that there is nothing classically 'heroic' about this hero. Goya was among the first – if not the first – artists to depict the anonymous people as heroes and makers of history.

The *Disasters of War*, as they eventually came to be called, had to wait until 1863 – thirty-five years after Goya's death – to be published. When the artist went into exile in France in 1824 – after the Spanish liberal revolution of 1820–1823, which restored the 1812 constitution, was put down by a new French invasion, ordered by Louis XVIII to restore Fernando VII to his throne – he left the plates behind in his house. The series as published ended with plates 78 and 79 which showed the death of Truth and suggested that should she try to rise again she would be struck down once more by Spain's forces of evil and reaction. But the final print which Goya designed for the series (82) during the last brief liberal period which ended again with reaction on the throne, was a vision of peace and plenty, a reaffirmation of his hope for mankind.[17]

---

* Though an eighteen-year-old pupil of his, León Ortega y Villa, was wounded in the fighting; and the royal painter Agustín Esteve and his pupil witnessed some of the events. His major-domo's circumstantial account of Goya going on the night of May 3 to the Montaña del Principe Pío to see the corpses by moonlight has been proven fictitious.
† See Chapter 3, p. 62.

THE COSTS OF THE WAR*

The conflict cost Spain some 215,000 to 375,000 missing population between those who died and those who were not born because of the war.† Added to this were material destruction, social disruption and the state's virtual bankruptcy. Beginning in 1808, just as some population growth was under way to recuperate the losses of the disastrous pre-war famine, yellow fever and malaria epidemics, the war put paid to the respite and worsened the crisis which had already cost the country between 350,000 and half a million missing population – a greater loss than during the war itself. The anti-French struggle, however, had one particularly negative outcome. At the start of the war youth of marriageable age, the sixteen to twenty-five-year-olds, had enlisted massively – and been massively slaughtered in the heavy defeats of 1808–1809; their loss seriously affected population growth long after the last of the war's survivors had died.

The wartime losses added to the even heavier pre-war losses resulted in a demographic haemorrhage of some 560,000 to 885,000 missing population – between six and ten percent of the late eighteenth-century total.‡ This was due as much to declines in the expected number of births as to adult deaths. The effects were especially notable throughout much of the rest of the century in the missing births of the potential children who were not born between 1800 and 1814.

The war had very diverse effects in different parts of the country. The worst hit were the two border regions at opposite ends of Spain: Cataluña and Extremadura. The former experienced a net loss of over seventy-five thousand of its pre-war population; the latter, which had already suffered sharply pre-war, close on sixty thousand (representing declines of 8.6 percent and 14.1 percent of their respective regional populations). Andalucia was the next largest with a loss of just under five percent. Castilla la Vieja, on the other hand, was outstanding in its wartime recuperation of the region's heavy population losses during the 1803–1805 famine; Castilla la Nueva was not as fortunate: its minimal war increase was insufficient to offset the pre-war famine loss. Conversely, Valencia's pre-war gain was more than enough to absorb limited wartime losses; while in Galicia, the Basque country and Navarra the conflict

---

* I gratefully acknowledge Professor David Sven Reher's guidance and help on the demographic computations, especially of missing population; any errors are of course my sole responsibility.
† The customary measure of deaths alone does not do justice to the war's disruption of life. Births or their lack were equally significant. The missing population's wide range is due to projecting two plausible annual population growth rates – one moderate, the other brisk – to compare an 'expected' population with the author's actual (weighted) total. On this basis, the missing due to the war ranged from about 2.4 to 4.2 percent of the eve-of-war population. (The missing, it must be observed, include those absent through flight, imprisonment or for whatever other cause; and the figures put forward should be taken as rough estimates. For further details of the computations see Appendix 5, 'The Human Costs of War (and Peace)'.
‡ The last reliable census of 1787 forms the basis of the author's weighted population of nine major regions from 1800 to 1814.

led to considerable – though not negative – declines in growth. (In the latter two regions, where the major losses occurred during Wellington's last campaign of the war, population growth declined by over two-and-a-half times in the Basque country and two times in Navarra. Galicia was less affected: the decline was held to just 13.5 percent.) The disparities between the two war-torn border regions were equally marked. Unlike Extremadura, Cataluña had not suffered from the 1803–1805 famine and had enjoyed reasonable demographic growth of nearly four percent from 1800 to the war's start. The conflict led to an increase in mortality of some sixty percent; a small rise in the birth rate could not compensate for such a massive loss. The high number of deaths was particularly pronounced in the war's first full year (1809) and again during the famine of 1811–1812. In addition the French sieges of four major towns (Gerona, Lérida, Tortosa and Tarragona) took their toll. Lasting longer in Cataluña than any other region, the war thus not only truncated earlier population growth but turned it into a significant loss. It was not until three years after the war ended that the population reached one percent higher than in 1800.

Over the first fifteen years of the new century Extremadura was one of the most severely affected by pre-war famine and the calamities of war. Its overall population losses were equally heavy in both, though wartime deaths in fact dropped by ten percent compared to the previous period. The problem lay in the low number of births. Even here there were significant intra-regional differences. The southern Badajoz province suffered during the conflict much more heavily than Cáceres to the north. The French and especially British sieges of Badajoz played their part: deaths rose by nearly twenty percent and births dropped by just over this amount. As a result of the pre-war and wartime losses, Badajoz province ended the war with nearly half of its 1800 population missing – an outcome unheard of anywhere else.*

Over nine major regions as a whole, the six years of war concluded with a minimal gain of 1. 1 percent in population.† This was somewhat better than the half of one percent loss in the pre-war's eight years, demonstrating that pestilence and famine were harsher on the population than armed conflict; but little comfort could be derived from the fact. Without the war and its accompanying losses, the population in the worst affected regions pre-war could have been expected to recuperate slowly; and, barring any new disasters, growth in the unaffected regions would have continued.

On the financial cost of the conflict things were little better. The central patriot treasury received 1,500 million reales during the war – six hundred from South America (though these were rapidly reduced from 1811 and the colonies' independence struggle); but this figure had little meaning overall since each regional junta's treasury kept the tax money it collected to finance its own army. Cataluña alone spent five hundred million on its military effort. Apart

---

* Badajoz province pre-war also suffered greater losses than Cáceres. But as the sample in each case was small the figures should be taken with caution.
† The apparent paradox was explicable by the fact that the more populous regions – Castilla la Vieja and Galicia especially – experienced population growth during the war while the smaller regions like Cataluña and Extremadura were the hardest hit.

from the money raised in taxes or received from the colonies, the real matter concerned the supplies the villagers provided, had requisitioned or exacted. When receipts were given it was very rare that these were ever paid. (Even British army receipts meant going to Lisbon and waiting weeks to receive the money. Hence a flourishing market in British debt developed, enriching those who had the money to pay villagers in deeply discounted cash on the nail). In fact, the national (patriotic) debt rose by some six hundred thousand million reales during the war which, with a couple of hundred thousand millions more, was cavalierly struck off the national debt by the government in power in 1834.[18] A large part of this money was owed to the rural population for supplies to the patriot armies.

These figures do not, of course, take into account the Bonapartists' tax income and expenditure on the war which, since it was nominally in control of the greater part of Spain from 1810 on, was certainly no less than that of the patriot government. There can be no doubt that in the main this was also extorted from villagers.*

*

Internationally the Spanish people's sacrifices in the war counted for little. The great powers – Austria, Prussia and Russia – considered themselves solely entitled, with Britain which had to no little extent financed their war effort, to determine the continent's post-Napoleonic fate. To the continental allies, it was their decisive military victories in central Europe and later France itself which had led to victory; in comparison Spain's participation – indeed the Peninsular War itself – was a sideshow, important no doubt in keeping the struggle alive but never capable alone of defeating Napoleon. In general, their view was hard to fault: Germany was the strategic military theatre, for it was there, and there alone, that Russia, Austria and Prussia could assemble their armies in force and threaten France. But their argument overlooked one significant fact. Had Napoleon been able to marshal the two hundred thousand troops still tied down in Spain, the continental allies might have found victory more difficult. A pacified Spain would also have provided Wellington with less propitious terrain from which to fight his way, finally, into southern France. As was observed earlier, the patriots were less concerned with Napoleon's overthrow than with throwing his brother off the Spanish throne and freeing their country from French military occupation. This awareness, as also that of the duplicitous role played by the 'desired' Fernando VII in captivity, and his signature to an anti-British pact to secure his return to Spain, doubtless influenced the allies' marginalization of the country from their political negotiations on a post-Napoleonic settlement. But even more important was the certainty that Spain had been bankrupted by the struggle and that the colonial independence movement would further ruin the country. For over two centuries Spain had

* As late as the mid-nineteenth century, villages were still trying to collect from the government monies owed for supplies provided to the patriot armies. (See Rosa Ros Massana, 'La formación d'un enclau industrial. La indústria tèxtil llanera de Béjar (1680–1850)' doctoral thesis, vol. 2, chap. 6, 1996.)

declined to a second-rate European power; in the past century, under the Bourbons, its international standing had depended almost exclusively on its ally France.

Although Spain had interests in Italy – the kingdoms of the Two Sicilies (Naples and Sicily) and Etruria (created by Napoleon and originally ceded to the son-in-law of the Spanish queen) – the allies and Britain paid no heed to these in their negotiations on the future of Europe. While Spain was officially represented at the Congress of Vienna, the Spanish delegate was excluded from the allies' inner councils.

After six continuous years of resisting the French occupation – longer than any of the allies experienced and often alone despite the alliance with Britain – Spain's international treatment was shameful. Reasons of state outweighed all recognition of the sacrifices the Spanish people had made in holding down great numbers of imperial troops which otherwise could have been unleashed to advance Napoleon's hegemonic designs.

*

Spain was ruined. Villages, land and livestock devastated. In Móstoles, scene of the proclamation on the May 2 rising in Madrid, of the sixty well-to-do farmers who had worked their lands pre-war, not a single one remained in 1815. The medium-sized farmers had been reduced to one-sixth of those in 1808. There had been no beggars on the outbreak of war; now there were 141.[19] There were scores of such townships and villages which suffered as greatly.

As late as 1817, for example, five years after the war effectively ended in Andalucía with the French withdrawal in 1812, Puerto Real, which had been in the imperial front line during the two-year siege of Cádiz, was still missing over half of its six thousand pre-war population. Over forty percent of its buildings and warehouses had been destroyed. Less than half of its former land was being cultivated, and only one-quarter of its olive trees were still standing. Six out of every seven of its large extent of pines had been cut down. The local authorities estimated that the total capital destruction amounted to over sixty million reales, and that its tax revenues had been reduced to one-third of their pre-war level.[20]

Whether in the 'front line' or not, many towns never recovered their earlier eminence. Alcalá de Henares, Cervantes' birthplace, a university town north-east of Madrid, had benefited greatly from the pre-war establishment of a royal textile factory in Guadalajara. This was abandoned during the war and Alcalá's inhabitants – especially women spinners who had worked at home – were left without other means than to eke out a living from agriculture. The township which in 1768 had a population of four thousand householders was reduced to twelve hundred in 1836.[21] Alcorcón, another town close to Madrid, which had begun pre-war to develop a glass manufacture, was ravaged by the war: three times as large before the conflict as it was after its end, the place never recovered.[22] Talavera which had enjoyed economic growth pre-war due to the establishment of a royal silk factory declined in population and importance from the time of the battle there.[23] Béjar, a town known for its woollens south of

Salamanca, never saw a major battle, yet it was an important communications centre. In 1809 alone, it was estimated that the town and the surrounding district paid 1,215,000 reales in woollens, supplies, contributions and impositions, nearly ten times its annual pre-war taxes. Apart from this, it was sacked by the French.[24] Though its woollens managed to survive the war, much of the pre-war artisanal production in other rural townships was either lost for good or suffered a serious economic setback and erosion of capital. In an impoverished country there was no market for goods. Antonio Iñigo, whose annual pre-war profit had been put at one thousand reales, was one of the many small manufacturers in Palencia, Castilla la Vieja, known for its production of woollen blankets. As he recorded:

> In more prosperous times I had a small woollens factory . . . today because of the great burden of billeting [French soldiers], the dearness of food and other causes which are well known, I am left without any capital. I have had to find work labouring in my brother's factory, with a day wage that is hardly enough to buy the bread needed [to keep my family alive].[25]

He was lucky to find work with his brother as a day labourer; great numbers of workers of both sexes were laid off and reduced to beggars during the war. It took two decades for the town to overcome the wartime crisis.[26]

On the land, livestock losses overall were incalculable. In Gerona, where in 1790 it was reported that most farmers had amongst their considerable farm animals a small flock of sheep whose lambs were so prized that that they were exported to Madrid and Valencia, in 1815 all that were left were thirty-five lambs, eighteen sheep, eight oxen, four cows, twelve goats and twenty pigs.[27]

On top of this a great number of villages had to sell part of their commons in order to pay taxes and imposts exacted by the French or Spanish armies, thus losing a source of income which pre-war had served to pay taxes and further impoverishing the already poor labourers and small tenants for whom these lands had often offered the only material life-saving expedient.

The post-war brought little or no relief: the depression which affected Europe at the end of the Napoleonic wars saw a large drop in agricultural prices which even further impoverished the already destitute Spanish villager.

*

It was the greatest irony of the war – a conflict replete with ironies – that at an enormous cost of lives and destruction and the almost certain loss of its colonies, patriot Spain had in the end fought to restore an absolutist monarchy. The people had risen to defend king, religion and fatherland; the liberals' attempt to create a parliamentary monarchy out of the conflict had not counted on the lower classes' necessary support, offering them little but the panacea of a market economy which would further destroy their traditional 'moral economy'. However resounding their great leap forward, the liberals abstractly believed that their constitution's fine words were sufficient: it was enough to have approved and incarnated them in print for their political reality to prevail.

This piece of political ingenuousness, which would be repeated more than once in Spain's subsequent history, led to the liberals' easy dismemberment – and repression – by military force at the behest of the most malign sovereign in modern times to occupy the Spanish throne. The war's final result was to set back the country economically, politically and demographically by at least three decades if not more.

Had the struggle been worth such an outcome? The response can be safely left to Goya. In an engraving of which there is evidence that the artist finally planned it as the last of the *Disasters of War*, a male corpse is seen half rising from a coffin. In his hands are a sheet of paper on which, as though inscribed by the dead man, is a single word. *Nada* – Nothing. The original caption repeats the word and adds: 'That is the Case.'

Epilogue

The political divide, which the war had visibly exposed, was demonstrated by the subsequent fate of a number of its participants. Those opposed to the absolutist restoration suffered harsh repression: imprisonment and exile at the least, execution at the worst.

Two well-known guerrilla leaders, El Empecinado and Juan Díaz Porlier, were hanged by Fernando VII for supporting the liberal cause. In Porlier's case for staging a military rising, in 1815 in La Coruña, to overthrow the regime; in El Empecinado's for fighting against it during the liberal revolution of 1820–1823. The fate meted out to the latter was particularly outrageous: captured, he was kept in a village cage, suffering absolutists' and rural illiterates' insults for eighteen months, before he was finally hanged.

A third renowned guerrilla chief, Francisco Espoz y Mina, was somewhat more fortunate: he escaped death but not failure in the struggle against absolutism. Immediately at war's end he rose against the reinstalled Old Order but, significantly, the majority of his Navarrese guerrilla officers refused to follow him, and Mina fled to his former enemy's nation, France. It was one thing to fight the French occupation; another for Mina's men (as it was for the military sergeants who betrayed Porlier) to disavow the divinely ordained throne for which they had fought.

Matías Calvo, the Aragonese cavalry sergeant in Mina's division, exemplified some of the guerrilleros' political and (this being Spain) regional problematic. At the end of the war, he and the bulk of the Aragonese rejected Mina's liberalism, and the wartime depreciation they felt they had suffered at the hands of the Navarrese; they deserted the division and put themselves at the command of the royalist, José Palafox, 'hero' of the Zaragoza defence, whom Fernando VII had appointed captain general of Aragón.

Lorenzo Calbo Rozas, the Suprema's enterprising merchant deputy, remained true to his political ideals; in the 1820–1823 revolution, which reinstated the 1812 constitution, he became a liberal deputy in the Cortes; Manuel Quintana, poet-founder of the *Semanario Patriótico* and author of most of the Suprema's proclamations, was released by the liberal revolution after six years of absolutist imprisonment and presided over the new government's Board of Public Education; while Bartolomé J. Gallardo, polemicist, Cortes librarian and bibliophile, who was condemned to death by Fernando's regime, managed to escape to England. (Over one thousand Spanish exile families were said to be living in London alone.) He returned to Spain to participate in the liberal revolution, was imprisoned after it and later condemned to internal exile; but his subsequent renown rested more on his uncompromising devotion to literary studies than on his politics. The (posthumous) publication of his bibliographical work on rare and curious Spanish books was a landmark in Spanish literary and cultural historiography.

After the allied victory at the battle of Vitoria (1813) some twelve thousand afrancesado families sought exile in France. Among them was Francisco Amorós, the former Bonapartist royal commissioner (whose set-to with the French General Thiébault was described in an earlier chapter). Unlike most of those who had formed part of the Bonapartist administration, he remained unrepentant. He, too, became well-known; his work in France on developing physical education as part of the state school's curriculum, a labour he had begun in pre-war Spain under Godoy, was widely adopted in his country of exile.

Under French pressure – Louis XVIII was politically wary of their presence in France – the afrancesados were amnestied by the liberal Spanish revolution. Those who returned had shortly to resume their exile when, at the Holy Alliance's behest, Louis invaded Spain to restore Fernando to his 'rightful' throne in place of the constitutional monarchy which, as a result of the revolution, he had been forced to accept.

Some of the leading patriot protagonists on both sides of the divide died before the end of the war. Among them, most notably, were Floridablanca, the Suprema's first president, as early as 1809; Gaspar Melchor Jovellanos who, in the sorry aftermath of the Suprema's demise, died in his native Asturias in 1811. In the same year, General Romana, who had hastened with his army in 1810 to Wellington's defence at the Torres Vedras lines before Lisbon, died in Portugal (of syphilis, it was said). In his obituary, Wellington accorded him the greatest honours of any Spanish general in the war.

As might be expected, the three major protagonists of these events – Manuel Godoy, Fernando VII and Josef Bonaparte – experienced differing fates. Refused permission by Fernando to return to Spain, Godoy lived for most of his remaining life in impoverished exile in Paris, his previous reputation as a 'despot' much relativized by liberals who had experienced the absolutist restoration.

With the brief exception of the liberal triennium, Fernando ruled as absolute king until his death in 1833, when he left the succession to his new-born daughter, Isabel; thereupon, his younger brother Carlos, who had shared Fernando's wartime reclusion in France, claimed the throne in the name of an apostolic Catholic absolutism and, backed by villagers in the north, where the guerrilla had found its greatest popular base, instigated the first Carlist civil war against the liberals on whose support Fernando's widowed queen regent,

María Cristina, had to rely. Though the Carlists went down to defeat in the five-year conflict, the anti-liberal cause refused to die with them; a century later, the military rising against the liberal second republic and the ensuing Spanish civil war (1936–1939), the gravest of all, demonstrated that absolutism in a modern authoritarian–clerical form remained alive in the sinews of Spanish society.

In the post-Napoleonic era, Josef Bonaparte chose a more peaceable course: he crossed the Atlantic to exile in the US – an option Napoleon rejected – to settle in New Jersey where, under the title of Count Survilliers, he lived for many years farming a couple of hundred acres in character with what he really was: a philanthropic country gentleman. Popular, it appears, amiable and cultured as always, he won his neighbours' affection; his success with women, which Napoleon had envied, had not abated: one of his female admirers, a young Quaker, bore him a child and, concerned for their future, Josef secured her a French refugee husband. Later, after a time in England, he retired to Tuscany where in 1844, at the age of seventy-six, he died in the company of his first (and only) French wife. Of Josef it could be said that he was one of the truly honourable (although ineffectual) protagonists of this long, often savage and, for both sides ultimately, cursed war.

Appendix 1

May 2, 1808, Rising, Madrid: Identified Combatants by Occupation/Gender, Casualties and French Executions

Juan Pérez de Guzmán's 1908 roll of dead and wounded has remained for a century (as it remains in this work) the basis of statistical calculations concerning the rising.[1] But the roll is unsatisfactory in more ways than one: it neither differentiates combatants from non-combatants, nor does it segregate the combatants killed or fatally wounded during the events from those executed during or after them. The second defect, recognized by Guzmán himself, is that the roll of 171 wounded – a ratio of one wounded to nearly 2.5 dead – clearly under-represents the numbers of the former.[2]

I have endeavoured in Table 1 to make good some of these deficiencies. I have excluded from Guzmán's roll a total of 92 non-combatant dead and wounded; wherever there was any doubt about their status, I included them as combatants. (I also deducted one apparent duplication among the wounded).[3]

At the same time, I have added to Guzmán's roll: 44 unwounded combatants, culled from witnesses to the actions of the dead and wounded in the official postwar submissions;[4] or to the mention of other uninjured combatants in these applications. Also added are 24 military who escaped unwounded from the artillery park. Another 54 unwounded combatants were prisoners from the city gaol, whose overall numbers I have increased by one to take account of a prisoner who escaped from another Madrid prison and was killed. I have also added three wounded combatants who are missing from Guzmán's list and, among the executed combatants, six hospital workers and three masons building the new Santiago church, none of whom Guzmán lists separately. I have also included as combatants the six excisemen who were executed since it must be assumed that they put up resistance before being captured; as well as two combatants subsequently executed in Leganés. Among the non-combatants executed, I have added two women, as Note 8 to Table 1 explains. In all 145 individuals.

TABLE 1

OCCUPATION/ GENDER	Combatants recorded: number & % of total (617)	Killed/fatally wounded & % of total (252)	Wounded & % of total (158)	Number % of all combatant casualties (410)	Uninjured & % of total (122)	Combatants executed & % of total (85)	Non-combatants executed (17)	Number of combatants & non-combatants executed & % of total (102)	Combatants as % of Madrid occupational strata
ARTISANS	91 (14.7)	36 (14.3)	19 (12.0)	55 (13.4)	10 (8.2)	26 (30.6)	2	28 (27.4)	0.6
SERVICES[5]	94 (15.2)	34 (13.5)	30 (19.0)	64 (15.6)	11 (9.0)	19 (22.3)	5	24 (23.5)	0.5
LABOURERS[6]	17 (2.8)	8 (3.2)	7 (4.4)	15 (3.6)	1 (0.8)	1 (1.2)	0	1 (1.0)	0.3
AGRARIAN[6]	7 (1.1)	5 (2.0)	2 (1.3)	7 (1.7)	–	–	1	1 (1.0)	0.2
WOMEN[7]	37 (6.0)	19 (7.5)	18 (11.4)	37 (9.0)	–	–	2[8]	2 (2.0)	–
LIBERAL PROFESSIONS	26 (4.2)	9 (3.5)	8 (5.0)	17 (4.1)	5 (4.1)	4 (4.7)	2	6 (5.8)	0.9
GENTLEMEN[9]	27 (4.4)	15 (6.0)	11 (7.0)	26 (6.3)	–	1 (1.2)	1	2 (2.0)	–
LADIES[10]	8 (1.3)	6 (2.4)	2 (1.3)	8 (2.0)	–	–	–	–	–
ADMINISTRATIVES	12 (2.0)	4 (1.6)	3 (2.0)	7 (1.7)	1 (0.8)	4 (4.7)	–	4 (4.0)	–
ROYAL PERSONNEL	22 (3.6)	9 (3.6)	2 (1.3)	11 (2.7)	2 (1.6)	9 (10.6)	1	10 (9.8)	–
EXCISE & TAX OFICIALS[11]	11 (1.8)	2 (0.8)	–	2 (0.5)	3 (2.5)	6 (7.0)	–	6 (5.8)	–
CLERGY	5 (0.8)	0	4 (2.5)	4 (1.0)	–	1 (1.2)	–	1 (1.0)	0.3
MILITARY	87 (14.1)	36 (14.3)	26 (16.4)	62 (15.1)	24[12] (19.6)	1 (1.2)	–	1 (1.0)	2.1[13]
VILLAGERS[14]	18 (3.0)	8 (3.1)	4 (2.5)	12 (2.9)	3 (2.5)	3 (3.5)	3	6 (5.8)	–
ADOLESCENTS	5 (0.8)	2 (0.8)	1 (0.6)	3 (0.7)	2 (1.6)	–	–	–	–
PRISONERS	57 (9.2)	2 (0.8)	1 (0.6)	3 (0.7)	54 (44.3)	–	–	–	–
BEGGARS	2 (0.3)	2 (0.8)	–	2 (0.5)	–	–	–	–	0.2
VARIOUS – UNSPECIFIED	91 (14.7)	55 (21.8)	20 (12.7)	75 (18.3)	6 (5.0)	10 (11.8)	–	10 (9.8)	–
TOTALS	617 (100)	252 (100)	158 (100)	410 (99.9)	122 (100)	85 (100)	17	102 (99.9)	–

Sources: Author, compilation of aggregates; AV, Legajos 2–326 to 2–329; Pérez de Guzmán, Madrid, 1908, 'Catálago Alfabético-Biográfico'; Jesusmaría Alia y Plana, 'El primer lunes de mayo de 1808 en Madrid' in Museo del Ejército, Madrid, 1992, pp. 105–138; Col Nicolas Horta Rodríguez, 'Represión en Madrid, mayo de 1808', Revista Historia Militar, No 38, 1975. pp. 49–75; Aniceto Ramos Charco-Villaseñor, 'El dos de mayo de 1808 Aclaraciones' in Revista Historia Militar, No. 2, 1958, p. 81, fn. 40.

From these re-calculated figures it will be observed that the ratio of wounded to killed has risen to 1:1.6. Despite the increase, this still remains an unsatisfactory basis on which to estimate an overall combatant figure; a proportion of three or four wounded for each person killed in street fighting would appear a more likely minimum; the average of this proportion, 3.5, seems reasonable in the circumstances.[15] The same factor should be applied also to the numbers of unwounded combatants.

However, the executed are similarly understated: it is known from parish records that 43 individuals were buried after being executed on the Montaña del Príncipe Pío but only 24 of these are recorded in Guzmán's roll; and there are grounds for believing that sixteen more unrecorded individuals were executed in the Prado. A factor of 1.5 applied to the executed would account for these extra numbers. Rounding up all figures to indicate that there is no pretension of providing exact numbers, the following provides an approximate combatant estimate:

Killed/fatally wounded:	250
Wounded: 3.5 × 160:	560
Executed: 1.5 × 85:	125
Non-wounded 3.5 × 120:	420
Total:	1,355

This hypothetical aggregate represented 0.8% of Madrid's 176,374 inhabitants, according to the Godoy census, which without doubt underestimated the population. (Most historians put the figure at or around 200,000.) It also lends credibility to Colonel Aniceto Ramos Charco-Villaseñor's estimate that 1,000 people must have taken part in the defence of the artillery park, if not in the park itself (where Guzman's figure of 100 defenders is patently wrong since nearly 250 men, defending the rear of the park, were at their posts when the French took the place), then in the surrounding streets in order to have held off the French attacks for even three hours.[16]

The number of total combatants identified represents about 45% of the estimated total.

VILLAGERS

The general assertion that great numbers of villagers had stayed over in Madrid from the day before, a Sunday, and participated in the rising or came in specifically to fight remains an open question. The identified number is small, 18 in all. (Only one group of villagers – from Fuencarral, just to the north of the capital – and led by a local priest, is known to have come specifically to Madrid to fight: the priest's enthusiasm was such that he brought his group to the capital on Sunday; but their numbers are not recorded and only the priest figures in table 1 under 'clergy'.)

In determining the status of villager, it is highly important to distinguish in the casualty listings between the word 'householder in . . .' or 'resident of . . .'

('vecino de' in Spanish) from the word 'place of origin' or 'native of' ('natural de'). A large proportion of the Madrid population had migrated from their places of origin to live and work in the capital: though 'natives' of other places, they had become Madrileños and were included in population figures as such. Equally, those 'natives' of villages near to the capital cannot be taken as non-Madrileño villagers who participated in the rising (as some over-eager researchers have done) simply because of the proximity to Madrid of their places of origin when, as far as is known, these 'villagers' lived in the capital.

A further source of confusion has lain in following Guzmán in not distinguishing between combatants and non-combatants: a number of muleteers who arrived at the city gates from nearby villages during the fighting have been identified as participants in the rising, especially as many of them met a tragic fate: seized by the French troops and searched, they were executed if carrying even a sack-sewing needle. But these victims of the rising (who are included in Table 1 as Non-Combatants Executed) did not have time to participate in the insurrection, even had they intended to.

In light of the small number of identified village combatants, two assumptions are possible. That – like the Madrid prisoners – villagers suffered a very low casualty rate and they therefore returned home unrecorded in casualty rolls; or that they rest unidentified among the 91 combatants of unspecified occupations and places of origin. On the unlikely assumption that the latter were all villagers, their participation – taken together with identified villagers – would reach some 18% of all recorded combatants, the highest single proportion of any group.

One piece of evidence does suggest that many of these unspecified combatants may have been villagers: only four of them were killed in the artillery park, while the majority died in the poor southwestern neighbourhoods which would have been more familiar to them than the park which had only opened the previous year.

Of the identified village combatants it is noteworthy that four came from Leganés under the lordship of marqués de Astorga, and two from places under the duque del Infantado's lordship – Manzares el Real and Miraflores de la Sierra; both nobles were leading Fernandistas. A further five combatants came from five other lordships around Madrid.[17]

NOTES

1. Pérez de Guzmán y Gallo, Juan, 1908: *El dos de mayo de 1808 en Madrid. Relación histórica documentada*, especially the 'Catálago Alfabético-Biográfico . . .' Madrid.
2. The reason for this, he suggests, is that most of the wounded were tended by their families at home in order to avoid French reprisals and therefore went unreported. To which it can be added that anyone in a position to do so avoided going to hospital where the chances of dying of a contracted disease unrelated to the original cause of admission were higher than those of remaining at home. In fact the majority of the rising's recorded deaths were of wounded individuals who subsequently died in hospital.
3. The criteria for excluding casualties as 'non-combatants' were: spectators wounded and killed in their own houses; those obviously going about their daily business in

the streets; those carrying out humanitarian tasks attending or giving extreme unction to the dying; those wounded or killed outside the city limits or as they entered the city gates; and adolescents unless it is specifically stated that they fought. Included as combatants are those killed or wounded outside the Palace in the first French cannonade; and all casualties in the streets whose personal files leave some doubt as to whether or not they fought.

4. Sworn witnesses to those making official applications in the immediate postwar period for the May 2 medal instituted for casualties of the rising.

5. Servants, inn porters, waiters and cooks, hospital attendants and male nurses, water-carriers, street porters, muleteers, carters and coachmen, small traders, and shop attendants, etc.

6. Madrid inhabitants engaged in agrarian, livestock or agrarian transformational occupations, such as charcoal burners.

7. Since the documents barely ever referred to their jobs I have relied almost exclusively on the humble neighbourhoods where these women lived to include them among the plebeian ranks.

8. The artillery park 'heroine' Manuela Malasaña and the non-combatant widow of an executed non-combatant who was herself subsequently executed in Alcalá de Henares.

9. 'Dons' of no known profession.

10. 'Doñas' of no known profession.

11. Resguardo del Estado y Rentas Reales.

12. Artillery and infantry officers and men known to have defended the artillery park.

13. Based on a garrison of 3,000 men.

14. Only those listed as householders ('vecinos') of villages outside Madrid are included. Excluded are individuals from Royal Palaces and estates outside of Madrid already accounted for under Royal Personnel, as well as one priest (Fuencarral), one surgeon (Valdemoro), one Revenue man (Vallecas), and an Army doctor (Chinchón) who have similarly been accounted for under their respective occupational headings.

15. In later set battles like those of Talavera (1809) and Vitoria (1813) the French killed to wounded ratio ran from 1: 6 to 1:8; but as many of those wounded in the streets of Madrid subsequently died, I have chosen a more conservative proportion.

16. Ramos Charco-Villaseñor, 'El dos de mayo de 1808, Aclaraciones' in *Revista Historia Militar*, No. 2, 1958, p. 81, fn. 40. Perez de Guzmán's categoric assertion that 4,000 forest guards in civilian clothes took part in the insurrection has been authoritatively disproven by Alia y Plana who demonstrates that this force numbered under 100 men in all, and states that there is no documentary proof to show that even this small number participated in the rising. Alia y Plana, *Museo del Ejercito*, Madrid, 1992, p. 122.

17. See *Relación de las Ciudades, Villas, Lugares, Aldeas, Granjas, Cotos redondos, Cortijos y Despoblados de España y sus Islas Adyacentes, 1801*, accompanying the *Censo de la población de España de el año 1797*, facsimile edition, Madrid, 1992.

Appendix 2

TABLE 2.1 Socio-occupational positions of 29 initial juntas' members, by region*

REGIONS	Local royal authorities: Number & % of total	Municipal authorities: Number & % of total	Military officers: Number & % of total	Clergy: Number & % of total	Administratives: Number & % of total	Co-opted elites: Number & % of total	Merchants: Number & % of total	Guild & other labouring classes: Number & % of total
SPAIN: 29 juntas, 585 members	86 (14.7)	140 (23.9)	107 (18.3)	138 (23.6)	21 (3.6)	61 (10.4)	13 2.2)	19 (3.2)
ANDALUCÍA: 7 juntas, 117 members	18 (15.4)	31 (26.5)	13 (11.1)	36 (30.8)	6 5.1)	10 (8.5)	3 (2.6)	0
ARAGÓN: 4 juntas, 52 members	4 (7.7)	15 (28.8)	3 (5.8)	22 (42.3)	2 (3.8)	4 (7.7)	1 (1.9)	1 (1.9)
ASTURIAS: 1 junta, 42 members	5 (11.9)	36 (85.7)	0	0	0	1 (2.4)	0	0
CASTILLA LA VIEJA: 4 juntas, 77 members	8 (10.4)	16 (20.8)	11 (14.3)	18 (23.4)	4 (5.2)	20 (25.9)	0	0
CATALUÑA: 4 juntas, 61 members	6 (9.8)	4 (6.6)	17 (27.9)	12 (19.7)	1 (1.6)	7 (11.5)	2 (3.3)	12 (19.7)
EXTREMADURA: 1 junta, 22 members	3 (13.6)	2 (9.1)	14 (63.6)	3 (13.6)	0	0	0	0
GALICIA: 3 juntas, 56 members	17 (30.4)	8 (14.3)	11 (19.6)	12 (21.4)	0	6 (10.7)	2 (3.6)	0
MALLORCA: 1 junta, 34 members	7 (20.6)	6 (17.6)	12 (35.3)	7 (20.6)	0	2 (5.9)	0	0
MURCIA: 2 juntas, 41 members	2 (4.9)	8 (19.5)	20 (48.8)	6 (14.6)	1 (2.4)	4 (9.8)	0	0
VALENCIA: 2 juntas, 83 members	16 (19.3)	14 (16.9)	6 (7.2)	22 (26.5)	7 (8.4)	7 (8.4)	5 (6.0)	6 (7.2)

Sources: I wish to thank Richard Hocquellet for his kindness in making available to me his doctoral thesis from which 20 of the 29 local juntas' figures have been calculated for the regional totals. (Hocquellet, 1999, vol 1, tables 2, 3, 4, 5, 6, pp. 98–99, 101–102, 105, 107–108, 111–112, 115.) I have added a further 9 juntas whose sources are given in parentheses in the following list of local juntas represented in the regional totals.
ANDALUCÍA: Sevilla, Córdoba, Granada, Cádiz, Almería, Málaga and Jaén. ARAGÓN: Zaragoza, Teruel (Gascón, 1908, p. 36), Huesca (Guirao & Sorando, 1995, p. 30), Albarracín, (Caruana Gómez de Barreda, 1959, p. 100). ASTURIAS: Oviedo. CASTILLA LA VIEJA: León, Zamora, Salamanca & Soria. CATALUÑA: Gerona, Vich (Ramisa i Verdaguer, 1993, p. 17), Tarragona (Moliner i Prada, 1989, p. 24), Barcelona Junta 'in exile' formed in Granollers, June 11, 1808 (Moliner i Prada, 1989, p. 22). EXTREMADURA: Badajoz. GALICIA: La Coruña, Vivero, (Donapétry Iribarnégaray, n.d/1991, p. 264), Tuy, (AHN, *Estado,* Legajo 75F/364). MALLORCA: Palma. MURCIA: Murcia, Cartagena (Egea Bruno, 1991, p. 1). VALENCIA: Valencia and Alicante.

*Excluding Castilla la Nueva for which full data is lacking.

As was observed earlier (see chapter 5), the titled nobility regained in the juntas a certain part of its former political power; and, despite what might have been expected, the Church's most anti-French sector, the religious orders in general, secured only a relatively small proportion of the clerical seats. As Table 2.2 demonstrates, of the co-opted elites who represented about one in ten of the total juntas' membership, nearly one-third were titled nobles. While clerics overall filled one in four of the juntas' places, the regular clergy formed only one quarter of the clerics' total.

TABLE 2.2   Titled nobility and regular clergy: junta membership, by regions

REGIONS	*Titled nobility:* Number & % of each region's members	*Regular Clergy:* Number & % of each region's members
ANDALUCÍA: 7 juntas, 117 members	6 (5.1)	5 (4.3)
ARAGÓN: 4 juntas, 52 members	1 (1.9)	9 (17.3)
ASTURIAS: 1 junta, 42 members	0	0
CASTILLA LA VIEJA: 4 juntas, 77 members	4 (5.2)	3 (3.9)
CATALUÑA: 4 juntas, 61 members	0	3 (4.9)
EXTREMADURA: 1 junta, 22 members	0	0
GALICIA: 3 juntas, 56 members	0	5 (8.9)
MALLORCA: 1 junta, 34 members	0	2 (5.9)
MURCIA: 2 juntas, 41 members	3 (7.3)	2 (4.9)
VALENCIA: 2 juntas, 83 members	5 (6.0)	5 (6.0)
REGIONAL JUNTAS: (585 members) total	19 (3.2)	34 (5.8)

Sources: ibidem.

Popular Social Change and Stasis

An increase in literacy (if the capability of signing the 1808 military enrolment is considered sufficient evidence) and a decline in illegitimacy were the most significant of the immediate changes, especially among the youngest age group, the sixteen to twenty-year-olds. The enlistments of Morón de la Frontera, southwestern 'Andalucía, and Igualada in Cataluña, provided evidence of comparative regional literacy. There was one proviso, however. In Morón there was good reason to believe that in general only volunteers from outside the township were required to sign and thus this category alone (of a total of 335 volunteers and 48 signatories) is included. As all the Igualada contingent were volunteers, the comparison stands.

TABLE 3.1 LITERACY OF VOLUNTEERS BY AGE GROUPS

	No. of volunteer signers & % of total volunteers	No. & % of total volunteer signers by age groups: 16–20	21–25	26–35	36–45	46–55
Morón district*	48 (14.3)	23 (47.9)	18 (37.5)	5 (10.4)	2 (4.2)	– –
Igualada	104 (20.4)	51 (49.0)†	22 (21.2)	23 (22.1)	5 (4.8)	2 (1.9)

Sources: AM, Morón de la Frontera, Legajo 659, *Enlistment roll, 1808*; AHM, Igualada, *Lista de afiliación de voluntarios, 1808;* Author/db: Morón & Igualada enlistments

It was noteworthy that in the 16–25 Andalucian age group literacy exceeded the Catalan equivalent by over 15%, probably demonstrating the effect of Godoy's rural school reform. But this was offset in Cataluña by the greater age 'depth' of literacy: from 26 to 55 years Catalan literacy surpassed Andalucian by over 14%. Moreover, artisans represented 69.2% of all Igualada signers and of these 38.5% were from Barcelona which provided 20.7% of all volunteers.

* Excluding Morón township.
† This age group in Igualada included one 14 and three 15 year-olds.

ILLEGITIMACY

The enrolment lists registered the enlisted and volunteer illegitimates in a straightforward manner: 'son of another (father)'. As the total enlisted and volunteers from Morón township and Puerto Serrano were almost identical (311 & 312) and those of unknown age represented 4.2% in both places, the figures afford a useful comparison between a relatively large Andalucian rural township and a small village some thirty kms off in the deep countryside; between a largely artisan group – 70% of the enlisted of known professions and trades in Morón – and Puerto Serrano's mainly agrarian enrolment. In turn these figures could be contrasted with the Catalan artisan and agrarian percentages by age groups in Igualada.

TABLE 3.2 ILLEGITIMACY BY AGE GROUPS

| No. illegitimates enlisted & % of their age group's intake: | | | | | | Ages un-specified | No. illegiti-mates & % total intake |
16–20* (born 1788–92)	21–25	26–35	36–45	46–55	56–65		
Morón	3 (4.2)	2 (4.4)	11 (13.3)	11 (15.7)	2 (11.1)	2 (22.9)	2	33 (10.6)
Puerto Serrano	20 (11.3)	11 (16.7)	8 (18.6)	2 (18.1)	1 (16.7)	–	2	44 (14.1)
Igualada: total	21 (7.2)	12‡ (10.3)	5 (6.1)	1 (10.0)	–	–	5	44 (8.6)
Igualada: agrarian	9 (7.2)	5 (8.9)	3 (8.8)	–	–	–	–	17 (7.7)
Igualada: artisans	9 (6.5)	6 (12.5)	2 (4.6)	1 (12.5)	–	–	–	18 (7.5)
(Barcelona artisans)†	5 (8.2)	3 (21.4)	1 (3.6)	1 (20.0)	–	–	–	10 (9.2)

Sources: AM, Morón de la Frontera, Legajo 659, *Enlistment roll, 1808*; AHM, Igualada, *Lista de afiliación de voluntarios, 1808*; Author/db: Morón & Igualada enlistments
* In Igualada, 15–20
‡ Artisans who had fled Barcelona and enlisted in Igualada. These are inclued in the Igualada total figures

A steady percentage decline of illegitimacy in the last half of the eighteenth century, particularly marked in the youngest age group, suggested that a moral change, already established and less surprising among the deeply religious Catalans, was also evidently taking place in Andalucía, fostered no doubt by the Church's determined reaction to the French Revolution. With the exception of Morón itself, the Catalan rate was significantly lower than in Andalucía; while agrarian workers showed higher overall rates – though only barely so in Igualada – than township artisans. On the other hand, the 109 Barcelona artisans demonstrated that, though in general declining, promiscuity in the metropolis among this category of the labouring classes was greater than in the Catalan countryside.

RELIGIOUS OBSERVANCE

INQUISITION TRIBUNALS

To ascertain whether any other significant religious or social changes occurred between the pre- and post-war which might be attributed to the conflict itself, the Inquisition's tribunals appear a good starting point. This repressive organization with its close vigilance of the population's religious and moral state could hardly fail to record such changes. Examination of ten tribunals' records over the whole country revealed, however, few surprising differences. Of the tribunals' score of accusations seven were selected for inclusion in the following table on the basis of covering both religious and social offenses.

Some of the accusations require explanation. As was noted in Chapter 12, 'propositions' were verbal expressions of a heretical, erroneous or scandalous nature. 'Soliciting' referred to secular and regular clergy who propositioned women either in the confessional or outside in the course of their religious duty. 'Irreverence/irreligiousness' were distinct categories which the author has subsumed under one for their relative similarity. (Irreverence was the accusation of an individual's lack of respect for the Catholic Church's dogma; irreligiousness was obviously the same though carried to a further degree.) The remaining categories are self-evident.

It must be stressed that the tribunals' figures refer to charges laid against individuals by Inquisition officials and anonymous informants. The accused had not necessarily been officially charged or brought before the Inquisition's courts. The post-war accusations refer as much to individuals' wartime as to their immediate post-war conduct.

As can be seen, 'Propositions', which formed the highest pre-war proportion, more than doubled during the war and immediate post-war for reasons outlined in Chapter 13. Though the national level of 'Irreverence/irreligiousness' sextupled, suggesting that 'verbal heresy' was accompanied by a rejection of

TABLE 3.3   INQUISITION TRIBUNALS* PRE- AND POSTWAR NATIONAL FIGURES & % OF TOTAL

Categories	1803–1807	1815–1817
Propositions	115 (54.8)	243 (60.6)
Irreverence/irreligiousness	2 (0.9)	12 (3.0)
Blasphemy	11 (5.2)	11 (2.7)
Soliciting	34 (16.2)	34 (8.5)
Bigamy	21 (10.0)	25 (6.2)
Forbidden books	25 (12.0)	31 (7.7)
Freemasonry	2 (0.9)	45 (11.2)
Total	210 (100.0)	401 (99.9)

Sources: See end of Appendix

* The 10 tribunals were: Barcelona, Sevilla, Córdoba, Granada, Murcia, Madrid, Logroño, Santiago de Compostela, Toledo and Valencia.

Church dogma and the Catholic faith per se, this was deceptive. Two regions, Murcia, where 'Propositions' rose by five times in the war and post-war compared to pre-war, and Andalucía where they quadrupled in the same period, alone accounted for 9 of the 12 national accusations of 'Irreverence/irreligiousness'. As was observed in Chapter 10, Murcia experienced a particularly conflictive start to the war and Andalucía (Sevilla especially where propositions rose more than six-fold) did not lag far behind. It should not be overlooked that 'verbal heresy' was the easiest accusation to make and the hardest to disprove, and provided therefore a simple means in the post-war of attempting to settle wartime vendettas.

LENT CONCEPTIONS

A second method used to assess changes in religious observance due to the war was the number of conceptions during Lent when the Church prescribed sexual abstinence. An overall view of the minimal changes, and their exceptions, are examined in Chapter 13, therefore it is only necessary here to explain the method used to compile Table 3.4 and the inevitable shortcomings involved. As the basic data consisted of *monthly* births, Lent conceptions were taken as baptized and recorded births nine calendar months later. Gestation of between thirty-eight and forty-two weeks is (today) considered normal; nine months from the beginning of February, March and April – the period in which Lent almost always falls – average 39.7 weeks, as close as could be achieved in the circumstances to the average term of pregnancy.

The forty-six days of Lent (from Ash Wednesday to Easter Saturday inclusive) often included some days of a month at the beginning or the end of the period (most usually in February or April) during which, in the absence of daily figures, it was impossible to calculate precisely the number of conceptions. The solution adopted was to multiply the average of backdated births for the month in question by the number of days covered by Lent; to the margin of error created by this method must be added another of greater significance. The recorded births ignore abortions, stillbirths and the newborn who died in the usual forty-eight hours before baptism, and thus understate reality.

In years when there was an increase or decrease in the percentage of year-on-year population growth – expressed in the table as relative natural growth (RNG) – it could be expected that Lent conceptions would similarly rise or fall. The interest in Table 3.4 lies therefore in those years when the two did not coincide. (To help the reader identify these, the figures in the table are followed by a plus or minus sign, indicating a rise or decline of the annual percentage in relation to the previous year.)

The changes in the Lent conception rate are admittedly often so small – no more than tenths of one percent – that they may statistically be the outcome of random results, as computer tests of their validity have demonstrated. However, the occurrence of certain annual rises and falls running counter to natural growth and which can be related to wartime events, especially the restoration of absolutism in 1814, indicate that in historical terms more than randomness was at stake.

TABLE 3.4　LENT CONCEPTIONS
Pre-War

Year	Andalucía %LC*	%RNG*	Castilla la Nueva %LC	%RNG	Castilla la Vieja %LC	%RNG	Cataluña %LC	%RNG	Extremadura %LC	%RNG	Basque Country %LC	%RNG	Valencia %LC	%RNG
1800	16.17	100.00	11.08	100.00	13.15	100.00	14.76	100.00	14.85	100.00	11.27	100.00	12.23	100
1801	13.06−	98.90−	9.53−	100.05+	14.26+	100.40+	13.07−	99.90−	16.01	98.90−	14.50+	101.90+	11.17−	100.00=
1802	13.18+	98.99+	10.73+	100.05=	11.40−	100.30−	13.34+	99.80−	11.09−	98.89−	10.00−	101.77−	15.06+	100.10+
1803	14.21+	99.59+	12.32+	98.40−	11.72+	97.22−	14.26+	100.30+	14.98+	99.59−	11.66+	101.35−	12.31−	98.50−
1804	14.46+	96.82−	9.81−	95.63−	11.56−	95.71−	14.84+	101.30+	12.36−	94.76+	13.31+	100.95−	10.81−	101.52+
1805	13.67−	99.15+	10.05+	97.45+	14.36+	99.25+	11.60−	100.49−	16.69+	95.77+	12.54−	101.88+	14.28+	100.70−
1806	13.04−	99.36+	10.21+	100.11+	12.00−	100.64+	12.48+	100.88+	12.37−	98.53+	10.17−	101.29−	12.85−	100.69−
1807	16.07+	99.89+	8.65−	100.87+	12.86+	101.71+	13.07+	101.07+	16.16+	98.74+	14.65+	101.83+	15.20+	100.49−
Average	14.23	99.09	10.30	99.07	12.66	99.40	13.43	100.47	14.31	98.15	12.26	101.37	12.99	100.25

+ and − signs indicate an increase or decrease in the figure compared to the previous year
Source: Author db/Demography, monthly births by regions, 1800–1817

War

Year	Andalucía %LC	%RNG	Castilla la Nueva %LC	%RNG	Castilla la Vieja %LC	%RNG	Cataluña %LC	%RNG	Extremadura %LC	%RNG	Basque Country %LC	%RNG	Valencia %LC	%RNG
1808	13.19−	99.57−	11.77+	101.40+	12.88+	101.57−	14.37+	100.19−	20.49+	100.12+	11.82−	100.81−	13.73−	100.98+
1809	11.70−	99.24−	11.12−	98.08−	9.28−	100.00−	7.17−	92.98−	20.03−	96.63−	9.98−	100.44−	13.40−	99.80−
1810	12.65+	98.26−	13.14+	100.65+	11.04+	101.65+	13.37+	100.41+	11.52−	97.11+	15.08+	101.68+	15.97+	100.78+
1811	13.74+	100.11+	11.80−	101.51+	14.74+	101.63−	17.83+	99.79−	17.45+	98.39+	12.56−	100.78−	14.99−	101.06+
1812	14.86+	98.12−	12.55+	99.47−	14.98+	100.40−	10.55−	96.18−	12.78−	95.09−	14.22+	100.60−	12.47−	96.94−
1813	13.59−	98.76+	12.20−	99.68+	13.16−	100.00−	14.03+	100.32+	16.78+	97.88+	14.54+	99.40−	12.58+	98.62+
1814	14.34+	100.91+	9.09−	100.96+	8.95−	101.29+	12.95−	101.60+	13.87−	99.86+	9.66−	100.52+	13.01+	101.40+
Average	13.44	99.28	11.67	100.25	12.15	100.93	12.90	98.78	16.13	97.87	12.55	100.60	13.74	99.94

Postwar

Year	Andalucía %LC	%RNG	Castilla la Nueva %LC	%RNG	Castilla la Vieja %LC	%RNG	Cataluña %LC	%RNG	Extremadura %LC	%RNG	Basque Country %LC	%RNG	Valencia %LC	%RNG
1815	14.50+	100.91=	10.59+	101.80+	12.95+	102.26+	14.59+	102.31+	14.92+	101.22+	15.52+	102.41+	14.84+	100.89−
1816	14.42−	101.01−	11.02+	101.87+	11.04−	102.21−	13.41−	101.75−	14.14−	101.47+	14.20−	102.01−	16.15+	100.68−
Average	14.46	100.96	10.81	101.84	12.00	102.24	14.00	102.03	14.53	101.35	14.86	102.21	15.50	100.79

Sources of Inquisition Tribunals' figures:
AHN: *Consejo de la Suprema Inquisición*, Cartas al Consejo.
ANDALUCÍA: Sevilla, Córdoba & Granada: Legajos 2477–78, 2543, 2699, 3066, 3721–2–3, 3726–7, 3730–1
BASQUE COUNTRY: Logroño: Legajos 2248, 3722, 3731, 3592, 4490
CASTILLA LA MANCHA: Toledo: Legajos 24, 37, 39, 44, 46–7, 70–1, 78, 82–3, 86, 89, 91, 96, 99, 108, 116, 128, 200, 205, 210, 214, 217–8–9, 220–1, 227, 230, 3719, 3720, 3722–3–4, 3726, 3730
CATALUÑA: Barcelona: Legajos 2177, 3721–22, 3731
GALICIA: Santiago de Compostela: Legajos 2941, 2543, 3720, 3730
MADRID: Legajos 2194, 2542–3, 3722, 3725, 3727, 3730, 3736, 4499
MURCIA: Legajos 2879–80; 3720, 3722, 3731, 3735
VALENCIA: Legajos 1795, 3723–4, 3727, 2730, 3732

* %LC = Lent Conceptions as a percentage of annual conceptions.
* %RNG = Relative Natural Growth, the year-on-year percentage population growth or decline.

Appendix 4

Guerrillas

The author's database of 751 guerrilleros (-as) is the foundation of the following tables.* (As the original sources on which it is based are inordinately long, they are given at the end of this appendix.) The db's purpose was to construct a social profile of the guerrilleros and en route to discover as much as possible about their numbers, the regions in which – and the reasons for which – they fought. The criterion for a guerrillero's inclusion in the db was that more than one fact other than name should be established about each. (Even so, existing information was so meagre that many of the data fields yielded information on only about one-third of the db's total; consequently each of the tables states the number and percentage of those in the db about whom this data is known.)

In order to compute guerrilleros' total numbers – a particularly difficult task because a considerable number of parties have no recorded figures, and of those that do, the numbers are not always of consecutive years – a special procedure was adopted: parties were first segregated into large, medium and small; thereafter, if various figures were given for different months in one year, the last month available was taken as the yearly figure; and where data existed for one year but not the next, it was assumed that the same numbers existed as in the prior year. While in the big parties, which dominated in numbers, this was of little general import since the addition or loss of some members did not fundamentally change the overall picture, in the medium and small parties

---

* The database does not include the Catalan and Galician irregulars for reasons explained in chapter 12. Some of the data offered here varies from that published by the author in 'Identidades sociales desconocidas. Las guerrillas españolas en la Guerra de la Independencia, 1808–1814', *Historia Social*, No. 46, Valencia, 2003, and a similarly titled essay in *International Journal of Iberian Studies*, Vol 16, No. 2, Bristol, 2003, pp. 81–99. This is due to the database's subsequent re-elaboration by statistician Paloma Botella for whose meticulous work on analysing and computing the figures the author wishes to express his gratitude. The major changes consisted of eliminating 61 names, the majority Galicians, and adding 64 previously not included of the 81 who were condemned to death by the extraordinary criminal tribunals and could, without a shadow of doubt, be identified as guerrilleros.

the effect was more significant. However, as the latter's members formed by 1811–1812 only one-sixth of those of the large parties the margin of error was reduced.

TABLE 4.1   START OF GUERRILLA ACTIONS*

YEAR	Numbers	% (of 216)
1808	54	25.0
1809	42	19.4
1810	73	33.8
1811	25	11.6
1812	21	9.7
1813	1	0.5
TOTAL	216	100

Source: Author, db/Guerrillas
* The commencement year is known for only 216 (28.8%) of the 751 recorded guerrilleros

TABLE 4.2   TYPES OF GUERRILLA PARTIES

Of the total guerrillero db of 751 members, 448 (59.7%) are recorded as having fought in one of three distinct types of guerrilla: partisans (those who raised parties without official permission); privateers (those having received civilian or military permission); and 'religious crusades' (parties led by or manned principally by clerics).

Types	Numbers & % (of 448)
Partisans	366 (81.7)
Privateers	54 (12.1)
Religious cruzades	28 (6.2)

Source: ibidem

TABLE 4.3   GUERRILLA PARTY STRENGTHS IN 1811 & 1812

1811	Large (over 1,000)	Medium (250–999)	Small (to 249)	Unknown category	Totals
Number &	16	11	29	56	112
average size	2,977.5	493.5	84.9	Nd	
Total					
guerrilleros	47,640	5,429	2,462	Nd	55,531
Total Foot &	41,250	4,069	1,148	Nd	46,467
average per party	2,578.1	369.8	39.6		
Total Horse &	6,390	1,360	1,314	Nd	9,064
average per party	388.2	123.6	45.3		
% Foot	86.6	74.9	46.6	Nd	83.7
% Horse	13.4	25.1	53.4		16.3

Source: ibidem

1812	Large (over 1,000)	Medium (250–999)	Small (to 249)	Unknown category	Totals
Number &	17	5	13	25	60
average size	2,719.4	910.0	114.3	(ND)	
Total					
guerrilleros	46,229	4,550	1,486	Nd	52,265
Total Foot &	39,630	3,625	1,040	Nd	44,296
average per party	2,331.2	725.0	80		
Total Horse &	6,599	925	446	Nd	7,970
average per party	388.2	185.0	34.3		
% Foot	85.7	79.7	70	Nd	84.8
% Horse	14.3	20.3	30		15.2

Source: ibidem

TABLE 4.4   NUMBERS & REGIONS OF
PRINCIPAL OPERATIONAL BASES: 1810–1812

The operational regions are recorded for 741 guerrilleros – 98.7% of the db's total of 751. (Many fought in more than one region as can be seen in Table 4.5: Guerrilla mobility. Here only their major base is given.) The numbers of regional residents (*vecinos*) recorded are 277 –37% of the db's total. Percentages are calculated on the recorded base figures, 741 and 277 respectively.

REGION*	Number of total recorded guerriller-os (741)	% of total recorded guerrilleros	Number & % of total recorded guerrilleros resident in region (277)	Population: Regional % of Spain's total†	Area: Regional % of Spain's total‡
Andalucía	143		45		
		19.3	(16.2)	17.7	17.8
Aragón	80		38		
		10.8	(13.7)	6.0	9.7
Asturias	25		7		
		3.4	(2.5)	3.4	2.2
Basque Country	32		17		
		4.3	(6.1)	2.9	1.5
Cantabria	17		7		
		2.3	(2.5)	1.4	1.1
Castilla La Nueva	101		35		
		13.6	(12.6)	11.7	17.8
Castilla La Vieja	218		85		
		29.4	(30.7)	14.5	20.2
Extremadura	19		4		
		2.6	(1.4)	4.0	8.5
Navarra	68		29		
		9.2	(10.5)	2.1	2.1
Valencia	38		9		
		5.1	(3.2)	7.8	4.7

Source: ibidem

* The provinces included of multi-provincial regions (and this remains true for all further references in this appendix) are: ANDALUCÍA: Sevilla, Huelva, Cádiz, Almería, Córdoba, Málaga, Granada y Jaén. ARAGÓN: Huesca, Teruel y Zaragoza. BASQUE COUNTRY: Álava, Vizcaya y Guipúzcoa. CASTILLA LA NUEVA: Guadalajara,

Cuenca, Ciudad Real, Toledo, and Madrid. CASTILLA LA VIEJA: León, Palencia, Burgos, Soria, La Rioja, Segovia, Salamanca, Zamora y Valladolid. EXTREMA-DURA: Cáceres y Badajoz. VALENCIA: Valencia, Castellón y Alicante.

† Forming 75% of the population of 10.4 million as given in the Floridablanca (1787) census. For reasons explained in the text, Galicia and Cataluña, which made up 21.5% of the population, do not figure in these tables; Murcia, the Balearic and Canary islands accounted for the remainder. The regions' populations included are as follows: ANDALUCÍA: 1.849.883; ARAGÓN: 623.055; ASTURIAS: 352.851; BASQUE COUNTRY: 306.388; CANTABRIA: 149.864; CASTILLA LA NUEVA: 1.218.642; CASTILLA LA VIEJA: 1.515.139; EXTREMADURA: 417.364; NAVARRA: 224.443; VALENCIA: 810.520.

‡ Because of the difficulties involved in calculating regions' exact extent under the Old Regime, the present political map has been used. The percentages are calculated on a national area of 492.463 Km². The regions' sizes are as follows: ANDALUCÍA: 87,599 kms²; ARAGÓN: 47,720; ASTURIAS: 10,604; BASQUE COUNTRY: 7,234; CAN-TABRIA: 5,321; CASTILLA LA NUEVA: 87,489; CASTILLA LA VIEJA: 99,269; EXTREMADURA: 41,634; NAVARRA: 10,391 and VALENCIA: 23,255. These regions form 85.6% of the present national territory.

TABLE 4.5   GUERRILLA MOBILITY

As in Table 4.4, of a db total of 741 guerrilleros whose regions of operation are known.

REGION	No. of guerrilleros who fought exclusively in the region	No. of guerrilleros who also fought in other regions & their % of each region's total	Other regions where they fought
ANDALUCÍA	141	2 (1.4)	1: Extremadura; 1: Murcia
ARAGÓN	71	9 (11.2)	1: Castilla La Vieja; 5: Navarra; 1: Navarra, Valencia; 1: Navarra, Basque Country; 1: Asturias, Cantabria, Navarra
ASTURIAS	23	2 (8.0)	1: Extremadura; 1: Navarra
BASQUE COUNTRY	27	5 (15.6)	1: Aragón, Navarra; 1: Asturias, Cantabria; 1: ARAGÓN, Cantabria, Castilla La Vieja; 1: Cantabria, Castilla La Vieja, Navarra; 1: Aragón, Cantabria, Castilla La Vieja, Navarra
CANTABRIA	8	9 (52.9)	2: Asturias; 3: Castilla La Vieja; 3: Basque Country; 1: Aragón, Castilla La Vieja, Navarra
CASTILLA LA NUEVA	84	17 (16.8)	2: Andalucía; 2: Aragón; 5: Castilla La Vieja; 7: Extremadura; 1: Andalucía, Murcia

CASTILLA LA VIEJA	176	42 (35.6)	3: Aragón; 18: Castilla La Nueva; 3: Extremadura; 2: Basque Country; 1: Aragón, Navarra; 3: Aragón, Castilla La Nueva; 2: Asturias, Cantabria; 2: Cantabria, Basque Country; 2: Asturias, Cantabria, Basque Country; 5: Cantabria, Navarra, Basque Country; 1: Asturias, Cantabria, Navarra, Basque Country
EXTREMADURA	15	4 (21.1)	4: Andalucía, Castilla La Nueva
NAVARRA	38	30 (44.1)	13: Aragón; 1: Castilla La Vieja; 1: Basque Country; 2: Aragón, Castilla La Vieja; 6: Aragón, Basque Country; 4: Castilla La Vieja, Basque Country; 2: Aragón, Castilla La Vieja, Basque Country; 1: Asturias, Cantabria, Castilla La Vieja
VALENCIA	37	1 (2.6)	1: Aragón, Castilla La Nueva
TOTALS	620	121 (16.3)	

GUERRILLEROS' SOCIAL PROFILE

Of the db's total number, the occupational status of 213 (28.4%) is recorded. Of these, 157 (73.7%) came from the privileged classes, 56 (26.3%) from the labouring classes. The Old Order's practice of recording those entitled to the appellation of 'don' (i.e. the educated or those of superior social status) and ignoring the labouring poor was evidently at work. To correct this defect, the author has resorted to a 'weighted' solution. Dons who would always have been recorded are expressed as a percentage of the total guerrillero db (751); the labouring classes as a percentage of those of known occupational status (213). The resulting percentages showed the privileged making up 20.9% and the labouring classes 26.3% of the guerrilleros.

Female guerrilleros: Nine women (or 1.2% of the db total) are on record as having been active members of a party.

TABLE 4.6   GUERRILLEROS BY OCCUPATION
LABOURING CLASSES

Categories	Numbers & % (of 213)
Agrarian:	33 (15.5)
–Farmer	24 (11.3)
–Day labourer	1 (0.5)
–Shepherd	7 (3.2)
–Market gardener	1 (0.5)
Artisan*	9 (4.2)
Transport	2 (0.9)
Outlaw†	5 (2.3)
Deserter, dispersed soldier	4 (2.0)
Other	3 (1.4)
Totals	56 (26.3)

PRIVILEGED CLASSES

Categories	Numbers & % (of 751)
Authority/Functionary	19 (2.5)
Clergy	62 (8.2)
Military: on active service in 1808‡	26 (3.5)
Military: retired in 1808 without known profession	14 (1.9)
Person of private means (*rentistas*)	8 (1.1)
Professional§	10 (1.3)
Student	10 (1.3)
Trade	3 (0.4)
Other	5 (0.7)
Totals	157 (20.9)

* Of the 6 whose trades were known, there was an iron-master, a tailor, a butcher, a shoemaker and 2 barbers.
† 4 smugglers, 1 bandit.
‡ Of the 12 who were officers, 1 was a brigadier, 2 were colonels, 1 a Lt. Col., 6 captains & 2 without recorded ranks.
§ 6 lawyers, 3 doctors and 1 apothecary.

TABLE 4.7   GUERRILLA PARTY LEADERS BY OCCUPATION

The occupational status of 121 (35.9%) of 337 db leaders is recorded, of whom 96 came from the privileged and 25 from the labouring classes. A similar 'weighting' as in Table 4.6 has been adopted (as has the subsequent percentage recalculation). The labouring classes' percentage is calculated on the 121 of known occupations, the privileged classes on the total number of leaders. Computed as absolute percentages, this showed the privileged with a clear majority over the labouring classes.

LABOURING CLASSES

Categories	Numbers & % (of 121)
Agrarian:	14 (11.6)
–Farmer	11 (9.1)
–Shepherd	3 (2.5)
Artisan	3 (2.5)
Outlaw	5 (4.1)
Sailor	1 (0.8)
Transport	2 (1.7)
Totals	25 (20.7)

PRIVILEGED CLASSES

Categories	Numbers & % (of 337)
Authority/Functionary	14 (4.1)
Clergy	40 (11.9)
Merchant ship's captain	1 (0.3)
Military on active service in 1808	17 (5.0)
Military retired in 1808 without known profession	9 (2.7)
Persons of private means	5 (1.5)
Professional	6 (1.8)
Student	2 (0.6)
Trade	2 (0.6)
Totals	96 (28.5)

TABLE 4.8   GUERRILLA SUBALTERN RANKS BY OCCUPATION

Of a db total of 294 lower rank guerrillas, the trades and professions of 58 (19.7%) are recorded, 12 of the labouring and 46 from the privileged classes. The same weighting system as in the previous two tables is used here: the labouring classes are expressed as a percentage of those of known trades (58) and the privileged classes as a percentage of the total number of lower ranks (294). The percentage recalculations (see Table 4.6 for the method used) demonstrated that the labouring classes more than made up for their minority of the leadership in their command of guerrilleros in action.

LABOURING CLASSES

Categories	Number & % (of 58)
Agrarian:	10 (17.2)
–Farmer	8 (13.8)
–Day labourer	1 (1.7)
–Shepherd	1 (1.7)
Artisan	1 (1.7)
Other trades	1 (1.7)
Totals	12 (20.6)

PRIVILEGED CLASSES

Categories	Number & % (of 294)
Authority/Functionary	3 (1.0)
Clergy	18 (6.1)
Military	12 (4.1)
Persons of private means	3 (1.0)
Professional	3 (1.0)
Student	7 (2.4)
Totals	46 (15.6)

TABLE 4.9   RANK AND FILE BY OCCUPATION

121 guerrilleros are recorded in the db as of unknown rank; it is probable therefore
that they had none. However, the professions and trades of only 34 (28.1%) of these
non-rankers, the guerrilla base, in other words, were known. The same weighting
system as before is used: the labouring classes are expressed as a percentage of the
rank-and-file of recorded occupations (34), and the privileged of the total of the non-
rankers (121).

LABOURING CLASSES

Categories	Number & % (of 34)
Agrarian	9 (26.5)
–Farmer	5 (14.7)
–Market gardener	1 (2.9)
–Shepherd	3 (8.9)
Artisan	5 (14.7)
Deserter, dispersed soldier	4 (11.8)
Other	1 (2.9)
Total	19 (55.9)

PRIVILEGED CLASSES

Categories	Number and % (of 121)
Authority/Functionary	2 (1.7)
Clergy	4 (3.3)
Military	2 (1.7)
Professional	1 (0.8)
Student	1 (0.8)
Trade	1 (0.8)
Other	4 (3.3)
Total	15 (12.4)

TABLE 4.10 PARTISANS BY OCCUPATION

Partisans were those who became guerrilleros without prior civil or military permission. The 'weighting' system has again been used: the labouring classes' percentage is calculated on the 98 partisans whose occupations are known (of a db total of 366 partisans: 48.7% of the db total guerrilleros recorded); the privileged classes on the db total of 366.

LABOURING CLASSES

Categories	Number & % (of 98)
Agrarian	18 ((18.4)
–Farmer	13 (13.3)
–Day labourer	1 (1.0)
–Shepherd	4 (4.1)
Artisan	3 (3.1)
Transport	1 (1.0)
Outlaw	5 (5.1)
Other trades	2 (2.0)
Total	29 (29.6)

PRIVILEGED CLASSES

Categories	Number & % (of 366)
Authority/Functionary	8 (2.2)
Clergy	19 (5.2)
Military	21 (5.7)
Persons of private means	6 (1.6)
Professional	7 (1.9)
Student	8 (2.2)
Total	69 (18.8)

TABLE 4.11 GUERRILLEROS BY AGE GROUPS

Only 76 (10.1%) of the db's 751 guerrilleros' ages are on record. The overall average was 25.9 years. Fifty percent of guerrilleros were between 18 and 30 years old, 25% under 18 and the remaining 25% older than 30. The youngest was 10 and the oldest 60.

Age	Number of guerrilleros	Percentage of total (76)
under 16	3	3.95
16–20	30	39.47
21–25	19	25.00
26–30	5	6.58
31–35	5	6.58
36–40	6	7.89
41–45	3	3.95
46–50	2	2.63
over 50	3	3.95

GUERRILLEROS BY AGE & OCCUPATION
LABOURING CLASSES

No ages are recorded for those occupations that do not figure in this table

Categories	Number & average age
Agrarian:	20; 22.8
–Farmer	15; 23.8
–Day labourer	1; 23
–Shepherd	4; 19.2
Artisan	3; 25.2
Outlaw	2; 39.0
Total & average age	25; 24.4

PRIVILEGED CLASSES

Categories	Number & average age
Authority/Functionary	3; 35
Clergy	1; 39
Military	10; 30.7
Persons of private means	2; 43
Professional	2; 40
Student	7; 18.1
Total & average age	25; 29.7

TABLE 4.12   CIRCUMSTANCES OF JOINING THE GUERRILLA

For only 99 (12%) of the 751 db guerrilleros are former personal experiences recorded which could account for fighting in a guerrilla. Objective circumstances, the first listed in the following table, are obviously not devoid of subjective judgements; for example, a dispersed soldier might not return to the army because he disliked its rigorous discipline, hunger, uncertain pay and almost certain defeat in open battle. The second category, however, records what can be considered more subjective conditions.

OBJECTIVE CIRCUMSTANCES	Partisans	Privateers	Religious Crusades	Unrecorded category	Total number & % (of 99)
Convention War veteran	7			2	9 (9.1)
Regular army volunteer, 1808	2			1	3 (3.0)
Failure of regular Spanish armies' strategy of fighting war	5			1	6 (6.1)
Dispersed soldier	11			4	15 (15.2)
Escaped prisoner of war in enemy-occupied zone		2			2 (2.0)
Escaped from prison in 'self-defence' against French	1				1 (1.0)
Escaped not to pay French exactions	1				1 (1.0)
Taken by force by a guerrilla party	1		3		4 (4.0)
Appointed by civilian authorities	9	2	1	1	13 (13.1)
Appointed by military authorities	2	1			3 (3.0)
SUBJECTIVE CONDITIONS					
Defense of home territory	8		6		14 (14.1)
For Religion and Fatherland	1				1 (1.0)
Juvenile day dreams on hearing of guerrilla exploits	1				1 (1.0)
Personal violence by French*	18		3		21 (21.2)
Escape from hated friar's condition	1				1 (1.0)
Asked and received civilian authorities' permission to form a party	1		2		3 (3.0)
Other	1				1 (1.0)
Total	70	5	15	9	99 (99.8)

* This category should be viewed with caution; many sources produced by Spanish historians during the nineteenth century Romantic period liked to insist on personal violence as the guiding motive for joining a party when a century later contemporary historians deduced more important reasons included in the table's other categories, for instance those who had fought the French revolution in the Convention War, the dispersed soldier or those appointed by civilian and military authorities.

TABLE 4.13   GUERRILLA DEATHS NUMBER & CAUSES

The fate of 179 guerrilleros – 23.8% of the total db – was recorded.

Causes	Number of guerrilleros (179)	% (of 179)
Killed in combat or on being taken prisoner	47	26.3
Sentenced to death by extraordinary crimes Tribunal	81*	45.2
Sentenced to death by French Military commission (drumhead court martials)	9	5.0
Sentenced to death without specifying whether by extraordinary crimes tribunal or French military commission	33	18.4
Killed without stating cause	3	1.7
Assassinated by afrancesados	2	1.1
Executed by patriot authorities or by guerrilla†	4	2.2

* Of these 13 (7.3% of the total) were known to have had their sentences commuted. As emphasized in chapter 17 there was no proof in many other cases that the sentences were carried out.
† 12 parties were recorded as having been dissolved, their members taken prisoner or their leaderships changed by the authorities because of their 'bad conduct'.

TABLE 4.14   GUERRILLEROS' POST-WAR
TRAJECTORIES AND POLITICAL AFFILIATION

As the guerrilleros' political affiliations were often only clearly revealed in the post-war struggles, the following table details the trajectories of 61 (8.1% of the total guerrillero db). However, as the table necessarily includes several who participated in more than one of the political movements – for example, royalists and later Carlists – the percentages of each category are not stated. The figures show that as compared to the guerrilleros who fought against the royalist insurrection during the liberal restoration (1820–1823) of the 1812 constitution, over double the number of guerrilleros sided with the royalist cause. On so small a sample, it is hazardous to venture any general conclusions. But possibly the sample demonstrated that the guerrilleros supported the pre-war monarchy, in whose name they had risen, without any of the liberal Cádiz constitutional restrictions on the king's sovereignty. This political option did not, however, exclude the serious reforms expected from Fernando's reign. If this interpretation were correct, it probably reflected public opinion at large.

To some extent this interpretation was borne out a decade later in the first Carlist civil war which pitted a moderate liberal government against a sui generis Catholic absolutism. The numbers of those ex-guerrilleros who supported the latter and those who fought against it was almost exactly reversed in comparison to 1820–1823. Though once again the figures on which to base a judgement were very small, it might be deduced that ex-guerrilleros, like most of the country, had by then come to accept a moderate liberal monarchy in face of an absolutist option.*

Remained in army	11
Returned to civilian life	15
Returned to previous outlaw life & condemned to death in absentia	3
Imprisoned after Fernando VII's first return to power (1814–1820)	2
Exiled by Fernando VII after his first return to power (1814–1820)	1
Went into exile after Fernando VII's first return to power (1814–20)	3
Fought as royalists against the liberal restoration of 1820–23	11
Fought against royalists during liberal restoration of 1820–23	5
Executed after Fernando VII's second return to power (1823)	1†
Took part in first Carlist war (1834–39) on Carlist side	3
Took part in first Carlist war (1834–39) on liberal/governmental side	6
	61

* An extreme case of this political transition was furnished by Saturnino Abuín ('El Manco'). Having escaped from gaol in Valladolid at the beginning of the anti-French insurrection, he formed a guerrilla party which later was amalgamated with that of El Empecinado whose subordinate commander he became. During the war he betrayed his leader and went over to the Bonapartist regime which rewarded him with its highest decoration and appointed him to lead a counter-guerrilla. At the end of the war he took refuge in France, and did not return to Spain until the liberal triumph of 1820 when he formed a royalist party to combat the liberals; defeated, he again fled to France. He returned to Spain with the French expeditionary military force which, in 1823, at the behest of the 'Holy Alliance', restored Fernando VII to his 'rightful throne'. Abuín was rewarded by Fernando with an army officer's command. But during the first Carlist war he sided with the liberal government.

† El Empecinado, who was captured, imprisoned and hanged in 1825 by Fernando VII's reinstalled regime after the brief liberal parliamentary restoration of 1820–1823 on whose side he had taken up arms against the royalist insurrection.

SELECT LIST OF SOURCES CONSULTED

Archives

AGS, *Papeles del Gobierno Intruso, Gracia y Justicia*, Legajos 1076–1197, various legajos*

AHN, *Estado*, Legajos 1–84 (Papers of the Junta Suprema), various legajos*

PRO, *FO & WO series*, Spain, Peninsular War, various reports*

Books and articles

Alexander, Don W., 1984: **Rod of Iron; French Counterinsurgency Policy in Aragón during the Peninsular War**, Wilmington

Anon., (attributed to Francisco Gallardo y Merino), 1886/1989: **Noticia de casos particulares ocurridos en la ciudad de Valladolid, año de 1808 y siguientes** (ed. Juan Ortega y Rubio), 1886, in **Valladolid, Diarios Curiosos (1807–1841)**; [facsimile edition, 1989] Valladolid

Ardit, Manuel, 1977: **Revolución liberal y revuelta campesina**, Barcelona

Arzadún, Juan, 1910: *Los guerrilleros en la Guerra de la Independencia* (talk given at the Ateneo de Madrid)

Barthèlemy, Rodolfo G de, 1995: **'El Marquesito' Juan Díaz Porlier,** Santiago de Compostela, 2 vols

Becerra de Becerra, Emilio, 1999: **Hazañas de unos lanceros. Hª del Regimiento de Caballería 10 de Lanceros de Castilla, según los papeles de Don Julián Sánchez Garcáia, el Charro,** Salamanca

Calvo, Matías, 2000: **El manuscrito de Matías Calvo** (ed. Marcén Letosa), Zaragoza

Carantoña Alvarez, Francisco, 1983: **La Guerra de la Independencia en Asturias,** Oviedo

Cassinello Pérez, Andrés, 1995: **Juan Martín, 'El Empecinado', o el amor a la libertad,** Madrid

Cueco Adrián, J. Mª, 1962: **Romeu. Héroe de la Independencia,** Sagunto

Cuesta, Josefina, 1995: *La memoria de un guerrillero: D. Julián Sánchez 'El Charro'. De la guerrilla local al concepto de guerrilla,* (in **Antiguo Régimen y Liberalismo, Homenaje a Miguel Artola**, vol 2, pp. 453–464), Madrid

* AGS. References to the guerrilla are scattered, at an approximate count, throughout over one-third of the 121 legajos of this series. In the AHN, guerrilla matters also appear in great numbers of the 84 legajos of the Junta Suprema's papers. Though the PRO references are less abundant, it is nonetheless materially impossible to provide a comprehensive list here of all those papers in the three archives which deal with the guerrilla.

Esdaile, Charles J., 1996.: *Heroes or Villains: Fresh Thoughts on La Guerrilla* (ll Semanario Internacional sobre la Guerra de la Independencia, 24–26 October, 1996), Madrid

Esdaile, Charles, J., 2004: **Fighting Napoleon: Guerrillas, Bandits and Adventurers in Spain, 1808–1814**, New Haven, London

Espoz y Mina, Francisco, (ed. Miguel Artola), 1851–1852/1962: **Memorias del general Don Francisco Espoz y Mina, escritas por él mismo**, Madrid

Fugier, André, 1989: **La Junta Superior de Asturias y la invasion francesa (1810–1811)**, Oviedo

Gil Novales, Alberto, 1998: **Diccionario biográfico español 1808–1813 (Personajes extremeños)**, Mérida

Gómez Imaz, Manuel, 1910: **Los periodicos durante la Guerra de la Independencia, (1808–1814)**, Madrid

Gómez Villafranca, Roman, 1908: **Extremadura en La Guerra de la Independencia**, Badajoz

Guirao Larrañaga, Ramón, 2000: *Guerrilleros y patriotas en el Alto Aragón*, Huesca

Hernández Sánchez-Barba Mario & Miguel Alonso Baquer (eds), 1986: **Historia social de las fuerzas armadas españolas**, Vol. 2: *Revolución nacional e independencia*, Madrid

Herrera Alonso, E, 1979: *Don Juan López Campillo: Guerrillero de Cantabria, La Guerra de la Independencia (1808–1814) y su momento histórico*, in **III ciclo de estudios históricos de la provincia de Santander,** vol. 11, pp. 483–491

Horta Rodríguez, Nicolás, 1967: *Aportación a la historia del guerrillero Don Miguel Díaz, Revista Historia Militar*, No. 23, Madrid

Horta Rodríguez, Nicolás, 1973: *Prólogo a un guerrillero, el sargento Sánchez, Revista Historia Militar*, No. 34, Madrid, p. 46

Horta Rodríguez, Nicolás, 1986: *Sociología del movimiento guerrillero*, in Mario Hernández Sánchez-Barba and Miguel Alonso Baquer (eds), **Historia social de las fuerzas armadas españolas**, 2: *Revolución nacional e independencia*, Madrid, 1986

Jiménez de Gregorio, Fernando, 1954: *Un guerrillero manchego de la Independencia: Manuel Ademuz, 'El Locho'*, in **Cuadernos de Estudios Manchegos**, primera época, no. 7, Ciudad Real, pp. 390–402

Lasa Esnaola, Fray José Ignacio, 1973: **Jáuregui el guerrillero (un pastor guipuzcoano que llegó a mariscal)**, Bilbao

López Pérez, Manuel y Isidoro Lara Martín-Portugués, 1993: **Entre la guerra y la paz, Jaén (1808–1814)**, Granada

Lovett, Gabriel H., 1965: **Napoleon and the Birth of Modern Spain**, 2 vols, New York

Martel y Abadia, Demetrio, 1887/1989: **Diario de Valladolid, que comprende desde junio de 1810 hasta fin de dicho mes de 1834**, in **Valladolid, diarios curiosos (1807–1841)** [facsimile edition], Valladolid

Natalio Rivas, Santiago, 1940: **El alcalde de Otivar, héroe en la Guerra de la Independencia,** no publication place given

Ortuño Martínez, M, 2000: **Xavier Mina. Guerrillero, liberal, insurgente,** Pamplona

Pardo de Andrade, M, 1992: **Los guerrilleros gallegos** [facsímile edition], La Coruña

Pascual, Pedro, 2000: **Curas y frailes guerrilleros en la Guerra de la Independencia**, Zaragoza

Rodríguez Zurro, Ana Isabel, 1997: *Colaboración y apoyo de la guerrilla y de la armada de Gran Bretaña durante la Guerra de la Independencia,* Investigaciones Históricas 17, Valladolid, pp. 161–163

Rodriguez-Solís, E., 1887: **Los Guerrilleros de 1808**, 2 vols, Madrid

Saiz Bayo, Santiago, 1988: **'El levantamiento guerrillero en la Guerra de la Independencia'**, *Revista Historia Militar*, No. 65, Madrid

Sánchez Fernández, Jorge, 1997: **La guerrilla vallisoletana (1808–1814)**, Valladolid

Sánchez Fernández, Jorge, 1998: **'Nuevas aportaciones a la biografia del guerrillero Saturnino Abuín (1781–1860),** *Researching & Dragona*, vol. III, n° 6, Madrid, pp. 4–9

Sánchez Fernández, Jorge, 1999: *Un episodio inédito de la biografia del guerrillero vallisoletano Saturnino Abuín,* *Argaya*, No. 18, pp. 20–22, Valladolid

Sánchez Fernández, Jorge, 2000: **¡Nos invaden! Guerrilla y represión en Valladolid durante la Guerra de la Independencia española, 1808–1814,** Valladolid

Tone, John Lawrence, 1994: **The Fatal Knot: The Guerrilla War in Navarre and the defeat of Napoleon in Spain,** North Carolina

Toreno, conde de, 1838/1916: **Historia del levantamiento, guerra y revolución de España**, Madrid

Torre, Joseba de la, 1991: **Los campesinos navarros ante la guerra napoleonica. Financiación bélica y desamortización civil**, Madrid

Appendix 5

Human Costs of War (and Peace)*

As was observed earlier (Chapter 19) deaths alone are not the most appropiate measure of the war's human ravages. They may indeed be misleading. It is difficult to distinguish between war-related deaths and deaths due to other causes; nor is it possible to estimate an 'expected' number of 'normal' deaths and then compare them to the actual number of deaths since there were hardly any 'normal' years between 1800 and 1814 upon which to base the estimate. But there is an even more pressing reason for rejecting a simple death count. Births – especially those which never occurred because of the conflict – are needed alongside deaths to assess the conflict's full human cost.

Before proceeding, a number of caveats must be entered about the author's 1800–1817 regional population database sample on which all the other computations are based. Recording some 300,000 inhabitants, the sample formed just over three percent of the total of the nine principal regions covered, according to the last reliable census (Floridablanca, 1787) before the war. But for some regions the percentage was smaller, given the material impossibility of sampling each region proportionately to its population. The solution adopted – to weight the sample (Tables 5.1A and 5.2A)† – created another problem. Because weighting required reliable population figures, and the only ones extant were those of the 1787 (Floridablanca) census, in effect the basis of the weighted tables became not that of mid-1800/mid-1801 (the unweighted sample's estimated base) but of 1787. It had therefore to be assumed, not unreasonably, that regional population distribution did not fundamentally change between the latter date and 1800.

* As acknowledged in Chapter 19, I am deeply indebted to Professor David Sven Reher, historian and demographer at the Complutense University, Madrid, for his help and guidance, most especially for suggesting that the crude sample data be converted into a weighted sample and for calculating the pre-war and wartime potential population losses. Needless to say, any errors are my responsibility.
† This consisted essentially of taking the sample's unweighted mid-1800–1801 estimated population figure and dividing it by the reliable (1787) census figure of regional populations. The resulting proportion was then applied to the sample's births and deaths to re-compute the mid-1800/mid-1801 population. The same process was used to re-calculate the mid-1807/mid-1808 estimated population on the eve of the war and the mid-1813/mid-1814 figure on the conflict's end.

Lacking a trustworthy (or any) figure for regional populations in 1800 these have had to be estimated on the basis of the unweighted sample;* on them depends the all-important population figure at the start of the war. The estimates run from mid-year to mid-year; births and deaths are of calendar years. Another objection, already referred to in Chapter 19, is that the sample did not account for inhabitants missing – through flight, imprisonment or for whatever other cause. For all of these reasons, the most that can be claimed for the figures advanced here is that they represent gross approximations.

That said, the weighted data unambiguously demonstrates that over the nine regions as a whole the pre-war disasters were more destructive of population than the war. This is most graphically illustrated by the potential population losses: pre-war 350,000 to 510,000 people (4.0 to 5.8 percent of the regions' 1787 population) can be estimated as missing compared to 215,000 to 375,000 (2.4 to 4.2 percent) in the war. The broad range of these losses is explicable by the method used in their calculation: two different growth rates which, had there been neither war nor pre-war demographic disasters, could have applied: a moderate 0.5% per year (near the eighteenth-century average growth rate) and a brisk 0.75% (close to that after the war). Using both these rates to compare the 'expected' population with the actual weighted sample provides a minimum and maximum range of the numbers of missing population.

While pre-war the nine regions experienced overall a small negative growth rate (as can be seen in Table 5.1A), the war ended with an also small but positive rate (Table 5.2A). However, the latter is distorted by the fact that the regions with smaller populations which were particularly punished by the conflict – Cataluña and Extremadura especially – are 'outweighed' by more populous regions (Galicia and Castilla la Vieja) which experienced positive wartime growth. As the tables below indicate, wide regional disparities existed during the war as they had pre-war.

Taken together, the first fourteen years of the new century saw a loss to the country of between 560,000 and 885,000 people (six to ten percent of the 1787 regions' weighted total). The latter figure is not far from the 800,000 estimated population loss for the period 1797–1814 proposed by the Spanish demographer, Vicente Pérez Moreda, lending the sample a certain credibility.† This highly negative situation was due as much to declines in the expected numbers of births as to adult deaths. The results of the downturn in births persisted throughout much of the nineteenth century and was especially visible in the decline of births of potential children of those who were *not* born in the 1800–1814 period.

* This was effected by using an average Spanish birthrate of 40 per 1000 at the time. Taking the average number of births for the three year period 1800–1802 and dividing this by 0.04 (the average birthrate) the mid-1801 population was arrived at. On the basis of the latter, the mid-1800 population was calculated by subtracting the cumulative *average* natural growth (births minus deaths) of 1801 and 1802. This resulted in the data covering one mid-year to the next. (In regions – most notably in Andalucía and Extremadura where birth rates were lower – the population estimate was probably too high, and in those with higther rates – Galicia was an example – too low.)

† Pérez Moreda, 'La evolución demográfica española en el siglo XIX (1797–1930). Tendencias generales y contrastes regionales', in Società Italiana di Demografia Storica (SIDES). *La popolazione italiana nell'ottocento. Continuità e mutamenti*, Bologna, 1985. See also Jordi Nadal, *Les grandees mortalités des anneés 1793–1812: effets à long terme sur la démographie catalane. Problèmes de mortalité*, Liege, 1963.

TABLE 5.1   SAMPLE: UNWEIGHTED POPULATION GROWTH PRE-WAR (1800–1807)

REGION	Mid-1800/ mid-1801 estimated population	Total Births (calendar years 1800–1807)	Total Deaths (calendar years 1800–1807)	Mid-1807/ mid-1808 estimated population	Net mid-1807/ mid-1808 natural growth over mid-1800/ mid-1801	% mid-1807/mid-1808 natural growth over mid-1800/ mid-1801
Andalucia – southwest	85,696	24,586	30,646	79,636	-6,060	-7.1
Basque country	20,254	5,814	3,479	22,589	2,335	11.5
Castilla la Nueva	74,740	18,528	23,962	69,306	-5,434	-7.3
Castilla la Vieja	37,958	9,320	11,132	36,146	-1812	-4.8
Cataluña	37,017	10,528	9,108	38,437	1420	3.8
Extremadura	8,889	2,325	3,566	7,648	-1241	-14.0
Galicia	9,594	2,929	1,495	11,028	1,434	14.9
Navarra	10,048	2,736	1,346	11,438	1,390	13.8
Valencia	12,870	3,715	3,456	13,129	259	2.0
TOTALS	297,066	80,481	88,190	289,357	-7,709	-2.6

Source: Author, db/*Demography*: Regional Population Growth, 1800–1817

TABLE 5.1A SAMPLE: WEIGHTED POPULATION GROWTH PRE-WAR (1800–1807)

REGION	Population 1787 census	Mid-1800/ mid-1801 sample population	Proportion of region's sample population to 1787 region's population	Sample births adjusted to regional size*	Sample deaths adjusted to regional size*	Sample mid-1807–1808 population adjusted to regional size*	Net new population	New growth rate
Andalucía, south-west	1,849,883	85,696	0.046	530,727	661,542	1,719,068	–130,815	–7.1
Basque country	306,388	20,254	0.066	87,950	52,628	341,710	35,322	11.5
Castilla la Nueva	1,218,642	74,740	0.061	302,101	390,702	1,130,040	–88,602	–7.3
Castilla la Vieja	1,786,449	37,958	0.021	438,635	523,915	1,701,169	–85,280	–4.8
Cataluña	886,624	37,017	0.042	252,165	218,153	920,636	34,012	3.8
Extremadura	417,364	8,889	0.021	109,165	167,434	359,095	–58,269	–14.0
Galicia	1,355,299	9,594	0.007	413,766	211,192	1,557,873	202,574	14.9
Navarra	224,443	10,048	0.045	61,114	30,066	255,492	31,049	13.8
Valencia	810,520	12,870	0.016	233,961	217,650	826,831	16,311	2.0
TOTALS	8,855,612	297,066	0.034	2,429,585	2,473,281	8,811,915	–4,3697	–0.5

Source: Courtesy David Sven Reher on basis of author's unweighted sample

* See Table 5.1 for original figures

TABLE 5.2 SAMPLE: UNWEIGHTED POPULATION GROWTH WARTIME (1808–1814)

REGION	Mid-1807/ mid-1808 estimated population	Total Births (calendar years 1808–1814)	Total Deaths (calendar years 1808–1814)	Mid-1813/ mid-1814 estimated population	Net mid-1813/ mid-1814 natural growth over mid-1808	% mid-1813/mid-1814 natural growth over mid-1808
Andalucía – southwest	79,636	27,189	31,122	75,703	–3,933	–4.9
Basque country	22,589	5,683	4,712	23,560	971	4.3
Castilla la Nueva	69,306	19,069	17,858	70,517	1,211	1.7
Castilla la Vieja	36,146	9,856	7,740	38,262	2,116	5.9
Cataluña	38,437	11,547	14,835	35,149	–3,288	–8.6
Extremadura	7,648	2,142	3,217	6,573	–1,075	–14.1
Galicia	11,028	3,261	1,841	12,448	1,420	12.9
Navarra	11,438	2,299	1,551	12,186	748	6.5
Valencia	13,129	3,855	3,924	13,060	–69	–0.5
TOTALS	289,357	84,901	86,800	287,458	–1,899	–0.7

Source: Author, db/Demography: Regional Population Growth, 1800–1817

TABLE 5.2A SAMPLE: WEIGHTED POPULATION GROWTH WARTIME (1808–1814)

REGION	Population 1787 census	Mid-1807/ mid-1808 sample population	Proportion of region's sample population to 1787 region's population	Sample births adjusted to regional size*	Sample deaths adjusted to regional size*	Sample mid-1813/mid-1814 population adjusted to regional size*	Net new population	New growth rate
Andalucía, southwest	1,849,883	79,636	0.043	631,580	722,940	1,758,522	−91,361	−4.9
Basque country	306,388	22,589	0.074	77,082	63,912	319,558	131,70	4.3
Castilla la Nueva	1,218,642	69,306	0.057	3,375,300	314,006	1,239,936	21,294	1.7
Castilla la Vieja	1,786,449	36,146	0.020	487,115	382,535	1,891,028	104,579	5.9
Cataluña	886,624	38,437	0.043	266,354	342,198	810,780	−75,844	−8.6
Extremadura	417,364	7,648	0.018	116,892	175,557	358,699	−58,665	−14.1
Galicia	1,355,299	11,028	0.008	400,764	226,252	1,529,812	174,513	12.9
Navarra	224,443	11,438	0.051	45,112	30,435	239,121	146,78	6.5
Valencia	810,520	13,129	0.016	237,989	242,248	806,260	−4,260	−0.5
TOTALS	8,855,612	289,357	0.033	2,598,188	2,500,083	8,953,716	98,104	1.1

Source: Courtesy David Sven Reher on basis of author's unweighted sample
* See Table 5.2 for original figures

Places included and sources: 'Courtesy' indicates data given voluntarily by originator; 'author/name', commissioned or data purchased by author; originators' name and publication, data used from printed sources.

ANDALUCÍA, South-West: *CÁDIZ:* Cádiz capital (Julio Pérez Serrano, **Cádiz, la ciudad desnuda. Cambio económico y modelo demográfico en la formación de la Andalucía contemporánea**, Cádiz, 1992); Jerez de la Frontera: (Author/Elena Quirós); *HUELVA*: Alájar (Manuel Moreno Alonso, *Vida y muerte en la Sierra de Huelva, Alájar, 1800–1899*, in **Actas del III Coloquio de Historia de Andalucía**, Córdoba, 1983, vol. III, pp. 203–216); *JAÉN:* Guarromán (Antonio J. Jiménez Torribio, **La población de un lugar de repoblación, Guarromán 1767–1900**, Sevilla, 1996, 2 vols); *SEVILLA*: Sevilla capital (L.C. Álvarez Santaló, **La población de Sevilla en el primer tercio del siglo XIX**, Sevilla, 1974); Constantina (Antonio Serrano Vargas & José Antonio Álvarez Pizarro, *Un análisis demográfico de Constantina en el primer cuarto del siglo XIX (1800–1825)*, in **Actas del III Coloquio de Historia de Andalucía**, Córdoba, 1983, pp. 217–231); Peñaflor (Manuel Jesús Fernández Naranjo, **Una aproximación a la demografía de una zona rural andaluza, Peñaflor 1613–1850**, Sevilla, 1991);

    BASQUE COUNTRY: *GUIPÚZCOA*: Andoaín, Ataun, Azcoitia, Azpeitia, Beasain, Cestona, Deva, Elgoibar, Errezil, Fuentearrabia, Guetaria, Hernani, Irún, Legazpia, Mondragón, Motrico, Oñate, Ordizia, Orio, Oyarzún, Pasajes de San Juan, Renteria, Soraluze, Tolosa, Urrestilla, Zarauz; *VIZCAYA*: Arrieta, Balmaseda, Baracaldo, Bilbao, Bausari, Ceberio, Erandio, Galdames, Getxo, Lezama, Portugalete, San Salvador del Valle, Santurce, Sestao, Sopelana; *ALAVA*: Vitoria (For all Basque figures, author/Manuel González Portilla, José Urrutikoetxea Lizarraga & Karmele Zarraga)

    CASTILLA LA NUEVA: *CUENCA*: Albadelejo del Cuende,, Belmonte, Buenache de Alarcón, Cervera del Llano, Leganiel, Motilla del Palancar, Olmeda del Rey, La Perajela, Priego, Puebla de Almenara, Valdemeca, Valdeolivas (Courtesy David Sven Reher; also Sven Reher, *Dinámicas demográficas en Castilla la Nueva, 1550–1900 Un ensayo de reconstrucción*, in **Actas del 11 Congreso de la Asociación de Demografía Histórica**, Alicante, April, 1990, vol III, pp. 17–75); Barajas de Melo, Huelves (Author/José Camacho Cabello); *CIUDAD REAL*: Almadén (Author/José Camacho Cabello), Argamasilla de Calatrava, Herencia, Villanueva de los Infantes (Sven Reher, **Actas**, Alicante, 1990); *GUADALAJARA*: Cereceda, Escariche, Hontanillas, Mantiel, Miraflores de la Sierra, Villanueva de Alcorcón (Author/José Camacho Cabello); Chiloches, Mochales (Sven Reher, **Actas**, Alicante, 1990); *MADRID CAPITAL* (María F. Carbajo Isla, **La población de la villa de Madrid: desde finales del siglo XVI hasta mediados del siglo XIX**, Madrid, 1987); *MADRID PROVINCE*: Colmenar Viejo, Griñon, Móstoles, Torrejón de Ardoz (Sven Reher, **Actas**, Alicante, 1990); *TOLEDO*: Añover del Tajo, Cuerva, Cedillo, Esquivias, Gálvez, Lominchar, Piedrabuena, Sonseca, Ventas (Author/Ramón Sánchez González). Navalucillos (E. Molina Merchán, **La población de los Navalucillos: siglos XVI–XIX. Estudio de historia demográfica de un municipio toledano, 1526–1985**, Toledo, 1990); Mascaraque, Orgaz, El Toboso, Valdeverdeja, Ypes (Sven

Reher, **Actas**, Alicante 1990); Almendral de la Cañada (Amalio Calvo Díaz and Agustín Moreno Fernández, *Evolución de la población en Almendral de la Cañada, Toledo (1612–1850)* in **1 Congreso de Historia de Castilla la Mancha**, Ciudad Real, 1988, Vol. VIII, pp. 5–10)

CASTILLA LA VIEJA: *BURGOS*: Briviesca, Quintanilla de la Mata, Sasamón (Author/Leonor Hernández), Pampliega (Ismael David Bahillo Santoyo, **Pampliega: Evolución Demográfica (siglo XVI–XX)**, Burgos, 1997); *LA RIOJA:* Abelda, Arenzana, Bergasa, Canales, Casalarreina, Grávalos, Laguna, Logroño, Munilla, Muro, Nájera, Rincón, Sotés, Villalba (Courtesy Mercedes Lázaro & Pedro A. Gurria); *PALENCIA*: Palencia capital (CSIC, Madrid); *SALAMANCA:* Aldehuela de la Bóveda & sus anejos: Bóveda de Castro, Castro Enríquez, San Julián de los Álamos, Tellosancho & El Villar de los Álamos; Barbadillo & sus anejos: Galindo, Perahuy, Santo Tomé de Colledo (Author/M^a. Pilar Brel); *VALLADOLID*: Fuensaldaña, Tordesillas (Author/ Leonor Hernández); *ZAMORA*: Bretó (Courtesy M^a. Pilar Brel)

CATALUÑA: *BARCELONA*: Arenys de Mar, Berga, Castellterçol, Igualada, Llavaneres (J. Nadal, **Bautismos, Desposorios y Entierros. Estudios de história demográfica**, Barcelona, 1992); Gelida, La Bisbal de Penedès, La Geltru, Monistrol d'Anoia, Pacs del Penedès, Sitges, St. Llorenç d'Hortons, St. Quinti de Mediona, St. Sadurni d'Anoia, Sta. Margarida i els Monjos, Sta. María de Mediona, Vilafranca, Vilanova, Vilobi del Penedès (Courtesy Francesc Muñoz Pradas, doctoral thesis & **Creixment demografic, mortalitat i nupcialitat al Penedès (segles XVII–XIX)**, Barcelona, 1990); El Papiol (Courtesy Carles Millas Castellvi); Pierola (Josep Térmens Samsó i Francesc Valls Junyent, *La Guerra del Francés en un poble de la comarca de l'Anoia, "Notas" del Dr. Pere Solanllonch, rector de Pierola*, **Miscellanea Aqualatensia**, No. 4, Igualada, 1987, pp. 113–151); St. Pere de Riudebitlles (Courtesy Angels Torrents Roses, doctoral thesis & **Transformaciones demografiques en un municipi industrial català: Sant Pere de Riudebitlles**, Barcelona, 1993); *GERONA*: Olot, Palamós, (Nadal, ibidem); *LERIDA*: Alpicat, Bellpuig, Seu d'Urgell (Nadal, ibidem); *TARRAGONA*: Aiguamurcia, Almoster, Brafim, Cabra, Constanti, Figuerola, La Selva, Monral, Perafort, Vallmoll, Vilallonga, Vila-Rodona, Vinyols (Author/Luis José Navarro Miralles)

EXTREMADURA: *CÁCERES*: Cambroncino, Casares de Hurdes, Ladrillar, Nuñomoral, Pinofranqueado, Vegas de Coria (José Pablo Blanco Carrasco, **Estructura demográfica y social de una leyenda. Las Hurdes en el Antiguo Régimen,** Cáceres, 1994), Plasencia (Author/José Antonio Sánchez de la Calle, **Plasencia. Historia y población en le época contemporánea (1800–1990),** Cáceres, 1994); *BADAJOZ*: Mérida (José Montero Omeñat, **La Población de Mérida (a la mitad del siglo XIX)**, Mérida, 1990), Talavera de la Reina (Author/Manuel García Cienfuegos)

GALICIA: Fifty places unspecified, the majority in La Coruña province (Baudillo Barreiro Mallón, *Demografía y crisis en Galicia durante el siglo XIX*, in **Actas de las I jornadas de metodología aplicada de las ciencias históricas**, Vol 111, Santiago de Compostela, 1975, pp. 477–503)

NAVARRA: *PAMPLONA*: Pamplona capital; Pamplona Merindad (Francisco Miranda Rubio, *Evolución demográfica de la Merindad de Pamplona de 1787 a 1817*, in **Príncipe de Viana**, XLI, 1980, pp. 97–134.); Valle del Roncal: Roncal, Urzainqui, Garde, Vidángoz, Burgui (Francisco Miranda Rubio, *Evolución demográfica del Valle de Roncal de 1788–1816,* in **Cuadernos de etnología y etnografía de Navarra, Pamplona,** Year IX, no. 27, Sep–Dec 1977, pp. 389–413)

VALENCIA: *ALICANTE:* Monóvar (Remedios Belando Carbonell, **Estudio demográfico de Monovar (siglos XIV–XIX),** Alicante, 1990); *CASTELLÓN*: Val de Almonacid (Courtesy Josep Ma. Pérez); *VALENCIA*: Aldaia, Benimodo, Tabernes Blanques (Courtesy Manuel Ardit, Seminari d'estudis sobre la població del País Valencià & *Les sèries vitals valencianes*, **Quadernes Valencians de població,** Valencia 1996, vol 1); Játiva (Author/Pilar Rovira)

Notes

PROLOGUE

1. González Alonso, 1988, in *Alianza*, vol 2, p. 378.
2. Artola, 1989, p. 80.
3. Ruíz Torres, 1988, p. 42.
4. José Alvarez Junco, 'The Nation-Building Process in Nineteenth-Century Spain', in *Nationalism and the Nation in the Iberian Peninsula*, (ed. Clare Mar-Molinero and Angel Smith), Oxford, 1996, pp. 89–106.
5. Aguilar Piñal, 1989, vol. 2, pp 57–71.
6. Callahan, 1984, p. 32.
7. Anes, 1976, pp. 80–81.
8. Callahan, 1984, pp. 39–41 and Pierre Vilar, 'Estructures de la societat espanyola cap al 1750. Algunes llicons del cadastre d'Ensenada', *Recerques*, I, Barcelona, p. 46, 1970, quoted Fontana, 1978, pp. 58–59; Anes, 1970, p. 292; Anes, 1976, pp. 71–72; Herr, 1958, p. 89.
9. Esteban Canales, 'Diezmos y revolución burguesa en España', in García Sanz and Garrabou, eds., 1985, pp. 245–274; Fontana, 1978, pp. 234–242.
10. Leandro Higueruela del Pino, *El Clero de Toledo desde 1800 a 1823*, Madrid, 1979, pp. 54 and 72, cited in Callahan, 1984, pp. 16–17.
11. Anes, 1976, p. 77; for Andalucía, Bernal, 1979, pp. 65–66.
12. Callahan, 1984, p. 21.
13. ibidem, 1984, p. 24.
14. Report of Diocesan Visitor, Juan Álvarez Lorenzana, to Cardinal Borbón, August 10, 1803, in Rodríguez López-Brea, 1996, p. 48.
15. Álvarez Santaló, 1988–1989, (1), pp. 578–579.
16. Callahan, 1984, p. 71.
17. Moral Sandoval, Introduction, 1989, pp. xlv–xvl for publication details; Herr, 1959, pp. 357–358 for Adam Smith; Marcelin Defourneaux, *L'Inquisition espagnole et les livres français au XVIIIe siècle*, Paris, 1963 for overall consideration of French books banned.
18. Domínguez Ortiz, 1976, p 40.
19. Domínguez Ortiz, 1991, p. 7.
20. Vicente Palacio Atard, *Fin de la sociedad española del antiguo régimen*, Madrid, 1952, p. 23.
21. Anes, 1976, p. 254.
22. Windler-Dirisio, 1995, and Carasco Martínez, 1995, for Medinaceli and Infantado respectively.

23. Anes, 1976, p. 124.
24. García Sanz, 1985, 'Introduccion', p. 21.
25. Elorza (ed.), 1971, p. 18.
26. For the period 1793–1797; see Cepeda Gómez, 1986, p. 159.
27. Esdaile, 1988, p. 22.
28. Roura i Aulinas, 1993, p. 157–158 for the proportions; Cepeda Gómez, 1986, pp 157, 178, 187 for officers' politicization.
29. Cepeda Gómez, 1986, Table, 'Personal del ejército entre los años 1788 y 1817', p. 160.
30. Floridablanca, 'Instrucción reservada . . .', cited Cepeda Gómez, 1986, p. 153 et seq.
31. Lt. General, Franciso Javier de Negrete, 'Estado en que se hallaba la Ynfantería Española en fines del año 1801 y principios del de 1802 . . . por el Ynspector de dicha arma . . .', cited in Andújar Castillo, 1991, p. 94.
32. R. Salas Larrazabal, 'Los ejércitos reales en 1808', Madrid, 1983, p. 432, cited by Enrique Martínez Ruíz in 'La presión de las guerras revolucionarias sobre el ejército español', VV.AA., 1991, p. 97.
33. Andújar Castillo, 1991, pp. 59–60.
34. On all these administrative problems, see Esdaile, 1988, pp. 3–4.
35. Cepeda Gómez, 1986, p. 165, explores this identity crisis.
36. Miguel Alonso Baquer, cited Cepeda Gómez, 1986, p. 165.
37. Varela, 1998, p. 230.
39. The phrase is the Rev. Josef Blanco's from his submission to the *Comisión de Literatos del Real Instituto Militar Pestalozziano*, 1807.
40. Cruz, 1996, pp. 45–47.
41. Franch, 1986, p. 283.
42. Álvarez Santaló, 1988–1989, (2), vol. 7, p. 254.
43. Alberto Marcos Martín, 1991, p. 29.
44. Molas, 1985, p. 245.
45. Soubeyroux, 1980, pp. 55 et seq.
46. ibidem, p. 106.
47. Guillamón Alvarez, 1981, p. 127.
48. J.F. Peyron, *Nuevo viaje en España en 1772–73*, in J. García Mercadal, *Viajes de extranjeros por España y Portugal*, Madrid, 1962, Vol III, p. 879.
49. Moral Roncal, 1998, p. 149, and Anes, 1976, p. 135.
50. Díez Rodríguez, 1990, p. 45.
51. José Coroleu, *Memorias de un menestral de Barcelona, 1792–1854*, Barcelona, 1946, p. 35.
52. These figures come from the signed minutes of guild meetings researched by Moral Roncal, 1998, p. 93. Tailors, wax chandlers, tanners, wig-makers and dressers, glove-makers, esparto weavers and coach-builders showed 90–100% of guild members signing. The details of books from the same author, p. 98.
53. Díez Rodríguez, 1990, p. 121, fn. 21.
54. To the Madrid Royal Economic Society which the government had entrusted with the task of reforming the capital's guilds.
55. Cited Moral Roncal, 1998, pp. 138–139.
56. Pérez Moreda, 1980, p. 228.
57. Cabarrús, *Cartas sobre los obstáculos que la naturaleza, la opinión y las leyes oponen a la felicidad pública*, written in 1792 to Jovellanos and published under the Bonapartist regime in Vitoria, 1808. Cited Sarrailh, 1985, p. 25.
58. Massimo Livi-Bacci's figures for Spain, cited Pérez Moreda, 1980, p. 144; for the French figure, ibidem, p. 145, fn. 28; the English figure from E.A. Wrigley and R.S. Schofield (eds.), *The Population History of England 1541–1871: A Reconstruction*, Cambridge, 1989, fig. 7.8, p. 235.
59. Pérez Moreda, 1980, pp. 156–159.
60. For Castilla la Vieja, see Alberto Marcos Martín, 'El mundo rural castellano del

siglo XVIII a la luz de algunos estudios recientes' in VV.AA, Madrid, 1990 (1), vol. 1, pp. 981–996. For Castilla la Nueva, María Dolores Marcos González, 'Castilla la Nueva y Extremadura', in Miguel Artola (ed.), *La España del Antiguo Régimen*, Salamanca, 1971.

61. Jovellanos, *Memoria sobre los espectáculos*, B.A.E. edition, vol. XLVI, p.494*b*, quoted in Sarrailh, 1985, p. 30.
62. ibidem, 1980, p. 174.
63. Andrés-Gallego, 1991, p. 138.
64. Ortega, 1993, p. 42.
65. ibidem, p. 18.
66. Ortega, 1983, p. 84.
67. Saavedra, 1994, p. 330.
68. Aguilar Piñal, 1989, vol. 2, pp. 57–71.
69. ibidem, vol. 2, p. 70.
70. Saavedra, 1994, pp. 331–332.
71. Egido, 1990, p. 774.

1. SPAIN AND THE FRENCH CONNECTION

1. Giles y Carpio, 1808, p. 22; and Sancho, 1896/1989, p. 11.
2. For example, Sancho, 1896/1989, p. 11 in Valladolid; Zaonero, 1998, pp. 37–38 in Salamanca.
3. According to Sancho, 1896/1989, p. 11, who gives this as a reason for their disciplined behaviour.
4. Anes, 1970, p. 421.
5. AHN, *Estado*, Legajo 46M/306–307. French army captain's report to General Dupont.
6. Robledo, 1997, p. 176, citing A. Grasset, *La guerre d'Espagne*, Paris, 1914.
7. Mercader Riba, 1952, pp. 235–237; Jover Zamora, 1958, pp. 52–53.
8. Cited by Fugier, 1930, vol. II, p. 383.
9. Fugier, 1930, vol. II, pp. 384–385 and 388–389; Mercader Riba, 1952, p. 236.
10. Jean Tulard, 'Les responsabilités françaises dans la guerre d'Espagne' in VV.AA., 1984, p. 3.
11. Farias, pp. 52–53.
12. Josetxo Urrutikoetxea, 'Mortalidad de crisis en la Guipúzcoa del siglo XVIII, la Guerra de la Convención', *Hernaroa. Revista de historia de Euskal Herria. Euskal Historiazko Aldizkaria*, no. 1, Bilbao, 1985, pp. 128–162.
13. See Ferrer, 1815–1818, vol. I, pp. 15–50.
14. Grasset, A, *La guerre d'Espagne*, Paris, 1914, pp. 403–408, cited by Hocquellet, 1999, p. 30.
15. Diego, 1992, in Enciso Recio (ed.), 1996, p. 244.
16. Antonio Fernández García, 'La sociedad madrileña bajo la ocupación francesa', in Enciso Recio (ed.), 1992, p. 589.
17. Diego, 1992, p. 246.
18. Tournon to Napoleon, March 13, 1808, in Marti Gilabert, 1972, p. 106.
19. Fontana, 1978, p. 62.
20. Alonso Alvarez, 1986, table 3.5, p. 42.
21. Lynch, 1993, p. 417.
22. Villanueva, 1825/1996, pp. 138–139. All page references are to the 1996 edition.
23. Agustí M. Vilà Galí, 'Una família de Franciac i les guerres amb França', *Quaderns de la Selva*, 5, 1992, Centre d'Estudis Selvatans. I have to thank Professor Antoni Simón i Tarrés for making these extracts from the diary of Felicià Thió Prats available to me.
24. Máximo García Fernández, 'Actitudes colectivas ante la muerte a fines del XVIII en Valladolid', in Molas Ribalta, Pere (ed.), 1991, pp. 211–227; and the same

author's 'Mantenimiento de los comportamientos religioso-culturales colectivos en las sociedades agrarias castellanas', in VV.AA., 1994, vol 2, pp. 707–724. See also Saavedra, 1994, pp. 331–332.
25. Anes, 1972, p. 176.
26. *Historia de Carlos IV*, Madrid, 1959, vol. II, pp. 54–55.
27. Cited F. Díaz Plaza, 'Los españoles ante la Revolución Francesa', in *Historia 16*, no. 159, Madrid, 1989, p. 40.
28. Elorza, 1989, p. 83.
29. The quotes are from Quintana's memoirs, written in prison in 1818, entitled *Memoria sobre el proceso y prision de don Manuel José Quintana en 1814*, Madrid, 1972 reprint, in *Quintana revolucionario*, ed. M.E. Martínez Quinteiro, pp. 45–46.
30. On Marchena, see Fuentes, 1989.
31. José María Blanco in an 1807 submission to the *Comisión de Literatos del Real Instituto Militar Pestalozziano*, cited by Moreno Alonso, 1989, pp. 244–245.
32. AHN, *Estado*, Legajo 3953, cited by Domergue, 1989, pp. 153–154.
33. Ángel Ossorio y Gallardo, *Historia del pensamiento político catalan durante la guerra de España con la Revolución Francesa*, Barcelona 1913 and 1977, p. 37, cited by Roura, 1989, p. 177.
34. Anes, 1976, p. 34.
35. For the letter, Varela, 1989, p. 63, fn. 18; Corona, 1957, p. 238.
36. Cited by Roura, 1993, p. 150.
37. Fr. Diego Josef de Cádiz, *El soldado católico en guerra de religión*, Barcelona, 1794, pp. 4–7.
38. Jordi Llimargas, 'El reclutamiento de 1795 en Cataluña y la Junta de la provincia. Una aproximación pólitica', in Butrón & Ramos (eds), 2000, p. 48.
39. For the exchange of correspondence between Guipúzcoa and the government, see E. Martínez Ruíz, 'Los paisanos en la Guerra de los Pireneos', in *San Martín en España*, Madrid, 1981.
40. Rubio Pobes, 1996, pp xvii–xix; Juan Gracia Cárcamo, *Mendigos y Vagabundos en Vizcaya, 1766–1833*, Bilbao, 1993; Portillo Valdés, 1989, pp. 239–282.
41. Ribechini, 1996, pp. 26 and 36–37.
42. Anon., 1794.
43. Ribechini, 1996, pp. 40–41.
44. Steven Englund, *Napoleon: A Political Life*, Cambridge, Mass., 2004, p. 343.
45. Anes, 1976, p. 421; also La Parra López, 1992.
46. Izquierdo, 1963, p. 71.
47. Alonso Alvarez, 1986, tables 3.6, 3.7 and 3.8, pp. 45–46.
48. Fontana, 1983, p. 44.
49. Herr, 1958, p. 396.
50. Lovett, 1965, vol. 1, p. 35.
51. Domínguez Ortiz, 1976, p. 513.
52. Herr, 1958, p. 395.
53. Hamnett, 1985, pp. 48–51.
54. Fontana, 1978, pp. 200–202.
55. Artola, 1983, pp. 148–149.
56. Hamnett, 1985, p. 57.
57. Herr, 1958, p. 397.

2. PRELIMINARIES OF WAR

1. Izquierdo, 1963, pp. 250–251 for the king's proclamation.
2. ibidem, pp. 209–210; according to an English observer, he showed 'little inclination to study, and still less to sports or amusements. He seldom marked the slightest preference or affection to such as were admitted to his company. Some little

aptitude to mathematics was observed in him, and he was said to take interest in the scientific part of fortification; but it was generally believed that he was weak both in character and intellect . . .' Holland, 1851, pp. 78–79.

3. Teófanes Egido, 'Oposición a Godoy: sátiras y motines', in *Homenaje a Antonio de Béthencourt Massieu*, Las Palmas de Gran Canaria, 1995, vol. 1, pp. 511–525.

4. Corona, 1957, pp. 330–333.

5. Izquierdo, 1963, pp. 240–245 for the letter.

6. Quintana's intellectually influential *Semanario Patriótico*, in particular the article, 'Relacion de los principales sucesos ocurridos en Madrid y las Provincias de España desde 31 de Octubre 1807 hasta el 1 de Septiembre de 1808', issue of Nov 17, 1808, is a good index of this.

7. *Colección de papeles interesantes sobre las circunstancias presentes*, 1808, Quaderno IX, pp. 257–292.

8. Izquierdo, 1963, pp. 298 and 369; Lovett, 1965, pp. 93 and 95.

9. Murat, *Lettres et documents pour servir à l'histoire de Joachim Murat*, Paris 1908–1914, vol. V, p. 298, cited by Izquierdo, 1963, p. 291.

10. Marti Gilabert, 1972, p. 58.

11. Anon., *Relato de la caida de Godoy . . .*, 1958, p. 486. Only one of the four copies gives the author's name: José de Ascutia; from his first-hand knowledge of Teba's movements, he was possibly used by the latter in some role during the events. A rabid anti-Godoyist, his account, lacking any literary pretensions, was originally written for an acquaintance in Cádiz.

12. ibidem, p. 488.

13. José de Arango, *Manifiesto imparcial y exàcto*, 1808, p. 12 and fn. (b).

14. Anon., *Relato de la caida de Godoy*, 1958, pp. 488–489.

15. Félix Torres Amat, *Sucesos de Aranjuez en marzo de 1808*, (diary from March 13 to 19, 1808), in Marti Gilabert, 1972, p. 121; and p. 140.

16. Alcalá Galiano, *Memorias*, p. 323.

17. Quoted in Marti Gilabert, 1972, p. 122.

18. Anon., *Revolucion de la Corte de España*, 1808, pp. 6–7.

19. Anon. (Kotska Bayo), 1884, vol. 1, p. 72.

20. J.G. d'Esmenard, prologue to French edition of the Principe de la Paz's memoirs, in Marti Gilabert, 1972, p. 135, fn. 193.

21. Cepeda Gómez, 1986, p. 166.

22. Anon., *Relato de la caida de Godoy*, 1958, pp. 489–490. Other witnesses, however, claimed that his guard did initially fire on the mob.

23. BL, *Eg* 384/122, Gil de Bernabé to Bernardo Iriarte, letter of March 21, 1808.

24. Alcalá Galiano, *Memorias*, Madrid 1886/1955, vol. 1, p. 326.

25. BL, *Eg* 384/132, unsigned letter to Iriarte, Aranjuez, March 22.

26. Anon, *Diario de lo ocurrido . . .*, 1808, entry of Saturday, March 19, 1808.

27. Escoiquiz, Juan de, *Memorias*, 1808/1957, first conference with Napoleon, no. 26, p. 123.

28. Torres Amat, *Sucesos de Aranjuez en marzo de 1808*, p. 166, in Marti Gilabert, 1972, p. 195.

29. Torras, Jaime, *Liberalismo y rebeldía campesina, 1820–1823*, Barcelona, 1976, p. 18.

30. BL, *Eg* 384/122, Bernabé to Iriarte, letter of March 21, 1808.

31. BL, *Eg* 384/115 et seq., Academy caretaker's report to Iriarte, unsigned, March 20, 1808.

32. Marti Gilabert, 1972, p. 209, fn. 344.

33. Hilarión Sancho, 1856/1989, p. 14.

34. Gallardo, 1886/1989, p. 121.

35. Zaonero, 1998, pp. 41–42.

36. José de Arango, *Manifiesto imparcial y exàcto*, 1808, p. 8; Toreno, 1838/1916, vol. 1, p. 64.

37. Seco Serrano, 1978, pp. lxlll–lxiv.

38. Herr, 1958. p. 359.

39. Fernández García, 1992, p. 590.
40. BL, *Eg* 384/142, unsigned letter to Iriarte, Madrid 25, 1808.
41. Diego, 1992, p. 250.
42. Mesonero, 1967, p. 14.
43. BL, *Eg* 384/142, unsigned letter to Iriarte, Madrid 25, 1808.
44. Lorenzo Villanueva, 1825/1996, pp. 232–233.
45. AHN, *Estado*, Legajo 22²G/14². One of a series of documents seized by Spanish patriots from the French consul's office in Cádiz after the anti-Napoleonic rising and subsequently translated for the Junta Suprema's benefit. Although written on hearing the news of Josef Bonaparte's ascension to the Spanish throne, the desire for the suggested reforms would have pre-existed this news. In terms of representing Spanish feelings at the time, the document is authenticated by its comment on the popular hatred Napoleon had aroused in Spain. Unsigned and undated, the report was probably written by the French consular agent, Carriere, in Jerez de la Frontera.
46. Pérez de Guzmán, 1908, p. 277; Escoiquiz, 1808/1957, p. 194.
47. Martínez Colomer, 1808, p. 21.
48. Diego, 1992, p. 265, fn. 39.
49. Artola, 1968, p. 6.
50. ibidem, p. 7; Lovett, 1965, vol. 1, pp. 104–105.
51. Artola, 1968, pp. 13–14.
52. Cevallos, 1808/1957, p. 160; the earlier quote on the 'mysterious obscurity' of Napoleon's plans is from ibidem, p. 159.
53. Toreno, 1835/1916, pp. 37–38; Cevallos, 1808/1957, p. 161.
54. Peréz de Guzmán, 1908, p. 226.
55. Anon, *Diario de lo ocurrido*, 1808, entry for April 1, 1808.
56. Diego, 1992, p. 250.
57. Anon, *Diario de lo ocurrido*, entry for April 27, 1808.
58. Lovett, 1965, vol. 1, p. 135.
59. Mesonero, 1967 p. 34.
60. Clerc, *Guerre d'Espagne. Capitulation de Baylen. Causes et conséquences*, Paris, 1903, p. 39; quoted in Morange, 1989, p. 28.
61. Diego, 1992, p. 251.
62. See chap. 3, p. 60.
63. BL, *Eg* 385/40–41v, *Noticias*, ms., undated, unsigned, but most probably written in Madrid around April 20, 1808.
64. Fernández García, 1992, p. 590.
65. ibidem, p. 623, fn. 11.
66. Pérez de Guzmán, 1908, pp. 285–286.
67. For Murat's letter, Izquierdo, 1963, p. 419; Alcalá Galiano, 1886/1955, p. 335.
68. Anon, *Diario de lo ocurrido*, April 23, 1808.
69. *Papeles de Cathaluña*, 1808, BUB/Ms 395: Letter unsigned and with unstated addresse, dated Madrid, April 22, 1808.
70. Cited Izquierdo, 1963, p. 417.
71. Diego, 1992, p. 252.
72. Izquierdo, 1963, p. 422.
73. Anon, *Diario de lo ocurrido*, April 30, 1808; in order to illustrate popular reaction to good news I have taken the liberty of extracting this quotation from a similar, though subsequent, piece of misinformation or rumour concerning Fernando's return to Spain.
74. ibidem, April 27, 1808.
75. Napoleon to Murat, letter of April 25, cited by Celso Almuiña Fernández, 'Las reacciones de la opinión pública', in Enciso Recio (ed.) 1992, p. 487.
76. Moraleda y Esteban, J., 1909, pp. 14 and 19–20.
77. *Carta de un oficial retirado a uno de sus antiguos compañeros*, dated Toledo, April 23 (BL, *Eg* 385/27–30 in a copy dedicated in Marchena's hand to Bernardo Iriarte).

See also Juan Francisco Fuentes, *José Marchena, Biografía política e intelectual*, Barcelona, 1989, pp. 227–229.

78. Anon, *Diario de lo ocurrido*, April 30, 1808.
79. The phrase is taken from Cevallos' report to the governing junta of April 22, see Izquierdo, p. 422.
80. Cevallos, 1808/1957, p. 163.
81. Elorza, 1970, p. 36.
82. Johann Gottlieb Heineccius, *Elementa juris naturae et gentium*, cited Herr, 1958, p. 177.
83. Escoiquiz, 1808/1957, Documentos, no. 26, p. 119.
84. idem, p. 126.
85. Artola, 1968, pp. 7–8; Lovett, 1965, vol. I, p. 115.
86. This is stated in an occasional paper of *Papeles tocantes a la guerra de España*, the Bernado Iriarte collection, and since Iriarte was at this time a member of the junta, can be supposed to have a certain authencity. (BL, *Eg* 385/38–38v).
87. Azanza and O'Farril, 1814/1957, p. 289; Artola, 1968, pp. 24–25.
88. Cevallos, 1808/1957, p. 168.
89. Artola, 1969, p. 35. For Fernando's letter, Izquierdo, 1963, p. 398–399; see also Lovett, 1968, vol. I, p. 118.
90. Cevallos, 1808/1957, p. 167; Izquierdo, pp. 411–413; Lovett, 1965, vol. I, p. 118. As only Napoleon, Carlos IV, the queen and their two sons were present at the meeting, all accounts are based on second-hand verbal information from the participants.
91. Anon. (Kotska Bayo), 1884, vol. 1, p. 169.
92. Las Cases, *Mémorial de Sainte-Hélène*, cited Tulard, 'Les responsabilités françaises dans la guerre d'Espagne', in VV.AA., 1984, p. 1.
93. ibidem, vol. 2, p. 731, cited ibidem, p. 4.

3. THE FIRST SHOTS OF THE WAR

1. Mor de Fuentes, 1957, p. 385.
2. Pérez de Guzmán, 1908, must be credited with having discovered his testimony.
3. AV, 2–327–18, Memorial of José Muñiz Cueto.
4. Mor de Fuentes, 1957, p. 385.
5. Blanco White, 1822, pp. 411–412.
6. Alcalá Galiano, 1878/1955, pp. 336–337.
7. Blanco White, 1822, p. 413.
8. Lovett, 1965, vol. 1, pp. 138–138; de Diego, 1992, p. 251.
9. AHN, *Libros de Gobierno de la Sala de Alcaldes de Casa y Corte*, 1808, vol. II/399, quoted by Pérez de Guzmán, 1908, p. 230; Bertrán de Lis, Vicente, 1851, pp. 32–37; Ardit, 1977, p. 121; Tone, 1994, p. 44.
10. Mor de Fuentes, 1957, p. 386; the author wrote that on going to the barracks he discovered that two thousand firearms had been distributed to the population.
11. AV, 2–327–18, Memorial of José Muñiz Cueto.
12. AHN, *Estado*, Legajo 41E/188–191.
13. The conde de Altamira, for example, a Fernandista noble and one of the richest men in Spain. See *Museo del Ejército* (ed.), 1992, p. 122.
14. Murat report to Napoleon, May 2, 1808, cited in *Museo del Ejército* (ed.), 1992, p. 120.
15. *Museo del Ejército* (ed.), 1992, p. 121. The long arm of the new regime he had been fighting to prevent caught up with him eventually. The fugitive, Luis Gonzalez, of Casarrubios, who had been sentenced in 1807 for sheep-stealing, was detained in 1810 in Carabanchel on suspicion of being one of a gang who had stolen seven head of cattle. It was held against him by the ruling Bonapartist regime that he had not returned to prison after the May rising. (AGS, *Gracia y Justicia*, Legajo 1086, *Sala de Alcaldes*, Madrid, July 9, 1810.)

16. AV, 2–326–9, Memorial of Francisco Matas.
17. AV, 2–326–8, 1816, Memorial of Agustin Perez de Hiriás. I have changed the third person singular, in which the memorial, like all others, is written, to the first person singular.
18. Museo del Ejército (ed.) 1992, pp. 121–122.
19. Mor de Fuentes, 1957, p. 385.
20. AV, 2–328–4.
21. Diego, 1992, pp. 256–257.
22. See Appendix 1.
23. Peréz de Guzmán, 1908, *Catálogo Alfabético-Biográfico*, p. 712.
24. Arango, Rafael de, 'El dos de mayo de 1808. Manifestación de los acontecimientos del Parque de Artillería de Madrid en dicho dia', Madrid, 1837, BN Vc^a 486–25. The author was the youngest brother of José de Arango, who wrote the *Manifiesto imparcial,* 1808, cited earlier.
25. Aunt's testimony in AV 2–238–22.
26. Jonas Castro Toledo, 'Clara del Rey, heroína del 2 de mayo', in *El Trijón*, Villalón de Campos, no. 21, Dec 1996. I am endebted to Jorge Sánchez Fernández, of Valladolid, for pointing out this article. See also AV 2–239–60.
27. AHN, *Estado*, Legajo 41E/88. *Memorial to Junta Suprema*, October 29, 1809.
28. Pérez de Guzmán, 1908, *Catálogo Alfabético-Biográfico*, pp. 654–695; 696, 701.
29. Diego, 1992, pp 256–257.
30. Pérez de Guzmán, 1908, *Catálogo Alfabético-Biográfico*, pp. 668–670, 673, 684, 687, 691, 708.
31. ibidem, p. 701.
32. AV 2–326–8, memorial of Celestino Espinosa.
33. Pérez de Guzmán, 1908, *Catálogo Alfabético-Biográfico*, p. 706.
34. AV 2–327–20.
35. Alcalá Galiano, 1886/1955, pp. 338–339.
36. Blanco White, 1822, p. 415.
37. AV, 2–326–9.
38. The Order of the Day, which announced that all those caught with arms would be executed and, among other repressive measures, that any place where a French soldier was killed would be burned to the ground, is reproduced in Pérez de Guzmán, 1908, p. 436; the proclamation, same author, pp. 436–438, fn. 2 from p. 436.
39. AGS, *Gracia y Justicia*, Legajo 1128, n.n. Entreaty of the 'unhappy actors of the Coliseo de la Cruz of Madrid', to José Bonaparte's government signed by a dozen players, Madrid, Dec 18,1810; also Entreaty of Manuela Carmona, the theatre's director.
40. Foy, Brussels, 1827, vol. III, p. 172.
41. Diego, 1992, pp. 256–257.
42. Deputy corregidor Pedro Pérez de la Mula – orders added to Móstoles proclamation, Talavera de la Reina, May 2 and 3, 1808 (from photocopy of original proclamation).
43. AHN, *Estado*, Legajo 3/74, Nov (no day's date) 1808. The quote was part of a recapitulatory account of events in Trujillo within the framework of congratulating the Junta Suprema on its formation.
44. Senior Justice Ciro de Meneses y Camacho – orders added to the Móstoles proclamation, Mérida, May 4, 1808 (from photocopy of original proclamation).
45. Toreno, 1838/1916, vol. 1, p. 242.
46. AHN, *Estado*, Legajo 3/34: El Cerro, in communication congratulating Junta Suprema on its founding, Nov 10, 1808.
47. AHN, *Estado*, Legajo 82B/193: Letter from Sanabría to Junta Suprema, Sevilla, Dec 12, 1808.
48. ibidem.
49. AHN, *Estado*, Legajo 53A/113: Sevilla town hall testimony to Hore, included in his

protest to the Junta Suprema after the latter confined him to his native Manchegan village on Oct 14, 1808.

50. AHN, *Estado*, Legajo 53A/101–117[4]: ibidem.
51. Artola, 1968, p. 70.
52. Napoleon, *Correspondance*, no. 13889, May 25, 1808, cited Lovett, 1965, vol. 1, p. 123.
53. Lovett, 1965, pp. 123–124.
54. AHN, *Estado*, Legajo 68F/279, Bishop of Orense to Sebastián Piñuela, minister of Grace and Justice, governing junta, May 29, 1808.
55. Such were the cases in Gerona and Salamanca, at least. See Simón Tarrès, 1985, p. 188 and Robledo, 1996, June 16, 1996, p. 34.
56. Artola, 1968, p. 76.
57. On this debate, see Muñoz de Bustillo Romero, 1991, capítulo preliminar; Jordi Solé Tura and Eliseo Aja, *Constituciones y períodos constituyentes en España (1808–1936)*, Madrid, 1988. Significantly, while denying its constitutional status, the latter authors include the Bayonne document in their work on Spanish constitutions.
58. I have used a contemporary printing of *Constitución del Reyno de España é Indias*, Perpiñan, n.d., in the above account. Muñoz de Bustillo Romero, 1991, provides a very useful analysis of the Constitution in the first part of her work which is also a study of its concrete application in three Andalucian townships. More general accounts can be found in Lovett, 1965, vol. 1, p. 126 et seq.; Herr, 1996, p. 75; Artola, 1968, p. 74 et seq.
59. Blanco White, 1988, pp 184–185.
60. Anon., 1808 (1).
61. Junta de Sevilla's proclamation *Españoles* of May 30, 1808. Reproduced in *Gazeta Ministerial de Sevilla*, June 15, 1808.
62. *La Felicidad de la España, Colección de papeles interesantes*, Quaderno IX, pp. 344–348.

4. DECLARATION OF WAR: THE NATIONAL RISING

1. AHN, *Estado*, Legajo 22[2]G/14[2]. Letter to the French consul general in Cádiz from an informant in Jerez, undated, translated into Spanish from papers seized in the consul's office after the rising.
2. AHN, *Estado*, Legajo 45[1]/174.
3. ibidem, Aspiroz to the Commerce and Agriculture junta, testimony of Vicente Cano Manuel, Regent of the Valencia audiencia.
4. de Juana and Castro, 1990–1991, p. 76.
5. Carantoña Álvarez, 1984, pp. 76–77.
6. ibidem, pp. 42–47.
7. ibidem, Appendix 1, pp. 191–193.
8. AHN, *Estado*, Legajo 83N/230–253, in particular 232–233, Lluesma and Rausell, memorial to the Valencian junta, Sept 20, 1808. In a later memorial to the Junta Suprema, they wrote: 'Exposing themselves to the greatest risks, they distracted the evil-minded from committing thefts or insulting people, distributing much money to attract people to the good party . . .', Memorial of March 22, 1809 (AHN, *Estado*, Legajo 83N/238).
9. Rico, 1811, pp. 14–15.
10. ibidem, pp. 19–27; Martínez Colomer, 1810, pp. 4–11.
11. Alcaide Ibieca, 1830, vol. 1, p. 5; Casamayor, 1908, p. 11, who says the French troops were coming from Madrid.
12. Alcaide Ibeica, p. 5.
13. ibidem, p .4.
14. Mariano de Pano y Ruata, *La Condesa de Bureta, doña María de la Consolación de Azlor y Villavicencio y el Regente don Pedro María Ric y Montserrat. Episodios y*

documentos de los Sitios de Zaragoza, Zaragoza, 1908/1947, pp. 116–117, cited Lafoz Rabaza, 1996, p. 76, fn. 179.

15. Alcaide Ibieca, 1830, vol. 1, p. 6.
16. ibidem, pp. 6–7.
17. Casamayor, 1908, p. 12.
18. ibidem, 1908, p. 12.
19. Toreno, 1838/1916, p. 57; Álvarez Valdés, 1889/1988, p. 62.
20. Álvarez Valdés, 1889/1998, p. 62, and Appendix 8, pp. 268–269.
21. AGMS, *Ilustres*, P-1, cited Pedro Rújula López, introduction to Palafox 1834/1994, p. 11.
22. Mariano de Pano y Ruata, *La condesa de Bureta, pp. 116–117, in Lafoz Rabaza, 1996, p. 76, fn. 179*.
23. Palafox's comments on Alcaide Ibieca's book, in Lafoz Rabaza, 1996, p. 75.
24. Alcaide Ibieca, 1830, vol. 1, p. 10.
25. Palafox, 1834/1994, p. 59. Ibidem for previous quotation.
26. Genovés Amorós, 1967, p. 44.
27. Ardit, 1977, p. 124.
28. Rico, 1811, pp. 14–15.
29. AHN, *Estado*, Legajo 83N/238². Lluesma and Rausell memorial to Junta Suprema of March 22, 1809.
30. Gómez Imaz, 1908, p. 94.
31. Velázquez y Sánchez, 1872/1994, pp. 58–59.
32. For the differing views, *Archives du Ministère des Relations Extérieures* (Paris), *Correspondance Consulaire*, La Corogne, t. 17, fol. 430, 2-IV-1808, cited by de Juana and Castro, 1990–1991, p. 76 and Carré Aldao, 1915, p. 12.
33. Toreno, 1838/1916, p. 64.
34. Giles y Carpio, 1808, entry of May 26, pp. 24 and 24a.
35. Mirtilo Sicuritano, 1814, pp. 58–59.
36. ibidem, p. 61 and fn. (a).
37. AHN, *Estado*, Legajo 30E/114². Plea to the Junta Suprema, Sevilla, Jan 12, 1809, to free her husband who had been imprisoned along with Tap by the Sevilla junta ten days after the successful insurrection.
38. AHN, *Estado*, Legajo 30E/116, undated, but Jan/Feb, 1809. Tap's and Esquibel's prison statements taken on the Junta Suprema's orders.
39. Cited in Barreiro, 1993, p. 67.
40. Antonio Benito Fandiño, *Oración funebre que, a la inmortal memoria del nunca bien celebrado español y heroico patriota don Sinforiano López Alia, víctima de la verdad y mártir de la justicia*, Santiago, 1821, cited in Martínez Salazar, 1953, pp. 39–40.
41. ibidem.
42. AHN, *Estado*, Legajo 43/10. Alcedo to Junta Suprema, La Coruña, Nov 2, 1808.
43. ibidem.
44. Rey Escariz, 1908, *La voz de Galicia*, cited in Carré Aldao, 1915, p. 17.
45. AHN, *Estado*, Legajo 74A/1, provisional general junta statement, May 31, 1808.
46. Gómez Villafranca, 1908, Appendix no. 8, p. 7.
47. Toreno, 1838/1916, p. 69.
48. Gómez Villafranca, 1908, *Declaración de D. Juan Gregorio Mancío*, p. 9.
49. ibidem, *Declaración del Sr. Provisor, D. Gabriel Rafael Blazquez Prieto*, p. 12.
50. ibidem, p. 13.
51. ibidem, *Declaración de D. Joaquín Vergara, Comandante del Regimiento Caballería de Bailén*, p. 16.
52. ibidem, *Declaración del Sr. Provisor, D. Gabriel Rafael Blazquez Prieto*, p.13.
53. Toreno, 1838/1916, p. 69.
54. Gómez Villafranca, 1908, *Sumaria actuada, Declaración de D. Manuel Huertas, Teniente Coronel*, pp. 15–16. Huertas was the captain general's adjutant and was by his side when he was killed.

55. Sancho, 1886/1989, p. 23.
56. AHN, *Estado*, Legajo 68D/162.
57. AHN, *Estado*, Legajo 64/20 and 64/170. Copy of Cuesta letter to León town councillors, May 29, 1808.
58. Anon, 1886/1989, *Noticia de casos particulares ocurridos en la ciudad de Valladolid*, pp. 123–124.
59. ibidem, pp. 123–124.
60. ibidem, pp. 124–125.
61. ibidem, p. 125.
62. AHN, *Consejos*, Legajo 5512/21; Sancho, 1886/1989, p. 22; Artola, 1968, p. 54.
63. Sancho, 1886/1989, pp. 22–23; Anon, 1886/1989, pp. 126–127.
64. Artola, 1968, p. 54.
65. Sancho, 1886/1989 p. 24.
66. AM de Cartegena, *Actas capitulares*, F-114-115, 14 May, 1808, in Piñar López, 1986, p. 232.
67. The following account relies mainly on Piñar López, 1986, pp. 227–235 and Egea Bruno, 1991, pp. 1–2.
68. AGMM, *Archivo de la Guerra de la Independencia, Legajo 2/3*, 'Extracto de los sucesos ocurridos en los Reinos de Valencia y Murcia durante la primera campaña de la Guerra de la Independencia', in Piñar López, 1986, p. 227.
69. Piñar López, 1986, pp. 241–242; Egea Bruno, 1991, p. 1.
70. Alcalá Galiano, 1886/1956 pp. 348–349.
71. See Charles Tilly, *The Vendée*, Cambridge, Mass., 1964, 1976, especially pp. 322–330.
72. Cited in Fontana, 1988, p. 148.
73. For the full proclamation, Pla Cargol, 1962, p. 28 fn.
74. Sarret y Arbos, 1922, pp. 12–13.
75. Testimony of a Manresa primary school teacher, José Freixa, cited in Sarret y Arbos, 1922, p. 22.
76. Cited in Sarret y Arbos, 1922, pp. 26–27.
77. Cardús, 1962, p. 24.
78. AM de Igualada, *Actas*, 1808–1809, fol. 21.
79. Segura, 1908/1978, vol. 1, pp. 597 and 602, fn. 1.
80. Saret y Arbos, 1922, p. 46.
81. Testimony of Manuel Casaña, royal customs inspector in Manresa, who is credited with the idea, Nov 3, 1809, cited in Sarret y Arbos, 1922, pp. 36–38.
82. Segura, 1908/1978, vol. 1, p. 605 and fn. 3.
83. Anon., cited in Blanch, 1861/1968, p. 64.
84. Carner, 1963 (2), pp 77–78.
85. Sarret y Arbos, 1922, p. 31.
86. According to Carner, 1963, p. 9.
87. In the absence of an adequate military study of El Bruch, I have used Segura, 1908/1978, vol. 1, pp. 607–618; Sarret y Arbos, 1922, pp. 32–38, and Blanch, 1861/1968, pp. 57–64.
88. Carner, 1963, p. 11; Blanch, 1861/1968, p. 63. The Swiss infantry suffered 320 and the cavalry 65 casualties; the Igualada sometent captured more than 30 horses.
89. Carner, 1963, p. 13; Fontana, 1988, p. 149.
90. Lérida junta, circular, June 9, 1808, cited by Moliner i Prada, 1989, pp. 29–30.
91. Moliner i Prada pp. 39–40 for the places.
92. Mercader Riba, 1953, pp. 14–15.
93. ibidem, p. 9.
94. Toreno, 1838/1916, p. 95.
95. AHN, *Estado*, Legajo 27D/252^1–252^2, Santa Cruz de Mudela parish priest's proclamation of Nov 7, 1808, calling on locals to enlist in the patriot army, and recalling their recent deeds. 'Without a Spanish army in sight', he began, the villagers had risen to fight the French. Also García-Noblejas, 1982, p. 85.
96. I take the figure from the Godoy census of 1797.

97. From 165,000 in June 1808, the figures rose to 300,000 in October of the same year, 354,000 in July 1811, and fell to 258,000 in October 1812, showing the reduction of forces due to the Russian campaign. Artola, 1968, p. 265. French figures were slightly different. In February, 1809, they recorded 288,500 soldiers (an effective strength of 194,000), with just under 20,000 holding garrisons in León, Castilla la Vieja, Álava, Vizcaya, Santander and Guipúzcoa. By the beginning of 1810, the French army numbered 360,600 men (287,650 effective strength). Oman, vol. 1, pp. 624–627; *Mémoires et correspondance politique et militaire du Roi Josef, publiés, annotés et mis en ordre par A. Du Casse*, Paris, 1854, vol. VII, pp. 134–137, in Hamnett, 1985, p. 89.
98. AHN, *Consejos*, Legajo 5519/21. Pedroches de Córdoba to Consejo, May 30, 1808.
99. ibidem.
100. AM de Murcia, Legajo 1303/1.
101. AHN, *Estado*, Legajo 3/78, Villanueva de la Serena junta's report to newly established Junta Suprema, Nov 8, 1808.
102. ididem.
103. Blanco White, 1822, pp. 431–432.
104. AHM, *Orihuela*, A.C., libro 103, in Hocquellet, 1999, p. 46.
105. See Jesús Millán, *Rentistas y campesinos, desarrollo agrario y tradicionalismo político en el sur del Pais Valenciano, 1680–1840*, Alicante, 1984, especially Chapter 2.
106. AHN, *Estado*, Legajo 3/55, Orihuela town hall statement welcoming Junta Suprema's formation, Nov 19, 1808.
107. AGP, *Caja* 14–2/59, letter from Pedro Oliva, Dominican friar, to Palafox, June 4 or 5, 1808, in Lafoz, 1996, p. 84.
108. AGP, *Caja* 5–13/2, letter to Palafox from Miguel de Sola, of Mallén, June 3, 1808, in Lafoz, 1996, p. 81.
109. Blanco White, 1988, p. 183 and p. 187.
110. Freixas letter of August 9, 1808, to unknown correspondent, in Benach i Torrents, 1968, p. 33.
111. ibidem, in Benach i Torrents, 1968, pp. 30–31 The following quotes from same source.
112. ibidem, in Benach i Torrents, 1968, p. 32.
113. *Llibre de notes i curiositats de Isidre Mata del Racó i Mir pagès, familiar del Sant ofici, del terme del Castell de Sant Pere de Subirats*, quoted by Benach i Torrents, 1968, pp. 34–35.
114. Toreno, 1838/1916, pp. 58–59.
115. García Noblejas, 1982, pp. 36–37. I do not include in this figure French military–civil assassinations which took place subsequent to Dupont's column advancing into Andalucía.
116. The expression is Blanco White's in 1822, p. 438.
117. Trillo y Borbón, 1890/1918, p. 82, para 164.

5. NEW SELF-GOVERNMENT: THE JUNTAS

1. *Colección de papeles interesantes*, 1808, vol. IV, pp. 283–287, n.d. but June, 1808.
2. Extracts of proclamations from the juntas of Galicia, Asturias, Manresa, Sevilla, Mallorca, Cartagena, Bilbao, Lérida, Cádiz, Granada.
3. *Diccionario de la Real Academia Española*, 1780 edition: 'Revolución: 1) El movimiento de la esfera celeste, dando una vuelta entera.'
4. 'Grito general de la nacion', *Demostracion de la lealtad*, 1808, vol. I, pp. 20–25.
5. *Coleccion de documentos interesantes*, 1808, Tomo 1, Quaderno Quatro, pp. 242–247.
6. AHN, *Estado*, Legajo 73F/207, Reino de Galicia (as the junta titled itself), June 6, 1808; AHN, *Estado*, Legajo 73D/160, Reino de Galicia, July 8, 1808; Martínez Salazar, 1953, p. 98.

534   NAPOLEON'S CURSED WAR

7. Proclama de Galicia, n.d., *Demostracion de la lealtad* , 1808, vol. II, pp. 123–125.
8. 'Declaracion de guerra al Emperador de la Francia Napoleon', *Demostracion de la lealtad*, 1808, vol. 1, pp. 103–105.
9. Quesada Montero, 1958, pp. 39–40.
10. 'Manifestacion política sobre las actuales circunstancias', *Aviso*, letter from Andújar, June 9, 1808, in *Demostracion de la lealtad*, vol. I, p. 102; Toreno, 1838/1916, p. 94.
11. Unsigned, undated, but 1808, *Coleccion de papeles interesantes*, 1808, Quaderno VII, pp. 177–198.
12. Muir, 1996, p. 35.
13. Lovett, 1965, vol. 1, p. 156.
14. Sherwig, 1969, pp. 198–199.
15. AHN, *Estado*, Legajo 76A³/3, Actas del Reino de Galicia, La Coruña, August 1808, acknowledging receipt of one million Spanish dollars; a further 500,000 duros (ten million reales) received on or about Sept 17, 1808 (AHN, *Estado*, Legajo 76A⁵/23).
16. ibidem, *Estado*, Legajos, 76A⁵/16, 76A⁵/43, and 76A⁸/45, Actas del Reino de Galicia, La Coruña, Sept 14, 23, and Dec 17, 1808. The junta informed Castilla and León that the ten million reales it had just received from Britain as the last instalment of its 26m reales was 'exclusively' for Galicia and that London had sent the former five million reales via Asturias. (See also AHN, *Estado*, Legajo 68A/66.) The junta was somewhat more generous with arms: it sent twenty thousand British muskets and three hundred thousand cartridges to Vizcaya and six thousand muskets to Santander in September 1808. The generosity was understandable in that these were 'frontline' provinces whose resistance would keep the enemy from Galicia's borders (Actas . . . La Coruña, Sept 17, 20 and 22, 1808, AHN, *Estado*, Legajo 76A⁵/24, /33 and /38).
17. Joaquín García Álvarez, Justice of La Robla to united junta, September 16, 1808, ibidem, *Estado*, Legajo 68A/67.
18. AHN, *Estado*, Legajo 72A/168, Reino de Galicia to Junta Suprema, La Coruña, Dec 21, 1808.
19. ibidem, *Estado*, Legajo 76A⁶/15–16, Actas del Reino de Galicia, La Coruña, Oct 4, 1808. The Reino refused their resignation.
20. For the following account see Rev. James Robertson, 1863.
21. ibidem, p. 64.
22. ibidem, pp. 68–72.
23. ibidem, pp. 76–81.
24. Juan Antonio Fabregue, letter to his brother, from aboard HMS *Edgar*, August 29, 1808 *Gazeta Ministerial de Sevilla*, Nov 15, 1808.
25. Toreno, 1838/1916, p. 127.
26. RAH *Manuscript*, 11–5–7, 9003, Letter 15, Guervos to his parents, Reus, 8 Feb 1809.
27. AM, Morón de la Frontera, Legajo 659; Alistamiento del partido de Morón de la Frontera, 1808. (Author's computations).
28. AM, Morón de la Frontera, Padrón vecindario, 1803, Legajo.369.
29. AHM, Igualeda: Lista de afiliacion de voluntarios, 1808.
30. AM, Alicante, *Armario 7*, caja 3, '*Informes 1703–1841*'
31. Proclama a los franceses', Sevilla, May 29, 1808, in '*Coleccion de papeles interesantes*, 1808, Quaderno 11, pp. 83–87.
32. Bando de la Suprema Junta de Sevilla, June 14, 1808, in *Demostracion de la lealtad*, 1808, vol. I, pp. 124–125.
33. Bando de Oviedo: 'A los Polacos, a los Italianos y a los Portugueses que militan en el exército frances,' Oviedo, July 12, 1808, in *Demostracion de la lealtad*, 1808, vol. III, pp. 107–113.
34. AHN, *Estado*, Legajo 9B/1–5, Edicto de la Suprema Junta Central, Sevilla, Feb 11, 1809.

35. ibidem, *Estado*, Legajo 13/6/4, Proclama de la Suprema Junta Central, no place, no date, but Sevilla, spring 1809.
36. ibidem, *Estado*, Legajo 33/182, 'Relación del Brigadier Mariano Renovales desde el Reyno de Navarra a la Junta Suprema', n.d. but autumn, 1809.
37. Barreiro, 1993, p. 78, puts the figure at 4.5 million reales. However, this seems not to include the two million reales donated to the Junta by the Archbishop of Santiago in November, 1808, which was paid, on the Junta Suprema's orders, to the Compañía de Filipinas. (AHN, *Estado*, Legajo 76A/7/18.)
38. Gómez Villafranca, 1908, Appendix, no. 16, pp. 24–30.
39. AM de Alicante, *Cabildos* 1808, Armario 9, Libro 103/133–140, sessions of June 12 and June 13, 1808; also Alvarez Cañas, 1990, p. 64.
40. AM de Alicante, *Cabildos* 1808, Armario 9, Libro 103/140 and 142–143, sessions of June 13 and 14, 1808.
41. ibidem, Libro 103/247–248, session of July 21, 1808.
42. ACA, Junta Suprema de Cataluña, *Sección de Diversos*, Caixa 3, *Officio sucesos de Manresa, 6 julio 1808, a la Junta de Lérida*, Manresa, July 8, 1808.
43. Sarret y Arbós, 1922, pp. 85–87.
44. Moliner i Prada, 1989, pp. 46–47.
45. ACA, *Sección de Diversos*, caixa 3/44, letter from Manresa criminal magistrates to the captain general and supreme junta of Cataluña, Manresa, Oct 1, 1808.
46. Sarret y Arbós, 1922, p. 80.
47. Lafoz Rabasa, 1996, p. 88.
48. J.M. Recasens, pp. 59 and 138–139; Moliner i Pradas, 1989, p. 42.
49. Bertrán de Lis, 1852, p. 13.
50. Rico, 1811, pp. 75–77.
51. Ardit, 1977, p. 127.
52. Martínez Colomer, 1810, p. 17.
53. Rico, 1811, p. 54.
54. Ardit, 1977, p. 126.
55. ibidem, p. 129.
56. ibidem, 1997, p. 130.
57. Martínez Colomer, 1810, pp. 34–37 on the friars' attempts to save the French.
58. Cited in Ardit, 1977, p. 131.
59. AHN, *Estado*, Legajo 83N/230–253; Ardit, 1977, pp. 131–132.
60. Ardit, 1977, p. 138. Ardit's account forms the general basis of these events' description.
61. Bando de Sevilla, May 29, 1808, in *Demostracion de la lealtad,* 1808, vol. I, p. 67.
62. Edicto de Sevilla, June 7, 1808, in *Demostracion de la lealtad,* 1808, vol. I, pp. 94–95.
63. Proclama de Cartagena, May 24, 1808, in *Demostracion de la lealtad*, 1808, vol. I, pp. 10–11.
64. Bando de Cartagena, May 26, 1808, in *Demostracion de la lealtad*, 1808, vol. I, pp. 12–13.
65. *Colección de documentos interesantes*, 1808, Tomo 1, Quaderno Quatro, pp. 242–247.
66. Moliner i Pradas, 1989, p. 52.
67. Oviedo arms factory, 52,466 (Canella Secades, 1908, p. 67); La Coruña, 40,000; Sevilla, 26,000; Zaragoza, 25,000.
68. AHN, *Estado*, Legajo 74A/26, for La Coruña junta's first call on June 1 for return of arms given to villagers; on June 15, the Galician junta published an edict calling on all those who had arms to hand them in immediately (Martínez Salazar, 1953, p.96); Sevilla, junta edict of May 29, 1808, in *Demostracion de la lealtad*, 1808, vol. I, p. 67; Cádiz junta edict of June 8, 1808, stating that it had already made repeated calls for arms to be turned in (ibidem, 1808, vol. I, pp. 99–100).
69. Decreto de la Suprema Junta de Sevilla, July 9, 1808, in *Demostracion de la lealtad*, vol. III, pp. 78–79.
70. AM de Alicante, *Cabildos*, Armario 9, Libro 103/173–173, June 22, 1808.

6. EARLY VICTORIES AND DEFEATS:
LESSONS OF THE POPULAR WAR

1. 'Consideraciones de un verdadero español a sus compatriotas', Madrid BL, *Eg* 385, vol. II, 97–100. The pamphlet, unsigned and undated, bears all the typographical hallmarks of Murat's Madrid press. Internal references situate it on the outbreak of war.
2. Anon, 'Prevenciones,' Sevilla, nd. (but June, 1808), in Delgado, 1979, pp. 79–84.
3. Oman, 1902/1995, vol. I, p. 142.
4. Lafoz, 1996, p. 149.
5. AHM de Zaragoza, *Archivo Palafox*, caja 8/21; Lafoz, 1996, p. 118 fn. 278.
6. ibidem, caja 3–2/23.
7. Alcaide, 1830–1831, vol. I, pp. 27–29.
8. ibidem, p. 115.
9. ibidem, p. 59.
10. ibidem, p. 65.
11. Rudorff, 1974, pp. 90–93.
12. Anon, 1808 (2), p. 220–221; Anon, 1808, (1), p. 38.
13. Anon, 1808 (1), pp. 41–42.
14. Neither side admitted to their casualties. Those of the French killed were the Spanish estimates: See Palafox's proclamation of June 16 (in fact written by intendente Calbo de Rozas who had remained in Zaragoza) on the outcome of the previous day's combat, in Anon 1808, (1), p. 46. Both Oman, 1902/1995, vol. I, p. 149 and Rudorff, 1974, p. 96, accept the figure. Rudorff, on whom I have relied heavily for the account of the fighting, gives the Spanish casualty figure without citing a source.
15. Anon, (2), 1808, p. 220.
16. Lafoz, 1996, p. 136, fn. 350.
17. Casamayor, 1908, p. 44.
18. Alcaide Ibieca, 1830–1831, vol. I, p. 86.
19. La Forest, 1905, pp. 97–98.
20. ibidem, p. 145, letter of July 6, 1808.
21. Rico, 1811, p. 243.
22. *Manifiesto*, Valencia, 1809, p. 7, fn. 9; Martínez Colomer, 1810, p. 92.
23. Rico, 1811, p. 247.
24. Boix, 1981, vol. III, p. 49.
25. Martínez Colomer, 1810, pp. 89–90.
26. Rico, 1811, pp. 265–266.
27. *Diairo de Valencia*, June 19, 1808.
28. *Gazeta de Valencia*, June 17, 1808, reproducing report from La Coruña of May 31, 1808.
29. ibidem, July 15, 1808.
30. Martínez Colomer, 1810, pp. 100–101; Rico, 1811, p. 262.
31. *Diario de Valencia*, July 8, 1808.
32. Both figures in Alcaide, 1830–31, vol. I, pp. 112–13.
33. Casamayor, 1908, p. 61. He is the only eyewitness who gives a cause for the explosion.
34. Marqués de Lazán, June 27, 1808, Zaragoza, reproduced in Alcaide, 1830–1831, vol. I, Nota 11, pp. 283–284.
35. Anon, (1), 1808, p. 60.
36. ibidem, p. 120.
37. Alcaide, 1830–1831, vol. I, p. 169.
38. Vaughan, 1809, p. 15.
39. Jacob, 1811, pp. 123–124.
40. Lafoz, 1996, p. 179, fn. 428.
41. Anon, (1), 1808, p. 73.
42. Vaughan, 1809, p. 19; Rudorff, 1974, p. 128.
43. Alcaide, 1830–1831, vol. I, p. 174.

44. Casamayor, 1908, pp. 83–84.
45. Anon, (1), pp. 111–112.
46. Alcaide, 1830–1831, vol. I, p. 171.
47. ibidem, Nota 14, p. 289.
48. Vaughan, 1809, p. 21.
49. Anon, (1), 1808, p. 85.
50. Cited in Rudorff, 1974, p. 147.
51. Rudorff, 1974, p. 149.
52. Lazán, *Primera campaña de verano de 1808*, ms, in Alcaide, 1830–1831, vol. I, Nota 18, pp. 293–297.
53. Anon, (2), 1808, p. 227.
54. Testimony of Capt. Alberto Langles, commandant of the Puerta del Sol gate, Aug 20, 1808, in Alcaide, 1830–1831, vol. I, Nota 21, pp. 310–302.
55. The figures are from J. Belmas, *Journaux des siéges faits ou soutenus par les français dans la Peninsule, de 1807 á 1814*, Paris, 1836, 4 vols, cited in Rudorff, 1974, p. 156.
56. Anon, (1), 1808, p. 110, fn. 1.
57. Belmas op. cit., in Rudorff, 1974, pp. 161–162.
58. Rudorff, 1974, p. 162.
59. Casamayor, 1908, p. 144.
60. ibidem, p. 165.
61. Vaughan, 1809, p. 29.
62. Anon, (2), 1808, p. 229 and p. 231.
63. Vaughan, 1809, p. 30.
64. Anon, (1), 1808, pp. 127–128.
65. AHN, *Estado*, Legajo 74ª/151. Proclama: 'Aragoneses y Soldados que Defendeis a Zaragoza,' Zaragoza, Aug 13, 1808.
66. Lafoz, 1992, p. 94.
67. Checa y Gijón, ms., Sevilla, 1808, p. 25.
68. Rafael Vidal Delgado, 'La batalla de Belén', in VV.AA., 1999, p. 52.
69. Saavedra, ms, July 8, 1808.
70. *Reglamento de ejercico y maniobras*, 1792: 'Only due to its excellent methods and gift for training recruits in the shortest possible time was such a surprising result possible', Girón, 1978, vol. I, p. 222.
71. Vidal Delgado, pp. 49 and 64.
72. Girón, 1978, vol. I, pp. 225–226.
73. RAH, ms., 11–5–7/9003, Guervos letter no. 1 to his parents, Bailén camp, July 22, 1808.
74. Robert W. Gould, *Mercenaries of the Napoleonic Wars*, Brighton, 1995, pp. 130–131; Rafael Vidal Delgado, 'La batalla de Belén', in VV.AA., 1999, p. 75.
75. Girón, 1978, vol. 1, p. 227.
76. Manuel López Pérez, 'María Luisa Bellido, la heroina de Bailén', in *Revista de Historia Militar*, nos 49 and 50, 1980–1981, pp. 59–79 and 51–67.
77. RAH, ms., 11–5–7/9003, Guervos letter no. 1 to his parents, Bailén camp, July 22, 1808.
78. BL, *Eg* 386/8–15 Castaños despatch to Sevilla junta, July 27, Andújar; Oman, 1902/1995, vol. I, pp. 201–202. Two of the line regiments – *Irlanda* and *Ordenes Militares* – which suffered heavy casualties and missing, were those with the highest number of new recruits.
79. Jesús de Haro Malpesa, 'La campaña de Andalucía y la batalla de Bailén en la historia y la historiografia españolas de los siglos XIX y XX', in VV.AA., 2001, p. 64, comments on the 'looting to which the defeated army was submitted without respect for the dead or the wounded'.
80. Muir, 1996, p. 34.
81. *Gazeta Ministerial de Sevilla*, July 23, 1808.
82. Cited in Jesús de Haro Malpesa, 'La campaña de Andalucía' in VV.AA., 2001, p. 65 fn. 40.

7. SOLDIERS AT THE FRONT
AND RURAL CONFLICT IN THE REAR

1. *Semanario Patriótico*, Sept 15, 1808.
2. Alcalá Galiano, 1886/1955, vol 1, p. 44.
3. ibidem, p. 44.
4. Ferdinand Whittingham, *A Memoir of the Services of Lieutenant-General Sir Samuel Ford Whittingham*, London, 1868, p. 45.
5. *Gazeta de Madrid*, Friday, August 26, 1808, pp. 1079–1080.
6. *Semanario Patriótico*, Sept 29, 1808.
7. *Diario de Madrid*, Thursday, Aug 25, 1808.
8. ibidem, Friday, Aug 26, 1808.
9. Hamnett, 1985, p. 68.
10. AHN, *Estado*, Legajo 43/44, Castaños to Martín de Garay, undated except for 'Madrid lunes', and probably after the Junta Suprema's formation on Sept 25.
11. *Diario de Madrid*, Thursday, Sept 1, 1808.
12. The Spanish historian, Miguel Artola, has claimed (Artola. 1968, p. 390) that Cuesta first made his proposal in Segovia to Charles Stuart, a British representative to the patriots, presumably with the idea of sounding out the British attitude to his plot. However, there is no mention by Stuart in his official correspondence for Sept–Nov, 1808, of such a meeting which, given the highly important political significance of Cuesta's proposals, is more than surprising. (Stuart's official correspondence from August to November, 1808, in PRO *FO* 72/58–59.) Toreno (1838/1916, p. 130) who had his information direct from Castaños, states that Cuesta's plan was to divide military and civil power, with the Consejo de Castilla exercising the latter.
13. AHN, *Consejos*, Gobierno Sala de Alcaldes, Legajo 1398, Aug 19, 1808.
14. Parish priest of Herrara del Duque to archbishopric of Toledo, June 2, 1808, cited by Higueruela, 1982, p. 183–184.
15. AHN, *Estado*, Legajo 52A/24. No doubt a pseudonymous name.
16. AM Carmona, *Libro 1153, Expedientes de Juntas Gubernativas desde 28 de mayo de 1808 a 29 de enero de 1810*, Actas de la Junta de 9 de junio, 1808.
17. AGMM *Fraile*, vol. 761. f. 125. Bando: *Escasez de jornaleros en el campo y abusos que derivan de esta falta*, Sevilla, June 19, 1808.
18. AM Carmona, *Libro* 1153, Actas de la Junta de 25 de junio, 1808.
19. AHN, *Estado*, Legajo 52A/85, anonymous letter from Don Benito to conde Floridablanca, president of the Junta Suprema, November 12, 1808.
20. ibidem, Legajo 52A/85.
21. ibidem, Legajo 61S/378 and 381, Sept 26, 1808.
22. On these events see Carantoña, 1983, pp. 90–101 and Alvaro Valdés, 1889/1998, pp. 178–184.
23. AHN, Legajo *Estado*, Legajo 61S/380, Sept 29, 1808.
24. ibidem 61S/381, Flórez Estrada and Blas Alexandro de Posada, printed address, Oviedo, Oct 6, 1808.
25. Álvaro Valdés, 1889/1998, p. 184.
26. AGS, *Gracia y Justicia, Papeles del Gobierno intruso*, Legajo 1183, nn. 'Meinadier memorial to King Josef,' Puerto Real, Sept 28, 1810.
27. ibidem.

8. FATHERLAND AND NATION:
A NATIONAL PATRIOTIC GOVERNMENT

1. AHN, *Estado*, Legajo 74A/19, Vigo junta to Reino de Galicia, July 21, 1808.
2. ibidem, Legajo 22^1C/35, Nov 15, 1808.
3. ibidem, Legajo 22^2C/87^2, Oct 3, 1808.
4. ibidem, Legajo 29C/47, anonymous letter to Junta Suprema, Nov 26, 1808.

5. ibidem, Legajo 52F/244, anonymous letter to Junta Suprema, Madrid, Nov 22, 1808.
6. ibidem, Legajo 28B/111, Junta Suprema to the Governor of the Sala de Alcaldes, Madrid, Nov 6, 1808.
7. ibidem, Legajo 28B/112, the Governor of the Sala de Alcaldes to Junta Suprema, Madrid, Nov 10, 1808.
8. ibidem, Legajo 53A/94–100, communications from Villaverde justice, Madrid corregidor and Martín de Garay, Nov 13–16, 1808.
9. Cited in Serane, 1977, p. 25.
10. The original text can be found in Delgado, 1979, pp. 295–300. The Valencian version was published in the *Diario de Valencia*, Supplement, Sunday, August 7, 1808, under the title *Catecismo, o Breve Compendio de las operaciones de España*.
11. Antillón, 1808, p. 5.
12. ibidem, 1808, p. 4.
13. Álvarez Junco, 2001, pp. 45–48; E.J. Hobsbawm, *Nations and Nationalisms since 1780*, London, 1990, p. 16.
14. *Representacion dirigida al ayuntamiento de una de las ciudades de Castilla La Vieja*, Valladolid, 1808, extracts of which are reproduced in Antillón, 1810, pp. 16–19. Extracts also in *Gazeta del Gobierno*, Sevilla, Sat, Dec 23, 1809. Perhaps because of the Junta Suprema's ban on republication of the whole article I have not been able to find the full original version.
15. Antillón, 1810, pp. 19–21.
16. AHN, *Estado*, Legajo 22^2D/1–10.
17. 'Puerto de Santa María – Proclama: La Junta de Gobierno a los habitantes de esta muy noble y leal ciudad,' June 7, 1808, *Demostración de la lealtad*, Cádiz, 1808, vol. 1, pp. 33–34; Delgado. 1979, p. 104.
18. *Demostración de la lealtad*, Cádiz, 1808, vol. 1, pp. 20–25; Delgado, 1979, pp. 70–76.
19. Capmany, 1808/1988, part 1, p. 90.
20. ibidem, part 2, p. 137.
21. Antonio Alcalá Galiano, *Indole de la revolución de España en 1808*, cited in 1988 introduction to Capmany.
22. ACA, *Junta Superior de Cataluña*, Sección Diversos, Caixa 2, f. 92, Recoder Memorial Aug 6, 1808. The following account is from the memorial, though I have taken the liberty of changing the third person singular in which most such petitions were written to the first person singular.
23. *Manifiesto que hace*, pp. 142–143.
24. AHN, *Estado*, Legajo 70D/84, Valdés, León junta president from Ponferrada, to Reino de Galicia, August 3, 1808.
25. Anon, 1808, *Gobierno pronto y reformas necesarias*, Madrid.
26. AHN, *Estado*, Legajo, 60G/134: testimony of unseated Valladolid deputies, Gabriel Huarte y Alegria and the Comendador (Commander) José Cavesa de Vaca, alleging that the second Castilla la Vieja deputy, Xavier Caro, who only arrived on the day of the Junta Central's foundation, had not been able to consult a printed version. Jovellanos, who was present as a deputy for Asturias, left only a rudimentary account of the proceedings. 'In these sessions, the credentials committee recognized – and all approved – the powers given to the provincial deputies, and a president [Floridablanca] and a secretary-general [Martín de Garay] having been named, and the form of oath having been agreed with all the other necessary measures, the decision was taken to proceed to the Junta's solemn inauguration on September 25.' Jovellanos, 1810/1992, p. 153.
27. According to José Miguel Caso González, 'Estudio preliminar' to Jovellanos, 1810/1992, p. ix; Martínez de Velasco, 1972, was unable to identify the social status of eleven deputies, p. 195.
28. Martínez de Velasco, 1972, pp. 195–196.
29. AHN, *Estado*, Legajo 3/53. Muros judge's communication to the Junta Suprema, Oct 23, 1808.

30. ibidem, Legajo 3/55, Olmos communication to the Junta Suprema, Nov 19, 1808.
31. ibidem, Legajo 28A/2 Junta Suprema order to Consejo de Castilla, Sept 30, 1808.
32. ibidem, Legajo 7C/48–53.
33. ibidem, Legajo 82B/251, Sevilla provincial junta to Junta Suprema, Sevilla, April 13, 1809.
34. PRO, *FO*, 72/59/p. 114, Stuart to Canning, Aranjuez, Oct 26, 1808.
35. AHN, *Estado*, Legajo 61S/382, Junta Suprema to Galicia and Asturias juntas, Aranjuez, Oct 9, 1808.
36. ibidem, Legajo 17/6¹/20, Junta Suprema statement, Aranjuez, Nov 7, 1808.
37. ibidem, Legajo 17/1¹⁰&¹¹, Calbo Rozas' personal letters to Martín de Garay, Madrid, both of Nov 6, 1808. Stuart recorded that two noble deputies had earlier been sent to Madrid to persuade the grandees to contribute, but without success. (PRO, *FO* 72/59/103–104, Stuart to Canning, Aranjuez, Oct 14, 1808.)
38. ibidem, Legajo 17/1¹¹, second Calbo Rozas personal letter to Martín de Garay, of same date, Madrid, Nov 6, 1808.
39. ibidem, Legajo 17/1³⁵, Calbo Rozas personal letter to Martín de Garay, Madrid, Nov 9, 1808.
40. ibidem, Legajo 17/1¹¹,¹³&³⁵, Calbo Rozas, personal letters to Martín de Garay, Madrid, Nov 6 and Nov 9, 1808.
41. PRO, *FO* 72/59 pp. 146–148, Stuart to Canning, Aranjuez, Oct 25, 1808.
42. PRO, *FO* 72/59/273, Stuart to Canning, Aranjuez, Nov 4, 1808.
43. AHN, *Estado*, Legajo 12A/1.
44. Diary of Sir Charles Vaughan, cited in Oman, 1902/1995, vol I, pp. 431–432.
45. AHN, *Estado*, Legajos 7C/48–53 & 67A/240, Junta Suprema communications of Nov 13 and Dec 10, 1808.

9. NAPOLEON'S 1808 OFFENSIVE

1. AHN, *Estado*, Legajo 34A/17, Junta Suprema order, Aranjuez, Nov 24, 1808.
2. Toreno, 1838/1916, p.146.
3. ibidem, Legajo 7C/23–24, Junta Suprema order to all juntas and captains general, Aranjuez, Nov 28, 1808.
4. García de León y Pizarro, 1894–1897/1953, vol. 1, p. 116.
5. AHN, *Estado*, Legajo 34A/20², advice to Junta Suprema, Madrid, Dec 1, 1808.
6. García de León y Pizarro, 1894–1897/1953, vol. 1, p.116.
7. Oman, 1902/1995, vol. 1, p. 469.
8. BL, *Eg* 385/181–182v, undated Iriarte memoir.
9. García de León y Pizarro, 1894–1897/1953, vol. 1, p.116.
10. AHN, *Estado*, Legajo 74A/88–89, sworn testimony of Domingo Traveso, Mondoñedo, Dec 26, 1808.
11. AHN, *Estado*, Legajo 74A/88–89, sworn testimonies of Francisco Cao y Cordido, and Fernando Baltar, Mondoñedo, Dec 26, 1808.
12. Lovett, 1965, vol. 1, p. 314.
13. AHN, *Estado*, Legajo 37E/156, testimony of the wife of Joaquín María Sotelo, the Supreme War Council solicitor who reached Extremadura: letter to Junta Suprema, April 12, 1809.
14. García de León y Pizarro, 1894–1897/1953, vol. 1, pp. 119–120.
15. The *Gazeta de Madrid* of Dec 11, 1808, published the decrees in full.
16. ibidem, *Suplemento*, Dec 18, 1808.
17. AHN, *Estado*, Legajo 45²/284, Letter from Castaños to Junta Suprema, Torre Milano, Dec 21, 1808.
18. ibidem, Legajo, 38/146, Calbo to Junta Suprema, Dec 8, 1808.
19. ibidem, Legajo 1I/10, Calbo de Junta Suprema, Aranjuez, Nov 24, 1808.
20. ibidem, Legajo 27B/158–159, correspondence between Junta Suprema and Plasencia cathedral chapter, Dec 11, 1808.

21. ibidem, Legajos 38C/130², Extremadura junta's reply to Sevilla, Dec 1, 1808; 38C/449, Jaén junta's 'Aviso al Público' on sending two delegates to the Córdoba meeting, Dec 4, 1808; 38C/450, Jaén junta to Junta Suprema, saying that its only intention had been to 'observe the sovereign intentions for the good of the motherland', and respecting its subordination to the Supreme Junta, Dec 9, 1808.
22. García de León y Pizarro, 1894–1897/1953, p. 124.
23. AHN, *Estado*, Legajo 34G/393, Junta Suprema to Badajoz junta, Dec 18, 1808.
24. *Gazeta de Madrid*, Dec 19, 1808. This letter was intercepted by the French among patriot soldiers' baggage and published in the Bonapartist Gaceta. Despite its source, and lack of address, the situation it describes appears authentic.
25. *Semanario Patriótico*, second period, Sevilla, July 20, 1809, 'Resumenes de los sucesos militares . . .', unsigned, but in fact written by Isidoro Antillón.
26. AHN, *Estado*, Legajo 46B/37³, Fernández del Castillo, Cáceres, to Junta Suprema, Sevilla, Dec 29, 1808.
27. ibidem, Legajo 7B/9, Junta Suprema order, Trujillo, Dec 9, 1808.
28. ibidem, Legajo 46B/37³, Fernández del Castillo, Cáceres, to Junta Suprema, Sevilla, Dec 29, 1808.
29. ibidem, Legajo 83K/137, Gregorio de Villamiel, Predicador General, to Junta Suprema, Cáceres, n.d. but after Almaraz bridge taken.
30. ibidem, Legajo, 7B/10, Junta Suprema to bishops, incomplete document, n.d. but before end of Dec, 1808.
31. *Gazeta de Madrid*, Dec 19, 1808. French intercepted letter. Angulo's following quote from same source.
32. Duque del Infantado, *Manifiesto de las operaciones del Ejército del Centro*, Sevilla, 1809, cited in Esdaile, 1988, p. 132.
33. AHN, *Estado*, Legajo 15/Box 1/1/37 and 39, Infantado orders of Dec 30, 1808, and Jan 2, 1809, Cuenca, repeated on Feb 10 and 13, 1809.
34. ACA, *Secció de la Guerra de la Independencia*, Diversos, vol. 20, Letter from Catalan junta to marqués de Villel, Tortosa, Jan 8, 1809; AHN, *Estado*, Legajo 31F/131.
35. Rudorff, 1974, p. 206.
36. Alcaide Ibieca, 1831, vol. II, p. 17.
37. Rudorff, 1974, p. 216.
38. AHN, *Estado*, Legajo 33/104.
39. Rudorff, 1974, pp. 188–189.
40. Casamayor, 1908/2000 p. 173, diary entry, Feb 13.
41. Alcaide Ibieca, 1831, vol. II, note 16, p. 332.
42. ibidem, pp. 163–164; Rudorff, 1974, pp. 226–227; Casamayor, 1908/2000, p. 167.
43. Alcaide Ibieca, 1831, vol. II, p. 158.
44. Rudorff, 1974, pp. 244–245.
45. Alcaide Ibieca, 1831, vol. II, pp. 187–189 gives the full text.
46. *Memoires du général Lejeune*, vol. II, Paris, 1895, cited by Rudorff, 1974, p. 262.
47. ibidem, cited by Rudorff, 1974, p. 263.
48. Heinrich von Brandt, *Souvenirs d'un oficier polonais. Scènes de la vie militaire en Espagne et en Russie, 1808–1812*, Paris, 1877, cited by Rudorff, 1974, p. 264.
49. Maestrojuan Catalán, 2003, p. 29.
50. Figures calculated from Castillo Valgañon, Ismael, et al, 'Evolución de la población de Zaragoza en el siglo XIX', *Revista de Historia, Jerónimo Zurita*, no. 57, Zaragoza, 1990.
51. On Moore's campaign in Spain, I have relied heavily on W. D. Davies, *Sir John Moore's Peninsular Campaign*, The Hague, 1974.
52. Zaonero, 1998, diary entry for Nov 1808, pp. 49–50.
53. AHN, *Estado*, Legajo 81L, cited in *Historia de Salamanca, IV, Siglo Diecinueve*, coordinador Ricardo Robledo, director José-Luis Martín, Salamanca, n.d., p. 60. The letter is signed S.J.C.

54. ibidem, Legajos 78/7/50 (food) and 76/7/6 (horses), Galicia junta orders of Oct 17 and Nov 5, 1808, La Coruña.
55. Moore to his brother, Salamanca, Nov 26, 1808, in James Moore, *Narrative of the Campaign of the British Army in Spain*, p. 44, cited in Davies, 1974, p. 110.
56. AHN, *Estado*, Legajo 83S, report from Commandant Juan Lozano de Torre to Junta Suprema, n.d.
57. *Journal of a Soldier of the 71st or Glasgow Regiment, Highland Light Infantry, from 1806 to 1815*, Edinburgh, 1819, p. 66, cited in Davies, 1974, p. 161.
58. R. Blakeney, *A Boy in the Peninsular War: The Services, Adventures and Experiences of Robert Blakeney*, ed. Julian Sturgis, London, 1899, pp. 49–50.
59. *Journal of 'T.S.' of the 71st*, p. 58, cited by Oman, 1902/1995, vol. 1, p. 567.
60. Blakeney, op. cit, p. 67.
61. A.M. Delavoye, *Life of Thomas Graham, Lord Lynedoch*, London, 1880, p. 295, cited in Davies, 1974, p. 233.
62. Blakeney, op. cit., pp. 92–93.
63. Ormsby, vol. II, p. 162, cited in Oman, 1902/1995, vol. 1, p. 577, fn. 1.
64. AHN, *Estado*, Legajo 16/8/36, Junta Suprema protest to British Secretary of State, Sevilla, Feb 9, 1809.
65. ibidem, Legajo 17/2/59, Sevilla, Feb 9, 1808.
66. Oman, 1902/1995, vol. 1, p. 582; Davies, 1974, p. 255.
67. These figures of losses at La Coruña from Davies, 1974, p. 250. The overall losses respectively from Napier, op. cit., vol. 1, p. 502, and Oman op. cit., vol. 1, p.648, Appendix XIII; Davies, 1974, advances no figure, but reports that on embarkation a number of regiments which had fought in the rearguard on the retreat had come through almost unscathed or had lost between ten and twenty percent of their strength; and states that it has often been noted that regiments which never fought showed heavier losses than the rearguard which was almost constantly engaged. 'Our army (officers and men) is only fit to fight, noways to bear the hardships of war', Colonel Thomas Graham wrote to his brother from La Coruña on Jan 13, 1808. (Davies, 1974, pp. 258 and 241.).

10. THE CONTAGION OF DEFEAT:
POPULAR REVOLTS AND LOCAL RESISTANCE

1. Seven in Lérida, five in Badajoz, two in Usagre, Extremadura, and one in Ciudad Real.
2. AHN, *Estado*, Legajo 31A/9, communication from Badajoz junta member to Junta Suprema, Badajoz, Dec 20, 1808.
3. ibidem, Legajo 31F/138, Tomás Veri, Junta Suprema's special commissioner in Cataluña, to Junta Suprema, Tarragona, Feb 16, 1809.
4. ibidem, Legajo 31B/21², interim investigators' report to Junta Suprema, Badajoz, Feb 13, 1809. Finally in May, 1809, four men were executed for their part in the assassinations.
5. ibidem, Legajo 31H/166, letter from Gonzalo Ximenez Carrion, a lawyer who had escaped from Madrid and reached Murcia just after the riots, to Junta Suprema, Murcia, March 23, 1809. It should be said that no other witness mentions this tax; though Jiménez Gregorio, 1947, p. 40, accepts it as one of the causes of the provincial junta's unpopularity.
6. This was certainly the educated classes' suspicion. See, for example, AHN, *Estado*, Legajo 31H/161, letter from Antonio García to Junta Suprema complaining that there had been nothing 'but a continuous revolution' in Murcia since Villar's appointment, Murcia, Feb 4, 1809. Valle testified also to his belief that the tumults had been 'set going by decent, perhaps powerful, subjects of the people'. The deposed intendente, Clemente Campos, had no doubt that there was a 'plot' to rid him of the junta's presidency. See AM de Murcia, Legajo 4068–11,

56/136r–138r for Valle's testimony, AHN, *Estado*, Legajo, 31H/171[1], 172, for Campos.

7. ibidem, Legajo, 31H/197, Villafranca to Junta Suprema, Murcia, Dec 29, 1809.
8. AM de Murcia, Legajo 4068–11, p. 51/98r–108r, Valle's declaration to investigating magistrate, Murcia, April 17–18, 1809.
9. AHN, *Estado*, Legajo 31H/171[1], 172, 173 and 174, Campos to Junta Suprema, Murcia, letters of Jan 1, 3, 7 and 18, 1809.
10. AM de Murcia, Legajo 4068–11, 51/98r–108r, Valle's declaration to investigating magistrate, Murcia, April 17–18, 1809.
11. ibidem, *Estado*, Legajo 4068–11, 38/5r–6r, episcopal palace porter's testimony, Murcia, Jan 13, 1809.
12. ibidem, Legajo 4068–11, 40/14r–16r, Marín's testimony to investigating magistrate, Murcia, Jan 18, 1809.
13. ibidem, Legajo 4068–11, 39/11v, Manuel Gómez's testimony, Murcia, Jan 18, 1809.
14. AHN, *Estado*, Legajo 31H/179, Bishop of Cartagena – whose diocesis included Murcia – to Junta Suprema, Murcia, Dec 30, 1808.
15. AM de Murcia, Legajo 4068–11, 42/30r–31r, Bishop of Cartagena to Villafranca, Murcia, Jan 26, 1809.
16. AHN, *Estado*, Legajo 16/9–10/58, new Murciano recruits' anonymous complaint to Junta Suprema, Murcia, n.d. but prior to March 29, 1809.
17. AM de Murcia, Legajo 4068–11, 51/198r–208r, Valle's declaration to investigating magistrate, Murcia, April 18, 1809.
18. ibidem, Legajo 4068–11, 47/68v–71r, Mariano Molina's (the lawyer-officer) evidence to investigating magistrate, Murica, March 11, 1809.
19. ibidem, Legajo 4068–11, 47/68v–71r.
20. ibidem, Legajo 4068–11, 45/56r–57r, Juan Muñoz Soler, volunteer sergeant on duty at the time of the guardhouse closure, to investigating magistrate, Murcia, March 3, 1809.
21. AHN, *Estado*, Legajo 52G/325, anonymous letter, n.d. to Junta Suprema, Murcia.
22. ibidem, Legajo 81A/79, Castillo Zapata to Junta Suprema, Murcia, April 29, 1809. It should be noted that Castillo Zapata was an ardent Villafranca supporter. Jiménez Gregorio, 1947, p. 53, fn. 16, believes that the writer was probably using a pseudonym.
23. Ardit, 1977, pp. 145–146.
24. For the rioters' actions, see AHN, *Estado*, Legajo 31C/43[2], report of Felix Jones, Cádiz military governor to Junta Suprema, Cádiz, Feb 24, 1809; on Villel's detention, his letter to the Suprema from the Capuchin friary of Feb 22, 1809, the first day of the riot, AHN, *Estado*, Legajo 31C/39; on Tap y Nuñez' release, his haranguing the crowd, and the Suprema's order for his new detention, AHN, *Estado*, Legajo 30E/124; on the riot in general, see the investigation into Villel's conduct, demanded by the Catalan deputy to clear his honour, AHN, *Estado*, Legajo 6A/14–108; Captain Joaquín de Miranda's comment on the city's 'lowest classes' in his letter of March 29, 1809, to Martín de Garay, the Suprema general secretary, AHN, *Estado*, Legajo 16/3[2]/4/58.
25. AHN, *Estado*, Legajo 31G/144, Junta Suprema order to Judge Bendicho, Sevilla, Dec 31, 1808.
26. ibidem, *Estado*, Legajo 31G/142, Bendicho to Junta Suprema, Almagro, Feb 20, 1809.
27. ibidem, Legajo 31G/153.
28. ibidem, Legajo 15[1]/15–18, 25, 47, 57, Bendicho to Junta Suprema, to junta provincial de Ciudad Real, and latter to Bendicho, Feb 27 – March 3, 1809.
29. Population figures from López-Salazar Pérez, 1976, pp. 245 et seq.
30. Cited in ibidem, p. 281.
31. AHN, *Estado*, Legajos 15/1/72, junta de Ciudad Real to Bendicho, Ciudad Real, Jan 25, 1809, and 63C/73, report from La Carolina junta to Suprema, March 7, 1809.
32. ibidem, Legajo 83T/578, Villanueva de los Infantes junta to Suprema, Aug 4, 1809.

33. ibidem, Legajo 63E/152–154, various reports to Bendicho and to Suprema on the Carrión de Calatrava incidents, March, 1809.
34. ibidem, Legajo 9¹, n.n., Junta Suprema to provincial juntas, Sevilla, Feb 13, 1809.
35. ibidem, Legajo 22²C/114³, report of Juan Antonio Francos to Suprema, Villacañas, Jan 1, 1809. The following account and quote are from the same source.
36. ibidem, Legajo 22²C/102, report of Clemente Terrón to Suprema, Torrejoncillo, Jan 5, 1809; Suprema's marginal note on report to inform General Cuesta to arrest the magistrates.
37. AGS, *Papeles del Gobierno intruso, Gracia y Justicia, Legajo* 3000², n.n. Francisco Amorós, police commissioner, to the duque de Campo Alange, Santander, Dec 1, 1808.

11. 1809

1. Author, db/Demography: Regional population 1800–1817: Castilla la Nueva, Castilla la Vieja. In the latter region, although mortality overall remained at its average, more under-sevens died in 1809 than in any other year between 1800 and 1817.
2. AHN, *Estado*, Legajo 66B/223, Chinchilla junta to Junta Suprema, (abstract), n.d. but certainly Jan–Feb, 1809.
3. ibidem, Legajos 17/9¹/7 & 17/10¹/47, Tomás Veri, Junta Suprema deputy and the latter's commissioner in Catalonia, to Suprema, Tarragona, April 6 and March 24, 1809.
4. ibidem, Legajo 82B/205, Sevilla junta to Junta Suprema, Sevilla, March 11, 1809.
5. Artola, 1968, p. 265.
6. AHN, *Estado*, Legajo 40/228, de la Cerda to Junta Suprema, Pueblanueva, Nov 27, 1809.
7. Higueruela, 1982, p. 175.
8. Artola, 1968, pp. 193–195; Lovett, 1965, vol. 1, p. 329.
9. AHN, *Estado*, Legajo 11/3, Finance Minister Saavedra's order, Sevilla, Jan 9, 1809.
10. ibidem, Legajo 7C/48–52, Junta Suprema decree, Sevilla, Jan 3, 1809.
11. ibidem, Legajo 9B/6–11, Tribunal of Public Safety to Junta Suprema, Sevilla, Feb 22, 1809.
12. ibidem, Legajo 44A/13, memorandum from Junta Suprema Secretary General, Garay, to the War Minister ordering him to propose the 'severest measures' to 'contain these abuses'. No place stated, though certainly Aranjuez, Nov 17, 1808.
13. ibidem, Legajo 2B/13–29/ n.n. Dec 29, 1809.
14. ibidem, Legajo 44A/148, Junta Suprema order on training, Sevilla, April, 1809.
15. ibidem, Legajos 4A/13 & 6B/44, Junta Suprema order on horses and batmen respectively, Sevilla, March 28 and Dec 2, 1809.
16. ibidem, Legajo 44A/178 & 178², correspondence between Junta Suprema and War Minister, Sevilla, May, 1809.
17. ibidem, Legajo 11/40, Jovellanos to Junta Suprema, Sevilla, April 5, 1809.
18. ibidem, Legajo 17/10¹/38, Junta Suprema to Tomás Veri, Sevilla, March 12, 1809.
19. ibidem, Legajo 67A/93 & 94, Badajoz junta to Junta Suprema, March 23, 1809, and latter's reply, Sevilla, March 24.
20. ibidem, Legajo 43/158, Junta Suprema to Cuesta, Sevilla, April 9, 1809.
21. ibidem, Legajo 67A/125, 134 and 135 of April 27, May 9, May 22, 1809 between Junta Suprema and Extremaduran junta, Cuesta and Suprema's military junta.
22. ibidem, |Legajo 16²/44–45.
23. ibidem, Legajo 16¹/44–45.
24. ibidem, Legajo 16¹/38–43 for Embite's full report of reaching and returning from Madrid, where he was from Feb 11–18, written on return, Sevilla, Feb 28, 1809.
25. ibidem, Legajo 16¹/26–27, unsigned letter formally addressed to Azanza, Madrid,

Feb 8, 1809, but according to Embite's Madrid sources in fact mainly written by Azanza.

26. ibidem, Legajo 16^1/32–36 and ibidem Legajo, 16^1/38–43, for report on his findings in Madrid, written on return, Sevilla, Feb 28, 1809..

27. ibidem, Legajo 16/8/45 Lieutenant Colonel José González de la Torre, commandant, Horcajo de los Montes, to Suprema Feb 19, 1809.

28. ibidem, Legajo 38C7/189$^{3\&4}$, Military governor, Badajoz, March 23 and 25, 1809.

29. ibidem, Legajo 24A/26, Sevilla Sala del Crimen to Martín de Garay; Feb. 17, 1809.

30. ibidem, Legajo 34D/226^4, Hurtado's note attached to a statement of work carried out in the week of March 6–12, 1809.

31. ibidem, Legajo 34D/214, report to Villel, the Junta Suprema's Cádiz representative and passed on by him to the Suprema, Cádiz, April 1, 1809.

32. ibidem, Legajo 34D/231^2, Ayamans to Junta Suprema, Cádiz, Jan 27, 1810.

33. See Maurizio Viroli, *For Love of Country, An Essay on Patriotism and Nationalism*, Oxford, 1997.

34. AHN, *Estado*, Legajo 74A/206, protest to corregidor and president of local junta, Vivero, June 28, 1808. Following quotes from same source.

35. ibidem, Legajos 60/189 on Grievance Juntas' creation; and 34E/345 on cases pending in Sevilla.

36. ibidem, Legajo 16/6–7/37, Gómez Romero to Junta Suprema, Puebla de Guzmán, April 8, 1809.

37. ibidem, Legajo 16/6–7/13, Gómez Romero to Junta Suprema, Higuera la Real, March 25, 1809.

38. ACR, *Guerra de la Independencia*, Diversos: Quintas, caja 71, s.n., July 3, 1809.

39. AHN, *Estado*, Legajo 44A/15.

40. Viadér, 1810, pp. 29–30.

41. AHN, *Estado*, Legajos, 7C/9 of Dec 3, 1808; 11A/2 & 27B/207, of Jan 3, 1809, clarified April 22, 1809; 6B/18 of May 5, 1809 and 46B/55 of Dec 9, 1809, record these Junta Suprema's orders.

42. AHN, *Estado*, Legajo 82C/335, Ecija junta to Sevilla junta, June 18, 1809.

43. ibidem, Legajos 15/1/2^5/54 and 46B/58.

44. Figueroa Lalinde, 1992, pp. 132 and 135; AHN, *Estado*, Legajos 76A/9, Galician junta to Junta Suprema, Jan 4, 1809.

45. ACA, *Guerra de la Independencia, Diversos*, Caja 71 n.n. Letter fom Valencia junta to Catalan junta, Dec 14, 1809.

46. Canales, 1988, p. 293.

47. AHN, *Estado*, Legajo 52F/276, letter to Junta Suprema, Aug 1809.

48. ibidem, Legajos 52F/262 and 52G/403, two anonymous letters from Benameji to Junta Suprema, Feb 4 and 16, 1809.

49. Maties Ramisa, 1993, p. 171.

50. Canales, 1988, pp. 278.

51. ibidem, p. 299.

52. ibidem, p. 279; Maties Ramisa, op. cit, p. 124; interestingly, the latter author has Rovira calling for conscription to resolve the problem.

53. AHN, *Estado*, Legajo 34C/148^4, Veri to Suprema, Tarragona, Jan 10, 1809.

54. Cardús, 1976, p. 117.

55. Canales, 1988, p. 276.

56. Bosch i Cardellach, 1815, diary entry of May 18, 1810; in Canales (ed.) version, p. 15.

57. AHN, *Estado*, Legajo 51A/26, Colonel Carbantes' memorial to Junta Suprema, Dec 30, 1809.

58. ibidem, Legajo 72A/106, Junta Suprema statement, Aranjuez, Nov 17, 1808.

59. Sherwig, 1969, pp. 198–199.

60. Miguel Martínez, 'Armamento y munición', in *Militaria-84*, 1984, p. 88.

61. AHN, *Estado*, Legajo 36M/293, Dátilo report of July 27 on the Oviedo arms factory processes, Sevilla, July 27, 1809.

62. ibidem, Legajo 36E/54, Granada junta report to Suprema, Oct 28, 1809.
63. ibidem, Legajo 36E/25, Granada junta report on arms factory to Junta Suprema, Granada, July 8, 1809.
64. ibidem, Legajo 36E/42, Junta Suprema order, Sevilla, Aug 14, 1809.
65. ibidem, Legajo 36M/276, Dátilo to Junta Suprema, Sevilla, June 12, 1809.
66. ibidem, Legajo 36L/346 & 349, Eguaguirre y Redín's submission to Junta Suprema, and latter's agreement, Sevilla, July 10 & 25, 1809.
67. These negotiations can be followed in AHN, *Estado*, Legajo 36M, especially documents 280–301.
68. AHN, *Estado*, Legajos 38D/338, 42A/129, 44B/421–222 give details of these salaries; both the latter two were also audiencia judges.
69. ibidem, Legajo 36E/61 'Estado de la fábrica de fusiles de Granada, en 31 de diciembre de 1809' – report to Junta Suprema.
70. ibidem, Legajo 35D/205, Vicente Maria de Maturana, Director General of Artillery, to Junta Suprema, Oct 18, 1809; a weekly arsenal return of Sept 30, 1809 (ibidem Legajo 37A/27^2) had already mentioned the workers' absence.
71. ibidem, Legajo 35B/14, Junta Suprema order, Sevilla, Jan 19, 1809.
72. ibidem, Legajo 36T/415^2, González's submission to Junta Suprema, Cádiz, Dec 12, 1809.
73. ibidem, Legajo 37E/156, Sotelo letter to Junta Suprema, Mérida, April 12, 1809.
74. ibidem, Legajo 37E/166, Junta Suprema's reply to Sotelo, Sevilla, April 21, 1809.
75. ibidem, Legajo 37E/170, Sotelo to Junta Suprema, Mérida, April 27, 1809.
76. Sotelo's biographical and political trajectory is derived from two sources: Manuel Ruíz Lagos, *Joaquín Sotelo, político y literato. Prefecto de José Bonaparte en la ciudad de Jerez de la Frontera*, Jerez de la Frontera, 1971, pp. 7–23; and his wife's long, chronological and reasoned submission in defence of her husband's patriotism, pre-war and during the war, to the enquiry, ordered by the Regency in 1812, into her husband's conduct over his abortive peace talks. Most of the details of his wartime vicissitudes, as well as this quote, are taken from her submission which can be found in AHN, *Estado* Legajo 37E/180.
77. The *Gazeta de Valencia*, of Sept 2, 1808, reported this in a despatch dated Aug 18, 1808, from Badajoz; and it was also published in the *Gazeta Ministerial de Sevilla*, Sept 23, 1808.
78. AHN, *Estado*, Legajo 37E/152, petition of Nov 23, 1808, Madrid.
79. ibidem, Legajo 37E/180.
80. ibidem, Legajo 37E/154, petition of María de las Mercedes Porres, Sotelo's wife, to the Junta Suprema, Cádiz, Jan 31, 1809.
81. ibidem, Legajo 37E/180, see note 29.
82. La Forest, 1905, vol, II, p. 171; Artola, 1989 (1), p. 133.
83. AHN, *Estado*, Legajo 37E/180, see note 29.
84. *Relación de los méritos, grados y ejercicios literarios del Licenciado en ambos derechos, D. Joaquin Ma Sotelo, AHN, Consejos*, Legajo 13, 361/43, cited in Ruíz Lagos, p. 15, see note 29.
85. AGS, *Papeles del Gobierno intruso, Gracia y Justicia*, Legajo 1038 n.n., report from Almagro to Cambronero, Bonapartist justice minister, Sevilla, May 12, 1810.
86. Rivas' trajectory can be followed in AHN, *Estado*, Legajo 29^2/306/306^4 and AGS, *Papeles del Gobierno intruso, Gracia y Justicia*, Legajos 1143 and 1157 n.n.

12. POPULAR TERRITORIAL LIBERATION STRUGGLES: GALICIA AND CATALUÑA

1. AHN, *Estado*, Legajo 13/6/1, Junta Suprema proclamation, *Pueblos de Galicia*, Sevilla, n.d.
2. ibidem, Legajo 22^1 A/11, Junta Suprema to its secretary of state, Aranjuez, Nov 16, 1808.

3. Barreiro, 1993, pp. 59–61.
4. ibidem, p. 60.
5. Villares, 1985, p. 120; Villares, 'A sociedade galega a inicios do século XIX' in *Militaria-84*, 1984, pp. 97–98; Barreiro, 1982, p. 92.
6. Saavedra, 1994, p. 26.
7. Barreiro, *Historia de Galicia*, Vigo, 1981, vol. IV, p. 242.
8. Barreiro, 1993, pp. 203–204.
9. Figueroa Lalinde, 1992, pp. 132 and 135; AHN, *Estado*, Legajos 76A/9, Galician junta to Junta Suprema, Jan 4, 1809; 42A/182, Romana to Suprema, Chaves, Feb 13, 1809.
10. AHN, *Estado*, Legajo 72A/81, Galician junta to counsul, La Coruña, Nov 2, 1809; Figueroa Lalinde, 1992, pp. 137–147; in fact they were not returned until 1810–1811.
11. Martínez Salazar, 1953, extracts of La Coruña's municipal council minutes and communications with the Galician junta, Aug 27 and Sept 1, 1808, pp. 98 and 102–103.
12. Posse, 1984, p. 116.
13. Barreiro, 1993, p. 90.
14. *Semanario Patriotica*, no. 4, Sevilla, 1809, report from Antonio Eiras on these events, cited in Barreiro, 1993, pp. 108–109.
15. ibidem, no. 14, p. 325, cited in Barreiro, 1993, p. 113.
16. *Diario de Santiago*, no. 49, 1809, cited in Barreiro, 1993, p. 109.
17. Donapétry, 1991, pp. 269 and 271; figures of French casualties and prisoners from same source.
18. Jesus de Juana y Xavier Castro, 'Apuntes sobre la Guerra de la Independencia en Galicia', in *Boletin Auriense*, Orense, 1990–1991, p. 79.
19. Donapétry, 1991, pp. 272–273.
20. Barreiro, 1993, p. 113.
21. *Militaria-84*, 1984, pp. 70–71.
22. Barreiro, 1993, p. 101; the preceding quotation, ibidem, p. 100.
23. José Fernández Neira, *Proezas de Galicia*, re-edited, 1984, p. 63, cited by Barreiro, 1993, pp. 101–102.
24. Jesus de Juana y Xavier Castro, in *Boletin Auriense*, op.cit. Orense, 1990–1991, pp. 87–88. Ney's aide de camp Lavevasseur wrote that Galicia's distance from the Spanish capital, the insurgents' and Romana's troops' actions 'left us totally isolated, without any news of France or even from Madrid, for six months'. This was a situation to which Napoleon's officers and troops were unused.
25. Barreiro, 1993, pp. 120–122; Figueroa Lalinde, 1993, p. 73.
26. Basil Hall, *Corcubión*, ed. J.M. Alberich, Exeter, 1975. Hall was the Endymion's lieutenant at the time and a witness to the events.
27. Arturo Lezcano Fernández, 'La División del Miño' in *Militaria-84*, 1984, p. 84.
28. General Martín de la Carrera, victory report, Santiago, May 23, 1809, cited in Barreiro, 1993, p. 124.
29. *Las memorias del mariscal Soult. Las tropas napoleónicas en Galicia, 1808–1809*, trans. Mark Zbigniew Guscin, La Coruña, 1999, pp. 80–81.
30. Manuel Rodriguez Maneiro, 'Batalla de Pontesampaio (Junio de 1809)', *Militaria-84*, 1984, p. 47–50.
31. Troncoso to Cornel, Couto, Aug. 28, 1809, cited in Martínez Salazar, 1953, pp 30–37.
32. Ramón Villares, 'A sociedade galega a inicios do século XIX' in *Militaria-84*, 1984, pp. 97–98.
33. AHN, *Estado*, Legajo 29^2E/40, Blake to Junta Suprema, 'indicating the thinking of the less barbarous of our enemies', Vich, Aug 29, 1809.
34. ibidem, Legajo, $17/10^1$/21 and 22, Junta Suprema to Reding ordering him to the relief of Zaragoza, Sevilla, Feb 9, 1809.
35. *Diario del Sitio*, vol. IX, pp. 390–391, copy of a letter from J. Pastor to a woman friend in Villanueva de la Geltru, May 11, 1809.

36. Oman, 1908/1996, vol. III, p. 22.
37. Fornas' ms. notes, Arteche, vol. VII, p. 458, quoted by Oman, 1908/1996, vol. III, p. 22; Pla Cargol, 1962, p. 222.
38. Simón Tarrés, 1985, p. 67.
39. ibidem, pp. 51, 153 and 47 respectively.
40. ibidem, pp. 214–215.
41. Pla Cargol, 1962, pp. 116–118 and 120.
42. *Diario del Sitio*, vol. X, copy of a letter from J. Pastor to a woman friend, pp. 393–395, op. cit., June 6, 1809.
43. AHN, *Estado*, Legajo 27A/84$^{1-3}$, Coupigny to Junta Suprema, Tarragona, Aug 28, 1809.
44. RAH, ms. 11–5–7, 9003, Carta 4, Guervos to his parents, San Andrés de la Barca, Nov 22, 1808.
45. ibidem, Cartas 11, 12 and 39, Guervos to his parents, Reus, Jan 10, 13 and Nov 22, 1809.
46. AHN, *Estado*, Legajo 34C/143, Army HQ, Tortosa, Aug 8, 1809, to Junta Suprema.
47. RAH ms. 11–5–7, 9003, carta 32, Reus, Aug 2, 1809.
48. Bosch i Cardellach, 1815, diary entry of March 20, 1809, in Canales (ed.) version, 1988, p. 13.
49. *Gazeta Extraordinaria del Principado de Cataluña*, 'The villagers of the Vallés,' April 9, 1809.
50. ACA, *Guerra de la Independencia, Diversos*, Caja 71, n.n., Granollers, August 19, 1809, to junta of Cataluña.
51. ibidem, *Guerra de la Independencia, Diversos*, Caja 71, n.n. one of the many testimonies offered by the Vallés justices in their communication to the Junta of Catalonia (see previous fn.).
52. ibidem, Caja 71/1, junta del partido del Vallès, ibidem Granollers, Aug 19, 1809, ('Sumario criminal contra unos Migueletes que intentaron robar un rebaño en el término de Mollet, é hicieron fuego contra el Bayle y Regidor del mismo Pueblo.').
53. ibidem, Caja 76, n.n. Report of March 29 and 31, 1810. Another report from the justice of Begues, province of Barcelona, to the Catalan Junta, of July 24, 1809 shows that the practice of smuggling food into Barcelona had begun earlier. 'In this place, armed men wearing the capes of the San Boy sometents frequently come to steal flocks of sheep . . . They drive them, it is commonly said, to Barcelona to sell to the French.' (ibidem, *Diversos*, Caja 71 n.n.).
54. St Cyr, *Campagne de Catalogne*, p. 98, cited by Oman, 1903/1995, vol. II, p. 76.
55. Blanch, 1861/1968, p. 195.
56. ACA, *Guerra de la Independencia, Diversos*, Caja 76 n.n., Antonio Borràs memoir to Catalan junta, Villafranca, Jan II 29, 1810.
57. ibidem, Caja 76, n.d., Josef de Calasanos, on behalf of the Mataro junta, to Catalan junta, Mataró, March 29, 1810.
58. AH de Girona, I 1.2.3., Legajo 10: Martiniano Clara to Gerona junta, Besalu, Nov 18, 1808; junta's decision contained in marginal note.
59. This was almost certainly an understatement. As remarked earlier, protests to the Catalan junta were conditioned by villages' and townships' geographical proximity, and so many of the more distant complaints would have been addressed not to it but to local juntas.
60. ACA, *Guerra de la Independencia, Diversos*, Caja 2, Sindico Personero de Olot to junta of Cataluña, August 30, 1809.
61. ibidem, *Guerra de la Independencia*, vol 30, 'Borrador de memoriales extractados y decretados por la junta de Cataluäna desde el 16 de noviembre de 1808 hasta 6 de octubre de 1810, sobre asuntos de Gracia y Justicia'; author's calculation on the basis of these documents from November 1808 to June 1809.
62. Mercader i Riba, 1978, p. 42.
63. Roura i Aulinas, 1984, p. 138, table XVI.

64. AHN, *EstadoGuerra de la Independencia, , Legajo 51C/219, report on risings' failures to Junta Suprema by three Barcelona inhabitants, Ignacio Regés, Ramon Alguér and Bruno Petrus, who had been involved in some of the later plots, Villanueva y Geltru, June 28, 1809*.

65. *Gazeta del Gobierno*, Sevilla, Aug 10, 1809 in a report from Barcelona, July 20, 1809; Blanch, 1861/1968, pp. 207–210.

66. AHN, *Estado*, Legajo 51C/219 – from the same report as cited in note 64.

67. Pla Cargol, 1962, p. 98.

68. Viadér, 1810, p. 11.

69. ibidem.

70. AHN, *Estado*, Legajo 34C/148[4], Veri to Suprema, Tarragona, Sept 11, 1809.

71. Pla Cargol, 1962, pp. 144–146; Oman, 1908/1996, vol. III, pp. 44–46.

72. Arteche, vol.VII, p. 579, quoting the diary of Dr. Ruíz. Cited in Oman, vol. III, p. 51.

73. Major General M. de Haro, of the Gerona defence, *Relación histórica de las defensas de Gerona en 1808 y 1809*, Madrid, 1820, p. 82, cited by Tarrès, 1985, p. 18.

74. Toreno, 1838/1916, p. 218.

75. AH de Girona, I, 1.2.3, Legajo 18, n.n.

76. Pla Cargol, 1962, pp. 149 fn:, 150, 154 and 163.

77. AH de Girona, I, 1.2.3, Legajo 18, Oct 12, 1809, n.n. This 'irregular conduct' came to a head when two Bourbón regiment infantrymen entered a junta member's house and demanded bread.

78. *Diario de Gerona*, Oct 5, 1808.

79. AH de Girona, I, 1.2.3., Legajo 18, Gerona junta to Alvarez for his agreement, Sept 28, 1809.

80. Pla Cargol, 1962, p. 169.

81. Nieto Samaniego, 1810, p. 161.

82. ACA, *Guerra de la Independencia*, diversos, Box 71, n.n., Josef Antonio Savalles to Catalan junta, Lérida, Nov 24, 1809.

83. Viadér, 1810, p. 13.

84. Pla Cargol, 1962, p. 180.

85. *Diario del Sitio,* vol. XII, p. 433.

86. ibidem, vol. XI, pp. 419–420, Nieto Samaniego, report to Alvarez, Nov 29, 1809; Pla Cargol, 1962, p. 172 fn.

87. *Diario del Sitio,* vol. XI, p. 418, Nieto Samaniego.

88. AH de Girona, VII, 1.1.1. Legajo 6, 'Fuerza efectiva que componen los individuos de los Colegios y Gremios de 16 á 60 años para el servicio de la plaza . . .' n.n., n.d., but probably late April, 1809. It should be noted that 91 market gardeners had their own guild. The document adds that there were a further 582 artisans and workers who were not affiliated to guilds making a total of 1,321 men.

89. Pla Cargol, 1962, pp. 194–195.

90. ibidem, p. 202 and 204; Oman, 1908/1996, vol. III, p. 60.

91. *Diario de Gerona*, vol. X, pp. 432–433; other authors give slightly different figures.

92. Cited in Oman, 1908/1996, vol. III, p. 59.

93. R. Alberich, 'La població de Girona a la fin del segle XVIII', *Treballs de Historia*, Girona, 1976, quoted in Tarrès, 1985, p. 67, for a modern demographic study of the military and civilian dead.

94. AHN, *Estado*, Legajo 38E/396, Junta Suprema to Blake, Sevilla, Oct 3, 1809.

95. Moliner i Prada, 1989, p. 53.

13. THE CHURCH AT WAR

1. *Colección de papeles interesantes*, 1808, Quaderno II, pp. 106–114. Undated, but 1808, prelate unidentified. The Sevilla Junta also issued a proclamation on June 7,

1808, calling for a 'general reform of customs', 'modesty of dress', 'the gravity, seriousness and honesty for which Spaniards have always been known and with which real Christians should distinguish themselves', as well as 'secret mortification and penitence to placate God's anger'. ibidem, p. 98.

2. AHN, *Estado*, Legajo 52E/207, unsigned, undated, but 1808.
3. Higueruela del Pino, 1982, pp. 26–28.
4. AGS, *Papeles del Gobernio intruso, Gracia y Justicia*, Legajo 1184, Bishop of Valladolid pastoral, undated, and letter to Sebastián Pinuela, justice minister of Bonapartist government, Valladolid, July 13, 1808.
5. Margarita Gil Muñoz, 'Discurso político-religioso de los sermones y honras fúnebres como vehículo de propaganda', paper presented to an AEGI seminar, May, 2003.
6. ibidem.
7. AHN, *Estado*, Legajo 22^2/G/6^2 for a draft of the circular which probably was never issued since it appeared in a file headed 'minutes not given effect to'; however it illustrated the Suprema's disillusionment with the Church's support.
8. AHN, *Estado*, Legajo 9E/4, Sevilla, March 15, 1809.
9. Sermons of 1809, cited in Callahan, 1984, pp. 90–91.
10. 'Memoria del obispo de Calahorra sobre mejoras de la legislación', Murcia, Oct 14, 1809, in Higueruela del Pino, 1982, p. 121.
11. AHN, *Estado*, Legajo 13/10, 'Exhortacion: Españoles de mi corazón', Sevilla, Dec 20, 1809.
12. ibidem.
13. ibidem Legajo 27B/176, Rivero to Junta Suprema, Sevilla, Oct 2, 1809; the Suprema nonetheless permitted the bishop to publish his diatribe on women's dress.
14. 'Sermones dedicados a inflamar las llamas del patriotismo con la doctrina de la Relgión y sostener los ánimos con confianza en el éxito', cited by Margarita Gil Muñoz, op. cit.
15. AHN, *Estado*, Legajo 27B/187, Bishop of Segovia to Junta Suprema, Horcajo de los Montes, May 17, 1809.
16. ibidem, Legajo 10C/1–16, Junta Suprema decree and preamble, Sevilla, April 12, 1809.
17. ibidem, Legajo E/n.n., letter to Suprema from Rev. Juan Vicente Gutiérrez, El Pedroso, June 14, 1809.
18. ibidem, Legajo 27A/43, Junta Suprema to parish priest of Bourguillos, Sevilla, April 6, 1809.
19. Higueruela del Pino, 1982, p 71, fn. 20.
20. AGS, *Papeles del Gobierno intruso, Gracia y Justicia*, Legajo 1089. n.n. The Bonapartist state announced on Dec 23, 1809 that it owed a total of 150,345 reales in regular orders' pensions which, at 2,200 reales per head, made 683.
21. ibidem, Legajo 1088, n.n. Madrid, Aug 18, 1809.
22. Higueruela del Pino, 1982, p. 68.
23. ibidem, p. 71.
24. R.J. Aymes, 'La notion du public', in 'La Revolution française: Ses consequences et les reactions du "public" en Espagne entre 1808 et 1814', *Annales litteraires de l'Université de Besançon*, no. 388, 1984/1985, p. 134.
25. AHN, *Estado*, Legajo 27A/66, letter to Junta Suprema, Carmona, Feb 6, 1809.
26. ibidem, Legajo 9^2E/n.n., letter to Junta Suprema from Prior Blas de los Dolores, Convento Del Carmen, El Coronil, June 10, 1809.
27. ibidem, Legajo 11A/58, Junta Suprema circular letter to all bishops, Sevilla, Dec 7, 1809.
28. ibidem, Legajo 14A/10^3/2–3, letter to Junta Suprema, Granada, Dec 21, 1808.
29. ibidem, Legajos 47B/79–80, first Junta Suprema instructions on Church treasure, Sevilla, April 4, 1809; and 'grief' at response, n.d., 1809.
30. ibidem, Legajo 21E/43^2, and 21B/31^2, Bishop of Cuenca to Junta Suprema,

Cuenca, Dec, 1809, and testimony of Bernardo Martínez, assistant priest of the parish of San Martín, Salamanca, who took the silver to Sevilla, n.d.
31. ibidem, Legajos 47B/79, 7C/48–53 and 9K/n.n. of various dates for the Suprema's orders.
32. ibidem, Legajo 27E/275, letter from abbot to Suprema, Oct 24, 1809.
33. ACA, *Guerra de la Idependencia, Diversos*, cajas 12 and 95, for the abbot's dispute, Dec 1809–Feb 1810; AHN, *Estado*, Legajo 27E/274 for his report to the Junta Suprema, Oct 24, 1809.
34. AHN, *Estado*, Legajo 47B/113–120, authenticated accounts of silver taken from each of the townships, Nov–Dec 1809.
35. Termens Samsó and Valls Junyent (eds), 1987, Solanllonch's notes V, pp. 143–148. Following quotes from same source.
36. Dr L.I.Y.L., *El justo. Memoria del joven Salvador Torrent, natural del lugar de Chirivella*, Cádiz, 1808.
37. AHN, *Estado*, Legajo 52G/330. Undated letter, signed G.D.F.J.P., addressed to the marqués de Astorga, the then Suprema's president.
38. ibidem, Legajo 52G/333, undated, unsigned letter to Suprema.
39. Higueruela del Pino, 1982, p. 196, citing the bishop of Salamanca's pastoral, p. 9, 1813.
40. ibidem, p. 196, bishop of Salamanca's pastoral, p. 9, 1813
41. ibidem, pp. 193–195, Lozoya parish priest's report to His Majesty, 1813.

14. ORIGINS OF THE GUERRILLA

1. *Colección de papeles interesantes*, 1808, vol. 5, pp. 329–336.
2. For a scholarly history of the word 'guerrilla' see Vittorio Scotti Douglas, 'Spagna 1808: La genesi della guerriglia moderna. Guerra Irregolare, "petite guerre", "guerrilla"', in *Spagna Contemporanea*, no. 18, 2000.
3. Louís Roura i Aulinas, '"Guerra pequeña" y formas de movilización armada en la Guerra de la Independencia', in José A. Armillas Vicente (ed.) *La Guerra de la Independencia*, Estudios, vol 1., Zaragoza, 2001, p. 281.
4. Cepeda Gómez, explores this identity crisis in his 'La época de Carlos IV: crisis del ejército real borbónico', in Hernández Sánchez-Barba and Miguel Alonso Baquer (eds), Madrid, 1986, p. 165.
5. Alonso Baquer, cited by Cepeda Gómez, op. cit., 1986, p. 165.
6. Cassinello, 1995, p. 62.
7. AHN, *Estado*, Legajo 11A/12: 'Instrucción que su Magestad se ha dignado aprobar para el corso terrestre', Sevilla, April 17, 1809.
8. Horta Rodríguez, 'Legislación guerrillera en la España invadida (1808–1814), *Revue Internationale d'Histoire Militaire*, no. 56, Madrid, 1984, pp. 157–194.
9. AHN, *Estado*, Legajo 51A/6, Alcalá Galiano to Garay, Junta Suprema general secretary, Sevilla, April 10, 1809.
10. Nicolas Horta Rodríguez, 'Aportación a la historia del guerrillero Don Miguel Díaz', *Revista Historia Militar*, no. 23, 1967, Madrid, pp. 31–75.
11. ibidem, 'Prólogo a un guerrillero, el sargento Sánchez', *Revista Historia Militar*, no. 34, 1973, Madrid, p. 46.
12. Cited in Sánchez Fernández, 1997, p. 18.
13. AGS, *Papeles del Gobierno Intruso, Gracia y Justicia*, Legajo 1145, n.n. papers captured on comandante Eraso, El Empecinado's subordinate, Guadalajara, 1811 n.d.
14. José Carlos y Javier Enriquez Fernández y Enriqueta Sesmero Cutada, 'Criminalidad y Guerrilla Vizcainas en la Guerra de la Independencia', in VV.AA.(3), 1990, pp. 245–255.
15. Domínguez Ortiz, 1976, pp. 402–4.
16. In a letter to Lord Holland in late 1809, cited in Miguel Artola, 1968, p. 429.

17. Massimo Livi-Bacci's figures in Vicente Pérez Moreda, *Las crisis de mortalidad en la España interior, siglos XVI–XIX*, Madrid, 1980, p. 144.

15. FROM THE BATTLE OF TALAVERA
TO THE SUPREMA'S DEMISE

1. Muir, 1996, p. 100.
2. AHN, *Estado*, Legajo $16/5^2/43$, report from Talavera agent to Captain Josef Maria Crivell, Sept 5, 1809. Original stress in letter, the rest of which is missing.
3. ibidem, Legajos 4A/65–79 and 67A/200–201 on Extremaduran conversations with Wellington and Junta Suprema's reaction, Aug 26–27, 1809.
4. ibidem, Legajo 4A/60–64, Sevilla, Aug 24, 1809.
5. ibidem, Legajo 47C/223, report from Rodríguez to Junta Suprema, Sevilla, n.d.
6. PRO *WO1*/237, private letter from I. Stuart to Castlereagh, London, Sept 11, 1809.
7. AHN, *Estado*, Legajo 67A/207, letter from Escamilla to Junta Suprema, Sevilla, Sept 7, 1809.
8. ibidem, Legajo $17/11^1/4$, letter from La Carolina junta to Junta Suprema, La Carolina, Aug 15, 1809.
9. Cruz, 1996, p. 43, table 2.5, 'Net assets of merchants in Madrid, 1750–1850'.
10. A. Gil Novales, *Diccionario biográfico del trienio liberal*, Madrid, 1991, pp. 116–117.
11. AHN, *Estado*, Legajo 11/17, Calbo to Junta Suprema, Sevilla, Dec 20, 1809.
12. ibidem, Legajo $17/1^{33}$, April 14, 1809.
13. Calbo Rozas, 1810, p. 1.
14. The article was published in *El Correo Político y Literario de Sevilla*, which the Junta allowed to reopen only after the appointment of a special censor to vet it.
15. AHN, *Estado*, Legajo 39C/84, Calbo to Garay, Monasterio, Aug 1, 1809.
16. ibidem, Legajo 39C/96, Extremaduran junta to Junta Suprema, Badajoz, Aug 12, 1809.
17. PRO *WO1*/237, private letter from I. Stuart to Castlereagh, London, Sept 11, 1809.
18. AHN, *Estado*, Legajo 39C/116,118,121, letters from Calbo to Garay, Suprema general secretary, Medellín. Aug 28, 29 and 30, 1809.
19. ibidem, Legajo 47A/3 and 4, Junta Suprema agreement with Fr. Puebla's report, Sevilla, April 18, 1809.
20. ibidem, Legajo $47A/16^1$, Francisco Matas to the General Superintendent of Hospitals, La Carolina, June 9, 1809.
21. ibidem, Legajo 47A/18, Lorenzo Pérez to Suprema, Úbeda.
22. ibidem, Legajo 47A/72. Report by Canga Argüelles, Valencia, Nov 1, 1809. The poor's contributions refer solely to two of the city's five administrative areas, El Mar and El Grao, for which detailed figures are available. El Grao was almost exclusively a popular area.
23. AHN, *Estado*, Legajo 30E/214–225, Fr. Pablo de Vélez-Málaga, June, 1809.
24. ibidem.
25. *Semanario Patriótico*, Sevilla, May 25 and June 1, 1809.
26. ibidem, Sevilla, June 22, 1809.
27. *El Espectador sevillano*, no. 38, Nov 8, 1809, cited by Hocquellet, 1999, vol. II, p. 450.
28. AHN, *Estado*, Legajo $22^2F/22$, proposal to Junta Suprema by two of its deputies, Sevilla n.d.
29. ibidem, Legajo 82B/288–289, Sevilla, Oct 17–18, 1809.
30. ibidem, Legajo $17/11^1/23$ & 31, reports by Ravé, Suprema deputy and commissioner to La Mancha army, to Junta Suprema, La Carolina, Oct 29, 1809; and from two La Carolina envoys to La Mancha, Nov 9, 1809.
31. ibidem, Legajo 38F/445, Aréizaga to Granada junta, Nov 15, 1809.
32. PRO, *FO* 72/98/31, Cádiz, Oct, 1810.

33. AHN, *Estado*, Legajo 17/11¹/32, Ravé, Santa Cruz de la Zarza, to Junta Suprema, Nov 16, 1809.
34. ibidem, Legajo 66B/184, 191, 193 and 201, reports from Cuenca junta and Cuenca townhall, to Junta Suprema, Nov 8–20, 1809.
35. Toreno, 1838/1916, pp. 230–232; Lovett, 1965, p. 235; Schépeler, vol. II, pp. 503.
36. AHN, *Estado*, Legajo 5D/38, Saavedra to Suprema's president, Sevilla, Jan 24, 1810.
37. ibidem, Legajo, 5D/n.n., Saavedra to Suprema's president, Sevilla, Jan 25, 1810.
38. ibidem, Legajo 5D/n.n. Suprema delegates' summons to Laodicéa, Jan 27, 1810.
39. ibidem, Legajo 17/1¹⁹, Dec 27, 1809.
40. Calbo Rozas, 1813, pp. 76–94.
41. Herr, 1996, p. 84.

16. 1810–1811

1. Oman, 1902/1995, vol. 1, pp. 624–627; *Mémoires et correspondance politique et militaire du Roi Josef, publiés, annotés et mis en ordre par A. du Casse*, Paris, 1854, vol. VII, pp.134–137, cited by Hamnett, 1985, p. 89.
2. Saíz Bayo, 1988, p. 120; Tone, 1994, 117–119; Artola, 1968, p. 265.
3. AGS, *Papeles del Gobernio intruso, Gracia y Justicia*, Legajo 1103, n.n. ms. copy of circular to all provincial magistrates, n.d. but summer, 1810.
4. Issue no. 6, p. 124, no date, but La Coruña, Sept 1809, unsigned article.
5. AGS, *Papeles del Gobernio intruso, Gracia y Justicia*, Legajo 1103, n.n. same circular as in fn. 3.
6. Cassinello, 1995, p. 264; Jorge Sánchez Fernández, 'El ejército contra las guerrillas: la jefatura militar frente al fenómeno guerrillero durante la Guerra de la Independencia', *Revista Historia Militar*, Madrid, no. 87, 1999, pp. 166–168 for the case of Gerónimo Saornil's accumulation of wealth.
7. Artola, 1968, pp. 232–233.
8. Muir, 1996, p. 125.
9. Cited by Glover, 1974, p. 133.
10. Artola, 1968, p. 235.
11. ibidem, p. 233.
12. Tone, 1994, pp. 104–105; Lovett, 1965, pp. 712–713.
13. A.L.F. Schauman, *On the Road with Wellington: The Diary of a War Commissary in the Peninsular Campaigns*, trans. A.M. Ludovic, London, 1924, p. 255.
14. Artola, 1968, pp. 237–238.
15. Muir, 1996, p. 128.
16. Glover, 1974, p. 148; Esdaile, 2003, pp. 330–331.
17. General Maximilien Sebastian Foy, *Vie Militaire de General Foy*, Paris, 1900, p. 85, cited by Michael Glover, *Legacy of Glory: The Bonaparte Kingdom of Spain*, London, 1971, p. 151.
18. AHN, *Estado*, Legajo 3003/2, Josef to Suchet, Córdoba, Jan 28, 1810.
19. AGS, *Papeles del Gobierno intruso, Gracia y Justicia*, Legajo 1109, n.n., Bujalance, March 25, 1810.
20. Napoléon No. 17111, Napoleon to La Forest, French ambassador in Madrid, Paris, Nov 7, 1810, cited by Lovett, 1965, *Napoleon–Correspondance de*, 32 vols, Paris, 1857–1870.
21. His trajectory can be followed in AHN, *Estado*, Legajos 8B/17–24/n.n; 17/11¹/23; 17/11²/31; 45¹/78–107 and 47B/113–120. AGS, *Gracia y Justicia*, Legajos 1078; 1083; 1086; 1094; 1103; 1106; 1143 and 1149.
22. BL, *Eg*, 388/f.39, Amorós to king, Burgos, July 30, 1809.
23. ibidem, 388/f. 89, Amorós to Thiébault, Burgos, Sept 12, 1809.
24. ibidem, 388/ff. 53–55, Amorós to Thiébault, Burgos, Aug 2, 1809.
25. ibidem, 388/ff. 94–95, Amorós to king, Burgos, Sept 14, 1809.

26. ibidem, 388/f. 83v, Amorós to king, Burgos, Sept 8, 1809.
27. ibidem, 388/ff. 83–84, Amorós to king, Burgos, Sept 8, 1809.
28. ibidem, 388/f. 110, Amorós to various ministers, Burgos, Sept 26, 1809.
29. *Carta Circular, que escribe un Patriota español a sus Paisanos*, Santiago, April 13, 1809, unpaginated but p. 3.
30. AGS, *Papeles del Gobernio intruso, Gracia y Justicia*, Legajo 1088 for initial decree, and ibidem, Legajo 1109, letter from Benito Redondo de Toledo, Paris, Aug 14, 1810.
31. ibidem, Legajo 1086, April, 1810; many of the other decrees can be found in Legajos 1088 for 1809, and 1109 for 1810.
32. ibidem, Legajo 1083 n.n. Madrid, 1809 n.d.
33. ibidem, Legajo 1128 n.n. Madrid, January 1811.
34. ibidem, Legajo 1122 n.n. Madrid, Dec, 1810.
35. ibidem, Legajo 1143 n.n. Madrid, Nov 1810, comte de Melito to justice minister in answer to latter's question as to whether the two justices to be assigned to Aranjuez could be paid out of the produce of the royal lands.
36. AGP, *Gobierno intruso*, C.75/20, Aranjuez, Jan 25, 1810.
37. ibidem, C.75/11, Añover del Tajo, April 3, 1811, Alcalde Leonardo Carmena's report to the Aranjuez intendant.
38. AHN, *Estado*, Legajo 3003[1], Urquijo to Miguel Azanza, Madrid, July 8, 1810 (intercepted letter), published in the *Gaceta de la Regencia*, Sept 7, 1810.
39. Muñoz de Bustillo Romero, 1991, pp. 282–284.
40. *Mémoires et correspondance politique et militaire du Roi Josef*, vol. VII, p. 493, cited by Lovett, 1965, p. 533.
41. Lovett, 1965, p. 535; Artola, 1989, p. 181.
42. Lovett, 1965, p. 371.
43. Herr, 1996, p. 85.
44. Toreno, 1838/1916, pp. 300–302.
45. See Claudette Dérozier, *La Guerre d'Independance Espagnol a travers l'estampe (1808–1814)*, vol. 1, Toulouse, 1974.
46. Toreno, 1838/1916, pp. 299.
47. *Diario de sesiones de las Cortes generales y extraordinarias, 1810–1813*, 8 vols, Madrid, no. 243, June 1, 1811, cited by Pérez Ledesma, 1991, p. 191.
48. Peris Serra and Gimeno Muñoz, 1993, p. 141.
49. Quoted in Ardit, 1977, p. 225, lawyer to Consejo de Castilla, July 2, 1814.
50. Report of the agricultural commission to the Cortes, February 1812, in Pérez Ledesma, 1991, p. 201.

17. THE INVISIBLE ARMY: GUERRILLA SUCCESSES AND FAILURES

1. *Memoires du comte Miot de Mélito*, vol. III, Paris 1874, cited by Artola, 1968, p. 260.
2. Tone, 1994, pp. 102–103.
3. ibidem, 1994, pp. 116–117.
4. Cited by Aymes, 1990, p. 58.
5. Col Lorenzo Ximénez, *Breve noticia del célebre partidario el Coronel Don Francisco Espoz y Mina*, Cádiz, 1811, quoted by Moliner i Prada, 2004, p. 56. Ximénez had been a French prisoner of war on his way to France when Espoz y Mina attacked the column on May 25, 1811, and freed him and a number of others.
6. Anon (attributed to Francisco Gallardo y Merino), 1886/1989: pp. 256–257.
7. PRO, *FO*/72/116/36v–37 and ibidem 116/47 et seq., the latter being Mina's own account sent to Brigadier-General Walker from the 'Camp of Honour of Navarra', June 12, 1811, and translated into English. Also Tone, 1994, p. 120.
8. Oman, 1911/1996, vol. IV, pp. 636–637.
9. Santiago Saíz Bayo, 'El levantamiento guerrillero en la Guerra de la Independen-

cia', *Revista Historia Militar*, no. 65, 1988, Madrid, p. 102; and José Carlos y Javier Enriquez Fernández, Enriqueta Sesmero Cutanda, 'Criminalidad y guerrilla vizcainas en la Guerra de la Independencia', in VV.AA., 1990 (3), p. 251.

10. *Archivo de la Real Chancellería de Valladolid*, Sala de lo Criminal, Pleitos 36–5, quoted by Sánchez Fernández, 2002, p. 150.

11. I am indebted to Jorge Sánchez Fernández for this information which exists in the Valladolid municipal archives for 1814 and was reproduced by Narciso Alonso, a local historian at the beginning of the twentieth century. Cortes documentation of the time suggests that they were part of the guerrilla movement which may be because of their spying activities or because they actually took part in some actions. (Sánchez Fernández letter to author.)

12. Intercepted letter, cited in Tone, 1994, p. 131.

13. Espoz y Mina, vol. 1, p. 86.

14. Alexander, 1984, p. 196.

15. Tone, 1994, pp. 141–142.

16. Alexander, 1984, p. 125.

17. ibidem, p. 237.

18. PRO, *FO/72/99/230*, letter from Sergeant Major Carré, Sevilla, April 8, 1810 (intercepted by guerrillas between Segovia and Madrid and passed on to marqués de la Romana in Badajoz, who in turn gave a copy to the British military representative).

19. Reynaud, 1992, p. 189.

20. Torre, 1991, p. 50, cuadro 4. This excellent study informs us equally on the guerrillas' exactions of its population. Tone, 1994, p. 159, fn. 46, gives the average annual product of agriculture, commerce and industry in Navarra in the period before the war as 71.6m reales.

21. Torre, 1991, 'Resumen totales', p. 91. This is based on the 116 towns and villages for which accurate data is available.

22. Reynaud, 1992, p. 88. The Bonapartist-set exchange rate to the franc was 3.56 reales.

23. M.A. Sánchez Gomez, *Cantabria en los siglos XVIII y XIX*, Santander, 1986, pp. 161–188; also the same author's 'Guerra de Independencia y presión fiscal extraordinaria: el caso de Cantabria', in VV.AA., 1990 (3).

24. AGS, *Papeles del Gobierno intruso, Gracia y Justica*, Legajo, 1146, n.n., Pedro Dárripe, Santander, March 6, 1811.

25. ibidem, Legajo 1085 and 1104 n.n. The Extraordinary Crimes Tribunal was about to judge an ex-Franciscan priest and companion of Mina when the latter took two French officers, a chief medical officer and five soldiers prisoner in Tafalla. Mina immediately proposed to exchange these for his companion and another guerrilla about to be tried with him. D'Agoult agreed. This 'serious affair', as the Bonapartist government termed it, subsequently led to a recommendation that the king order d'Agoult not to permit the recurrence of such events which disturbed public order. Jan–Feb, 1810, Pamplona–Madrid.

26. Sánchez Fernández, 1997, p. 31.

27. T. Pérez Delgado, 'Salamanca en la Guerra de la Independencia: el vivir de una ciudad', in *Los Arapiles. Encuentro de Europa*, Salamanca, p. 186.

28. These songs are reproduced from a variety of sources including J. Gella Iturriago, 'Canciones de la Guerra de la Independencia', in *Estudios de la Guerra de la Independencia*. vol. II, Zarazoza, 1966.

29. All Matías Calvo's quotes are from Marcén Letosa's published transcription, *El manuscrito de Matías Calvo*, Zaragoza, 2000.

30. Andrés Martín, *Historia de los sucesos militares de la División de Navarra y demas acontecimientos de este Reyno durante la última guerra contra el Tirano Napoleón*, 2 vols, Pamplona, 1953, vol. 2, pp. 53–54, quoted in Tone, 1994, p. 208 fn. 4.

31. Tone, 1994, p. 135; Alexander, 1984, p. 159.

32. French person in vulgar Spanish, from the provençal 'gavach', or crude speaker, according to the dictionary of the Real Academia of the Spanish language (ed. 21,

1998), applied to French troops as a synomyn for cowardice in Aragonese. *Vocabulario Básico Bilingue* by A. Martínez, Huesca, 1997.
33. Oman, 1914/1996, vol. V, appendices, 'The Scovell ciphers', pp. 611–618.
34. AHN, *Estado*, Legajo, 10/1/32, and *Gazeta de Madrid*, Saturday, April 29, 1809.
35. AGS, *Papeles del Gobierno intruso, Gracia y Justicia*, Legajo 1121, n.n. Guadalajara Prefect Diego Gallari to justice minister, June 26, 1811.
36. ibidem, Legajo 1122 n.n.
37. ibidem, Legajo, 1148. n.n. Treasury minister report to police minister, Manuel García Pardo, July 23 (no year).
38. Reynaud, 1992, p. 86.
39. AHN, *Estado*, Legajo 68A/53. On Sept 7, 1808, the united juntas of Castilla, León and Galicia informed the Sevilla junta that 'due to the French treatment of Spanish prisoners, justice demands the use of reprisals on the French troops your army has taken (at Bailén)'. Lugo, Sept 7, 1808.
40. Tone, 1994, p. 87.
41. ibidem, pp. 110–111.
42. ibidem, pp. 128–129.
43. PRO *FO* 72/94/134–135, regency request to British resident minister Henry Wellesley, Cádiz, March 23, 1810.
44. ibidem, *FO*72/116/31, White to William Hamilton, La Coruña, June 5, 1811.
45. ibidem FO72/132/77, Alicante, Sept 3, 1812.
46. Ana Isabel Rodríguez Zurro, 'Colaboración y apoyo de la guerrilla y de la armada de Gran Bretaña durante la Guerra de la Independencia', in *Investigaciones Históricas*, 17, Valladolid, 1997, pp. 161–163.
47. AGS, *Gobierno Intruso, Gracia y Justicia*, Legajo 1130, n.n., letter from Aldamar to justice minister, Santander, July 10, 1810.
48. Alexander, 1984, p. 239.
49. Lazo, S., *Memorias del alcalde de Roa. Don Gregorio González Arrán 1788–1840*, Roa, 1995, p. 24.
50. Farias, *Memorias de soldados franceses durante la Guerra de la Independencia*, p. 326, quoted Lovett, 1965, p. 683.
51. Alexander, 1984, p. 237.
52. ibidem, 1984, p. 161.
53. Cassinello, 1995, p. 161. Point 33 of El Empecinado's 'Response to the Guadalajara junta's representations'.
54. Espoz y Mina, 1851–1852/1962, vol. 1, p. 21.
55. Tone, 1994, pp. 18–19.
56. Torné i Domingo, 1990, pp. 50–51.
57. VV. AA. *Victoires, conquêtes, désastres, revers et guerres civiles des Français*, Vol. XIX, Paris, 1820, cited by Reynaud, 1992, p. 98.
58. Suchet to Reille, who had taken command of Aragón while Suchet was engaged in the siege of Tortosa, June 11, 1812, cited by Reynaud, 1992, pp. 117–118.
59. Suchet to Marshal Berthier, Nov 22, 1810, cited by Reynaud, p. 118.
60. Marshall Bessières to French minister of war, San Sebast-ián (intercepted) quoted by Tone, 1994, p. 141.
61. AGS, *Papeles del Gobierno Intruso, Gracia y Justicia*, Legajo 1076 n.n.
62. Martínez Martel y Abadía. 1887, pp. 385–394.
63. Muñoz de Bustillo Romero, 1991, p. 276.
64. Ribechini, 1996, Document 15, pp. 165–170.
65. Tone, 1994, p. 126.

18. 1812–1814

1. AGS, *Papeles del Gobierno intruso, Gracia y Justicia*, Legajo 1146, n.n., San Martín neighbourhood police commissioner report to police minister, March 16, 1811.

2. AV, Legajo 2–136–22, quoted by Espada Burgos, 1968, p. 603.
3. AGS, *Papeles del Gobierno intruso, Gracia y Justicia*, Legajo 1146, n.n., San Martín neighbourhood police commissioner to police minister, Jan 17, 1811.
4. ibidem, Legajo 1145 n.n., Maravillas neighbourhood police commissioner to police minister, Sept 19, 1811.
5. ibidem, Legajos 1145, 1146, 1148, 1150, 1151 for various reports on gambling.
6. ibidem, Legajo 1146 n.n., San Geronimo neighbourhood police commmissioner to police minister, reports of Feb 10 and 12, 1812.
7. ibidem, Legajo 1146 n.n. Scrap of paper giving the theatre's takings on these two days.
8. ibidem, Legajo 1151, n.n., report from El Barquillo neighbourhood police commissioner to police minister, Madrid, April 29, 1812.
9. ibidem, Legajo 1151, n.n., San Geronimo neighbourhood police commisioner to police minister, Madrid, Jan 16, 1812.
10. ibidem, Legajo 1145, n.n., Judge León de Sagasta, who had collaborated with the Bonapartist regime from the beginning and in Feb 1811 had been been appointed judge of the first instance in Madrid, to police minister March 22, 1812.
11. Anes, 1976, p. 259.
12. AGS, *Papeles del Gobierno intruso, Gracia y Justicia*, Legajo 1145 n.n. Official list of all foodstuffs and their prices on May 11, 1811; same Legajo, secret police report on wheat prices paid in the Madrid grain market on May 11, 1812.
13. ibidem, Legajo 1146, n.n., report to interior minister, Madrid, March 1, 1812.
14. Miot de Mélito, Paris, 1874, vol. III, p. 210.
15. Mercader Riba, 1971, p. 301; Mirta Núñez Díaz Bacart, 'Beneficiencia bonapartista para la hambruna madrileña', in *Ciencia e independencia politica* (ed. A. Gil Novales), Madrid, 1996, pp. 147–161.
16. AGS, *Papeles del gobierno intruso, Gracia y Justicia*, Legajo 1145, n.n. Police minister's report to the president of the Madrid extraordinary crimes tribunal and the commandant of the royal gendarmerie to the police minister, Madrid, April 10, 1812. Also Mercader Riba, 1971, p. 302.
17. AGS, *Papeles del gobierno intruso, Gracia y Justicia*, Legajo 1145, n.n. Madrid secret police report of April 3, 1812.
18. ibidem, Legajo 1151, n.n., Madrid secret police report of April 16, 1812.
19. ibidem, Legajo 1151, n.n., Madrid secret police report, May 5, 1812.
20. ibidem, Legajo 1145, n.n., Report of the San Lorenzo neighbourhood police, April 12, 1812.
21. ibidem, Legajo 1145, n.n., Madrid secret police report of May 11, 1812.
22. ibidem, Legajo 1145, n.n., Madrid secret police report of June 1, 1812.
23. *Mémoires et Correspondance du Roi Josef* IX, 4–6, Josef to Marshal Berthier, Madrid, May 4, 1812, cited by Mercader Riba, 1971, p. 305.
24. Mesonero Romanos, 1967, pp. 91 et seq.
25. Toreno, 1838/1916, p. 409 gives this figure.
26. Alexander, 1984, p. 150.
27. PRO, *FO/72/*115, Wellesley correspondence p. 26, reports of Oct 28 and Nov 8, 1811.
28. ibidem, *FO/72/*114, Wellesley correspondence pp. 8v–9, report from Sevilla of Oct 4, 1811 and *FO/72/129*, pp. 132/132v, agent's reports of Jan 21 and 24, 1812.
29. ibidem, *FO/72/129*, Wellesley's correspondence, p. 1 et seq., Cádiz, Jan 13, 1812.
30. ibidem, *FO/72/*115, Wellesley's correspondence, p. 274 & *FO/72/*129, p. 198v, reports from Sevilla agent, Dec 19 and Dec, 5, 1811.
31. *Gaceta de Sevilla*, Friday, Nov 15, 1811, cited by Moreno Alonso, 1995, p. 239.
32. Moreno Alonso, 1995, p. 240; see also PRO, *FO/72/*129, Wellesley's correspondence, pp. 132–132v, Sevilla patriot agent's report of Jan 21, 1812.
33. PRO, *FO/72/*114, Wellesley's correspondence, pp. 8v–9, Sevilla, Oct 4, 1811.
34. *Gaceta de Sevilla*, Tuesday, May 7, 1811, cited by Moreno Alonso, 1995, p. 238.
35. PRO, *FO/72/*113, Wellesley correspondence, pp. 146 et seq., Wellesley to the

marques of Wellesley, Cádiz, Aug 31, 1811; and ibidem, pp. 3–7v, Colonel Green to Wellesley, aboard HMS Invincible off Arens de Mar (sic), July 11, 1811.

36. Ardit, 2003, 'Guerra de independencia y lucha antifeudal' (lecture), p. 5.
37. Ardit, 1977, pp. 148–154 gives a detailed account of the intrigues.
38. PRO, *FO/72/98*, Wellesley correspondence, pp. 9–11, Doyle to Henry Wellesley, Valencia, Oct 16, 1810.
39. ibidem, *FO/72/*113, p. Wellesley correspondence, pp. 19 et seq., Cádiz, August 10, 1811.
40. Ardit, 1977, pp. 159–161.
41. Arteche, 1868–1903, vol. XII, pp. 362–363.
42. This and all the following quotations are from Brother Pelegrin Benavent, who related his experiences succinctly in a report after the war, which is cited textually in Ricardo Blanco, *Los Albores de la España fernandina*, Madrid, 1968, pp. 25–36.
43. Mercader Riba, 1971, pp. 278–287; also the same author's *Barcelona durante la ocupación francesa (1808–1814)*, Madrid, 1949.
44. ACA, *Dominación Napoleónica*, Sección Diversos, Caja I, Legajo 1/1, Jan 1813.
45. ibidem, Caja IV/1, Legajo 5, Préfêt du Ter, Gerona, Dec 22, 1812; ibidem, *Dominación Napoleónica*, Caja V/3, Legajo 5, Les Cirses to Préfêt du Ter, Figueras, Nov 16, 1812, Legajo. 5; ibidem, *Dominación Napoleónica*, Caja VII/1, dossier 10, illegible to Préfêt du Ter, Palamós, May 1, 1812.
46. PRO, *WO/269/*17, Colonel Green, British military adviser to the Catalan army, put the army's total armed strength at 26,100 of whom 15,500 were infantry and 630 cavalry and a further 10,000 armed reserve or militia, and 600 men from the irregular partidas. Unarmed: infantry 4,800, cavalry 360, reserve or militia 28,000, General total, 58,900 infantry, 990 cavalry. Colonel Green to Lord Liverpool, Vich, Jan 1812 At the same time he estimated the French strength at 17,000 infantry and 1,400 cavalry (ibidem, *WO/269/*19).
47. ibidem, *WO 269/*359–362, Codrington to Lacy, HMS *Blake* off Villa Nueva, March 9, 1812.
48. ibidem, *WO 269/*397–400, Codrington to Lacy, HMS *Blake*, off Arenys del Mar, March 23, 1812.
49. Artola, 1968, p. 274, Oman, 1902–1995, vol. 4, pp. 638–642; vol. 5, pp. 82–84; vol. 6, pp. 741–745.
50. Artola, 1968, p. 278.
51. Muir, 1966, pp. 199–202, whose account of Ciudad Rodrigo and Badajoz I have basically followed.
52. Mesonero Romanos, 1975, pp. 91–92.
53. Fernando Jiménez de Gregorio, 'La Villa de Madrid en la guerra por la independencia: dos sucesos en el año 1812', *Anales del Instituto de Estudios Madrileños*, vol. XXI, pp. 435–447, Madrid, 1984.
54. PRO, *FO 72/*129, Wellesley correspondence, pp. 187–187v, Madrid, Jan 24, 1812.
55. AGS, *Papeles del Gobierno intruso, Gracia y Justicia*, Legajo 1145, n.n. Madrid, April 3, 1812.
56. Lovett, 1966, vol. II, p. 464, and Herr, 1996, pp. 87–88 give the best resumé of the constitution in English.
57. Pérez Ledesma, 1991, pp. 183–186.
58. AD de Toledo, *Borbon*, Legajo 41, Dr Ortega y Canedo, vicar of Ciudad Real, to Nicasio Tomás, Siruela (Badajoz), June 13, 1811 and ibidem, Almadén, 1813, quoted by Higueruela del Pino, 1982, pp. 154 and 159.
59. Herr, 1996, pp. 88–89.
60. Morange, 1989, p. 79.
61. Toreno, 1838/1916, p. 410.
62. See the biographical studies of Juan Marqués Merchán, *Don Bartolomé Jose Gallardo, Noticia de su vida y escritos*, Madrid, 1921, Pedro Saínz Rodríguez, *Bartolomé J. Gallardo y la crítica de su tiempo*, Madrid, 1986 and Alejandro Pérez Vidal, 'La recepción del pensamiento de los "ideólogos" en la España de Carlos IV:

la obra juvenil de Bartolomé José Gallardo', in VV.AA. 1994 (1), vol. II, pp. 1052–1064.

63. Gallardo, 1838, pp. 129–132.
64. See Prologue, p. xvi.
65. Hamnett, 1985, pp. 165–167.
66. Lovett, 1966, p. 471.
67. Azucena Pedraz Marcos, 'La cuestión religiosa en los periódicos de la Guerra de la Independencia' citing *El Sensato*, no. 73, Jan 21, 1813, in *Ciencia e independencia política* (ed. A. Gil Novales), Madrid, 1996, pp. 327–331.
68. Toreno, 1838/1916, p. 444.
69. Lovett, 1966, p. 479–480; Toreno, 1838/1916, pp. 450–51; Artola, 1968, p. 452.
70. This case, of which much of the early investigatory documentation still exists, has been extensively explored by the Spanish anthropologist María Tausiet in her book, *Los Posesos de Tosos (1812–1814). Brujería y justicia popular en tiempos de revolución*, Zaragoza, 2002. I must thank her for allowing me to quote extensively from the book, and to William Christian for bringing it to my notice in the first place. (The page numbers cited are from the book.) The interpretations within the war's setting, however, are exclusively mine and Tausiet bears no responsibility for them.
71. Tausiet, 2002, p. 57.
72. Alvar Monferrer. *Els endimoniats de la Balma*, Valencia, 1997, cited by Tausiet, fn. 54, p. 57.
73. Cases cited by Tausiet, 2002, fn. 53, p. 58.
74. ibidem, pp. 36–39.
75. ibidem, p. 41.
76. ibidem, p. 95, Commissioner Bernard's report of Dec 4, 1813, Cariñena.
77. ibidem, p. 106, Commissioner Bernard's report, n.d.
78. ibidem, pp. 64–65, citing the priest Francisco Marcos' report of 1817.

19. MILITARY VICTORY AND POLITICAL DEFEAT

1. Muir, 1996, pp. 262–265.
2. Pierre Gassier and Juliet Wilson, *The Life and Complete Works of Goya* (2nd English edition), New York, 1981, p. 223.
3. Muir, 1996, pp. 264–271.
4. Sánchez Fernández, 2002, p. 124, fn. 383.
5. Ardit, 1977, p. 228.
6. Lovett, 1966, p. 815.
7. ibidem, p. 819.
8. PRO, *FO* 72/160/12, Madrid, March 25, 1814; also *The Diary and Correspondence*, 1930, pp. 70–71.
9. Muir, 1996, p. 211.
10. PRO, *FO* 72/129/213, Wellesley correspondence to Castlereagh, Cádiz, March 10, 1812.
11. Lovett, 1966, p. 832.
12. Muir, 1996, p. 305. Barcelona was not finally freed from French occupation until May 28, 1814 – the longest of any city in Spain, having lasted continuously for six years. Suchet lost his outlying fortresses of Lérida, Mequineza and Monzón in mid-February 1814, thanks to a ruse as cunning as any Napoleon's generals had used to take Spanish fortresses at the beginning of 1808: faked patriot orders to withdraw bearing Suchet's forged signature were delivered to their French officers in command who obeyed them.
13. Gassier and Wilson, 1981, p. 210.
14. Elie Faure, introduction, Francisco de Goya, *The Disasters of the War*, London, 1937, p. 8.

15. Gassier and Wilson, 1981, p. 160.
16. ibidem, p. 206.
17. ibidem, p. 220.
18. Fontana and Garrabou, 1986, pp. 97–104.
19. Higueruela del Pino, 1982, p. 169, parish priest's communication, n.d., 1815.
20. *Estado comparativo y demonstrativo del la riqueza territorial de que se componia el vezindario de la Villa de Puerto Real en el año del 1808 antes de la invasion de los enemigos en 1810*, ms., BN, (R.63225).
21. Sherwood, 1988, p. 64.
22. ibidem, 1988, p. 64.
23. Higueruela del Pino, 1982, pp. 167–168.
24. Rosa Ros Massana, 'La formación d'un enclau industrial. La indústria tèxtil llanera de Béjar (1680–1850)', doctoral thesis, vol. 2, chap. 6, 1996.
25. Pablo García Colmenares, *Evolucion y crisis de la industria textil castellana, Palencia 1750–1990*, Madrid, 1992, p. 144.
26. ibidem, p. 150.
27. Simon Tarrès, 1985, pp. 125–126.

Bibliography

Aguilar Piñal, Francisco, 1989: 'Predicación y mentalidad popular en la Andalucía del siglo XVIII', in Álvarez Santaló, C. Buxo et al., 1989 (3), vol 2, pp. 57–71

Alexander, Don W., 1984: **Rod of Iron: French Counterinsurgency Policy in Aragón during the Peninsular War,** Wilmington

Alía y Plana, Jesusmaría, 1992: 'El primer lunes de mayo de 1808 en Madrid,' in Museo del Ejército (ed.), 1992, Madrid

Alianza, 1988: **Enciclopedia de Historia de España,** 7 vols, ed. Miguel Artola, Madrid

Alonso Alvarez, Luis, 1986: **Comercio colonial y crisis del antiguo régimen en Galicia (1778–1818),** La Coruña

Alvarez Cañas, Maria Luisa, 1990: **Cambio político y crisis del Antiguo Régimen en Alicante (1808–1814). La Guerra de la Independencia en Alicante,** Alicante

Álvarez Junco, José, 2001: **Mater Dolorosa. La idea de España en el siglo XIX,** Madrid

Álvarez Santaló, León Carlos, 1988–1989 (1): 'La Iglesia y el estado' in Domínguez Ortiz (ed.), 1988–1989, vol 7, pp. 542–582

———, 1988–1989 (2), 'Economía y sociedad en el siglo XVIII', in Domínguez Ortiz (ed) 1988–1989, vol 7, pp. 209–318

Álvarez Santaló, León Carlos, Buxó, María Jesús and Rodríguez Becerra, S. (eds.), 1989 (3): **La religiosidad popular,** vol. 2, **Vida y muerte: La imaginación religiosa,** Barcelona

Andrés-Gallego, José: 1991: **Historia general de la gente poco importante, América y Europa hacia 1789,** Madrid

Andújar Castillo, Francisco, 1991: **Los militares en la España del siglo XVIII: Un estudio social,** Granada

Anes, Gonzalo, 1970: **Las crisis agrarias en la España moderna,** Madrid

———, 1972: **Economía e 'Ilustración' en la España del siglo XVIII,** (2nd ed.), Barcelona

———, 1976: **El Antiguo Régimen: los Borbones,** (2nd ed.) Madrid

———, (ed.), 1990: **Informes en el expediente de ley agraria,** Madrid

———, 1996: 'Del "Expediente de ley agraria" al *Informe* de Jovellanos,' in García Sanz and Sanz Fernández, (eds), 1996, pp. 69–103

Anon. (generally attributed to Kotska Bayo, Estanislao), 1884: **Historia de la vida y reinado de Fernando VII de España,** Madrid

Ardit, Manuel, 1977: **Revolución liberal y revuelta campesina,** Barcelona

———, 1981: 'La rebellia camperola en la crisi de l'Antic Règim (1801–1823)' in VV. AA., 1981, pp. 45–53

Armillas Vicente, José A. (ed), 2001: **La Guerra de la Independencia: Estudios,** Zaragoza

Artola, Miguel, 1968: **La España de Fernando VII** (vol. XXVI of **Historia de España,** ed. Ramón Menéndez Pidal), Madrid

————, 1983: **Antiguo Régimen y revolución liberal,** (2nd ed.) Barcelona

————, 1989 (1): **Los Afrancesados,** Madrid

————, 1989 (2): 'Las declaraciones de derechos y los primeros textos fundamentales galos en los orígenes del constitucionalismo español', in Moral Sandoval, Enrique, 1989, Madrid, pp. 73–87

Atienza Hernández, Ignacio, 1987: **Aristocracía, poder y riqueza en la España moderna. La Casa de Osuna, siglos XV–XIX,** Madrid

Aymes, Jean-René, 1973–1990: **La Guerre de Independence Espagnole (1808–1814),** Paris

———— (ed), 1989: **España y la Revolución francesa,** Barcelona

Barreiro, Xosé R., 1982, **Los orígines del pensamiento reaccionario y liberal en Galicia (1808–1833),** Vigo

————, 1993: **Galicia Historia,** Tomo VII, Historia Contemporánea Politica (siglo XIX), Chapters 1, 2 and 3: 'De la Revolución francesa (1789) a la Guerra de la Independencia (1808)'; 'El levantamiento contra los franceses' and 'Conquista y liberación de Galicia (1809)', La Coruña

Barthèlemy, Rodolfo G. de, 1995: **'El Marquesito'. Juan Díaz Porlier, general que fue de los ejércitos nacionales (1788–1815),** 2 vols. Santiago de Compostela

Benach i Torrents, Manuel, 1968: **El corregidor Lluis Freixas i la Guerra del Francès a Vilafranca, 1808–1813,** Vilafranca del Penedès

Bernal, A.M., 1979: **La lucha por la tierra en la crisis del antiguo régimen,** Madrid

Bilbao, Luis María, & Fernández de Pinedo, Emiliano, 1988: 'Artesanía e industria' in Alianza, 1988, vol 1, pp 137–151

Blanch, Adolfo, 1861/1968 (facsimile): **Historia de la Guerra de la Independencia en el antiguo principado,** Barcelona

Boix y Ricarte, Vicente, 1981: **Historia del País Valenciano,** vol III, Madrid/Barcelona

Butrón Prida, Gonzalo, and Ramos Santana, Alberto (eds.), 2000: **Intervención exterior y crisis del Antiguo Régimen en España,** Huelva

Callahan, William J., 1984: **Church, Politics, and Society in Spain, 1750–1874,** Harvard

Candau Chacón, Mª Luisa, 1994: **El Clero rural de Sevilla en el siglo XVIII,** Sevilla

Canella Secades, Fermín, 1908: **Memorias asturianas del año ocho,** Oviedo

Cannon, John, 1995: 'The British Nobility, 1660–1800' in Scott, H.M. (ed), 1995 pp. 53–81

Carantoña Alvarez, Francisco, 1984: **La Guerra de la Independencia en Asturias,** Oviedo

Cardús, Salvador, 1962: **Historial de la Guerra Napoleònica a Terrassa, Heroic sacrific d'un patriota exemplar,** Terrassa

Carr, Raymond, 1966: **Spain 1808–1939,** Oxford

Carré Aldao, Eugenio, 1915: **El Alzamiento contra los Franceses en Galicia, 1808–1809,** Madrid

Cassinello Pérez, Andrés, 1995: **Juan Martín, 'El Empecinado', o el amor a la libertad,** Madrid

Catalá Sanz, Jorge Antonio, 1995: **Rentas y patrimonios de la nobleza valenciana en el siglo XVIII,** Madrid

Castro, Concepción de, 1987: **El pan de Madrid. El abasto de las ciudades españolas del Antiguo Régimen,** Madrid

Cepeda Gómez, José, 1990: **El ejército en la política española (1787–1843),** Madrid

————, 1986: 'La época de Carlos IV: crisis del ejército real borbónico' in Hernández Sánchez-Barba, Mario, and Alonso Becquer, Miguel (eds), 1986, Madrid

Chartier, Roger, 1991: **The Cultural Origins of the French Revolution,** (trs. Lydia G. Cochrane), Durham and London

Corona, Carlos, 1957: **Revolución y reacción en el reinado de Carlos IV,** Madrid

Cruz, Juan, 1996: **Gentlemen, Bourgeois and Revolutionaries: Political Change and Cultural Persistence among the Spanish Dominant Groups, 1750–1850,** Cambridge

Cúndaro, Fr. Manuel, 1833/1953: **Historia político-crítico militar de la plaza de Gerona en los sitios de 1808 y 1809,** Gerona

Davies, D. W., 1974: **Sir John Moore's Peninsular Campaign,** The Hague

Delgado, Sabino, 1979: **Guerra de la Independencia: proclamas, bandos y combatientes,** Madrid

Derozier, Albert, 1975: **Escritores políticos españoles, 1780–1854,** Madrid

Díaz Torrejón, Francisco Luis, 2001: **Osuna Napoleónica, 1810–1812,** Sevilla

————, 2004: **Guerrilla, contraguerrilla y delincuencia en la Andalucía napoleónica (1810–1812),** vol 1, Ronda

Diego, Emilio de, 1992: 'Madrid: de Fontainebleau al Dos de Mayo', in Enciso Recio (ed.), Madrid

Díez Rodríguez, Fernando, 1990: **Viles y mecánicos, trabajo y sociedad en la Valencia preindustrial,** Valencia

Domergue, Lucienne, 1989: 'Propaganda y contrapropaganda en España durante la Revolución francesa' in Aymes, ed., 1989

Domínguez Ortiz, Antonio, 1976: **Sociedad y estado en el siglo XVIII español,** Barcelona

———— (ed.), 1988–1989: **Historia de España,** vol. 7, **El reformismo borbónico (1700– 1789);** vol 9, **La transición del Antiguo al Nuevo régimen,** Barcelona

————, 1991 (1): 'La nobleza en la España del siglo XVIII' in Saavedra & Villares (eds), Barcelona, Vol 1, pp. 1–15

————, 1991 (2): 'Los comerciantes en la sociedad andaluza de la Ilustración', in García-Baquero González (ed.), Cádiz, Vol 1, pp. 191–206

Donapétry Iribarnégaray, Juan, n.d.1991: **Historia de Vivero y su concejo,** Vivero (facsmile)

Egido López, Teófanes, 1990: 'La religiosidad de los españoles (siglo XVIII)' in VV.AA, 1990 (1), Madrid, Vol 1, pp. 767–792

Eiras Roel, Antonio, 1982: 'Problemas demográficos del siglo XVIII', in VV.AA., 1982, Taragona

Elorza, Antonio, 1970: **La ideología liberal en la Ilustración Española,** Madrid

————, 1989: 'El temido Árbol de la Libertad' in Aymes (ed.), 1989

Enciso Recio, Luís Miguel (ed.), 1996: **La burguesía española en la edad moderna. Actas del Congreso Internacional,** Madrid/Soria, 1991: Valladolid/Madrid

———— (ed.) 1992, **El Dos de Mayo y sus precedentes. Actas del Congreso Internacional,** Madrid

Enríquez Fernández, José Carlos, 1996: **Costumbres festivas y diversiones populares burlescas, Vizcaya, 1700–1838,** Bilbao

Esdaile, Charles J., 1988: **The Spanish Army in the Peninsular War,** Manchester and New York

————, 2003: **The Peninsular War: A New History,** London

————, 2004: **Fighting Napoleon: Guerrillas, Bandits and Adventurers in Spain, 1808– 1814,** New Haven and London

Farias, 1920: **Memorias de la guerra de la independencia, escritas por soldados franceses,** Madrid

Fernández García, Antonio, 1992: 'La sociedad madrileña bajo la ocupación francesa', in Enciso Recio (ed.), 1992, Madrid

Fernández, Roberto (ed.), 1985: **España en el siglo XVIII. Homenaje a Pierre Vilar,** Barcelona

Fernández del Pinedo, Emiliano, 1982: 'Coyuntura y política económicas' in Tuñón de Lara (ed.), 1982, chaps 1–8

Figueroa Lalinde, Ma. Luz, 1992: **La Guerra de la Independencia en Galicia,** Vigo

Fontana, Josep, 1978: **La quiebra de la monarquía absoluta, 1814–1820** (3rd revised ed.), Barcelona

————, 1979, **La crisis del Antiguo Régimen 1808–1833,** Barcelona

————, 1983: **Cambio económico y actitudes políticas en la España del siglo XIX,** (5ᵗʰ ed.), Barcelona

————, 1988: **La Fi de L'Antic Regim i la Industrialització 1787–1868. Història de Catalunya,** vol V, Barcelona.

————, 1991: 'Burguesía e Ilustración: mitos y realidades', in García-Baquero (ed.) 1991, pp 17–28

Fontana, Josep and Ramón Garrabou,, 1986: **Guerra y hacienda La hacienda del gobierno central en los años de la Guerra de la Independencia (1808–1814),** Alicante

Franch, Ricardo, 1986: **Crecimiento comercial y enriquecimiento burgués en la Valencia del siglo XVIII,** Valencia
Fuentes, Juan Francisco, 1988: **Si no hubiera esclavos no habría tiranos. Proclamas, artículos y documentos de la revolución española (1789–1837),** Madrid
————, 1989: **José Marchena. Biografía política e intelectual,** Barcelona
Fugier, André, 1930: **Napoléon et l'Espagne,** 1799–1808, 2 vols., Paris
Gallego Burín, Antonio, 1922/1990: **Granada en la Guerra de la Independencia. Los periódicos granadinos en la Guerra de la Independencia,** Granada
García, Máximo & Bartolomé Yun, 1997: 'Pautas de consumo, estilos de vida y cambio político en las ciudades castellanas a fines del Antiguo Régimen', in José Ignacio Fortea Pelser (ed), 1997: **Imagines de la diversidad El mundo urbano en la corona de Castilla (siglos XVI–XVIII),** Santander
García-Baquero González, Antonio (ed.), 1991: **La burguesía de negocios en la Andalucía de la Ilustración,** 2 vols, Cádiz
García Gutiérrez, Patrocinio, 1991: **La ciudad de León durante la Guerra de la Independencia,** Valladolid
García-Noblejas, José Antonio, 1982: **Manzanares. Guerra de la Independencia,** Madrid
García Prado, Justiniano, 1953: **Historia del alzamiento, guerra y revolución de Asturias,** Oviedo
García Sanz, Ángel, 1985: 'Introducción' in García Sanz, Ángel, and Garrabou, Ramón (eds) vol. 1, 1985, Barcelona
————, 1986: **Desarrollo y crisis del Antiguo Régimen en Castilla la Vieja,** Torrejón de Ardoz, Madrid, (2nd ed)
García Sanz, Angel, & Ramón Garrabou, (eds), 1985: **Historia agraria de la España contemporánea, Vol 1. Cambio social y nuevas formas de propiedad (1800–1850),** Barcelona
García Sanz, Ángel, & Jesús Sanz Fernández, (eds) 1996: **Reformas y políticas agrarias en la historia de España,** Madrid
Gascón, Domingo, 1908: **La provincia de Teruel en la Guerra de la Independencia,** Madrid
Gay, Peter, 1977: **The Enlightenment: An Interpretation: The Science of Freedom,** New York
Genovés Amorós, Vicent, 1967: **Valencia contra Napoleón,** Valencia
Glover, Michael, 1974: **The Peninsular War 1807–1814: A Concise Military History,** Newton Abbot
Gómez Arteche, José, 1868–1903: **Guerra de la Independencia. Historia militar de España de 1808 a 1814,** 14 vols, Madrid
Gómez Imaz, Manuel, 1908: **Sevilla en 1808,** Sevilla
————, 1910: **Los periódicos durante la Guerra de la Independencia,** Madrid
Gómez Villafranca, Román, 1908: **Extremadura en la guerra de la independencia,** Badajoz
González Alonso, Benjamín, 1988: 'La Justicia' in Alianza, vol 2, Madrid
González-Pola de la Granja, Pablo, 1994: **Sargadelos 1798. Un motín en la Galicia de finales del Antiguo Régimen,** La Coruña
Gould, W, 1995: **Mercenaries of the Napoleonic Wars,** Brighton
Guerrero, Ana Clara, 1990: **Viajeros británicos en la España del siglo XVIII,** Madrid
Guillamón Alvarez, Javier, 1981: **Honor y honra en la España del siglo XVIII,** Madrid
Guirao, Ramón & Luis Sorando, 1995: **El Alto Aragón en la Guerra de la Independencia,** Zaragoza
Hamnett, Brian R, 1985: **La política española en una época revolucionaria, 1790–1820,** Mexico
Hernández Sánchez-Barba, Mario & Alonso Baquer, Miguel (eds), 1986: **Historia social de las fuerzas armadas españolas,** Vol II: **Revolución nacional e independencia,** Madrid
Herr, Richard, 1958: **The Eighteenth Century Revolution in Spain,** Princeton
————, 1996: 'The Constitution of 1812 and the Spanish Road to Parliamentary Monarchy,' in **Revolution and the Meanings of Freedom in the Nineteenth Century,** (ed. Isser Woloch), Stanford
Higueruela del Pino, Leandro, 1982: **La Diócesis de Toledo durante la Guerra de la Independencia Española,** Toledo

Hocquellet, Richard, 1999: **Du Soulevement patriotique á la Souveraineté nationale. La première phase de la Révolution Espagnole, 1808–1810,** 2 vols, Doctoral thesis, Université Paris I – Panthéon Sorbonne

Holland, Lord Henry Richard, 1851: **Foreign Reminiscences** (ed. Henry Edward Lord Holland), New York

Iglesias Rodríguez, Juan José, 1991: 'La inversión industrial burguesa en el Cádiz del siglo XVIII. Las oportunidades perdidas' in García-Baquero (ed.) 1991, vol II, pp 87–98

Izquierdo, Manuel, 1963: **Antecedentes y comienzos del reinado de Fernando VII,** Madrid

Jiménez de Gregorio, Fernando, 1947: **Murcia en los dos primeros años de la guerra por la independencia,** Murcia

Jover Zamora, José María, 1958: 'La Guerra de la Independencia española en el marco de las guerras europeas de liberación,' **Historia de la Guerra,** vol 1, Zaragoza, 1958, pp. 41–165

La Forest, Comte de, 1905: **Correspondance du Comte de la Forest, ambassadeur de France en Espagne, 1808–1813** (ed. Geoffroy de Granmaison), 5 vols, Paris

Lafoz Rabaza, Herminio, 1992: **José de Palafox y su tiempo,** Zaragoza

————, 1996: **La Guerra de la Independencia en Aragón, del motín de Aranjuez a la capitulación de Zaragoza, (marzo 1808 – febrero 1809),** Zaragoza

La Parra López, Emilio, 1992: **La alianza de Godoy con los revolucionarios. España y Francia a fines del siglo XVIII,** Madrid

————, 1994: 'La central y la formación de un nuevo ejército. La Junta Militar (1808–1809)', VV.AA, 1994 (2), vol. 3: 'Política y cultura'

Laspra Rodríguez, Alicia, 1992: **Intervencionismo y revolución. Asturias y Gran Bretaña durante la Guerra de la Independencia (1808–1813),** Oviedo

Llombart, Vicent, 1996: 'El Informe de ley agraria y su autor, en la historia del pensamiento económico', in García Sanz and Sanz Fernández (eds), 1996, pp. 105–159

Lorente Toledo, Luis, 1993: **Agitación urbana y crisis economica durante la Guerra de la Independencia. Toledo (1808–1814),** Toledo

López Pérez, Manuel & Lara Martín Portugués, Isidoro, 1993: **Entre la guerra y la paz. Jaén (1808–1814),** Granada

Lovett, Gabriel H., 1965: **Napoleon and the Birth of Modern Spain,** 2 vols, New York

Lynch, John, 1993: **Bourbon Spain, 1700–1808,** Oxford

Maestrojuán Catalán, Francisco Javier, 2003: **Ciudad de vasallos, nación de héroes,** Zaragoza

Marcos Martín, Alberto, 1991: 'Historia y desarrollo: el mito historiográfico de la burguesia. Un apunte sobre la transición al capitalismo,' in Enciso Recio (ed.), 1991, pp. 15–34

Marqués Merchán, Juan: 1921: **Don Bartolomé José Gallardo. Noticia de su vida y escritos,** Madrid

Marqués Planagumá, Jose M., 1959: 'Libro de resoluciones capitulares de 1807 a 1812, resoluciones concernientes a la defensa de la ciudad', in same author's 'La iglesia de Gerona en la defensa de la ciudad durante los sitios de 1808 y 1809', **Anales del Instituto de Estudios Gerundenses del Patronato,** (ed. José Ma. Quadrado), Gerona

Marti Gilabert, Francisco, 1972: **El motín de Aranjuez,** Pamplona

Mateos y Sotos, R, 1910: **La provincia de Albacete en la Guerra de la Indepencia,** Albacete

Martínez Salazar, Andrés, 1953: **De la Guerra de la Independencia en Galicia,** Buenos Aires

Martínez San Celedonio, Felix Manuel, 1991: **Bajo dos banderas. Calahorra, 1808–1813, Guerra de la Independencia española,** Calahorra

Martínez Shaw, Carlos, 1991: 'La burguesía mercantil andaluza. Actividad económica y proyección institucional,' in García-Baquero (ed.) 1991, vol 2, pp. 15–32

Martínez Torrón, Diego, 1995: **Manuel José Quintana y el espíritu de la España liberal,** Sevilla

Martínez de Velasco, Angel, 1972: **La formación de la Junta Central,** Pamplona

Meléndez Gayoso, Antonio, 1991: 'Las aspiraciones de los burgueses segovianos a finales del siglo XVIII. Su comportamiento frente al status social de los privilegiados', in Enciso Recio (ed.), 1991, pp. 439–454

Mercader Riba, Joan, 1971: **José Bonaparte rey de España, 1808–1813. Historia externa del reinado,** Madrid

————, 1978: **Catalunya i l'imperi Napoleonic,** Montserrat

Militaria-84, **Las guerras napoleónicas en Galicia. 175 aniversario,** 1984, La Coruña

Molas Ribalta, Pere, 1970: **Los gremios barceloneses del siglo XVIII,** Madrid

————, 1985: **La burguesía mercantil en la España del Antiguo Régimen,** Madrid

————, Pere, (ed.) 1991: **La España de Carlos IV,** Madrid

Moliner i Prada, Antoni, 1981: **Estructura, funcionamiento y terminología de las Juntas Supremas Provinciales en la guerra contra Napoleón. Los casos de Mallorca, Cataluña, Asturias y León,** doctoral thesis, Universidad Autónoma, Bellaterra

————, 1989: **La Catalunya resistent a la dominació francesa, la Junta Superior de Catalunya, (1808–1812),** Barcelona

————, 2004: **La Guerrilla en la Guerra de la Independencia,** Madrid

Moral Sandoval, Enrique, (ed.) 1989: **España y la Revolución Francesa,** Madrid

Moral Roncal, Antonio Manuel, 1998: **Gremios e Ilustración en Madrid (1775–1836),** Madrid

Morange, Claude, 1989: 'La "Révolution Espagnole" de 1808 a 1814. Histoire et ecritures', in **La Révolution Française. Ses conséquences et les réactions du 'public' en Espagne entre 1808 et 1814,** 1989, Paris

————, 1990: 'El conde de Montijo. Apuntes para su biografía y reflexiones en torno al protagonismo del "partido" aristocrático en la crisis del Antiguo Régimen' from same author's **Siete calas en la crisis del Antiguo Régimen español,** 1990, Alicante

Morell i Torrademè, Josep, 1994: **Demografia de Reus i la seva àrea de mercat a l'època moderna,** Tarragona

Moreno Alonso, Manuel, 1989: **La generación española de 1808,** Madrid

————, 1995: **Sevilla Napoleónica,** Sevilla

————, Manuel, 1997: **Los españoles durante la ocupación napoleónica. La vida cotidiana en la vorágine,** Málaga

Muñoz de Bustillo Romero, Carmen, 1991: **Bayona en Andalucía El estado Bonapartista en la prefectura de Xerez,** Madrid

Muir, Rory, 1996, **Britain and the Defeat of Napoleon, 1807–1815,** New Haven and London

————, 1998, **Tactics and the Experience of Battle in the Age of Napoleon,** Yale

Murphy, Martin, 1989: **Blanco White: Self-banished Spaniard,** New Haven and London

Museo del Ejército, (ed.) 1992: **Madrid, el 2 de mayo de 1808. Viaje a un dia en la historia de España,** Madrid

Olaechea R., 1969: **El conde de Aragón y el 'partido aragonés',** Zaragoza

Olivé Serret, Enric, 1998: **Els Moragas. Història íntima d'una família de notables (1750–1868). Privacitat i família en la crisi de l'antic règim a Catalunya,** Tarragona

Oman, Sir Charles, 1902/1995: **A History of the Peninsular War,** 7 vols., London & Mechanicsburg, PA

Ortega, Margarita, 1986: **La lucha por la tierra en la Corona de Castilla: el expediente de Ley Agraria,** Madrid

————, 1993: **Conflicto y continuidad en la sociedad rural española del siglo XVIII,** Madrid

Peña Guerrero, María Antonia, 2000: **El tiempo de los franceses. La Guerra de la Independencia en el suroeste español,** Almonte (Huelva)

Perez de Guzmán y Gallo, Juan, 1908: **El dos de mayo de 1808 en Madrid. Relación histórica documentada,** Madrid

Pérez Moreda, Vicente, 1980: **Las crisis de mortalidad en la España interior, siglos XVI–XIX,** Madrid

Peris Serra, María Francisca, & María Desamparados E. Gimeno Muñoz, 1993: 'Conflictividad antiseñorial en el campo valenciano', in Sarasa Sánchez & Serrano Martín (eds.), vol IV, 1993, Zaragoza

Piñar López, J.J., 1986: 'Cartagena en los inicios de la Guerra de la Independencia, 1808', in I^{ero} **Concurso de Historia de Cartagena,** Cartagena, pp. 207–332

Pla Cargol, Joaquín, 1962: **La Guerra de la Independencia en Gerona y sus comarcas,** Gerona/Madrid

Portillo Valdés, José M., 1989: 'El País Vasco. El Antiguo Régimen y la Revolución', in Aymes (ed.) 1989

Quesada Montero, Enriqueta, 1958: **La actuación de la Suprema Junta de Sevilla a través del diario de su presidente,** Sevilla

Ramisa, Maties, 1993: **La guerra del francès al corregiment de Vic, 1808–1814,** Manresa

Recasens Comes, José M^a., 1965: **La revolución y Guerra de la Independencia en la ciudad de Tarragona,** Tarragona

Reher, David Sven, 1990: **Town and Country in Pre-Industrial Spain: Cuenca, 1550–1870,** Cambridge

Reynaud, Jean-Louis, 1992: **Contre-guerilla en Espagne (1808–1814). Suchet pacifie l'Aragón,** Paris

Ribechini, Celina, 1996: **De la Guerra de la Convención a la Zamacolada: Insumisión, matxinada, dispersión,** San Sebastián

Robledo, Ricardo, 1996: **Salamanca, ciudad de paso, ciudad ocupada, la Guerra de la Independencia,** Salamanca

Rodríguez López-Brea, Carlos M., 1996: **Frailes y revolución liberal. El clero regular en España a comienzos del siglo XIX (1800–1814),** Toledo

Rodriguez-Solis, E., **Los guerrilleros de 1808** 2 vols Madrid

Roura i Aulinas, Lluís, 1984: **L'Antic Régim a Mallorca. Abast de la commoció dels anys 1808–1814,** Palma de Mallorca

————, 1989: 'Cataluña y la Francia de la Revolutión, in Aymes, (ed.) 1989

————, 1993: **Guerra Gran a la ratlla de França. Catalunya dins la guerra contra la Revolució Francesa, 1793–1795,** Barcelona

————, Lluís, 2001: '"Guerra pequeña" y formas de movilización armada en la Guerra de la Independencia', in José A. Armillas Vicente (ed.) **La Guerra de la Independencia. Estudios,** vol 1., Zaragoza, 2001, p. 281

Rubio Fernández, María Dolores, 1989: **Elecciones en el Antiguo Régimen. La reforma municipal de Carlos III en Alicante, 1766–1770,** Alicante

Rubio Pobes, Coro, 1996: **Revolución y tradición. El País Vasco ante la Revolución liberal y la construcción del estado español, 1808–1868,** Madrid

Rudorff, Raymond, 1974: **War to the Death: The Sieges of Saragossa, 1808–1809,** New York

Ruíz Torres, Pedro, 1985: 'El País Valenciano en el siglo XVIII La transformación de una sociedad agraria en la época del absolutismo', in Fernández, Roberto (ed), 1985, pp 132–248

————, 1988: 'Economía y sociedad en la crisis del Antiguo Régimen', in Domínguez Ortiz, (ed), Vol 9, 1988

Saavedra, Pegerto, 1994: **La vida cotidiana en la Galicia del Antiguo Régimen,** Barcelona

Saavedra, Pegerto & Ramón Villares, 1985: 'Galicia en el Antiguo Régimen. La fortaleza de una sociedad tradicional', in Fernández, Roberto (ed) 1985, pp. 434–504

————, (eds), 1991: **Señores y campesinos en la península ibérica, siglos XVIII–XX,** 2 vols., Barcelona

Sáinz Rodriguéz, Pedro, 1986: **Bartolomé J. Gallardo y la crítica de su tiempo,** Madrid

Sánchez Fernández, Jorge, 1997: **La guerrilla vallisoletana, 1808–1814,** Valladolid

————, 2000: **¡Nos invaden! Guerrilla y represión en Valladolid durante la Guerra de la Independencia española, 1808–1814,** Valladolid

————, 2002: **Valladolid durante la Guerra de la Independencia española, 1808–1814,** Valladolid

Sánchez Jara, Diego, 1960: **Intervención de Murcia en la Guerra por la Independencia,** Murcia

Sarasa Sánchez, Esteban & Eliseo Serrano Martín, (eds), 1993: **Señorío y feudalismo en la península ibérica,** 4 vols, Zaragoza

Sarrailh, Jean, 1957: **La España Ilustrada de la segunda mitad del siglo XVIII**, Mexico-Madrid-Buenos Aires

Sarret y Arbòs, Joaquin, 1922: **Manresa en la Guerra de la Independencia**, Manresa

Scott, H.M., (ed.), 1995: **The European Nobilities in the Seventeenth and Eighteenth Centuries**, London

Seco Serrano, Carlos, 1978: **Godoy. El hombre y el político**, Madrid

Segura, Rev. Joan, 1908/1978 (facsimile): **Historia d'Igualada**, 2 vols., Barcelona/Igualada

Serano Montalvo, Antonio, 1958: 'El pueblo en la Guerra de la Independencia. La resistencia en la ciudades', in VV.AA., 1958, Zaragoza

Serone, María Cruz, 1977: **Oratorio y periodismo en la España del siglo XIX**, Madrid

Sherwig, John M., 1969: **Guineas and Gunpowder: British Foreign Aid in the Wars with France**, Cambridge, Mass.

Sherwood, Joan, 1988: **Poverty in Eighteenth Century Spain: The Women and Children of the Inclusa**, Toronto

Simón Tarrès, Antonio, 1985: **La crisis del Antiguo Régimen en Girona**, Bellaterra

Tausiet, María, 2002: **Los Posesos de Tosos (1812–1814). Brujería y justicia popular en tiempos de revolución**, Zaragoza

Thompson, I.A.A., 1995: 'The Nobility in Spain, 1600–1800' in Scott (ed.), 1995, pp. 174–236

Toreno, conde de, 1838/1916: **Historia del levantamiento, guerra y revolución de España**, Madrid

Tone, Lawrence John, 1994: **The Fatal Knot: the Guerrilla War in Navarre and the defeat of Napoleon in Spain**, North Carolina

Torre, Joseba de la, 1991: **Los campesinos navarros ante la guerra napoleónica. Financiación bélica y desamortización civil**, Madrid, 1991

————, 1992: **Lucha antifeudal y conflictos de clases en Navarra, 1808–1820**, Bilbao

Tuñón de Lara, Manuel (ed.), 1982: **Historia de España**, vol VII, **Centralismo, Ilustración y agonía del Antiguo Régimen, 1715–1833** (2nd ed.), Madrid

VV.AA., 1958: **La Guerra de la Independencia española y los sitios de Zaragoza**, Zaragoza

————, 1981: **La invasió napoleonica, economia, cultura i societat**, Bellaterra

————, 1982: **España a finales del siglo XVIII**, Taragona

————, 1984: **Les Espagnols et Napoléon. Actes du Colloque International d'Aix-en-Provence, 13–15 de Octobre, 1983**, Université de Provence

————, 1988: **I Congreso de Historia de Castilla-La Mancha. Actas,** vols VIII and IX, Toledo

————, 1990 (1): **Coloquio Internacional Carlos III y su siglo. Actas,** 2 vols., Madrid

————, 1990 (2): **Repercusiones de la Revolución Francesa en España. Actas del Congreso Internacional celebrado en Madrid 27–30 noviembre 1989**, Madrid

————, 1990 (3): **El Jacobinisme: reacció y revolució a Catalunya i a Espanya, 1789–1837. Actas del Colloqui Internacional**, Barcelona

————, 1991: **Les Révolutions Ibériques et Ibéro-Américaines à l'Aube de XIXe siècle. Actes du Colloque de Bordeaux, 2–4 juillet, 1989**, Paris

————, 1994 (1): **El mundo hispánico en el siglo de las luces. Actas del Coloquio internacional. Unidad y diversidad en el mundo hispánico**, 2 vols, Salamanca

————, 1994 (2): **Antiguo Régimen y liberalismo. Homenaje a Miguel Artola**, 3 vols, Madrid

————, 1999: **La Batalla de Bailén. Actas de las primeras jornadas sobre la batalla de Bailén y la España contemporánea**, Jaén

————, 2001: **Bailén y la guerra contra Napoleón en Andalucía. Actas de las segundas jornadas sobre la batalla de Bailén y la España contemporánea**, Jaén

Varela, Javier, 1988: **Jovellanos**, Madrid

————, 1989: 'La elite ilustrada ante las nuevas ideas. Actitudes y contradicciones' in **España y la Revolución Francesa**, Moral Sandoval, Enrique (ed.), Madrid

Vaughan, Sir Charles Richard, 1809: **Narrative of the Siege of Zaragoza**, London

Vázquez de Prada, Valentin, 1992: 'Los motines de 1766 en España. Una cuestión a debate', in Enciso Recio (ed.) p. 103 et seq.

Velázquez y Sánchez, José, 1872/1994: **Anales de Sevilla de 1800 a 1850,** Sevilla

Vilar, Pierre, 1987: **Cataluña en la España moderna,** 3 vols, Barcelona (Spanish translation of **La Catalogne dans l'Espagne moderne. Recherches sur les fondements économiques des structures nationales,** Paris, 1962)

————, 1982: **Hidalgos, amotinados y guerrilleros. Pueblo y poderes en la historia de España,** Barcelona

Villares, Ramón, 1985: **Historia de Galicia,** Madrid

Wellesley, Henry, 1930: **The Diary and Correspondence of Henry Wellesley, First Lord Cowley, 1790–1846,** (ed. Col the Hon. F.A. Wellesley), London

Yun Casalilla, Bartolomé, 1993: 'Consideraciones para el estudio de la renta y las economías señoriales en el reino de Castilla (s. XV–XVIII)' in Sarasa Sánchez, Esteban & Serrano Martín, Eliseo (eds.), 1993, Vol. 2, pp 11–45, Zaragoza

ESSAYS AND ARTICLES

Abbad, Farid, 1977: 'La Confrerie condamnée ou une spontaneité festive confisquée' in **Mélanges de la Casa de Velazquez,** Vol. XIII, Paris

Canales, Estebán, 1988: 'Patriotismo y deserción durante la Guerra de la Independencia en Cataluña', in **A Revolução Francesa e a Península Ibérica,** **Revista Portuguesa de História,** Vol XXIII, Coimbra

Carner, Antonio, 1963 (1): 'Los treinta dias del mes de junio de 1808. Síntesis histórica y documental', Igualada

————, 1963 (2): 'Leyenda e historia de las batallas del Bruch. Las batallas del 6 y 14 de junio de 1808 no fueron acciones espontáneas del paisanaje en armas', **Revista de Historia Militar,** No. 12, Madrid, pp. 73–89

Carrasco Martínez, Adolfo, 1995: 'Estrategías y actitudes aristocráticas en España a finales del Antiguo Régimen', **Historia Social,** No. 23, 1995, Valencia, pp. 65–78

Caruana Gómez de Barreda, Jaime, 1959: 'La sierra de Albarracín durante la Guerra de la Independencia', **Teruel,** No 21, Jan-Feb, 1959, pp. 93–134

Díez Rodríguez, Fernando, 1984: 'Los papeles del correjero' in **Estudis d'història contemporània del País Valencià,** Valencia

Egea Bruno, Pedro, 1991: 'Cartegena durante la Guerra de la Independencia. La actuación de la Junta de Gobierno (1808–1810)', **Agua,** Autumn issue, pp. 18–19, Murcia

Espada Burgos, Manuel, 1968: 'El hambre de 1812 en Madrid', **Hispania,** no. 110, Madrid

Juana, Jesús de & Castro, Xavier, 1990–1991: 'Apuntes sobre la Guerra de Independencia en Galicia', in **Boletín Auriense,** años XX–XXI, Ourense, pp. 75–89

La Parra López, Emilio: 'Los derechos del hombre. Aceptación en España de las declaraciones francesas', in **Estudios de Historia Social,** nos. 103–109

López-Salazar Pérez, Jerónimo, 1976: 'Evolución demográfica de la Mancha en el siglo XVIII', **Hispania,** No. 133, Madrid, pp. 233–299

Mercader Riba, Joan, 1950: '¿La junta igualadina de 1808–1809, gobierno faccioso?', in **Miscellanea Aqualatensia,** Igualada

————, 1952: 'España en el Bloqueo Continental', in **Estudios de Historia Moderna,** Vol II., pp. 233–278, Madrid

————, 1953: 'La ideologia dels Catalans del 1808', **Anuari de l'Institut d'Estudis Catalans,** Barcelona, pp. 3–16

Mercader Riba, Joan, Josep Ma. Torras i Ribé, 1970: 'Assaig sobre les oligarquies socials d'Igualada en el segle XVIII. Discurs llegit en la XX Sessió Plenària del CECI, 2 de juliol del 1967', Igualada

Moliner i Prada, Antonio, 1985: 'La Junta de Alicante en la Guerra del Francés', **Trienio, Revista de Historia,** no. 6, pp. 37–73, Madrid

Morange, Claude, 1983: 'El conde de Montijo durante la guerra de la Independencia. Apuntes para su biografía', in **Trienio, Revista de Historia,** no. 2, pp. 3–41

Pérez Ledesma, 1991: 'Las Cortes de Cádiz y la sociedad española', in *Ayer*, no. 1, 1991

Robledo, Ricardo, 1997: 'Los franceses en Salamanca según los diarios de la biblioteca universitaria (1807–1813)', *Salamanca, Revista de Estudios*, 'Las guerras en Salamanca (ss XVII–XX)', no. 40

Rodríguez Zurro, Ana Isabel, 1997: 'Colaboración y apoyo de la guerrilla y de la armada de Gran Bretaña durante la Guerra de la Independencia', *Investigaciones Históricas 17*, Universidad de Valladolid, pp. 161–171

Ruíz Torres, Pedro, 1987: 'Patrimonios y rentas de la nobleza en la España de finales del Antiguo Régimen,' in *Hacienda Pública Española*, nos. 108–109, Madrid

Saiz Bayo, Santiago, 1988: 'El levantamiento guerrillero en la Guerra de la Independencia', *Revista Historia Militar*, no. 65, Madrid

Sánchez Fernández, Jorge, 1999: 'Un episodio inédito de la biografia del guerrillero vallisoletano Saturnino Abuín', *Argaya*, no. 18, pp. 20–22, Valladolid

Soubeyroux, Jacques, 1980: 'Pauperismo y relaciones sociales en el Madrid del siglo XVIII', *Estudios de Historia Social*, nos. 12–13, pp. 7–227, Madrid

Térmens Samsó, Josep, Francesc and Valls Junyent, 1987: 'La Guerra del Francés en un poble de la comarca de l'Anoia. "Notas" del Dr. Pere Solanlloch, rector de Pierola', **Miscellanea Aqualatensia**, no. 4, 1987, pp. 113–151, Igualada

Windler-Dirisio, Christian, 1995: 'Las reformas administratives de la aristocracía española en el contexto del absolutismo reformista,' in *Historia Social*, no. 23, 1995, pp. 79–99, Valencia

PRINTED PRIMARY SOURCES

Alcaide Ibieca, Agustín, 1830–1831: **Historia de los sitios que pusieron a Zaragoza en los años de 1808 y 1809 las tropas de Napoleón,** 3 vols, Madrid

Alcalá Galiano, Antonio, 1886/1956: **Memorias de D. Antonio Alcalá Galiano,** Madrid

————, 1878/1956: **Recuerdos de un anciano,** Madrid

Alvarez Valdés, Ramón, 1889/1988: **Memorias del levantamiento de Asturias en 1808,** Gijón

Anon.: **Lo que pasó en la Coruña el 29, 30 y 31 de Mayo de 1808** (ed. Antonio Rey Escaríz), May, 1908, *La Voz de Galicia*, La Coruña

Anon., 1808 (1): **Memoria de lo mas interesante que ha ocurrido en la ciudad de Zaragoza, con motivo de haberla atacado el ejército francés,** 1808, Madrid (BN VE/787–28)

Anon., 1808 (2): **De una carta de Zaragoza fecha el 13 del present mes de Agosto de 1808,** *Colección de papeles interesantes sobre las circunstancias presentes*, vol II, Cuaderno 13, pp. 213–235

Anon., 1808 (3): **Gobierno pronto y reformas necesarias,** Madrid

Anon.: **Relato de la caida de Godoy por un testigo presencial:** Sept–Dec, 1958 (ed. A. Rodríguez-Moíno): *Revista de Estudios Extremeños*, Vol XIV, pp. 477–492

Anon., (attributed to Francisco Gallardo y Merino), 1886/1989: **Noticia de casos particulares ocurridos en la ciudad de Valladolid, año de 1808 y siguientes** (ed. Juan Ortega y Rubio): 1886, in **Valladolid, Diarios Curiosos (1807–1841)** pp. 115–375, [facsimile edition, 1989] Valladolid

Anon., **Libro de Apuntes de un Alcalaino (1809–1814),** *Revue Hispanique*, vol. 1, pp 169–258, New York, Paris, 1914

Antillón, Isidoro, 1808: **¿Qué es lo que mas importa a la España? Discurso de un miembro del populacho,** Teruel, Cádiz, n.d., (BN R60527)

————, 1810: **Cuatro verdades útiles a la Nación, estractadas de algunos escritos españoles,** Palma (BN. 60885)

Artola, Miguel, (ed), 1957: **Memorias de tiempos de Fernando VII,** Madrid

Azanza, Miguel José & Gonzalo O'Farril, 1814: **Memoria de D. Miguel José de Azanza y D. Gonzalo O'Farril sobre los hechos que justifican su conducta política desde marzo de 1808 hasta abril de 1814,** in Artola (ed.), 1957

Bertrande Lis, Vincente, 1851: **Los Gobiernos y los intereses materiales, o sean Apuntes históricos sobre varias cuestiones importantes (1ª y 2ª parte),** Madrid

————, Vicente, 1852: **Apuntes biográficos o sea Apéndice a los folletos titulados, "Los Gobiernos y los intereses materiales",** Madrid

Blanco White, Josef, 1822: **Letters from Spain** (under pseudonym, Don Leucadio Doblado), London

————, 1988: **Autobiografía de Blanco White** (ed. and translated by Antonio Garnica), 2nd edition, Sevilla; first published posthumously in English in 1845 as **The Life of the Rev. Josef Blanco White, written by himself with portions of his correspondence,** 3 vols (reprinted 1971)

Bosch i Cardellach, Antoni, 1815/1988: **Resumen de lo sucedido en la villa de Bràfim (situada en la carretera de Barcelona a Valls, a dos horas de esta y a cuatro de Tarragona) en todos los años de la última guerra con Francia y su intruso gobierno,** *BUB*, ms. 481, (published as 'Una visió més real de la Guerra del Francès: la història de Bràfim d'en Bosch i Cardellach', ed. Esteban Canales Gili, *Recerques*, no. 21, Barcelona, 1988)

Bourgoing, J. Fr., 1808: **Modern State of Spain,** London, (trans. from French edition of 1807)

Calvo, Matías, 2000: **El manuscrito de Matías Calvo, memorias de un monegrino durante la Guerra de la Independencia** (transcribed & ed. Juan José Marcén Letosa), Zaragoza

Calvo Rozas, Lorenzo, 1810: **Reformas y Medidas propuestas en 1809 para la organizacion y buena asistencia de los exércitos y Aviso Interesante por los que han hecho servicios á la Patria en la presente guerra nacional,** Cádiz

————, 1813: **Representaciones que en el año de 1810 dirigió desde su prision D. Lorenzo Calvo de Rozas al Consejo Interino, y proposiciones que en 1808 y 1809 hizo a la Suprema Junta Central, para asegurar la libertad y el bien estar de sus conciudadanos,** Madrid

Capmany, Antonio, 1808/1988: **Centinela contra franceses,** Madrid/London

Casamayor, Faustino, 1908: **Los Sitios de Zaragoza, diario de Casamayor** (ed. José Valenzuela La Rosa), Zaragoza

Censo de 1797 'Godoy': 1992, Madrid (facsimile)

Cevallos, Pedro: 1808: **Exposición de los hechos y maquinaciones que han preparado la usurpación de la corona de España y los medios que el Emperador de los Franceses ha puesto en obra para realizarla,** in Artola (ed.), 1957, pp. 155–185

Colección de papeles interesantes sobre las circunstancias presentes: 1808, ed. J.A.M. (2nd edition), Madrid, Quadernos I–IX

Colección de documentos interesantes, que pueden servir de apuntes para la historia de la revolucion de España, por un Amante de las glorias nacionales: 1808, Madrid

Colección de decretos y ordenes de las Cortes de Cádiz: 1820/1987 (facsimile), Madrid

Constitucion del Reyno de España é Indias, Perpiñan, n.d. (but probably 1808–1809)

Coroleu, José: 1946: **Memorias de un menestral de Barcelona, 1792–1854,** Barcelona

Demostracion de la lealtad española Colección de proclamas, órdenes, discursos, estados de ejército, y relaciones de batallas publicadas por las Juntas de Gobierno, o por algunos particulares en las actuales circunstancias: 5 vols, 1808, Cádiz.

Elorza, Antonio, (ed.), 1971: **Pan y Toros y otros papeles sediciosos de fines del siglo XVIII,** Madrid

Domingo Palomar, Juan, (ed.) 1894: **Diario de un patriota complutense en la Guerra de la Independencia,** Madrid

Escoiquiz, Juan, 1808: **Idea sencilla de las razones que motivaron el viaje del Rey don Fernando VII a Bayona,** in Artola (ed.), 1957, pp. 189–226

Espoz y Mina, Francisco, 1851–1852/1962: **Memorias del general Don Francisco Espoz y Mina, escritas por él mismo,** 2 vols, (ed. Miguel Artola), Madrid

Ferrer, Raymundo, 1815–1818: **Barcelona cautiva, ó sea diario exacto de lo ocurrido en la misma ciudad mientras la oprimieron los franceses, esto es, desde el 13 de febrero de 1808 hasta el 28 de mayo de 1814,** Barcelona, 5 vols. published, 2 vols. ms.

Gallardo, Bartolomé J: 1838: **Diccionario Crítico-Burlesco,** Madrid

García de León y Pizarro, José, 1953?: **Memorias,** Madrid

J. de A. (José de Arango), 1808: **Manifiesto imparcial y exacto de lo mas importante ocurrido en Aranjuez, Madrid y Bayona,** Cádiz/Madrid (BL, *EG* 385/66–96)

Libro de resoluciones capitulares de 1807 a 1812, resoluciones concernientes a la defensa de la ciudad (de Gerona), 1959: in Marqués Planagumá, José M, 1959: *La iglesia de Gerona en la defensa de la ciudad durante los sitios de 1808 y 1809, Anales del Instituo de Estudios Gerundenses del Patronato* (ed. José Ma. Quadrado), Gerona

Manifiesto de los procedimientos del Consejo Real en los gravisimos sucesos ocurridos desde octubre del año próximo pasado: 1808, Madrid,

Manifiesto que hace la Junta Superior de Observación y Defensa del Reyno de Valencia, de los servicios y heroycos esfuerzos prestados por este desde el dia 23 de mayo de 1808, en favor de la libertad é independencia de la nacion, y de los derechos de su augusto y legítimo soberano, El Sr. D. Fernando Septimo, de eterna memoria: 1809, Valencia,

Martínez Colomer, Vicente, 1808: **El filósofo en su quinta,** Valencia

————, 1810: **Sucesos de Valencia desde el dia 23 de mayo hasta el 28 de junio del año 1808,** Valencia

Martínez Martel y Abadía, Demetrio, 1887: **Diario de Valladolid que comprende desde Junio de 1810 hasta fin de dicho mes de 1834,** Valladolid

Mesonero Romanos, Ramón, 1967: **Memorias de un setentón,** Madrid

Miot de Mélito, comte, 1874: **Mémoires de,** vol 3, Paris

Mirtilo Sicuritano (pseudonym of Nicolas Tap y Nuñez Redón), 1814: **Apuntes para la historia de España,** 2nd edn, Madrid

Mor de Fuentes, José, 1957: **Bosquejillo de la vida y escritos de D. José Mor de Fuentes** in Artola (ed.) 1957, pp. 375–428.

Moraleda y Esteban, J., 1909: **Sucesos notables ocurridos en Toledo durante la Guerra,** Toledo

Nellerto (pseudonym of Juan Antonio Lorente), 1814–1816: **Memorias para la historia de la revolución española con documentos justificativos,** Paris

Nieto Samaniego, J.A., 1810: **Memorial histórico de los sucesos más notables de armas y estado de la salud pública durante el último sitio de la plaza de Gerona,** Tarragona

Palafox, José de, 1834 ms.1994: **Memorias,** (ed. Herminio Lafoz Rabaza), Zaragoza

Pérez Villamil, Juan, 1808: **Carta sobre el modo de establecer el Consejo de regencia del reyno, con arreglo á nuestra constitucion,** Madrid

Perich i Viader, Antoni, 1911: **Narració de los sis anys y quatre meses que los franceses han estat en Cathalunya, contant de los primers de febrer de 1808, fins al primers Juny, 1814** in *Unes memories de la guerra de la Independència,* J Pella i Forgas, *Boletin de la Real Academia de Buenas Letras de Barcelona,* vol VI, 1911, pp. 1–6, 420–430 & 479–501

Pons Anguera, Antoni, 1988: **Libro de varias cosas sucedidas en esta villa y algunos parages de Cataluña,** (ed. Pere Anguera), Reus

Posse, Juan Antonio, 1984: **Memorias del cura liberal don Juan Antonio Posse con su Discurso sobre la Constitución de 1812** (ed. Richard Herr), Madrid

Principe de la Paz (Godoy, Manuel), 1956: **Memorias críticas y apologéticas para la historia del reinado del señor D. Carlos IV de Borbón,** 2 vols, Madrid

Quintana, Manuel José, 1872: **Memoria sobre el proceso y prision de don Manuel José Quintana en 1814,** (written 1818), in **Obras Inéditas,** Madrid, reprinted in M.E. Martínez Quinteiro, 1972: **Quintana revolucionario, Estudios, notas y comentarios de texto,** Madrid

Ribera, Dr. Pere, 1992: **Una crònica de Tárrega poc coneguda: el manuscrit del Dr. Pere Ribera** (ed. Gener Gonzalvo i Bou), *URTX* No. 4, Urgell

Rico, Fr Juan, 1811: **Memorias históricas sobre la revolución de Valencia,** Cádiz

Robertson, Rev. James, 1863: **Narrative of a Secret Mission to the Danish Islands in 1808** (edited from the author's ms. by his nephew, Alexander Clinton Fraser)

Sancho, Hilarión, 1896/1989: **Diario de Valladolid, (1807–1841)** in *Valladolid, Diarios Curiosos (1807–1841)* pp. 11–111; [facsimile edition, 1989] Valladolid

Schaumann, Friedrich, 1925: **On the Road with Wellington, the diary of a war commissary in the Peninsular campaigns,** New York

Schépeler, Col Berthold von, 1829: **Histoire de la Révolution d'Espagne et de Portugal**, 3 vols, Liége

Serrat, Mossèn Isidre, 1958–1960: Rector de Comià (Osuna), **Diario** (1776–1815), (ed. Miquel Furriols) in *Ausa*, Vol 3, No. 23, Vich

Termens Samsó, Josep, & Francesc Valls Junyent, (eds.), 1987: **La Guerra del Francès en un poble de la comarca de l'Anoia. 'Notas' del Dr. Pere Solanllonch, Rector de Pierola, *Miscellanea Aqualatensia***, No. 4, 1987, Igualada, pp. 113–151

Torné i Domingo, Francesc, 1990: **Los veinte años de inscripción, una visió carlina de les turbulències de la primera meitat del segle XIX, Reus 1800–1853** (ed. Pere Anguera), Reus

Trillo y Borbón, Juan, 1890/1918: **Libro en donde están apuntadas todas las novedades acaecidas en esta ciudad de Xerez de la Frontera desde el año 1753, y algunas otras que han ocurrido fuera de ella**, Jerez

Viadér, Dr Josef Antonio, 1810: **Memoria sobre las enfermedades que han afligido á los moradores y guarnicion de esta plaza de Gerona y demas pueblos de su departamento desde junio de 18108 hasta ultimos de febrero de 1810**, Gerona

Villanueva, Joaquin Lorenzo, 1825/1996: **Vida Literaria,** London, 1825 (ed. Germán Ramírez Aledón), Alicante, 1996

Zaonero, Joaquín, 1998: **Libro de noticias de Salamanca que empieza a rejir el año de 1796 (hasta 1812)** (critical edn by Ricardo Robledo), Salamanca

ARCHIVES

ACA: Archivo General de la Corona de Aragón
AD de G: Archivo Diocesano de Girona
AGMM: Archivo General Militar de Madrid
AGMS: Archivo General Militar de Segovia
AGP: Archivo General de Palacio
AGS: Archivo General de Simancas
AH de DIP: Archivo Histórico de la Diputación de . . .
AHM: Archivo Histórico Municipal de . . .
AHN: Archivo Histórico Nacional
AM: Archivo Municipal de . . .
ARV: Archivo del Reino de Valencia
AV: Archivo General de la Villa de Madrid
BL, *Eg*: British Library, Egerton Collection
BN: Biblioteca Nacional
BUB: Biblioteca Universitaria de Barcelona
PRO: Public Record Office
RAH: Biblioteca de la Real Academia de Historia

MANUSCRIPT SOURCES

Anon., 1794: *Noticias sobre la entrega de San Sebastián . . . y resto de Guipúzcoa hasta Tolosa a los franceses*, Bilbao, unpaginated, 19 Aug, 1794 (BN R63300²)

Anon., 1808: *Papeles de Cathaluña*, **BUB** (ms. 395)

Anon., 1808: *Rebolucion de la Corte de España* in **Relaciones diversas de los tumultos ocurridos en Aranjuez, Madrid y Cádiz los dias 18, 25 y 26 de marzo,** 1808 (BN R62628)

Anon., 1808: *Diario de lo ocurrido en Aranjuez desde el dia 13 de marzo*, unpaginated, 1808 (BN R60334)

Anon., n.d. *Diario del sitio de Gerona del año 1809 recopilado por . . . De documentos y piezas relativas*, 13 vols., Gerona

Checa y Xijon, José, n.d: *Documentos del coronel retirado en Sevilla, Dn. José de Checa y Xijon,* (BN R62746)

Daoíz, Martin Vicente de, 1808: *Fragmentos de cartas escritas a su primo,* Sevilla, (BN R/ 62739)

Estellés, Josef, n.d. **Diario**: untitled, 139 pp. unnumbered sewn sheets, without cover, ARV (*Propiedades Antiguas,* Legajo 423)

Giles y Carpio, Fr. Manuel, 1808: *Quaderno de Noticias raras de diferentes años . . . Quaderno primero: lo sucedido en todo el año de 1808* (BN R/62734)

Guervos, Francisco, *Cartas personales enviadas por Francisco Guervos a sus padres desde el campo de batalla, concretamente desde julio de 1808 hasta 1815, en que muere con veintitantos años por las secuelas de las heridas y el padecimiento de la guerra,* BRAH (ms. 11–5–7 9003)

Saavedra, Francisco Arias de, *Diario de las operaciones de la Suprema Junta de Sevilla, desde su formación hasta la instalación de la Regencia* (in fact notes for a diary that was never compiled), Fondo Saavedra, Caja *56–4,* Archivo histórico S.I., 'Provincia de Andalucía', Facultad de Teologia de Granada. Granada

NEWSPAPERS

Diario de Gerona
Diario de Madrid
Diario de Valencia
Gazeta de Madrid
Gazeta del Gobierno, Sevilla
Gazeta Ministerial de Sevilla
Gazeta del Principado de Cataluña
Gazeta de Valencia
Gaceta de Zaragoza
Semanario Patriótico

REFERENCE WORKS

Alsina, Claudi, 1996: **Diccionari de mesures catalanes,** Barcelona (BN: 10/33899).

Emsley Clive: 1993: **Napoleonic Europe,** London

Haythornwaite, Philip J., 1996: **The Napoleonic Source Book,** London

Valcárcel, A.: **Tablas de reducción de medidas, pesos y monedas del antiguo sistema de Castilla al moderno y del moderno al antiguo, conteniendo además las tablas de reducción de precios mandado X** (sic) **observar desde 1° de julio de 1880,** Madrid, 1883 (BN: 1/307)

Valcárcel, A.: **Diccionario métrico para reducir unidades del antiguo sistema al moderno y del moderno al antiguo con una simple multiplicación,** Madrid, 1867 (BN: 2/324485)

Index